Powers of theory
Capitalism, the state, and democracy

ROBERT R. ALFORD
University of California, Santa Cruz

ROGER FRIEDLAND
University of California, Santa Barbara

H. Kim
May 1986

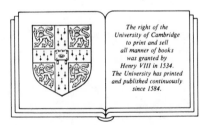

The right of the
University of Cambridge
to print and sell
all manner of books
was granted by
Henry VIII in 1534.
The University has printed
and published continuously
since 1584.

CAMBRIDGE UNIVERSITY PRESS

Cambridge
London   New York   New Rochelle
Melbourne   Sydney

Published by the Press Syndicate of the University of Cambridge
The Pitt Building, Trumpington Street, Cambridge CB2 1RP
32 East 57th Street, New York, NY 10022, USA
10 Stamford Road, Oakleigh, Melbourne 3166, Australia

First published 1985

Printed in the United States of America

Library of Congress Cataloging in Publication Data
Alford, Robert R.
Powers of theory.
Bibliography: p.
1. Capitalism   I. Friedland, Roger.   II. Title.
JC325.A49   1985   306'.2   84–23197
ISBN 0 521 30349 4 hard covers
ISBN 0 521 31635 9 paperback

For Gloria, comrade-in-arms

For the light in Debra's eyes

Contents

Contents

PART IV: THEORY, POLITICS, AND
CONTRADICTIONS IN THE STATE

Tables and figure

Tables

Figure

Preface

Three major historical developments frame theories of the state in Western capitalist democracies: first, the rise of capitalism as a form of social production, resulting in an explosion of the productivity of human labor; second, the expansion of bureaucratic states as power structures maintaining police and military control over potentially rebellious populations and reproducing the conditions for capitalist accumulation; third, the establishment of democratic institutions providing vehicles for political participation by and representation of ordinary citizens.

The fundamental distinction among capitalism, the state, and democracy is the axis around which debates within and among three major theoretical perspectives – which we shall term "pluralist," "managerial," and "class" – have revolved. Our purpose in this book is to delineate the mode of inquiry of each perspective, review its partial character, and then offer a synthetic framework for a more comprehensive theory of the state.

Our subtitle is a conscious gloss on Joseph Schumpeter's classic, *Capitalism, Socialism and Democracy*, an exemplar of the managerial perspective. By defining socialism as centralized state control of the economy, and democracy as elite competition for mass support, Schumpeter rejected the historical vision of democratic socialism as an economy in which production is socially controlled and a polity in which public participation is genuine and equal. Also, the phrase indicates our view that the state mediates between capitalism and democracy.

Although each perspective has immediate ideological and political implications, we purposely focus mainly upon the analytic potential of each. Each perspective interprets the history, structure, and functions of the state very differently.

The theoretical perspectives contain incompatible world views about the relations among society, institutions, organizations, and individuals. But neither can any one perspective even potentially claim to provide the basis for an exalted General Theory of the State. Each theoretical perspective has a distinctive but limited "power": a home domain of analysis within which its classic examples are tours de force. Advocates of each perspective sometimes argue that its interpretations can be modified to comprehend all of the phenomena that other perspectives try to explain, and do it better. We argue, instead, that the assumptions of other perspectives are thereby rejected silently or reinterpreted in another language. What appears to be the resolution of intellectual conflict is silent domination by one or another perspective, which is manifested in institutional power over the conditions of intellectual debate.

We present this work not merely as an academic exercise. The adequacy of social theory limits our understanding of the potentialities of human history and our chances of realizing our dreams or avoiding our nightmares. For this reason theoretical differences evoke great passion. In this volume we confront the differences among three theories of the state, an institution that has embodied the wildest hopes and fears of human beings for several centuries. Guardian of the national will, powerful bureaucratic tool, and instrument of capitalist power – each image evokes different historical possibilities. Here we shall analyze not the possibilities but the theories by which we might better comprehend them.

Acknowledgments

This book has been a decade in the making. It originated before our collaboration began (see Alford 1975b). We began to work together in the wake of intense conversations that lasted for miles walked along Lake Mendota in Madison, Wisconsin. Our initial studies together concerned theories of political development (Alford and Friedland 1974) and the sources of political power (Alford and Friedland 1975). From those studies evolved a decision to write this book together. Other work and the exigencies of professional careers and personal lives have prevented its completion until now, despite continuing strolls in the Los Angeles and Santa Barbara hills and the Santa Cruz redwoods. In writing this book, we walked many miles. In the process, the book grew longer and our friendship deeper.

But the book would never have been finished without the personal and intellectual support and often brutally frank criticism offered by many friends, colleagues, and students. Reviewing our files of letters and recalling the conversations bring home forcefully the generous criticisms we have received. A mere list of names cannot possibly convey the warmth of our feelings about the persons mentioned. Some may have actually forgotten their contributions, which date back as much as a decade.

First, we must mention Frances Fox Piven, who has read and reread our drafts more times than she would care to remember. For her friendship and determination to improve our work we are grateful. Others who have commented on versions of various chapters, and upon whom we bestow the customary absolution, include Michael Aiken, Allen H. Barton, Linda Bergthold, Michael Brown, Dudley Burton, Nancy Di-Tomaso, G. William Domhoff, Graeme Duncan, Susan Eckstein, Gosta Esping-Andersen, Peter Euben, Richard Flacks, Bill Friedland, Norman Glickman, Wally Goldfrank, Alexander Hicks, Richard Child Hill, Patrick M. Horan, Al Imershein, Ira Katznelson, David Kettler, Michael Kimmel, Maria Los, Paul Lubeck, Paul Luebke, Steven Lukes, Michael Mann,

Wendy Mink, John Mollenkopf, Kenneth Newton, James O'Connor, Claus Offe, Chris Pickvance, Marshall Pomer, Marc Renaud, Alice Robbin, Sidney Tarrow, Charles Tilly, Hayden White, Erik Olin Wright, James D. Wright, and Will Wright.

Important research assistance was rendered in Santa Cruz by Robin Cowan, Eric Fredell, Peter Ibarra, Linda Kimball, Libby Sholes, and Todd Shuman. A year at the Netherlands Institute of Advanced Study in the Humanities and Social Sciences provided indispensable free time for the first author to work on the penultimate draft. The Division of Social Sciences at the University of California at Santa Cruz provided material and moral support for this project almost since its inception. And we deeply appreciate the efforts of the Division word-processing staff, who have patiently and accurately inserted myriads of changes into multiple successive versions made possible by modern computer technology.

Last but not least, we thank Sue Allen-Mills of Cambridge University Press for her faith in the potential of the manuscript.

Introduction
State and society in theoretical perspective

The appropriate powers of the state in Western societies have become a crucial source of political conflict and a topic for theoretical debate. The scope of democratic participation, the capacities of public bureaucracies, the inefficiencies of a regulated capitalist economy, state responses to fiscal crises and structural unemployment have become hotly contested public issues. These political conflicts resonate in the seemingly more dispassionate world of academic discourse. As a result, the state has once again become a central topic for research and theoretical reassessment.

The state and theory

The modern concept of state was formed during the period from the thirteenth to the sixteenth centuries and represented a decisive shift away from the idea of the ruler maintaining his state to the notion of a separate legal and constitutional order – the state – which the ruler had an obligation to maintain.

One effect of this transformation was that the power of the State, not that of the ruler, came to be envisaged as the basis of government. And this in turn enabled the State to be conceptualized in distinctively modern terms – as the sole source of law and legitimate force within its own territory, and as the sole appropriate object of its citizens' allegiances. [Skinner 1978a, p. x]

Therefore, the state is a more fundamental concept than government, because it is not merely the specific regime in power at any one moment – the governing coalition of political leaders – but also the basis for a regime's authority, legality, and claim for popular support.

Political theorist Quentin Skinner goes on to argue that political life itself "sets the main problems for the political theorist, causing a certain range of issues to appear problematic, and a corresponding range of questions to become the leading subjects of debate." But these "ideological superstructures [are not] a straightforward outcome of their social

1

base," since the "intellectual context in which the major texts were conceived" have an important impact on both the included and excluded ideas (Skinner 1978a, p. xi). Skinner uses as an example John Locke's silence on the subject of the prescriptive force of the English Constitution; Locke's silence makes sense only when we know the leading issues of his day. As we shall see in later chapters what is *not* treated in a work is as theoretically significant as its explicit assumptions and hypotheses. Silence carries the corollary that the expected audience will accept or be blind to the absence of treatment of certain issues as historical realities.

According to Skinner, by the beginning of the seventeenth century the "concept of the state – its nature, its powers, its right to command obedience – had come to be regarded as the most important object of analysis in European political thought" (Skinner 1978b, p. 349). The transition to the recognizably modern usage of the term "state" first occurred in France. Skinner argues that this happened because the "material preconditions for such a development were all present: a relatively unified central authority, an increasing apparatus of bureaucratic control, and a clearly defined set of national boundaries" (p. 354). In other words, the state had to exist before the concept of the state could become accepted.[1]

Skinner advocates that concepts be analyzed dialectically as ideologies, in order to connect their historical and theoretical use to political behavior and political practice (1978a, p. xi). Such a method does not presuppose that ideas are not useful or true or that they must mislead ordinary people. It does presume that concepts must be located within the context of a theoretical perspective in which they are used to describe and explain phenomena they abstract from reality. In addition, they play specific social and political roles in the life of the society.

Theories of the state have tended to derive from one or more major theoretical perspectives. The pluralist perspective, which dominates university research and public discourse in the United States today, emphasizes political consensus and the peaceful, evolutionary character of political modernization. Pluralist theories have been criticized by what we shall call the managerial perspective (or elite theory), which maintains that an alliance of elites in military, executive, and corporate bureaucracies has been taking power from traditional democratic institutions of legislatures, parties, and elections. And both perspectives have been challenged by the neo-Marxist class perspective, which sees the state as

---

[1] For a comprehensive review of the relative importance of the idea and the institution of the state in continental Europe in comparison with the Anglo-American countries, see Dyson 1980. Dyson goes so far as to argue that the English-speaking political tradition is "stateless" because it lacks a "historical and legal tradition of the state as an institution that 'acts' in the name of public authority" (p. viii).

determined by its role in a capitalist society. The managerial and class perspectives were always more alive in Europe than in America, because of more centralized state intervention and strong labor and socialist ⌐ political movements in the former. In the United States today, these traditions remain more marginally located. But the basis for a pluralism ✓ of theoretical debate has been laid.

Our main concern in this book is to develop a synthetic framework out of which a new theory of the state can be constructed from these three perspectives, rescuing and integrating the major contributions of each. Each perspective has something to offer to the understanding of the state: The pluralist perspective contributes to a partial understanding of the democratic aspect of the state; the managerial perspective contributes to an understanding of the state's bureaucratic aspect; and the class perspective helps explain the state's capitalist aspect.[2]

Our core argument is that each theoretical perspective on the state has a home domain of description and explanation. That is, the meaning of "state" depends upon whether the vantage point for analysis is individuals, organizations, or societies and also upon the fundamental assumptions made about the relationships among those levels of analysis. Their problematic relationship to each other makes the state an "essentially contested concept" (Gallie 1956). In this introduction we define the home domains of the three perspectives and outline their distinctive views of society, state, power, and politics.

We have not isolated any essence of the state independent of the theoretical perspectives. By superimposing, as it were, the perspectives on each other by means of a language both derived from and critical of each of them, we hope to enrich the powers of theory to understand the state in Western societies. Clarity on the theoretical issues may contribute to a more precise understanding of the potential for new leaders, policies, and social movements to significantly challenge the drift into economic crises, political and cultural repression, and war. We do not

---

[2] Our distinctions among perspectives are common in the social science literature, although the central descriptive terms vary. Sociologist Colin Crouch (1979) called them the "class," "elite," and "interest group" theories; sociologist Randall Collins (1968) the "Marxist," "Weberian," and "functionalist" views of politics; economist Robert Haveman (1973) the "radical political economist," "vested interest," and "pluralist" views. Political scientist Theodore Lowi (1968) distinguished the "social stratification" school that makes the "straightforward Marxian assumption that there is one-to-one relation between socioeconomic status and power over public decision" from the "power elite" school that focuses on the major "orders" of society ("military, industrial and political hierarchies") and the "pluralist" model exemplified by David Truman's *Governmental Process* (1951). English Marxist Perry Anderson (1980, p. 51) distinguished among theories that saw the source of social and political order in "norms and values" (Talcott Parsons), in the "command of a coercive state" with the "capacity to exercise violence" (Jean-Paul Sartre), and in the "dominant mode of production" (Louis Althusser).

believe that theories create politics. Theories motivate people to act and
rationalize those actions afterward. Actions are understood in certain
ways and are believed to have certain kinds of consequences. If the
theory is correct and the conditions under which the action takes place
are compatible with the theory, the intended outcomes are more likely
than not. In this respect, theory has powers.

The home domain of each perspective

The pluralist perspective's home domain is the political behavior of individuals and groups and the influence their interactions have on government decision making. The empirical focus is upon interactions among
citizens, representatives, and officials, particularly as these generate controversial issues that must be decided. The structure and functions of
public and private organizations and the class relations that underly
them are taken as given. Only the interaction of visible actors – whether
individuals or groups – on the political stage is taken into account.
Immediate outcomes are explained by the interaction among the skills,
preferences, and resources of the participants. The resulting political
situations or "events" constitute the core of the pluralist home domain.
This surface of politics glitters with issues and conflicts over who will
be elected, who will be appointed, who will decide, who will resign or
be fired, who gets arrested, tried, and convicted. The headlines portray
these events with a heavy emphasis on the ever-changing cast of char-
acters in the spectacle, or, to change the metaphor, the shifting players
in the political game.

Issues and conflicts are normally contained within the limits of organizational structures and class alignments in a given historical period.
But if individuals, groups, and leaders refuse to remain within the rules
of the game and develop alternative values by which to govern, the
political arena may explode. Mass movements, disruptive demonstrations, rebellions are evidence of a lack of social integration and political
consensus. An explosion of participation is seen as a pathological lack
of appropriately developed political institutions. The pluralist home domain is thus the realm of "normal politics" in which individual actions
in concrete situations can be observed.

When widespread political participation and group competition are
possible, and only "dispersed inequalities" (Dahl 1961) exist in a democratic decision-making system, pluralist concepts are appropriate. Because citizen participation and group contest for influence are not always

possible and democratic institutions are not always effective, the pluralist perspective has serious analytic limits.[3]

The managerial perspective's home domain of explanation is that of single-state organizations, or "interorganizational networks" seen as constituting the state. Such a unit of analysis assumes that organizations have a significant degree of autonomy from society and the individual and group relations that compose them. The empirical focus is upon organizational structures – both inside and outside the state – and the domination of the elites that control their relationships. Immediate outcomes of controversial issues do not necessarily reveal anything about the structure of those organizations. Rather, the managerial perspective focuses on the ways these organizational structures of power protect themselves both from unorganized participation and from the kinds of issues that they cannot manage or control. Explosions of participation are the result of temporary shifts in the balance of organizational power, fragile moments when the structure of state domination has crumbled.

When the organizational boundaries of the state are clear and state bureaucracies have the capacity for control necessary to achieve their goals, the managerial perspective is appropriate. To the extent that the state is bureaucratic and has achieved both sufficient autonomy from and control over the economy and the culture to rationalize its internal operations, managerial concepts are useful. Because state autonomy, control, and rationality are limited in every Western society, the utility of managerial concepts are also limited.

The class perspective's home domain is the relationship among capitalism, the state, and democracy. The social relations between labor and capital are contradictory and ultimately depend for their stability neither upon societal consensus nor upon state legitimation but upon class power to maintain the institutional boundaries between capitalism, the state, and democracy. Explosions of participation – in the voting booth, in the factories, or in the streets – are treated as manifestations of societal contradictions. Modes of production evolve via the contradictory social relations that simultaneously reproduce ideological hegemony and create the conditions for societal transformation via class struggle.

Under historical conditions in which human labor is sold to private

---

[3] The pluralist perspective assumes, we think correctly, that democratic institutions maximize the possibilities for political participation and for all groups to influence state behavior. However, the pluralist perspective, like the class and managerial perspectives, is applicable to societies without such democratic institutions to the extent that political participation is possible at all.

owners of the means of production who exploit that labor to accumulate
capital, and capital accumulation and class struggle shape state policy,
concepts from the class perspective are useful. To the extent that capitalism limits both the efficacy of democracy and the rationality and autonomy of the state bureaucracy, the class perspective is appropriate. It
must, however, be adapted to take account of powerful state intervention into the economy and the seemingly paradoxical rise of trade unions
and working-class parties without socialist transformation in advanced
capitalist societies, as well as nonclass factors in both state and society.

Our view of the state

Each perspective's home domain emphasizes a particular level of analysis: For the pluralist perspective it is the individual; for the managerial,
the organization; and for the class, society. We believe that an adequate
theory of the state must incorporate all three levels of analysis.

The state must be understood first in terms of the contradictory relations among its capitalist, bureaucratic, and democratic aspects, which
constitute the state at the societal level beyond the visible appearances
of legal structures, governmental decision making, and political behavior. Second, the state also can usefully be seen as composed of organizational networks, as structures that differ in their political and legal
capacity to control internal and external resources: funds, personnel,
and political support. Third, the state is also a decision-making arena
within which multiple groups contend for influence, with varying outcomes depending on what interests are at stake, how successfully they
mobilize, and the specific mechanisms of access of those making political
demands upon political leaders.

Our principal task in this book is to analyze the contribution of specific
empirical and historical works that exemplify each theoretical perspective. We shall use each perspective as a source of critical judgment, to
show the logical and empirical disjunctures that appear when different
levels of analysis are not properly distinguished. Almost no works selected for analysis exhibit concepts or hypotheses drawn from only one
perspective.

We limit ourselves primarily to theories and empirical studies of states
in societies considered modern, industrialized, and capitalist. How these
characteristics are related to each other and how they are changing are
the subjects of intense theoretical debate. Although our mode of inquiry
can be applied to societies other than the capitalist democracies in West-

ern Europe and North America, we will not, except in passing, consider studies of non-Western or either precapitalist or socialist societies.[4]

Power and contradictions in the state

Each perspective locates a primary level of analysis at which power operates. For the pluralist perspective, power is situational and is measured by influence over the outcomes of conflictual participation. For the managerial perspective, power is structural and is observed in the capacity of politically biased state and corporate organizations to dominate each other. For the class perspective, power is systemic and is inferred from the reproduction of exploitative social relations.

These levels of power are similar to what Steven Lukes has called the dimensions of power. According to Lukes, the "one-dimensional view of power involves a focus on *behaviour* in the making of *decisions* on *issues* over which there is an observable *conflict* of (subjective) *interests*, seen as . . . policy preferences, revealed by political participation" (1974; p. 15; italics in original). This is the pluralist view of power as influence.

The two-dimensional view, Lukes says, "incorporates into the analysis of power relations the question of the control over the agenda of politics and of the ways in which potential issues are kept out of the political process" (p. 21). In our terms, this is the managerial view of power as domination.

The three-dimensional view, Lukes argues, compensates for the focus on decisions (whether taken or not taken) in both one- and two-dimensional views. The three-dimensional view emphasizes the way in which power is exercised in the absence of any political conflict at all, to benefit the real interests or different elements of the population *without any political participation*. Lukes describes the origins of this form of power in several rather general ways, as "social forces," "institutional practices," "collective forces," "social arrangements" (1974, pp. 22, 24). In Lukes's opinion, the three-dimensional view of power adds to the other

---

[4] Some important theoretical debates concern the development of less advanced states as laboratories by which to understand the history of the West. Many controversies have occurred over whether or not the underdeveloped Third World countries can be expected simply to repeat the emergence in Western societies of democratic, bureaucratic, and capitalist states. Such "modernization" was one of the chief tenets of the pluralist perspective in the 1950s and early 1960s. The stability of many undemocratic regimes, the inability of many new nations to create stable bureaucratic state structures, and the unwillingness of many of these societies to follow the capitalist path has fundamentally challenged those premises. We shall not deal with the controversy directly, although we believe that most of the arguments concerning the new states are still couched in the language of one or more of the theoretical perspectives on Western states.

two views the critical element of showing how the very wishes and perceptions of the population – their political consciousness – are shaped or stunted, so that their real interests are not served; they are not even aware of other possibilities. The "normal" functioning of a particular social order creates "submission and intellectual subordination" among a population. In our language, this is the class view of power as hegemony.

Every contemporary political situation, we believe, always involves all three levels of power and cannot be fully understood without a synthetic analysis incorporating all three. Their relative importance in consciousness and action depends upon specific historical and political conditions. The meeting of the president's cabinet, for example, to decide whether or not to invade Vietnam can be seen as simultaneously involving all three levels of power. Its situational component is the contest within a group (the cabinet) for influence over decisions. Personality factors, overt and covert bargains, career contingencies, and political skills all play a role in the immediate outcome. Its structural component is the conflict between government agencies – the army and navy, civilian and military, executive and legislature – over resources and the role of legitimate proponent of a popular policy (or opponent of an unpopular one). The decision would be seen as a competition for national prestige in a balance of power between nations or as an opening gun in a future electoral contest between competing parties.

The systemic component of the decision to invade Vietnam is the historical context of socialist development elsewhere in the world, which has long-term consequences for the possibility of reproducing capitalism in the United States. The decision at this level of analysis would be seen in terms of its consequences for international capitalist control over raw materials and labor markets in the Far East, and for the power of capitalism to expand into less developed areas of the world economy to compensate for domestic tendencies toward economic crisis. The exclusion of dominated classes from access to the decision would be taken for granted, partly because of the systemic consequences of the decision.

Such an event cannot therefore be understood adequately in terms of pluralist concepts of "decision-making" in groups or in terms only of the managerial language of "institutional conflict" between organizations. The context of a world system of capitalist production creates the historical conditions in which certain institutions exist and therefore decision-making situations become more or less probable. As we shall argue in Chapter 17, it is a mistake to collapse levels of analysis (and therefore levels of explanation) into each other.

Although each perspective takes one level of analysis and thus one level of power as primary, each perspective recognizes that power has multiple sources. Accordingly, within each perspective there is an internal debate on the conditions under which the organizational instruments of the state are shaped either by their societal function or by political action. The functional and political relations between state and society, which constitute the central contradiction in the state within each perspective, are charted in Table 1. In the first three parts of this book, we analyze the aspect of the state and the contradiction within it that each perspective takes to be central.

In the pluralist perspective, moderate democratic participation (Chapter 4) within a consensual political culture (Chapter 3) leads to a governable state. Situational participation must occur within a functioning consensus. The tension between *participation* and *consensus* is mediated by the party system and by governmental leadership socialized to balance between group demands and the public interest. Excessive participation or a breakdown of consensus creates the key issue of the *governance* of the society. Then, Chapters 5 and 6 present the pluralist perspective on the bureaucratic and capitalist aspects of the state.

In the managerial perspective, bureaucratic centralization dominates the overall historical development of the state in industrial societies (Chapter 8). Powerful organizations and interests irrationally fragment the state at a time when the technical capacity of an autonomous state to monitor a fast-changing, increasingly complex society is most critical, creating a conflict between private and public rationality (Chapter 9). New, "corporatist" forms of interest aggregation arise to manage this conflict between *centralization* and *fragmentation*. The central issue for the state is *elite capacity* – finding mechanisms that can coordinate both pressures toward centralization and the capacity of organized interests to fragment state authority. Then, Chapters 10 and 11 present the managerial perspective on the democratic and capitalist aspects of the state.

In the class perspective, capitalist accumulation constrains state structure and state policy (Chapter 13). Class struggle – resistance, protest, revolt, or simply the strategic withdrawal of labor power – challenges the hegemony of the production relations between capital and labor (Chapter 14). The actual and potential power of the working class must be subordinated to the requirements of crisis management by the state. This contradiction between the imperatives of *capital accumulation* and *class struggle* is mediated by state fiscal dependency upon taxation of private incomes and by the structural segregation of functions critical to capital accumulation from those functions that absorb working-class political struggles. This contradiction within the society as a whole leads to the central issue for the state: the constant possibility of economic and political crises. Then, Chapters 15 and 16 present the class perspective on the democratic and bureaucratic aspects of the state.

Within each perspective, the contradictions between societal functions

Table 1. *Power and contradiction in perspectives on the state*

Level of power	Theoretical perspective		
	Pluralist	Managerial	Class
Situational power Specific strate-gies of political action to influ-ence govern-ment decisions	Voters and di-verse groups compete for in-fluence in politi-cal situations	Organizational elites use re-sources at critical junctures	Agents of capital and labor strug-gle in historical conjunctures
Structural power The internal or-ganization of the state	The state is a highly differen-tiated mosaic of agencies and programs acces-sible to influence	The state is an autonomous, coercive, techno-cratic administra-tion with legal authority, nego-tiating with pri-vate organiza-tions	The state has a distinctive form that reproduces capitalist social relations
Systemic power The societal functions of the state	A consensual value system de-fines the bound-aries of state action	A complex, changing society creates technical and resource constraints on the state	Capitalist tend-ency to economic and political cri-sis limits the he-gemony of both state and capital
State structure			
in the state (functional versus political relations)	Tension between *consensus* and *participation*	Conflict between *centralization* and *fragmentation*	Contradiction be-tween *accumula-tion* and *class struggle*
Central issue for the state	Governance	Elite capacity	Crisis
Central types of politics	Liberal and conservative	Reform and reactionary	Socialist and fascist

Note: In each perspective, all three levels of power are regarded as important, although each perspective focuses upon one level of power as primary. In each, the structure of the state is a consequence of both policy responses to political demands and societal constraints upon state structure.

and the historical possibilities for political action are accommodated, managed, or mediated by the structure of the state. The state is seen as the thermostatic instrument for reproduction of the social order, as an agency managing social conflict, or as a potentially explosive focus of societal contradictions.

In Chapter 17 we stand back from the perspectives and deal with the underlying issue of powers of theory to analyze the state in society. We shall use our exposition and critique of each perspective to consider the requirements for an adequate framework for a theory of the state in Western societies.

In Chapter 18 we use this theoretical framework to consider critically the types of politics that seek to control the state. The dominance of particular strategic coalitions must be understood in the context of specific historical conditions that create the possibilities for particular kinds of political actions.

In Chapter 19 we analyze the internal and external contradictions in the state. Our argument is that at the societal level of analysis the state in these societies is best understood in terms of contradictory relations among capitalism, bureaucracy, and democracy. These relations can only be explained historically. In brief, capitalist growth requires autonomous bureaucratic and democratic institutions and yet limits their functioning. The capitalist, bureaucratic, and democratic aspects of the state are insulated from each other and yet depend upon each other for their own internal functioning. Power at the societal level inheres in contradictory institutional interrelationships.

By this argument we do not mean to imply that bureaucracy requires either democracy or capitalism or that democracy requires capitalism or bureaucracy. We believe that the relations among these three institutional logics are both symbiotic and historically limited. One of the fundamental silences of all three theoretical perspectives – one that is perhaps inevitable – concerns the limits and conditions of these relations.

The logics of capitalism, bureaucracy, and democracy

A concrete example may help clarify the logics of capitalism, bureaucracy, and democracy and make clear that our distinctions are not purely academic but apply in public discourse. By a "logic" we mean a set of practices – behaviors, institutional forms, ideologies – that have social functions and are defended by politically organized interests. Individual actors may not be aware of these logics.

In 1979 a conflict erupted over whether or not a California state agency (the Department of Transportation, CALTRANS for short) should sell homes it had acquired several years before back to the local residents –

some of whom still lived in the same houses – at below-market prices. (A planned freeway had been abandoned.) While approval was being debated by the agency, inflation pushed housing prices up past the point where the residents could afford to buy them back. Which should prevail – the logic of capitalism (market prices), the logic of bureaucracy (agency jurisdictions), or the logic of democracy (the rights of citizens to participate in critical decisions)?

The actual headline of the *Los Angeles Times* article (January 22, 1979) that described the incident illustrates the logic of democracy: NEIGHBORHOOD FIGHTS FOR ITS HOMES. The implication of this headline was that community residents have an inalienable right to maintain their neighborhood and to appeal to their legislative representatives for support on that basis. Their political participation therefore has a claim superseding bureaucratic rules and law, as well as any market rights. The community residents called upon the state bureaucracy to "understand the simple fact" that they were only protecting their basic human rights and asked them to act as if they were "public servants," recognizing the supreme value of what people need in their daily lives. The community residents activated the city council, their representatives in the state assembly, and even other state agencies to support their appeal to CALTRANS to allow repurchase of their homes at below-market prices.

If the *Times* had chosen to emphasize the logic of capitalism, the headline might have been: PUBLIC MONEY USED TO PREVENT MARKET COMPETITION IN HOUSING. The market values had already risen on the houses. Because the residents no longer owned them, they had no special claim on the housing if they did not have the income to purchase or rent them when they came back on the market. Markets are impersonal and should operate independently of state action. The state should not interfere with the housing market, which will in the long run operate efficiently to increase the supply of appropriately priced housing if only freed to operate. CALTRANS acted appropriately in building highways as an infrastructure for transportation but should only use the market to deal with the new situation by having the houses appraised and sold at the market price to the highest bidder.

If the *Times* had chosen to emphasize the logic of bureaucracy, STATE AGENCIES ASKED TO BREAK THE LAW might be the headline. State agencies cannot single out a particular group to benefit from its actions, unless that benefit is spelled out in the relevant legislation. Otherwise, as a CALTRANS spokesman said, they might get into endless lawsuits. And the state agency must not act outside the framework of its enabling legislation, precisely in order to render the agency more accountable to the public. Delays may indeed occur, because agencies must follow orderly procedures within the law, even if individuals and families are hurt by the delays. Other state agencies that became involved could afford to be critical of CALTRANS because their own procedures and rules were not involved, but they would suffer the same delays if their own internal operations were being challenged. "These things take time," when a new set of rules is being established. Agencies cannot operate as if every decision were unique but must make decisions in a way that will maximize the chances of routinizing future similar decisions. The delays caused now may speed up similar disposals of property if a set of rules can be devised that covers most contingencies. One bureaucracy (the Department of Housing and Community Development, pleading for the below-market sale) cannot simply ask another (CALTRANS) to use its own internal decision-making rules because the rules of one agency have an internal coherence – whether politically or administratively decided – that cannot instantly be changed without consideration of the consequences.

As events developed, a coalition developed among the residents (via the Route 2 Tenants Association), a state agency (the Department of Housing and Community Development), a community organization (the Los Angeles Community Design Center), and representatives of two legislatures (the state senate and the Los Angeles City Council), against another state agency (CALTRANS). The courts (in this case, the attorney general functioning as a judge) supported the coalition by ruling that the tenants' claim to their homes overrode market-value housing prices as well as Article XI of the state constitution, which provided that highway trust funds cannot be used for anything except highway purposes.

The content of the *Times* article was consistent with the headline, favoring the logic of democracy. Criticizing the logic of capitalism, the writer referred to "windfall profits," as if profits were bad. Criticizing the logic of bureaucracy, the writer referred to "bureaucratic babble," as if most legal and official language were nonsense. The community was described as an "occupied territory," as if the official state agencies did not have legitimate jurisdiction over the entire population and territory of California. If written from the point of view of the logic of capitalism or bureaucracy, the article would have used a totally different rhetoric, potentially evoking quite different responses in its readers.

Conclusions

Our argument, as we have already said, assumes that there is some validity in all three perspectives. Our concern is not with the politics of language – with the ideological content and uses of words to convince and mystify – but rather with the language of politics – the different ways in which theories of the state are conveyed by the language in which they are couched, and the way language itself carries the content of the theories. What is seen and what is said are related. Both are theoretically constructed.

1

Theoretical perspectives as modes of inquiry

The home domain of each theoretical perspective comprises a particular level of analysis, world view, and method.[1] In addition, each perspective has a distinctive view of key societal dimensions, the state, and its most important relations with society. Table 2 summarizes these elements of the mode of inquiry of each perspective. We shall show through detailed critical examination of actual empirical inquiries where the analysis is strong on a particular home domain and how it becomes weak when it leaves that domain without the appropriate conceptual adjustments.

Our own position is that individual interests, motivations, and perceptions can never adequately explain individual behavior. Both organizational and societal factors must be taken into account in explaining variations in rates of individual behavior occurring in different types of situations. But the reverse is not possible – one cannot explain organizational or societal processes by theories of individual behavior or social interaction. Nor can organizational relations explain the totality of social relations.[2]

---

[1] What we are calling "world view" the late Alvin Gouldner called "domain assumptions" in his critical work on American sociology (1970). Gouldner's own domain assumptions led him, unfortunately, to consider sociology a far more autonomous intellectual and theoretical system than is warranted (chaps. 2, 13). His own work "resonates," to use one of his favorite words, much more broadly with social theory in general. Gouldner artificially and unnecessarily limited his critique to sociology.

[2] Sociologist Jeffrey Alexander has recently distinguished the "metaphysical environment" (which we call the world view) from the "empirical environment" (which we call the level of analysis) of science. He correctly refuses to make a sharp and qualitative distinction between them. Without suggesting that this is a rigid continuum or hierarchy, Alexander uses such words as "models," "concepts," "definitions," "classifications," and "propositions" to designate the intermediate stages between world view and level of analysis. As he says, every specific actual statement is influenced by metaphysical presuppositions, even when those are completely implicit (1982, p. 4). Because our concern is with applying these epistemological concepts to substantive analyses of the state in Western societies, we shall not deal in detail with this issue.

15

Table 2. *Theoretical perspectives and elements of a mode of inquiry*

Elements of a mode of inquiry	Home domain of each perspective		
	Pluralist	Managerial	Class
Level of analysis	Individual	Organizational	Societal
World views (relations between levels)			
Functional relations	Integrated social system	Rationalized structures	Mode of production
Political relations	Interactions and exchanges	Organizational conflict	Class struggle
Method	Interrelated processes in open systems	Dominant causes within structures	Contradictory relations within a totality
Central societal process	Differentiation in a modernizing society	Rationalization of a mode of domination in an industrializing society	Accumulation within a capitalist mode of production
Key dimension of society	Cultural (values)	Political (power)	Economic (class)
Relation between state and society	Interdependent, both cooperative and tensionful	Interorganizational, subject to both authority and conflict	Inter-institutional, both hegemonic and crisis-ridden
Key aspect of the state	Democratic	Bureaucratic	Capitalist

Levels of analysis

Each perspective distinguishes in its own way among three levels of analysis: individual, organizational, and societal. Each perspective regards one of the levels as central and interprets the other levels from the vantage point of that level. This is the limit of each perspective's powers, exercised in its home domain.

The societal level refers to the interinstitutional relations within and between whole societies. The concept of "institution" refers to a pattern of supraorganizational relations stable enough to be described – polity, family, economy, religion, culture. Each perspective has its own concepts to describe the societal level, although it is the home domain only for the class perspective. The concepts "social formation," "world economy," and "political economy" portray a total society (or even a global system of societies). The societal contradictions of class, a concept presuming interinstitutional relations, are seen as imprinted in the operation of all institutions.

Within the pluralist perspective, the concepts "modern," "social structure," or "culture" convey an image of society as an aggregate of interacting individuals socialized into cultural values and engaging in diverse communications and exchanges, especially in markets. In the managerial perspective, the concepts of "industrial society" and "institutional realm" convey an implicit image of a society as a set of organizations commanded by elites, within a complex environment in which resources are scarce.

The organizational level refers to the formation and operation of formal, bounded bureaucratic structures within a society. Such contrasting concepts as formal versus informal, complex versus simple, bureaucratic versus patrimonial, private verses public, legal versus illegal, large versus small, and centralized versus decentralized are all used to compare attributes of organizations. Each theoretical perspective empirically recognizes organizations, and the state qua an organization, but they are the theoretical home domain only of the managerial perspective. In the pluralist perspective, organizations are seen as associations based on voluntary choice, as aggregates of individuals, as coalitions of interest groups, but not as instruments of domination. In the class perspective, they are seen as agents of class interests, as the embodiment of the relations between capital and labor, or as surrogates for more powerful class forces but are not themselves powerful and autonomous actors. Both pluralist and class perspectives would argue that the assumption of organizational autonomy reifies the unit of analysis, because the matrix of group or class relations that generate organizations is ignored.

Within and between organizations and societies, individuals act in wonderfully diverse ways: living and dying, loving and building, buying and selling, fighting and making peace, forming friendships and coalitions, joining and leaving groups. The interactions of individuals within small groups and concrete situations constitute the individual level of analysis. Through individual competition and reciprocal interaction, roles are filled and the system of roles and norms governing their performance is continuously differentiated. Although each perspective recognizes individual actions, the individual level is theoretically primary only for the pluralist perspective.

For the managerial perspective, individuals are seen as part of the masses, as clients and members, or as elites – officials occupying a formal position within an organization or enjoying informal, unofficial power. In the class perspective, individuals are either agents of classes, "bearers" of class relations, or occupants of class locations. The distinctive qualities of individual consciousness and the dynamics of interaction are not theorized, although they are empirically recognized.

World view

A world view consists of the assumptions within a given perspective about the relations among levels of analysis. Each perspective analyzes individuals, organizations, and societies via a special image of their relations. In each perspective, there is a tension between the emergent logic of the social system as a whole (the functional approach) and the purposeful actions of those units composing the system (the political approach).

Functional approaches assume highly constrained if not completely determined relationships among levels of analysis. In addition, they assume that the individual, organizational, or societal process can be analyzed independently of its composition or context. Public-choice theories, for instance, assume that the interactions of individuals in markets can be generalized across diverse institutional settings. Structuralist organizational theories assume that abstract qualities of technology and tasks or goals can account for general configurations of organizational authority. Functionalist Marxists argue that the dynamics of a mode of production can be understood independently of the content of state policy and the contingent outcomes of political conflict, because these are in the last analysis determined by the logic of capital. The two principal attributes of the functional approach – the lack of autonomy of levels of analysis and the positing of their "laws of motion" independently of context or composition – are related, because a pure functional approach reifies the central level of analysis.

A pure political approach, by contrast, makes the opposite assumptions on both counts, holding that the levels of analysis have autonomy and that the relations among them are open and contingent. Typically, the interactions among individuals, organizations, and classes are seen as explanations of the ways in which markets, states, and societies change. These interactions are contingent on changing historical circumstances, which make it impossible to ascribe laws of structure, function, or change to a particular level of analysis per se. In addition, political approaches tend to focus on the tensions, conflicts, and contradictions within social relations rather than argue that a structure or system has functional properties that can be independently described. Thus different levels of analysis are approached in a more historical, open-ended manner.

Political pluralist analyses focus on the unique historical contingencies that actors must take into account in deciding how to realize their preferences in political and economic marketplaces, especially political and economic entrepreneurs with new public and private goods. Political managerial analyses assume that organizational elites make strategic choices that shape public and private organizations and reshape the organizational alliances that compose state power structures. Political class analyses assume that historically contingent patterns of class struggle decisively affect capitalist development, as well as the probability of economic crises and societal transformation. Corporate technologies and social production are shaped by the history of class struggle. But these are debates *within* the respective world views.

The pluralist view, whether functional or political in emphasis, is that social systems are constituted by the interdependencies among individuals who occupy roles differentiated by function and integrated by values. Yet the individual actions and exchanges by which this system is created have the potential to transform the normative basis of that system.

In the generic managerial view, a society is composed of dominant organizational structures and increasingly dominated by one bureaucracy, the state. Individual behavior can best be understood in terms of positions and resources within organizations. Yet the power conflicts by which organizations are rationalized have the potential to transform the institutional structure of society.

The fundamental argument of the class perspective is that societies are reproduced by the material constraints inherent in a mode of production. Organizations can best be understood as agents of class interests, and individuals as owners, workers, or occupants of contradictory class locations. Yet, even when class struggle is channeled into forms that spur the development of the forces of production and compel the state to attempt to regulate the system, it retains the capacity to revolutionize the social relations of production.

Such world views are broader than the concept of "paradigm" made popular by philosopher of science Thomas Kuhn (1962), but they partake of the same qualities: a set of assumptions that become taken for granted by the investigator as the parameters or the context of a concrete analysis. What is *not* looked at – the "silence" of the inquiry – can be as important as what is explicitly argued on the basis of evidence.

Whether different levels of analysis are integrated by values, controlled by dominant structures, or potentially transformed by the contradictions of a mode of production usually remains a latent assumption in concrete empirical studies. Most works on the state do not take an explicit stand on these issues. Their world view remains implicit. Some would even reject the necessity of explicit discussion of these issues,

assuming that establishing valid relations among concepts and data –
not to mention the heavy labor of gathering relevant data – is difficult
enough without worrying about such "philosophical" issues. Critically
evaluating the presuppositions of empirical inquiry is sometimes rejected
as either ideological or outside the boundaries of science. We believe,
on the contrary, that the assessment of the validity of empirical generalizations is furthered by an understanding of the world view underlying
them.

The concept of "level of analysis" is itself an abstraction, of course.
The "individual" is abstracted from real, living human beings in order
to define social roles or identities. An "organization," similarly, is inferred from the artifacts that mark its existence: laws creating a program,
the physical location of an office, a letterhead announcing its identity.
"Societies" and their contradictions, equally, are not visible but are inferred from their presumed causes and consequences. Nevertheless, the
distinction among levels of analysis helps clarify the differences among
the theoretical perspectives on the state.[3]

This concept neglects an important distinction between levels of analysis and levels of abstraction, as Table 3 demonstrates. We have ignored
the unique entities at each level of analysis except as empirical references,
in order to theorize the relations between instances of institutional types
and systemic entities at each level of analysis. Our conceptual framework
would have been overloaded – it is complex enough – if we had attempted to take account of this distinction at every point, but we do not
believe that it would have affected many important arguments.

How the relations between levels are theorized in both "directions"
depends on one's world view. The directions in which constraints and

---

[3] The significance of the distinction among levels of analysis goes beyond that of theoretical
clarity. We argue that it is critically important in assessing the significance of empirical
research. Some recent studies claiming to conduct quantitative research within a Marxian
world view have conflated the levels of analysis. (See Alexander 1982, for a detailed
critique of conflation.) An example is a study of the correlation of attitudes toward
criminal injustice with race and occupation (Hagen and Albonetti 1982). The dependent
variable is the attitudes toward equality of treatment of accused criminals by different
segments of the state (police, law enforcement officials, judges, courts, juries). The
authors found that blacks were more likely to perceive criminal injustice than whites
and that unemployed persons were more likely to do so regardless of race. The theoretical
explanation is entirely social-psychological, in terms of individual perceptions, sensitiv-
ities, consciousness, and experiences appropriate for their data at the individual level.
The study translates standard survey and census classifications into Marxist language
but shifts levels of analysis. Unemployed persons become the "surplus population";
officials, managers, professionals, and proprietors become the "professional-managerial
class." Nonowning skilled and unskilled workers become the "working class." Theoretical interpretation of their interesting findings is misleading if the characteristics of
individuals are aggregated to form a concept of class at the societal level. Conversely,
pluralist analyses have always used the term "class," but in the sense of stratification:
multiple hierarchies of status, income, occupation, education, and so on.

Table 3. *Levels of analysis and levels of abstraction*[a]

| Level of analysis | Level of abstraction | | |
	Unique entity	Instance of an institutional type	Systemic entity or generic process
Individual	Roger Friedland	Sociologist	Intellectual
	Ronald Reagan	President	Presidency
	Lee Iacocca	Executive	Capitalist/ businessman
Organizational	Friedland family	Families	The family
	General Motors	Corporations	Capital
	United Auto Workers	Trade unions	Labor
	Department of Housing	Federal agencies	State bureaucracy
Societal	Americans	Nations	Culture
	United States	States	The state
	"World capitalist economy"	Social formations	Mode of production

[a] We are indebted to Erik Olin Wright for forcefully calling to our attention the distinction between levels of analysis and levels of abstraction. Processes as well as units can be classified in the same way. The Flint sit-down of 1936 is an instance of a strike and also of collective disruption or class struggle, depending on one's world view, which includes a theory of comparative instances and historical consequences.

determinations are assumed to flow and how much autonomy the properties of each level are believed to have from the properties of other levels *define* one's world view and influence both the choice of empirical data and the labels one places upon them. They do not *determine* the data, however. This scheme does not therefore imply that theories are immune from empirical confirmation or disconfirmation.

Method

Each perspective also has a typical method of inquiry. Frequently, in the course of an inquiry, the theoretical assumptions that justify the choice of particular types of data and their interpretation are left implicit. In subsequent chapters, we shall show from detailed analysis of particular works how the method flows from a focus upon a particular level of analysis and world view.

For the pluralist perspective, multiple processes interact within a system or subsystem. The social system can be observed in the actions of individuals in interaction. In the functional approach, the actions and perceptions of individuals and groups inside and outside the state are used to make inferences about the requirements of a social system. In the political approach, explanations are sought in terms of historically variable beliefs and actions. National political cultures imprinted in individuals reflect past group conflicts and the conditions of origin of a nation, such as frontier opportunities and the absence of a feudal agrarian structure in the formation of the American nation. Both great leaders and the actions of political entrepreneurs affect the trajectory of a national political system, and in this sense the system and its politics are interdependent.

Pluralist inquiries are likely to be concrete, focusing upon specific actions, using language that has become common sense about the influence of motives and intentions in situations. Attitude surveys of the perceptions and values of leaders and voters are frequent. Sampling is necessary in order to discover the typical variable characteristics of groups and populations.[4]

For the managerial perspective, dominant causes are sought for structures of significant variables. Comparative analyses of complex organizations attempt to specify the causes and consequences of state structure and policy. It is assumed that public organizations, including whole national states, can be compared. In the functional variant of managerial inquiries, organizations are treated as systems determined by technology, tasks and environment. "Input–output" models assume, for example, that organizational attributes lead to greater or lesser outputs and that these outputs can be measured. Sometimes the entire state–society relation is analyzed as an interorganizational system with particular structural attributes.

In the political variant, key informants are used to locate the strategic decisions made by elites that decisively shape the structure of the organizations over which they exercise control. Organizational structures, including the state, reflect the historical and thus contingent conditions of their origin, and these structures do not automatically adapt as those conditions change (Stinchcombe 1968). Further, state elites make strategic decisions to raise particular issues, mobilize particular constituencies, or intervene in particular ways in the operations of private

---

[4] The pluralist method can be either qualitative or quantitative. Narrative historiography relies upon a qualitative method, highlighting the actions of named individuals in unique situations. Survey analysis relies upon a quantitative method that analyzes the responses of anonymous individuals assigned various social attributes (income, sex, occupation, for example). Both are pluralist, in the sense that the implicit world view is frequently that the imputed actions, beliefs, and values of individuals are the primary level of analysis, with organizational and societal contexts seen from the vantage point of individuals, or ascribed to them as a membership, in an environment that creates incentives or pressures for certain kinds of perceptions, beliefs, and behaviors.

organizations that are not mechanically determined by the tasks, technologies, or environment of the state (Child 1972). Organizational histories and strategic decisions of elites are of extraordinary importance.

Central to the class perspective is the method of dialectical materialism, which assumes that man's productive relationship to nature and the resultant relationships with other human beings form the essential character of entire societies, and therefore the state. The origin of these social relations is obscured, which leads them to be reified, because conventional meanings and institutionally enforced definitions tend to distort proper conceptualization. Because of the contradictory nature of class societies, particularly capitalist societies, explosive ruptures – riots, strikes, crises, and revolutions – reveal the inner logic of society. During such historical moments, latent contradictions are revealed, and transformation of seemingly eternal and unchanging truths seems possible. Such moments are critical units of observation for the class perspective, clarifying the essential character of the social relations that define a mode of production.

In political class approaches, the patterning of class struggle in different capitalist societies at various historical conjunctures is the central object of analysis. These patterns shape the dynamics of a mode of production and the resultant forms of state behavior, as well as the transformations between modes of production and types of states. In functional class approaches, institutional practices and society–state relationships are assumed to reproduce capitalist society. Class struggles only reveal the socially structured possibilities of what can be achieved within the limits of a mode of production, including the possibility of transformation to another mode of production. The considerable variation among capitalist states with the same mode of production and the same level of development of productive forces is regarded as relatively unimportant, giving typical functional class analyses a highly abstract quality.

Central societal process

Each world view makes certain assumptions about the central societal process, which differs from each perspective and within the context of which each perspective sees all other processes. These assumptions determine how society – and the state – is defined (as modern, industrial, or capitalist) and define the relationship among different levels of analysis. They also delineate those conditions that lie outside the home domain of a given perspective and are therefore presumed to be transitory, abnormal, accidental, or simply not appropriate for analysis. The conditions not theorized tend to be the ones that are the central focus of the other perspectives.

Processes of individual and group political participation are the central focus only for the pluralist perspective. Neither the managerial nor the class perspective focuses upon individual and/or group actions as a theoretically important problem. Ironically, the class perspective has never successfully developed a theory of "class-for-itself," involving as it does an explanation of group identification and individual adult political socialization, as distinct from "class-in-itself," which is based on objective interests grounded in relations of production.

The structure of organized power inside and outside the state is central only for the managerial perspective. Neither the pluralist nor the class perspective has ever made the state, qua state, a central object of theoretical inquiry. For both, the state is conceptualized as either a reproductive organ of the social order or a medium that either aggregates preferences or mediates class struggle. Under particular historical conditions, the state may assume great importance, not because it has become a core theoretical object but because it has come to be ungovernable or a source of crisis.

The central focus of the class perspective is interinstitutional contradictions and their dialectical transformation through class struggle. Only class theory has developed a political economy in the sense of a systemic theory of state–society relations. For pluralist theory, "political economy" refers to the generalization of market relations to political phenomena, as in its preoccupation with theories of social choice or public choice. Or, institutional realms are assumed to be sufficiently differentiated that they can be analyzed in isolation. Managerial theorists do not derive a societal logic from their organizational studies of state agencies, private firms, or agency–firm relations.

The societal conditions that each perspective explains in systemic terms are regarded as abnormal, special, or historically transitory by the other perspectives, which assign them a secondary causal status. From a pluralist perspective, societal consensus and government representation of differentiated groups are explained by historical processes of modernization. In both managerial and class perspectives, popular identifications with the state or with local political party organizations are products of elite manipulation or false consciousness deriving from the illusory universality of the capitalist state.

From a managerial perspective, the increasing rationalization of the state, its centralization and growing control over society, derives from the historical process of industrialization. From a pluralist perspective, it is a pathological development, an overstepping of the proper functions of government and a failure to restrain the private interests of public bureaucrats. From a class perspective, it represents a desperate attempt to manage the contradictions of capitalism and may even presage a transformation of the institutional structure of society away from democracy or even toward socialism.

From a class perspective, capitalist accumulation and class struggle leading to economic crisis represent the core historical process. From pluralist and managerial perspectives, class formation, noninstitutionalized social movements, and crisis are pathological. For pluralism, they indicate blockages to individual opportunity and differentiation or lack of representation. For the managerial perspective, they indicate an ill-constructed state structure or strategic failures of control by state elites. Class struggle and economic crisis are not systemic for either the pluralist or the managerial perspective.

As we shall show in Chapter 18, these societal conditions are also those that are most propitious for particular types of politics. Because of the power of particular theories to make sense of those conditions, politics tend to have specific theoretical content.

Dimensions of society

Each perspective also has its own interpretation of three fundamental dimensions of society: cultural, political, and economic. The cultural dimension of society is central to the pluralist perspective, whose explanations refer to cultural values and beliefs that pattern and give meaning to the interactions of individuals. Organizations and societies and their political and economic dimensions are interpreted from the standpoint of individuals socialized into a culture. The pluralist perspective stresses the values that inhere in patterns of social relations. Deeply felt and widely shared values are seen as necessary to sustain the essential quality of an institution over time.

The political dimension of society is central to the managerial perspective because it focuses on the power relations within and among networks of organizations and the elites who command them. A "party" or "power structure" consists of a relatively permanent alliance mobilizing resources to achieve certain goals, an important one being the preservation of the power structure itself. Individuals and societies and their cultural and economic dimensions are interpreted from the standpoint of resources managed by elites. The managerial perspective also stresses the buttressing of political relations by legal authority and organizational resources. Legality reinforces a pattern of social relations if the authority of the state – via the police or the army – enforces a claim or punishes a violation of a rule.

The economic dimension of society is central to the class perspective, whose analysis centers on the class relations deriving from the mode of production historically developed in a society. A "society" consists of the social relations deriving from the material conditions of human life. Organizations and individuals and the political and cultural (ideological) dimensions of society are interpreted from the standpoint of their consequences for the reproduction or the transformation of class relations and the mode of production. The class perspective stresses the ways in which given patterns of social relations both reinforce and undermine the social order and are thus contradictory.

The state and society

Each perspective has its own version of a debate over whether the state is an "entity" or a "relation." This in part turns on the degree to which a state must be seen as a set of organizations separate from society. If the state is an entity, with legal authority and a monopoly on legal violence, then one can legitimately refer to public and private spheres and distinguish among the state, the economy, and culture. This language presupposes the existence of the state as a separate set of institutions, organizations, or functions, which are affected by interest groups, elites, or class agents.

The opposite view, again with its particular version within each perspective, is of the state as a "relation," expressing values, interests, and imperatives that cannot be understood in any meaningful way except as part of the whole society. The state may appear to be a relatively autonomous set of institutions and organizations (legislatures, courts, administrative agencies, executive bodies), but even such legal entities are an outcome of forces that cannot be understood if the problem is already defined away by assuming the state to be an autonomous entity. The boundary line in law and politics that distinguishes lawful and legitimate action from unlawful and illegitimate action is seen itself in this view to be the changing outcome of common values, elite strategies, or class rule. The boundary between public and private spheres of authority is regarded as the continuous focus of group demands, elite conflict, and class struggle.

The power of concepts

As this compressed summary of the contrasts and similarities between these theoretical perspectives indicates, the key concepts in each perspective refer to historically developed usages that have come to symbolize different aspects of social life. Our position is close to that of Raymond Williams, the English cultural historian, who asserts that the critical analysis of key concepts is an exploration of the vocabulary of a crucial area of social and cultural discussion, which has been inherited within precise historical and social conditions and which has to be made at once conscious and critical – subject to change as well as to continuity – if the millions of people in whom it is active are to see it as active: not a *tradition* to be learned, nor a *consensus* to be accepted, nor a set of meanings which, because it is "our language," has a natural authority; but as a shaping and reshaping, in real circumstances and from profoundly different and important points of view: a vocabulary to use, to find our ways in, to change as we find it necessary to change it, as we go on making our own language and history. [1976, pp. 21–2; italics in original]

Williams holds a class perspective on the politics of language; he says that "many crucial meanings have been shaped by a dominant class." Language not only is shaped by class interests but also is subject to active struggle and reflects "profoundly different and important points of view" (p. 21). Concepts are historical. The choice of concepts therefore contains political judgments.

In this view, concepts are properties of the social relations of production of knowledge. Concepts are historically transformed under specific conditions that vary with the class location of both writer and audience. Paradigms of inquiry become part of the substructure of meanings, which may disappear into the underpinnings of a discipline as its ideology. The very institutional differentiation of "economics" from "history" and from "sociology" is evidence of the way the historical development of capitalist society creates special languages that render certain kinds of intellectual problems invisible. Divisions of intellectual labor thereby reinforce institutional structures. If those problems were made visible by definitions using critical concepts, they would create opposition to the dominant institutions of the society.

The pluralist perspective, by contrast, sees language as an incremental and consensual evolution of usages, as the creation of a common cultural tradition conveying shared meanings and values. Concepts are indicators of events or behaviors. The power of a concept is its influence, its ability to persuade readers or listeners that it is true or to win in a debate over the logic or evidence of another argument. A concept is more powerful if people argue over its meaning and someone succeeds in defining it in ways to which others consent. Dictionaries represent a majority vote about common usage that decides which meanings are standard and which idiomatic or obsolete.

The managerial perspective sees language as an instrument, as a resource for human beings to use in dealing with a complex world. Accordingly, definitions of concepts have rational authority. Concepts constitute the building blocks of a structure of interrelated explanations that have greater or lesser utility or impact. Scientific, intellectual, philosophical, and literary elites enforce a paradigmatic structure of explanation, which sometimes controls even the information-gathering capacities of non-elites. Concepts become part of the legitimate and even mandatory vocabulary of analysis within sectors of a field. Articles in journals, papers read at professional meetings, the appropriate language of a grant proposal, the criteria for tenure are the communication channels for the power of concepts. Critics of the "democratic" approach to the construction of dictionaries argue that there are criteria for "good English" that can be defined by an intellectual elite.

Works written from any one of the perspectives can (and do) contain the whole range of concepts, but each concept has a different logical status within the argument. Concepts are sometimes regarded as neutrally descriptive, without theoretical content, and sometimes as explicitly and self-consciously theoretical, containing the core commitments of the perspective. In such cases, the perspectives become genuine paradigms of inquiry.[5]

A theoretical category is one that is logically associated with the central assumptions of a perspective, and an empirical category is one that is not theorized but is used simply to locate phenomena that are not part of the home domain of the perspective. The theoretical categories of one perspective are the empirical categories of the others, and the theoretical categories of the others tend to be regarded either as jargon or as ideology.

The meanings of a given concept must therefore be understood in both their empirical and theoretical contexts. The context of the argument, the assumptions underlying the choice of level of analysis, the implicit rules of inference connecting evidence to concepts constitute the historical meanings of a concept, independent of their uses by a given writer. Each concept associated with a perspective has a central meaning identified with a particular theoretical perspective but also peripheral meanings associated with other perspectives. The core concepts of a perspective have both theoretical and empirical status; the peripheral concepts have only empirical status and are used to describe or recognize phenomena that must be taken into account but are not central to the perspective.

Because each perspective has its own specific explanatory focus, what

---

[5] One must avoid being confused by the use of terms that are a core part of another perspective. Although the core pluralist word, for example, is "governance," sometimes "popular rule" is used by pluralists. The point is that the pluralist meaning is that orderly procedures exist for the selection of leaders and that those leaders, while they are in positions of authority, enjoy the consent of the governed. Using the managerial or class term "rule" may imply hard-nosed assessment of the realities of power, control, and command by those leaders, as long as they occupy the command posts of the state. If the use of the term is within a pluralist world view, "governance" could be substituted, with a gain in clarity. The reasons for using particular concepts have to do with the politics of theory, which is outside our scope.

may seem to be an empirical debate is often a deeper theoretical or political conflict extending beyond an overt disagreement over interpretation of evidence. Works mostly within one perspective tend to introduce concepts from other perspectives, which they do not themselves theorize, in order to deal with gaps or silences within their own framework.

We believe that the appearance of intellectual conflict is a misleading way to identify the critical fault lines in the geography of social theory. The most intense conflicts usually occur between persons who share the same fundamental assumptions. In intellectual life, as in religious groups and political parties, the sharpest polemics are reserved for the heretic and the dissenter. Sharp debate is therefore frequently an indication not of difference but of similarity. Intense debates, usually within a perspective, occur about the relative importance of one or another factor or historical process. These debates are evidence that the perspectives are not monolithic.

Core concepts in each perspective are "essentially contested" in the sense that they do not, and cannot, have unequivocal definitions. Each essentially contested concept comes to have multiple and internally contradictory meanings, which are given to it by societal interests with a stake in its definition. The three senses in which concepts are contested correspond to the three perspectives. First, concepts compete for influence to be the most useful terms to describe different phenomena. Concepts are used to aggregate individuals and events into general terms: "President Reagan" and the "presidency," the "Democratic Party" and "political parties," "Diablo Canyon antinuclear demonstration" and "antinuclear movements." Debate occurs over the usefulness of terms and the truth of hypotheses. The issue is whether or not the abstract descriptions of presidential control over nominations or the role of the police in demonstrations accords with the specific events and behaviors they purport to describe or the range of variation the generalizations subsume. This is a measure of the influence of the concepts on the choice of the most useful word.

Second, concepts come to be part of dominant or subordinate paradigms. Clusters of terms come to control discourse when a particular school of thought dominates a university department, a professional association, or a government agency. The language of a discipline, a bureaucracy, an ethnic group, or a subculture consists of an interrelated set of assumptions, which are seen partly as identifying the membership of the group. The "ingroup" language rejects other concepts because they belong to the outsiders, the enemy, the other faction. The response to contestation lies in isolating one's language from the potential conflicts within it (and one's group) and selecting one set of meanings to dominate, leaving other potential meanings for other groups to defend. Language comes to have its home territory, just like a state, and indicates membership in a collectivity that enforces usages.

Third, concepts come to be part of the taken-for-granted foundation of a culture or society. Some words are simply not questioned until the fundamental social conditions that gave rise to their meaning and usage change, and suddenly they become problematic and difficult. A recent example is the discovery of a linguistic bias toward male hegemony which was pervasive until challenged by the feminist movement. Such concepts are essentially contested precisely because they are *not* the subject of continuous debate over their usefulness (that is, how much influence a concept should have), nor do they form part of the repertoire of dominant usages in a network of interrelated concepts. Such concepts have systemic power.

Certain concepts have such a heavy historical weight of meanings – connotations, assumptions, hypotheses – buried in them that their use almost commits writer and reader to the implicit (and all the more powerful because of that implicitness) theory about the causes and consequences of the phenomena alluded to by the concept. The term "power," for example, has three fundamental meanings, one associated with each perspective, which we have called influence, domination, and hegemony. Frequently a writer will slide from one meaning to another, partly to gain the maximum explanatory leverage on a problem. An explanation will appear more powerful if more aspects or factors can be hidden in a single word. But multiple meanings may also be a tactical victory for one's theory if another argument can be sneaked in by way of plausible concepts rather than an explicit argument. The point is that unambiguous definitions and the consistent use of words is an abstract power of theory; in the real world of debate and contestation such theory may have no power at all.

Capitalism, the state, and democracy

Core concepts of each perspective tend to have different terms of reference for the other perspectives. The term "capitalism," for example, is the central aspect of the state only for the class perspective. When pluralist theorists use the word, it refers to market activities and incentives. For managerial theorists, it is a specific form of organizing and controlling industrial production. The term "state," central to managerial theorists, often carries, for pluralists, a negative image of a powerful organization immune from democratic accountability and, for class theorists, the image of an apparatus constrained by the requirements of capital accumulation. "Democracy," central to pluralist theorists, is usually qualified by the adjective "bourgeois" by class analysts who wish to stress the distortions of democracy under capitalism and is seen by managerial theorists as either a symbol of legitimacy or as a set of organizations (legislatures, political parties) with their own internal structures of power.

We cannot resolve conceptual issues by definitional fiat, because the issue is an epistemological argument about the nature of the whole in relation to the parts. Concepts charted in the Glossary are therefore not definitions in the usual sense, nor are they alternative words for the same meanings. This argument may seem circular, because we are using concepts drawn from each perspective to describe the others. Ultimately, there is no escape from that circle unless we introduce a completely new language that is grounded nowhere, which has its own distinctive drawbacks.

We do not wish to beg the question by building in a bias toward one set of assumptions or another in our own choice of descriptive concepts, although of course we have a theory about the state in society. Our temporary solution, simply in order to construct an analytic scaffolding to begin our argument, is therefore to refer sometimes to "capitalism," "the state," and "democracy," which implies that capitalism and democracy are external to the state, constituting societal forces that press upon it to act in certain ways. These are the implicit views of the class and pluralist perspectives, emphasizing the power of capitalism and of democracy to dominate state structure or to influence state decisions. The managerial perspective, stressing the strength and autonomy of powerful organizations both inside and outside of the state, accepts this external separation with the opposing premise that the state can resist or can overcome those pressures in important ways.

The notion of the capitalist, bureaucratic, and democratic *aspects* of the state conveys, admittedly in a crude way, the assumption that there is no simple way to describe this complex field of relationships, their origins, and their outcomes. Thus, in different contexts, we refer both to aspects of the state and to capitalism, the state, and democracy. The notion of "aspects" signifies our assumption, which is somewhat different from those of any of the classic perspectives, that we must find a theoretical language that recognizes the partial truth of each perspective but also their partial blindness to the other aspects and how they must be taken into account in a fully adequate explanation.[6]

It should now be clear why we resist the appeal to "define our terms."

---

[6] We sometimes use "democratic state" instead of "aspect," or sometimes just "democracy," simply to shorten key phrases, but we do not mean to imply that there are three states or that one aspect captures the totality.

Just because every definition commits one to a theory, we can say only that every contested concept contains within it contradictory aspects. Our exposition in the following chapters of the different "translations" of the capitalist, bureaucratic, and democratic aspects of the state into the vocabulary of each perspective is intended to demonstrate that point. Defining a word in one way or another is a fateful choice, because it allows one to recognize or ignore one or another potential aspect of reality.

Conclusions

Only recently has the state qua state again become an object of serious theoretical work within any of the perspectives. The discovery by theorists of each stripe of democratic ungovernability, of autonomous state power, and of the political specificity of economic crisis has renewed theoretical attention on the state. A wide variety of empirical and historical studies of the role of the state have been made. We reduce the complexity of their different topics, concepts, and units of analysis to three ideal-type perspectives, which we believe represent the underlying similarity of world view among arguments seemingly quite different on the surface.

Our basic argument is that the elements that are most useful from each perspective are those that are drawn from its home domain: the special combination of a level of analysis, world view, and aspect of the state. Although a particular world view is likely to be associated with a particular level of analysis and to focus on a certain aspect of the state, some of the most interesting and complex studies, as we shall see in later chapters, are those that use a particular world view to analyze a level of analysis not within the home domain. Such synthetic analyses, we believe, contribute to a more powerful theory of the state in society.

PART I

The pluralist perspective

2

State and society in pluralist perspective

The pluralist perspective could have been called by several other names, "democratic," "behavioral," "individualistic," "functionalist," or "market," each of which would signify an emphasis and set of issues within the perspective. We chose "pluralist" because it is a common term in the literature, and it states the essential assumptions of the world view in one word.

The pluralist home domain

Within the pluralist home domain, the constitutive units of both organizations and societies are individuals, whose *preferences* (motives, grievances, tastes) and *values* (accepted norms, personal commitments, beliefs and perceptions) are the irreducible unit to which other levels of analysis must ultimately be referred. Individuals take action and join groups compatible with their preferences and values. Interactions and exchanges among individuals form all of the diverse social entities of a modern society.

Organizations (voluntary associations, pressure groups, state agencies, political parties, and even firms) represent aggregates of individuals in diverse ways, respond to different preferences among individuals, and remain in existence as long as they retain enough support. The multiple relations among groups and organizations normally generate a societal consensus through the communication of preferences and values, the formation of public opinion, and the responsive actions of leaders.

Individual behavior is divided into that which conforms to the values that integrate the society and that which deviates from them. There are major debates among its adherents over the conditions for change of values, and the best way to socialize individuals into the appropriate values necessary for social stability. But social change always involves changing individuals – their values, preferences, and participation.

35

Once one has chosen to view society as a collection of interdependent and differentiated individual roles and activities, one can then analyze any unit of analysis in isolation, assuming its boundaries are functionally determined. An organization, a community, a group can be examined apart from the whole, as if it represents or is a sample of the whole. Or it can be studied as if it were a whole, because all social systems operate according to universal functional requirements.[1]

With respect to the state, the paradigmatic questions that characterize the home domain are: How are government decisions influenced by group participation? What are the consequences of participation for the stability of democratic norms and values? How are political institutions constituted from multiple roles and values? What are the consequences of dissent, of lack of support, of a lack of trust or low sense of efficacy of political institutions? How are individuals socialized into democratic values?

Some research in the pluralist perspective focuses directly upon the conditions for and the consequences of democratic behavior. Others assume that those conditions more or less exist in societies that can be classified as democratic because they have certain institutional features, and that the functioning of those institutions can be analyzed *as if* they had democratic properties. This is particularly true for those institutions presumed to function as agents of or in response to mass participation: voting, elections, parties, legislatures. The pluralist perspective assumes that decision-making processes within the state take place primarily under circumstances of individual political equality and freedom. When those conditions are approximated, then the pluralist concepts referring to the democratic aspect of the state at the individual level are useful.

A comprehensive account of the state in Western societies is problematic for pluralists because these conditions are not always, or even frequently, met and also because to give such an account the pluralist vocabulary must be extended beyond its home domain. Sometimes pluralists assume that a democratic political culture pervades the whole society, is available to every individual, shapes democratic attitudes and behavior, and is an internalized object of loyalty. Other levels of analysis, both societies and organizations, are seen as multiple clusters of micro-groups, open rather than hierarchical, influenced by individual motives that use the symbol of legality and citizenship for purposes of persuasion. Such assumptions, we believe, are misleading, if not seen as merely one aspect of one level of analysis.

---

[1] *Union Democracy* by Lipset, Trow, and Coleman (1956) and Dahl's *Who Governs?* (1961) are classic examples of analyses that assume that an organization and a community can be analyzed as if they were examples in microcosm of democratic societies.

The pluralist world view

The pluralist world view is that modern societies are integrated by a differentiated value system. Individuals are normally socialized to accept both societal values and organizational goals. Deviant behavior occurs, but mechanisms of social control normally function to keep deviance within bounds that do not threaten societal integration. Tensions among individuals, organizations, and societies may develop when values are inconsistent and socialization is imperfect. Tensions can normally be resolved by communication, by further differentiation, which insulates tensions, or by problem-solving and tension-reducing activities by political leaders. Governmental institutions mediate many of these relations.

The functional approach within the pluralist perspective regards individuals as roles, institutionalized within the social system. The political approach regards individuals as persons incompletely defined by their roles. The multiplicity of group memberships contributes to individuality. Egoistic jockeying for advantage is rendered benign by common values and their institutionalization.

Within sociology the most general and systematic statement of the pluralist world view is that of Talcott Parsons. Although evolving over many years, his basic assumptions remained remarkably consistent.[2] We have chosen his work with Neil Smelser, *Economy and Society* (1956), as a classic pluralist view of the state.

Parsons's world view begins with individuals in interaction. A social system is "the system generated by any process of interaction, on the socio-cultural level, between two or more 'actors.' The actor is either a concrete human individual (a person) or a collectivity of which a plurality of persons are members" (Parsons and Smelser 1956, p. 8). Individuals thus "participate" in functionally integrated interaction systems. Organizations, institutions, and societies are built up from successive layers of individual interactions in segmented roles. The fundamental feature of a society is its quality of differentiation, because a society – by definition – is composed of a "network of differentiated subsystems in very complex relation to each other" (p. 9). A social system is "always characterized by an institutionalized value system" (p. 16). Values are something held by individuals. A functional imperative of a system is maintaining "individual motivations to conformity with institutionalized role expectations" (p. 17).

---

[2] Jeffrey Alexander gives a detailed analysis of Parsons's world view. "Parsons envisioned a reformed society as one of voluntarily cooperating and solidary individuals for whom the state would play a rather secondary role . . . universalizing these American characteristics into the basis for democratic society in general" (1983, p. 386).

Such a position does not entail the reductionist view that society is nothing but individuals. Here Parsons and Smelser contribute to a perennial debate within the pluralist perspective over the problem of whether or not society is an aggregate of individual preferences (utilitarian individualism), represented by the argument that "individual happiness is the sum of satisfactions and community happiness is the sum of individual happiness." Parsons and Smelser argue instead that one must start from the "institutionalized value system of the society and its various functional subsystems" (1956, p. 32), not from the individual. Despite their disclaimer, their epistemology is still individualistic, because it refers back to individual roles and the role orientations of individuals as the ultimate test of whether values play a role in the social system. No matter how complexly integrated into larger social systems, Parsons regards organizations and institutions as functionally integrated by means of values that individuals have internalized as a result of their experiences in institutions of primary socialization, preeminently the family. In a later book, Parsons expresses the core assumption even more explicitly: "a major tenet of modern sociological theory [that is, Parsons's theory] [is] that a system of value-orientations held in common by members of a social system can serve as the main point of reference" for the analysis of that system (Parsons 1960, p. 172). And values are unmistakably a characteristic of individuals. "[V]alues are in the first instance commitments of the individual personality" and must be "grounded" in *"existential beliefs," "motivational needs,"* and relations to others (p. 174; italics in original).

Institutions are a secondary level of analysis, because they derive from individuals and cultural values. Institutions are defined as the "ways in which the value patterns of the common culture of a social system are integrated in the concrete action of its units in their interaction with each other through the definition of role expectations and the organization of motivation" (Parsons and Smelser 1956, p. 102). This definition is enclosed in quotation marks in the original, indicating its carefully thought out and formal character. The key words pertain to characteristics of individuals, because only they can have "role expectations" and "motives." And the reactions of individuals to the deviance of others are psychological, not institutional. It is individuals who enforce social norms upon those who violate role expectations. Indignation, anxiety, concerns for security are "typical" psychological reactions to the violation of role expectations. Thus the "functioning of a unit in an interaction system ultimately depends on the motivation of the individual actors participating in the unit" (p. 50).[3]

---

[3] Sociologist Peter Blau, in *Exchange and Power in Social Life* (1964), builds up a theory of organizations and social structure from individual relations, following in this line of

Another excellent example of the pluralist world view is Raymond Boudon's *Logic of Social Action* (1981). "The logical atom of sociological analysis... is the individual actor" (p. 17). This principle of methodological individualism is explicitly applied to the state, which appears in various empirical examples. The relations between the British cabinet and the imperial German government, for example, are interpreted as a "system of interaction" of two sets of individuals (p. 25). And such a statement as "Germany prefers the costs of war to those of submission" is interpreted as referring to a "many-headed actor provided with a mechanism of collective decision-making – the German government" (p. 37).[4]

The pluralist world view of society includes both functionalist and political variants. Parsons is the best example of the former approach, George Homans of the latter. Homans regards behavioral psychology and economic assumptions about the cost–benefit calculations individuals make in deciding whether to do something or not as the key to the "elementary forms of social behavior" (1961). He explicitly rejects Parsons's view of society: "There is no functional prerequisite for the survival of a society except that the society provide sufficient rewards for its individual members to keep them contributing activities to its maintenance, and that it reward them not just as members of that society but as men" (p. 384). The individual level of analysis is constitutive of the society.

Another political approach starting from individuals is so-called rational choice theory, long popular in economics but recently applied to macrosociological problems of "group solidarity, social order, and collective action" (Hechter 1983, p. 10). The concern is explicitly to offer an alternative to traditional normative and structural (those we call functional) explanations of social phenomena.

The pluralist world view in general, however, emphasizes the self-regulating nature of a modern society, based on individuals acting in their own interest and accommodating themselves to the actions of other individuals. Shared values govern their interactions. A tension between

---

argument from George C. Homans, whose *Social Behavior: Its Elementary Forms* (1961) he explicitly credits. In later work Blau analyzes societies as a "multidimensional space of different social positions among which a population is distributed" (1977, p. 4).

[4] Boudon defines sociology itself, interestingly, as simply another form of social action, as a constrained choice by individuals. Sociology itself is defined by "that implicit definition shared by a majority of sociologists." Consensus thus defines the field of sociology. Individual sociologists participate by choosing for their studies among various differentiated social units (Boudon 1981, pp. xiv, 1). Boudon also reinterprets Marxian categories in pluralist terms. An instance of a "system of interaction," for example, which he labels as "Marxist," is a situation in which "the capitalist group inflicts damage upon the proletarian group, leading to a reaction by the latter" (p. 127).

private purpose and public interest indicates a failure of normative integration in the functionalist variant of pluralism and a problem of "ex-
ternalities" for nonfunctionalist exchange theories. Variations in
democratic institutions are explained by the varying strength of a democratic political culture, coupled with wise leadership, the growth of an
educated middle class, and the diffusion of democratic values into all
social institutions.

A society's economy tends to be viewed either as an environment
within which democratic politics occurs or as an entire social system
whose functioning parallels that of the larger society. In the first case,
the economic structure provides variable levels of resources with which
government can respond to the demands of the public and affects the
level of expectations to which the government is subject. Rising income,
intergenerational mobility, and technological innovation typically are
seen as reducing the popular pressures to which the government is
subject. Alternatively, the economy is a miniature society functioning
to satisfy preferences that, although differentiated, derive from core
societal values of individualism, achievement, and equality upon which
democratic governments are also based.[5]

Economic organizations are created where market exchanges between
individuals are insufficient to achieve collective action (Arrow 1974; Williamson 1975). Organizations survive to the extent that their members
derive sufficient benefit from them that they contribute to their survival
(Scott 1981). Internally, organizations are viewed as shifting coalitions
of interest groups who bargain for influence to shape the organization
according to their own values (Cyert and March 1963). Power flows to

[5] An example of the power of a world view to shape, and sometimes eliminate, perceptions
of other theories is Samuel Huntington's distinction between four different "images of
American politics." He criticizes three of them for being too "structural" and for failing
to see the importance of ideas as shaping social structure. All four of them are variants
of the pluralist perspective. The "class-conflict" theory emphasizes the "continuing
conflict between the few who are rich and the many who are poor," that is, individuals
who differ in some social characteristic. The "consensus" theory stresses the "consensus
on middle-class values." His "pluralist" theory emphasizes the "competition among
interest groups" and also has variants itself: a "process" version, which focuses upon
large numbers of relatively small interest groups, and the "organization" version, which
focuses on the dominant role of a small number of "large well-organized groups in
shaping public policy" (1981, p. 7). None of these, Huntington argues, gives enough
weight to "political ideas and values" (p. 11), but they do stress economic interests and
the relatively permanent group structure of American society. Huntington argues that
the United States enjoys a "unique consensus on and commitment to liberal, democratic
and egalitarian political values," which lead to the political "disharmony" that is the
subject of his book. His important contribution is to recognize the contradiction between
consensus and participation in the democratic state. The relevant point here is that all
four of the theories of American politics are internal debates within the pluralist perspective. He has translated some central managerial concepts into pluralist language,
but the silence on the class perspective is deafening.

those groups that are most important to the survival of the organization, a value that all members share (Hickson et al. 1971).

The state

Pluralist theorists frequently do not refer to the state at all. The classic concept of the state is inconsistent with the view that the entire society and its governing institutions are becoming modernized, as we shall see later in this chapter. The notion of a state implies a monolithic, hierarchical, and centralized structure, which pluralists reject either on political or on theoretical grounds. Instead, pluralists normally refer to the "political community" (De Grazia 1948), the "political system" (Easton 1965a, 1965b), the "polity" (Long 1962), or the "pluralist system" (McFarland 1969). Those varied terms suggest multiple sources of authority, institutions differentiated according to function (rule making, rule enforcing, rule adjudicating), and an open, accessible government. Talcott Parsons, in one of his last published articles, refers to a "single system of law" that regulates a population pursuing a "highly variegated set of interests" and enjoying "constitutionally guaranteed rights in a variety of spheres of freedom." Parsons calls this a "pluralistic" line of theorizing and contrasts it to what he sees as the main alternative: Marxism (1979, p. 448).[6]

Values

The pluralist world view assumes the state is integrated by values, is an institution chosen by individuals, and is functional for society. This view of the state goes back to Aristotle. The first sentence of *The Politics* is: "Our own observation tells us that every state is an association of persons formed with a view to some good purpose" (1962, p. 25). In some of the more extreme versions of the pluralist world view, the state is even defined by values. Political scientist David Easton, for example, defines the "political system" as the "most inclusive system of behavior in a society for the authoritative allocation of values" (1965a, p. 56).

Which values are most congruent with social order and governmental stability is a subject of considerable debate among pluralists, sometimes

---

[6] Norbert Elias defines "rule" in a highly differentiated society as "no more than the special social power with which certain functions, above all the central functions, endow their occupants in relation to the representatives of other functions." Further, "social power . . . corresponds . . . solely to the degree of dependence of the various interdependent functions on one another." The state is the "supreme organ of coordination and regulation" of these social functions. "Changes in the social power of the central functionaries . . . are sure indications of specific changes in the system of tensions within the society at large" (1982, p. 165).

related to their liberal or conservative political stance. Liberal pluralists tend to emphasize the importance of individual choice, of rights of participation, of government action to guarantee equality of opportunity, of representing all groups' interests in government decisions. Conservatives tend to emphasize minimizing "demand overload" in the interests of relieving the burden of decision making on political leaders, holding political demands within the boundaries of the consensus at any given time, and political culture as a moderating and limiting influence. Underlying this debate, however, is the common pluralist assumption of the centrality of values as a source of integration of society and state.[7]

Although values are central, pluralists tend not to explain their historical origins and variation but rather use values to explain other phenomena. Just as neoclassical economics takes the preferences of consumers and producers to be exogenous variables that are not explained, pluralist analysts of the democratic state take the values of voters to be an irreducible referent to explain political action.

Democratic stability is furthered by the congruence of values of different institutions. One theoretical statement argues that democratic values in families, community, and workplaces are conducive to democratic politics (Eckstein 1961). Political stability is assumed to be more likely where all institutions are permeated by the same societal values. One typical statement is that "high performance by any political system requires that the authority patterns of governmental institutions closely resemble those of less inclusive social units, notably those that socialize citizens and recruit and train political cadres and elites" (Eckstein and Gurr 1975).[8]

Pluralist concern with the impact of political culture on democratic stability is evident in S. M. Lipset's First New Nation (1963). He argued that the value system of a nation is one important factor stabilizing democracy. The stability of democracy in the United States, Britain, Canada, and Australia and its instability in France and Germany are explained by their dominant political cultures. Specifically, the values of achievement, egalitarianism, universalism, and specificity tend to support democracy, and the United States exhibits those values "more than any other modern noncommunist industrial nation" (p. 213). France,

---

[7] M. J. C. Vile argues that because the "values that characterize Western thought are ... potentially contradictory ... the nature of the governmental structures through which decisions are arrived at is critically important for the actual content of these decisions." There has therefore been a "continuous concern with the articulation of the institutions of the political system, and with the extent to which they have promoted those values that are considered central to the 'polity' " (1967, p. 1).

[8] See also Almond and Verba's discussion (1963) of the role of families in political socialization.

though exhibiting many of these values, did not succeed in creating a "value consensus among the key social groupings" after the French Revolution of 1789. Lipset agrees with Eckstein (1961) that democratic instability in Germany was caused by inconsistency between the authoritarian norms found in nongovernmental institutions, including the family, and the democratic political institutions.

Individuals

In the public-choice version of pluralism, law is seen as a choice of individuals: "Man . . . chooses deliberately to impose constraints on his own behavior" by a system of law (Buchanan 1975, p. 107). The state is an "enforcing agent," needed because of "conflicts among individual interests" (p. 12). One of the most important enforcements needed is the "protection of individual rights to do things" (pp. 12–13).

The pluralist assumption is that organizations and societies are constructed by individuals who choose to believe or are persuaded to act as if there are rules, norms, and values to which they should conform and in which they must believe. This view can be a potential corrective to a tendency to reify "the United States" or "capitalism" or "democracy" or "our country." Pluralists who stay within the home domain need not assume that the interactions of a small group of individuals are governed by the same factors as larger, more complex systems. But sometimes the language of "choice," "action" and "decision," or even "talking" is applied to states, as if they were individuals. The headlines, "Lebanon says," or "Israel blames," or "The United States wants," are pluralist metaphors for the state, extrapolating from individuals to states and identifying the state with society.

Functions

In the pluralist perspective, the state's main function is either to serve as a neutral mechanism to aggregate preferences or to integrate society by embodying consensual values. These are variants of the functional approach. In the former view, the state is seen as a provider of "collective goods" and politics as a conflict over processes of social choice (Benjamin 1980). The state is the "microdecision unit," which does what "society decides" (Auster and Silver 1979, pp. 1–2).

Political scientist Karl Deutsch has argued that it is useful to look upon government not as an instrument of power but rather as a mechanism of "communication," as the key mechanism steering the society (1963, p. ix). He emphasizes feedbacks, games, responsiveness, and the consequences of all of these processes for system integration (pp. xiv, xvi–xvii). In this view, it is not really important exactly what a state does;

what is important is that political leaders be able to meet the changing situations they must deal with flexibly, with due regard for the consequences for stability and order.

When the state functions properly to generate a normal political process, the interests of state and society are identical. In an indirect way, political scientist Ted Gurr has defined what is normal by defining its opposite, political violence: "all collective attacks within a political community against the political regime, its actors – including competing political groups as well as incumbents – or its policies" (1970, pp. 3–4). Political violence is a "threat to the political system in two senses"; such incidents "challenge the monopoly of force imputed to the state in political theory," and they are "likely to interfere with and, if severe, to destroy normal political process" (p. 4).

Here, under the guise of neutral definitions for empirical research, Gurr has inserted a theoretical bias toward the pluralist world view. He assumes that violence is not a "normal political process" but an abnormal one and that a challenge to the exercise of force by the state is a "threat to the political system." He thus identifies the state with the political system, thereby assuming that the state functions as it should in a differentiated society (see also Huntington 1968). Here one could ask why the political system (in the pluralist sense of the basic values of political leaders and voters) could not be saved either by challenging the state's use of force or by using force against a state that was violating the basic values of the citizenry. These questions, however, remain unasked as long as the political system is equated with the state.

The implicit state

To some pluralists, the state is no more than another nonmarket institution resulting from aggregated individual choice, without any societal function, power, or rule. This is an implicit concept of the state. The issue of whether or not the state is the central integrating institution, not to mention a dominant coercive organization or executive committee of the ruling class, is simply ignored. This is one of the silences of pluralism.

Economist Kenneth Arrow maintains that "the government is . . . only one of a large number of collective institutions. It is distinguished from the others primarily by its monopoly on coercive power" (Arrow 1974, p. 25). All such institutions "share the common characteristics of the need for collective action and the allocation of resources through nonmarket methods," not only government but also political parties, revolutionary movements, universities, and churches. Without assuming that market and nonmarket processes necessarily cooperate to produce a socially optimal result, Arrow argues that "when the market fails to achieve an optimal state, society will, to some extent at least, recognize the gap, and nonmarket social institutions will arise attempting to bridge it. . . . this process is not necessarily conscious" (Arrow 1963, quoted in Hirschman 1970, pp. 18–19). Here the state ("nonmarket institution") is performing the function society needs. Overall social needs (the public interest, the optimal equilibrium – the language varies) are realized via public actions when private actions do not suffice. Another economist, Oliver Williamson, regards "market" and "nonmarket" organizations as the two major possibilities in modern society. The state is merely one of many types of organizations of the nonmarket form. (Hospitals, universities, and foundations are other examples.) The state is disaggregated and has properties and variable characteristics (1975, p. 8). Alternatively, Williamson (1981) refers to different forms of "governance structures," assuming that any type of organization has one, including the state.[9]

A rather different example of the implicit state is continuous reference to empirical instances of the state while excluding it from theoretical status. The state, in Neil Smelser's work on collective behavior, is the object or cause of collective behavior. In connection with "crazes," when people "rush with sound and fury toward something they believe to be gratifying" (1963, p. 170), Smelser refers to American political conventions (p. 183), the fusion of Protestant churches with European states (p. 187), and British government debts (p. 188). Panics, in which people may flee because of their "hysterical beliefs" (p. 131), are linked with meetings of the Federal Reserve Board (p. 162), air force sonic booms, and New York air raid drills.

More directly related to the state are "hostile outbursts," meaning "participants" are "attacking someone considered responsible for a disturbing state of affairs" (Smelser 1963, p. 226). Presidential calling of the troops (p. 233), British cabinet authority, the Nazi government (p. 234), and the French Estates-General (p. 245) are also mentioned in other contexts. But the type of collective behavior with the most serious implications for the stability of the core values of a society is the value-oriented movement, a "collective attempt to restore, protect, modify, or create values in the name of a generalized belief" (p. 313). Examples are the French and Russian revolutions and national independence move-

---

[9] Williamson (1981) is mainly concerned with whether transactions are internalized within a firm (a "governance structure") or are externalized between firms (a "market"). He never mentions the state and the legal system specifically but claims at the end that his work integrates economics, organization theory, and contract law. The assumption is that the state is a stable environment within which firms can freely decide whether or not to buy each other out. Williamson rejects power as an explanation of their decisions.

ments in South Africa and Indonesia, events that affect the structure of the state if anything does. All of these examples are theorized in terms of components of *individual* action; the state remains implicit. Value-oriented movements involve "a reconstitution of values, a redefinition of norms, a reorganization of the motivation of individuals, and a redefinition of situational facilities" (p. 313). Even the latter, which might seem to denote the structural or objective conditions of individual action, is defined as whatever "the actor utilizes as means" (p. 24). Thus the state enters the analysis as an empirical category but remains theoretically implicit.[10]

A perfect example of the implicit state is George C. Homans's theory of "elementary social behavior" (1961). No noun remotely resembling a synonym for "government" or "the state" appears in the index, although many empirical examples are drawn from cases labeled "M.I.T.," a "Federal agency" (p. 390), an "Air Force base" (p. 289), "government," "national loyalties" (p. 388). Homans recognizes that "complex institutions" arise that cannot be understood in terms of exchange behavior between individuals but argues merely that processes of "elementary social behavior" will reassert themselves, particularly when those institutions break down, in "disaster, revolution, or defeat in war." But such breakdowns have no theoretical significance, because they are only the context within which individual behavior occurs.[11]

---

[10] An excellent example of the implicit state is found in Blau and Duncan 1967. Although the Census Bureau, the National Science Foundation, and several state universities sponsored and funded the project, the preface treats the book as a series of individual choices of problem, design, and interpretation of data by the authors, with the help of other individuals, of course. However, in their concluding discussion, the findings suddenly become relevant to the "political stability of American democracy" (p. 436). The "policy implications" are defined as something "we" (the democratic citizenry) should do about discrimination against Negroes. They regard their book as a contribution of "knowledge essential for effective action programs to better social conditions." Because all occupations are treated as theoretically equivalent, opportunity is defined as incremental movement upward and downward on a series of dimensions of stratification. The role of the state is thus limited to assuring equality of opportunity for individuals to move into the occupations of their choice. The role of the state in structuring opportunities and the positions to which they apply is also not analyzed. Thus, for example, no distinction is made between occupational attainment in public and private sectors. Here the pluralist world view has become a political ideology that conceals liberal politics under the seeming neutrality of scientific method.

[11] The state is implicit in experiments in which individuals are given choices of ways to make money within an "opportunity structure" established by the experimenters. Individuals are treated as if they were isolated actors able to make choices on the basis of cost–benefit calculations. The experimenters (like a state) establish the conditions under which individuals can freely choose to participate. In the conclusions of one such study (Cook et al. 1983), the authors say that "exchange networks" can be seen as operating according to a "decentralization" principle, forming "systems organized around multiple foci of power." These foci "can be viewed as 'regional centers' of power, like petty kingdoms in an encompassing empire" (p. 302). The authors then allude to a study of a state: charismatic kingship in Baltistan.

and individual worth, economic growth will be slow and halting or forced and unstable.

In the pluralist perspective, rationalization, which is an organizational phenomenon in the managerial perspective, is transformed into a normative attribute of individuals. Thus Wilbert Moore saw modernization as the "institutionalization of rationality," defined as the "normative expectation that objective information and rational procedures will be applied in pursuit or achievement of any utilitarian goal" (Moore 1964, cited in Valenzuela and Valenzuela 1978, p. 20). Thus, in the pluralist perspective, the calculus of rationality is something that is acquired in the process of modernization, not an inherent attribute of individual decision making (Valenzuela and Valenzuela 1978).

Modern values are diffused by the differentiation and mobilization of the society. Villages and cities become connected through the mass media, the exchange of products, labor migration, and secular education. Exchanges – of products, of labor, of ideas – lead to an increasingly elaborate social structure. The society increasingly depends upon individual choice to fill the new roles that are constantly developing. With this growth comes more competition but also more intricate webs of interdependence. Modern values make change, competition, and interdependence both possible and necessary. Such values gradually extend to a larger fraction of the population and are essentially similar in every modernized sector of society, not just the economy.

Political participation

The pluralist perspective stresses the historical development of universal suffrage for every adult in every Western society, with minor exceptions, as both a cause and a consequence of the democratic aspect of the state. Both voting and certain forms of nonelectoral participation (letter writing, membership in delegations, demonstrations) are possible in all Western societies. In addition, political parties, trade unions, and various types of voluntary associations can usually be freely organized and can play a role in formally representing the interests of various segments of the population. The rights of citizenship have become valued and legal, although they are not always used and are sometimes violated. These rights of participation constitute the essence of the democratic aspect of the state for the pluralist perspective.

The modern values that underpin economic markets also make possible the expansion of democratic participation. The freedom of the market – the ability to dispose of one's property or one's labor without regard to status – rests on democratic civil rights and vice versa. Indeed, welfare provisions for unemployed workers were originally seen as an infringement upon their civil rights. Historically, citizenship meant property rights, even before the right to vote was extended to those persons who had acquired their property through the market. Gradually, citizenship was extended to the state from its original protection of individual property rights in the market, and eventually to protection from the market (Bendix 1964).

Democratic citizenship rights are rooted in common values among both leaders and citizens. These values define the scope of political consensus on the public interest, as expressed in actions by the state. Democratic politics follows from these values, rights, and the institutions that embody them. Individuals and social groups convey their preferences to political parties. Parties aggregate the varied preferences into issues. Depending on complex processes of coalition formation, sometimes an electoral majority forms around an issue and a proposed legislative decision. Sometimes an interest group or party can mobilize enough popular support to persuade unwilling leaders to pass a law that they do not want. It is assumed that a clear and intense majority preference will ultimately become public policy, expressed in both legislative decisions and administrative implementation. A positive policy response by political leaders will integrate new social groups into the political system, if their values and preferences can be expressed as part of majority public opinion or legitimate minority opinion. A continuous upward and downward flow of information and responses must occur among citizens, elected officials, and public agencies.

Orderly and limited political participation is critical to maintain democratic government. Beneath the diversity of groups' demands must lie a binding value consensus. The values shared by citizens must establish a stronger bond than those that divide them. In a stable democratic state, public opinions of events tend to change in the same direction for all social groups, even if there are sharp initial group differences in beliefs. This is evidence of consensus. Groups accept compromises as the price of maintaining the system intact. Fair competition in the political market will enable an eventual response to all groups, if they respect the limits of realistic response.

Under normal circumstances, a belief in the importance of citizen participation is diffused throughout the society, from corporate presidents to neighborhood activists. Individuals can feel that their participation would have an impact even if they do not participate, because the slack in the system allows it to respond to potential demands.

Modernization is both a necessary condition for the emergence of a democratic state and a source of pathological influences that can undermine it. Modernization involves the continuous creation of new needs and therefore new political demands mobilized by interest groups and political parties. Consequently, new sources of tension develop over which groups and issues can gain access to political leaders.

The timing of the admission of new groups to the political arena determines whether political participation stemming from new forms of group conflict will undermine or strengthen the democratic aspect of the state. The process of modernization carries both promise and danger for the peaceful development of a democratic state. On the one hand, such changes as increased education, social mobility, higher incomes, increased literacy, and increased communications generate moderate and informed participation. Education produces political tolerance, inculcates the value of participation, and generates beliefs in democratic norms. Social mobility, together with rising incomes and job security, encourages working-class political moderation by generating long-term perspectives on the possibilities of social change, which will benefit the individual and his or her family. Literacy and mass communications reduce the isolation of social groups likely to espouse extremist politics and erode pockets of traditionalism opposed to participation or hostile to modern society and politics. On the other hand, the incomplete destruction of premodern bases of social organization (territory and regionalism, ethnicity, religion) maintains cross-pressures. Representation of nonmodern interests also provides the basis for the acceptance of modern politics by those remaining traditional groups, such as clerics and aristocrats. A quasi-traditional deference to governmental leaders provides another basis of support for democratically elected officials.

Dangers thus exist in the modernizing process. Extremely rapid social change dislocates people from their communities and produces a tendency toward extremism. Even where there is little individual dislocation, rapid change may induce rising expectations, which the political system cannot satisfy (leading to what Durkheim called "anomie"). When established leaders resist demands for participation, new groups may use force to gain access, generating revolutionary movements and reducing both the responsiveness of traditional leaders and the allegiance of disappointed potential new leaders. In situations where class, ethnic, religious, and territorial identities reinforce rather than cross-cut each other, political parties may find it difficult to compromise because of the extremism of their political base.

Even modern values have a negative potential, because they tend to be individualistic and self-interested. Individuals increasingly try to maximize their personal gains through the channels available to them. Although such individual motives are well adapted to the functioning of economic markets, they can be dangerous for the social cohesion of the democratic state. When expectations rise more rapidly than the society is able to satisfy them, political extremists may emerge who violate the political norms, proposing alternative values and threatening to over-throw the democratic state.

The democratic aspect of the state is thus the consequence of popular participation when supported by a political culture that encourages re-sponsiveness by political leaders to legitimate demands. Moderate par-ticipation is furthered by values of political trust and compromise, inculcated through subtle processes of political socialization in family, school, church, and community, and by responsible leadership that tan-gibly responds to political demands. Political socialization also develops the proper balance between support of political leadership and demands upon it.

Political development

The pluralist perspective views the growth and differentiation of the state as a process of political development. Developed states are com-posed of governmental institutions created by leaders who were social-ized into a modern political culture. The state grows incrementally as public and private leaders respond to the political demands of ever more diversified interest groups. The state is regarded as a separate set of institutions, mediating among economic interest groups, preserving so-cial order, and supporting the central values of political and economic freedom.

Western states originated in the activities of "nation builders," political leaders who created a national identity. Once their work is done and developed political institutions are in place, the need for major structural change in the state disappears. Political decisions and leadership policy responses to issues can become incremental adjustments within the con-stitutional framework of the state. Political conflict then occurs – in a healthy democratic political system – mainly over the choice of alter-native leaders to govern and over specific decisions of the state, not over basic structures.

The modernization process, by creating a complex economic and social structure of differentiated groups and interests, also creates the basis for a highly differentiated state structure. The complexity of the social structure generates ever-new political demands, and the state is appro-priately differentiated into multiple programs and agencies in response. A certain degree of duplication and overlapping of functions occurs, which is regarded as both inevitable and even desirable by pluralists. Democratic accessibility may be achieved at the price of bureaucratic rationality.

State institutions derive their governing capability from their ability to represent popular preferences and to aggregate them into policies that reflect the preferences of some and the values of all. Because of the enormous diversity of preferences pressed upon the state, policy making tends to be both differentiated and incremental. Policies are made separately for senior citizens, for the handicapped, for unemployed mothers, for redundant workers, for blacks, for Indians. In the parliamentary arena, this welter of groups and their demands may help to soften strong ideological conflict, although sometimes it may also lead to demand overload. Today's allies may be tomorow's enemies and vice versa. Given this situation of shifting political alignments, cooperation and compromise across party lines are essential if a regime capable of governing is to continue.

A central source of tension in a democratic political system, given this normal process of representation, is the difficulty in defining and pursuing the public interest. This difficulty is particularly problematic when a few people benefit greatly from a particular policy but most are marginally hurt. The process of representation makes it difficult to mobilize around diffuse but common interests. For this reason, flexible and responsible executive leadership is particularly important. Given the enormous amount of narrow pressure-group activity, political leaders must be socialized within a public-regarding ethic and an orientation to the long-range interests of the community. This orientation can be furthered by recruiting leaders from highly educated groups and by organizing the political system so that key governmental roles require previous public service before persons take office.

The internal organization of the state thus develops in response to the demands of political parties and interest groups, representing aggregates of group and individual interests. Political development involves a structural differentiation of government functions – rule making (usually by legislatures), rule adjudicating (usually by courts), rule implementation (usually by bureaucratic agencies). Democratic institutions, with their elaborate procedures for representation, are well suited to modern societies because they protect the governance functions of the state while assuring a continuous upward flow of citizen demands. Because of the speed of social change, continuous feedback must take place between society and state. In the pluralist perspective, modern society cannot be administered; it must be governed.

The pluralist perspective makes certain assumptions about the conditions under which a democratic state can be relatively stable and the society governable. First, reasonably consistent and stable *economic growth* is required. Furthermore, the benefits of that growth must be distributed fairly. Most people must have a sense of opportunity, either for themselves or for their children. If economic growth slows, if unemployment becomes high, if inflation rises steeply, one important set of conditions for the operation of the democratic aspect of the state is weakened: belief in individual achievement and opportunities. The state's stability not only depends on its economic performance but is rooted in public trust in the state's neutrality and commitment to the public interest and the appropriate individual motivations. If this trust erodes, then economic declines can have a serious impact on the effectiveness of the state.

Second, people must have access to *information* about the policies to which candidates are committed, the alternative policies the government could adopt, and the likely consequences of alternative decisions, so that they can choose when to try to influence political leaders. Without information, participation is blind and meaningless.

Third, bureaucracies must be *responsive*. They must be able to implement the decisions made by legislative bodies and accountable political leaders. If administrative agencies become insulated from public opinion and political leaders, if they start building empires of their own, another condition for the effective functioning of a democratic state is undermined.

A fourth set of conditions is *cultural*. The political culture must be one of moderation. People must be willing to accept decisions that are made through established procedures and must use established channels themselves when they attempt to influence decisions. Democracy requires that its citizens trust their governmental leaders, a trust based on shared values.

The managerial and class perspectives challenge the existence of these conditions for genuine democracy and question the significance of cultural values as causal factors in the origin and stability of democracy.[13]

Consensus versus participation

Within the democratic state, pluralists recognize a tension between consensus and participation. This tension is expressed in many ways: institutionalization versus participation, public interest versus private preferences, power versus responsiveness, social choice versus individual values. The theoretical tension corresponds to a division of labor within the perspective, reflected in our two chapters on the democratic state, one focusing upon consensus, the other upon participation.

The most problematic aspect of societal modernization is the tendency for political participation to increase faster than political institutionali-

---

[13] See Collier 1978 for a summary of the literature criticizing the relationship between economic modernization and political democracy assumed by the early development theorists. Collier focuses upon the work of Guillermo O'Donnell, whose contrast between "modern" and "bureaucratic-authoritarian" regimes in Latin America is grounded in a theoretical argument similar to ours, with the important exception that he links the development of bureaucratic-authoritarian states to the domination of foreign capital.

zation. Where expectations rise more quickly than the opportunities provided by economic development, newly mobilized social groups turn to political participation (Huntington 1968, pp. 54–6, 380). Where political institutionalization is weak, it is difficult for the demands of newly mobilized political groups to be aggregated through legitimate channels. Where political organizations are not autonomous, new social groups gain political access "without becoming identified with the established political organizations or acquiescing in the established political procedures" (p. 21). Rapid expansion in the scope of political participation can easily weaken the coherence of political organization unless new political leadership is socialized to accept the rules of the game (pp. 22–3). In a noncomplex political system, the absence of multiple access points makes the absorption of newly mobilized social groups politically difficult (pp. 18–19).

Where political institutionalization is strong, political participation regularizes intergroup relations, creates new bases of common interest and identity, and provides new opportunities for individual mobility (Huntington 1968, pp. 68–71, 397–403). Institutionalization means that participants, presumably both the governed and their leaders, "come to value" political organization "for its own sake" (p. 15). "In politically advanced societies, loyalty to . . . more immediate social groupings is subordinated and subsumed into loyalty to the state" (p. 30). Political participation becomes more than a means to aggregate parochial interests and thereby adjust the policies of the government to the interests of the governed; it becomes the basis of social order itself, if it occurs within a consensus on basic institutions.

Robert Dahl defines the tension as a "dilemma" between autonomy and control in pluralist democracies, focusing upon organizations in Western democratic states. Organizations face the problem of whether or not to "foster the narrow egotism of their members" in their attempt to represent their members' interests. If they do, however, it may be "at the expense of concerns for a broader public interest" (Dahl 1982, p. 1). Given the imperative of the public interest, organizations must be controlled somehow.[14]

Mancur Olson focuses upon the tension between common interests and preferences within the "developed democracies." His main thesis is that the "behavior of individuals and firms in stable [democratic] societies leads to the formation of dense networks of collusive, cartelistic,

[14] Dahl contrasts his own view with that of Ralf Dahrendorf and Isaac Balbus, who, he says, emphasize domination and subjection as the essential meaning of power, control, and influence (1982, p. 22). Dahl argues that power should be viewed as varying over an indefinitely large range of values – a pluralist view of the incremental possibilities of change of power between individuals and organizations.

and lobbying organizations that make economies less efficient and dynamic and politics less governable" (Olson 1982, from the flyleaf). That can happen "even if all the individuals in the electorate have the same preferences as before" (p. 47). Olson starts from the individual level of analysis in defining the "preferences" for democracy.[15] The divisiveness created by individuals, groups, and associations participating in various ways to realize their preferences is not offset by the "common interests [consensus] that all or most of the people in a nation or other jurisdiction share [and that] can draw them together" (p. 47).

A recent analysis of the tension frames the problem as a debate between pluralist political theory and social choice theory. Nicholas R. Miller argues that there is a fundamental tension between "collective rationality under majority rule" and "pluralistic preference profiles" (1983, p. 740). He argues that, although a "pluralist political system does *not* authoritatively allocate values in a stable fashion," the consequence need not be instability. Rather, "the pluralist political process leads to unstable political choice," which in turn "fosters the stability of pluralist political *systems*" (p. 744; italics added). Miller thus resolves the tension by arguing that there cannot be "one cleavage of overwhelming salience," such as a class division between capital and labor. To put the same point another way, in a pluralist society "preferences on one issue are independent of how other issues are resolved." A system of "cyclical majorities" will prevail, in which there are constantly shifting "preference clusters" on different issues, producing an unstable political process but a stable political system.

The tension has also been conceptualized as a trade-off between governmental responsiveness and governmental power. Almond and Verba (1963) locate the mechanisms to resolve the tension within the civic political culture, whereas others stress the critical role of two-party systems and political leadership.

A two-party system allows political parties to perform simultaneously representative and integrative functions, especially where "it is based on an elaborate, cross-cutting solidarity structure, in which men and groups are pulled in different directions only by their diverse roles and interests" (Lipset 1963, p. 308). Two-party systems also tend to provide for "generalized leadership" because, at any given time, the party in

---

[15] Olson views democracy as a process of collective decision making made possible through a variety of choice mechanisms, the most significant of which are majority vote or elected leadership. He follows Kenneth Arrow in this definition. Democracy is inherently a choice process through which the members of an association can express their preferences (Olson 1982, p. 55). A society for Olson is merely a particularly "heterogeneous group." Because of its heterogeneity, consensus on goals and collective actions is more difficult to achieve than among homogeneous groups.

power "temporarily becomes identical with the state" (p. 311). The legitimacy of the party rests on its ability to function as a "national government" and to moderate its factional ideology in the course of creating public policy, while simultaneously representing an electoral majority.

The tension is also resolved if political leaders are appropriately socialized to be oriented to the "public interest." But differentiated political institutions must exist that are capable of creating leaders who identify with the interests of the political institutions themselves. Political slack created by a widespread sense of political efficacy and trust in leadership reduces the likelihood of an overload of political demands and allows the flexibility necessary for leaders to mediate the tension between maintaining consensus and allowing participation.

Conclusions

Both the definition of the essential tension within the democratic aspect of the state between consensus and participation and the postulation of mechanisms that can resolve this tension are part of the pluralist world view. The bureaucratic and capitalist aspects of the state are either not theorized or are redefined in ways that either support the democratic state or become problems to be dealt with by further differentiation, further modernization, further economic growth, or – in extremis – by reducing participation if consensus is threatened.[16]

The tension, paradoxically, is postulated but neglected, because un-

---

[16] Although S. M. Lipset regards the Weberian and Marxian traditions as important intellectual sources for political sociology, he reinterprets them into a pluralist world view. Bureaucracy "can be viewed as one of the major mechanisms of integration in the political order" (1960, p. 52). The bureaucratic norm that a "member of a bureaucracy is an impartial expert rather than an interested party" is seen as a mechanism that can make the continuity of democratic government possible during periods of turnover in political offices. Because bureaucratic procedures "tend to reduce conflicts to administrative decisions by experts" and thus remove "issues from the political arena," bureaucracies play "major mediating roles." He concludes that these are just several of the ways "the pressures to extend bureaucratic norms and practices constitute an important strength for democratic consensus" (p. 52). Similarly, although Lipset gives credit to Marx for recognizing fundamental conflicts in modern societies, he mostly criticizes his theory from a pluralist standpoint. Marx "was unconcerned with society's need to maintain institutions and values which facilitate its stability and cohesion" (p. 45). Furthermore, "Marx was completely uninterested in safeguards against state power, or the need for the division of powers, or the protection of judicial guarantees, or a constitution, bill of rights, and other democratic mechanisms." The theoretical reason, he argues, was that Marx postulated a fundamental opposition between capitalist society, torn by conflict, and communist society, integrated by consensus. Democracy is in Lipset's definition a "social mechanism for resolving the problem of societal decision-making among conflicting interest groups with minimal force and maximal consensus" (p. 49).

derstanding its origins requires an analysis of bureaucratic domination and class rule. Most empirical analyses within the pluralist perspective assume "normal politics," that is, that a balance has been struck between a consensus on basic values and open participation.

3

The democratic state and consensus

In the pluralist perspective, the democratic aspect of the state is primary. Healthy democracy can prevent pathological tendencies toward bureaucratic rigidity and class conflict. Stable democratic institutions depend on a consensual political culture. The content of this political culture – the values and beliefs of citizens and leaders – is based on nonpolitical processes in the economy, family, community, and religion. These values come to be reflected in the political and governmental institutions of the society. In this chapter we examine the pluralist view of the role of political culture and consensus in maintaining democratic stability.

Democracy

Pluralists tend to view democracy as a set of procedures and processes. Robert A. Dahl defines democracy as a system in which all citizens have free opportunity to (1) formulate their preferences, (2) signify their preferences to other citizens and to the government through both individual and collective action, and (3) have their preferences weighted equally in the conduct of the government (1971, p. 2). Dahl qualifies his definition by asserting that no existing society meets all of those conditions. The definition thus is an abstract concept of democracy as a property of any "political system," to which any existing society could be compared. This analytic procedure isolates the democratic aspect of the state from the other aspects of the state so that it becomes a variable that then can be correlated with other variable properties of the society while the other aspects are held constant.

Dahl offers a "minimum" definition of democracy: "democratic theory is concerned with processes by which ordinary citizens exert a relatively high degree of control over leaders" (1956, p. 3). But, by defining the whole as "democracy" and making the basic distinction between "citizens" and "leaders," he assumes that these two roles are the most important ones. Although he agrees that no existing political system is fully democratic, his model of democracy allows him to assume that the bureaucratic and capitalist aspects of the state normally operate under conditions in which democracy can function.

Dahl is aware of this assumption and discusses the "division of labor" within democratic systems.

There is a need for bureaucracies of permanent experts to formulate alternatives and to make the most of the staggering number of decisions that a modern government must somehow make. These bureaucracies must be highly specialized among themselves since they perform highly differentiated tasks: they compete and conflict with one another and with other official groups in the system. [1956, p. 136]

This is the pluralist assumption of functional and mutually competitive bureaucracies. However, when Dahl applies the model to American society, elites come into view. In early American legislatures

legislative supremacy meant not so much the dominance of the people as it meant control over policy by the relatively small elites of wealth and status who were able to control one or both branches of the legislature. The rules . . . were rigged in favor of some groups and against others. [P. 139]

Elites and domination are recognized empirically and historically but are not theorized.[1] Dahl does not deny economic and social inequalities and the way they bias political institutions. But such biases are deviations from the theoretical model, problems to be compensated for by various political and economic mechanisms.[2]

Dahl clearly equates the democratic model with the American political system.

So long as the social prerequisites of democracy are substantially intact in this country, it appears to be a relatively efficient system for reinforcing agreement, encouraging moderation, and maintaining social peace in a restless and immoderate people operating a gigantic, powerful, diversified, and incredibly complex society. This is no negligible contribution, then, that Americans have made to the arts of government – and to that branch, which of all the arts of politics is the most difficult, the art of democratic government. [1956, p. 151]

In a later book Dahl examines what he calls the "social prerequisites of democracy" in more detail. He analyzes the economic conditions that are associated with a state that approximates democratic conditions: a polyarchy. Not surprisingly, the countries that are "fully inclusive polyarchies" are almost all capitalist democracies (1971, p. 248). But what

[1] See Dahl 1961 for a similar historical argument.
[2] Dahl maintains that the men at the Constitutional Convention in Philadelphia were also realists about the rules they were creating for the conduct of American government. They knew, that is, that "the rules must operate within the limits set by the prevailing balance of social forces" (1956, p. 141). Dahl does not say what those social forces were. Systematic consideration of the capitalist aspect of the state was outside his scope because of the implicit assumption that capitalism was not a problem for democracy.

is significant is that Dahl equates an "advanced economy" *not* with capitalism but rather with industrialization, urbanization, high levels of education, high levels of information available to a population, and the distribution of key "political resources and political skills to a vast variety of individuals, groups, and organizations." Even if income is unequally distributed, political resources must be relatively equal if a "pluralistic social order" is to be conducive to a democratic political system. And a "political subculture" must exist with "norms that legitimate negotiating, bargaining, logrolling, give and take, the gaining of consent as against unilateral power of coercion" (p. 77). Such economies are likely to be productive because workers are not operating under compulsion. Democratic politics thus feed back to the economy, increasing economic efficiency and supporting the conditions that then further stabilize democracy.[3]

Political scientist Robert Jackman asserts that "most analysts [have incorporated] notions of stability into the definition of democracy itself" (1975, p. 99).[4] Although he argues that this assumption is the result of "confusion," it seems more likely to us to be an intrinsic element of the pluralist world view. Despite his point, Jackman comes close to saying that, even if stability is not an aspect of democracy, it is a closely correlated consequence, because an institution that is responsive to the needs and demands of the population (thus presumably more democratic) will be better able to adapt itself to changing circumstances and thus survive.[5]

Political culture: the societal level

For the pluralist perspective, one important condition for democratic stability is found in the content and functions of *political culture*. A na-

---

[3] The empirical findings that support Dahl's argument treat the democratic aspect of the state as the key dependent variable and separate out characteristics of the economy as independent variables. Although this empirical procedure makes it difficult to see the ways in which the capitalist aspect of the state is intrinsically related to its democratic aspect, it also separates the economic conditions for democracy from capitalism per se. Dahl's analysis thereby becomes relevant to a world view that does not accept the equation of democracy with capitalism. His data support the conclusion that societies with relatively high income equality, equal dispersion of political resources, and high access to all forms of information are more likely to be democratic. Noncapitalist societies with these characteristics could maintain democracy.

[4] Jackman notes that S. M. Lipset has emphasized the "uninterrupted continuation of political forms" as an important aspect of democracy and cites Deane Neubauer's work (1967) as one of the few exceptions.

[5] Jackman's empirical work centers on the key pluralist hypothesis that democratic institutions increase social equality. He accepts the basic differentiation of society into "political" and "economic" dimensions that are empirically measurable. Such factors have external rather than internal relations with each other, enjoying causal autonomy as subsystems of a total society.

tional political culture comprises the fundamental beliefs and values held by both citizens and leaders concerning the importance of democratic processes and institutions. A political culture develops from nonpolitical processes of socialization in the family and other primary groups. The *content* (what people believe and want), *strength* (how much they believe and want something), and *homogeneity* (how much people agree about what they believe and want) of a political culture will vary considerably from society to society. These variations are held to affect the emergence and stability of democracy.

How does the political culture contribute to the emergence of the democratic aspect of the state? Here we call upon one of the classic studies of political culture: Almond and Verba's *Civic Culture* (1963). Although their work is based on contemporary survey data from 1,000 persons in each of five countries, the authors argue an essentially historical hypothesis about the impact of political culture. Almond and Verba's primary concern is to assess the type of political culture that is most supportive of a democratic state, specifically why Britain and the United States became relatively stable and effective democratic states whereas Italy and Germany experienced instability and ineffectiveness. (We shall not deal with their data on Mexico, the fifth country.)

A national political culture, according to Almond and Verba, is "the political system as internalized in the cognitions, feelings, and evaluations" of a population. Individuals have different kinds of orientations to politics and the political systems: knowledge (cognitive orientations), feelings (affective orientations), and opinions (evaluational orientations). These orientations are directed at both input institutions (political parties and elections) and output institutions (legislatures, police, welfare, and tax departments).

Political orientations are of three types: *parochial*, when people are simply apolitical; *subject*, when output orientations are developed but not input ones; and *participant*, when both output and input orientations are developed (Almond and Verba 1963, pp. 17–19). A subject culture rests on a passive political self-concept among citizens, and a participant culture rests on an active political self-concept. A political system can be characterized by the mix of orientations found among social groups. A civic culture, the type most conducive to democracy, is composed of a balanced mixture in individuals of all three orientations.

Besides looking for a correlation between political culture and the stability of democracy, Almond and Verba want to find the distribution of parochial, subject, and participant political orientations within each nation. They reason that where political structures and political cultures were not in balance political instability would result.

Almond and Verba find striking national differences in individual political orientations among the four countries. In the United States, Britain, and Germany, citizens were more informed and opinionated about politics than they were in Italy. Citizens in the United States and Britain were more likely to mention their pride in governmental institutions spontaneously and felt freer to discuss politics than did the Germans and Italians (1963, pp. 102, 122). General support for the political system was higher in the United States and Britain than in Germany and Italy (p. 68). American and British respondents were more likely than Germans and Italians to believe that the "ordinary man" should be "active in his community" (p. 176). More Americans and Britons than Germans and Italians said that they would "try and influence" their local and national governments on a hypothetical issue (pp. 184–5, 191, 194).

The national samples also varied in the proportion of individuals who believed that they could influence governmental decisions through political action ("citizen competence") or through administrative appeal ("subject competence"). In the United States, citizen competence was considerably greater than subject competence, in contrast to Britain where both were about equal. In Germany, citizen competence was lower than in either the United States or Britain, whereas subject competence was relatively high. Finally, in Italy, both citizen and subject competence were low (Almond and Verba 1963, p. 218). Almond and Verba explain these variations by historical differences in political development. The low level of subject competence relative to citizen competence in the United States is explained by the early mobilization of popular political participation, which considerably reduced the autonomy of administrative agencies and courts (p. 223). The high level of subject competence relative to citizen competence in Germany is explained by the historical accession of the middle class to economic power without political power (p. 227).[6]

With respect to nonpolitical social relations and their effect on politics, Almond and Verba discover sharp contrasts among these nations. In the United States and Britain, interpersonal trust and generosity were found to be high. People who reported themselves to be trusting of others were more likely to see informal political groups as a means of political influence (1963, p. 285). In Germany and Italy, on the other hand, these nonpolitical "overarching social values" (p. 285) were less extensive and did not facilitate informal political group formation. Almond and Verba conclude that a nonpolitical social consensus on basic

---

[6] It is significant that Almond and Verba use the term "class" only in historical references. "Group," "subgroup," "primary group," and "voluntary association" are some of the contemporary theoretical references.

values makes democracy possible. Social cohesion not only increases the nonpolitical resources available to the individual for political influence but also mutes the divisiveness of political cleavages within political parties and family, neighborhood, and work groups (pp. 294–9).

The pluralist view that societal values permeate all institutions and that a democratic state requires democratic values in all institutions is also derived from findings about nonpolitical authority patterns in family, school, and workplace. Americans and Britons were more likely than Germans or Italians to participate in family, school, and workplace. Such participation increased their sense of political competence (Almond and Verba 1963, pp. 330–8).[7]

Almond and Verba analyze the characteristics of the political cultures that foster the stability of a democratic state. They argue that a political culture that fosters continuously high levels of political participation cannot be stable, because it does not allow governments to acquire the double capacity to govern effectively and to respond to the needs of the governed. But bureaucratic decisions must also be constrained by their responsiveness to the demands of the citizenry. The political cultures of the United States and Great Britain, Almond and Verba argue, are distinctive because they balance this tension between the capacity of leaders to govern and their democratic responsiveness.

A civic culture contributes to democratization in two ways. First, it reduces active political participation while maintaining its potential. In both the United States and Britain, there was a substantial discrepancy between high political competence and relatively low levels of *actual* political participation (Almond and Verba 1963, pp. 479–81). Half of the U.S. respondents agreed that "the ordinary man ought to take some active part in the affairs of his community," but when asked what they "do in their free time," only about 10 percent mentioned community activities (p. 480). If there is mutual trust, this discrepancy frees political leaders from having to deal with high levels of participation. The everpresent potential for future political participation (sometimes called "slack" in the political system) prevents political leaders from taking advantage of this situation.

The continuous interaction between citizen participation and leader-

---

[7] Even the internal politics of families impinged upon the larger politics directed at the state. In the United States and Britain, females participated politically as much as males, whereas in Germany and Italy they participated much less than men. The authors argue that American and British families tend to be less male-dominated, and political issues are discussed in a more democratic manner between the parents. As a result, not only do children learn that women can participate in politics, they learn to accept political controversy as normal, because they have observed political disagreements between their parents (Almond and Verba 1963, pp. 325, 391, 397–9).

ship response leads to withdrawal of most citizens into a consensual passivity that reinforces both their sense of political competence and the legitimacy of the political system (Almond and Verba 1963, pp. 484–7). Almond and Verba argue that this inconsistency between norms and behavior is maintained by the ability of political leaders to keep "significant" issues out of the political arena by quick responsiveness to social needs (pp. 482–4).

Second, socialization of both leaders and citizens into nonpolitical cultural values enables citizens to trust leaders, thus reducing political polarization, and also provides citizens with the resources for the potential mobilization of informal social groups for political influence. A nonpolitical and consensual social structure constitutes the basis for the differentiation of a democratic state that can stay both effective and legitimate. The nonpolitical elements of the civic culture – multiple social groups intervening between citizen and state, particularly primary groups of friends, neighbors, and family – protect both citizens from the state and the state from citizens (Almond and Verba 1963, pp. 489–93).

Almond and Verba explicitly interpret their data to provide guidance not only to new nations in the twentieth century but also to "many older nations that have for a long time been attempting to create a stable pattern of democratic institutions." They say that merely writing a constitution with democratic guarantees or forming a political party to mobilize the masses is not enough. "The development of a stable and effective democratic government depends upon more than the structures of government and politics: it depends upon the orientations that people have to the political process – upon the political culture" (1963, pp. 497–8). Political culture thus plays an indispensable role in the evolution of democratic states. "The core processes of modernization – education and industrialization – create a democratic opportunity" but by themselves do not ensure a democratic state. Their assumption is that one can project backward from contemporary attitudes to discover the historical importance of political culture.[8]

---

[8] Some studies analyze deviant cases, such as a country that apparently violates some of the essential conditions for democracy yet remains democratic. The Netherlands, for example, has stable democratic institutions but a fragmented political culture, thereby violating Almond and Verba's hypothesis that a homogeneous political culture best sustains democracy. Political scientist Arend Lijphart's study (1975) analyzes the ways in which leaders of tightly organized ethnic, religious, party, and class blocs cooperated with each other to maintain democracy from 1917 to about 1967 (see p. 208). In the revised edition of his 1968 study, Lijphart notes that since 1967 increasing homogeneity of political culture has actually produced problems for Dutch democracy (Lijphart 1975). Lijphart explains this pluralist paradox by the unevenness among the various blocs of the move toward a homogeneous political culture, disagreements among political leaders, and the emergence of small splinter parties demanding more participation. Participation is in tension with consensus.

Almond and Verba assume that the politics of the civic culture in Western democratic states is influenced by the participation of ordinary citizens rather than organized by elites or ruled by classes. The civic culture makes possible an adaptive tension between state and civil society, between cleavage and consensus. The genesis of a civic culture is seen in an incremental process of political development of institutions, most strikingly in the United States and Britain.

Given this concept of democracy, Almond and Verba recognize a tension between participation and consensus.[9] Almond and Verba call this the need for a "power/responsiveness" balance, which is a normative way of resolving the contradiction by asserting that some way must be found to balance the opposing requirements of the democratic state. The "civic culture" provides the answer to this contradiction by postulating a balance of political orientations among individual citizens. "The need for elite power requires that the ordinary citizen be relatively passive, uninvolved, and deferential to elites" (1963, p. 478), thus solving the "power" half of the equation. The deferential orientation has its roots in traditional cultural values.

Conversely, enough people must be "participant" in their orientation to support the "responsiveness" side of the balance. At the institutional level, Almond and Verba suggest that competing parties are the main mechanism maintaining an adequate balance. But the primary requirement of democratic stability for most individuals is the appropriate mix of orientations.

Almost two decades after the publication of *The Civic Culture*, Almond and Verba edited a volume entitled *The Civic Culture Revisited* (1980). They deny that they had argued that political culture is the basic cause of political structures, including the state. Such a charge is incorrect, they say, arguing that

throughout the study the development of specific cultural patterns in particular countries is explained by reference to particular historical experiences, such as the sequence of Reform Acts in Britain, the American heritage of British institutions, the Mexican Revolution, and Nazism and defeat in World War II for Germany. It is quite clear that political culture is treated as both an independent and a dependent variable, as causing structure and as being caused by it. [P. 29]

This defense is irrelevant, because citation of specific historical events

---

[9] Political scientist Harry Eckstein has suggested that a democratic political system requires a blending of apparent contradictions – he calls them "balanced disparities" – if it is to function effectively. On the one hand, a democratic government must govern; it must have power and leadership and make decisions. On the other hand, it must be responsible to its citizens. For if democracy means anything, it means that in some way governmental elites must respond to the desires and demands of citizens. (From Almond and Verba 1963, p. 476, summarizing Eckstein's unpublished argument.)

does not entail any kind of inferences about causation. Their argument is an example of an epistemology that explains phenomena either by individual behavior or by historical events. In both cases "structural" causes are disaggregated as if the level of analysis of individuals and specific events contains self-evident causes.

Verba's "personal postscript" to the 1980 volume is remarkably evasive about a reconsideration of the theoretical framework of the 1963 volume, given the reversal of many predictions about modernization. As he says, in the two countries exemplifying the civic culture (the United States and Britain), there has been a "steady erosion of confidence in the government." He explains this development by specific events: Vietnam and Watergate in the United States, and the British government's "incapacity to deal with severe economic strain." But these specific events have nothing to do with the theoretical causes originally advanced to explain the emergence and stability of democratic political cultures. Almond summarizes those causes from the original study as follows: "education, the democratization of nongovernmental authority systems in the family, the school, and the workplace – general trust in one's fellow citizens" (Almond and Verba 1980, p. 399).

These factors summarize once again the pluralist image of modernization. Verba does not call this theoretical underpinning of the original study into question as a result of the reversal of historical support for it. Instead, individual events now explain the deviation. Another author in this volume, Dennis Kavanaugh, writes that the chapter on Britain paid "little attention to the possible determinants of the culture [and contained] ad hoc comments on British history" (Kavanaugh 1980, p. 133). Arend Lijphart, on the other hand, defends Almond and Verba against the accusation that they explain structure by culture. Rather, he argues, they look at culture and structure as "separate variables in a complex, multidirectional system of causality" (Lijphart 1980, p. 49). There are thus several ways of salvaging the pluralist world view. First, regard culture as the most important explanatory factor. If that fails, view culture as one factor among a complex multidirectional system. As a last resort, fall back on unique historical events to explain deviations. The fundamental assumption is that culture reflects history and historical events reflect the interaction of culture and structure. Causality adheres to the individual level of behavior and events.

The findings in such studies as *The Civic Culture* are interpreted by their authors only in terms of an aggregate political culture but can be seen otherwise as the expression of societal contradictions at the level of individual political orientations. Subject orientations are those toward the bureaucratic aspect of the state: acceptance of the legitimacy of the commands of officials installed according to established procedures. Citizen orientations are those toward the democratic aspect of the state: Participation is encouraged and rewarded both with tangible benefits (programs, subsidies, food stamps) and with symbolic benefits (the feeling of having done one's duty as a citizen). But what Almond and Verba call parochial orientations might be defined as those toward the capitalist aspect of the state, at least from the point of view of the ordinary citizen. Some realms of social and private life are perceived as having no relevance to legitimate democratic politics, that is, one's existence as a producer and consumer, worker and owner, in a capitalist society. Almond and Verba see such attitudes as "parochial" or "apolitical" behavior. Such orientations may indeed be necessary for the stability of the contradictory logics of such a society. Certain parts of it must be seen as irrelevant to one's responsibilities and privileges as a democratic citizen.

Almond and Verba argue that inconsistencies of orientations within individuals help stabilize the political system. The balance among subject, citizen, and parochial orientations is possible partly because citizens believe that they can in fact have an impact if they choose to participate. Similarly, the existence of the norm of participation is a source of pressure upon political leaders to be responsive, because they can anticipate that participation will punish them politically if they are not responsive to some degree. "A citizen within the civic culture has, then, a reserve of influence" (1963, p. 481). Two functional gaps are necessary, one between a high perception of potential influence and a lower level of actual influence and another between a high sense of obligation to participate and a lower amount of actual participation. These gaps maintain the balance between leadership power and responsiveness, on the one hand, and citizen activism and passivity on the other. The lack of salience of politics for most people allows these contradictory orientations to be maintained by individuals.

The authors have no evidence from their survey that would allow them to infer such functional gaps: The gaps follow from their theoretical assumption of system interdependence and the need for a balance of political orientations at the individual level. Reinterpreted, the point is consistent with our postulate of contradictory logics at the societal level. The penetration to the individual level of the contradictions among democratic (citizen), bureaucratic (subject), and capitalist (parochial) aspects of the state helps to sustain the institutions of these societies. Shorn of the assumption that it is only democratic institutions that are being sustained, such orientations may indeed stabilize a society composed of contradictory institutions.

This keystone of the pluralist empirical literature can thus be reinterpreted to show the way that the potential impact of democratic participation can be blunted in such societies. Exaggerating the democratic aspect of the state, Almond and Verba fail to see how so-called parochial or apolitical orientations serve to preserve the split between the state and society. Many potential political issues arising from the individual concerns of workers, community members, family members, and consumers seem to be nonpolitical and are separated from the issues that can legitimately be the source of political demands. Participation has been integrated into a politics that provides access while limiting it. Such studies as *The Civic Culture* provide empirically accurate but theoretically limited accounts of how such orientations serve to stabilize the political system.

Modernization and democracy

Rather than analyze individual beliefs and actions, some pluralists have studied social and economic factors assumed to underlie the political cultural basis of democracy. A frequent empirical approach is to correlate indicators of democracy (as measured by stable elections and peaceful changes of governments) with other characteristics of modern societies such as wealth, energy consumption, industrialization, literacy, and education.[10]

These associations are explained in terms of political culture. For example, a high level of education in a society is correlated with democracy because education "broadens man's outlook, enables him to understand the needs for norms of tolerance, restrains him from adhering to extremist doctrines, and increases his capacity to make rational electoral choices" (Lipset 1960, p. 56). Economic development (wealth and industrialization) permits "those in the lower strata to develop longer time perspectives and more complex and gradualist views of politics" (p. 61). Thus, wealth and industrialization create the conditions for the democratic state by creating persons with a predisposition to democratic attitudes and behavior. In these studies there are typically no direct measures of political culture. Instead, political culture is an unmeasured intervening variable, which theoretically interprets the relations between the independent variables of economic development and education and the dependent variables of stable elections or peaceful transfers of power.

Legitimacy is another social factor favoring democracy. Legitimacy is "the capacity of the system to engender and maintain the belief that the existing political institutions are the most appropriate ones for the society" (Lipset 1960, p. 77). A major test of legitimacy is whether or not a common "secular political culture" exists: national heroes (George Washington), a revered flag, a national anthem, rituals (Fourth of July),

---

[10] S. M. Lipset's *Political Man* (1959) is an early correlation study, but the tradition has continued, as evidenced by a 1979 article by Kenneth A. Bollen on the same topic.

and so on. Another test is whether or not the high status of conservative groups (such as the monarchy) is maintained in the period of transition to democracy.

Legitimacy is seen as compensating for the government's ineffectiveness. In the Great Depression of the early 1930s those governments, such as Britain and the United States, that enjoyed high legitimacy remained democratic in spite of their ineffectiveness in countering unemployment, whereas Germany and Italy went fascist because they were not legitimate. The ability of the democratic state to partake of a larger societal consensus not only sustains the legitimacy of the government but reduces the likelihood of irreconcilable political conflicts among citizens and leaders.

Legitimacy and consensus may be only consequences of stability, not causes, because they are aggregated individual attitudes and beliefs, which can have societal effects only when mediated through institutional arrangements. The assumption that unmediated cultural values can be causal factors is an important component of the pluralist world view.

Collective goals: the organizational level

Talcott Parsons's definition of power as the achievement of collective goals can be translated readily into an equation of consensus with democracy. "Power is the generalized capacity to mobilize the resources of the society, including wealth and other ingredients such as loyalties, 'political responsibility' etc., to attain particular and more or less immediate collective goals of the system" (Parsons and Smelser 1956, p. 49). This definition may seem at first glance to be inconsistent with Parsons's emphasis upon individuals as the primary level of analysis. But "collective goals" are those held by a plurality of members of the system or subsystem, because a collectivity is a plurality of persons. The equation of power with the mobilization of resources for collective goals leads easily to an institutional mechanism for integrating individual values into a consensus on goals: the democratic state.

Among mainstream economists, the view of the democratic state is more latent than in sociology and political science. This is partly due to their assumption that the political system can simply be taken as given. But in several works that deal with the conditions of social choices, the matter has been dealt with explicitly.

Economist Kenneth Arrow's "impossibility theorem" (1951) is a good example of the tension within the democratic aspect of the state. Arrow argues that in a "capitalist democracy" it is impossible to develop criteria that will maximize social welfare. He postulates a system in which individuals are free to choose among alternatives. The historical origins and organizational forms of those alternatives are not theoretically problematic.

Arrow's assumption that there is a consensus in the society establishes at the outset the criteria for an appropriate theory about the relations between social choice and individual values.[11] The term "social choice" indicates the pluralist world view that the society as a whole through some untheorized process chooses government structures and the policies those structures generate.[12]

Arrow offers two modes of ordering individual preferences by social choice. Either a "dictator" makes the choice as to whose preferences to satisfy, or "they might be determined by a majority vote of the individual members of the society." Arrow rejects the possibility of dictatorship, reflecting his assumption that democracy enjoys the support of the population. Once establishing that characteristic of the state and society, he postulates that there are two main mechanisms for making social choices: voting and the market. These are regarded as theoretically equivalent, because voting is used to make political decisions and the market to make economic decisions. This conceptual distinction is quintessentially pluralist, not only because of the division of society into separate political and economic spheres but because of the equation of voting and the market as devices for aggregating preferences.

Furthermore, Arrow assumes that "individual values are taken as data and are not capable of being altered by the nature of the decision process itself." Exogenous preferences is a "standard view in economic theory" (1951, p. 7). Arrow says that "the problem of achieving a social maximum derived from individual desires is precisely the problem which has been central to the field of welfare economists" (p. 3). This formulation ignores the ways in which elections, parties, and legislatures, not to mention state bureaucratic agencies, shape individual preferences. He simply assumes, following the theoretical model of economics, that "individuals in our society are free to choose, by varying their values, among the alternatives available" (p. 28).[13]

---

[11] One recent citation on this point will show that this assumption remains important: Democracy requires a "prior agreement among citizens on a set of rules" (Usher 1981, p. viii).

[12] Basic textbooks in economics usually summarize uncritically the Arrow theorems. See, for example, Henderson and Quandt 1971, pp. 284–7; and Quirk and Saposnik 1968, pp. 107–12.

[13] It is beyond our scope here to summarize the details of his five axioms, which together allowed Arrow to argue that it is impossible theoretically to define a social welfare function. It is relevant to note, however, that the empirical examples that illustrate the process of choice are elections in clubs and competitive foot races, all examples where participants are equal and the choice to enter the association or the game or leave it is a free one.

We see the same residual definition of the state by the consensual limits of the market in another well-known work on welfare economics. William Baumol asserts that "the essence of a democratic government may then be the voluntary acceptance of a central agency of intimidation designed for the attainment of the desires of the public" (1965, p. 57). Government, in this view, represents the interests of the whole, counterposed to individuals seeking to maximize their own interests. A democratic government is that limited government which carries out only those activities in the common interest that cannot be performed by free markets. Baumol in the introduction to his 1965 edition calls Arrow's work a "fundamental contribution" and a "basic work" on the theory of "group choice" (p. 39).

Another standard work on public finance, by economists Richard and Peggy Musgrave, also summarizes Arrow's work, saying that "determination of the budget plan through voting is a special application of the general problem of social choice" (Musgrave and Musgrave 1959, p. 116). The Musgraves discuss authoritarian versus democratic social choices, asserting that the latter is a method that reflects the "preferences of the constituent members of the group" (p. 118). And, "given our particular value judgment, the normative theory of budget planning must be democratic." The Musgraves agree with Arrow's conclusion that representation and consensus are ultimately in tension, because "there can be no social-welfare function that always meets both the doctrine of voter's sovereignty and . . . the minimum conditions of collective rationality" (pp. 119–20). The conditions can be met, the Musgraves assert, when the possible social choices are not mutually exclusive, when they can be represented by a continuous series of variable choices, and when all voters have a strong preference for one alternative. These are the classic pluralist images of a healthy democratic system in which compromise is possible and voters cluster around liberal and conservative parties functioning within a general consensus.

Support for legislatures

The key organizational instrument of democracy, and therefore a major target of group political demands, is an elected government, whether city council, state legislature, or national parliament. The political consensus at any given time (public opinion about spending for health care or for space exploration or for tax cuts) defines the general limits of legislative action. Political leaders – mainly those vulnerable to electoral defeat – must respond to those legitimate preferences that are expressed within the political consensus.

An empirical study of the cultural bases of political support for an

American legislature illustrates the pluralist analysis of democratic state organizations (Patterson, Hedlund, and Boynton 1975). Legislatures are assumed to represent voters and their political demands. Support for legislatures is assumed to contribute to the stability of the democratic state.[14]

Social status is highly associated with political support, regardless of leadership position. Better-educated, higher-income persons are more likely to support the legislature. Lobbyists, party leaders, and influential citizens – called "influence agents" or "linkage groups" – have much higher social status than ordinary citizens. Their support for the legislature is accordingly much higher.

Social gaps – inequalities of income, education, occupational status – are treated by the authors as empirical facts but are not theorized. The historical forces generating a *system* of inequality lying behind the seemingly neutral indexes of individual socioeconomic status have no theoretical significance. The silence of the study on the question of the meaning of one of its most important empirical findings is a key indication of its world view. The term "social class" is used (Patterson et al. 1975, p. 208) but is only an aggregate summary term for multiple, correlated characteristics of individuals.

It might be argued that social status is correlated with support by citizens because governing elites or ruling classes benefit from such an ideology; or, that institutions generate ideologies supporting them. The historical conditions that contribute to their stability cannot be inferred from the legitimating ideologies. Such an argument is consistent with the empirical findings offered by Patterson et al. but not with the pluralist world view.

"Influence agents" were inferred by Patterson et al. from *perceptions* of which of thirteen groups actually had influence and which ought to have influence. Private interest groups (chambers of commerce, farm

---

[14] In 1966 and 1967, University of Iowa political scientists interviewed 1,000 residents of Iowa, all but four of the 185 members of the Iowa legislature, nearly 500 persons nominated by legislators as politically knowledgeable, half of the 200 Iowa county party chairmen, and 100 lobbyists. A core index of "political support" was composed of seven questions and two dimensions. "Compliance" was based on four questions as to whether the respondent agreed that citizens ever have a right to break the law. "Institutional maintenance" was composed of three questions as to whether the legislature should be abolished or have its powers reduced. Persons who did not believe in breaking the law and who did not want to abolish the legislature were regarded as "supporting" the legislature. Other measures were of political culture ("pride in Iowa"), "traditionalism" (attitudes toward change), and "instrumental liberalism" (attitudes toward the welfare state). All of the groups of respondents were lumped together, as if they were equal in influence and in the significance of their opinions. Because issues were not given content, the empirical assumption was that analysis could neglect the *content* of politics while analyzing the *process* of support.

bureaus, National Farmers Organization, banks, insurance companies) are all lower in perceived influence than public groups (experts, the governor, party leaders, voters) and lower than labor, which was tied with party leaders in the legislature. "Labor, banks and insurance companies display the highest difference in means [influence], having more influence than they should" (1975, pp. 127–8).

"Linkage groups" were seen as generating political support, although the actual behavior of the political parties, lobbying groups, and pressure groups was not studied. V. O. Key provided their argument that linkage groups

> could constitute a distinctive political subculture sufficiently independent and diverse to provide the pluralism necessary for the democratic formula, sufficiently active and involved to be able to acquire and exploit access to both the narrower circles of political leadership and the wider circles of political participation and sufficiently imbued with common motives and norms to maintain and promote public trust, restraint in the exploitation of public opinion, and etiquette in the conduct of opposition politics. [Key 1961, pp. 536–40; Patterson et al. 1975, p. 75]

The emergence of a social structure composed of multiple linkage groups was related to the development of a more competitive and differentiated party system.

> Public demands on the state and local governments [in Iowa] have become more complex, reflecting the increasing needs for services and the liberalization of traditional practices felt by an ever-growing urban population. The political interest group structure of the state has shifted from dominance by the Iowa Farm Bureau Federation to a more pluralistic pattern in which no one organized group can exert an overwhelming influence on political affairs [Patterson et al. 1975, p. 23]

Thus there has been an "irregular but steady increase in party competition within the legislature" (p. 23). Economic development led to a proliferation of interest groups and then to more party competition.

The finding that private corporations (banks, farmers' organizations, insurance companies) are perceived as having more influence than they should have is viewed as an anomaly by the authors, who have no theory of the bases of institutional power. All thirteen types of groups are regarded as potentially equal in influence, simply because of the methodological device of including thirteen different types of groups in the same question and asking respondents about their relative influence (both "have" and "ought"). The resulting rank order conveys the impression that respondents agree with the theoretical decision to classify the groups *as if* they were potentially equal in influence and that perceptions are an adequate substitute for measures of actual control of institutional resources. The empirical decision to measure individual perceptions fits the pluralist conception of power as influence. Power becomes subjective and consensual.

Paraphrasing John Stuart Mill, the study concludes that "a legislature, the centerpiece of representative government, must, among other things, have substantial support in the mass public if it is to survive as a representative institution or if it is to perform the functions of representation effectively" (Patterson et al. 1975, pp. 21–2). This is, of course, the classic pluralist image of the relationship among public opinion, political culture, and democratic stability.

In this study, there is no historical or structural context. A single state legislature in the United States in the 1960s is treated as if its functioning revealed something about all representative organizations in the United States, whether city councils, state legislatures in other states, or Congress itself. Iowa is treated as if it were an autonomous political system, without a particular relation to the larger state, let alone to the capitalist system. This is typical of the pluralist world view that differentiated subsystems can be analyzed as if they revealed the logic of the entire society.

Another clue to the world view is the assumption that political institutions require support to survive, support provided by the beliefs of individual citizens and members of interest groups. Patterson et al. characterize their own work as expanding the boundaries of legislative research by paying more attention to its "representative function" than to its "legislative function" (1975, p. 8). But the authors substitute the symbolic function of political support for the tangible function of serving real interests.

Patterson and his colleagues distinguish several types of legislative research, which provide a convenient summary of pluralist approaches to organizations. "Institutional" studies describe the formal structure of legislatures, their legal powers and procedures for passing laws. Such studies contain "an implicit conception of the legislative institutional structure as a set of effective, channeling constraints that shape and pattern the behavior of legislators in important ways" (1975, p. 4). "Process-oriented" researchers reverse this emphasis; they take the "institutional character of the legislature for granted and concentrate on the activity transpiring within its framework," that is, the process through which "legislation emerges as the product of legislative activity, and how" (p. 5). One concern of process research has been with who wins and who loses particular contests within the legislature, using documents, roll-call votes, legislator biographies, and details about interest group and party involvement in particular decisions.

Patterson et al. explicitly note that the institutionalists assume that the processes function normally and vice versa. They recognize the intellectual division of labor within the pluralist perspective. As they put it, "Institutionalists found no reason to investigate the actions of legislators presumed to be rationally and individualistically judging the desirability of alternative proposals that seem to appear before them mainly through the operation of formal rules and procedure." On the other hand, "process-oriented research often appears to assume that legislators' behavior consists mainly of essentially passive, neutral reactions to demands, pressures, and influences put on them by such extra institutional actors as pressure groups, political party agencies, administrators, and executive agencies" (1975, p. 6).

The third type of research, into which their own work falls, is "behavioral," which usually focuses "attention on the persons and activities of legislators themselves." This work adds interest groups ("linkage agents") and voters to the diverse connections between representatives and the represented. Patterson et al. have isolated the "citizen role" as a key source of support for the legislature as a state organization.

Alienation versus efficacy and trust: the individual level

There have been few attempts to assess empirically the key pluralist tenet that consensus both exists and is necessary for the stability of democracy. One of the few such studies concludes that the only empirically well-confirmed hypotheses are those that find alienated persons likely to have lower social status and to participate less (Wright 1976, p. 3). Sociologist James D. Wright starts from the individual level of analysis, reanalyzing numerous public opinion surveys dealing with alienation (the presumed opposite of consensus) and participation. He points out that there are practically no investigations of the phenomenon and that those that exist are seriously flawed methodologically. Even more important, no criteria have ever been offered as to how much alienation would threaten democracy. "[T]he 'necessary amount' of consensus can be defined by whatever level happens to exist in a stable democratic state. Thus, the texts (on alienation) vacillate between stylistic exaggeration and conceptual tautology" (p. 63). Even those empirical efforts to specify the theory comment on the difficulty of translating the theory into testable empirical hypotheses.

Wright provides a devastating critique of the pluralist assumption that consensus is necessary for democratic stability. He notes, for example, that although Almond and Verba found that a quarter of Americans did not believe that they could do anything about an unjust national law the authors did not find it necessary to consider whether or not such alienation was dangerous to the civic culture. They offered no criteria for how much consensus was enough (Wright 1976, p. 64).[15]

Wright argues that all of the theories about the importance of political culture and consensus for democratic stability are inherently implausible. Why are such "vast quantities of trust" needed, if these are already stable democracies? Why isn't simple effectiveness enough? He suggests that the view derives from the assumption of unlimited appetites by the masses. To offset these appetites, a combination of "participatory potential" (what Dahl calls slack in the system) and the early inculcation of an allegiance immune to the actual behavior of political leaders is needed (Wright 1976, pp. 58–9).

Wright argues against this view, holding that

> there is no persuasive evidence that political alienation and discontent among the mass public pose a serious threat to democratic stability, in contrast to the consensus claims. Second, since the major observable consequence of mass disaffection with government is a decline in political interest and withdrawal from political activity, mass alienation is more threatening to democratic representation than to democratic stability.

The primary " 'problem' of the modern democracy, is therefore, not one of deactivating the masses, but of creating mechanisms that facilitate mass participation" (1976, p. 59). In effect, Wright is calling for pluralists to remain true to the original definition of democracy as a mechanism for allowing popular influence, participation, and representation.

Wright also reanalyzes some of the political socialization research, discovering that a substantial minority of the population (and a majority of less well-educated workers) does not accept "regime norms." Among eighth-graders from low-socioeconomic-status families, only 41 percent had a sense of political efficacy. "Upper SES children are apparently instructed from an early age that voting is important, participation useful, political activity likely to get results" (1976, p. 75). Although class theorists might argue that these data demonstrate that the working class is not socialized into the norms of bourgeois democracy, Wright is making an even more fundamental empirical point. Socialization is neither effective nor does it have consequences for political behavior. He reviews the evidence on a variety of presumed consequences of alienation (negativism, extremism, lack of participation, radical right ideologies) and finds it both scanty and trivially related (pp. 77–85). There is little evidence to support the fundamental argument that when citizens do not trust their government democratic stability is undermined. The absence of such research is indicative of a silence within the pluralist perspective.

---

[15] Wright is concerned with political alienation, not alienation in general, and with the two dimensions usually distinguished: *efficacy* (associated with participation) and *trust*.

Certain empirical relationships are taken as so self-evident, because of fundamental theoretical assumptions, that either no research is conducted on them or a lack of evidence is ignored.

It is important to emphasize that Wright, although critical of the empirical findings concerning political efficacy and trust in government, is theoretically committed to democratic participation and the potential good sense of ordinary citizens. He rejects the pluralist argument on empirical grounds while accepting the measures as the best available. He shows that alienation (or lack of efficacy political trust) is not correlated with extremism and antidemocratic behavior. At least half of the American electorate does not trust the government and does not believe that its participation has an impact. In other words, half of the American population is not included in the " 'great consensus' that allegedly sustains and facilitates democratic government" (1976, p. 116).[16]

We go further in arguing that the "political trust" scale can be reinterpreted, as attitudes toward the state.[17] "Government" is mentioned in all five of the standard items (the "people running the government" in three, whether "big interests run the government" in one, and just "the government" in the fifth). All five items tap into the general belief, or lack of it, that political leaders are inefficient (do not know what they are doing, make mistakes, waste money) and corrupt. Rather than political trust, such measures might well be interpreted as political realism, or even cynicism. High "distrust" may reflect a view of the state as an autonomous instrument of political and economic power, acting in the interests of those persons who run it, and not very efficiently at that.

The pluralist image of the state – as an entity that can be trusted – is quite naturally held by higher-status persons who participate more because they benefit more. Their participation induces a belief that government is effective and responsive. The description of the measure as one of political trust thus indicates the pluralist world view underlying the empirical procedures. Only individuals can be trusted, not governments or corporations.

We also can reinterpret the index of political efficacy. Government is

---

[16] Note that these data were all available in the period of celebration of American democracy in the 1950s. Herbert Marcuse and C. Wright Mills were wrong in presuming that most Americans supported the regime and its leaders.

[17] Empirical measures of "trust in government," similarly, assume that opinions can be aggregated for the whole society to form a measure of consensus on governing institutions. See, for the most recent and most comprehensive survey of the data on "confidence" and "trust" in government, business, and labor, Lipset and Schneider 1983. The authors conclude that, although confidence in all institutions has fallen, it is not a legitimation crisis, because most people distinguish between the "admirable functions" of American institutions and the personal, even dramatically corrupt, behavior of the individuals who run them.

again mentioned in three of the four items, but in all cases as an object of political participation and understanding. Having a say, thinking about government actions, being able to understand government action, voting – all refer to the potential impact of one's concerns, thoughts, actions upon government and public officials. If one believes that one has a say, if one can understand that voting matters, one is taking a pluralist perspective on the efficacy of participation. If elites or ruling classes control the state, however, democratic participation has only minimal impact on government policies, precisely because participation must be moderate and compromising and must not challenge the state or capitalism. Even if one does not agree with managerial or class skepticism about the limits of democracy, the opposite is not true, that absence of such beliefs constitutes a lack of efficacy. Rather, it may indicate a quite different image of democracy, that conventional political participation does not work, that people are misled, or that politicians simply ignore what people want.

Although Wright does not do this, these empirical data can thus be used for nonpluralist conclusions. That better-educated persons participate more and have "pluralist" beliefs in the efficacy of standard mechanisms of political participation may only be a sign of their commitment to capitalist democracy and institutions, a sign of the capacity of socializing institutions to create beliefs appropriate to their class consequences.

Socialization of leadership

Given the pluralist world view, the appropriate socialization of political leaders is also crucial to the stable functioning of the democratic state. "The political elite can be leaders and *representatives* only if there are mechanisms within the culture which foster the kinds of personal motivations that lead men to perceive and strongly support their interests within a political system which has relatively well-defined rules" (Lipset 1963, p. 208; italics in original).

Although the term "elites" is frequently used to describe individual roles in pluralist analyses, the term "leaders" can be substituted with a gain of conceptual clarity. Almond and Verba say (and we make the change) that leaders "may be recruited from particular political subcultures to perform bureaucratic, military, executive and other political roles" and that "the process of induction and socialization into these roles produces different values, skills, loyalties, and cognitive maps." They use Germany and France as examples: "[T]he bureaucratic and military elites were traditionally recruited from the aristocratic and authoritarian subcultures. In addition, the role socialization of these elites reinforced the antidemocratic tendencies and were significant obstacles to the emergence of homogeneous participant cultures" (1963, pp. 29–30). Thus, leadership decisions are heavily influenced by their role socialization and values. Almond and Verba do not offer any evidence for these historical hypotheses. In the context of their empirical study of five contemporary political cultures, these hypotheses are casual speculations at the margins of their analytic concerns.[18]

A major empirical study of "public opinion and American democracy" (Key 1961), based on Michigan Survey Research Center data, is filled with theoretical arguments about the nature and consequences of leadership socialization into democratic values but contains no evidence on that point. Key's classic study is based on the assumption that democratic governments must function with consensus not only on institutions but, if possible, on issues. Key's argument makes a number of distinctions among types of consensus – permissive, decision, concurring – the details of which are not important here. The important point is that he explicitly assumes that "the circles of leadership, the political activists of the society, constitute what might be called a 'political subculture.' . . . [They] may be carriers of the political culture or holders of the basic consensus on modes and styles of action, even though they may be sharply divided on the issues of the day" (p. 51). Key cites data from an earlier study by sociologist Samuel Stouffer, which found that "community leaders – public officials, party county chairmen, presidents of chambers of commerce, presidents of labor unions, and other community functionaries – rated on the average far higher on a scale of tolerance than did the rank and file of the citizenry" (Key 1961, p. 52). Key assumes without any data that the appropriate socialization of political leaders into democratic values occurs and has significant consequences for democratic stability.[19]

A later study adds some data, arguing similarly that the values and

[18] An early inventory of the literature on political socialization (Hyman 1959) dealt almost entirely with "subgroup differentiation" (age, occupation, sex, education, and so on) of the political orientations of citizens, although the author placed great theoretical importance on the study of "historically important political figures" and "political actors with lesser roles in history." Psychodynamic factors in the behavior of these "elites" could be studied biographically and also by inference from such data as roll-call votes of legislatures (p. 11). Hyman's underlying assumption was that the "psychology . . . of minor political actors" could be inferred from "statistical records of their decision behaviors." In other words, the actions of state organizations can be used to infer the individual attitudes and values of their members.

[19] Dahl and Key's statement of the pluralist problem of democratic consensus laid the basis for a number of subsequent empirical studies. The title of one conveys the theoretical framework precisely: Agreement and the Stability of Democracy (Budge 1970). Based on interviews with members of Parliament and potential voters in London, the study included an assessment of the "political stratum's support for democratic principles" (chap. 11).

attitudes of political leaders are particularly important in understanding democracy (Putnam 1973, p. 160). Putnam says explicitly that he was concerned with the implications of the different components of the "attitudes, values and habits" of political leaders for the "responsiveness, stability and effectiveness of British and Italian democracy" (pp. 237–8). Using interviews with 176 members of the British House of Commons and the Italian Chamber of Deputies, Putnam disaggregated the general concept of political culture into three main themes that compose a political culture: "political style, cognitive predispositions, and operative ideals" (p. 4). This solidly pluralist method takes a central concept referring to individuals and converts it into dimensions, then into measurable variables, which are finally empirically associated with each other in a way that assumes their autonomy as psychological subsystems.[20]

Putnam's conclusions were that, despite differences between Italian and British politicians (the latter were more "tolerant, trustful, open-minded and flexible" than the Italians in their attitudes toward political opponents), ideological polarization (the opposite of consensus) was declining in both countries. He attributed this to social and economic "progress" (read: modernization). "Increased economic productivity, greater consumer affluence, more widespread educational opportunities, increased social and geographical mobility, the creation of a new mass culture – all these changes in the environment of politics have provided the context in which attitudes toward partisan opponents could soften" (1973, p. 69). But Putnam assumes without evidence that consensus on democratic principles has an impact on the state. The bureaucratic state hardly appears, except in such offhand assertions as "the growth of government intervention in social and economic affairs increases the incentives for political participation" (p. 235). And capitalism appears only as a healthy producer of education, income, science, and technology.

An even more recent empirical study includes bureaucrats as well as politicians, both at an individual level of analysis (Aberbach et al. 1981). The study expands the scope to seven countries (the United States, Britain, France, Germany, Italy, the Netherlands, and Sweden). As in the previous study, the capitalist economy and bureaucratic state are regarded as contexts within which individuals believe, perceive, and act. The guiding assumption is that a central answer to the question, "How can the complex modern state be governed democratically?" involves the "norms and values that guide decision makers" (p. 170). And the

---

[20] This is the pluralist totality observed in the individual human being. Putnam recognizes this by saying that his analytic purposes required him to "pull apart the individual strands in a man's carefully woven fabric of political ideas and ideals" (1973, p. 237).

study found, in fact, that "support for pluralism is rather high among European elites" (p. 179), measuring pluralism by an index composed of answers to questions about political liberties, freedom of political propaganda, acceptance of conflict among interest groups, and accept-ance of the important role of political parties. Although Aberbach et al. see the tension between the problem of governing via consensus and of allowing participation, they still assume that "since all of the countries in this study are representative democracies – 'polyarchies' in Dahl's terminology – we anticipate that their leaders will, by and large, support both basic democratic values . . . liberty (or contestation) and equality (or participation)" (p. 173).

These brief citations are only samples of the literature on the beliefs and attitudes of political and administrative leaders that reflect the as-sumption that it is important to socialize them into democratic values. Such studies of individual attitudes and beliefs are not typically linked to institutional analyses of capitalism or bureaucracy.

Conclusions

The democratic aspect of the state is primary for the pluralist perspective. A moderate, compromising political culture is an indispensable support for democracy. Such a political culture is a cause, a consequence, and a hallmark of democracy. But, curiously enough, there are few empirical studies of political culture that offer criteria as to how much and under what conditions consensus is necessary for democratic stability. One important work (Wright 1976) questions the very existence of consensus, either as an empirical reality or as necessary for the stability of the political system. Nevertheless, this theoretical component of the pluralist world view lies beneath much empirical inquiry. A core assumption of the pluralist perspective is that measures of individual attitudes and behavior can be aggregated together and regarded as an attribute of the society as a whole: its "political culture." Culture, values, and societal norms and other closely equivalent concepts are regarded as indicating important causal factors in their own right. Thus they do not have to be associated with elite domination and class rule in order to have causal efficacy.

In this chapter we have dealt with studies that stress the functional rather than the political side of pluralism, those that emphasize the role that a consensus on common values plays in stabilizing democratic states. In Chapter 4 we turn to the other side of the intellectual division of labor, to examine studies of participation.

4

The democratic state and participation

The democratic state, in pluralist perspective, is influenced by multiple forms of citizen political participation within the limits of a consensus on the boundaries of state action. Public opinion and voting are explicitly modes of individual influence. Social movements, interest groups, and political parties aggregate individual preferences and values into political demands, which are presented to agencies of government. Noninstitutionalized participation such as demonstrations, riots, and rebellions is seen as a deviant form of political behavior. Although social movements typically begin outside the normal channels of political representation and may become pathological, in healthy democracies they are also mechanisms to create new political parties or to force existent parties to adapt to the demands of previously unrepresented groups.

Various analytic categories delineate forms of individual action within diverse group contexts. A. O. Hirschman's well-known essay *Exit, Voice, and Loyalty* (1970) is a good example of an attempt to go beneath such substantive categories as protest, voting, and public opinion to discover more generic modes of individual action. In democratic political systems individuals enjoy combinations of options. Either "voice" (the expression of preferences via political action) or "exit" (a decision to leave the group, organization, or political unit) must be available. "Loyalty" is a residual characteristic of those who stay. It is an ad hoc category, not theoretically grounded. The conditions necessary for people to speak out, leave, or be loyal can be investigated in any social unit. Democracy is most likely when both exit and voice are available. Hirschman includes "voluntary associations, competitive political parties, and some business enterprises" as the kinds of social units that "react strongly" to both exit and voice. Those that react to neither are "parties in totalitarian one-party systems, terroristic gangs, and criminal gangs," that is, social units with conditions incompatible with democracy (1970, p. 121). The mechanisms of exit, voice, and loyalty help to achieve stability within a societal consensus,[1] but only voice constitutes participation.

Political participation in the pluralist sense derives from diverse individual and group interests. Ideally, multiple roles pull individual citizens in opposite directions and moderate the stratagems of leaders anxious to achieve power (Lipset 1960, pp. 32, 88). If nonparticipants are less committed to democratic procedures (Lipset 1960, p. 102) and political leaders can respond in anticipation of potential participation (Dahl 1961; Almond and Verba 1963, p. 487), a low level of participation in politics is not a fundamental flaw in the system. High levels of political participation may actually reveal social and political instability, indicating a lack of coherence between the values of social groups and their political representatives (Berelson, Lazarsfeld, and McPhee, 1954). Different citizens and social groups bring different resources to bear in their political participation. What is important is that different *kinds* of resources are "dispersed unequally." Dahl (1971, p. 87) argues that "actors badly off with respect to one kind of political resource stand a good chance of having access to some . . . partly offsetting political resource." Lack of wealth can be compensated for by time, energy, political skills, or popularity.

In this political version of the pluralist perspective, power is *situational*; it derives from the actions of individuals and groups in specific political situations. Political power is observed in the outcomes of specific actors' attempts to influence state actions. Frequently, pluralists even define political participation in terms of its intended impact on public leaders. Verba and Nie (1972, p. 2) define political participation as "activities by private citizens that are more or less directly aimed at influencing the selection of government personnel and/or the actions they take." Power is seen in the resolution of controversial decisions in competitive elections, parliamentary votes, and policy arenas. The indicator of an individual's power was the number of victories in such contentious community decisions (Dahl 1961). Not only are political preferences revealed by political participation, but interests are defined by the subjective expression of preferences.

---

[1] Hirschman contrasts his own approach with that of Milton Friedman who, he says, like most economists, has a "bias in favor of exit and against voice" and criticizes the democratic process as "cumbrous political channels." Hirschman notes that exit has "in the political realm . . . been labeled desertion, defection and treason" (1970, p. 17). He argues that both mechanisms must be recognized as important and recommends the economic concept to political scientists and vice versa. This is a debate within the basic pluralist world view that the two spheres, market and nonmarket, are related to each other externally, rather than those relations together constituting some larger whole. Niklas Luhmann's view (1977) that politics and markets are separate contexts of action reflects the same assumption.

These are only a few samples of the pluralist argument that the primary source of power is political participation, empirically inferred from individual influence over publicly controversial decisions of the state. In our view, this political definition of power is inconsistent with the functional definition of power (also pluralist) as the capacity of a system to achieve collective goals. We know of no study where both types of power are simultaneously investigated empirically. The intellectual division of labor within the pluralist perspective leaves this tension between the functional requirements of consensus on collective goals and the political requirements of allowing open participation an unresolved theoretical issue, although it is empirically recognized as the political problem of governance facing leaders.

Social movements and party systems: the societal level

Social movements are seen as noninstitutionalized forms of political participation, arising when demands cannot be met through normal channels. Because they either arise from or call into question the changing relationships between institutions, they must be analyzed as a societal phenomenon. Social movements force governments to adapt to societal change, but violent societal transformation is prevented by democratic party competition. A party system is thus a key mediating institution between state and society.[2] When tamed by the pragmatic requirements of winning electoral victories, even revolutionary movements become reformist governing parties.

The institutionalization of a social movement

The farmers of Saskatchewan, Canada, were the core of a social movement that became an interest group, then a political party, and finally the government. The history of the farmers' movement is a nearly unique example of an explicitly socialist party winning electoral power in North America. From a pluralist perspective it is a success story for the democratic state and political culture (Lipset 1950).

Ever since the Civil War, the wheat farmers of North Dakota and

---

[2] For a classic study of the shifting electoral majorities of different parties in American history, see Burnham 1970. Following upon the work of V. O. Key, Jr., Burnham analyzed the major "critical realignments" of American party politics since the nineteenth century. In his words, "realignments are themselves constituent acts: they arise from emergent tensions in society which are not adequately controlled by the organization or outputs of party politics as usual, escalate to a flash point; they are issue-oriented phenomena, centrally associated with these tensions and more or less leading to resolution adjustments. . . . They are involved with redefinitions of the universe of voters, political parties, and the broad boundaries of the politically possible" (that is, the existing consensus) (p. 10).

Saskatchewan have been subject to sharply changing world prices for wheat, as well as to uncertain weather, and thus an unpredictable crop. They have depended upon bankers for expensive loans for equipment, upon elevator companies for storage facilities, upon railroads to ship their grain. Continuously in debt, complaining of high freight rates and the monopoly of the grain elevator companies, the wheat farmers organized demonstrations, interest groups (grain growers' associations), cooperatives (wheat pools, elevator cooperatives), and finally political parties (the Non-Partisan League in North Dakota and the Cooperative Commonwealth Federation in Saskatchewan) in their own defense. The CCF was formed in Saskatchewan in 1932 after the socialists convinced others that a political party, and not merely an economic interest group, was needed to defend the farmers' interests. The CCF won a provincial majority in 1944 and held governmental power until 1964. (It later changed its name to the New Democratic Party.)

The social and political structure of Saskatchewan was relatively unstratified, and there were myriad voluntary and elective positions in various organizations. Rural Saskatchewan was socially a "one-class" community, differing little in income and status. A "series of major social and economic challenges [required] the establishment of a large number of community institutions to meet them" (Lipset 1950, p. 246). This mass participation provided widespread political education in various community organizations.

Although the CCF was based on a specific social class of farmers, the leaders adapted their movement to beliefs already present. Socialism was downgraded, and the religious and moral aspects of their program played up, in order to achieve majority support. Once in power, the CCF promised to guarantee farmers that they could not lose their land because of debt, to strengthen cooperatives, to make collective bargaining mandatory and outlaw various antilabor practices, to raise the minimum wage and teachers' salaries, to establish free hospitalization, and to establish or purchase public utilities and some industrial enterprises.

Most of these programs were hardly socialist, but the political and social conditions under which they were announced still led to serious compromises. The guarantee of land to the farmer conflicted with proposals to nationalize land. The cooperatives favored larger farms and thus farmers with more capital. The strengthening of labor and the raising of wages reduced the competitiveness of the provincial economy. No attempt was made to turn over more decision-making authority to workers within economic enterprises. The attempt to establish socialized medicine lost completely, due to the objections of the doctors. The government-run industries could not compete effectively with privately owned ones.

Political compromise for the CCF programs also stemmed from the technical requirements for efficient administration of increasingly complex governmental tasks. Sufficient authority had to be delegated to expert administrators to enable them to carry out their tasks. Although this managerial argument seems to be inconsistent with the democratic requirement that the electorate be able to choose between alternative major policies to be carried out by technical experts, Lipset argues that the democratic constituency as a whole can "change the policies and the personnel of the bureaucracy," a pluralist premise (1950, p. 324). However, because the stability of the CCF government and leadership rested upon support from its political base of farmers, the growing gap between the state bureaucracy and the party leadership became a "problem."

Wheat farmers, cabinet ministers, local businessmen, civil servants, and CCF party officials were the diverse actors whose specific economic and political interests led to their participation. Although these groups were unequal in income, time, information, political skills, and experience, inequalities of these political resources were assumed to be relatively uncorrelated, and therefore different resources could potentially compensate for each other.

It is assumed that, in a democratic state, if the grievances of a group are severe enough; it can express its demands to the appropriate political leaders and get a response sufficient to be persuaded to limit demands to those that do not threaten democratic stability. Political demands must be limited to those that accept the legitimacy of *all* other groups in the society. Challenge to private property is ruled out in practice, as is a socialist movement capable of achieving more than an extension of the welfare state.

The evaluation of the impact of social movements upon the democratic state rests upon subjective factors. The "general climate of opinion determines what is radical or conservative at a given time and place. The introduction of major changes in the economy may not necessarily be radical for one community, though similar reforms would outrage the sentiments of other regions" (Lipset 1950, p. 271). Thus, the character of a political movement is judged by reference to the sentiments of the population at the time. This is yet another way of expressing the pluralist view that the consensus existing at any given time among major groups in the society is the ultimate judge of the democratic or undemocratic character of a popular movement or leadership actions.

In *Agrarian Socialism* (1950), Lipset studies a relatively homogeneous social group: wheat farmers who differed little in income and status. Social equality reinforced democratic participation. The chances for oligarchy were reduced because leaders had few incentives to manipulate their resources in order to stay in office. The implication is that severe economic inequality undermines the possibility of genuine democracy. Without relatively equal income and status, the political institutions of democracy become fictitious. They are emptied of democratic content, because the social preconditions do not exist that could allow them to become mechanisms of true representation of individuals and groups.

The choice of a one-class region as a research site to test propositions about the social bases of democracy is consistent with a pluralist world view. Though acknowledged explicitly, the homogeneity of the population is regarded simply as another "factor" to be either controlled or allowed to vary. A "subsystem" of the society is isolated for study in a way that makes systematic collection of empirical data possible. Because it is difficult to study a complex, differentiated society as a whole, a "sample" is selected from that society that will adequately "represent" major characteristics. One can then generalize to the society as a whole.

Lipset's empirical focus upon a specific social movement ends by generalizing to "democratic societies," as if the specific study is a sample of the universe of such entities. The pluralist image of society as an aggregation of increasingly more differentiated parts contains the assumptions that these parts can be studied in isolation from each other, that they are a microcosm of the whole, and that the whole is a healthy democratic system.

Agrarian Socialism omitted events and forces at societal or world levels. Depressions, wars, national policies, even court decisions affecting the possibilities of certain kinds of political action, are treated as exogenous events that must be taken into account by political actors within the CCF and Saskatchewan but are not a theoretical problem. Democratic politics is thus abstracted from its historical societal context. The CCF movement is seen as a response to an event – the economic depression of the 1930s – a leftist tendency that became successfully embedded in a political party and then in a government. This government carried out certain reforms but was restrained by its commitment to electoral victory from carrying out its socialist program. Democracy functioned to deradicalize the social movement by institutionalizing it as a political party.

The general and explicit theory is that group interests give rise to political demands and organizations that respond to those demands, present them to authoritative bodies, and attempt to gain influence in government. The original group interests that give rise to organizations defending those interests become inconsistent with the actions of the organizational leadership, which *must* be given autonomy if the organization is to continue its existence.

The implicit image is that this process is repeated endlessly in the history of democratic states. Left–right swings in response to economic crisis or prosperity, popular response to a leftist party, the institution-alization of reforms and their acceptance by conservative elements, the transformation of a leftist party into a governing coalition and a sponsor of incremental change are seen as *eternal* processes, fated to be repeated again and again in a healthy democracy. New dissatisfactions will occur, and then new parties and forms of participation will arise, only to become absorbed in the shifting consensus as participation becomes institutionalized.

From a class perspective, in contrast, movements such as the CCF are interpreted as potential challenges to capitalism. A movement someday may arise with the kind of ideology, leadership, and popular support that would replace the social relations of production with new forms of economic ownership and political control. The Cooperative Common-wealth Federation is seen as a momentary episode in a long struggle to replace capitalism with a more humane form of society. The absorption of the farmers' movement into the existing political and economic in-stitutions is explained by the specific history of class struggle and by the institutional position of the state in a capitalist democracy.

From a managerial perspective, the fate of the CCF is explained by the tendencies toward bureaucratization of social movements, the ca-reerism of organizational elites, and the complexity of the tasks facing state elites in industrialized societies. These are not inconsistent expla-nations, because they rest upon quite different comparative and histor-ical contexts and levels of analysis.

Party systems: a key mediating institution

As indicated above, political parties are a key mediating institution be-tween society and state in the pluralist perspective, because they ag-gregate individual preferences into programs with potential majority appeal and create leaders of a potential government. The recruitment of party leadership, the beliefs of party activists, and the bases of party support have thus been the topics of much pluralist research. That party leaders must subject themselves to the discipline of maintaining an elec-toral majority is seen as a source of stable democratic governance. The conditions under which a few (if possible, two) large political parties circling around the Center seek majority support have been a central concern for pluralists.

A recent major study of twenty-seven "contemporary democracies" contains an almost classically pluralist analysis of political parties (Powell 1981, 1982).[3] G. Bingham Powell's award-winning book *Contemporary*

---

[3] One chapter of Powell's 1982 book is a summary of the 1981 article we focus on. The article, like the book, is based on the "full universe of 'working' democracies of over one million citizens in the late 1960s" (1981, p. 878).

Democracies defines democracy in terms of individual rights to participate and the accountability of political leaders to citizens (1982, p. 1). He grounds his argument in the previous work of such scholars as Lipset, Almond and Verba, Lijphart, and Dahl. All of the defining characteristics of democracy are individual characteristics – "what people want," "voters can choose," "adults can participate" (1982, p. 3) – expressed in institutional arrangements that give these individual rights some meaning: elections, freedom of the press, and political parties.

Powell's concerns are with participation, modernization, economic development, social cleavages, and political performance. Riots are defined as "large numbers of citizens acting out of control in an unplanned disorganized fashion, and destroying property." Deaths by political violence sometimes result from riots but are "more frequently the outcome of systematic armed attacks by terrorists." A third indicator of the breakdown of order is "suspension or replacement of the national regime," which takes place "usually through actions of the military or the chief executive" (1982, p. 21).

The key variables used by Powell for classifying party systems are both derived from aggregated characteristics of individuals: whether or not voting led to a majority for a party or party coalitions in half or more of the elections during the period of the data (1967–76) and whether or not social group memberships were closely linked to parties. Four types of party systems resulted: "aggregative majority" (low linkage, party majority), "responsible majority" (high linkage, party majority), "fractionalized" (low linkage, no party majority), and "representational" (high linkage, no party majority). These are all subtypes of democratic party systems. Both the state structure and the economy are theoretical givens.

The stability of the state is an implicit criterion for Powell's classification of parties, because "extremist" parties were excluded from the definition of democratic party systems. This index prevents looking at the possibilities of change or transformation of the system from *both* left and right by assuming that all radical changes are equivalent dangers to democracy. The index also assumes that the wide range of state structures in these societies are all "democratic," and these variations need not be taken into account.

Powell uses his typology of party systems to investigate the debate within the pluralist perspective over the types of relations among individuals, social groups, and parties that best serve democratic stability. (Political "performance" is almost a synonym for democratic stability.) Powell argues that each type of party system has been seen as associated with political performance. According to Powell, Lipset, Downs, Truman, Almond, and Epstein argue that "aggregative majority" parties perform best. Schattschneider, Burns, Duverger, and Sartori argue for "responsible majority" parties because they increase citizen control over policy. "Citizen majorities can choose between more clearly defined policy packages" (Powell 1981, p. 863). Furthermore, such authors argue that the pressures to generate majorities keep extremists in check while mobilizing social groups to support the parties. This position has been criticized by Rokkan, Lijphart and Epstein. "Representational" parties have been seen by Daalder, Lehmbruch, and Jackman as enhancing stability because of the inability of any social group linked to a party to gain control of the state, or because of the importance of elite-negotiated accommodations. The important point here is not the empirical detail. The issue of the consequences of different relations among individuals, social groups, and parties for democratic stability is a debate within the pluralist perspective, regardless of which relationship is found to be strongest.

Two of the "performance" measures are also aggregated from individual data: voting turnout and the numbers of deaths due to political violence. Another is a characteristic of individuals in leadership positions in the state: the tenure of the chief executive of the state. A fourth, the length of time the party or parties in the government commanded a legislative majority, is not the same as a party majority, defined as the proportion of elections generating a majority. Thus the stability of the top leadership of the state is a measure of high performance and is seen as either a consequence or an attribute of democratic stability.

Powell makes causal inferences from correlations. But it is quite possible, to take a few of the above examples, that government instability may have increased political extremism, not the opposite. "Executive control" may be an indicator of elite cohesiveness, not of democratic performance. More riots may have generated extremist voting, not the opposite. Also, there is no *content* in anything the parties advocated or what governments did, or in the indicators of party strength or political system performance, consistent with the pluralist stress on process and procedures. Perhaps most important, however, almost one-third of the twenty-seven states in the study lost their democratic qualities in the ten years it covered. Democracy was abandoned in Chile, the Philippines, and Uruguay and was "temporarily suspended" in India, Ceylon, Lebanon, Turkey, and perhaps Jamaica. These events are empirically recognized but not theorized. Also, the study accepts as given the specific ways voters are linked to social groups or to types of parties. The systemic or structural factors explaining the form of the party system are not analyzed, another indication of the pluralist world view.

Interest groups and parties: the organizational level

Organizations within the pluralist perspective represent the aggregated preferences of individuals, formed into voluntary associations and interest groups. Those two concepts reflect the pluralist view perfectly: Individuals are assumed to be free to join and to exit associations and are assumed to form groups based on common interests.

"Interest group" is a concept theorized only within the pluralist perspective, although empirically recognized by the others.[4] Interests can be separated. Groups form to represent and aggregate individual interests. Groups are autonomous from the state. Multiple interests arise from deep within a differentiated society. Governmental decisions are influenced by multiple interests (Rose 1967). Interest groups mediate between individuals and the state, screening and aggregating demands so that they can be responded to by the state without "demand overload." Interest groups arise, become strong, and disappear as a result of the changing values and preferences of individuals.[5]

When pluralists look at democracy inside organizations, the problem is seen as one of maintaining internal diversity and perhaps competition between leaders in order to offset the tendency toward oligarchical rule. But when they look at the function of interest groups in a democratic state, their concern shifts to the ways in which leaders of such groups represent the interests of their members within the larger political system, assuming homogeneity of interests. This analytic tension is evaded by defining the same unit of analysis as an organization when internal democratic processes are of concern but as an interest group when its external role in a democratic state is the empirical focus. When the implicit level of analysis shifts, key concepts change.

Pluralists typically assume that all social units are potentially democratic, whether communities (Dahl 1961), organizations (Lipset, Trow, and Coleman 1956), or societies (Powell 1981), and that one can generalize from microstudies of small groups, communities, and organizations to societies. Even seemingly hierarchical bureaucracies are seen

---

[4] The term is used descriptively in the managerial and class perspectives. Regardless of the perspective, coalitions of interests into organizations of many kinds making demands upon the state, whether called pressure groups, political factions, sectors of capital, the military, the corporate rich, or the executive, are empirically recognized as pervasive features of contemporary states.

[5] A recent pluralist study of individual participation is Parker 1983. A survey of voluntary association members in Indianapolis asked questions about "official" participatory roles (holding office) and "unofficial" roles (raising money, telephoning, and so on). Many of the thirty-two "voluntary organizations" sampled were related to the state; they were drawn from "health or mental health, legal or criminal justice, neighborhood or community, and general civic action" groups. Neither societal nor organizational contexts are dealt with either theoretically or empirically. The public–private distinction is not even mentioned. Pluralists also debate whether interest groups originate from a "societal disturbance" (David Truman) or from "entrepreneurial skill" (Robert Salisbury), according to Jeffrey M. Berry. Berry conducted a survey of eighty-three interest groups in Washington, D.C., and concluded that Salisbury was right (Berry 1978).

as a welter of factions within offices, departments, branches, and professions, each attempting to shape the organization to serve their individual and group interests (Bacharach and Lawler 1980). A society does not differ fundamentally from its parts.

Take, for example, a study of democracy in the International Typographical Union (Lipset et al. 1956). The preface says that the "larger objective of this book ... is to illuminate the processes that help to maintain democracy in the great society by studying the processes of democracy in the small society of the ITU" (p. xi). And "the ... extension of democracy in an industrial society requires the extension of control by men over those institutions they depend upon" (p. 462). The conditions necessary for democracy are thus the same at any level of analysis. But, although the authors hold that labor unions have potential power to defend their members against the "tremendous state power inherent in a collectivist society," the book contains no argument justifying the inference that internal organizational democracy creates effective barriers to bureaucratic domination. Whether or not any given organization should be democratic is not an issue for them, nor are the conditions analyzed under which some kinds of organizations come to be a battleground for democratic participation and others are peaceful oligarchies.

The book starts with two basic observations. First, in most organizations, few members participate in decision making. Few people vote, few attend meetings, few run for office, few challenge leaders, even where there is a formally organized and legitimate machinery for participation. Second, in most organizations, leaders hold office for a long time, even when democracy is the official ideology.[6] The International Typographical Union was an exception to the rule. A two-party system had been established for a long time, and a regular interchange of top officials occurred as one party was voted out and the other in. Why didn't the normal pattern of elite domination of most organizations exist in the ITU? The answer is revealing of the pluralist approach to organizations and of the way in which the analysis is generalized to democratic states.

In most organizations, according to Lipset et al., oligarchy is normal because leaders control communications to members and can present

---

[6] This is the classic argument of the "iron law of oligarchy," presented in 1915 by the German sociologist Robert Michels in his *Political Parties* (1962), a study of the German Social Democratic Party. In this party, which advertised its commitment to democracy, oligarchy prevailed. It is interesting to note that Lipset's definition of democracy assumes frequent changes of leadership, whereas Powell, summarized earlier in this chapter, assumes that stable leadership is a measure of democratic performance. This reflects nicely the tension between representation and governance in the pluralist world view.

themselves as the only ones able to truly represent their interests. Second, leaders come to have a monopoly of expertise, because they gradually accumulate information and skills. Third, leaders have a tremendous interest in maintaining their positions, because in most organizations leaders are better paid and have higher status than rank-and-file members. Lack of participation by members is thus a consequence of a self-reinforcing vicious circle, even in organizations where democracy is an explicit goal. Members come to accept the existing leaders because they do not see any alternative channels open to them to influence the decisions of the organization or the choice of leaders.

The ITU was an exception. Leaders did not monopolize communication to the members, because printers have access to presses and can print leaflets and newsletters. Leaders did not have a monopoly of expertise, because printers are literate and have time to read and talk about internal politics. Leaders did not have a great stake in office, because their status and income were not much greater than those of the rank-and-file members who were highly paid craftsmen. Competitive elections and parties were therefore possible.

Once in existence, a successful history of party competition became self-reinforcing. Party loyalties developed, and channels of communication opened between competing leaders and their supporters. Alternative leadership pools developed in the local shops: Experienced officials went back to the shops but remained a resource for their party and for new recruits hoping for office. Union democracy became a reality.

Surveying members in several locals, the study discovered within the union political culture a strong commitment to the party system, a lot of interest in union politics, widespread participation and information, and an "occupational community" – dense networks of social contacts among members outside of the shop. The preconditions for democracy are low stratification, high information, and dispersed political skills. If lacking, they must be compensated for by a political culture of moderation and compromise, so that the have-nots will not tear down the fragile structure of democratic institutions to wrest away some of the privileges of the haves.

The authors' failure to consider the relationship between organizations and societies, however, makes it difficult to extrapolate from one level of analysis to another. The authors admit that the union was weaker externally because of its internal democracy. It could not negotiate as effectively with employers because union leaders had to calculate the potential electoral effects of their bargaining behavior. Some kinds of issues could not be brought to the bargaining table, because the opposition party would seize upon it as a betrayal of fundamental commitments. Internal democracy had real costs, even from an organizational standpoint.

More importantly, internal competition weakens an organization's power to compete within a larger democratic political system. Paradoxically, a democratic state may *require* undemocratic organizations. Effective competition at the societal level may exist only if the leaders of rival organizations enjoy enough unchallenged support to be able to negotiate binding agreements with other organizations. This paradox is not recognized, because the relations between levels are not problematic.

Also typical of the pluralist world view is an absence of discussion of the concrete benefits of democracy. Rights of participation are assumed to carry with them the potential consequence of tangible rewards, or else they are their own reward. The categories of analysis are free of content. The distribution of benefits to the membership is not a systematic part of the analysis. But the interests of members of a democratic union may not be as well served as they are by a bureaucratic oligarchy. An internally pluralist system may result in stalemate and in periodic internal political crises that prevent leaders from having the capacity to act in accordance with the interests of the majority of members. Whether or not this is true, the issue is not dealt with. The theoretical reasons are that pluralism is equated with democracy and that democracy is seen as a possible choice for almost any organization.

Opinions, voting, and protest: the individual level

Individuals in a democratic state have diverse ways of expressing their preferences and values. Pluralists recognize three major mechanisms: public opinion, voting in elections, and – where institutionalized mechanisms are unresponsive – protest.

Public opinion

For public opinion to function in a democratic state, individuals must have the capacity to understand their interests and to act on them, within the constraints of cultural values. The political system, in consequence, is assumed to provide reasonably undistorted information about the consequences of one's participation. That there are few pluralist studies of the causes and consequences of biased or unequal access to information is a significant silence.

Public opinion is formed by the diverse experiences of individuals in their families, in their communities, and in their workplaces. Their political identities – whether they see themselves as conservative, liberal, or radical, or identify themselves as a Democrat or a Republican – are formed in childhood, through political socialization. Historical events leave their imprint on successive cohorts of voters who reach political maturity during periods of war, depression, religious revival, or political quiescence. In a healthy democratic political culture, political attitudes and beliefs are created that are not extremist or intolerant, or easily manipulated.

Given individual political identities, the political system must be open enough to diffuse information to interested persons, allowing them to form opinions about the alternative candidates and issues facing the electorate in the next election. Opinion leaders who communicate information and suggest action form a key link between political leaders and the electorate. They tend to be the best-informed and most interested persons in different groups, and they play a key role in shaping general public opinion.[7]

In a democratic political culture, public opinion shifts back and forth within a range that does not exceed the limits of responsible actions by political leaders.[8] The active citizens who are most influential accept those realistic limits. Their beliefs (as "opinion leaders") shape the political expectations of others. The opinions of various "publics" (groups with interests in specific issues) combine three elements: concern with issues, loyalty to a party, and commitment to a candidate.

Public opinion is attributed a major role in both the growth of government and attempts to cut back the expansion of government in many Western nations. A constantly broadening base in public opinion is seen as underlying the frequent electoral majorities that favor welfare-state programs. Public opinion surveys show that most people believe that the disabled, the elderly, children, families with a large number of children, and the unemployed deserve some basic level of subsistence and

---

[7] A classic study, which set the framework for a generation of subsequent studies, was *Personal Influence* (Katz and Lazarsfeld 1955), which applied a market model to personal interaction, networks of communication, small groups as socializing influences on individuals, and the emergence of opinion leaders. Focusing upon "climates of opinion" in groups, it treated "public affairs leaders" as equivalent to fashion, movie, and market leaders. The book dealt only with leadership, groups, and influence; politics, power, class, and domination were not mentioned – to say nothing of elites or organizations.

[8] The journal *Public Opinion*, published by the American Enterprise Institute for Public Policy Research, is mainly written from within the pluralist world view. A typical article, by one of the editors, Ben J. Wattenberg, argues that "participatory politics" tends to "self-correct" the system, which makes "today's politics healthy." "[P]articipatory democracy has helped to open up our lives, helped spark the engine of our economy, helped improve the quality of life, helped toughen our resolve in a dangerous world." His discussion of the 1984 presidential election campaign focuses upon the individual characteristics of candidates, using the sports metaphors of a game or a race, typical pluralist images.

that the government is the only agency capable of providing that support, even if indirectly through the expansion of private employment. Once the government is seen as the provider of last resort, a cycle of rising expectations begins. People get services and payments and want more.

Public opinion drives state growth. The numerical dominance of relatively deprived persons in any democratic state implies a permanent potential public opinion majority supporting income redistribution by public spending. Strategists of both the Left and the Right accept this basic political premise.

The importance of public opinion in a democratic political culture has led to an accumulation of public opinion surveys measuring the attitudes, behavior, and values of citizens. Every citizen is viewed as an equal participant in such surveys, and in this respect the random sampling techniques of surveys parallel the equality of citizens in elections. Similarly, the surveys accept as given the social categories that people group themselves into; or, rather, they use the social categories that are found to be correlated with voting and opinion. Opinions are simultaneously seen as originating from political socialization into group identification (race, religion, occupation, region, even party) and as autonomous in the sense that individuals are free to choose their opinions.

An example of this type of analysis is found in a work based on University of Michigan surveys done in the 1970s (Miller and Levitin 1976). The authors regarded the emergence of roughly one-quarter of the American electorate as "New Liberals" to be evidence of an emerging basis in public opinion for the expansion of liberal and welfare programs.[9] The New Liberals

now represent about 24% of the electorate and are potential sources of great support for liberal candidates. The young New Liberals may be the portion of the electorate most crucial in determining the outcome of future elections. If the trend . . . continues, each succeeding cohort will be . . . more liberal on social and political concerns than the previous cohort. Liberal candidates will therefore have a growing constituency that is bound together by a common ideology. Furthermore it is an ideology that does not tie these voters to a particular party. [P. 224]

---

[9] Miller and Levitin (1976) classified as New Liberals those persons who believed in solving problems of poverty and unemployment rather than using force to put down urban unrest; who supported freedom to protest on college campuses rather than the use of force to quell it; who advocated protecting the rights of accused criminals rather than stopping the crime without regard for the rights of the accused. New Liberals were also relatively sympathetic toward marijuana users and people who go to rock festivals and relatively unsympathetic toward the military, the police, and white domination of blacks. Miller and Levitin assumed that such attitudes would predict the political behavior of these individuals.

Such a study points to a fundamental ambiguity in the pluralist perspective on public opinion. On the one hand, if such a cluster of opinions as "new liberalism" has become a genuine political force, it must not be easily influenced by political events and momentary circumstances. Political beliefs must be reasonably firm, or they are not worth studying as a *cause* of political behavior. If such opinions are mere will-o'-the-wisps, swayed by a charismatic candidate or the latest headlines, they are meaningless, except as collective behavior. Far more important would be the study of the strategies of political leaders. The pluralists hold that public opinion – and by extension the political culture that underlies public opinion – must be relatively impervious to elite manipulation. Public opinion is meaningless for democracy unless the conditions exist under which it can be freely formed, freely expressed, and freely acted upon.

On the other hand, public opinion must not become rigid and inflexible. "Ideological" is the pejorative term in this context. "Ideologues" are inflexible and uncompromising. Their beliefs do not allow them to take into account the political accommodations required of political leaders.

If American public opinion supports the expansion of welfare-state programs, why is the welfare state so undeveloped in the United States as compared to Europe? Political scientist Anthony King argues that differences in public opinion cannot explain these variations but differences in political culture do. He notes that "as far as one can make out, popular majorities at most times in all of our five countries have desired – often greatly desired – the extension of existing social services and the establishment of new ones. . . . American mass public seems to differ hardly at all in this connection from the mass publics of other countries" (1973, p. 412).

King argues that Americans believe, unlike Europeans, that the state should play the role of referee rather than manager of the marketplace. Americans tend to define freedom negatively, as freedom from the intrusions of the state, rather than positively, as freedoms made possible by state intervention (see also Sharpe, 1973a, 1973b). This antistatist political culture, with its philosophical roots in the writings of John Locke, hinders the state from providing goods and services. American officials and citizens see the state not as an instrument to be used to achieve collective purposes but as a potentially dangerous actor to be relied upon only as a last resort. They are caught between support for specific welfare-state programs and a more general distrust of government institutions. This distrust of government restrains the growth of government welfare programs in the United States. A general antistate political culture overrides the specific content of public opinion.

Such a debate over the relative role of public opinion and political culture in shaping the growth of the democratic state is contained within the pluralist world view. The relative importance of opinion versus culture in influencing leadership behavior and government decisions would seem to be a central empirical issue for the pluralist perspective. It has not been investigated, to our knowledge, partly because mechanisms of accommodation – responsible political leadership and compromising public opinion – are assumed to exist in democratic societies that will reconcile the tension between consensus and participation. Although this assumption allows pluralists to avoid the empirical issue, only the pluralist perspective treats the internal structure of public opinion as a theoretical issue.

A recent analysis has actually suggested the theoretical distinction between "climate" (political culture) and "weather" (public opinion). The general level of rainfall and the average temperature constitute the "climate," whereas the "weather" is situational – the stormy, windy, or sunny days that may occur in almost any climate.[10] Sociologist James Davis (1980) used the metaphors, summarizing responses to survey questions asked repeatedly between 1972 and 1978. In those years, the National Opinion Research Center's General Social Survey asked identical questions of a sample of 1,500 respondents, beginning with the prelude: "We are faced with many problems in this country, none of which can be solved easily or inexpensively. I'm going to name some of these problems, and for each one I'd like you to tell me whether you think we're spending too much money on it, too little money, or about the right amount" (Davis, 1980, p. 1132).

Such a question makes quite a few pluralist assumptions: Solutions to problems exist and can be arrived at incrementally (that is, by spending varying amounts of money). Majority public opinion ("we") can decide to change the amounts of money spent. Each problem is separate and can be treated as if it allows an independent decision about how much money to spend on it, the government's budget being the aggregate of such decisions.

Davis never uses the concept of state, but "we" also means the government deciding to spend. Space, environment, health, cities, education, arms, foreign aid, welfare, and drugs – all the "problems" asked about involve massive public expenditures. The methodological assumptions of such surveys, as we have already noted, mirror the image

---

[10] Pluralist analysts are fond of weather metaphors: the "firestorm" of public response to the firing of Elliott Richardson by Nixon in 1973; the "meteors" of participation that flame into action and just as quickly burn out (Wildavsky 1974); the "climate of opinion" that creates a cold or a hot environment for political leadership; the "changing political winds" in which hapless leaders slowly twist and turn.

of elections in the democratic state. Each individual is weighted equally, and each one's "participation" (reported opinions) is democratically equal.

Surveys from 1972 to 1978 showed that two patterns of change were operating: "a slow long-term trend toward liberalism in the opinion climate plus a sharp, short-term shift toward conservatism in the opinion weather" (Davis 1980, p. 1129). As the population grows younger and becomes better educated, its basic political attitudes are becoming more liberal on such problems as " 'protecting the environment,' 'solving the problems of the big cities,' 'improving the nation's health' . . . all of which remained top in priority throughout the early 1970s" (pp. 1132–7). Support for education, welfare, and abortion did not change, despite a conservative trend in support of arms expenditures. Support for expenditures to fight high crime rates was high and unchanging in the six-year period. Also, the proportion of individuals identifying themselves as liberal or conservative in their general political stances did not change. Davis's view of the political "climate" was that "the essentially liberal rank order of the items remained much the same from 1973 to 1978" (p. 1138).

The model used by Davis differentiates between two types of factors affecting public opinion: "situational" and "group" factors, which correspond to generic sources of weather and climate. The variable "year" is an empirical surrogate for the changing political situation. The events taking place between 1972 and 1978 suggest the context for the shifting weather: Nixon's visit to China, Watergate and Nixon's subsequent pardon, the end of the Vietnam "adventure," the decline of real income, and Carter's victory.

More stable group characteristics such as age and education were also used as independent variables indicating the bases of the climate of political culture. The assumption is that the population has the same relationship to problems that potentially affect all of them equally. Different groups experiencing different "political situations" have equal analytic status.

The index Davis uses regards as significant not the actual content of opinion but the balance between extremes of opinion. He subtracts the percentage of respondents who say that "too much" money is being spent for crime, health, or arms from the percentage who say "too little," to arrive at the summary measure. A value of 1.00 meant that everyone answered "too little"; a value of zero would indicate equal proportions saying "too little" and "too much." Negative 1.00 meant unanimity for "too much."

The difficulty with this index is that the same score would have been obtained if all respondents had said the expenditure was about right and none objected to the present level, or if one-third had chosen *each* alternative. These striking variations are completely ignored by the index, although they include most of the realistic alternative possibilities. Davis's index assumes that the balance between persons favoring more or less expenditures is the important abstraction, leaving out of account the great middle grouping the index tacitly assumes to be satisfied with the status quo.

An alternative interpretation of the same data would add the proportion satisfied with the status quo to the percentage that says that more expenditures on essentially "liberal" policies and programs are needed. Using such a measure, the American electorate is overwhelmingly committed to the public goals of health, education, "improving the conditions of blacks," and "solving the problems of big cities." Between 1972 and 1978 the proportion of Americans agreeing that at least the right amount was being spent by the government or that more was needed to solve those four problems never dropped below a full three-quarters of the electorate. Support for expenditures that would "improve and protect the environment" climbed from 40 to 50 percent whereas support for welfare expenditures vacillated sharply, rising and then falling to about 40 percent in 1978. These findings are not necessarily inconsistent because welfare expenditures might well be seen by some liberals as a poor substitute for improving the ill health, unemployment, and poor education that give rise to a need for welfare programs.

Voting and political issues

In the pluralist perspective, elections are assumed to significantly influence decisions by government officials. When such democratic institutions are buttressed by a democratic political culture, majority support becomes a prime source of consensus behind a given public policy. The search for programs that will appeal to a potential majority of the electorate is common to parties covering the whole political spectrum.[11]

Both candidates and voters are assumed to be free to choose their issues and parties on the basis of their political preferences. Issue, party, candidate, and vote are all contingent choices for the individual citizen. Although pluralist analyses of voting are aware that issues tend to be multiple and interrelated, that a candidate's stand on an issue is ambiguous, and that issues change in salience, these problems are seen as complicating the voting choice but not as preventing the use of a choice

---

[11] Studies of voting focus upon variations from election to election and from one community or constituency to another. They include surveys that ask the population – both voters and nonvoters – why they vote, which party they identify with, which candidates they favor, which issues they regard as important, their political attitudes and beliefs, their interest in politics, plus such social characteristics as religion, ethnicity, occupation, marital status, and income.

model of voting behavior. Full information is assumed to be available to voters. If it is not, it is an empirical issue that does not pose any theoretical problems.

Candidates must decide to offer themselves; parties must select candidates; candidates and parties must choose the issues to present to the voters; citizens must decide whether they will vote on the basis of party, issue, or candidate. When the problem is posed in that way, the complexity is tremendous, and detailed investigation seems needed of the empirical relations among these separate choices. Once one has focused upon a particular election, with an outcome contingent upon the complex relations of diverse individual voters to candidates, issues, and parties, then the problem is defined in a way that requires a pluralist method to explain action and outcomes.

The classic voting studies focused very narrowly on what determined the individual voting decision and on when the individual made up his mind to vote.[12] One's group memberships (being a Catholic or a Protestant, a worker or an employer, a southerner or a northerner), one's party identification (whether one thought of oneself as a Republican or a Democrat, and how strongly), the appeal of a particular candidate, or the issues one thought significant in the election were the central factors empirically investigated in the classic voting studies in the 1950s and early 1960s.

A study of American voting behavior published in 1976 is an example of both the strengths and the weaknesses of pluralist analyses of voting and elections (Nie et al., 1976).[13] The study defines the role of the state as follows: "Government, above all democratic government, depends on the support of the citizenry. It also depends on the ability and capacity of the political process to reconcile conflicting forces" (p. 2). Those "conflicting forces" are never analyzed, being simply the raw material on which the political process acts. The authors themselves, however, are critical of some elements of the pluralist perspective as well as some of the classic findings of voting studies. This study is an important con-

---

[12] The Columbia school of voting studies, based in sociology, emphasized the group memberships and affiliations that were correlated with different types of party choice. (See Berelson et al. 1954.) The Michigan school, based in political science, emphasized the more "political" aspects of choice – the variations among loyalties to party, commitment to certain issues, and support for individual candidates as factors explaining voting behavior. (See Campbell et al. 1960.)

[13] This "third-generation" voting study was based on fifteen national surveys conducted between 1939 and 1974, using a total of more than 30,000 respondents and the best data available: the Michigan Survey Research Center's regular election studies and several National Opinion Research Center and Gallup surveys. Because of the extensive data over time, the authors were able to aggregate the surveys of individual voters and consider the changing support for parties.

tribution to an understanding of American politics; it also bears witness to the internal debates within the pluralist interpretation of voting.

Stable party identification and therefore party support, whether as a Republican or a Democrat, were seen by pluralists in the 1950s as a source of stability for the democratic state. Different issues and candidates did not easily shake citizens from their basic party identification, and this gave flexibility to political leaders because voters were relatively unconcerned with specific issues. Citizens' party identification derived from early political socialization.

A major historical trend discovered by *The Changing American Voter* (Nie et al. 1976) is the decline of party identification among the American electorate. By the early 1970s, the proportion of voters identifying themselves, either strongly or weakly, as a Democrat or a Republican had dropped to only about one in four voters for each party. Nearly four in ten regarded themselves as independent in politics, and even those who remained partisan were more likely to defect from their party's candidate in the voting booth. This trend was away from any party, not from one party to another. This erosion of the traditional base of support for the two major parties poses a problem for the pluralist contention that strong party identification is a source of democratic stability.[14]

Further, along with the weakening of party identification, voter attitudes toward issues have become more consistent along a left–right continuum, according to Nie et al.[15] The remarkable increase in attitude consistency from the 1950s to the 1970s suggests to the authors that new issues arising in the 1960s have been "incorporated by the mass public into what now appears to be a broad liberal-conservative ideology. Liberals on traditional issues tend to be more liberal on new issues; conservatives are more conservative on these issues" (1976, p. 123).

The impact of both of these trends was felt on voting behavior. Although party identification became steadily less influential on the choice of a presidential candidate from 1956 to 1972, a voter's liberalism or conservatism had increasing impact on his or her evaluation of the stand of a candidate on issues. Both parties are therefore subjected to the

[14] A recent study explains the decline of voting turnout between 1958 and 1978 as largely due to the "combined impact of two attitudinal trends: the weakening of party identification and declining beliefs about government responsiveness, that is, lowered feelings of 'external' political efficacy." Both independent and dependent variables are at the individual level of analysis. (See Abramson and Aldrich 1982, p. 502.)

[15] "Left" or liberal positions were defined as favoring welfare, integration of blacks, and big government; opposing the cold war; favoring civil rights for criminals; and legalizing marijuana. Whereas only one-quarter of the population between 1956 and 1960 fell into the most consistent left or right category, more than 40 percent did by 1973, with the biggest change being registered between 1960 and 1964. These findings are consistent with those of Miller and Levitin, summarized earlier.

immediate electoral pressure of public opinion on issues. If voting is no longer mediated by party loyalty or blurred by inconsistent policy preferences, issues will be immediately reflected in the behavior of voters.[16]

The Changing American Voter does not analyze the shifts in the actual majorities favoring different kinds of policies, nor does it attempt to consider whether or not at any given time there is a majority of public opinion favoring "liberal" or "conservative" public policies. This position is defended not in theoretical but in methodological terms; the data would not bear such a comparative and historical interpretation. But it is in line with the pluralist view that a consensus around the Center, vacillating slightly from left to right, is the important political fact, not the actual content of the policies favored by the American electorate.

The concept of "issue" used in *The Changing American Voter* is a given, as if issues suddenly appear in front of the electorate and have a homogeneous and unproblematic meaning. Given a national political culture, issues emerging within it have a common meaning. But, despite the centrality of the concept, "issue" is never defined. Sometimes issues are alternative policies, sometimes a process generating policies or even a group aware of a set of policies benefiting them. Foreign policy in the Eisenhower period did not penetrate personal lives; in the Vietnam period it did. Inflation was a "discontent" issue in the 1970s but was presumably a traditional economic issue in the Truman years. The analytical content of an issue is not theoretically important because of the concern with how the mass electorate *perceives* "the most important problem facing the nation" and how these perceptions are *defined* as "political issues." The handsomely democratic disavowal of any intention to impose meanings on individual respondents allows survey responses to be aggregated into summary measures.

Pluralists do not analyze the changing content of issues, because they assume the efficiency of political markets, in which preferences are the ultimate source of political change. How the content of political issues

---

[16] An important finding of *The Changing American Voter* is that even less well-educated persons in 1972 had more attitude consistency than the college-educated in 1956 (Nie et al. 1976, p. 144). The original finding of low attitude consistency among the less educated was used by Philip Converse (1964) to demonstrate their cognitive incapacity, that is, their inability to make consistent political judgments. The opposite finding in 1973 was used not to challenge this hypothesis but only to argue that "the growth of attitude consistency within the mass public is not the result of increases in the population's cognitive capacities brought about by gains in educational attainment" (Nie et al. 1976, p. 150). In other words, the connection between education and cognitive capacity was not presumed to exist. Education became an *index* of cognitive capacity. To demonstrate that education is not important in predicting issue consistency is an important finding, which challenges the pluralist image of one of the important conditions of political modernization.

is shaped by organizational strategies or institutional contradictions is not considered theoretically.

Their measure showing the distribution of the population's political beliefs (see Nie et al. 1976, fig. 8-5) implies that the actual proportion of centrists as well as liberals and conservatives has changed. The term "centrist" suggests a measure of a center position in some left–right continuum, but that is not in fact the measure. Persons who gave middle choices on the issue questions (p. 144, n. 14) are included as well as persons who gave an extremely liberal answer on one issue question and an extremely conservative answer on another. The measure may actually be one of inconsistency, not of centrist political beliefs. The table therefore cannot be used to infer that the proportion of actual liberals or conservatives has changed, only that, with respect to the distribution of political attitudes within the 1956–73 period, individuals have become more *consistently* liberal or conservative. By ignoring the content of the issue (the actual political position taken), the authors assume that an aggregated "consensus" (the summation of individual beliefs into a single statistic) is the appropriate basis for comparison. Interestingly, they do not define a theoretical concept for the average distribution of beliefs for the entire period but simply use the statistical distribution as a base line from which to construct deviations of individuals and years.

The implication is that the content of beliefs does not matter, that what matters is the individual deviation from the measured and presumably consensual "center" at any given time. The actual distribution of liberal and conservative attitudes is not given, although the authors imply that the continuum shifted. By omitting this finding, they further imply that the consistency measure can be interpreted as a polarization of actual attitudes. Continuous shifts of attitudes from liberal to conservative can be tolerated by a democratic political system, but polarization of persons around the left and right extremes – *regardless of the political contents of those poles* – is a dangerous political development.

One of their conclusions is that, "as the Republican center collapses, the center of gravity moves right" (Nie et al. 1976, p. 199). This metaphor is not appropriate for a measure partially based on issue *consistency*, because it implies that the data can be interpreted as a genuine move to the left or right, which is not the case. The moves from left to right and back again have been standardized out of the data. Their measure is one of *relative* conservatism or liberalism, indicating the political stance of a group in relation to the population as a whole. But the authors imply that a group in some absolute sense becomes more liberal or more conservative.

This anomaly is, we suggest, not due to carelessness on the part of the authors (they are aware of the arbitrariness of their indicators); it

rests on a theoretical resolution of the pluralistic tension between consensus and participation. Individuals and groups are *supposed* to seek a
balance between satisfying their own preferences via participation and
accepting the consensual limits necessary to democratic stability. In the
absence of theoretical attention to this problem, the result is ambiguity
in the construction of key empirical indexes.

Analyzing an issue spectrum as Left, Right, and Center in the absence
of substantive analysis about the *content* of the issues reflects the classic
pluralist assumption that elections in a democratic state swing back and
forth from left to right. The empirical procedures bias the data in favor
of an interpretation that "only centrists can win" (Nie et al. 1976, p. 339),
although the authors are reluctant to draw that conclusion. If the spectrum shifts, then this still may be true, but the "center" candidate is
more left or right than before. Abstracting left, right, and center from
the content of politics makes the conclusion that only centrists can win
seem plausible but begs the question of just what the political competition is all about. Their conclusion of a "leftward drift of the public in
recent years," if true, suggests that candidates who earlier would have
been on the left extremes of the political spectrum are now closer to the
center. They also argue that "candidates can also move the public one
way or the other on the issue scale" (p. 343), although without any
evidence on the impact of candidate and party activity upon the electorate. What causes the public to shift is a question outside the scope
of their book. Vietnam, urban unrest, welfare are not discussed anywhere substantively but are taken as the salient issues of the day for
candidates, parties, and voters.

The left–right spectrum itself is assumed not to change. Like the measure of issue consistency, the device of statistically removing substantive
shifts of left or right policy preferences and measuring each voter in
relation to the entire population is based on the tacit assumption that
the political spectrum shifts so little that it is not important to assess
whether or not the actual content of voter preferences has become more
"liberal" or more "conservative." But, in fact, the spectrum itself might
shift so that a stand formerly seen as "far right" or "far left" is no longer
perceived by voters as so extreme. Because the authors have no theoretical antenna to detect these shifts, they accept the subjective perceptions of their respondents as the basis for constructing the left–right
spectrum. Their assumption is that *all* voters were available to respond
to candidates, issues, or party appeals, that their behavior could be
changed by the right appeals, and that moderate shifts of voting back
and forth from left to right constituted the full range of political choices
available.

Consistent with the division of intellectual labor within the perspective, the actions of parties and candidates are not analyzed. Although Nie et al. suggest that parties and candidates try to present themselves as centrist and try to define the opposition as extremist, this abstract possibility is not integrated into a discussion of alternative possible strategies of political elites. It is a peripheral and casual speculation.

Despite their lack of analysis of the historical role of American parties, Nie et al. are willing to conclude that the decline of the political parties as the "stabilizing forces in American politics . . . might lead to a more volatile electorate willing to follow a demagogic extremist" (1976, p. 290). If the electorate becomes volatile, the pluralist view is that parties, even new ones, must be a moderating force, restraining an electorate potentially willing to follow extremist political leadership. This argument is simply a restatement of the pluralist assumption about the functions of voting for the democratic state.[17]

The social control of protest

In a properly functioning society, people are socialized to want what they have a chance of getting. Accordingly, protest and political violence occur when a yawning gap emerges between expectations and real opportunities. It is not the most needy who rebel but those who cannot get what they have been led to expect they should have. According to those who hold to this theory of "relative deprivation," rising expectations or sudden loss of economic position generate aggression against the powers that be (Davies 1962; Gurr 1970). Indeed, because governmental leaders are eager to amass the votes that disaffected constituencies might deliver, they sometimes play their own part in these rising expectations.

Several studies have examined the hypothesis that there is a relationship between deprivation and political violence. One of the best known is Ted Gurr's *Why Men Rebel* (1970). Essentially it is a social-psychological theory of the way people respond to relative deprivation – the "perceived discrepancy between men's value expectations and their value capabil-

---

[17] Much pluralist research tends to fuse the relations between political parties and the electorate, assuming such a close (and functional) connection that changes in the electorate are assumed to be immediately reflected in changes in the party system and vice versa. The assumption of a functional linkage allows empirical research on it to be neglected. Political scientist John R. Petrocik points this out in his study of party realignment in the United States. Summarizing the literature, he notes that "almost any shift in party-related phenomena has been treated as evidence of a realignment. Changes in incumbency rates, electoral oscillation, defection rates, correlations between issue preferences and vote choice, and turnout, to name just a few, have served as indicators of a realignment, and even as evidence for whether the party system will survive in anything like its present form" (1981, p. 3).

ities" (p. 13). In other words, when people do not get what they expect they become angry and frustrated.

The basic data that Gurr uses to infer a connection between relative deprivation and political violence are mostly indirect ecological correlations. Few of the empirical correlations directly relevant to the theory were available. The studies he cites (1970, pp. 62–6) show that (1) high wheat prices and high unemployment "corresponded with the severity of overt mass protest in England between 1790 and 1850"; (2) variations in bread prices and the extent of mob violence were associated in revolutionary France; (3) the frequency of lynching in the American South varied weakly with indexes of economic well-being; (4) voting for Communist parties in Western Europe was correlated with per capita income in the late 1940s; (5) "extremist voting" in nine countries in 1928–30 was correlated with the percentage of the labor force that was unemployed; (6) organized group violence in Latin America in the 1950s was correlated with the rate of economic growth; (7) economically discontented Iranians were found in the late 1940s to be more likely to take extreme left or right political positions; and (8) unemployed Cuban workers were more likely to support Castro before the Cuban Revolution. He regards as the most "persuasive evidence" a fourteen-nation survey in the 1960s that found that the degree of discrepancy reported by respondents between their actual value positions (what values they were actually receiving in their lives) and their "ideals for the good life" was correlated 0.59 with the "magnitude of turmoil" between 1961–5 in the fourteen countries.

None of these data is direct evidence for the hypothesis Gurr wants to support: Relatively more deprived individuals are more likely to engage in political violence. In order to demonstrate his proposition, it would be necessary to compile a sample of instances of political violence and show that those persons engaging in more violent acts felt a greater gap between what they wanted and what they got than those engaged in less violent acts. Those who refrained from violence should perceive an even smaller gap, controlling for other relevant individual characteristics. Or, one could construct a sample of *persons* and show that persons who felt relatively more deprived engaged in more political violence (however the two variables were measured) than persons who felt relatively less deprived. Gurr's largely ecological correlations cannot necessarily be explained by social-psychological factors.

Gurr's types of political violence are also not psychological but structural. He distinguishes among *turmoil* ("unorganized political violence, with substantial participation, including violent political strikes, riots, political clashes, and localized rebellions"), *conspiracy* ("organized violence, with limited participation, including . . . assassinations, small scale terrorism . . . guerrilla wars, coups d'états, and mutinies"), and *internal wars* ("organized political violence with widespread population participation, designed to overthrow the regime or dissolve the state . . . including large scale terrorism and guerrilla wars, civil wars, and revolution") (1970, p. 11). But his explanatory variables are social-psychological: relative deprivation, aggression, perceptions, frustration, aspirations. Most of these types of violence are organizational or societal phenomena and cannot adequately be explained by psychological variables, except within a pluralist world view.

Another indication of the pluralist perspective on protest is Gurr's definition of political violence itself, which we have already cited: "all collective attacks within a political community *against the political regime, its actors . . . or its policies*" (pp. 3–4; italics added). It is significant that the violence engaged in by the regime itself is not included: the political repression of voting by blacks in the American South or the legal repression of strikes (before unions became legal in the 1930s). Violence is abnormal, is outside the established repertoire of political capabilities. Violence is endemic only when the institutionalization of political demands, expectations, and responses has disintegrated.[18]

Pluralists offer a specific interpretation of political protest. Protest, particularly violent protest, is seen as a breakdown of the normal social control mechanisms in the society, such as deeply held beliefs in the health of the economy, the responsiveness of political leaders, and the values of family, community, and religion. "Social control" in the pluralist sense refers to a loss of self-regulation by social groups, not to the use of force or repression by the state or other social institutions. When individuals are torn loose from their normal attachments to other individuals, their family, their church, their community, a "mass society" is created (Kornhauser 1959). Traditional norms that socialize individuals to obey weaken. Persons become anomic, losing a firm sense of their identity as social beings and of the rules that govern their behavior. Under such circumstances, the combination of social disorganization and

---

[18] A recent survey of attitudes in five countries (the United States, the United Kingdom, the Netherlands, Austria, West Germany) toward political action focused on whether "direct action" (that is, protest or demonstration participation) is approved or disapproved and on whether the respondent would participate or not. The conclusion was that protest action has increased and that citizens in these countries are increasingly approving of such noninstitutionalized political participation. The author's interpretation is that the concern of more and more citizens has shifted from order and security to concerns with equality and freedom of speech. Approval of protest was more evident among the educated youth than among others. This might be called a "left" pluralist position, focusing upon noninstitutionalized participation but still basing its analysis upon individual opinions and attitudes as a predictor of political behavior. Ian Budge's review of the book argues that its conclusions rest too heavily on the assumption that attitudes toward protest measure protest behavior itself. (See the *American Political Science Review*, March 1981, and Barnes et al. 1979).

individual frustration can lead to violence. The isolation of individuals from the core values of the society reduces respect for leaders. If rapid social change leads to a breakdown of contact between leaders and social groups, leaders in turn make more mistakes, become complacent and less responsive to popular needs. Such leaders are likely to engage in more repressive actions when protest does occur, which frequently leads to more protest. Rapid social change not only disrupts the relation between expectations and opportunities but also tends to disrupt the regulation embedded in daily life. When social life is unregulated, the rewards for conformity are absent.

Breakdown in social control also derives from a failure to build a truly national political culture in which the government has legitimacy, despite its failure to fulfill all the expectations of particular groups. To build legitimacy and governing capacity, the government must be capable of absorbing new groups as their mobilization catapults them into the political arena. The government must have the capacity to absorb the participation of new groups into legitimate channels, to socialize their leaders into the rules of the game, to build autonomous agencies capable of handling new demands, and to widen political parties to incorporate new constituencies (Huntington 1968; Rokkan 1970). Increasingly in the modern world, a national community is forged within political institutions. Political protest is likely to be the voice of those who want access to the political system but have been excluded, not those who want out. Thus, in those European countries where the state repressed rising working-class organizations, there is today a more ghettoized working-class political culture, one more likely to resort to protest or violence. The stability of governmental institutions requires that new groups be incorporated and their political participation channeled into both democratic and bureaucratic procedures. Repression of new groups is a reflection of the weakness of the government rather than its strength and ability to govern.

A definition of the research question as who does or who does not get involved in nonviolent political protests biases the conclusions as well as the method toward the pluralist perspective. A recent example of an empirical study allegedly testing Mancur Olson's "logic of collective action" model against the "resource mobilization" model converts the latter into the individual level of analysis by redefining the structural variables favored by Charles Tilly and others into situational variables characterizing individuals. Olson's model (1965) states the tension in the democratic aspect of the state: Most individuals have little personal stake in collective action that serves the public interest, and therefore most individuals will allow others to act on their behalf, as "free riders." But the possibility of participation or "activism" exists. Walsh and Warland (1983) test this theory by interviewing activists and free riders in the Three Mile Island area after the nuclear accident there. The authors conclude that an additive model combining all factors is the appropriate one, consistent with a pluralist method. The theoretical issue is squarely within the pluralist world view, because it turns on whether social solidarity and networks of interpersonal communication influence individuals to take political action or whether the key factor is such social psychological factors as perceptions of and reactions to grievances.

Conclusions

In this chapter we have focused upon studies dealing with various forms of participation, to show the intellectual division of labor within the pluralist perspective. Its silent assumption is that there is an interdependence between a consensual political culture and the modes of political participation that can influence state policies. Political leadership must mediate the tension between consensus and participation.

The problem of governance occurs when the conditions specified by the pluralist perspective are not present. Either leaders are not responsive enough to preferences, expressed either in institutionalized channels in the form of public opinion or voting or in noninstitutionalized channels such as protest, or citizens are demanding more than leaders can provide at any given time.

A fundamental set of conditions for governance includes a growing economy, allowing enough slack so that every group can get at least partly what it wants, and a reasonably efficient government, capable of perceiving and responding to political preferences organized and presented to it. In our words, the democratic state rests upon preconditions in the bureaucratic and capitalist aspects of the state and society. In Chapters 5 and 6 we confront the weakness of the pluralist perspective in analyzing both bureaucracy and capitalism. Pluralists interpret bureaucratic power and class rule within the pluralist world view, that is, they apply the concepts derived from the pluralist home domain to institutions and levels of analysis that cannot be understood adequately with those concepts.

5

The pluralist perspective on the bureaucratic state

The operations of democratic institutions define the bureaucratic aspect of the state in the pluralist perspective. Programs, funding, and leadership of state agencies are subject to shifting currents of public opinion and electoral choice. Bureaucrats are vulnerable to removal; programs are subject to cuts. Within the state, bureaucracies compete with each other for support and resources, like any other interest group. Even the internal operations of such organizations are not "bureaucratic" in the usual pejorative sense of being rule-bound and inflexible. Rather, bureaucracies are seen as coalitions of individuals maximizing their own benefits. Bureaucracies are highly political, shot through with personal communications and favors, and possess cultures just like communities and ethnic groups. Bureaucracies are established as a result of a collective choice to implement social values and ultimately arise from the diverse perceptions and needs of individuals. Bureaucratic centralization is not seen as a structural imperative but is an impermanent social choice. A continuous tension exists between the possibilities of centralizing decisions to serve the public interest or decentralizing them to serve the preferences of particular constituencies.

Bureaucracies themselves reflect the pluralism of governing institutions. Each has its own history, surviving crises of leadership succession by virtue of having become identified with values of the population and becoming institutionalized. Bureaucratic organizations are natural social organisms, with a life history of growth, development, and decline. If they become structures of elite domination or instruments of class rule and lose their identification with the central social values, they become vulnerable to both internal and external challenges. The rate and type of bureaucratization are regulated by the changing requirements of governance.

Pluralists can thus empirically recognize "bureaucrats" and "bureaucratic organizations" but theorize them as representing individual interests, executing important functions, or carrying out tasks decided

112

upon by representative bodies. Robert Dahl's recent discussion of pluralist democracy (1982, p. 27) shows the disquiet he feels with the term "organization," which he regards as too "hard-edged," an appropriate pluralist critique of the managerial concept. He prefers the Tocquevillean term "association," or even "group" or "subsystem." But he regards the "government of the state" as an organization in this sense, thus assimilating the bureaucratic state to the pluralist world view.

Bureaucratization and democracy

The bureaucratic aspect of the state becomes an indispensable arm of democracy when clear lines of authority can be drawn between *political* leaders (usually elected) and *administrative* officials (usually appointed). Then different sectors of the state can be held accountable, electorally and legally, for their actions. Political goals resulting from leadership assessment of public opinion can then be separated from the administrative techniques to implement them. But democracy must still be safeguarded by full rights of participation and full access to information about the behavior of officials.

This functionalist public administration position believes public bureaucracies can be efficient when operating simply to administer the policies decided by elected officials. Another, more political viewpoint considers bureaucracies to be the creations and agents of political constituencies. In works such as those by the political scientist Aaron Wildavsky (1974), bureaucratic decisions are treated as quasi-electoral in character. That is, the aggregated weight of preferences from various publics determines decisions, with bureaucratic actors functioning as agents of both internal and external constituencies. Bureaucratic policies are made in the context of electoral politics, because bureaucratic officials know that their decisions, reputations, and careers are subject to ratification by various constituencies. Bureaucrats are not insulated from external influences and able to make cool and rational decisions. They do not manage resources by calculating the most efficient way to achieve legally mandated tasks. Bureaucrats operate, instead, in a goldfish bowl of other agencies, legislative pressure, and interest group surveillance.

Pluralist analyses locate bureaucracies within an environment that is open to multiple influences. These influences are an aspect of the democratic political process. In the United States, the constitutional framework defining the democratic state separates powers among local, state, and national governments, among legislative, executive, judicial, and administrative branches of government, and among relatively weak political parties. This multiplicity of jurisdictions, functions, tasks, and legal powers creates an open and competitive system. Its very openness is seen as the essence of democracy by many pluralists and as an effective barrier to centralization. In the United States, authority is not easily centralized, because of both the importance of decentralization in the political culture and the multiple points of access to decision making, which reflect and sustain that value.[1]

Some pluralists regard bureaucracy as a technical problem of implementing decisions made by a democratic process. Liberal economists like William Baumol argue that there may be defects in the information available for rational decision making and that "because of the extreme complexity of the task an administrative agency can never make the technical interstitial arrangements necessary for the most efficient pursuit of the desires of the members of the economy" (1965, p. 199). Like most economists, Baumol assumes that democratic social choice assures that bureaucracies ultimately respond, through some never-analyzed process, to majority preferences. He says that some economists (he mentions Nicholas Kaldor and John Hicks) postulate that "reorganization" of society or state will compensate those who are worse off as a result of a given social "innovation." He assumes, as do most economists, that innovations happen when people want them. And he says that it is true that where a "permitted reorganization is possible the community could . . . do better for itself" (p. 163).

Baumol is here debating with other economists the theoretical alternatives available for assessing the price people are willing to pay for social change. He assumes that society-wide values are embedded in the concept of "community" and that the role of government agencies is not theoretically problematic. Baumol says "the role of government [is] that of assisting the members of the community to attain their own aims with maximum efficiency." Under some circumstances, it then "becomes the task of government to override the decisions of the market" (1965, pp. 55–6). Although markets are the best way to express the preferences of individuals, an overall societal consensus on what is in the interest of everyone may lead to state action to realize common interests that are not realized by social choices made in private markets.

Economist Kenneth Arrow, similarly, assumes that the implementa-

---

[1] One empirical study of bureaucratic centralization within the pluralist perspective regards organizational culture as the central independent variable. The study focuses on the forty-eight public assistance organizations in the United States from 1936 to 1970 (Weed 1977). Prior to 1936, "localistic" administrations were states with no statewide welfare organization whereas "pluralistic" administrations had such statewide organization. In 1970 "centralized" administrations were those in which the local welfare office director was appointed by the state, local government financed all of the administrative costs of local offices, and there was no local welfare board. The level of centralization was partly explained by the beliefs and values of the top administrators, which Weed called "administrative ideology."

tion of social choices by the state is a minor and theoretically trivial issue. Despite his rejection of a formal social welfare function, he argues that the ultimate ends of individuals may be limited enough by biology and culture that such a function can be formed. If so, "then the social ordering of social decisions should be based on the social ordering of social ends plus the use of scientific and statistical methods to limit the amount of ignorance in passing from decisions to ends and to limit the effects of the remaining ignorance" (1951, pp. 87–8). He immediately mentions this as a problem relevant to the efficiency of "centralized and decentralized planning." As more facts become available to central planners, there may be less uncertainty about the relationship between decisions and ends, and he suggests that it may be possible to develop a "rational method of planning against uncertainty" (p. 88). He takes it for granted that bureaucracies could adequately implement both social ends and individual preferences.

Bureaucratic functions and institutions: the societal level

The pluralists reinterpret the intellectual tradition stemming from Max Weber, which stresses the bureaucratization and rationalization of the world. Parsons and Smelser, for example, cite Weber as believing that "all social systems tend toward progressive rationalization relative to a given set of values" (1956, p. 291). Parsons and Smelser then say that they "would like to reformulate the process of rationalization as the tendency of social systems to develop progressively higher levels of structural differentiation under the pressure of adaptive exigencies" (p. 292). Viewing rationalization as the adaptation of structures to functions incorporates Weber into their pluralist world view without dealing with his own theoretical context, which stresses the power of bureaucratic domination and the state's monopoly of legitimate violence.[2]

Similarly, Parsons's treatment of formal organizations assimilates them to his world view that a society is integrated by interdependent functions (1960). The premise is that bureaucratic organizations arise to carry out societal functions. A defining characteristic of an organization is "primacy of orientation to the attainment of a specific goal," seemingly a neutral definition. But Parsons then postulates that one must analyze an organization from two points of view: its "values" (the "cultural institutional" point of view), and the "group" or "role" point of view, which takes "suborganizations and the roles of individuals participating

---

[2] All that Parsons and Smelser cite from Weber here is Parsons's own introduction to the *Protestant Ethic*, Parsons's translation of the *Theory of Social and Economic Organization*, and Parsons's own views on Weber as expressed in *The Structure of Social Action*.

in the functioning of the organization as its point of departure" (p. 20). Bureaucratic organizations are defined in terms of their values, which derive from the individual roles that compose them and the society whose functions they serve.

More recently, German sociologist Niklas Luhmann has also interpreted the bureaucratic aspect of the state from within a pluralist world view. In one of his few references to the bureaucratic state per se, Luhmann's position is similar to Parsons's but more political. He regards the political system as a functional subsystem, "specializing in the formation and manipulation of power" (1979, p. 168). But power cannot be confined to that exercised by specifically "political" or "state" institutions, because power based on land ownership, property, education, religion, the family, the financial system also continues to exist outside the political system. The state does have a special role, because it is able to base itself on "permanently superior physical violence," which allows a "certain systematization and specification of purpose," but the state does not completely monopolize power.

Luhmann sees this core problem in pluralist terms. The state ("the political system") must be kept from usurping power belonging to other insititutions. Other institutions must in turn be kept within their own functional boundaries, partly because they tend to try to take over political power to augment the power peculiar to their function. This is his premise about the functional relations among different institutional orders.

His interpretation of the functioning of state bureaucracies reveals his pluralist world view. Social order rests in part on the capacity of high-level civil servants to influence the opinions of lower-level ones (Luhmann 1979, p. 195). And this interpretation is consistent with his argument about the choices available to those subject to power. If subordinates do not accept the political opinions of higher officials, power has been eroded, and a fundamental condition for the operation of the bureaucratic aspect of the state (that is, "decision making and transmission") has been challenged. The stability of governing institutions largely rests upon consensus among administrative officials, political leaders, and their staffs.

Pluralists typically assume that different lateral functions are associated with differentiated structures within a society integrated by common values. Luhmann, for example, with respect to the specific problem of the relation between participation and democracy in organizations, argues that the "human relations" school of organizational management and control cannot work, because it imports the principle of "love" into the sphere of "power" (1979, p. 181). Luhmann says that the error lies in "collapsing different levels of system formation and this error is faithfully repeated in the amalgamation of participation and democracy." He sees bureaucratic organizations as a "technicized power which may be used free of context and is capable of innovative initiatives" (p. 183). Bureaucratic organizations therefore cannot be analyzed with the same vocabulary as should be used for democratic individual participation. In his language, forms of "communication and interaction which are less technical, more concretely focused and more context-dependent [constituting] aggregations of influence arising from intensified interaction" should not be mixed with bureaucratic forms. There are thus appropriate "power games" for the "small world of interaction and for the large world of organization" (pp. 183–4).

Luhmann is arguing appropriately, we believe, that the "small world" of interaction of individuals is the appropriate level of analysis for pluralist concepts and that the "large world" of organizational structure is the appropriate level of analysis for managerial concepts. But he remains within the pluralist world view because he views society as functionally and structurally differentiated and as normatively integrated.

Institutionalization: the capacity to govern

From a pluralist perspective, the bureaucratic aspect of the state evolves as the capacity to govern. Political scientist Samuel P. Huntington's influential book, *Political Order in Changing Societies* (1968), marked a decisive break with prior theories of political modernization. Much previous work viewed the modernization of political institutions as one aspect of a unitary process of societal modernization. Political development was a teleological construct that charted the movement of traditional politics and society toward some multidimensional and functionally interdependent end point (Lerner 1958; Apter 1965). Huntington argues, by contrast, that economic and societal modernization does not necessarily produce modern political institutions; on the contrary, they often produce political decay. Huntington abandons the search for a unilinear and functional set of stages through which all political systems have to pass. Rejecting the concept of political development as a universal process, he argues for a more generic process: political institutionalization, the process through which organizations and procedures acquire value. In our terms, "institutionalization" means the development of bureaucratic capacity to govern, from a societal standpoint.

Huntington's opening line forcefully divorces the conceptual content of political development from Western parliamentary forms. "The most important political distinction among countries concerns not their form of government but their degree of government." Huntington argues that the United States, Great Britain, and in certain crucial respects the Soviet

Union are similar because they enjoy "an overwhelming consensus among the people on the legitimacy of the political system," as well as

strong, adaptable, coherent political institutions: effective bureaucracies, well-organized political parties, a high degree of popular participation in public affairs, working systems of civilian control over the military, extensive activity by the government in the economy, and reasonably effective procedures for regulating succession and controlling political conflict. . . . If the Politburo, the Cabinet, or the President makes a decision, the probability is high that it will be implemented through the government machinery. [1968 p. 1]

Institutionalization depends upon four key characteristics of a stable bureaucratic state: adaptability, complexity, autonomy, and coherence. *Adaptability* is the ability of political organizations to survive environmental challenges such as the succession of a new generation of political leaders or changes in organizational function. *Complexity* is the degree of horizontal and vertical structural differentiation of governmental and political organization. "Complexity may involve both multiplication of organizational subunits, hierarchically and functionally, and differentiation of separate types of organizational subunits" (Huntington 1968, pp. 17–18). *Autonomy* refers to governmental and political independence from particular social groups. The extent to which an organization can "exist independently of other social groupings and methods of behavior" increases its value to its members and also its own autonomous interests. *Coherence* refers to the degree of consensus with which active participants regard the functional boundaries and the procedures of political and governmental organizations. The relations between these components of institutionalization are only problematic within the pluralist world view.

Huntington also equates the process of institutionalization with the public interest, identifying common values with the purposes and goals of the bureaucratic state. "The capacity to create political institutions is the capacity to create public interests [which can be defined] in terms of the concrete interests of the governing institutions. A society with highly institutionalized governing organizations and procedures is more able to articulate and achieve its public interests" (1968, p. 24).

Huntington's approach is classically functionalist. Political institutionalization represents a process of the differentiation of an autonomous governing subsystem. Political institutionalization becomes necessary because of the breakdown of traditional authority relations, the difficulty of achieving "political community" among increasingly conscious and active social groups that proliferate with modernization, and the consequent tendencies to anomie and alienation (1968, pp. 8–9, 36–8, 397). Political institutionalization becomes possible because the diversification of politically competitive social groups allows political parties and governmental organizations to establish independent and distinct interests from those "social forces" whose political participation they organize (pp. 11, 20). For example, a "political party . . . that expresses the interests of only one group in society – whether labor, business, or farmers – is less autonomous than one that articulates and aggregates the interests of several social groups. The latter type of party has a clearly defined existence apart from particular social forces. So also with legislatures, executives, and bureaucracies" (p. 20). Political organizations are defined by the functions they serve. In complex societies, for example, the achievement of "community" becomes increasingly dependent on politics (p. 9). A shattered social community is reconstituted at a political level (pp. 312–13). "A political organization or procedure . . . is an arrangement for maintaining order, resolving disputes, selecting authoritative leaders, and thus promoting community among two or more social forces. . . . The more complex and heterogeneous the society . . . the more the achievement and maintenance of political community become dependent upon the workings of political institutions" (pp. 8–9).

Political institutions are therefore the medium to achieve a consensual normative order for modern societies. On the one hand, governmental institutions "reflect" the common norms and interests of a society and are thus their "behavioral manifestations" (Huntington 1968, p. 10). On the other hand, political institutions become the only possible means to "define and realize" these common norms and interests (pp. 24–8). Huntington analyzes a successful revolution, for example, as a process in which excluded groups are politically mobilized faster than existing political institutions can absorb them and their demands, and this is followed by rapid institutionalization of new political organizations (p. 256).

If political institutions have the function of achieving political community in a complex society, then it is not surprising that Huntington defines "the public interest" as the interest of public institutions (1968, pp. 25–7). Because governing institutions have their own distinctive set of interests, they derive their legitimacy not simply from their ability to represent the interests of diverse social groups but from their ability to take actions that both reflect their own institutional interests and contribute to political stability (pp. 25–7, 433). Governments are able to legitimate themselves to the extent that their policies "strengthen" their institutions (pp. 25–6). The bureaucratic state, in the pluralist view, is not the supreme instrument of social control but only one among many different governing institutions, whose flexible relationships and mutual integration are necessary for a stable society and political system.

Bureaucratic cultures and responsiveness: the organizational level

There are a variety of pluralist approaches to bureaucratic organizations inside and outside the state. First, authority relations are seen as a

generic form within social units (Eckstein and Gurr 1975). Second, bureaucratic agencies are seen, within a democratic context, as vulnerable
to cooptation by internal and external constituencies necessary for their
support (Selznick 1949). Third, agencies are seen as developing their
own internal cultures, which defend them both against attempts to reorganize them and against attempts to shift their goals (Seidman 1980).
Fourth, agencies are subject to the political priorities of elected officials
seeking to influence the flow of benefits to voters prior to elections (Tufte
1978).

Authority relations

The generic concept of bureaucratic social relations is that of authoritative
roles and authority relations, not in the Weberian sense of coercive
domination but in Parsons's sense of the acceptance by subordinates of
the rightfulness of the commands they are given and of the system in
which they are a part. Political scientists Harry Eckstein and Ted Robert
Gurr explicate the concept of "authority" (1975, p. 31). They criticize
the traditional emphasis of political science on the structures of the state
that enjoy legal authority. They define the state as "those formally organized structures of societies that specialize in the exercise of 'sovereignty' as that term has been understood roughly since the early 17th
century: specialized organizations that make laws and implement them,
resolve conflicts arising under them, and have a uniquely 'legitimate'
right to do so" (p. 4).

This definition significantly modifies Weber's organizational view of
the state by omitting violence as a state monopoly and adding an emphasis on state functions.[3] Eckstein and Gurr note that, as "the boundaries between state organizations and other structures for carrying on
government and politics weakened, another objection against the focus
on state organizations emerged" (1975, p. 5). Because the state is no
longer a distinctive institution, a common language must be found to
analyze both public and private organizations. The key integrative concept is that of "authority relations."

Eckstein and Gurr apply their concept of authority relations to the
British welfare state (1975, p. 115), focusing on the effect of growth in
the "volume and variety of governmental activities" on the "complexity
of the British Governmental structure." They observe an increase in the
number of ministries, of departments within ministries, and other types

---

[3] Eckstein and Gurr assimilate Weber to a pluralist world view by emphasizing his concepts
of legitimacy and authority, not those of power and domination (1975, pp. 202–4). His
categories of action (affective, cognitive, habitual), they say, may be taken to indicate
"general values."

of both spatial and functional committees, standing committees, and interdepartmental coordinating committees. Their assumption is that such bureaucracies enjoy widespread consensus on common goals, where subordinates accept both those common goals and the legitimacy of direction by superordinates. Eckstein and Gurr not only reject the older pluralist tradition with its focus upon the legal framework of the state, they also criticize Parsons's and Easton's assumption that the state has the main function of "maintaining social order" (1975, p. 7).

Eckstein and Gurr thus defend a particular position within the pluralist world view, arguing for "structural" concepts that do not fall into the trap either of defining the subject in terms of the Western state or of too rigidly focusing on "public" government. Their final decision is to define an "authority pattern" as a "set of asymmetric relations among hierarchically ordered members of a social unit that involves the direction of the unit" (1975, p. 22). "Direction" has four aspects: (1) the management of the goals and means of the unit by the proper allocation and coordination of roles and activities; (2) the assignment of special rights and responsibilities to "superordinates" who exercise actual control by aggregating and processing inputs from subordinates; (3) the backing of prescriptions by superordinates with sanctions, which are explicit guides to action, not just habit; (4) diffuse perceptions of the rightfulness or justice of the overall "constitution" or pattern of direction of the social unit. Other social units that do *not* have asymmetrical (hierarchical) relations are not the appropriate object of political inquiry.

This is a pluralist definition of authority. First, diverse social units are seen as existing within a differentiated social whole, which is not theorized but taken as a given. Second, individuals are members of a unit and identify to some extent with the activities of the units. The implication is that the identification is a positive one, as the phrase "define the self by the collectivity" suggests. Identifying with the social unit and getting satisfaction from its achievement of goals are seen as basic properties of an authority system, not as variables. Third, social units as a whole are seen as having commonly accepted values rather than being conflictual or contradictory. If members or subgroups seek different goals, this is seen only as a variable within larger units of analysis enjoying common values.

Fourth, everyone in the social unit is assumed to accept the hierarchical relations between superordinates and subordinates. Some segments are "thought of as 'superior' to others" (Eckstein and Gurr 1975, p. 17). Hierarchy, according to Eckstein and Gurr, is often "simply a matter of implicit perceptions," sometimes a matter of formal organization charts, but in either case there is an assumption of consensus among members on which segments are lower or higher in the hierarchy. Consensus on the hierarchical structure becomes a defining feature testifying to the very presence of an authority pattern, not a variable requiring analysis. Fifth, the concept of "direction" assumes, in addition, essential agreement on the part of the members about the procedures and consequences of the directing activities.

A "social unit" has (1) an identity of its own, separate from those of its members, (2) "recurrent and patterned" interactions, (3) members who identify themselves partly in terms of the unit (for example, a professor at Princeton), (4) goals distinct from those of the members, (5) a division of labor or differentiated roles attuned to the goals. This is a pluralist definition, because autonomous entities that have properties or variables are simply assumed to exist. "Societies" are even defined as a "very large number" of social units with authority patterns (Eckstein and Gurr 1975, p. 23). The problems of analyzing the relations at the societal level among the state, society, and economy, however conceived, are eliminated at one conceptual stroke by the way the characteristics of social units are defined.

A pluralist world view is therefore embedded in the fundamental conception of the unit of analysis and its properties. The view of bureaucracy emphasizes individual commitment to values and the common goals shared by all members of a hierarchical social unit. The distinction between "asymmetric" and "symmetrical" also stems from the pluralist world view. Authority relations, by definition, are asymmetrical, because they involve hierarchical relations among superordinates and subordinates. Symmetrical relations are likely to be analyzed by economics, the field preeminently concerned with "instrumental symmetries in social relations." Free markets are analyzed by the "public choice" literature (Eckstein and Gurr 1975, pp. 31–3).

Here we see the division of intellectual labor within the pluralist perspective. The discipline of politics specializes in the study of the asymmetric relations called authority patterns. Economics specializes in the study of symmetrical relations called markets.[4] This division of labor makes it difficult to study the transformation of relations from asymmetric to symmetric, or the conditions under which certain kinds of relations *become* symmetric or asymmetric. Eckstein and Gurr even say that the relative fruitfulness of the different approaches can be settled after the fact by "competition between contending approaches" (1975,

---

[4] Quite aside from whether or not markets reflect free choices among equals, this position reflects the pluralist epistemological assumption that intellectual problems are identified with disciplines whose practitioners have freedom to choose the problems they wish to investigate.

p. 32). Scientific markets establish the value (for example, the usefulness) of an approach.

When they apply their basic concepts to various theoretical problems, influence, via participation, becomes a key concept: "attempts to affect behavior and the actual effects of the attempts" (Eckstein and Gurr 1975, p. 53). Via group and personal action, sometimes indirect and impersonal, subordinates can influence behavior of superordinates. In line with their pluralist world view, Eckstein and Gurr believe that there "probably is a general relationship between social development and greater participation" (p. 200). Development ("growing mastery over the environment") requires more and more knowledge, and that implies "seeing a need to participate and to acquire the skills necessary to form and use organizations for that purpose" (p. 200). Organizations are thus formed in modern societies for common purposes to reflect and transmit the growing importance of participation. Bureaucracies are only a particular form of asymmetrical social relationship.

Cooptation by constituencies

Because public bureaucracies in a democratic society are themselves open and democratic they must respond to external constituencies. Philip Selznick's study (1949) of the efforts of the Tennessee Valley Authority to develop a local base of support and the resulting impact on its internal decision-making processes is an example of the cooptation of a bureaucracy by an external constituency.

TVA was a "relatively autonomous public corporation free in important aspects from the normal financial and administrative controls exercised over federal organs. . . . a broad vision of regional resource development – in a word, planning – informed the conception, if not the actual powers, of the new organization" (Selznick 1949, p. 5). Selznick's concern is to show how the original concept of TVA as a rational instrument for economic and regional planning was undermined by the democratic commitments of TVA's leadership, which led them to establish linkages with local leaders and interest groups. The mission of the organization was transformed in the process.

The political culture of TVA, or, in Selznick's terms, its "administrative doctrine," was not a managerial statement of rational principles of organization but rather a statement of beliefs and values. David E. Lilienthal, the first administrative head of TVA, said that he wanted to administer TVA according to the principle of "people participating in the decisions of their government actively and with considerable zeal." Such administration would result in an "increase in freedom and . . . corresponding increase in responsibility and discipline. . . . decentralization of administration [is] a method of securing the participation of the people of the Valley in the TVA undertaking" (quoted in Selznick 1949, p. 19, from a 1942 speech).

In order to respond to local demands and involve local participants, TVA demanded administrative autonomy with respect to personnel and fiscal decisions from the federal government. TVA wanted exemption from civil service regulations, freedom from control by the General Accounting Office, and freedom to apply revenues to current expenses – in effect, to be as autonomous as an ordinary business corporation.[5] This philosophy of administrative leadership led to an attempt to be close to the grass roots in the several states affected by the activities of TVA.

Selznick emphasizes the internal political culture of the organization and the impact of external constituencies' participation on the policies and procedures of the organization. No sooner is an organization created than "problems arise from the need for some continuity of policy and leadership, for a homogeneous outlook [his term for culture], for the achievement of continuous consent and participation on the part of the ranks" (1949, p. 10).

His conclusion is that TVA was "coopted" by cooperation with external interest groups, specifically the "farm leadership" (1949, p. 145). "Cooptation" was defined by Selznick as the "process of absorbing new elements into the leadership or policy-determining structure of an organization as a means of averting threats to its stability or existence" (p. 13). The substantive goals of the organization, the rationality of its use of resources, the strategies of its elites are not theoretical issues. Cooptation for Selznick does not have the contemporary meaning of the undermining of organizational goals from their rational origins. Rather, cooptation is a part of the compromises necessary to maintain democratic participation in the formulation of goals and means in a bureaucracy.

Concretely, Selznick found that the local farm leadership and the regional land grant colleges exercised crucial veto power over programs and also influenced the implementation of other programs in their own interests. In Selznick's interpretation,

the unacknowledged absorption of nucleuses of power into the administrative structure of an organization makes possible the elimination or appeasement of potential sources of opposition. At the same time, as the price of accommodation, the organization commits itself to avenues of activity and lines of policy enforced by the character of the coopted elements. . . . there will be pressure for the or-

[5] Note that, from the point of view of top political elites, these TVA powers increased fragmentation. TVA, to quote David Lilienthal, was the "boldest and perhaps most far-reaching effort of our times to decentralize the administration of federal functions. If it succeeds . . . we shall have added strength to the administrative defenses which protect the future of our beleaguered democracy" (quoted in Selznick 1949, p. 26, from a 1939 speech made immediately after the German army had invaded Poland).

ganization as a whole to adapt itself to the needs of the informal relationship. [1949, p. 217]

He concludes, somewhat regretfully, that "specific programmatic and administrative imperatives, rather than general considerations of democratic policy, determine the form of intervention at the grass roots" (p. 219). The contradiction between the democratic and the bureaucratic aspects of the state is evident in the various ways in which the internal rationalizing imperatives of TVA administrators, regardless of David Lilienthal's visionary rhetoric, overrode the seeming commitment to genuine democratic participation.

With this caveat, Selznick's argument is that the bureaucratic aspect of the state cannot ultimately be centralized because the state is also open and vulnerable to diverse interests making demands for various benefits. Such bureaucratic responsiveness introduces what appear to be irrationalities, but they are a necessary price to maintain democratic responsiveness.[6]

Agency cultures

Quite aside from its responsiveness to external constituencies, the state is also seen as internally pluralistic in the sense that it consists of many agencies with different functions and internal cultures. A study by political scientist and former federal budgetary staff member Harold Seidman (1980) is an excellent example of an analysis of "agency cultures."[7]

Seidman's study focuses upon the failures of attempts to reorganize the federal government, because of resistance from "professional guilds" and the "vertical functional autocracies" that have developed. Seidman is ambivalent about the way in which bureaucracies resist change. On the one hand, organizations must develop an internal esprit de corps,

---

[6] Some pluralists, notably economists, therefore consider the state an inefficient mode of decision making, and they conclude that market allocation of resources through prices is an adequate substitute for many public decisions and policies.

[7] A recent empirical study of agency cultures deals with 150 metropolitan juvenile courts. The authors say that "the dominant value orientations of differing systems of justice are represented by observable structural correlates" (Stapleton, Aday, and Ito 1982, p. 550). They conceive of juvenile courts as " 'open systems' reacting to exogenous events and adapting to strain through the gradual introduction of new elements" (p. 559). They stress the options open to the judge and the probation officer. They can choose whether or not to refer, release, or counsel an offender. The prosecutor can participate in those decisions. The offender has rights. One of their major findings was that "centralization of authority" was furthered by the "control and distribution of organizational rewards – for example, hiring and firing, promotions, and incentive rewards" (p. 553). Individuals act within an organizational structure that is taken for granted. Here the bureaucratic aspect of the state is the unexamined context within which a differentiated function of the democratic state – justice – is carried out. The capitalist aspect – the class bias in who is arrested, for what, and with what outcomes – is totally absent, given the world view that juvenile justice is a "loosely coupled set of subsystems" (p. 560).

a defensive culture that resists external control in order to maintain morale. On the other hand, wider goals cannot be realized unless the broader vision of executive leadership can prevail over the patterns of behavior (almost traditional, in a Weberian sense) that are dominant in long–established public agencies.

Seidman argues that managerial language has become the political culture of bureaucracy. "Custom, culture, and role all require OMB [Office of Management and Budget] officials openly to profess their faith in 'economy and efficiency' as the prime goals of organization and re-organization" (1980, p. 12). But the reality is far different, according to Seidman. A variety of pluralist factors undermine the most committed efforts to rationalize the state.

First, the reasons for reorganization have little to do with bureaucratic rationalization and therefore cannot be expected to have that conse-quence. Seidman gives an impressively long list of the reasons for re-organizing an agency or department: (1) to respond to pressures for immediate answers to a complex problem that the old agency has been unable or unwilling to provide; (2) to dump an unwanted official con-veniently; (3) to bypass a troublesome congressional committee; (4) to create an impression of neatness and order; (5) to create an impression that something is being done about a problem; (6) to create public sup-port; (7) to contain and disorganize the opposition; (8) to conceal budg-etary expenditures by removing them from the budget through the establishment of public corporations (highway and housing funds); (9) to save a program with little appeal by renaming and reorganizing it (the Microbiological Research Agency became the Allergy and Infectious Disease Treatment Agency); (10) to enhance the agency's status in the outside community by establishing an image of professionalism (the National Archives and the Fire Academy) (1980, pp. 24–39). Reorgani-zation is seen as a cover for the actions of multiple actors creating tem-porary coalitions to serve their own interests. Such reorganizations have nothing to do with the managerial image of rationalization. Rational-ization is an ideology for pluralists, just as participation is an ideology to managerialists.

Second, "agency cultures" encourage bureaucracies to respond to their presumed legislative and programmatic mandates. "Each agency has its own culture and internal set of loyalties and values which are likely to guide its actions and influence its policies" (Seidman 1980, p. 19). Once in existence, each agency then seeks out a political base of support in other parts of the state and in external constituencies. These agency cultures are critically important because bureaucracies are not and cannot be neutral, rational, instrumental organizations.

Shared loyalties and outlook knit together the institutional fabric. They are the foundation of those intangibles which make for institutional morale and pride. Without them, functions could not be decentralized and delegated with the confidence that policies will be administered consistently and uniformly. But because people believe what they are doing is important and the way they have been taught to do it is right, they are slow to accept change. [p. 19]

Seidman gives several examples of how programs were effectively killed by being assigned to a "hostile" agency, and how frequently new agencies are established (quite rationally, from the point of view of sponsors of a new program) to create their own staff and establish their own programmatic commitments.

Third, rationalization depends upon an assessment of what is being and can be accomplished by a given agency or program. The basic difficulty of assessment is that state programs have multiple purposes and consequences, quite aside from their titles. Programs or legislation labeled "urban," "education," "energy" have multiple components, partly because they were passed in legislation written to attract a majority congressional coalition. The resulting agency and program are responsive to numerous constituencies and may actually be internally inconsistent, leading to continuous tensions.

As a result of these factors, the state exhibits a marvelous growth of organizational forms. Seidman devotes half of his book to an analysis of the reasons for their existence. The reality of organizational pluralism within the state is conveyed by his list: . . . "executive departments, independent agencies, assorted commissions, boards, councils, authorities, wholly-owned corporations, mixed-ownership corporations, 'captive' corporations, institutes, government-sponsored enterprises, foundations, establishments, conferences, intergovernmental bodies, compact agencies, and a wide variety of interagency and advisory committees" (1980, p. 22). Seidman emphasizes the point that "the differences among these institutional types are more a matter of convention and tradition than legal prescriptions." He does not mean that the distinctions have no political or policy significance, only that each type has its own history as it develops an institutional identity. "Institutional type can be crucial in determining who controls – the President, the Congress, or the so-called 'special interests' " (p. 22).

Fourth, genuine rationalization is impossible because of the character of Congress as a congeries of particularistic interests. Congressional power is divided among sixteen committees and ninety-seven standing subcommittees, each of which has its own "culture, mode of operations, and set of relationships to executive agencies subject to its oversight, depending upon its constituency" (Seidman 1980, p. 42). Congressional staff members "develop alliances with the executive branch bureaucracy and the bureaucracies representing interest groups" (p. 43) in the so-called iron triangle, a nearly irresistible coalition of different interests inside and outside the state. Any attempt at comprehensive planning to integrate different policies that impinge upon each other (housing and transportation, for example, or subsidies for different types of energy production) is fragmented, reflecting the fragmented congressional system. Each subcommittee has its own fiefdom of jurisdictions, procedures, and prerogatives that it jealously safeguards. The consequences turn sincere attempts at bureaucratic rationalization into a shambles.

The flow of benefits

Recent research within the pluralist perspective argues for bureaucratic responsiveness to electoral threat, showing that even the internal operations of public bureaucracies are affected by the electoral calculations of Congress and the president when faced with an upcoming election. Both Social Security payments and veterans' benefits increased more (13 percent) in election years than in nonelection years (8 percent). Most of the election-year increases occurred relatively close to the election, rather than at the beginning of the year (Tufte 1978). In election years the administrative discretion over the implementation of programs makes it possible for "those government agencies sending out checks [to] accelerate the processing of new beneficiary applications, the payment of retroactive benefits, and the initiation of new programs" (p. 39). The use of the flow of benefits to voters near elections assumes that voters will remember in the election what the President and Congress did for them yesterday, rather than blame their leaders for the overall level of unemployment and inflation.

A critique of Tufte (Brown and Stein 1982) argues that there is no relationship between elections and transfer payments and that presidents cannot manipulate either the economy or the bureaucracy as easily as Tufte concludes. The authors use survey data to show that voters who directly benefited from some government actions did not behave politically as Tufte predicted. This is a debate within the pluralist perspective on the issue of how the behavior of individual voters is influenced by the actions of political leaders attempting to control administrative actions.

Bureaucratic roles: the individual level

A major pluralist explanation of bureaucratic centralization is at the individual level. Favored by economists, it stresses individual skills and tastes for leadership. Centralization, economist Oliver Williamson (1975) argues, is most likely in an "integrated" task group and least likely in an "unrelated" task group. He summarizes Kenneth Arrow's logical argument about the conditions under which organizational centralization is likely. Because individuals must interact in integrated task groups (by definition), a joint decision on what individual activities should be is superior to individual decisions. An optimum decision depends on information. Because transmission of information is costly, centralization is more efficient. It is therefore also cheaper for a central individual or office to make a collective decision and transmit it. This explanation of centralization presupposes consensus among the individuals on what is to be done as well as a consensus on the procedures to be used to select the individuals who make the decisions.

The latter assumption is clear from another part of Williamson's argument and from that of an older economist, Frank Knight, whose work *Risk, Uncertainty, and Profit* (1965) Williamson cites. Both emphasize that individual factors explain the choice of individuals who become the leaders or coordinators. Because

processing and decision-making talents are not widely distributed, efficiency will be served by reserving the central information collection and decision-making position to the one or few individuals who have superior information processing capacities and exceptional oratorical and decision-making skills. Something of an elite thereby results. . . . not only does the peak coordinator enjoy the power which authority and expertise accord him but having more complete information gives him a strategic advantage over everyone else. The peak coordinator has inordinate influence over both the value and factual premises of other members of the group. . . . Simple hierarchy effectively obtains. [Williamson 1975, pp. 52–3]

Note that leadership status and influence derive from the needs of the group itself, internal consensus on the tasks and on the procedures by which leaders are to be selected, and the special leadership qualities of individuals. If such a "simple hierarchy" rests upon group recognition of the leadership qualities of individuals and upon agreement on the tasks to be achieved, then presumably the hierarchy can be changed if the group changes its mind. In this instance, a leadership hierarchy – an incipient bureaucracy – is the direct result of core aspects of democracy itself.

Another pluralist explanation of bureaucratic behavior interprets it in terms of the varied situational contexts in which individuals function in organizations and attempt to realize their interests. A classic example is Aaron Wildavsky's study of the federal budgetary process (1974).

The budgetary process

Wildavsky's study is explicitly an explanation not of the federal budget but of the "budgetary process," an entirely different thing. Significantly, he refers to the "participants" in the budgetary process but not to the

factors that explain the budget. He admits in the preface to the second
edition of his *Politics of the Budgetary Process* (1974) that he does not deal
with the nearly one-quarter of federal spending not allocated through
the normal budget process. As he says, "some $60 billion in tax subsidies
– money allowed to remain in private hands because of special tax provisions – [is] funneled through the House Ways and Means Committee,
and . . . still more [is] mandated through the 'backdoor' of the Treasury
under the aegis of legislative committees" (p. xvi).

The federal budgetary process illustrates how bureaucratic roles function to facilitate the responsiveness of legislatures to multiple constituencies (Wildavsky 1974). First, executive agencies develop budgetary
requests, then the Office of Management and Budget (OMB) cuts them,
then the president presents the budget to Congress, and ultimately the
Congress, through its committees and subcommittees, makes decisions
authorizing programs and appropriating expenditures.

Wildavsky's study of the federal budgetary process emphasizes the
roles created by varying positions within state institutions – agency
officials, congressmen, OMB officials, party leaders, and interest group
representatives. Individuals jockey and maneuver for relative advantage. The executive agencies play advocacy roles, seeking to defend their
own programs and projects. Other agencies, such as OMB, play "cut
the budget" roles, defining those roles as watchdogs of public funds,
as cutting out waste, as eliminating obsolete and unpopular programs.
Wildavsky argues that if and when both the advocacy and the cutting
roles are played properly a balance can be maintained between responding to political demands and holding down state expenditures in the
public interest.

The complexity of the multiple and simultaneous decisions that must
be made requires a division of labor. Nobody can consider all of the
consequences of the decisions they must make in the short time available
and with the skimpy information they can obtain. Congress delegates
its authority to committees, they in turn to their subcommittees, each
of which considers the annual budget requests of several government
agencies. The real decisions are made in the subcommittees, most of
whose decisions are accepted by their committees and then by the Congress as a whole. This gives a few individual congressmen – the chairmen
of key subcommittees – enormous power. The combination of long tenure in office and the claim of such tenured members to key chairman-
ships gives them considerable experience with the programs "their"
agencies run and also contributes to the stability and continuity of Congress as an institution (Polsby 1968).

The result is the annual budget game. The key players are agency representatives, congressmen on the relevant committees, and staff members in the OMB. The political consensus at any given time – public opinion, as estimated by congressmen for tax cuts or spending for health care or space exploration – defines the general limits of spending. Within these limits, political actors have leeway to calculate options and to develop strategies that maximize their interests. The system depends for its effective functioning on all political actors defining their preferences and advocating them strongly and effectively.

The outcome of such processes is normally the incremental expansion of the state: gradual extensions of old programs and additions of new agencies so that the budgets of governments will tend to grow at an annual rate of about 5 to 10 percent. Crises and social disturbances – wars, depressions, revolts – may necessitate nonincremental new programs, which sharply increase the budget, and such programs are seldom abandoned when the crisis is over. Incremental outcomes are generally a result of the combination of the openness of a democratic political system to group demands and the lack of any mechanism "above politics" that can limit spending on new programs.

Wildavsky focuses closely upon the social psychology of individual participants in the political, legislative, and administrative processes of budgeting. At innumerable points, he uses language that implies motives, perceptions, beliefs, incentives, biases of the participants. Congressmen are "losing faith" in the appropriations process. The president "insists" that he need not spend. Congressmen "feel" that the financial situation has got out of control but "respect" the presidential statements more than their own. The president's budgets are announced with an "air of confidence." Congressmen are "interested," "concerned," "unhappy," "want credit," "do not wish to face consequences," are "ambivalent." Politicians and civil servants are "assured and comfortable" but sometimes "worry" others.

The verbs he uses are largely active ones and can be divided into two kinds, those relating to *formal* actions (legal, administrative, statutory) and those relating to *informal* actions (political, strategic, tactical). Examples of formal verbs are: prepare, recommend, decide, notify, submit, instruct, send, spell out, check, deliver, present, analyze, authorize, appropriate, bind, appeal, adopt, approve, veto, pass, sign, audit, issue, apportion. Examples of informal verbs are: discuss, expect, urge, get together, bring, consider, agree, challenge, discourage, desire, request, talk, meet with, estimate, justify. The distinction stems from his emphasis on the importance of discovering the situations under which the "rational person," the "one who manipulates the few variables under his control to good effect," can act (Wildavsky 1974, p. 229). The job of pluralist policy analysis is to show the individuals involved how to act in a complex situation where information costs are high and there are few options.

These verbs scattered throughout indicate Wildavsky's emphasis on political actors: the calculations and strategies, the wishes and desires, the interests and concerns of individuals who must work within a political, legal, and administrative structure they cannot change. The attempts to change that structure through such devices as "program budgeting," Wildavsky regards as ill fated: Either they will produce the undesirable consequence of centralizing power and reduce the available political choices or they will not work at all, wasting considerable time and energy and increasing frustration and cynicism. Role-based social-psychological characteristics of individual bureaucrats and political leaders are seen as the best explanation for their behavior.

Wildavsky hardly refers to any structural or historical reasons why programs come about in the first place, why Congress is so unwilling either to resist demands for programs or to support additional programs to raise revenues for them. He poses the paradox: "Why do Congressmen who vote for their share of spending increases express unhappiness with the collective results of their individual actions?" (1974, p. 209). Consistent with his focus upon individual actors in contingent situations, he also focuses upon the inconsistency of their attitudes, preferences, and belief. No analysis is offered of the conflicts within structures or the contradictions between institutions that might create these inconsistencies. Similarly, he nowhere refers to any societal factors that might produce demands for programs, expenditures, taxation of various kinds. Only when they publicly appear in the forms of specific actual program or dollar requests does he take them into account in his analysis. The "government" as a whole is a congeries of highly differentiated institutions separate from the society and subject to all kinds of pressures.

The key assumption, casually stated, is that "the American political system works to assure that every significant interest has representation at some key point" (Wildavsky 1974, p. 130). Rose (1967) and Dahl (1961) also view the normal condition of "political man" as apathy. But specific, focused, and widespread grievances can be expressed and heard. This classic pluralist image assumes a process in which "bargaining takes place among many dispersed centers of influence. . . . Since there is no one group of men who can necessarily impose their preferences upon others within the American political system, special coalitions are formed to support or oppose specific policies" (Wildavsky 1974, p. 131).

Thus there is no direct competition between the interests at stake. The interests are mediated by political agents whose stakes are different. The political careers of agents – maintaining their positions and influence –

are at stake but not the specific interests affected by their decisions. This allows a moderate politics of compromise, precisely because the interests directly affected are not present in the decision-making process. Negotiations take place privately, allowing both hard bargaining and ultimate compromise.

Wildavsky appeals to the general social value of "mitigating conflict" as a reason for supporting incremental budgeting. But he does not consider the social costs of *not* reducing conflict or how that changes the outcome of budgetary processes. He appeals to those values he assumes to be widely shared, those he agrees with, those he believes will be useful to support his argument. In other words, his argument is also a thoroughly political one, designed to influence people's thinking to accept the realism and desirability of incremental budgeting, the reduction of conflict, and the positive functions of political bargaining.

The structure of the state is taken as given, as the environment that constrains the calculations of the participants, as the "elementary facts of life," as if the state were a biological organism. Just as Rose (1967) regarded the economic and political structures as not changeable by any conceivable political coalition, political changes are only due to a shifting political consensus. Wildavsky (1974) refers to the "contemporary climate of opinion," the "pressing and recognized needs of the times," which become "obvious to all." Growing unemployment "requires" measures to put people to work.

Wildavsky knows that statistics about unemployment, or average income, or the infant mortality rate, do not "require" any policies until they become embodied in political demands. Objective trends are seen as independent, exogenous causal forces that constrain and shape the actions of participants in the budgetary process but are outside the scope of his inquiry.

Wildavsky's argument is a good example of the two basic kinds of explanations relied upon by pluralists. On the one hand, there are exogenous, seemingly politically neutral forces, such as wars, depressions, epidemics, or "social disturbances" and "upheavals" (Peacock and Wiseman 1961), that change all of the calculations and strategies of political actors but are not subject to change by political action. On the other hand, there are situational, "political" processes under the control of or at least subject to influence by political actors. These two types of factors are seldom brought together analytically or theoretically, although the consequences of the decisions made by political actors continuously alter the structure or the environment – the bureaucratic state – within which political actors make their new calculations and devise their latest strategies.

Conclusions

Democratic competition in a "preference market" provokes organizational responses. Bureaucratic organizations are defined in terms of the
values they serve. Although the economic interests of influential groups
may coincide with those of the state, they are not seen as the major
force that generates political institutionalization. Nor are the interests
of the government decided by their most powerful offices or their ability
to dominate potentially recalcitrant citizens. Rather, institutionalized
governments are seen as independent of the instrumental control of any
particular elite or class and function to achieve political community in
a differentiated social order. The potential interest of governmental institutions in their own power is rendered benign by the theoretical assumption that the principal governmental function is to create political
community and that larger democratic processes suffuse bureaucratic
operations. State power is a consequence of democracy, normally not a
threat to it.

Bureaucratic rationalization is impossible because of the information
costs of comprehensive planning. Decisions based on assessment of the
general consequences of major alternatives is not feasible, due to the
time and energy limitations of decision makers, the lack of data bearing
on alternative decisions, and the political costs of considering even major
alternatives. Opening up political and administrative consideration of
major alternatives to full discussion activates the political resources of
actors who have the power to block any decision to get what they want.
Rather than attempting genuine bureaucratic rationalization, leaders must
rely upon a general consensus (a "sense of the meeting") that can envelop most existing programs in an aura of acceptability. This allows
leaders to concentrate on both the most precarious new programs and
crises of effectiveness of old ones. If a general atmosphere of consensus
does not envelop most programs, reducing the sheer burden of decisions
to be made, "demand overload" occurs. The stability of leadership in
particular and the political system in general is threatened (Easton 1965a).
Democratic governments cannot command the various components of
decision making or control the potential consequences of those decisions
with precision (Crozier, Huntington and Watanuki 1975). If they do,
they violate their own basic values.

Within the pluralist home domain, such analyses of the process of
political bargaining and negotiations within and between and among
bureaucracies are powerful and persuasive. If they are extrapolated, and
claim to be general explanations of the structure and institutional role
of the bureaucratic state, they become misleading. The requirement of
consensus can be reinterpreted as both an ideological weapon of elites

and an instrument of class struggle in a more synthetic analysis of bureaucracy. If not only the logic of democratic culture but also the logics of bureaucratic domination and capitalist accumulation are theorized, then pluralist concepts explaining internal bureaucratic processes are useful.

6

The pluralist perspective on the capitalist state

The pluralist perspective on the contemporary capitalist aspect of the state does not, for reasons that should be clear by now, use the language of class, of capitalism, and frequently not even of the state. But the relations between business and government are seen as of critical importance nonetheless.

It is important to emphasize at the outset that pluralists can empirically recognize capitalists, but they are seen as representing individual economic interests. When the term "capitalist" is used, it could be redefined as "businessman" in the sense of an occupation, with a gain of theoretical clarity. "Business" is a generic category, covering multiple differences or similarities of economic interests. Similarly, the term "worker" or even "labor" may be used, but this signifies an individual social location with multiple and sometimes loosely intercorrelated attributes such as occupational prestige, income, and education. Where these individual attributes intercorrelate and are labeled a "class," the meaning is still not within the class perspective if the latent world view is not one of capital–labor relations within a mode of production.[1]

The way in which class relations are absorbed into a pluralist world view is exemplified (among many examples that could be chosen) by this theoretical point from a seven-nation survey of "participation and political equality."

For Marx, economic position as indicated by one's relation to the means of production represented the dominant dimension of stratification that deter-

---

[1] A typical pluralist world view of class is found in Olson 1982. He says that the word "class" is an "extraordinarily loose, emotive and misleadingly aggregative term that has unfortunately been reified over generations of ideological debate. There are, of course, no clearly delineated and widely separated groups such as the middle class or the working class, but rather a large number of groups of diverse situations and occupations, some of which differ greatly and some of which differ slightly if at all in income and status" (p. 84). At the individual level of analysis, his point is absolutely correct, but it has no relevance to the societal concept of class because it disaggregates a societal-level phenomenon into individuals and groups.

mined, in the long run, all other stratification patterns. Weber, on the other hand, stressed the distinction among economic, political and social stratification hierarchies. Positions on such hierarchies can vary independently of each other. One individual or group may be more politically influential than another but less well off in economic terms. [Verba, Nie, and Kim 1978, p. 2]

The emphasis on the individual level of analysis translates class into stratification or "economic position." Power becomes influence. A mode of production is reduced to markets.

Because a key pluralist concept is of the economy as a market, implying free choices by individuals, another example of the relation of markets to the state may clarify the point. Harrison White defines markets as "self-reproducing social structures among specific cliques of firms and other actors who evolve roles from observations of each other's behavior" (1981, p. 518). He assumes that the key economic actors in markets are individuals and that one can abstract the operations of markets from both the state and the economy. A market is an "act" that must be "got together." White is aware of the metaphorical nature of his argument and discusses alternative metaphors, but in any case "the actors are making effective decisions on the basis of tangible observations of the actions of their confreres" (p. 526).

A stable – and untheorized – state environment allows these market choices to be made. White hardly mentions the state except as a context for individual action ("U.S. markets"). He assumes that firms are privately controlled and engage in free decisions about when to enter a market. The state is a source of definitions of industry used by firms and business journals. Firms are described as "legal corporations." In his only substantive reference to the state, he takes issue with microeconomic theory for not explaining markets well, arguing that "Law, in particular antitrust law, seems to shape the concepts [that analyze markets] more than does microeconomic theory" (White 1981, p. 541).

Values and functions in the economy: the societal level

Pluralist reinterpretation of the capitalist aspect of the state utilizes the division of intellectual labor between economics and the other social sciences, mirroring the institutional differentiation of the society. The "economy" can function because the "government" accepts its limited role and vice versa. Although, from the point of view of economic actors, taxes, subsidies, and regulation change their incentives for action, the state and the economy are seen as differentiated, precisely the pluralist image of institutional relationships. Tensions are created between institutions because of differences of function or values and failures of communication. These interinstitutional discrepancies account for change

(Baumol 1965, pp. 51, 183–97). Debate thus centers on how much the state needs to interfere with markets in order to safeguard the public interest.

In the work of economist Milton Friedman (1962), the state is indispensable in order to guarantee the freedom of persons to sell their property (including their labor) to others and to ensure that contracts will be honored. The rest of the programs added by the modern welfare state, partly as a result of its democratic character, are not merely superfluous but dangerous, because they interfere with the free market allocation of resources. Left alone, the market will make the most efficient use of scarce labor and capital.

For other economists, the distinctive properties of the capitalist state disappear into the universal properties of "social choices," much as the distinctive properties of the bureaucratic state disappear into "authority patterns" (Eckstein and Gurr 1975). Kenneth Arrow, for example, describes alternative social preferences in terms of "various particular decisions actually made by the government, such as tax rates, expenditures, antimonopoly policy, and price policies of socialized enterprises" (1951, p. 87). Social choices about capital investment by private firms are never mentioned, but the inference is that individuals have exactly the same potential rights to participate in those social choices as they do in elections.

Pluralists all recognize inequalities of income and wealth but do not link them to any pervasive consequences of the capitalist economy and state. Economist William Baumol is a good example. He appeals to a general consensus on social goals and values as the way to rectify inequality. "The general problem of maldistribution of resources seems to be one that is amenable to amelioration by a system of bounties and taxes as long as *we have some fairly good idea* of its direction and magnitude" (1965, p. 103; italics added). Who "we" are and how "we" could affect change in the distribution of wealth, income, and services are not discussed. Given a democratic society, "we," presumably the state, will somehow redress the worst "maldistribution." The main assumption is that the state is democratic because of equal rights to participate via voting. The corollary is that the economy is also democratic because similar principles of social choice operate through the market.[2]

---

[2] The world view of conservative pluralism is visible in a work by the philosopher Robert Nozick (1974), who contrasts his own view to that of Marx. Nozick's is one of those important works that explicitly deals with points of view far removed from his own, in part because the book is a record of his evolution toward a neoconservative political philosophy. Nozick's concern is to restore the assumption that the "choice" a worker makes in subjecting himself to capitalist control for part of his day is "voluntary," rather than determined by a system of class relations enforced by a capitalist state (pp. 253–64.).

Talcott Parsons and Neil Smelser, as one would expect in a work called *Economy and Society* (1956), take a pluralist view of the capitalist aspect of the state. They rely upon Durkheim for "classical discussions" of the "central economic institution" of "contract." (p. 104). Even seemingly non-value-oriented economic exchanges like contracts are defined by values: "the formal and informal rules by which those engaged in contracts are regulated" (p. 105). "[I]n the interests of stability, ego and alter must constitute parts of a single social system. . . . there must be some kind of *integration* and some kind of *common value pattern* which they share" (p. 109; italics in original).

The system goal of an economy is defined by "maximizing utility or the economic value of the total available means to want satisfaction" (Parsons and Smelser 1956, p. 20). Individual wants and their satisfaction can be aggregated to become system goals. The optimum condition is defined by maximal satisfaction of what people (or collectivities) want as consumers. And goals are defined as whatever "situational objects" (assuming an institutionalized value system) maximize "the stability of the system" (p. 17).

"State" and "economy" are seen as related but differentiated structures. "The development of 'big government,' such a conspicuous phenomenon of modern society, is, therefore, by no means incompatible in principle with the continuing growth of a nonsocialistic economy" (Parsons and Smelser 1956, p. 288). Parsons and Smelser appeal to seemingly commonsense observations about the growth of both the state and the economy, as if those facts were not theoretically problematic. Economic growth *means* stability. Structural differentiation of the state from the economy implies societal integration, but the point is not argued.

The availability of labor is taken for granted, as a resource available to the "economy." An "underlying commitment to work," independent of the sanction of unemployment, is a factor of production analogous to technology. Those factors "behave like land in the physical sense" and therefore can be grouped with land for economic analysis. They are "governed" by an institutionalized system of "values" and hence are associated with the pattern-maintenance subsystem of the society – particularly the family. "Such values will, within limits, be acted upon wherever appropriate, independent of cost" (Parsons and Smelser 1956, p. 26). Capitalism and the capitalist aspect of the state are defined by the value system that generates individual motivations both to work and to support core social institutions.

In his slightly later work on societies, Parsons further challenges other perspectives on ownership and control of modern corporations. For large industry, the "structural fusion . . . of the firm . . . with the owning lineage has been broken," and the firm is now a "structure of occupational roles" (1960, pp. 112–13). Because of this structural change, the most "crucial" change since Marx analyzed industrial capitalism, Parsons suggests that the " 'free enterprise' sector of the industrial economy" is no longer " 'capitalistic' at all" (p. 113). Rather, "functions are performed overwhelmingly in occupational roles" that are hierarchically arranged.[3]

This argument does not make Parsons a managerial theorist. Bureaucracy is the appropriate form of organization only for specific functions. Bureaucratic rationalization is not an overwhelming social force penetrating more and more institutions. Bureaucracies are still subject to differentiated societal functions integrated by values. Parsons makes an explicit analogy between the newly bureaucratized industries and "democratic-bureaucratic political organizations" (1960, pp. 114–15). In the former, owners have been replaced by a fiduciary board of directors, who are entrusted with other people's money. In the latter, "top political authority has been placed in the hands of popularly elected officials." In both cases, the top of the bureaucratic structure cannot itself be bureaucratic but must carry out specific functions according to societal values. Correlatively, the "government of industrial enterprises is approximating that of universities, hospitals, and other 'nonprofit' organizations in our society" (p. 114).

Parsons is not arguing that total harmony exists. The two types of organizations, industrial-bureaucratic and democratic-bureaucratic, are "successfully integrated, though not without strain" (1960, p. 115). Tensions exist between different types of organizations, because of differences of functions, but in a mysterious and untheorized way such that they are somehow fully integrated into the society.

Parsons argues that America's "cultural tradition . . . has emphasized economic values – an emphasis on enterprise and production in an activist sense" (1960, p. 206). Implementing these values, specialized organizations – the large corporations – have developed, led by corporate executives. Leadership is an essential function in all social systems, which, with their increase of scale and their functional differentiation, tend to become more specialized. "[W]ithin considerable limits . . . the emergence of the large firm with operations on a nation-wide basis [is] a 'normal' outcome of the process of growth and differentiation of the economy" (p. 207). Parsons asserts that the giant corporations have power (defined as the "generalized capacity of a social system to get things done in the interest of collective goals" [p. 181]) because they represent

---

[3] Parsons argues that this fits Weber's model of bureaucratic structure, and it does, but reinterpreted within a pluralist world view that sees such bureaucracies as simply another structure with distinctive functions, as opposed to Weber, who argued that bureaucracies are autonomous structures.

the basic economic values of the society. He says that, "given the nature of industrial society, a relatively well-defined elite or leadership group should be expected to develop in the business world" (pp. 211–12). But this leadership group functions in the economy, not in politics or in the society as a whole, which recruits and socializes different leaders.

Although it allows more tension between institutional orders than does Parsons, the much later work of Niklas Luhmann (1979) also assumes that corporate leadership is functional. Luhmann simply accepts the class structure of a capitalist society as a given, regarding "capital" as the function of the economy "to bring about . . . the elementary conditions for organized work to be possible" (p. 176). In a peculiar footnote he says that he knows full well that "there is a correlation between the economic situation and political participation of people and above all we do not dispute that division into social classes demands such as a correlation" (p. 197). The social "codes" (norms) directed against converting money into power are "so heavily institutionalized that even scientists become angry about such correlations and call for counter measures, instead of taking them as a sign of order and enjoying them" (p. 197). The class structure comprises a set of economic and social institutions exogenous to political power. The institutional differentiation between "money" and "power" is protected by "normative barriers."

Luhmann does refer to capitalism, but as a substantive example, not as a theorized concept. Thus he says that the "differentiation between societal systems and organized social systems [our distinction between the societal and organizational levels] . . . has the effect . . . of uncoupling organizational power from the political power formed in the societal system" (1979, p. 177). Luhmann recognizes the different types of power associated with different levels of analysis, but within a world view that focuses upon interdependent functions rather than contradictory logics or dominant structures.

Political scientists Eckstein and Gurr (1975), it will be recalled, define the "government" as the authority pattern of the "most inclusive" social unit, avoiding definitions of the state in terms of either a monopoly of coercion or the function of maintaining order. But they neglect the possibility that the capitalist economy may be an authority pattern even more inclusive than government, both because it is less publicly accountable and because of its "transnational" character. "Corporations" are mentioned as social units (p. 16), but the only empirical examples given are governments that legislate, administer, adjudicate, lobby, or aggregate votes. Production, consumption, employment, marketing, and labor control are not mentioned.

Eckstein and Gurr appreciate the possibility of including economic organizations under the general rubric of "authority patterns" but do not do so consistently. The relation of "buyer and seller," for instance (assuming "free" market conditions), is an example of a symmetrical relationship of equality and thus is not an authority pattern. They assume that a specific relationship of actors can be isolated from its organizational and societal context. Simply postulating a free market makes pluralist assumptions about the conditions under which buyers and sellers can enter markets. If genuinely free markets exist only under quite limited historical conditions, then their seemingly neutral analytic decision is based upon an implicit world view concerning the societal context of "buying" and "selling."

Eckstein and Gurr recognize certain phenomena empirically but not theoretically. When they refer to Alvin Gouldner's study (1954) of a strike in a gypsum plant, workers, managers, and strikers appear as empirical categories, but the only theoretically relevant terms are "individuals" and "groups" (Eckstein and Gurr 1975, p. 85). References to crowded conditions in German families, economic scarcity, and "regimented" workplace experiences are all seen as empirical instances of a subcategory of authority patterns (p. 57). Ghettos, dirty work, and degraded castes are empirical categories; the theoretical reference is to "social distance" variables.

Another instance of empirical but not theoretical recognition of capitalism is their point that certain kinds of factors may affect authority patterns but are "contingent situational influences" (Eckstein and Gurr 1975, p. 406). The example given is that the particular authority pattern in a factory may "reflect the fact that there is a depression or a period of special scarcity of the commodities on which operations depend." Conditions in the capitalist economy are regarded like the weather in Holland, constantly changeable and unpredictable and thus not capable of being incorporated into the explanatory framework. Here they exclude these phenomena after having made the explicit decision to confine their attention to "authority patterns" in "social units," either "governmental" or "nongovernmental." Once having done that, it is natural to regard economic depressions or the market position of an industry as contingent and situational. Eckstein and Gurr's pluralist world view regards depressions and market shortages as events to be recognized but that need not be theorized.

Eckstein and Gurr explicitly refer several times to Marxist ideas about capitalism but transform those ideas into variables related to authority patterns. Stratification has likely effects on "all aspects of authority" (1975, p. 420). Capitalists seeking profits are described as superordinates seeking authority. The exploitation of labor is seen as the psychology of subordination.

Political leadership and economic growth

Economic modernization is generated by acts of entrepreneurship. Productivity surges because of the rewards given to technological innovation, saving, and long-term investment. Profit is a return to entrepreneurial risk, not exploitation. But the state must be involved. In the initial stages of economic takeoff, political leaders have a critical role, because of the deferred consumption necessary to create the infrastructure of future growth. Princeton historian C. E. Black says that in the early stages of economic development

a large investment in producer goods... will result in more rapid economic development but will impose a heavier burden on the population.... Some political leaders are prepared to demand maximum sacrifices of the people in the interest of the rapid development of producer goods.... economic development depends to a great extent on the intellectual and political aspects of the process, the growth in knowledge and the ability of political leaders to mobilize resources [in addition to the purely economic aspects of modernization]. [1967, p. 19]

Sociologist S. M. Lipset, in *The First New Nation* (1963), discusses the deep involvement of the new American state in the economy. "Direct government financing of economic activities which required large sums of capital occurred in many states" (p. 51). In Pennsylvania, for example, for its first forty years there was considerable "direct state participation in ownership as a means of facilitating economic development.... The *doctrine of 'laissez-faire' became dominant only after the growth of large corporations and private investment funds reduced the pressures for public funds*" (p. 52; italics in original). State involvement in the economy reflected the actions of public leaders in the public interest. "All claims to a legitimate title to rule in new states" must win acceptance through the demonstration of effectiveness. "The loyalty of the different groups to the system must be won through developing in them the conviction that this system is the best – or at least an excellent – way to accomplish their objectives" (pp. 45–6).[4]

In the pluralist world view, capitalists were entrepreneurs whose success derived from their particular role orientations, status group membership, and common material interests. Paul Mantoux's historical study

---

[4] Some pluralists question the role of government in the nineteenth century in facilitating economic growth. Economic historian Frank Tipton argues that "the bureaucrative elites of 19th century Germany and Japan were much less successful in stimulating economic development than has been traditionally asserted. Direct government investment was neither extensive nor successful. Government-sponsored institutional change, notably in financial structures, had little if any beneficial impact" (1981, p. 139). The lesson he draws is that "centralized economic administration" by the state does not promote modernization.

(1961) of the Industrial Revolution emphasizes the individual qualities of the great English entrepreneurs, such as Matthew Boulton, Josiah Wedgwood, and John Roebuck, members of the same group of innovators sharing a similar consciousness. A capacity to organize and to turn "other people's inventions to practical results" was their distinctive quality. Mantoux describes Josiah Wedgwood as a man "whose practical ability works in harmony with the highest intellectual and moral qualities, and whose productive ability has not self-interest for its sole object but to do honor to the class to which they belong" (p. 388). Other entrepreneurs were "tyrannical, hard, sometimes cruel; their passions and greed were those of upstarts." Mantoux distinguishes the dissimilar elements that had gone into the making of the English manufacturing class and the unequal moral value of its members. Mantoux sees all of these individual manufacturers as members of a group sharing common economic interests, utilizing the state for their own benefit. Although he uses the term "class-consciousness," he means an aggregation of individual economic interests into a group identity.

The rights of citizens ("Englishmen") to participate in legislative decisions; how participation originates in individual needs; the growth of voluntary associations around diverse interests in a community; the uniting of individuals with specific economic interests for political action to serve their needs – all of these pluralist elements are seen in Mantoux's interpretation of the political role of the emerging capitalists in relation to the English state of the eighteenth century.

Sociologist Neil Smelser (1959) regards social system requirements and societal values as the general explanation for the role of the state in creating a working class during industrialization. Factory Acts by the British Parliament are seen as a functional mechanism for "handling" social disturbances over the introduction of technology and over child labor in a way that reintegrates the social order in the least damaging way.

Smelser's concern is with the structural differentiation of the family in response to the replacement of handloom weaving by machine weaving in England in the early nineteenth century. Factory operatives

reacted immediately and fiercely to this pressure in a number of disturbed social movements . . . a series of vigorous but unsuccessful strikes to resist the improved machinery; a commitment to the ten-hour agitation of the 1830's, one effect of which would have been to preserve the old work structure; a prolonged attempt to subvert the Factory Act of 1833, which threatened to separate the labor of adult and child even further; and a brief though intensive flirtation with the Utopian cooperative movement. [1959, p. 406]

Within the class perspective, this process would be described as working-class resistance to the commodification of the family's labor and to state efforts to increase the power of capital in the labor process. Smelser, however, describes the same process in very different terms.

Parliamentary investigation of the factory question represented a process of "handling and channeling" the disturbed elements of factory agitation. . . . Factory legislation between 1833 and 1847, in its turn, gradually eased the family structure into more differentiated directions. . . . The working class family which emerged about the time that the ten-hour day became normal was more specialized than the factory family of a quarter-century earlier; the economic performance of adults and children was segregated definitively. [1959, p. 407]

Such an empirical description probably could be agreed to by persons with any theoretical perspective. But Smelser did not refer to the "state" at all as a theoretical category. Factory legislation – acts of the state – was regarded as evidence of different stages of social response to "disturbances." Parliamentary investigation was described as "handling" the disturbance by "mechanisms of social control" (1959, p. 408). This was his *theoretical* interpretation of the action by the state. The potential "explosiveness" of the disturbance is "brought into line" by "police activity, governmental investigation, public debate, and journalistic commentary." Other stages refer to "more positive steps of encouraging ideas, specifying lines of social action, and translating these ideas into definite social experiments" (p. 406).

In Smelser's general view of reintegration and social control, these stages are all linked to cultural values. Action by the state is interpreted as a "covert handling of these tensions and a mobilization of motivational resources for new attempts to realize the implications of the existing value system" (1959, p. 15). Another action by the state is defined as " 'responsible' implementation of innovations . . . carried out by persons or collectivities which are either rewarded or punished, depending on their acceptability or reprehensibility in terms of the existing value system" (pp. 15–16). Still another example of state activity is in connection with disturbances around technological innovation in textiles. Overproduction and competition between different companies triggered a demand for action by Parliament. Parliament thus "acted as a 'handling' agency in a period of disturbance. It received all the complaints and recommendations from a distressed group, studied them, allowed some but cancelled others. In the meantime other agencies were involved in 'channeling' energy toward solutions consonant with the performance centered value-system" (1959, p. 113).

Here the concepts of capitalism, the working class, exploitation, factories, strikes, and the state have empirical but not theoretical status. Although Smelser recognizes that "the working classes suffered the most basic kinds of physical and psychological deprivations in the industrial revolution" (1959, p. 398), his concern is not with explaining why misery sometimes erupts into disturbances but with developing a model of how disturbances are integrated into the overall process of structural differentiation of both family and economy.

This study shows that state organizations are seen as performing economic functions within a societal value system. Only the specific historical actions of the state that have consequences for the institutionalization of values are central. Similarly, pluralists recognize the existence of capital accumulation and class formation as empirical categories but, as in the case of Smelser, theorize them as structural differentiation of new institutions and values, not as the development of the social relations of capitalist production.

Democracy and the market

For pluralists, one of the central issues is whether or not democracy has an impact on the market economy. Given the presumed importance of values of equality and the prediction of convergence between different modernizing institutional orders, it is natural that pluralists have been concerned with the impact of democracy on the distribution of income and living conditions (see Marshall 1964, for example).

An important strand of empirical literature is the quantitative comparative studies of the impact of "democratic performance" upon various social policies. Almost universally, such studies find that Western societies are more democratic, more egalitarian, more stable than other societies. But the very procedure of lumping states such as the United States and Britain together with Barbados and Trinidad assumes that the world population of states can be treated as if they were potentially equivalent social systems. The assumption that choosing "countries" or "governments" as units of analysis is theoretically neutral is a pluralist one, analogous to the assumption that one can "sample" communities, groups, organizations, as if they were self-contained social systems whose properties can be measured and compared.

An excellent example of this kind of research is Robert Jackman's study (1975) of the impact of democratic institutions on economic welfare and state program benefits in sixty noncommunist countries, including undemocratic ones. By measuring "democratic performance" in countries that do not have it, he assumes that they are potentially capable of achieving it, that there are no fundamental systemic or structural barriers to their becoming democratic that prevent a meaningful comparison.

Jackman's measure of democratic performance combines four components: the percentage of adults voting in a recent election, the competitiveness of political parties (ranging from no parties to a multiparty system with "no limitations on extremist party activity" (1975, p. 64), the existence of a "general acceptance of the 'rules of the game,' " and, finally, freedom of the press. All of these aspects of the democratic state are procedural in character, that is, they refer to processes and possibilities, not to actual consequences, particularly who benefits from state policies. The democratic machinery they measure is assumed to ensure the representation of popular interests within the state structure. The index contains the pluralist assumption that a political consensus on accepting the "limits on the struggle for power" (p. 64) actually works – that it does lead to genuine responsiveness to popular interests and needs.

The "social welfare index" (physicians per million, live births per thousand births, calorie consumption per capita, protein consumption per capita) is intended to "tap *actual* distributions of material goods rather than efforts to achieve more equalitarian societies" (Jackman 1975, p. 22; italics in original). But a per capita measure includes no information on the distribution across the entire population. Jackman is aware of this criticism and argues that there is an "upper limit or ceiling on the extent to which elites can monopolize consumption of these commodities" (p. 22). Thus he assumes that higher scores reflect more "egalitarian distributions" than lower scores. This is a "trickle-down" theory of the provision of public goods.

The measure of "social insurance program experience" includes whether or not a country had (and for how many years) family allowances; unemployment insurance; old age, invalidism, and death benefits; and work-injury, sickness, or maternity insurance borne by the state. As with the previous index, Jackman does not claim that these programs imply social equality but says that they imply "policy *efforts* at greater equality" (1975, p. 14; italics in original). This is the pluralist assumption that such programs represent an *intention* on the part of political leaders to move toward greater social and economic equality when such programs are passed. By simply accepting the "proclaimed intentions" of political leaders at face value, he equates public statements of officials with their real goals and in fact slides over into an assessment of the likely consequences of the programs as furthering social equality.[5] Regardless of the intentions of leaders, such state programs could be interpreted from a class perspective as part of the socialization of the costs of production necessary for the reproduction of labor power, or from the managerial perspective as devices to maintain state control over a

---

[5] An interesting exercise would be to rename Jackman's empirical indicators within a different world view and reinterpret the empirical findings accordingly. The Social Insurance Program Experience Index could be renamed "Expansion of the Welfare State," and the Social Welfare Index could be called "Level of Reproduction of Labor Power."

population, an elite strategy that has nothing whatsoever to do with social equality, either by intention or consequence.

In the pluralist perspective, there is a debate as to whether political development affects the distribution of material goods. Jackman argues that the relationship between democratic performance and distribution is spurious, as both change in direct response to patterns of economic development. Economic modernization is assumed to lead to an ever more equitable distribution of material goods, just as it fosters more democratic political procedures.

Business and corporate power: the organizational level

The role of corporate power has increasingly been debated within the pluralist perspective. Some pluralists, such as Grant McConnell (1966) and Charles Lindblom (1977), have argued that American democracy and the political culture that sustains it are insufficient to counter the rise of organized economic power. Corporate power increasingly challenges democracy, reducing the impact of political participation and biasing the democratic process.

McConnell rejects a class image of society. "American politics has been largely free of class divisions. . . . There has indeed been a profound consensus on the large issues that in other countries have been subject to the overriding fact of class conflict . . . the really persistent thread of conflict has been among units smaller than class," namely, strongly organized economic interest groups (1966, pp. 25–6). But the content of American political culture, he argues, has led paradoxically to the seizure of state power by such groups. Liberty, small units of association, a dislike of law, an ideology of freedom, individualism, and competition, a federal, decentralized state structure are all components of American values (pp. 52–3, 89–90, 92). Small communities and small constituencies guarantee freedom, social solidarity, and fellowship. But, under contemporary conditions of corporate power, organized interest groups are able to use that "ideology of small units" to serve their own interests. The ideology ignores "questions of *power* within the unit of organization" (p. 115). McConnell believes the public interest must be served by organizing national political constituencies around national parties and national issues.

The realities of corporate power derive from a failure to organize inclusive national political parties. Here McConnell echoes the thinking of Samuel Huntington (1968), who argues that democratic machinery is meaningless without the existence of institutionalized party competition as a determinant of state policy. Without party competition, democracy inevitably will lead to the control of the government by narrow groups of economic elites. Thus McConnell locates the sources of corporate power in the failures of democracy rather than in any contradiction among democracy, state, and capitalism. Corporate power is not rooted in a theory either of class rule or of elite domination. The structures and culture of democracy have not yet been adapted to the realities of corporate power and organization, which have blurred the boundary line between public authority and private power. Democracy has been undermined but not irretrievably.

McConnell blames the naiveté of the pluralist image of the democratic state for the quiet invasion by private economic power. In the case of regulatory agencies such as the Civil Aeronautics Board and the Federal Communications Commission, for example, nonpartisan, professionalized agencies were created based upon a "simple insistence upon the virtue of administrators as wardens of the public interest" (1966, p. 50). Failure to take account of the realities of corporate power led inexorably to their capture by the largest segments of the industries they were supposed to regulate.

McConnell's view is that in some of those cases the industry itself demanded regulation, in order to reduce internal competition to a minimum, but that "for the most part . . . popular desire for regulation in the public interest (as seen in Progressive terms) was the more important and the more consistent motivation" (1966, p. 281). These agencies are now firmly established with that "degree of solidity and seeming immortality known only to old-line government bureaus" (p. 282). They are frequently subject to criticism because of their lack of responsibility to any publicly elected authority, their lack of consistent criteria for decisions, their bias toward certain segments of the industries they are supposedly regulating, and their inefficiency.[6] McConnell argues that all of these criticisms are probably just but that saying "Bring them under control," "Get them to define standards better," or "Reorganize them" merely asks that the problem be solved by solving the problem. Rather, "delay, inefficiency, and indecision" are all related to the clear functions of their present mode of operations for the sectors of industries that control them.

The very independence of the regulatory commissions made them vulnerable to business influence, which seems paradoxical in view of the fact that they were not originally set up to be creatures of industry. Both formally and in reality the commissions are "more independent

[6] McConnell gives many examples of their arbitrary operations. The Civil Aeronautics Board has no understandable criteria for assigning routes to various airlines and has discriminated against surface transportation companies that are trying to begin air transportation. The Interstate Commerce Commission has interpreted "identical regulations on rate structure differently for the railroads and for the motor carriers" (1966, p. 286).

than many other agencies." This independence flowed from the progressive impulse to separate government agencies from potential influence by corrupt partisan politics. Unfortunately, what was achieved was not "freedom from all politics, but freedom only from party and popular politics. The politics of industry and administration remained" (McConnell 1966, p. 289). Standards could not be developed by the commissions, and they could not be independent of political influence: This was the fallacy of the progressive vision of the possibility of government regulation of private business.

These few examples illustrate why, in McConnell's view, business avoids electoral politics. "[W]hile a certain fiscal policy or the election of a particular Presidential candidate might appear advantageous to a given industry group, much more reliable and direct benefits may be gained by using available resources of influence to create a governmental administrative agency to care for the industry's interests vis-a-vis the public" (1966, p. 293). Thus the lack of business participation in elections does not mean that business interests are not represented in state policies. Direct influence as an interest group is far more politically effective than trying to mobilize voters.[7]

The most important aspect of this process is the "conquest of segments of formal state power by private groups and associations" (McConnell 1966, p. 162). As McConnell describes the typical stages of the process, local economic interests become organized nationally, capturing the policies of a public agency. The public agency then gains autonomy from the larger political process by becoming an independent regulatory agency. Close clientele relations are established with the outside private interests that benefited from or participated in the agency's establishment in the first place. McConnell argues that the private groups are likely to be oligarchic internally, with the stronger members controlling the behavior of the weaker members in a manner reminiscent of the iron law of oligarchy. "Given the oligarchic tendencies of organization, the private group will find itself exercising the compulsion the public official avoided. . . . the process exposes the members of the private groups to the vagaries of a power in which the compulsive force and authority of the state have been joined to the informal and social power of the private groups and from which no recourse may be possible" (p. 163). The public

---

[7] The symbiosis of the largest corporations in an industry and "its" governmental agencies is a perfect solution for two problems. Control over the industry is maintained by the leverage not merely of market power but also of legal power. The ever-present potential of genuine public control over the industry is avoided by preempting the possibility of regulation, through the ideal device of controlling the very agency supposed to regulate the industry.

agency controlled by private interests has usurped public authority. Such a development

makes a mockery of the vision by which one interest opposes another and ambition checks ambition. The large extent of autonomy accorded to various fragments of government has gone far to isolate important matters of public policy from supposedly countervailing influences. Moreover, the picture of government as mediator among different interests is falsified to the extent that government itself is fragmented and the various fragments are beholden to particular interests. [P. 164]

The merger or blurring of "private" and "public" power, McConnell argues, has undermined the image of a democratic system in which an independent state mediates the activities of private associations.

Other theorists within the pluralist world view are similarly skeptical of the empirical hypothesis that public opinion and electoral majorities are the major forces shaping public policies and that corporate power can be kept from controlling the state. Political economist Charles Lindblom ends his controversial book *Politics and Markets* (1977) with a paragraph on the private power of the giant corporations.[8]

Enormously large, rich in resources, the big corporations... command more resources than do most government units. They can also, over a broad range, insist that government meet their demands, even if these demands run counter to those of citizens expressed through their polyarchal controls.... They are on all counts disproportionately powerful, we have seen. The large private corporation fits oddly into democratic theory and vision. Indeed, it does not fit.

Although the political power of the giant corporations does not fit the pluralist image of the appropriate sources of political participation, corporations claim the political rights of individuals. "[T]hey do not disqualify themselves from playing the partisan role of a citizen – for the corporation is legally a person" (Lindblom 1977, p. 356). If they have political resources no other organizations, let alone individuals, can match, then treating corporations as if they were individual citizens from the point of view of their political rights produces a fundamental inequality of participation in the political system.

Corporate power is therefore a direct challenge to the pluralist postulates of equality of representation and the primacy of individual participation. Such a conclusion is disquieting to scholars profoundly

---

[8] Lindblom, in the preface, says that his classification of basic processes is different from the four distinguished in *Politics, Economics, and Welfare* (written with Robert Dahl in 1953), because he now wishes to make "more of a fundamental distinction between hierarchy and the other three [price system, bargaining, and polyarchy] all of which represent forms of mutual adjustment rather than approximations of unilateral control" (1977, p. x). In our terms, he recognizes that the three were variants of a pluralist perspective. The book was controversial (it was sharply criticized in the *Wall Street Journal*), partly because of the challenge to some central pluralist ideas.

committed to democratic values and a pluralist image of democracy. But, although McConnell and Lindblom empirically recognize corporate power, their theory is rooted in the logic of democracy, not in that of bureaucracy or of capitalism. Corporate power is seen simply as a pathological development, undermining the conditions of democracy, one that can be reversed by a stronger national party system, for instance. In our view, the phenomena McConnell and Lindblom have described can best be interpreted as a contradiction between democracy and capitalism.

A more typical pluralist image of the role of business is that state action benefiting corporations is a consequence of the correspondence of the values of entrepreneurship with the values shared by most of the population. Sociologist Arnold Rose, for example, writes that "the actions of government to aid business . . . should not be construed as indicating business domination of government [because] government can improve the economic health and other aspects of the welfare of the entire society by engaging in certain actions that business also particularly wants" (1967, p. 124).

Similarly, a recent theoretical analysis of urban policy making by political scientist Paul Peterson (1981) argues that local governments cannot increase the welfare of their residents independently of local business because they lack the power to control the flow of labor and capital. Because economic development policies enhance the ratio of public benefits to tax burdens for the average local taxpayer, they cannot be used to judge the power of those business actors whom they explicitly benefit. Inferences about local business power based on programs such as urban renewal, highway construction, or zoning are therefore "probably pointless" (p. 47). This approach has been criticized for depoliticizing economic growth (Friedland and Palmer 1984).

Political scientist David Truman emphasizes that the political influence of business corporations stems from their being regarded as favored "defensive groups," whose interests lie in the functioning of existing institutions and their continued functioning, not in their change. Such defensive groups (doctors are another example) have an advantage in political situations because of the strength of "vested relationships" and also the "opportunities for delay or obstruction offered by existing legislative processes." Business corporations are favored defensive groups, much more so than labor unions, not only because people are "accustomed" to their patterns of behavior but also because these patterns include "roles highly valued by large segments of the society" (1971, p. 354).

Pluralists assume that businessmen have both prestige and a socially valued role, which give them a special position in the political process.

But pluralists argue that businessmen are rarely united in the political arena, that politics in capitalist democracies tends to be fragmented on an issue-by-issue basis, and that the larger population can use its most important resource – the vote – to offset whatever business power does exist; hence, McConnell's call for the political mobilization of national constituencies. Political scientist Robert Dahl (1961) recognizes the great economic power of business and the political power of its resources, as we have already noted, but believes that popular electoral majorities can offset the influence of wealth in democracies. All large organizations, including labor, are seen as possessing such resources, and, to the extent that they have them, they are capable of exercising political influence over government decisions. In certain situations, the combined resources of organizations other than business may be able to challenge the interests of business. Business can be defeated if an issue commands widespread public support and becomes the object of electoral mobilization, and if a majority of Congress believe that their offices will depend upon their vote on the issue. Within the context of political issues that challenge neither elite domination nor class rule, this pluralist argument is valid.

Pluralists attempt to refute empirically class and managerial perspectives by discovering government decisions where a dominant elite or class interest group participates and loses. Rose (1967) pointed to the American Medical Association's loss in the battle over Medicare. Polsby (1963) noted the defeat of a leading business in Middletown, Indiana, on several important issues. Pluralists have discovered that the major determinant of elected national officials' behavior is party affiliation (Rose 1967, pp. 32, 86), that Democratic presidential victories have thwarted business-supported Republican candidates (p. 34), that political leaders are not likely to have business backgrounds, and that even businessmen do not necessarily act in the interests of business when in public office (pp. 116–27). Because the data are at the individual level, these studies have little bearing on alternative hypotheses about the operations of structural and systemic power.

Citizenship rights: the individual level

How can a political culture that emphasizes the rights of citizens be compatible with a capitalist economy fostering inequalities of wealth and privilege? British sociologist T. H. Marshall's classic answer (1964) to that question is that individual citizenship is the functional equivalent of economic equality.

For Marshall, democracy is an institutionally differentiated status of citizenship, that is, a set of legal rights and duties bestowed on individuals who are full members of a national community. Surveying 250 years of British history, Marshall argues that the substantive content of rights and the proportion of the population enjoying citizenship status have continuously increased. Marshall argues that this phenomenon was intrinsically related to the concomitant development of capitalism (1964, pp. 77; 92–3). And, until the twentieth century, citizenship was normatively consistent with capitalist social organization. Citizenship consisted of universal rights to own and exchange property, without regard to social or legal status. Civil rights constituted the potential basis of a universal status of citizenship but at first were granted only to men of property.

The extension of such rights was essential to the consolidation of a class system based on property and education as opposed to legal status. During the eighteenth century, the courts struck down the Elizabethan Statute of Artificers, which reserved certain occupations to certain classes, as well as local regulations that reserved town employment for its own residents (Marshall 1964, pp. 76). The equal and free status of citizenship provided the legal and moral bulwark for the emergence of contract as the primary basis of economic organization, allowing market forces alone to govern the movement of labor, land, and capital. Thus, according to Marshall, the status of citizenship, which was confined to civil rights, "provided the foundation of equality on which the structure of inequality could be built" (p. 88).

Social rights at that time were completely dissociated from the status of citizenship. Those who fell outside a political community defined by property had no claim on the state. Initially, social rights had been part of a broad state program of regulation whose destruction was marked by the defeat, at the end of the eighteenth century, of the Speenhamland system of poor relief. This system had offered a guaranteed minimum wage, family allowances, and rights to work or maintenance, rights that were achieved again only late in the twentieth century (Polanyi 1957). Marshall explains that this national system of poor relief decayed because it infringed on the civil rights of citizens to negotiate contracts for work at locations and under conditions of their free choice (1964, p. 79).

The Poor Law of 1834 gave social rights to noncitizens, to nonmembers of the economically defined political community. The early Factory Acts, which improved industrial working conditions for all, referred legally only to women and children and "meticulously refrained from giving this protection directly to the adult male – the citizen par excellence" (Marshall 1964, p. 81). The normative logic of a civil-rights-based status of citizenship led to the development of social rights as an alternative, rather than an addition, to the citizenship status. State relief to those unable to compete in the labor market involved an abrogation of individual duties and rights of free contract. Paupers were stripped of civil rights by confinement in workhouses. Receipt of welfare required an abdication of citizenship, rather than being its confirmation. Significantly, Marshall does not discuss the extensive state aid given to property owners. Citizen rights gave the individual, therefore, "as part of his individual status, the power to engage as an independent unit in the economic struggle and made it possible to deny to him social protection on the ground that he was equipped with the means to protect himself" (Marshall 1964, p. 87).

Marshall explains that the enfranchisement of the working class did not destroy capitalism, as Marx had earlier predicted, because citizenship was part of a process of political integration. The status of citizenship requires a collective loyalty to "a civilization which is a common possession." The struggles to extend the status of citizenship and the rise of nationalism reflected the emergence of a consensual political culture, a culture that capitalist markets promoted.

Working-class electoral participation was then used to create new rights within the political community rather than to challenge directly the causes of economic inequalities that made those rights necessary. The resultant extension of public services to ever larger proportions of the population was both cause and consequence of a consensual political community. Marshall argues that the growth of public services was a mechanism of income equalization not between classes but between individual members of the political community, all of equal political status. Thus the welfare state was organized around a universal status of citizenship rather than a specific class relation or authority relation. Its expansion derived from the common political culture undergirding citizenship.

Similarly, the emergence of a policy of fair wages extended the social rights of citizenship and intruded on the contractual agreement of buyers and sellers. The politicization of income inequality and the equalization of real income through public service expansion threatened to make market inequalities "economically functionless." Whereas capitalist property once defined the civil rights of citizenship, social citizenship now defines the limits of capitalist property rights. Whereas the political community was once economically defined, the economy is now politically reordered according to the social rights of citizenship. This uneven development of civil, political, and social rights, argues Marshall, made democracy historically compatible with capitalism.

What Marshall's analysis implies is that the rise of citizenship created forms of political integration that undercut the possibility of radical working-class political organization and socialist ideology. A universalistic

state, a consensual political culture, the suppression of the market in
the service of social rights – each rendered the organization of class
conflict more difficult.

The historical development of state policies is hidden within the evolution of political culture.

Citizenship is a status bestowed on those who are full members of a community.
All who possess the status are equal with respect to the rights and duties with
which the status is endowed. There is no universal principle that determined
what those rights and duties shall be, but societies in which citizenship is a
developing institution create an image of an ideal citizenship against which
achievement can be measured and towards which aspiration can be directed.
The urge forward along the path thus plotted is an urge towards a fuller measure
of equality, an enrichment of the stuff of which the status is made and an increase
in the number of those on whom the status is bestowed. [Marshall 1964, p. 92]

The origins of that "ideal citizenship" remain unanalyzed. The causes
of changes in political culture remain theoretically exogenous. For Marshall, the logic of the development of individual citizenship rights is
governed by societal values rather than by the rhythm of class struggle
or the requirements of bureaucratic legitimation. Institutional differentiation of a status of universal citizenship has progressively intruded on
the rights and roles defined in the capitalist market place. The democratic
aspect of the state has overridden the capitalist aspect of the state. A
democratic political culture becomes one mechanism for reconciling the
contradiction between democracy and capitalism.

Conclusions

For the pluralist perspective, business is not the central interest that
must be served by the capitalist state but merely one of a number of
interest groups, whose special impact on the state is created by the
affinity of its interests with the fundamental values underlying social
institutions. In a sense, this is a pluralist version of the structuralist
school of the class perspective. This version argues that government
actions need not be directly dictated by agents of capitalist interests. The
economic health of capitalism benefits the adaptive capacity of a society
in general, not merely its businessmen. Service to the public interest
can be equated with the interests of business. This equation is not seen
as ideological, as it is in both class and managerial perspectives.

To the pluralists, capitalist development involves continuous differentiation in which new roles (owner, worker, manager, consumer) must
be created and individuals socialized and recruited into them. This is
not always a smooth, continuous process. Institutions – polity, economy,
family – evolve unevenly. Capitalist development creates groups that
violate political norms, demand new institutional relationships (worker

control of investment, for example), or make unrealistic demands on government resources. These crises are seen as the result not of capitalism per se but of a failure of social control and imperfect social integration. The institutions of the state play their own special role in "handling" the social disturbances that have resulted when ordinary people reject their new function as workers. Pluralists recognize the existence of political and economic tensions, even crises, but attribute them mainly to individual unwillingness to accept realistic limits or to the pathologies of private representation of intensely interested groups.

Epilogue: the problem of governance

"Demand overload," a phrase first used by political scientist David Easton (1965a), occurs when the state cannot handle democratically derived political demands. The capacity of the political system and its leadership to handle multiple and complex decisions simultaneously is sorely tested by the location of the state in the midst of competing, overlapping, inconsistent, and expensive demands for new programs and expenditures but seldom for the elimination of old ones. Political leaders and agency officials are continuously off-balance, unable to manage their programs efficiently because they are constantly devising new ones or attempting to justify and rationalize the old ones. This is a contradiction within the democratic aspect of the state.

In the 1970s a number of pluralist analysts, faced with mounting problems of governance, particularly fiscal crisis, began to stress the inherent limits to democracy. When democracies offer the population tangible benefits, these responses raise expectations, which lead to demands for still more benefits. According to Samuel Brittan, democracy is now endangered in Great Britain by "excessive expectations . . . generated by the democratic aspects of the system" (1977, p. 130). The system appears to be in crisis, not because there is too little democracy but because there is too much democracy, particularly economic democracy. This is a retreat from the progressive extension of citizenship rights envisaged by T. H. Marshall (1964).

A second factor explaining problems of governance in the pluralist perspective is a pathological development within the state itself when the bureaucratic autonomy required for governance grows too strong and unresponsive. Public bureaucracies sometimes manage to attain such a degree of budgetary and political autonomy that they become almost invulnerable to challenge. State budgets rarely are reexamined to discover whether or not a given program or agency serves its presumed public purpose. When coupled with dwindling tax revenues caused by the decline of economic growth, itself seen as engendered by overregulation, and other government interference with the operation of the market, the autonomy of the state can be itself a source of crisis.

A third factor is the result of the first two: a crisis of confidence in public opinion. The inability of the state to meet the multiple demands of social groups and the successes of state bureaucracies in insulating themselves from political and administrative accountability can lead to a breakdown in the "civic culture," manifested by mistrust of government and dwindling participation.

With this argument, we have come full circle in the pluralist world view. The structural and systemic powers of the state and the economy are explained by individual beliefs, perceptions, and values, aggregated into cultures, organizations, and societies. Solutions to problems of governance, as well as the causes, are found in changing individuals. As we shall argue in our concluding chapters, we believe that the pluralist mode of inquiry is not satisfactory to explain bureaucratic domination and class rule. But, conversely, bureaucracy and capitalism cannot themselves be understood without taking into account how a democratic political culture creates individuals who increasingly demand participatory rights in all institutions.

PART II
The managerial perspective

7

State and society in managerial perspective

The managerial perspective could have been called the "elite" or the "bureaucratic" perspective, alternate emphases within the perspective. The term "managerial" emphasizes the organizational base of elites and their control of the state. The strategic activities of elites are stressed, rather than static entities, such as a bureaucracy or an elite structure.[1]

The managerial home domain

The managerial home domain contains organizational structures that have different resources for domination of each other and of the society. The state is first and foremost the dominant *organization* of society. Elites compete for control of their environment, propelled by the organizational requirement of reducing external uncertainty. Conflicts between them can be understood without resorting to the societal-level concepts of contradiction or differentiation. Society is conceived either as an uncertain interorganizational power structure shaped by the history of elite strategies, the political version, or as itself an organization writ large, the functional version.

Which structures are dominant depends on the success of different elite strategies of controlling organizations and shaping the activities of members, clients, opponents, and supporters. These organizations are the instruments of dominant elites, not natural systems whose members have a common interest in their survival (Scott 1981). An organization's

[1] See Krasner 1984 for a review of a number of important books, mostly within the managerial perspective. Krasner is critical of the pluralist or "behavioral" perspective and offers an alternative "statist" perspective. He does not assess works within the class perspective. According to Krasner, the statist perspective emphasizes "rule and control" rather than allocation, sees the state as a powerful actor in its own right (rather than merely reflecting societal characteristics), emphasizes institutional constraints, and focuses upon conflict over rules of the game, not on plays in the game. He argues, as we do, that a pluralist theory is associated with empirical and behavioral methodology and with the rejection of the state as a central theoretical concept.

internal structure is determined by strategies of control, utilizing available technology and extracting resources from other organizations in the environment. Organizational goals include the survival of the organization. Varieties of bureaucratic structure are also closely related to their interorganizational relations. Considerable debate goes on about the conditions under which managers gain the autonomy to make strategic choices (Lawrence and Lorsch 1967). Conflicts arise among elites, both within and between different organizations, over control of resources and jurisdictions. These conflicts are managed by elite negotiations, concessions, legal orders, and sometimes force. Out of these conflicts, some organizational forms survive and others do not. Organizations also try to manage external uncertainty through mergers, joint ventures, and a myriad of other arrangements with other organizations upon which they are dependent or which they wish to control (Pfeffer and Salancik 1978).

Societal properties are seen as environmental resources or constraints for organizational elites, establishing conditions under which organizations survive and operate. Individuals must be induced or coerced into the appropriate beliefs that will lead to conformity to rules or appropriate degrees of initiative and discretion. Individuals within an organization must accept its procedures as establishing legitimate limits for their own behavior (the "zone of discretion"). Individuals outside any specific organization ("citizens," for example) must believe in the effectiveness of sanctions by the police and the courts and thus obey orders by legitimate state officials.

Both societal and individual conditions are assumed to exist that allow the emergence of organizations that have – within limits and with important variations – the following characteristics: (1) specification and justification of tasks, (2) criteria of accountability for performance and sanctions for failure to perform, (3) technical capabilities, (4) procedures for selecting personnel according to ability to perform a given task and procedures for rewarding or removing them, (5) a hierarchy of officials charged with implementing the tasks and carrying out these requirements. Organizational goals are strategic choices and do not reflect societal values.

Regardless of how much these conditions are violated in practice, the key analytic contrast is between this model of essentially bureaucratic organization and other types ("clan," "patrimonial," "feudal," "sect," "voluntary") whose organizing principles are not bureaucratic in character. Thus the core research questions concern the societal conditions that facilitate the bureaucratization of the state (planning, coordination, centralization, integration, policy formation) and rationalize the internal processes within state organizations. At the individual level of concern are the structural conditions under which members, clients, employees, or officials will behave in ways compatible with the achievement of organizational goals, given limits on individual rationality and self-interest.

Thus the pluralist question about who wins in situations allowing multiple influence (that is, the conditions for participation) is transformed into the managerial concern with how state policies are controlled (the conditions for rationalization). Organizational elites must be able to structure the decision-making process in such a way that some social problems become political issues whereas others cannot and that some interests have access to relevant centers of public authority and others do not. Specific decisions and the question of who influenced them are less important than the structural biases of the organizations in which those decisions are taken.[2]

The environment within which state organizations function is recognized, but is not theorized at a societal level. The use of state authority by private organizations or vice versa is a contingent outcome of organizational strategies. Recent work using a "population ecology" model of organizational survival attempts to develop a theory of the probability of different types of organizational existence within a "population" of organizations (Aldrich and Pfeffer 1976; Hannan and Freeman 1977; Aldrich 1979). The model deemphasizes the ability of organizational elites to make strategic choices, favoring an explanation by environmental selection of certain organizational forms. That model, however, does not explain the emergence of organizational niches – locations in a societal environment – apart from characteristics of organizations themselves. By focusing on organizations that lack the power to control their environments, to shape the niches, the model neglects the role of organizations in structuring society. The societal environment is only conceptualized as an abstract set of resources.

In general, political and administrative elites are seen as increasingly managing the state and the economy and not merely responding to political and economic markets. The democratic machinery of represen-

---

[2] March and Olsen have recently launched a major critique of the pluralist perspective, arguing that "most contemporary theories of politics" define it as the "aggregate consequences of individual behavior." Action is the "result of choices based on calculated self-interest" (1984, p. 734). Their alternative is to emphasize "formally organized social institutions," particularly those that have become "larger, considerably more complex and resourceful and prima facie more important to collective life." They assert that the rediscovery of institutions such as the state is due to the "modern transformation of social institutions," i.e., due to historical forces that have resulted in the fact that "most of the major actors in modern economic and political systems are formal organizations, and the institutions of law and bureaucracy occupy a dominant role in contemporary life" (p. 734).

tation has to a large extent become fictitious as the society and state have become more complex and the criteria for effective decisions have become more technical. As the state has become more powerful, it has superseded class interests, or can override them in its own interests. Bureaucratic command of corporations and unions and the negotiation of elites of business, labor, and state agencies have become the most important realities in the state, not the rule of a capitalist class. The central historical focus of the managerial perspective is on the issue of how varying elite strategies of domination have shaped the emergence of the bureaucratic aspect of the state.

The bureaucratic aspect of an industrial state is thus central for the managerial perspective because of its stress upon the increasing autonomy of the state and the efficiency and domination in both the economy and the state of large-scale bureaucratic forms of organization. As we have already seen, bureaucracies are limited by popular values and majority preferences in a pluralist perspective. As we shall see later, they are constrained by the logic of capital in a class perspective. Bureaucracies do not have the potential for autonomous domination that they have in the managerial perspective.

The managerial world view

The managerial world view sees an industrial society as a network of controlling and subordinate organizations, each commanded by elites who attempt to manage resources and extend their domain of control.[3] New forms of domination have replaced older capitalist structures. Corporate and managerial power has become more important than capital or a capitalist class in structuring the relations between state and economy. And the pluralist view of an increasingly differentiated society composed of individuals is also misleading.[4]

The imperative of rationalization stems from the growing complexity of the society, which depends more and more upon scientific knowledge, technical capacity, and administrative expertise. The division of labor cannot be left to the unseen hand of the market. Corporations, unions, banks, universities, research organizations, and state agencies must each

[3] French sociologist Raymond Aron in a series of lectures given in 1955 said that "instead of capitalism I have chosen industrial society (or technical, scientific or rationalized society) as the principal historical concept" (quoted in Bell 1973, p. 73).

[4] Sociologist James S. Coleman argues that the pluralist view of society as a vast aggregate of persons occupying roles is obsolete. The "very structural elements" of which society is composed have become an array of "corporate actors" (1974, pp. 13–15). These new structural entities that compose society include not only business corporations (the preeminent model) but also churches, trade associations, trade unions, professional associations, towns and cities, and others. See also Tilly 1978, p. 26.

be organized rationally and then coordinated to make resources available for the efficient management of the society.

Our principal exemplar of the managerial world view is the work of sociologist Daniel Bell. His well-known work on postindustrial society (1973) and subsequent extension of the argument (1976) postulates three different "institutional realms": "polity" (or political system), "culture," and "social structure." These categories are asserted to compose a society and are not further theorized. Bell presents the scheme only as a "standpoint" from which "models can be generated and theories developed" (1973, p. 112).

Each institutional realm has an "axial principle," and the logic of each contradicts the others. Axial principles are the legitimating principles for different institutions, and their conflicts constitute the society and help explain its structure and changes. The word "contradiction" in the title of Bell's 1976 volume may suggest the class world view, but he rejects the view of society as a "web of relations" (p. 9). His conception of axial principles reflects the managerial world view that the relations between institutions can best be interpreted as conflicts between controlling and subordinate structures.

Bell says that he is writing a book about changes in the social structure, from industrial to postindustrial society, not about the polity or about culture. Consistent with his world view that there are no systemic relations, Bell says that there is no necessary correlation between changes in the social structure and changes in the culture or political system. He thus distinguishes his own world view from class and pluralist ones. He rejects the assumption, which he associates with both Marxism and Parsons's functionalism, that "society is a structurally interrelated system and . . . one can understand any social action only in relation to that unified system" (1976, p. 10). He disagrees both with the Marxist principle of totality transformed through the "process of commodity production and exchange" and with the pluralist view from Durkheim to Parsons that society is "integrated through a common value system" (p. 10). With reference to his more specific argument about the state, Bell distinguishes his perspective both from pluralists such as Aaron Wildavsky (1974) and William Niskanen (1971), who focus on the " 'internal' politicking of budget setting" and from such Marxists as James O'Connor (Bell 1973, p. 221).

Bell associates himself with Weber and Schumpeter in his critique of Marx. He argues that industrial societies are evolving not from capitalism to socialism but "towards some form of statism and bureaucratic society" (1973, p. 80). Bell accepts the Weberian focus on "political order" (p. 84) and the potential rationality of social planning by the bureaucratic state. Bell cites Weber approvingly as the source of the view that bureaucracy follows from the "imperatives of functional rationality" in industrial society, whether capitalist or socialist (p. 41). Although fully aware of the ambiguities of rationalization, Bell holds up the rationalizing and economizing principle as the key to postindustrial society.

In the post-industrial society, production and business decisions will be subordinated to, or will derive from, other forces in society; the crucial decisions regarding the growth of the economy and its balance will come from government, but they will be based on the government's sponsorship of research and development, of cost-effectiveness and cost-benefit analysis; the making of decisions, because of the intricately linked nature of their consequences, will have an increasingly technical character. [P. 344]

The codification of theoretical knowledge is thus penetrating more and more institutions and creating a new basis for political decisions. This argument is based upon premises about the bureaucratic and technical rationalization of the society, which are illustrated by a set of plausible empirical examples.

Bell argues that "functional rationality" is the axial principle of the social structure in postindustrial societies, yet his examples refer to organizational and not societal factors (1973, p. 13). The increasing "bureaucratization of science" and "specialization of intellectual work" pose "management" problems for the political system. The political order has become the central source of social change, and the culture and the economy have accommodated themselves to this development, although they still create management dilemmas. The logic of rationalization penetrates other spheres of the postindustrial society, characterized by a service economy, "preeminence of the professional and technical class, . . . the centrality of theoretical knowledge, . . . the control of technology, [and] the creation of a new 'intellectual technology' for decision-making" (p. 14). Bell conceives of the society as if it were an organizational system tending toward rationalization that can be achieved only by the most powerful, inclusive organization, the state.

Bell sees his own analysis as exemplifying the power of the new intellectual elite shaping the new society. His argument is a theoretical rationale for his own impact on policies of the state, through the "social indicators" movement in the Russell Sage Foundation and the National Science Foundation. The book justifies efforts to gather new types of data on the social consequences of state policy in such areas as health, education, welfare, and urbanization, analogous to the established economic indicators on income, employment, and inflation.[5]

---

[5] An assumption about the possibility of rationality in a bureaucratic state is seen in the use of the "volume and kinds of information that the government collects and publishes" as an empirical indicator of "the ability of the government to adopt complex policies" (Flanigan and Fogelman 1971b, p. 444). Use of such an indicator involves a set of man-

Bell's main argument provides a legitimating ideology for science policy and for social indicators, and it is significant that the book does not give any evidence on the actual uses of science in making social policy. Data on the explosion of scientific research and on the growth of government are not evidence for the impact of science on policy. Despite the concrete examples, the argument about potential technical determination of public policy is not documented by any relevant research data but is only a statement of his world view.

Bell challenges the importance of interest group activity as an explanation of government policies. Such a view is "astonishingly out-of-date" (1973, pp. 308–10). He regards the corollary concept of the politician as a broker mediating between interests as equally obsolete.[6] He presents his own argument to the effect that three fundamental changes have become decisive factors shaping national policy: (1) the way foreign policy requirements have centralized resources "in the hands of a national administration" (p. 311), (2) the way that the need to anticipate and direct social change has led to an "emphasis on planning" in order to increase productivity from scientific innovation, and (3) the further consequence of both of these factors in increasing the technical component of decision making, in order to manage the national economy. The overall consequence has been the enormous centralization of power in the hands of the executive branch of the state in all Western societies. This is the managerial world view.[7] Interest group politics and the resulting brokering function of politicians seeking to build electoral majorities are historically obsolete because of the powerful forces that have centralized the state.

Bell, finally, offers a substantive justification of the domination of the

---

agerial assumptions. First, the greater the amount of information collected, the greater is the amount of relevant information available to decision makers; second, the available information is actually used by decision makers and is highly correlated with the rationality of state policies.

[6] Bell (1973, pp. 310) quotes V. O. Key, Jr., and Robert Dahl and cites Earl Latham and David Truman, as well as Adam Smith, as supporting these concepts.

[7] Another coherent statement of the managerial world view is that of Henry Jacoby. His view of the bureaucratization of the world asserts that every "member of contemporary society is part of a large conglomerate whose self-expression . . . depends on the operation of complicated governmental machinery" (1973, p. 1). In a debate within the managerial perspective, Jacoby argues with Weber's rational view of bureaucracy. "What characterizes our age is precisely the forceful transformation of rational administration into the irrational exercise of power, the lack of clearly defined limits to coercion, and the increasing competence of a state which arrogates independence to itself" (p. 2). The issue is the nature of power and the degree of rational legitimation. Both positions accept the fundamental reality of bureaucratization. Jacoby interprets both Marx and Tocqueville from that point of view, not granting any other possible world views. The economy is seen as based on technological innovations reshaping the "economic foundation of the 'new industrial state' " (p. 209).

state as a bureaucratic organization. "The power of the state (and indeed, its possible autonomous role) is the central fact about modern society" (1976, p. 228). The state has expanded through the need to manage the economy, to subsidize science and technology, and to create a welfare state and conscious social policy.

Centralization has taken place within the state at various levels and within each level. One recent study concludes: "As the role of the federal government in national life has expanded, the center of gravity of the powers it exercises has gradually shifted, from the legislature in the first half of the 19th century to the judiciary in the second half of the 19th century, to the executive and administration in the 20th century" (Freedman 1978, p. 3). Freedman notes that one-third of the federal administrative agencies were created before 1900, another third between 1900 and 1930, and another third by the New Deal and after. The expansion of bureaucratic agencies occurred under both Republican and Democratic regimes. Bureaucratic centralization was not a result of party policy.

Freedman's summary of the general impact of the expansion of federal bureaucratic functions and their penetration in almost every area of social life shows the organizational level of analysis:

the federal administrative process . . . embraced more than sixty independent regulatory agencies as well as perhaps several hundred administrative agencies located in the executive departments. Administrative agencies exercise regulatory responsibilities in scores of important and sensitive areas. The decisions rendered by the federal administrative agencies were many times the number rendered by the federal courts and probably affected the lives of more ordinary citizens more pervasively and more intimately than the decisions of the federal courts. In virtually every relevant respect, the administrative process has become a fourth branch of government, comparable in the scope of its authority and the impact of its decision-making to the three more familiar constitutional branches. [1978, p. 6]

Ralf Dahrendorf's work, *Class and Class Conflict in Industrial Society* (1959), is another important exemplar of the managerial world view. His concept of class is Weberian, not Marxist, because it is based on authority as a "universal element of social structure," more general even than property or status (p. 168). Dahrendorf defines classes as "social conflict groups, the determinant of which can be found in the participation in or exclusion from the exercise of authority within any imperatively co-ordinated association" (p. 138). The economic bases of group formation are seen as important mainly if they affect the exercise of authority. Powerful and autonomous organizations, mainly those of the state and industrial production, are the main agents of societal power. The rights of managers to command and expect obedience have become as important as those of owners to receive profits, partly because of the fragmentation of authority groups ("classes"). He argues that "the lasting determinant of social conflict is the inequality of power and authority which inevitably accompanies social organization" (p. 64). These will persist after most economic and status inequalities have been eliminated, Dahrendorf believes.

Dahrendorf also explicitly contrasts his own "coercion theory" with Parsons's "integration" theory. Rather than sharing common values, a social structure must be seen as dominated by those positions within every social organization that are "entrusted with a right to exercise control over other positions in order to ensure effective coercion" (1959, p. 165).

Power and structure

In the managerial perspective, power derives from the organization of authority in which decisions are made, that is, structures. The ability to create effective organizations outside the state transforms social groups into dominant interest groups with the capacity to control or create particular forms of state organization, securing continuous access to the centers of power. Because dominant interests and the state organize around each other to secure reciprocal access, the internal organization of the state and the external organization of dominant interest groups tend to be homologous. The internal structure of the state is seen as a powerful cause of external political organization and political consciousness, limiting the kinds of issues that gain access to the political arena. The structure of the state affects the level and the effectiveness of different social groups' political participation; thus it is itself a source of power. Even definite and focused policy preferences by some groups may find no organizational channel for participation.

Like the other perspectives, the managerial perspective postulates a conflict between functional constraints and political action as bases of power. On the one hand, societal change has become ever more complex and interdependent, requiring overall coordination and planning. On the other, organized interest groups increasingly concentrate their resources seeking bases of technical expertise for their autonomy. Despite these different emphases, all of these variants of the managerial perspective share a common view of the nature of power in industrial societies. A typical recent argument is that of Anthony Giddens. Power relations are "regularized relations of autonomy and dependence," that is, of "subordinate and dominant actors" (1979, p. 6). "Resources are the media through which power is exercised, and structures of domination reproduced" (p. 91). The concept of "structuration" is used to coopt the pluralist emphasis on action and agency. Giddens advocates the concept of a "duality of structure" which unifies and interprets both "personality" and "society" (pp. 69–70).

Although the concept of contradiction is seemingly central to Giddens, it is interpreted as significant only at the organizational ("structural") level. After a brief discussion of contradictions he moves to "power, control and subordination," criticizing Weber's theory of bureaucracy for neglecting the ways in which subordinate actors can exercise some control. Giddens reserves the concept of power for the organizational level. "Contradiction is . . . connected to power only via domination, as the form in which resources are structured within the reproduction of social interaction. Domination and power are closely tied, but the connections between domination and conflict are mediated through power relations" (1979, p. 145).

In his summary critique of the Marxist view of class, Giddens argues that Marx did not acknowledge the importance of the fact that "all class . . . societies are *administered societies* . . . in which centralized control of 'knowledge' or 'information' is a medium of domination" (1979, p. 162; italics in original). A fundamental assumption for Giddens is that the "structural characteristics of class . . . societies . . . are basically governed . . . by the connections between authority and property" (pp. 162–3). This assumption that the primary principles of all institutional realms are those of authority, domination, or administration reflects his managerial world view. Giddens defines class relations in terms of power and domination, in the managerial sense of those words.[8]

---

[8] It is beyond our scope here to discuss the subtle distinctions Giddens draws among "structure," "system," and "structuration," involving rules, resources, and the capacities of actors to achieve their will (not their values, preferences, or needs). All these distinctions are within the managerial perspective. Giddens distinguishes his view of power from that of both Marx and Parsons. As he says, Marx analyzed power as a "specific property of class relations rather than as a feature of social interaction in general" (1976, p. 111), and Parsons emphasizes the internalization of norms by actors as a form of power in interaction. Giddens himself views power as capacity, as the possession of resources, specifically authority and force as key resources, or relevant "technical knowledge." Power need not imply conflict, when power holders act legitimately. In Giddens's most recent elaboration of the theory of structuration, his world view is even more explicit. "Structuration" has three principal dimensions: signification, legitimation, and domination (1984, p. 186). Signification refers to "symbolic orders" and "modes of discourse" and always has to be "grasped in connection with domination and legitimation" (p. 31). Also, "domination is the very condition of existence of codes of signification" (p. 31). Giddens subsumes Marx's argument about the historical relation between money and capital in the capitalist mode of production to the suprahistorical principles of structuration, an approach quite different from the epistemology of the class perspective. The structural principles of signification, legitimation, and domination are to be found in any institutionalized system of power, and Marx's theory is a special case rather than the reverse.

Society, state, and organizations

Society is dominated by organizations, and the state is the central organization, in the managerial world view. Sociologist Alain Touraine asserts that "our society . . . is dominated by the power and secrecy of the great decision-making apparatuses, by the . . . importance of control, manipulation, and repression" (1977, p. 157). Touraine distinguishes his own perspective from pluralist and class views. Because he is "constantly mindful of the *fact of domination*," he stands in "strenuous opposition to the neo-liberal sociologies of influence and strategy" (p. 170; italics in original) and thus to the central arguments of the pluralist perspective (pp. 42–3). Touraine criticizes the pluralist assumption that "social order is . . . achieved . . . by the efficient functioning of representative institutions" by asserting that although "the field of negotiations and representative institutions is widening [it] does not permit us to conclude that a society is a political market, that power is no more than influence, and that no structural limits exist to negotiations" (pp. 42–3).

Because his "central theme is that of conflicts, not . . . contradictions," Touraine stays aloof from "those sociologies critical of the established order" (1977, p. 170), that is, the class perspective. Touraine (1971, pp. 6–7) says that "social domination" is now more important than "economic exploitation." His distinction among three forms of social domination illustrates a theoretical issue found only in the managerial world view. First, "social integration," in which the "individual is pressured into participating – not only in terms of his work but equally in terms of consumption and education – in the systems of social organizations and power which further the aims of production" (1971, p. 7). Note that participation is not autonomous, as pluralists would see it, but is "pressured." The second form of domination is "cultural manipulation," because "influence over needs and attitudes must also be controlled." The third form of domination is "political aggressiveness." A society composed of "interlocking agencies, dominated by great politico-economic organizations, is more than ever oriented toward power and strictly political control over its internal functioning and its environment" (1971, p. 8). The state is "an apparatus of social management defined by that certain degree of integration of the political system, social organizations, and field of historicity" (1977, p. 464).

Sociologist Frank Parkin, in *Marxism: A Bourgeois Critique* (1979), explicitly contrasts his view of the state with both class and pluralist perspectives.

Pluralist theory . . . has little room in its explanatory model for a social agency so heavily laden with the trappings of power. Power in the pluralist model is a political resource that does not readily lend itself to such storage and concentration; rather, it is subject to continuous dissipation and self-cancellation through the push and pull of competing veto groups. [P. 119]

But Parkin reserves his sharpest criticism for the Marxist assumption that the state is principally an agent of class rule and counterposes the essentially Weberian view that the "state is founded on a separate and possibly competing basis of power to that of social classes" (p. 126). That basis is bureaucracy, and the state bureaucracy is a "powerful stratum distinct from social classes" (p. 127). He notes that some recent Marxists such as Poulantzas have grappled with the expansion of a "relatively autonomous state" and the problems that poses for the classic image of a class-dependent state and says that "a state that operates as a unified entity, and in accordance with a logic of its own, does not seem to be at a far remove from a state acting in its own corporate interests" (p. 128).[9]

Sociologist Randall Collins asserts that "what we call a society is nothing more than a shifting network of groups and organizations held together by one or both of these two principles – coalitions of interests, or dominance and submission" (1968, p. 51). Collins explicitly rejects the notion that a society is integrated by common values, as held by Durkheim and Parsons, and he also rejects the Marxist view that the "state" and the "society" derive from some overall imperatives of the class relations of production. Rather, the political and economic spheres are seen as "independent but interacting orders." Dominant and subordinate structures must be understood as a "struggle over economic resources" and outcome of conflict over the apparatus of domination. The "polity is first of all (both historically and theoretically) an organization" (p. 49).

The organizational context also dominates individual behavior. According to Collins, "an individual can dominate others over any extended period of time only by organizing a network of mutual expectations among them" (1968, p. 52). Collins rejects the explanation of power by "disembodied values, floating in the 'political culture.' " On the contrary, "individuals will orient to [values] only if they know that other

---

[9] Parkin criticizes the assumption that "whatever autonomy the state enjoys is . . . circumscribed in the long run by the parameters of class-based power" (1979, p. 128). But he cites several works within the Marxist tradition, notably one by British Marxist Perry Anderson, as implicitly adopting an organizational level of analysis for their concrete historical studies. Parkin argues that "the essential feature of this type of account is that the dominant social class of the epoch is counterposed not against an abstraction called the state, but against a definable political elite with specific interests of its own which has *control* of the agencies of state" (p. 131; italics in original). Parkin assumes that a different level of analysis is tantamount to adopting a different world view, which is not the case.

persons, and especially the most powerful persons, are also oriented to them. Hence the important values are those that are publicly *expressed* by individuals who clearly occupy places in dominant political institutions" (p. 52). Organizations create values; values do not create organizations.

Collins argues that "it is in organizations that social classes acquire their distinctive outlooks; class cultures are the effects of organizational positions" (1975, p. 347). Social classes are not important unless represented by organizations, and this explains the specific functions and forms of both politics and the state.

Politics begins to fall into greater order when we ... focus on the organizational weapons over which men struggle. The broad outlines of the state can be treated as a question of military and governmental administration; democratic politics in party, community, legislature, or national government can be explained as a special version of general organizational processes. [P. 347]

Historian and sociologist Charles Tilly distinguishes his organizational level of analysis from a pluralist model derived from Durkheim. He calls his approach a "polity" model of the relations between "contenders" (competing elites) and "governments" (1978, p. 231). For Tilly, government is a coalition of ruling elites. He also distinguishes his approach from Dahl's emphasis on the relations between "citizens" and "leaders" (Dahl 1961).

Tilly says that the state is an "organization, controlling the principal means of coercion within a given territory, which is differentiated from other organizations operating in the same territory, autonomous, centralized, and formally coordinated" (Tilly, ed., 1975 p. 638). Tilly dismisses the argument of several pluralists – Phillip Cutright, Talcott Parsons, David Apter, and Samuel Huntington – as either ahistorical, vague, obsolete, or just plain wrong. He notes that Apter's book *The Politics of Modernization* contains "absolutely no discussion of the organizational structure of states" (Tilly, ed., 1975, p. 617).[10]

The state for sociologist Theda Skocpol "is ... a set of administrative, policing, and military organizations headed, and more or less well coordinated by, an executive authority" (1979, p. 29). States are "actual organizations controlling (or attempting to control) territories and people" (p. 31). States operate within the "context of class-divided socio-

---

[10] Interestingly, however, Tilly claims that his analytic framework is consistent with a class perspective. After presenting an unexceptionable summary of Marx's major methodological injunctions (1978, pp. 12–15), he argues that Marx provides a theory of collective action, which we believe to be a large extrapolation. He refers to "conflicts of interest," which translates Marx's societal concept of class struggle into managerial language. Also, to infer that "social classes and their representatives are the principal actors in politics" for Marx is not accurate. Social classes as such are not political actors for Marx, nor can they have "representatives" in any direct sense.

economic relations, as well as within the context of national and international economic dynamics." Then she concedes something to the democratic aspect of the state by saying that the state is only part of "overall political systems," which include "institutions through which social interests are represented in state policymaking" or through which "nonstate actors are mobilized to participate in policy implementation." But she draws a boundary around her concept of the state, refusing to extend it in the democratic direction, by repeating that "the administrative and coercive organizations are the basis of state power as such" (p. 29).

For Skocpol, state interests in internal order and external defense determine its relationship to dominant classes. State enforcement of the authority of dominant classes derives from state and not class interests. She contrasts her view of the international system with that of Wallerstein (reviewed in Chapter 16, herein), arguing that one cannot explain the international structure of state organizations by the requirements of world capitalism. "The international states system as a transnational structure of military competition was not originally created by capitalism." It is *"interdependent* in its structure and dynamics with world capitalism, but not reducible to it" (Skocpol 1979, p. 22; italics in original).

These several examples of the managerial view of the state and society show that neither capitalism nor democracy is viewed as the decisive force shaping the state. Organizational power is increasingly the most important force that explains the direction of change in both state and society.[11]

Capitalism, democracy, and the state: the managerial view

In the managerial perspective, the capitalist economy is seen as a process of industrialization, democracy as an outcome of elite competition, and the state as largely subject to the forces of bureaucratic rationalization. In this section, we use the language of the managerial perspective to state its view of the relationships among industrialization, elite competition, and bureaucratic rationalization. We do not cite specific works

[11] An important recent work on the sociology of the state is Badie and Birnbaum 1983. It criticizes most recent sociology for neglecting power and domination in general and the state in particular. It is critical both of the "neofunctionalist" school exemplified by Parsons and others who accept the "differentiation paradigm" (p. 48) and of the class theorists like Claus Offe who hold that the state is "relatively autonomous" (p. 58). Their typology of states, which ranges from strong (France) to moderate (Prussia and Great Britain) to weak (the United States), emphasizes the degree of bureaucratization and centralization of the state but recognizes the historical and cultural variations between both society and state.

because we are bringing together the logical elements of the managerial world view.

Industrialization

Industrialization is characterized by the growing role of knowledge as a critical factor in production, coupled with bureaucratic rationalization of both production and distribution. The control of economic growth by large-scale bureaucratic organizations – corporations, scientific research institutes, banks, and government agencies – is made possible and necessary by new communication technologies, economies of scale, and the growing role of organizational power as a source of profits. Bureaucratic structure is a rational response to advanced, large-scale technology. The growing organizational complexity of the society requires both corporate and state planning by the technocracy – a technically and scientifically trained corps of experts. The anonymity of the market and the formal and legal equality of employees in labor markets and of buyers and sellers in commodity markets create an important precondition for bureaucratization of the economy and consequently managerial flexibility in the efficient allocation of labor and capital. Increasingly, social inequality derives from the structure of organizations and not from differences in individual values and skills.

Industrialization involves rationalizing production, the adjusting of technical and organizational means to the end of efficiency. With the growth of technical knowledge and the enormous economies that can be achieved through the application of science to production, the economy becomes increasingly large-scale and complex. As organizations grow in size and complexity, the functions of ownership become progressively less important and those of management more important. Early capitalists were both owners and managers. Although their heirs may still own vast amounts of property and stocks, decision-making power has devolved to professionally trained managers. Access to information, capacities to shape human needs, and the power to coordinate and plan become more important than ownership in determining organizational power.

Bureaucratization of the economy occurs because of the need for reliability and accountability in multiple complex transactions. Corporations try to reduce market uncertainty by replacing the market with monopoly control or with state regulation. The rise of large-scale corporations and interlocking directorates, providing interorganizational coordination outside the market, increases the importance of authoritative regulation by the state to supplant the self-regulation of the market. The state, therefore, must itself become more bureaucratized, to regulate the industrial bureaucracies and also to provide the political conditions in which those bureaucracies can continue to organize the economy.

Elite competition

In the managerial perspective, democracy is seen as a consequence of elite competition for popular support, mainly through the competition of political party elites seeking electoral backing and of other elites seeking political power. Mass participation is made possible by a proliferation of organizations dependent upon mass membership and support: trade unions, political parties, interest organizations of many kinds (professional, scientific, commercial, industrial, labor, voluntary, cultural). Participation is mobilized by organizational elites rather than by individual preferences or class interests and is constrained by tendencies toward oligarchy within such organizations. Elites use the power conferred by their office to control access to information, which their clients, constituents, or members might use against them. Elites shape public opinion by controlling the selection of issues and managing participation.

Where democratization is possible because of elite competition, political cleavages are based increasingly on the differences of access to bureaucratic authority. The natural tendency of organizations to develop hierarchy and monolithic rule is restrained by their need to maintain popular support. The organizations these elites control, whether political parties, labor unions, or public bureaucracies, are also restrained in their drive to power by competition with other organizations for resources.

Democratization also can be understood as a strategy of state elites to gain control of their external political environment. The multiplication of politically oriented organizations threatens the domination of state elites. Conflict among labor unions, corporations, and state agencies themselves renders the political environment of dominant elites increasingly unpredictable. Elections provide the state with a new basis of legitimacy to secure citizen compliance to its commands and to reduce the vulnerability of the top elites to direct political manipulation. Elections also standardize the transfer of rule. This is one managerial interpretation of the reasons for elite acceptance of the democratic aspect of the state.

From one standpoint within the managerial perspective, mass democracy may be related to state expansion, which compels ever greater resources to be extracted from the society. Democratic rights are a means by which the state can secure access to new societal resources – food supplies, men for its armies, capital for the public debt, income for the treasury. The extension of democratic rights may be the political price the state must pay to social groups in order to get access to the resources those groups control. Mass democracy becomes possible when mass political support – expressed by military conscription, taxation, or labor – becomes necessary, or when the state lacks the repressive capacity to exact such resources without popular legitimacy.

Political interests that are not organized find it very difficult to secure access to the strategic elites located within the state. Sometimes, of course, party and other elites may mobilize groups on the basis of potential interests. Unorganized interests are a resource to secure support in elections and legitimation for ruling coalitions of elites. Political parties make strategic choices about which groups would be most advantageous to mobilize. The competition between party elites allows unorganized group interests potential access, albeit limited, to the centers of power. Where elite coalition rather than competition occurs, unorganized interests are likely to be effectively shut out of the political system.

As the economy becomes increasingly dominated by large-scale organizations, the political representation of economic interests also takes place via conscious coordination among those organizations (corporations, labor unions, state agencies) rather than by an open competition among their elites. In such corporatist states participation is highly organized, and elites control the political action of their social base, rather than the other way around. Elite competition in a corporatist regime moves out of the parliamentary arena because the crucial political bargains are increasingly made outside legislatures.

The expansion of public bureaucracies leads to the emergence of state personnel as a separate and significant elite. Bureaucratization of the state limits the scope of decision making by legislative elites either to incremental changes in allocations among agencies or to the creation of new agencies. The substantive purposes of existing agencies cannot be changed easily, so two or more overlapping agencies may be created because of the inability to change the behavior of existing agencies. The problems of interagency coordination become important administrative and political issues. This in turn reinforces the power of the executive as the only location in the state potentially capable of mobilizing enough political power to change the internal commitments of the state bureaucracies.

Thus the bureaucratization of the state furthers elite competition by adding new organizations in the state that become quasi-autonomous political actors in their own right. Bureaucratization almost by definition means creating stable political bases for different elites in labor, corporate, and state organizations. The state is not simply the manager of the economy or the regulator of conflicts but has its own internal dynamic of elite competition.

Rationalization

In the managerial perspective, the rationalization of the state is a necessary accompaniment to industrialization and elite competition. The growing technical requirements of managing an economy composed of large firms whose interrelations are decreasingly regulated by the market necessitate centralization of both executive and administrative functions, with a corresponding decline in the importance of legislative and party politics. Despite their dwindling importance, even the internal functioning of legislative bodies is subject, however, to rationalization and bureaucratization.

Rationalization of the state occurs in many ways. Planning agencies staffed by experts (Office of Management and Budget, for example) attempt to develop long-range plans to deal with problems that may not be the current object of interest group demands. Unfortunately, interest group demands are likely to be raised in parochial and short-run terms, which must be responded to with compromises inconsistent with the rational management of some resources.

Rationalization also occurs as the state is progressively centralized in order to integrate programs fragmented both horizontally in separate agencies and vertically in separate levels of government. Executive agencies gradually take over control of policy making from legislatures. The central government takes increasing responsibility from local and regional governments for raising revenues and setting public policy priorities. Subnational governments are charged with the implementation of centrally determined policies. Both horizontal and vertical integration involve forms of centralization.

Regardless of the functions served by various parts of the rationalized state bureaucracies, either the state in general is seen as a set of relatively independent bureaucratic organizations, each with its own interests and bases of domination, or the state as a whole is seen as a single giant organization, with a budget and component departments. Legislatures, given the short-term tenure and lack of professional training of the members, increasingly lack the information or the skills to develop public policies that will serve state interests. The institutional requirements of maintaining partisan legislative majorities and state executive authority are increasingly in conflict. A party must get elected, and a state must maintain control over the economy and the society. State rationalization of the economy through planning may therefore alienate large blocs of the electorate and undermine support for elected officials.

Further, strong interdependencies develop between public agencies and private organizations. Private organizations are increasingly delegated public authority. The success of both public and private organizations comes to depend upon a continuous and reciprocal flow of information, personnel, and material resources. Growing state intervention in the economy has increased the dependency of the state upon the behavior and personnel of the private organizations on whose operations the state interferes. This explains why legislative institutions become subsidiary in the actual policy-making process, dominated by bureaucratic executives who implement policy inside and outside the state.

The structure of the state is itself seen as a powerful cause of political organization by limiting the kinds of issues that can gain access to the political arena. The structure of the state, not merely group and class interests outside the state, selects demands that can be handled by government and defines the legitimate issues and participants. The most powerful groups and organizations are those that establish government agencies that routinely serve their interests, often without even having to participate directly in government decision making. Nondominant groups cannot then alter the distribution of power merely by choosing new officials.

All bureaucracies are able to achieve a measure of autonomy because of their internal control over expertise and the information upon which outsiders depend. But the state's autonomy rests ultimately upon its monopoly of the legitimate use of coercion within the territory over which it claims sovereignty. This unique access to the instruments of coercion makes economic elites dependent upon the state. The rise of standing armies and the development of ever more technically sophisticated weaponry, backed up by global logistics and supply systems, require the state to rationalize its operations. To sustain such a repressive capacity, the state must increasingly extract resources from the society, for example, obedience, taxes, food, scientific knowledge, which also lead to a vast administrative system both to collect the resources and to ensure that the society is capable of producing them.

Economic growth is an environmental constraint upon state domination. In its search for resources, the state may dramatically alter the pattern of economic growth that might have otherwise taken place. If the society is unable to produce the resources necessary to protect state power, the state may intervene to assure them itself, through expropriation, conquest, subsidy, state enterprise, or taxation. Such state interventions are interpreted in the managerial perspective both in terms of the dominant interests they are likely to favor and in terms of the interests of the state itself.

The drive to rationalize the internal organization of the state qualitatively shifts the scope and character of government. Rationalization of the economy and the state favors increasing bureaucratization because of the superior speed, precision, and efficiency with which bureaucratic managers pursue their tasks. With rationalization, the state becomes more professionalized, as civil service regulations control personnel selection and performance, and more bureaucratic, as agencies grow and the need for coordination becomes imperative.

Rationalization is both a logic of efficiency and a strategy of legitimation. When conflict occurs within or between state agencies, the officials who can most plausibly claim that their program of actions and their proposed plan of organization fit the mandate of their agency or conform with previously accepted policies will win their budget increase, avoid a cut, have their programs approved, have new staff appointed. In this sense, rationalization is both an organizational and an elite strategy.

To the extent that bureaucratic agencies successfully insulate themselves from "political processes," the logic of rationalization may well apply. If the bureaucracy has become politicized – either by a change of overall political leadership or by the vulnerability of a particular agency or program to powerful interest groups and segments of public opinion – then rationalization is mainly an elite ideology rather than a set of rules governing the internal behavior of the organization. Red tape, overlapping and conflicting jurisdictions, and empire building are a few of the organizational pathologies that interfere with the logic of rationalization and are of continuous theoretical and empirical concern to those accepting a managerial world view.

Bureaucratization is facilitated by elite competition. Elites must solidify their political support by building internal political parties within organizations with stable social bases. Bureaucratization protects internal governmental elites from outside political interference, but it also protects the interests being served by the agencies from easy attack. The complexity of the state allows bureaucratic officials to sidestep demands, refer them to other agencies, enmesh the applicants or the challengers in complex interagency negotiations that finally cool them out, and in other ways prevent access to internal decisions by any outside interests except those that still benefit from the agency's functioning. In this way the competition among agency heads within government for fiscal support leads to further bureaucratization of government.

To summarize, bureaucratization of the state is explained in the managerial perspective by the varying effects of industrialization, elite competition, and the generic process of rationalization. The technical requirements of industrialization reflect the functional emphasis within the world view. The power interests of elites to reduce mass participation and its potential threat to elite domination reflect the political emphasis. But the common assumption is that economic growth through industrialization creates large-scale organizations, which need mass membership and loyalty. Technically determined political decisions expand the state but also reduce the incentives for and the consequences of political participation. Thus economic growth ultimately make political participation less necessary and even dangerous for rational decision making, except insofar as participation provides elites with information about danger points in the level of mass support. Rationality is seen in the functional version of the managerial perspective as a genuine consequence of bureaucratic organization, in the political version as a manipulative ideology of social control used by dominant elites to control the masses.

Bureaucratic functions versus elite strategies

The schematic summary above should not be taken as evidence of consensus within the managerial perspective. A major debate concerns which elites (whether economic, administrative, political, professional, intellectual, or scientific) will control which resources and institutions. And there is conflict over the relative importance of technologies, administrative strategies, and scientific discoveries for the changing domination of different elites. Given our focus on the state, we cannot summarize either the history or the nuances of these arguments.[12] But an argument between C. Wright Mills and Daniel Bell illustrates both the terms of the argument and the common ground of the world view.

C. Wright Mills's book *The Power Elite* (1956) distinguished three hierarchies of powerful organizations: corporate, military, and executive. Mills argued that national power now resides in the economic, political, and military "domains" or "orders." In each of the three, the "typical institutional unit has become enlarged, has become administrative, and, in the power of its decisions, has become centralized."

The economy... has become dominated by two or three hundred giant corporations, administratively and politically interrelated, which together hold the keys to economic decisions. The political order... has become a centralized executive establishment.... The military order... has become the largest and

---

[12] This debate goes back to the classic forebears of the managerial perspective, who differed among themselves concerning the conditions and stability of elite domination as well as its desirability. Vilfredo Pareto (1963) stressed the "circulation of elites," with "lions" (charismatic leaders) being appropriate for political and revolutionary transitions and "foxes" (organizers and bureaucrats) being appropriate to administer an established regime. Gaetano Mosca (1939) emphasized the "political formula" – the ideology that could convince the masses to support a ruling elite. Robert Michels (1962), a German Social Democrat, investigated the "iron law of oligarchy" – the tendency for even committed democrats who become the rulers of a political party to buttress their rule by suppressing mechanisms of intraparty democracy. For a contemporary argument, see Bachrach 1967.

most expensive feature of government, and...has all the grim and clumsy efficiency of a sprawling bureaucratic domain. [P. 7]

In all of these domains, "the means of power at the disposal of decision makers have increased enormously; their central executive powers have been enhanced; within each of them modern administrative routines have been elaborated and tightened up" (p. 7). Expertise and appointed officials have become increasingly important in the state.

Under the weight of bureaucratic centralization and institutional collusion among the state executive, the military, and corporations, Mills believed that liberalism increasingly lost its relevance as a political philosophy, becoming a rhetorical cover for organizational power (Horowitz 1983). Under the technical complexity of planning and the growing power of organizations, public life seemed to be collapsing. The old middle class, the bourgeois bulwark of democracy, had been reduced to status-conscious functionaries. When decisions are made by nonelective experts, public opinion ceases to matter either to government officials or to the citizenry. The population, according to Mills, retreats to private life and the anxieties of status.

Daniel Bell criticizes Mills for not developing a theory of which institutional realm might dominate others, for not specifying a method by which a power structure might be inferred, and for neglecting the cultural or ideological sources of elite power and unity (or disunity). According to Bell, Mills's "big decisions" involve foreign policy. Domestic policies are largely ignored (see Bell 1958; Horowitz 1983). In addition, Bell criticizes Mills's political judgment about the consequences of Soviet policy and the foreign policy decisions of U.S. leaders.

Despite the critique of The Power Elite by Bell, Mills and Bell share the same world view. Political and economic power is now wielded by giant organizations, and democratic institutions have become secondary. Both accept the reality of elite domination of industrial societies, differing on who the elites are and on where and when they function adequately. They differ about which controlling structures operate effectively under what conditions. Bell stresses the technocratic/scientific elites and the centrality of theoretical knowledge. Mills emphasizes the political bureaucrats, the economic managers, and the military. Bell and Mills represent the functional and political versions of the managerial world view.

Conclusions

As this example demonstrates, the representatives of the managerial world view whom we have briefly summarized do not agree among themselves on the causes of bureaucratic power, although they agree that organizational relations define the primary level of analysis from which societies and individuals must be understood.[13] Our purpose is not to reconcile their arguments or to argue for one position among them but rather to show the common ground upon which they stand. They agree that the dynamics of industrial societies can best be explained by the power of giant organizations controlling the political and economic resources of society and commanded by different elites. The mechanisms of domination may differ, but the emergence of organizational – and specifically state – domination is the preeminent historical development, which takes primacy over both capitalism and democracy.

As we have already seen in several contexts, the managerial world view contains two images of the bureaucratic state, a functional one, emphasizing the technical capacities of organizations to manage complex tasks and a more political and less benign one, emphasizing the capacity of powerful organizations to dominate those groups whose interests do not conform to the goals of elites. Centralization and rationalization of the state are frequently accompanied, in the latter version, by an expanding means of coercion over potentially rebellious populations.

In Chapters 8 and 9 we analyze exemplary works within the managerial perspective that differ in their emphasis on the capacity of the bureaucratic state to effectively centralize and rationalize its operations or on the capacity of powerful elites to fragment the state. The resulting conflicts create dilemmas for elites and crises of capacity to rule, leading to alternative organizational strategies of centralization and decentralization.

[13] Dennis Wrong's (1979) eloquent defense of the managerial world view explicitly disagrees with the class perspective, holding that "only social institutions embodied in concrete organizations can be said to have and to exercise power" (p. 255). Wrong says that he is committed to the "organization paradigm" rather than to the "class paradigm" and argues that "organizations, not classes, are the collective historical actors in contemporary advanced industrial societies." (p. 255)

8

The bureaucratic state and centralization

Building a state apparatus with sufficient power to defend itself against other states and planning an increasingly complex society compel the centralization of the state, in the managerial perspective. To gain greater control over the society, the central state must achieve dominance over its subnational units. To offset the forces of fragmentation imposed by dominant interest groups and their bureaucratic allies within the state, power must increasingly move out of the parliamentary arena into the hands of the executive. Rationalization requires centralization.

Whether the bureaucratic state is capable of controlling democratic participation and of managing the capitalist economy, while simultaneously maintaining internal rationality, is a central issue. How such a state has emerged and the conditions for its control by political, administrative, and economic elites are also central problems within the managerial world view. Class conflicts and crises of legitimacy are seen as problems to be managed by the appropriate elite strategies, not as way stations on the path to modernization or as endemic features of capitalism. The "society" remains indistinct, either as a set of external constraints or as "problems" defined by elites.[1]

---

[1] Political scientist John Zysman, in an important case study (1983), assumes that the economy can "function routinely" only if political and institutional arrangements are "stable." If there is no "stable settlement" of the distribution of the costs and benefits of economic growth, then "distributional battles will interrupt the routine functioning of the marketplace and make the institutions of the economy – such as the structure of finance and labor relations – the scene of overt political conflict" (p. 309). He assumes that the state can control the stability of such settlements by "consciously shaping the market to impose a particular distribution of the costs and gains of growth; by permitting the market to allocate them with only limited government intervention or compensation; or by negotiating an explicit settlement between the producer groups" (p. 309). Zysman is critical of the "state as neutral mediator in the public interest" school of pluralism. Financial institutions and decisions are inherently "political" in the sense that they are subject to conflict by affected organized interests. "In periods of economic adjustment,

The historical establishment of bureaucratic states: the societal level

The establishing of centralized bureaucratic states controlling a continuous territory and monopolizing the means of coercion within it provided their political and administrative elites with control over resources and therefore considerable autonomy. Nascent political elites in Western Europe used a variety of stratagems to build a central state apparatus capable of dealing with the expansive territorial claims of other states and managing their own frequently recalcitrant populations. The probabilities of state survival were slim. Whereas Europe of 1500 had about five hundred independent political units, in the Europe of 1900 only twenty-five remained (Tilly, ed., 1975, p. 15).[2]

The national bureaucratic state emerged as the dominant form in Western Europe. Although other alternatives were possible (a centrally controlled empire, a theocracy, a political trade network, or a feudal structure) (Tilly, ed., 1975, p. 26), several factors facilitated its emergence. The relatively homogeneous culture of Europe as a whole allowed easy shifts of control of territory from one state to another. The weakness of traditional kinship-based communities allowed both the separation of the state from these communities and the cooptation of traditional elites. Lastly, the openness of the European periphery, vulnerable to the stronger central states, allowed external imperial expansion of the nascent states (pp. 27–31).

The survival of any given nation-state was contingent upon the synchronized growth of the means of both coercion and surplus extraction. Here surplus means not unpaid labor but the resources extracted from a population. The frequent wars made heavier taxation necessary, and the increased means of coercion required state centralization. The state's efforts to generate the revenues, the food, and the personnel to finance, feed, and staff its increasing bureaucracy generated intense popular

when conflicts about control and organization of the economy and society are fought out in marketplace arenas as much as in electoral or legislative settings, financial institutions reveal clearly that they are allocative institutions – the scene and instrument of political conflict – whose behavior is not simply a technical but a political matter" (p. 308). Here the state is a conscious actor and can impose solutions to the problem of who will bear the costs of economic growth. Accumulation as an imperative beyond the reach of any conceivable mobilization of political or legal force and class struggle as a potential disruptive force that cannot be permanently controlled by the state do not appear in his analysis.

[2] The essays collected in the volume edited by Charles Tilly, *The Formation of National States in Western Europe* (1975), take a particularly managerial view of the process of state formation. Points from the essays by Ardent, Braun, Finer, and Rokkan are taken from that volume. See also Mann, 1979.

opposition in the form of tax riots, food riots, and sometimes civil war. These reactions in turn stimulated further expansion of a centralized coercive apparatus.

In general, military organization followed a uniform evolution among the European states (Finer 1975, p. 99). Ad hoc armed groups became a permanent standing army; unpaid obligatory service became paid volunteer service. Semiprivately controlled armies (mercenaries and marketable military commissions) commissioned by the king became publicly controlled armed forces. These changes in military organization were costly to the state. In order to secure the funds necessary centrally to control a powerful military force, princes and kings usurped tax-granting authority and intervened to cement existing class structures or create new ones. In this argument, elite strategies resulted in new administrative and financial institutions, thereby shaping the direction and pace of economic development and laying the foundation for bureaucratic rationalization.

These factors also explain variations among Western states in the degree of centralization. Different elite strategies resulted in a more highly centralized state in Germany than in Britain. The comparison provides a good example for our point. In seventeenth-century Brandenburg-Prussia, the elector (the ruling prince) was able to create a centrally controlled standing army, financed by taxes that were partially administered by the elector's own paid officials. A system of military commissars first developed in the Thirty Years' War protected the interests of the prince against mercenary commanders (Braun 1975, pp. 268–75). In 1667 the elector first effectively used troops unilaterally to impose taxes, particularly excise taxes on the towns (pp. 270–1). This suppressed the traditional self-government of the municipalities and destroyed the representative Estates (deliberative assemblies incorporating those segments of the population that had acquired legal liberties or privileges) (Tilly, ed., 1975, p. 22). Once an administrative staff was in place, these excise taxes were easily expandable. Large revenues, in addition, from the elector's own holdings and a centrally controlled standing army made the destruction of the quasi-representative Estates possible.

In order to secure the support of the Prussian landed aristocrats (the Junkers), the elector solidified a feudal agrarian structure, fiscally strained the cities while exempting the Junkers, and incorporated the nobility into the militarized administrative structure. In order to secure an initial grant from the Estates of Brandenburg, which convened in 1650, Frederick William (the Great Elector) had both guaranteed a noble monopoly on land and consolidated serfdom (Finer 1975, p. 136). An initially reluctant nobility was forced, by police power if necessary, to send their sons to state military training, thereby replacing previous contract systems of recruitment and office appointment (p. 141). By increasing the prestige, regularity of employment, and pay of the military, the electors eventually assimilated the nobility into the military state. To secure mass military recruitment, the elector managed to fuse the lord–officer and the peasant–soldier relationships, thereby attaching the coercive power of the state to agricultural production. Under the new military system established by Frederick William, "the noblemen who were the officers of the army or whose sons were, provided their own serfs and led them into the field for military service; trained them; and controlled them," returning them to work on the farm each year after spring maneuvers were over (p. 142; see also Braun 1975, p. 277).

Given the low level of commercialization of both agriculture and urban industry in Prussia, the burden of taxation was very high. In 1688 the Prussian tax rate was twice that of France per capita, and France then was more heavily taxed than England (Finer 1975, p. 140). Without a well-developed agricultural market, the taxation of the peasantry was extraordinarily difficult. For several reasons – the increasing importance of the logistics of war, the difficulties of securing food in a weakly monetized agrarian economy, and the exemption of the Junkers from taxation – the central elites had increasingly to intervene in the organization of the food supply (p. 139; Braun 1975, p. 301). But, the administratively complex system also slowed the rate of agricultural innovation of new crops and techniques.

The resulting dependence of the central Prussian state on an excise tax on the cities and towns may have not only directly hindered commercial development but also indirectly hindered it through the extensive regulation of trade necessary to monitor existent trade flows and to try to create new commerce (Finer 1975, p. 138). Thus Braun argues:

The Prussian "administrative machinery," armed with the confidence of possessing the know-how and the means to shape the economy and society in the right fashion, hampered economic development in practice, as government not only regulated and minutely controlled the economic sphere from above, but also entered the field of production and commerce by itself, setting up a host of governmental enterprises in various sectors. Quite often these enterprises proved to be unprofitable, despite the fact that they enjoyed many special privileges and advantages. [1975, p. 300]

To summarize, the Prussian state's capacity, given a weakly commercialized agrarian sector, to extract the surplus necessary to support a standing army and administrative apparatus was dependent upon that army and apparatus. In turn, a strong Prussian state impeded agricultural commercialization, reduced capital accumulation, and prevented the development of a powerful bourgeoisie. In this view, state interests structured the development of class relations.

In sharp contrast to Prussia, in England – the argument runs – the failure of the crown centrally to control the means of coercion made the survival and extension of parliamentary rule possible. In England the ability of the gentry and the mercantile classes to continue to control administration and finance prevented the centralization of political authority typical on the Continent. In contrast to Prussia and France, the English crown had to rely on justices of the peace for local administration. These agents of the central administration were unremunerated gentry and men of property.

In the sixteenth and seventeenth centuries the English crown had at its disposal not a powerful standing army but a politically unreliable shire militia summoned and officered by unpaid gentry and noblemen (Finer 1975, pp. 117–21). The monarchy lacked an independent apparatus for internal repression. These same gentry and noblemen controlled the revenue sources of the crown through a tax-granting parliament, which also increased their political power.

To secure revenues, the crown attempted to bypass Parliament by increasing customs duties, securing forced loans, and granting commercial and manufacturing monopolies, thereby alienating the emergent bourgeois class (Braun 1975, pp. 267, 264). The gradual emergence of an absolutist administration in Stuart England was undermined by the revenue requirements of war. The Scottish rebellion in 1638 forced the crown to obtain external funding. With the crown unable to secure loans from the emergent bourgeoisie in the City of London or extraordinary grants of revenue from Parliament, or even to hold the military support of a significant segment of its militia, the stage was set for a civil war that established parliamentary supremacy (pp. 259–68; Finer 1975, p. 117).

Strong agricultural commercialization, facilitated by the enclosures and a land tax, allowed the agricultural sector to bear the bulk of direct taxes (Braun 1975, pp. 302–3). A domestic supply of food for the new urban labor force was created. Because food did not have to be imported, balance-of-payment problems did not exist and industrial raw materials could be imported (pp. 302–3). This in turn generated a high volume of commercial trade that was also relatively painless to tax (Ardant 1975, p. 202). In 1694, Parliament created the Bank of England, which obtained credit and loans using state revenues as security. This assured bourgeois influence in the state well before the bourgeoisie was granted the franchise in 1832. The Bank itself served as a bureaucratic apparatus to accumulate public surpluses through taxation, which were then transferred into capitalist hands.

Whereas the Brandenburg-Prussian state of 1740 had no debt but drew nearly one-half of its revenues from the crown's properties, the English state spent 34 percent of its expenditure for debt (a figure that rose to 56 percent by 1786) (Braun 1975, p. 294). The emergence of debt finance presupposed a capital market based on the existence of a bourgeoisie. The assumption of the public debt by a Parliament controlled by gentry and nobility made the state dependent on the bourgeoisie but also secured capitalist material interest in the parliamentary system (Finer 1975, p. 123). In turn, the extension of commerce and industry in England increased the value of participation in the state for the bourgeoisie and gave them the resources necessary to purchase that participation (Ardant 1975, pp. 217, 231).

The histories of Brandenburg-Prussia and England illustrate the argument that varying elite strategies affected the pattern of state centralization. In Brandenburg-Prussia, the geopolitical requirements of state formation created a standing army that facilitated administrative standardization directly as a military strategy and indirectly through the large fiscal demands the military was able to impose on the society it controlled. The state froze the agrarian social structure, fiscally constrained the development of an urban bourgeoisie, and made subsequent economic development in Germany contingent upon high levels of state action.

In contrast, the absence of a standing army in England not only hindered administrative centralization but allowed the development of a fiscal structure (property taxes and debt finance) that further encouraged strong commercialization in town and country. Resource extraction by the state was easier, producing an apparatus that, paradoxically, had less autonomy from the emerging capitalist class but more access to the economic resources being generated by capital accumulation.[3]

This version of the managerial perspective focuses upon the capacity of armies controlled by state elites and the way that coercive capacity conditions their strategic options and class alignments. In this approach state elites are highly political actors, governed by narrow institutional interests and oriented to maximizing their structural power. A more functional version, which stresses the state's role in national develop-

---

[3] An empirical study of military technology and the rise of bureaucratic states found a relationship between the size of armies and the growth of government expenditures in Europe in the fifteenth and sixteenth centuries (Bean 1973). The author, an economic historian, argued that "the increased effectiveness of infantry resulted in a shift in the production function of defense so that the minimum efficient size of the state was increased and the centralized state was given a greater advantage over the decentralized state. ... the way in which [this concentration of power] occurred probably determined the pattern of economic growth in Europe. The changes in the art of war practically guaranteed the weakening of the feudal nobility, the concentration of power within each state, and the reduction of the number of states" (pp. 220–1).

ment within a general managerial world view, is political sociologist Stein Rokkan's explanation of the rise of central state organizations.

For Rokkan, the geopolitical location of each nascent nation-state within Western Europe helps explain variations in "center formation and periphery incorporation" (1975, p. 575). Four factors are seen as important: the distance from Rome, the distance from trade routes, the concentration of landholdings, and the cultural homogeneity of the population.

The distance northward from Rome indicated the potential impact of Roman law on legal unification and of the supraterritorial Catholic Church. The northern territories were able to break with the Rome-based Catholic Church, thereby effecting a fusion of national state and church. In the Reformation countries of the North, particularly the Lutheran monarchies, not only was religion nationalized but the national vernacular was legitimized as languages of both worship and statecraft (p. 581). In the South, by contrast, the Catholic Church retained its supraterritorial character and "acted as a brake on all efforts to build up strong national identities" (p. 581). However, in the Counter-Reformation empires (Hapsburg and Iberia), the state, acting on behalf of a supranational church, was not able to enforce cultural standardization or to create a nation out of culturally diverse territories.

Rokkan writes: "Spain has to this day remained a state and not a nation: the Catalan and the Basque peripheries have for centuries refused to identify with the power center in Castile and have on several occasions been on the brink of secession" (1975, p. 580). By contrast: "The Protestant centers of the far North could pass quickly from state-building to nation-building . . . and could develop unified cultures well before the era of mass politics" (p. 581).

The second factor was the geopolitical distance west and east from the central belt of trade route cities from northern Italy to Flanders and the Baltic. These cities grew as trade developed between the Orient, the Mediterranean, and the North Sea. Those territories to the east and west of the central urbanized trade belt were able to engage in earlier and more effective center formation than those territories within the trade belt. Rokkan writes:

The decisive thrusts toward the formation of nation-states came at the edges of the Old Empire, first on the seaward fringe, much later on the landward side. . . . The cities of the trade route belt from the Mediterranean to the North Sea and the Baltic were for centuries strong enough to thwart all efforts of military-administration. [1975, p. 576]

The central trade route territories developed short-term confederations of city states such as the Hanseatic League. Strong conquest centers grew up at the edges of the trade belt due to the greater "geopolitical loads" experienced by state elites close to the trade belt where a more powerful and expensive state apparatus was required. Comparing France, at the edge of the belt, and England, far from the belt, Rokkan notes that France not only took longer to consolidate its territory but also generated an absolutist regime that continued into the nineteenth century. "France was *closer* to the central trade belt and had to build up a much stronger apparatus to define its national territories; England was *at a safe distance* from the central area and did not have to build up a monolithic apparatus to delimit a distinctive system" (p. 587; italics in original). In part, state formation was easier far from the trade belt because it was only there that strong national or regional systems of law were developed. Within the trade belt itself, Roman law customarily dominated as a method of carrying out intersocietal exchanges (p. 584).

The third factor affecting center formation was the concentration of landholdings deriving from the consolidation of feudal agrarian structures, and the fourth was the ethnic and linguistic distinctiveness of the population conditioned by the emergence of vernacular languages along with the decline of cross-ethnic communication in Latin. These factors all affected the varying success of elites in building a centralized and bureaucratized state apparatus, separate from traditional institutions and capable of consolidating control over its territory, extracting resources from its subject population, and regulating interaction across its borders. In Rokkan's stage theory of nation-state formation, the state apparatus had to be created ("penetration") and a national identity forged ("standardization") well before the masses could be turned into citizens ("participation") and become able to use the state to redress material inequalities ("redistribution").

Nation-building elites are seen as autonomous actors, like the political organizations representing social classes or the religious organizations with which they allied or opposed. The autonomy of the state from external social forces is not treated as a historical variable by Rokkan. State autonomy is simply assumed. From the very beginning of the history of the state, nation builders are distinguished as separate actors. This conceptual device is consistent with the selection of the contemporary bureaucratic aspect of the state as dominant, the contemporary territorial boundaries of the states as final, and the contemporary form of the party structure as frozen. If present nations are in their final form and if in some sense the historical process was aiming for this form, then it becomes convenient to postulate a set of historical actors – nation-building elites – whose historical role it was to build the contemporary nation-states (Alford and Friedland 1974).

Rokkan assumed the autonomy of the state elites only during the early historical stages, however. In the early period of nation building, state elites had independent interests and alliance options. The closer his analysis comes to the present, however, the more the state is conceptualized as a relatively neutral medium for the aggregation of interests – a more pluralist conception of the state. A curious tension appears in Rokkan's analysis between the concept of the developed state and the historical agent that created that state. The state was transformed, but the analytic categories do not reflect the transformation.

Centralization: the organizational level

Once bureaucratic states became dominant in Western societies, industrialization created pressures for further centralization.[4] Centralization of the state is an important factor explaining the expansion of public expenditures and the linkages between the state, corporations, and labor.

As the central state increasingly regulates the economy its role in the transfer of income and the provision of services expands. One managerial study of the growth of welfare-state spending has also examined the impact of state centralization (Wilensky 1975, 1976). Wilensky analyzed the percentage of gross national product (GNP) spent on welfare programs, social security, and welfare expenditures per capita and their growth in sixty-four states, including all Western ones. In his analysis state expenditures are not a result of bargaining between interests or a result of crisis management to guarantee capital accumulation but a consequence of rational decisions by political elites allocating scarce resources, often against the preferences of the citizenry. The state is an organization.

Given the pressures to provide public services in rich countries, "political elites . . . have only a few broad fiscal alternatives" (Wilensky 1975, p. 59): increasing direct or indirect taxes, increasing social security contributions by either employers or employees, reducing tax cheating, increasing the efficiency of state programs, cutting benefits or holding down their increase. Taxation is seen as a strategy at the disposal of elites seeking to manage the political reaction to their decisions to expand the welfare state. Only "foolish" elites rely on visible taxes, because they

---

[4] An important recent example of historical analysis of the building of the U.S. bureaucratic state is Skowronek 1982, which focuses upon three case studies of the civil administration, the army, and business regulation. Skowronek's basic premise is that "states change (or fail to change) through political struggles rooted in and mediated by preestablished institutional arrangements." State building is "most basically an exercise in reconstructing an already established organization of state power" (p. ix). Skowronek is explicitly critical of the pluralist view that the state can be analyzed as a functional adaptation to social needs. The history of the American state was "not simply a gradual accretion of appropriate governmental responses to environmental problems" (p. viii). Skowronek also distinguishes his approach from the neo-Marxist view that "American state development is framed by an ongoing struggle to reconcile political democracy with support for the private economy" (p. viii).

provoke backlash against welfare-state expansion. Wilensky found that the resources available to elites (as measured by GNP) was the most important correlate of the level of social security spending in sixty countries. Economic growth makes "countries with contrasting cultural and political traditions more alike in their strategy for constructing the floor below which no one sinks" (p. 27). The states in industrialized societies also keep their citizens alive longer, creating both a growing political base (the aging population) for pensions and health care and a need for such programs. The richer countries also started their programs earlier, so that natural processes of expansion had more time to operate.[5] The states in rich industrialized societies respond to "similar problems of providing economic and career incentives and maintaining political order under conditions of the general push for equality and social justice and specific concern about the aged" (p. 49). Their responses typically establish similar levels of social security and welfare systems and thus lead to similar levels of government spending.

Wilensky's argument assumes that welfare effort is a genuine goal of elites and that expenditures for programs called "welfare" and "social security" actually provide services that improve the welfare and security of the population. Wilensky assumes that there is a reasonably high correlation among rhetoric, intentions, and implementation, that is, state actions are rational. Wilensky agrees (1975, p. 96) that there are few data on the actual consequences of state spending. Some analysts have argued that subsidies and payments of various kinds help not the poorest segments of the population but rather the already better-off, who have the information, political skills, and capacity to secure the benefits. If critics of welfare spending are right, then explanations are weak that presume a connection among spending, the goals of elites, and benefits for the poor. Given the regressiveness of indirect taxation, the kind least likely to provoke welfare backlash, according to Wilensky's own data, the redistributive character of welfare spending may actually vary inversely with its level.

Elite strategies manage the backlash against welfare spending. Wilensky merges four components of political action into his composite backlash index: parties ("electoral successes of social or political movements"), interest groups (presence of "large, well-staffed, and well organized movements," whether national or regional in scope), protest

---

[5] Wilensky gives credit to Wildavsky's pluralist explanation of *internal* political and administrative processes within democratic states that lead to gradual growth of state spending (Wildavsky 1974). But, he argues, these processes do not explain the large variations *between* such states.

("clear anti-welfare state component in strike or collective demonstration of nationwide significance"), and public opinion ("diffuse backlash sentiments") (1976, pp. 58–60).

These reactions to welfare spending are not regarded as mechanisms of political representation as in a pluralist view, because neither the impact nor the conditions of these different types of political action are of concern. Wilensky is concerned only with the conditions of successful *elite strategy* – reliance on invisible taxes and centralized control – not with the conditions under which different types of participation to challenge spending can be made effective.

Wilensky concludes that a few strong parties in a long-established constitutional order "bottle up" discontent (1976, p. 37), a view that emphasizes the control function of parties, not their representative function. Neither the content of the party's demands nor the Left or Right orientation of its policies is used, only the number and strength of parties. Parties are seen as organized components of the ruling regime. Their capacity to form a government, their control over the legislature, and their stability are the main theoretical concerns.

State centralization is measured by how much the central government spends as a percentage of total government revenue, whether there is a unitary or federal government, and whether the central government appoints provincial, district, and local officials. In his earlier study, Wilensky shows that more centralized governments spend more. "Political elites who embrace the welfare state in centralized polities can better overcome resistance to the necessary taxes and expenditures than elites in decentralized polities" (Wilensky 1975, p. 52). Legislatures are seen as playing symbolic roles, absorbing the political energies of mass publics, but not finally making the major decisions on the expenditures of public funds. Legislatures ratify decisions taken elsewhere, either inside the dominant bureaucracies, by political elites in the executive branch, or in the quiet negotiations between major economic interest groups and state elites. Wilensky finds that how legislatures are organized makes no difference in the level of public expenditures but that there remains a strong *positive* relationship between centralization (measured by the power of the central government to appoint officials) and social security spending in nineteen advanced states.

Wilensky strengthens his argument by showing that two pluralist factors and one class factor do not affect welfare spending. He rejects the argument that democratic political structures allow demands for more social security to be politically effective, finding that liberal–pluralist political systems do not spend more for social welfare than nonpluralist systems.[6] The correlations are much lower than those among

---

[6] Drawing upon a study by political scientist Jean Blondel, Wilensky classifies sixty-four states as *liberal democratic* (examples are the United States and Sweden), *authoritarian*

GNP, the age of the population, and the age of the welfare system. Wilensky concludes that the type of "political system is a weak predictor of major components of public consumption spending" (1975, p. 18).

Wilensky also rejects the pluralist argument that a societal consensus on the proper role of government in furthering equality determines the actual level of services provided. Consensus was measured by the extent to which the dominant party coalition in a country supports welfare programs.[7] No correlation was found between this measure and the level of social security spending.

Wilensky also rejects the class argument that whether an economy is centrally planned (socialist) or organized by markets (capitalist) should predict the level of welfare spending. He cites a study by Frederic Pryor, which compares seven communist and seven capitalist countries. When "factors other than economic systems are held constant, [the countries] are indistinguishable by their public expenditures for health and welfare and converge between 1956 and 1962 in their spending for education" (Wilensky 1975, p. 20). Wilensky concludes that the "economic system is irrelevant" as a factor determining social welfare expenditures, arguing that capitalist and socialist nations face similar problems of managing their economies, creating "economic and career incentives," and "maintaining political order" (p. 49).

Wilensky's analysis of the state is not at the individual level of analysis because it does not analyze specific political *situations*, does not deal with specific *decisions*, and does not deal with the *interactions* of political actors.[8] Actions, decisions, and events are converted into probabilities, which are regarded as the consequences and causes of organizational properties, such as centralization. Thus the "strength of organization of the working class" is aggregated from voting turnout figures in several elections. Political behavior in electoral situations is converted into an

---

populist (Mexico and Syria), *authoritarian oligarchic* (Spain and Portugal), or *totalitarian* (the USSR and East Germany). The criteria used to make these distinctions are (1) "the degree to which the mass of citizens participate in decision-making" and (2) "the degree to which the state allows or encourages the voluntary action of numerous autonomous groups" (1975, p. 21).

[7] Data were taken from thousands of pages of descriptions of the positions of political parties on six different major issues – providing for social welfare, redistribution of wealth, economic planning, government ownership of the means of production, allocation of resources to armed forces, and equality of opportunity – plus "official rhetoric in party platforms, campaign literature, press releases, speeches, newspaper reports" (Wilensky 1975, pp. 42–5). Each of twenty-two countries was rated on "the ideological stance of the ruling parties or dominant coalitions . . . from 1950 through 1965."

[8] An analysis of pension policy in Britain and the Soviet Union criticizes Wilensky for ignoring the ideological factor in policy making. The "values and beliefs and a catalog of objectives" of policy makers are "key forms of influence in policy formation" (Mitchell 1983, pp. 181, 178). Mitchell criticizes "deterministic" approaches to policy analysis, such as Wilensky's, and argues that the "industrial determinism fundamental to the prediction

organizational attribute of the society and thus part of the environment of the state (Wilensky 1976, p. 52).[9]

The process of centralization

Once bureaucratic states are established, centralization seems inexorable in the managerial perspective. An example of the process of bureaucratic centralization is a quantitative analysis of 215 city, county, and state finance agencies in the United States from 1966 to 1972 (Meyer 1979). Almost all of these organizations grew in size between 1966 and 1972, and as they grew they became more complex, adding divisions, levels, and sections. As they became more complex, the personnel procedures became more formalized. Meyer regards his index of formalization as a measure of Weber's concept of bureaucratization: whether employees are hired according to uniform personnel codes; whether written regulations determine promotions; if probation for new employees is more than six months; if the head of the department is appointed rather than elected; and the proportion of employees covered by civil service regulations. Even in the relatively brief six-year period, all finance departments became more bureaucratized.

Finance departments are a key component of any bureaucratic structure because they have a critical managerial function: budgeting, administering fiscal services, and controlling expenditures. The bureaucratization of local finance departments is clearly related to the central state's drive for rationalization. The pressure of "increasing federal intervention in local government personnel practices" (Meyer 1979, p. 161) began back in 1882 with the Pendleton Act that created the U.S. Civil Service Commission. That act did not mention state or local government but created the precedent extended in 1939 and then again in 1970 with the Intergovernmental Personnel Act. Each of these pieces of legislation aimed to take "politics out of administration by requiring impersonal procedures for the selection and advancement of employees" (p. 161).

---

of convergence [between socialist and capitalist states] theoretically excludes ideology as a relevant factor in policymaking" (p. 197). Mitchell refers to Khrushchev's and Brezhnev's beliefs as well as Beveridge's and Thatcher's as explanations of particular shifts in welfare benefits, an individual level of analysis far different from Wilensky's (pp. 182, 188–90).

[9] Wilensky's focus is consistently at the organizational level, although the data are for societies. He assumes that the state is an organization and that centralized organizations will create linkages with each other. "Peak associations" and their "command posts" are assumed to develop networks of communication and exchanges of resources. He called those variables "linkages," although none of the data refers to linkages. This measure reflects the assumptions that government, business, and labor organizations, when controlled from the top, will interact and have an impact on state policy.

Historical trends in local agency organization since the beginning of the twentieth century extended the managerial principle of operations to local government. The oldest agencies (1930s or earlier) were likely to be called comptroller departments and were limited to financial control: "to certify whether a proposed expenditure is allowed by the budget." The newer agencies, called finance departments (established in the 1940s and 1950s), also had the "responsibility . . . to raise . . . money if it is not available." The "department of administration," the latest form, "may be consulted to determine whether the project is the most cost-effective means of attaining long-run objectives" (Meyer 1979, p. 135). This gradual expansion of goals from accounting to fiscal control and finally to planning by the core managing agency of the local state is an aspect of its gradual rationalization. Although all departments were becoming more bureaucratized, Meyer found a clear indication that the newer departments with broader managerial functions were more bureaucratized than the older ones.

As the finance departments (his general term for all such agencies) grew and assumed more responsibilities, they simultaneously were challenged by other departments, which competed to take over fiscal functions. Other growing departments wanted fiscal autonomy, their own data-processing operation, and other attributes of bureaucratic power and prestige. This process indicates a tendency toward fragmentation as well as decentralization. The distinction between financial and non-financial policy making became blurred as the budgetary implications of new functions became clearer.

Meyer's study is important partly because he has data on the structural features of organizations that enable him to explain some of the correlates of public-sector bureaucratization over time. For example, what he calls environmental demand factors (measured by the total amount of funds a finance department administered and the number of employees of the city or county – thus the sheer number of tasks confronting the department) usually were closely related to the size of the finance department. The more tasks to be accomplished, the larger the department. However, where the top elite positions in the department had continuity in authority and greater autonomy, environmental demand was almost unrelated to size. In other words, where elite positions are "stable, autonomous of higher authority, and insular from it, organizational structures have high predictability over time" (Meyer 1979, p. 124). Stability was indicated by the number of years the head of the department had held office; autonomy, by being elected or selected by civil service procedures rather than being appointed; and insularity, by the department head's spending less time with higher officials. Bureaucratization was reduced if the administrative elites had more continuity of authority and more autonomy. Meyer's study shows that the issue within the managerial perspective as to whether elites shape structures or structures select elites is not a simple one; both are true under specific conditions.

Elites and masses: the individual level

Nowhere has the image of the growth of giant bureaucracies controlled by elites and dominating society been more vividly presented than in C. Wright Mills's *Power Elite*. This book, published in 1956, revived the classic tradition of Max Weber in a period in the United States when dominant institutions seemed invulnerable to challenge. Mills focuses upon how managerial elites convert publics into masses. He holds that the command posts of the society are composed of three major bureaucratized elites: the corporate rich, the military establishment, and the political executive. The power elite – those few men who hold the top positions in those three hierarchies – is sustained by complex networks of social contacts.

Hierarchy, control, and coordination at the top is matched by subordination, passivity, and helplessness at the bottom. A "mass society" has been created by the breakdown of attachments by individuals to valued social groups of all kinds – religious, ethnic, community, neighborhood, even class. Individuals and families have become socially isolated, atomized, and fragmented. This process is the corollary of extreme bureaucratization of work, politics, education – every institution of significance has lost organic connections to the "underlying" population. At the top, the power elite is able to control the major decisions affecting the life of the population. Also, through its control of the mass media, it manipulates the preferences of the masses.[10] Thus the "mass" society, a result in the pluralist perspective of insufficient organization of intermediary groups, is here seen as the natural result of a centralization of bureaucratic power in both the economy and the state.

Mills himself explicitly rejects both pluralist and class theories. The chapter entitled "The Theory of Balance" dismisses the "romantic pluralism" of David Riesman as a view that "confuses, indeed it does not even distinguish between the top, the middle, and the bottom levels of power" (Mills 1956, p. 244). The veto groups – an image of the dispersal of influence over many decisions to many groups, able to veto if not to command – elevated by Riesman to the substance of power in America are dismissed by Mills as the "semi-organized stalemate . . . of the middle levels of power" (p. 244).

---

[10] A convenient source for the debate around Mills's thesis is contained in a collection of readings edited by G. William Domhoff and Hoyt Ballard, *C. Wright Mills and the Power Elite* (1968).

Power has thus been lost not only by individuals and families but also by the "middle levels" of organization: Congress, voluntary associations, trade unions, small businessmen, the middle class. Decisions get lost in fruitless battles in Congress or between various interest groups. Leaders of these associations either lose touch with their members, if they become a peripheral part of the power elite, or else must accept their impotence.

Mills also rejects a class theory. The term "ruling class," he argues, confuses political power ("ruling") with economic power ("class") and thus does not allow enough autonomy to the political or military orders (1956, p. 277). Mills says that he rejects the "simple view that high economic men unilaterally make all decisions of national consequence." This "simple" view is a caricature of the class perspective; and Mills is using it as a straw man. He also says that "only in the often intricate ways of coalition do [the elites of the executive branch of government, the corporations, and the military] make up and carry through the most important decisions." Then he says that he is considering the "higher circles . . . in terms of power," that is, a political phenomenon rather than a class or economic phenomenon. The "bourgeois" democracy that results from the subordination of electoral politics to the requirements of capitalism in the class perspective is here seen as the result of domination of executive, military, and economic elites.

This is a crucial theoretical ambiguity in Mills because, on the one hand, he defines the power elite as separate hierarchies, and power as essentially of three distinct types – economic, political, military – and, on the other hand, he shows the close relations among the three hierarchies: the interchange of personnel, borrowings of status, social contacts, intermarriages, and common sources of recruitment. A principal reason why Mills may have rejected the concept of a ruling class was that he did not see the working class as an active agent in the transformation of capitalism to socialism and in fact saw no organized force as potentially capable of challenging the dominant institutions of the society. His theoretical ambiguity is linked to the lack of any theory of the societal contradictions of capitalism, despite his radical rhetoric and politics. Systemic power does not exist for Mills. Power is manifest in organizational form with elites commanding resources.

Mills assumes, without arguing the point or giving any evidence, that the major decisions of the power elite have been against the objective interests of the great majority of the American people. Mills does not consider the content or actual historical consequences of any concrete decisions; he only asserts that the powerful are capable of making decisions with little popular check or channels of significant public influence.

Robert A. Dahl's seminal study of New Haven, Connecticut (1961), was meant in part as a rebuttal to Mills's argument. Dahl's critique of

Mills starts with the pluralist assumption that power is manifest in the outcomes of disagreement over public political choices. Given that definition, a ruling elite exists where there is a well-defined group, in a fair sample of decisions, whose preferences run counter to other groups and whose preferences prevail over other groups. Dahl says that this might be too weak a test of an elite, because if an elite exists, and we fail to identify the right group for which to test the elite hypothesis, then we will not find the elite. He says that it is the burden of the elite theorist to specify which group it is and to show that its preferences prevail. On the other hand, this definition and test might be too strong if the members of the ruled groups are indifferent to the various alternative outcomes, for then it would seem as if the group whose preferences prevail has power.

Dahl (1958) eliminates this possibility by requiring as a condition for the existence of a "key political issue" that it involve actual disagreement on policy preferences. This is a critical exclusion because it presents a version of the "consensus" thesis of pluralism in the guise of the indifference of the public. Dahl says that an elite exists if the decisions were made by an elite and the indifferent majority "fell into ready compliance with an alternative that had nothing else to recommend it intrinsically" (quoted in Domhoff and Ballard 1968, p. 33). Dahl's position also assumes that it is a true indifference to perceived alternatives and not a failure to be able to perceive channels through which some kind of effective challenge can be mounted.

Mills's managerial approach focuses on control over "big decisions," mostly the military and foreign policy decisions that presumably structure the parameters within which other decisions are or are not made. These decisions are taken at the executive level and are not within the grasp of congressional politics, the middle level of power.

Dahl's study of New Haven starts from a pluralist world view in the attempt to answer Mills. By studying one city, he assumes that one can infer the structure of the whole by analyzing its local parts. By studying controversial governmental decisions as the location of power, Dahl assumes that publicly visible issues subject to legislative control are the best test of power. For Mills, Dahl's study was a nonsequitur. A study of controversial issues of potentially minor importance at the lower levels of power was not an appropriate challenge, regardless of what was found.

Mills's position isolates the power of elite decision from the systemic context of the interests those decisions serve and focuses upon an abstract and ahistorical image of bureaucratic hierarchies, with command posts at the top. Mills is led into a theoretical and methodological quicksand in which both pluralist and class theorists have attempted to bury him. On the one hand, class theorists have viewed his network of elites as constituting a ruling class (Domhoff 1978). On the other hand, pluralists have used various samples of public decisions to show that there is no cohesive elite that dominates all major issues (Polsby 1963). Without an understanding of the contradictions in the interinstitutional structures that these elites command, we will not have a theoretical basis for isolating the big decisions, specifying the conditions under which elite coalitions are possible or necessary, and also understanding the historical conditions under which democratic publics might control state policy.

Conclusions

We have reviewed disparate studies within the managerial perspective, differing in their level of analysis but sharing the assumption that the role of the bureaucratic state must be understood in terms of a hierarchy of centralized organizations and their elites, attempting to rationalize the state, in both senses. Most of these studies underplay the conflicting pressures toward state centralization and the counterpressures toward its fragmentation. The next chapter deals with the problems created by this conflict and the dilemmas faced by society and state as a result of crises of elite capacity, as defined within the managerial perspective.

9

The bureaucratic state and fragmentation

Fragmentation is the other side of state centralization, indicating a loss of elite capacity to rule and, in extreme situations, leading to revolutionary transformations of state power. In this chapter we deal with managerial analyses of state fragmentation at each level of analysis.

Breakdown of elite capacity: the societal level

In the managerial perspective, the ultimate form of fragmentation is the emergence of multiple centers of state authority, which can degenerate into civil war and/or revolution (Tilly 1975). Managerial analysts debate the organizational characteristics of the state that expand or limit its structural power – that is, the size and capacities of the army or how much control dominant classes have over state revenues. Issues within the perspective also revolve around the comparative importance of the ideology of revolutionary elites based in dissident regions or cities as compared with the internal cohesion or fragmentation of state elites as the structural factors leading to revolution.

The managerial explanation of civil war and revolution differs dramatically from a focus on the role of struggle between ascendant classes based on developing productive forces and declining classes based on obsolete relations of production (see Zeitlin 1984). It also differs sharply from an emphasis on the perils of too rapid modernization relative to political development, the absence of normative consensus between leaders and led, and popular expectations that rise too rapidly (Gurr 1970).

States and Social Revolutions by Theda Skocpol (1979) contains an important state-centered theory of social revolution. In Skocpol's richly textured explanation of three successful social revolutions – the French in the late eighteenth century, the Russian in the early twentieth century, and the Chinese in the mid-twentieth century – the strength of the state, seen as a potentially autonomous bureaucratic organization, is a key factor. The impetus for state autonomy lies in the necessity to maintain a monopoly of coercion in order to manage conflicts with other states.

Skocpol defines a social revolution as a coincident transformation in state and class structure. Such changes in these three states were brought about by the weakening of the state in the face of competition from more advanced states and economies abroad and the consequent creation of opportunities for revolt by subordinate classes. The inability of the state to respond to these external challenges was due in part to the power of the dominant classes to block the modernization of agriculture and in part to the bureaucratization of the state. The so-called bourgeois revolution of France began as a revolt of the aristocrats, as did the peasant revolution of China. Facing competition from other states, these states also confronted a politically powerful landed upper class. The conflicts between state and upper class immobilized the state, opening the way for more popular revolts from below.

Skocpol's argument is that ultimately the class structure depends upon state power. Once that state power is shattered, the class structure is open to challenge from subordinate classes. The requisites of state power – organizational autonomy and access to societal surplus – collide with the material interests of the dominant class. Thus the Marxian logic of class struggle leading to societal transformation is replaced by Skocpol with conflicts not only between states but also between state and classes, including conflicts with the dominant class. Political contradictions are more important than class contradictions.

Class relations within a mode of production are therefore evaluated for their contribution to state power, not for their internally contradictory properties or their genetic tendencies toward societal transformation. Conflict between states affects the pattern of economic development, as do the structure of the state and the manner in which it extracts resources from the society. The most important products of social revolutions are more centralized and bureaucratic states with enormous capacities for mass mobilization and industrialization. Where state breakdown coincides with class-based revolts from below, conditions are ripe for the creation not only of a new state but also of a new society.

Skocpol is concerned to specify the structural determinants of successful social revolutions, as opposed to failed social revolutions – political transformations not accompanied by equivalent change in social structure.[1] She rejects those explanations of social revolution that em-

---

[1] There is a methodological problem in Skocpol's research design. Her dependent variable is successful revolution, defined as simultaneous transformation of state and class structures accompanied by class-based revolts from below. Thus she incorporates an independent variable into the definition of the dependent variable, and she "samples" on the dependent variable, "successful social revolution," rather than on the relevant in-

phasize the values or ideologies of revolutionary movements, elites, or classes. "The fact is that historically no successful social revolution has ever been 'made' by a mass-mobilizing, avowedly revolutionary movement" (1979, p. 17). Another theoretical reason for rejecting a voluntarist approach to social revolution is to avoid assuming that state authority rests upon a consensual, normative order.

The case of the French Revolution exemplifies her approach. The absolute monarchy under Louis XIV in the seventeenth century faced military competition from other European powers, particularly the British. France was defeated in a series of wars and was unable to protect its seaborne commerce. To increase the resources for military mobilization of both an army and a navy, the French state would have had to increase the resources it extracted from the society. Increasing its tax revenues required an increase in agricultural productivity and urban commerce. Such economic development was blocked by the way that the absolutist state incorporated the aristocracy, both as unproductive owners of offices and as beneficiaries of seigneurial rights. The result was heavy taxation on the peasantry coupled with tax exemptions for propertied moneyed elites, fragmented landholdings, continuous investment of surpluses in public offices, and a slow-growing internal market for domestic manufacture. In addition, because the French state used feudal structures as instruments of administration, its capacities for centralized control were limited and its dependence on the consent of dominant classes was acute. Because the state allowed the owning classes to convert wealth into power, both the production of wealth and state power were undermined.

Attempting to finance its military operations, the state taxed heavily, borrowed from private financiers, and sold offices. The insufficiency of these measures forced the state to try to rationalize the tax structure in order to eliminate many of the fiscal privileges of the landed and the wealthy who had been incorporated within the French state itself. These privileged elites began to resist the state's reforms through the mechanism of the *parlements*: urban judicial corporations that had the right to register opposition to royal edicts. Their agitation – and their mobilization of popular support – was the first factor in the revolutionary situation.

The second factor came in the aftermath of the War for American Independence, as the result of which the French crown had finally ex-

---

dependent variables: internationally disadvantaged state position, state breakdown, or class-based revolts from below. Her argument does not therefore demonstrate the conclusion that it is possible to have revolutionary situations (defined by the independent variables) without successful social revolutions (defined as transformations of political and class structures).

hausted its capacity to raise revenues to pay for its astronomical debts. Because it had absorbed large numbers of wealth owners into the state apparatus, it could not politically write off its debts. Ironically, the state's revenue requirements had organized the dominant propertied class. "In short, when its unquenchable penchant for war carried the eighteenth-century Bourbon monarch into an acute financial crisis, it faced a socially consolidated dominant class. This class was dependent upon the absolutist state and implicated in its international mission. Yet it was also economically interested in minimizing royal taxation of its wealth and capable of exerting political leverage against the absolute monarchy through its institutional footholds within the state apparatus" (Skocpol 1979, p. 64). In this argument, the state is seen as organizing the dominant class. The source of state crisis is not a class contradiction but a political one. The requirements of state power incorporated a dominant class in a way that undermined itself.

As the fiscal crisis of the state worsened, the monarchy proposed ever more radical tax reforms, such as taxation on all lands without respect to the feudal status of the owner. The parlements demanded that the king summon the defunct Estates-General, last summoned in 1614, in order to represent their interests in royal decision making. Because army officers were also drawn from the same class background as those who now challenged the king's authority, they refused to repress resistance. The significance of the calling of the Estates-General was not only that it politically fragmented the property-owning classes but that the political divisions it unleashed destroyed the "administrative system of the Old Regime" (Skocpol 1979, p. 65). The major struggle at this point, Skocpol argues, was not over the class structure but over the state structure.

This erosion of state control provided the third ingredient necessary for a revolutionary situation – class-based revolts from below. In their internal struggles, what Zeitlin calls differing "segments" of the dominant class (see Chapter 13, herein) mobilized the popular classes and formed urban militias. Power devolved to municipal assemblies, fragmenting the French state and making it impossible, even for the National Assembly, to implement policies or collect revenues.

When the Constituent Assembly met in 1789, it was faced with peasant revolts across France. The revolts were precipitated by a bad grain harvest, which caused bread prices to rise sharply. Not only had the state administration's capacity for coercion collapsed, but the king himself invited the peasantry to participate in the preparation of a list of local grievances to be presented by deputies for the Third Estate. "Overall, the repressive forces were uncoordinated and not decisively deployed, thus encouraging the peasant revolts and resistance spread across the country" (Skocpol 1979, p. 124). What began as limited bread riots spread

to an attack upon the exactions of the French state and upon the seigneurial system in general. Once the peasant revolts began, this polarized the dominant class, making it impossible to consolidate a "liberal"
parliamentary revolution. Again, we see the argument that the state
plays a role in class organization, not vice versa.

What structural factors accounted for the capacity of the peasantry to
rebel in France? First, the French peasantry owned a substantial amount
of land and controlled production. Second, the peasants maintained
communal institutions, such as common lands and rules regarding crop
rotation. Third, through their village assemblies, they had a forum for
collective discussion and decision making.

The interaction between the breakdown in central state authority,
precipitating a national political crisis, and the organizational capacities
for revolt from below engendered a social revolution in France. The
political crisis generalized the challenge to the class structure. Whereas
class theorists have analyzed the French Revolution in terms of the
vanguard role of the bourgeoisie, with decisive consequences for the
development of capitalism, Skocpol's analysis centers on the capacities
of the elite who exercise state authority and the state-building consequences of the revolution. Marginal elites, not ascending classes, engineered these social revolutions.

In France, the revolutionary leadership increasingly came not from
the rising commercial families or from Paris but from administrative and
professional families living in provincial towns. Skocpol argues that in
all three revolutions the class-based revolts eroded the power of landed
upper classes. By so doing, they allowed a more centralized and bureaucratic state to be constructed based upon higher levels of mass
mobilization.

The bureaucratized state that emerged consolidated some of the preconditions for capitalist development, such as the elimination of guild
and estate barriers to national markets. Such a state was able ultimately
to halt the process whereby accumulated wealth was invested unpro-
ductively into public offices. That the state accomplished these changes
was due, she argues, not to the power of the bourgeoisie but to the
conditions and consequences of its own power. Thus the destruction of
seigneurial rights and the universalization of private property in the
countryside also destroyed the constraints on the bureaucratization of
the state. Private ownership of land, without consideration for state-
dependent status, was a way to eliminate the parcelization of sovereignty
and to create a citizenry that was equal before the law. Private ownership
served to achieve total state sovereignty and to increase its access to
societal resources.

The revolution also brought with it the disruption of foreign trade, the destruction of large numbers of the wealthiest entrepreneurs, and the reinforcement of a peasantry standing astride a fragmented French countryside. All these were enormous impediments to capitalist growth. Finally, the revolution failed to provide the parliamentary governmental form desired by the bourgeoisie. As Skocpol points out, "France provides poor material indeed for substantiating the notion of a bourgeois revolution that supposedly suddenly breaks fetters on capitalist development" (1979, p. 177).

The wars that attended the revolution provided both the opportunity and the incentives to restructure the relationship between state and society once again, first by the Montagnards and then by Napoleon Bonaparte. The goals of state elites were to centralize and bureaucratize the state and army, to regulate the economy, to mobilize masses of men, and to extract enormous amounts of societal resources. Whereas the first transformations were achieved with the aid of popular revolts from below, these later transformations were won through violent repression of popular revolts, often of the same groups. Under Napoleon, nationalist military mobilization radically changed the tactics of warfare and increased the efficacy of a professionalized army. Skocpol explains popular nationalism not by consensual values but by the logic of state formation. The state created by the revolution "in the name of the People, demanded goods and services on a far more massive scale than royal agents had ever been able to command" (1979, p. 203, cited from William McNeil, *The Shape of European History* [New York: Oxford University Press, 1974], p. 154).

Skocpol's concern is to establish the power and the autonomy of a coercive and centralized state as an independent causal force and the breakdown of the capacity of state elites as the fundamental cause of revolution. Neither class contradictions, the decline of legitimate authority, nor shifts in the "ideological self-conception" of key actors can account for social revolution, according to Skocpol (1979, p. 42).[2]

Her case study of France illustrates how she combines theoretical and empirical elements from all of those explanations. She asserts that as a result of the "formation of an alliance of powers pledged to stop its expansion," the French state suffered setbacks. This explanation of the weakening of the French state by an unexplained historical event would seem to be the kind of factor that a structural argument would not include

[2] When criticizing liberal (pluralist) and Marxist (class) theories of the state, Skocpol argues that both of these seemingly disparate views reduce the state to social forces and conflicts. Neither grants the state autonomy. Skocpol uses managerial language to describe the basic disagreement betwen pluralist and class theories: The issue between them is defined as the "means the political arena distinctively embodies: fundamentally consensually based legitimate authority, or fundamentally coercive domination" (1979, p. 25).

(Skocpol 1979, p. 54). Another instance of a situational explanation is the assertion that in 1789 the "quarrels within the dominant class . . . culminated in a victory for the Parisian National Assembly" (p. 67). That event had the consequence of the "sudden devolution of control over the means of administration." Here a situational factor had a structural consequence: decentralization of the state from royal administration into the "decentralized possession of the various cities and towns" (p. 67). Skocpol does not regard explanations in terms of specific actions and events in situations as theoretically relevant but recognizes them empirically.

Similarly, sometimes she calls upon social-psychological factors. The army officers were "reluctant" to suppress resistance, and this "helped to trigger spreading administrative chaos and military breakdown" (Skocpol 1979, p. 64). Here a social-psychological factor led to a structural change in the state. She explains their reluctance by a structural fact: the links of the army officers socially and economically to the dominant class. The psychology of the army was a result of their class membership and connections. Such an argument is an interpretation of the significance of class at the organizational and individual levels.

At the organizational level of analysis, Skocpol sees multiple connections between class and state. For example, a major source of resistance to new taxes that the French king wanted to impose came from "those wealthy, privileged groups that were simultaneously socially prominent and strategically ensconced within the state machinery" (1979, p. 61), notably the parlements. Here is an example of how class interests manifest in organizational form cannot be separated from the actions of the state. Her argument depends upon the politically relevant actions of segments of the dominant class, located both inside and outside the state.

Although Skocpol rejects the theoretical argument that the loss of legitimacy of authority is an important factor in revolution, analogous processes are recognized empirically. "News of the monarch's financial peril precipitated a general crisis of confidence within the dominant class" (1979, p. 64). The dominant class was "no longer confident" and "wanted" a representative body – a social-psychological interpretation of intentions and beliefs that has descriptive but not theoretical status in her argument.

Skocpol's important study indicates the difficulty of moving from "historical" explanations in terms of specific individuals and their intentions and actions, in all of their contingency, to "structural" explanations (the strength of the state, the interests of dominant classes, or the capacity for resistance of dominated classes). Although Skocpol recognizes that multiple levels of analysis need to be taken into account in explaining crisis and revolution, her own theory focuses on the breakdown of elite capacity and failures of the bureaucratic state.

Fragmentation of the state: the organizational level

Because the state does not control the resources necessary to carry out essential tasks and because state elites frequently want to dissociate themselves from the consequences of those tasks, organizational units of the state are sometimes decentralized or are able to resist centralization. The resulting tendency toward fragmentation establishes structural limits on the capacity of central elites to rule.

Once a bureaucratic agency is created, its internal drive toward rationalization leads toward autonomy, even if it is a formally subordinate department or division within a larger organization. On the one hand, it seeks out constituencies independent of the superordinate organization, and, on the other, it strives to monopolize resources without which the superordinate organization cannot function or to gain control over resources – including legal ones – that are not easily manipulated by the superordinate organization.[3] The conflictual process of lawmaking that occurs in most democracies also allows public agencies considerable autonomy, given the fragmentation of groups with potential interests in the agency's operation. The result is a tendency toward fragmentation in all aspects of the bureaucratic state, according to a principal argument in the managerial perspective.[4]

Vertical fragmentation is illustrated by the decentralization and then recentralization of two federal agencies. Horizontal fragmentation is exhibited in the divisions between executive, department, and program within the federal government.

---

[3] The case of Robert Moses and his insulation of the Triborough Bridge Authority and many other agencies in New York City from the demands of even the president of the United States is instructive in this regard. (See Caro 1974)

[4] Another example of a contradiction in the bureaucratic state is the conflict between attempts to enforce accountability and the "displacement of organizational goals" (Attewell and Gerstein 1979). Attewell and Gerstein argue that national attempts to control local agencies have real effects but not those that are intended. Analyzing several methadone clinics in California, they found that federal pressure to develop measurable indicators of program performance in order to justify a renewed cycle of funding led to practices in relation to clients that undermined the presumed goals of the program. Methadone treatment became an adjunct of heroin addiction when addicts were allowed to move in and out of the program and to switch from heroin to methadone at public expense. This study is an important example of the internal consequences of conflicting bureaucratic goals, a direct example of the consequences of fragmentation.

Vertical fragmentation in the federal state

Both fragmentation and centralization are dynamic properties of the state.[5] A case study of this dynamic process is analyzed in Walter Williams's *Government by Agency* (1980), a study of federal implementation. The political compromises between different groups inside and outside the state produce extremely ambiguous legislation but also give public agencies considerable leeway to define what the programs should in fact be. Once a political compromise is worked out in Congress and an ambiguous piece of legislation is passed, the inconsistencies have to be dealt with by the administrative agencies. The resulting organizational conflicts between different agencies and even within agencies reflect, we believe, the contradiction between the democratic and bureaucratic aspects of the state.

Williams observes that the 1960s saw the creation of a "host of new social programs in the areas of manpower training, education, community action and development, and the delivery of social and health services" (1980, p. 1). His study does not treat the popular or class origins of these programs, only the problems they posed for state management. At first these programs were highly centralized. Detailed regulations specified the functions of regional and state staffs of the federal agency. This centralized managerial strategy did not work. "As very detailed cures failed to solve the problems, new programs directed at new categories of recipients were developed. Complexity in programmatic and administrative terms characterized these services. . . . Political and organizational problems beset these federally funded and administered, but locally operated programs" (p. 1).

The "New Federalism" of Presidents Nixon and Ford was, Williams says, a double strategy of "decategorization" (the consolidation of "specific programs under a single heading") and "decentralization" (the shift of responsibility and authority from the "headquarters units of federal agencies to organizations in the field") (1980, p. 6). His study analyzes the attempts to implement this decentralization strategy between 1973 and the advent of the Carter administration in January 1977. Specifically, he deals with the regional and field staffs of the Department of Labor (DOL) and the Department of Housing and Urban Development (HUD), which he calls the "administrative and support" component of the state. This intermediate bureaucratic structure is "where the message of the top decision makers must be translated into operational terms" (p. 4). Most studies, he argues, concentrate upon visible big decisions made

---

[5] For an important case study of attempts in the 1960s to decentralize the State Department and the recentralization that followed, see Warwick, et. al, 1975.

by the president and Congress or the impact of specific program and agency operations in cities and local communities. "In between, the grayish hue of bureaucracy and the tediousness of regulations and fiscal procedures get ignored."

An alleged decentralization of manpower programs occurred when the old Manpower Development Training Act (MDTA) was replaced by the Comprehensive Employment Training Act (CETA), introducing a new center of power, local government, as the "prime sponsor" of programs. Established local organizations operating manpower programs had long had direct relations with the federal agencies funding those programs, and those relations were disrupted when local governments gained access to funding (Williams 1980, pp. 72–3). Local governments directly received the federal funds and then contracted with individual employment and training projects.

Within the federal bureaucracy, the lowest level was the "field reps," the persons in contact with the prime sponsors and the projects. The "area operations office," the line unit responsible for CETA, was above them. The next level was the Regional Employment and Training Administration, composed of two suboffices that were the main source of staff services: the Office of Program and Technical Services and the Office of Administration and Management Services. Above the regional office was the assistant secretary of housing and urban development in charge of the Employment and Training Administration (ETA).

Both of the laws Williams examined were

shaky, unclear compromises between the Nixon administration, which expressed the intent to turn programs over completely to state and local governments, and the Democratic Congress, which was reluctant to give up so much federal power. That initial congressional intent was unclear and made agency interpretations of national intent difficult, thereby placing a heavy burden on headquarters and regional offices. [1980, p. 7]

Although CETA was advertised as a major change from previously more centralized MDTA programs, in fact there was little substantive change at the operating level. A National Academy of Sciences (NAS) evaluation on the first three years of CETA concluded that "there has been little change in basic program design. Sponsors were inclined to continue the kinds of programs they inherited" (Williams 1980, p. 85). The report also said, however, that "local control of programs has resulted in tighter program management, greater accountability, and more rational delivery systems. . . . However the shift of program control scrambled the relationships among government jurisdiction and among the local institutions that deliver manpower services" (NAS report, quoted in Williams 1980, p. 86). Decentralization altered the political and bureaucratic relations among local, state, and federal components of the state.

Recentralization began almost immediately, as indicated by the pulling back of power not only from the prime sponsors to the regional office but from the regional office to the national headquarters in Washington (Williams 1980, pp. 75–6). The national headquarters wanted information from the regional offices to help them make policy but did not want the regional offices actually to make decisions. Williams cites a key paper by a manpower program official:

> With CETA, the Congress and the national bureaucracy had ... increased the flexibility and the power of state and local governments. Almost without a pause, they immediately began actions to effectively reverse that decision and regain the power they had just given up. CETA was not being singled out for discrimination; it was simply being subjected to a common practice observed throughout intergovernmental relations. Under whatever heading one cares to choose, be it "carrying out the provisions of the Act," "meeting national goals, priorities and standards," "protecting the prime sponsor," or "in order to meet the informational needs of the Congress," the erosion of block grant flexibility under CETA was inevitable [paper by Robert McPherson, quoted in Williams 1980, p. 77].

The legislative requirement of decentralization was also fictitious with respect to the requirements of "citizen participation" in the implementation of the community development block grants (CDBG). Williams quotes a Brookings Institution study on the impact of the participation requirement: "citizen participation [was shaped] to fit their own [local government] objectives and preferences, both substantially and procedurally. . . . local officials were supportive of citizen participation because they had the opportunity to control it and use it as they saw fit" (1980, p. 118). Thus local elites could, with covert support by federal bureaucrats, make it appear as if there were significant local participation in the implementation of the CDBG program. Williams (and the Brookings report) points to the contradiction between expanding participation and the goals of the program to conduct "broader, more comprehensive planning for community development" (p. 120), specifically for the needs of the poor in the cities. The more participation was encouraged, the broader the benefits to different groups. Given local autonomy to allocate CDBG funds, the middle class, not the poor, would receive the bulk of the assistance if participation were encouraged.

The program led to the further bureaucratization of the state. The availability of funds for a new program required local governments to become more bureaucratized. Those cities with an established and experienced professional staff got much more than the inexperienced, that is, less bureaucratically organized, cities. And even though the program began as a legislatively mandated decentralized structure, Williams's study documents the seemingly inexorable pressure to recentralize the program. The Department of Labor gradually required more and more information and imposed more regulations upon the prime sponsors of CETA programs. Decision making within the federal hierarchy itself became more centralized.

Williams's other case study of how the structure of HUD affected the implementation of the CDBG program is a good example of bureaucratic fragmentation. A major analysis of HUD by the accounting firm of Coopers and Lybrand describes the fragmented structure of HUD as follows:

Regional administrators and area office directors find themselves dealing with many-headed hydra when looking to Washington for direction. The Office of the Deputy Under Secretary for Field Operations provides the general line policy directives. But at the same time, assistant secretaries speaking directly to their counterparts at both the regional and the area office level can give conflicting policy statements based on their own particular programmatic orientation.... HUD has liaison staff in each of the programmatic areas at the national level, and each staff has a continuing relationship with its regional and area counterparts. Added to this confusion is the fact that each assistant secretary represents a specific interest (i.e., community planning and development or housing management) and often policy developed by one assistant secretary directly contradicts that of another, leaving field staff in the unenviable position of trying to implement conflicting directives. [Quoted in Williams 1980, pp. 90–1]

Staff members adapted to the existence of "three separate organizational levels mirroring each other as to functions" (Williams 1980, p. 92) by bypassing the normal channels of bureaucratic communication simply in order to find out what was going on at the local levels. Trustworthy contacts had to be found, whether in local government, the area office, the regional office, or national headquarters. Because "regional and area offices are forced to follow two different lines of authority" (they are responsible to both the secretary and the under secretary and also to assistant secretaries who have specific program responsibilities), a special liaison office (the Office of the Deputy Under Secretary for Field Operations) was established in an attempt to coordinate and mediate directly contradictory directives. Such an office, the report asserts, would have been completely unnecessary except for the fragmented structure of HUD.

Williams's study gives details of the conflicts within, between, and among agencies, levels, divisions, and bureaus over whether to emphasize management (the selection, training, and evaluation of staff) or structure (the number of levels, the division of tasks, and the allocation of responsibilities). Several of the in-house evaluation studies summarized by Williams recommended two strategies. Management changes would entail leaving the structure intact and improving the level of experience and skills of the staff personnel at different levels. Structural changes would entail also reorganizing to improve communication up and down the hierarchy, to clarify lines of responsibility, and to simplify the span of control of different officials. This argument illustrates the conflict between elite and structural conditions for rationality.

With the advent of the Carter administration, a wholesale reorganization of HUD appeared to take place. The duplication of authority and overlapping of jurisdictions in the three-tier structure were eliminated – on paper – after an authoritative decision by Secretary Patricia Harris. Assistant secretaries were now to override the regional administrators. During the implementation process, however, the regional administrators somehow remained in place. Williams speculates that this office may have served as a conduit for direct information to the secretary, bypassing the bureaucratic link between the assistant secretaries responsible for programs and their area offices. Or perhaps it was decided that "lopping off an entire layer of an agency" by abolishing the regional administrators would have devastated agency morale by reducing the number of higher positions to which staff could aspire (1980, p. 138).

This case is an example of the overarching goal of rationalization being subverted by the incentives created by career opportunities within fragmented parts of the organization. These factors at the organizational level of analysis are treated as independent of any societal requirements. The issue is defined as whether cycles of centralization and decentralization are better explained by the dynamics of bureaucratic structures or by the strategies of political elites. Williams's argument is that the goals of legislation will be better served by agency management strategies, specifically by "increased local commitment to performance objectives and capacity to perform in the field" (1980, p. 21). The social agencies are described as "large-scale public organizations (bureaucracies) characterized by a long, hierarchical chain of command," which presents "power problems" for political elites (he calls their elites "decision domain political executives") (pp. 12–14).

Williams's typology of agency resources and functions shows how the managerial perspective is sensitive to the internal complexities of the bureaucratic state. Agency resources include funding authority, political and organizational clout, organizational and programmatic techniques, information and how to use it, managerial and staff skills, all of which create "capacities or potential capacities" for management. Agency functions include (1) approval (specifying how legislation and administrative directives are to be carried out and how conditions for a particular grant will be determined); (2) information development and analysis, to monitor and evaluate performance; and (3) technical assistance, "provision by one administrative unit to another administrative . . . unit" of supportive services aimed at improving the other unit's "administrative, organizational, or programmatic techniques and procedures" (Williams 1980, p. 16). Assistance can be further divided into procedural versus substantive technical assistance and compliance versus advisory assistance. These categories all refer to alternative strategies for rationalizing the state bureaucracy in the face of pervasive structural tendencies to fragmentation.

Williams treats the economic conditions that triggered the legislation as an exogenous factor that defines the problem faced by policy makers. Thus he says that "the growth of the new categorical programs was in response to unusually large unemployment rates, especially for youth" (1980, p. 76). An indicator of some trend must be noticed by an elite (professional, political, or administrative) and defined as a "problem." The problem must be seen as discrete, with boundaries, about which the state can do something: conduct research, design a program, create an agency, pass a law, offer a subsidy, a service, or a payment. The state policy must be a rational response (that is, empirically based) to the problem. The problem must be attributed to specific causes that can be dealt with by the agency. The consequences of the "treatment" must be measurable by rational evaluation techniques. All those conditions must exist before the problem (unemployment, poverty, housing, energy) can be subjected to bureaucratic action within the state.

The organizations composing the state thus come to shape the definition of the appropriate problems that bureaucratic agencies can manage. In the internal debates within HUD, the idea of setting up a three-tiered structure at the national level was presented as rational, even if the outcome was a compromise with the career interests and political motives of elites. Although bureaucratic rationality requires distinctive agency jurisdiction over specific tasks and policy areas, this requirement builds fragmentation into the interorganizational system. In our terms, this is an internal contradiction within the bureaucratic state.[6]

Horizontal fragmentation

The state can also be analyzed as a horizontal complex structure, with each unit being part of the organizational context within which other units must operate. Studies of bureaucratic units (departments and agencies) and their programs frequently take the structure of the state for

---

[6] Williams also fails to consider the possibility that the fragmentation he observes is peculiarly a problem of the agencies concerned with social welfare programs, those most vulnerable to political surveillance and criticism. Pluralist politics surrounding the agencies may account for much of the continuous reorganization. This "structural segregation" of different kinds of benefits and functions is a reflection of the contradiction between democratic and capitalist aspects of the state. (See Friedland, Piven, and Alford 1977.)

granted, reflecting the assumption that organizations can be regarded as homogeneous decision-making entities.

The budgetary process in the federal government has been analyzed by John Padgett, empirically focusing upon twenty-five separate programs in a series of HUD budgets from 1967 to 1970 (urban renewal, Alaska housing, Federal National Mortgage Association, open space, and twenty others). Padgett analyzes data concerning cuts in the twenty-five HUD programs at different stages of the "planning cycle" for each budget: (1) the "preview stage" (May to August of each year), the period when each department sends its next year's budget to the Office of Management and Budget (OMB); (2) the "ceiling stage," when OMB budget examiners prepare ceilings for each department; and (3) the "formal agency request" stage in September. Cuts occur at several stages: (1) the regular cut from preview to formal agency request stage; (2) the more stringent so-called band cuts; (3) the OMB director's review stage (October to December); and (4) "ratchet" cuts by OMB to get the totals back into line. After the cuts, departments have a chance to appeal. The cycle concludes in January with the submission to Congress of the president's budget (1981, pp. 85–6).

Three organizational units of the bureaucratic state are involved: the "executive," charged with making policy decisions; "departments" charged with "administration and support"; and agencies with specific "operations." Executive (presidential) policies are based on "Keynesian economics on the macroeconomic front and 'balance of power' or Cold War ideology on the foreign policy front" (Padgett 1981, p. 83). These national policies are the "structural parameters" of decisions from the point of view of the internal budgetary process.

In agencies, "decision making centers on the administrative determinations of 'proper' allocations necessary to fund individual program 'needs.' Technical, legal, administrative and efficiency issues reign" (Padgett 1981, p. 80). Agency requests are formulated by decision-making processes that are independent of each other and are determined by internal negotiations between staffs within the agency. Externally, these internal conflicts may or may not be seen but are condensed into their outcome: the budget line items. At the "middle level of organizational aggregation," "decision making centers on the distributional determination of relative spending priorities among programs" (p. 80). The pluralism of the internal politics of agencies of concern to Wildavsky (1974) is not dealt with by Padgett, whose focus is on the outcome controlled by the dominant faction within the agency.

Padgett is concerned theoretically with one factor in each unit of the bureaucratic state: (1) the legal structure of a given program, which determines how controllable budget increases or cuts can be; (2) the organizational priorities of the departments; and (3) the overall fiscal targets of the executive branch of the state. Empirically, he focuses only on the second factor, taking as given the fiscal target of the budget and regarding the legal requirements of a particular program as varying randomly or probabilistically according to specific situational factors.

Within each unit, "politics . . . have been aggregated and compressed into a single piece of information": the dollar figure assigned to a budget item, program cost, a proposed cut, a limit on a total (Padgett 1981, pp. 80–1). From the perspective of each agency, that dollar figure is an input into their own decision-making process, and they have only limited political and legal power to alter it. That premise operates at even the highest levels of formal decision-making authority. Similarly, the "legal and technical constraints" on a given agency compress a complicated history of past decision making into a set of perceived alternatives: the immediate parameters of decision making. A complex bundle of political decisions compressed into a few budget numbers leads to a sequential search strategy for ways of bringing program, department, and total numbers into the limits set by other levels of the bureaucratic hierarchy.

Padgett specifies various theoretical models of budget cuts and estimates them empirically. The data support his hypothesis that "most programs most of the time receive fairly small cuts" (1981, p. 99), an observation consistent with Wildavsky's and other incremental studies of budgeting. But he finds that "radical and even 'catastrophic' " cuts (from the point of view of the affected program) are equally routine, statistically speaking (p. 99). Drastic budget cuts are to be expected occasionally from a statistical distribution that results from situations where multiple and content-free decisions must be made by bureaucratic elites. Padgett says radical budget cuts are the "structural consequence of controllability and policy priority heterogeneity, which induces differential sensitivity among programs to aggregate fiscal and foreign policy events" (p. 99). When the Reagan administration cut domestic social programs and increased the military budget, for example, the parameters of internal budget-cutting decisions shifted for the decision makers in HUD and OMB.

Thus each organizational unit within the state (executive, department, and agency) operates with a different strategy to rationalize (in both senses) the decisions appropriate for their level. The result is a complex system of bureaucratic politics, without any necessary rationality to the whole. The "politics perspective is more that of many different institutional actors pulling simultaneously in many different directions than it is that of the budget as a rational instrument for central planning and control" (Padgett 1981, p. 80).

This conclusion seems superficially like a pluralist interpretation but is actually a "political" version of the managerial perspective. Padgett rejects the "competing incrementalist model." But he also disagrees with the position he identifies with public finance economists of the "state as manager." Their central image is that of a "central authority rationally allocating relatively pliant resources in accordance with macroeconomic policy, program policy priorities and efficiency criteria" (1981, p. 76). He also rejects the explanation of budgetary decisions as a reaction to outside demands, whether from external interest groups or from a dominant class. His own alternative perspective is that "The state, in the realm of budgeting at least, is such a buffered and inertial bureaucratic system that external political demands are reflected within it at best only at the time of legislative birth of new programs and at the extreme margins of discretionary expenditure growth" (p. 78). The system is deterministic because of "organizational stability and bureaucratic standard operating procedures" (p. 77). His position is not inconsistent with the public finance economists' view of the state as manager because their perspective is from outside the state bureaucracy. The empirical focus shifts from one organizational unit to another, but the world view is the same: organizational elites developing strategies to rationalize their decisions, under both internal and external constraints.

Padgett rejects the allegedly Weberian model of a "unified central command system in which policy is set on high and is then implemented below" as "highly misleading" (1981, p. 114). He offers a model of the state as a relatively autonomous bureaucratic system with its own internal dynamic, with several competing elites located within a fragmented federal state. Executive, departmental, and agency elites have different organizational resources, and their strategies are affected by the conditions existing at different levels of the hierarchy. His model, we believe, is not inconsistent with a more nuanced view of bureaucratization as a *tendency* toward centralized and hierarchical decision making. The legitimation of bureaucratic decisions will at least be framed in the rhetoric of rationality.[7]

---

[7] Padgett's emphasis on the politics of fragmentation is consistent with the discovery that bureaucracies lack the coherence that Weber's ideal type of bureaucratization seemingly implied. Size, formalization, hierarchy, differentiation, complexity, legal authority, and efficiency have been found not to be correlated highly. Even such seemingly "hard" indicators of organizational structure as their size are ambiguous. Hood and Dunsire, in their study of sixty-nine British central government agencies (1981), found it very difficult to define a department, apparently a clear and measurable concept. Lists constructed for political, legal, constitutional, budgetary, fiscal, management, and parliamentary purposes were all different. For example, there were 450 audit categories, 480 budget estimates, 100 "blocks" for cash control, 24 parliamentary departments, and 69 "estimates departments" that had a vote in the budget estimates of 1976 (pp. 40–7). The fragmented state creates problems for research that are all too easily assumed away in the process of gathering and interpreting empirical data.

Political and bureaucratic dilemmas: the individual level

An important analysis of elite actions in a fragmented bureaucratic state is Graham Allison's study (1971) of alternative interpretations of the Cuban missile crisis – the U.S. blockade of Cuba in October 1962, followed by Soviet withdrawal of missiles. Allison distinguishes three theoretical models and derives different predictions of the course of events from them. Model I ("Rational Actor") is analogous to the pluralist world view. Models II and III correspond to the functional versus political versions of the managerial perspective. Model II he calls the "Organizational Process" model. It emphasizes the "outputs of large organizations, functioning according to regular patterns of behavior" (p. 6). Model III he calls the "Governmental (Bureaucratic) Politics" model. It explains events as the "resultant of various bargaining games among players in the national government.... Predictions are generated by identifying the game in which an issue will arise, the relevant players, and their relative power and skills" (pp. 6–7).[8]

Although Allison focuses on individual actions (by President Kennedy, for example), political decisions (whether or not to blockade the Soviet fleet), and specific events, he rejects individual motives as an explanation and disagrees with the extrapolation of individual characteristics to nations. Model I, he says, explains behavior, after the fact, as a "value-maximizing choice" (1971, p. 246). Model I assumes that both the blockade and the withdrawal can be explained adequately in terms of Soviet and American "intentions," as if states make choices that flow from their values and purposes. Allison cites Henry Kissinger's work as typically misleading: "We added the atomic bomb to our ar-

---

[8] A similar analysis using different terms is Hugh Heclo's *Government of Strangers* (1977), which deals with relations between the "political executives" and the "bureaucracy" in the United States. Heclo is dealing with alternative strategies of elites faced with a fragmented state (he calls it "compartmentalized"). The executives supposedly controlling the bureaucracy are "transient, structurally divided, largely unknown to each other, and backed by a welter of individual patrons and supporters. Held vaguely responsible for the actions of the government's huge organizations, these national political executives are too plentiful and have too many diverse interests to coordinate themselves. But ... they are ... too few and too temporary to actually seize control and operate the governmental machinery." These executives face a "spectrum of high-level bureaucrats and semipermanent figures through whom executives must lead. This immensely larger number of bureaucratic officials is not so much fragmented as compartmentalized by agency and program. Most can be expected to have far more organizational and political experience than their political superiors" (pp. 242–3). The "disparities between what is required for effective working relations and what is likely to occur in executive politics suggests *structural weakness* that cannot be cured simply by urging political executives to try harder or become more skilled in the statecraft of political administration" (p. 243; italics added). Heclo is describing an internal contradiction in the bureaucratic aspect of the state.

senal." And "we" must define the "nature of a peace consistent with our values" (pp. 25–6). Allison rejects such explanations as being appropriate only for individual actions, not for state policies.

Allison's work is a powerful critique of such an identification of states with individuals, the hallmark of an extreme pluralist world view, completely outside its home domain. However, "the analogy between nations in international politics and a coordinated intelligent human being" is influential (1971, p. 252). He notes that even when participants in American policy debates are fully aware of the bargaining that goes on in arriving at their own decisions they assume that other nations can be treated as if their policies are decided by rational individuals. Allison says that Model I analyses try to explain "bad outcomes" by "bad intentions" and explain bureaucracies in the same way. Or, alternatively, bad outcomes may be explained as "aberrations from the normal processes of government" (1971, p. 265).

Allison does concede something to pluralist Model I. Under certain very limited conditions, Model I provides the "broader context, the larger national patterns" of national values, the "objectives" within which the applicability of Models II and III must be established. "For explaining actions where national security interests dominate, shared values lead to a consensus on what national security requires, and actions flow rather directly from decisions, Model I is useful" (p. 276). In this limited respect, Allison agrees with an element of the pluralist world view that the societal totality is defined by values. But his assertion that "overarching ideas or the climate of opinion" help explain major differences in state policy (1971, p. 258) is puzzling, because popular demands and public opinion play almost no role in his analysis. Societal values must be filtered through the perceptions and beliefs of elites before they become effective in policy making. In the Cuban missile crisis, decisions lay in the hands of "organizational elites," not public opinion, Congress, or a political party, and thus not "democratic leaders."

Model II emphasizes the organizations composing the state. What are the "repertoires, programs, and SOP's [standard operating procedures] . . . these organizations have for making information . . . available, . . . for generating alternatives [and] for implementing alternative courses of action?" (Allison 1971, p. 257). The unit of analysis for Model II is an "organizational output" (p. 256). Model II thus is the functional side of the managerial perspective, stressing centralization, organizational goals, coordination, implementation, administrative feasibility, and control. State decisions result from goals. The state is seen as an organization with outputs. "For explaining the specific characteristics of a governmental action performed by a large organization, Model II is most powerful" (p. 276). But Allison also regards Model II as inadequate.

Model III supplements the other two, and Allison argues that it is the most accurate image of how decisions are actually made in a bureaucratic state. In our terms, Model III illustrates how bureaucratic fragmentation reduces the capacity of political elites to rule. What we call fragmentation Allison calls the "bargaining games" of elites located in different hierarchies within the state. In detail, he recounts the inability of President Kennedy to implement even a direct and clear order, because of "sticky" bureaucratic routines. "Established, rather boring, organizational routines determined hundreds of . . . seemingly unimportant details – any one of which might have served as a fuse for disaster . . . each provided a source of potential friction between leaders and organizations" (Allison 1971, p. 139). Authoritative orders to remove Jupiter missiles from Turkey were issued by Kennedy as well as the Joint Congressional Committee on Atomic Energy, not to mention the National Security Council, via an action memorandum. Nothing happened. An official in the State Department who happened to be negotiating with the Turkish government simply decided not to remove the missiles.

A Model III analyst would "expect much pulling and hauling, and consequently large errors as a result of innumerable small slips" (Allison 1971, p. 270). Model III focuses upon "political activity toward competing goals" of component bureaucracies (p. 276). Elite attitudes, largely stemming from their organizational position – army, political, or bureaucratic careers – decisively shaped the advocacy of a particular stand when the alternatives had to be faced (p. 263). Major policy shifts in the state occur not when elites have a "change of heart" but when there is a "change of effective power within the central circle" (p. 263).

This emphasis upon the political and organizational context within which individuals negotiate denies the ultimate rationality of the policy-making process. Organizations are power bases for individual elites. Their strategies cannot be explained by societal values or class interests, but neither can they be explained by organizational functions.

Model III is thus a political version of the managerial perspective at the individual level of analysis. "Decisions that emerge from intra-governmental debate at the highest levels are the stuff of Model III" (Allison 1971, p. 276). As Allison defines the "bureaucratic politics orientation," such decisions are a process of "bargaining along regularized circuits among players positioned hierarchically within the government" (p. 144). The players are not potentially equal in resources because of their position in organizations. In Model III, the "action is located in the bureaucratized machine that is the executive, or administration" (p. 279).

A major premise of Allison's analysis is that "large organizations that function according to routines, and politics among individuals who share power, are inevitable features of the exercise of public authority in mod-

ern society" (1971, p. 266). Bureaucracy is inevitable, as well as bureaucratic rigidity. "Where these organizations are forced to deal with
problems that are not well understood – for example, poverty – their
performance is likely to appear sluggish and inappropriate to external
critics, and their patterns of behavior are likely to seem encrusted and
incapable of change" (p. 266). Allison goes on to discuss how to improve
the capabilities of "analysts" and "operators" within the bureaucratic
state, in other words, the policy-making elites.[9]

Conclusions

At one extreme, the image of a fragmented bureaucratic state is close to
the pluralist perspective, in which public agencies are seen as performing
multiple and differentiated functions. The difference lies in the underlying world view, which may not be explicit in any given analysis.

For managerial theorists, fragmentation limits rationalization, because
of the drive for power by bureaucratic elites, the capture of agencies by
dominant interest groups, and the contradictions within a bureaucratic
state. From a functional point of view fragmentation is a problem to be
managed. From a political vantage point it reflects elite conflict. But in
neither managerial view can state fragmentation be interpreted as the
differentiation produced by a robust democratic system or as bureaucratic anarchy analogous to and derived from capitalist commodity
production.

[9] Because Allison's three models did not include a class perspective, it is relevant to
mention a class analysis of the Cuban missile crisis, which saw it in the context of a
"postwar world order integrated into an economic system under United States leadership" (Shoup and Minter 1977, p. 199). The strategic policies necessary to maintain the
boundaries of the "free world" against "Soviet aggression" set the "context for decisions
in such crises as that of the missiles in Cuba in October 1962" (p. 200). The Council on
Foreign Relations, linked to the "largest and most internationally oriented sector of the
U.S. capitalist class" (p. 9), formulated "an activist, hard-line policy" (p. 206). An empirical analysis of the Cuban missile crisis from within the pluralist home domain is
provided in Irving Janis's *Groupthink* (1982). Janis is concerned with the social-psychological processes of group decision making and how individuals influence them.

10

The managerial perspective on the capitalist state

The managerial perspective subordinates the capitalist aspect of the state to the bureaucratic aspect. The relations between the "state" and the "economy" are defined as those between organizations commanded by elites. They are structures in conflict, not functions in tension or aspects of a contradictory system. Capitalist society is not the key level of analysis.[1]

The managerial critique of class analysis

Many theorists within some variant of the managerial world view have developed their ideas in a conscious critique of Marxism, challenging the functionalist version, which sees the state as the executive committee of the bourgeoisie. Authority relations have replaced class relations; political power has superseded economic power; industrialization has transcended capitalism.[2] Forces of production become resources of en-

---

[1] See Poggi 1978 for a clear and succinct sociological analysis of the state from a managerial world view. Poggi recognizes the "logic of profit," but that logic is a feature of the private economy, not the total society as in the class perspective. Poggi emphasizes the monopoly by the state over "society-wide, generalized coercive power" and the way the "state is constituted to exercise rule over society" (p. 135). Poggi is critical of the pluralist view of the "liberal state," regarding it as historically obsolete, but he also criticizes the class view that "the state's institutional principles are instrumental to bourgeois class dominance within the society" (p. 119). He regards the latter argument as "correct but somewhat partial," because it underplays the growing autonomy of the coercive and bureaucratic power of the state apparatus. Although Poggi says that he recognizes the "evolving dynamic of the capitalist economic system" (p. 122), that system is not dealt with as an object of theoretical analysis, although it is seen as historically and empirically real.

[2] But, frequently the class perspective is reinterpreted into managerial terms. Sociologist Tom Bottomore, for example, offers three answers to the question: "What causes have brought the state into existence and assure its future development?" (1979, p. 70). The first is that social functions have become more "differentiated" as human societies have become "larger and more complex," creating a need for a superior authority in society capable of regulating conflicts of interest among individuals and groups and of representing in some fashion the 'general interest.'" A second explains the state as the "imposition of the rule of one group of people upon another by conquest." A third, which he regards as derived from Marx, is that the state comes into being and is main-

ergy and information.[3] As the theoretical vocabulary changes, so does the world view.

French sociologist Raymond Aron emphasizes the pervasiveness of a political class or ruling elite, regardless of who owns the means of economic production. Aron says that "the operation of the state apparatus is never independent of the social classes but yet is not adequately explained by the power of only one class" (1966, p. 203). The " political class" is a "narrow minority who actually exercise the political functions of government." "Ruling class" is a managerial redefinition of the concept to mean "those privileged people who, without exercising actual political functions, influence those who govern and those who obey, either because of the moral authority which they hold, or because of the economic and financial power they possess" (p. 204). A ruling class in Aron's sense exists when the elites of various powerful organizations – industry, trade unions, political parties – exercise "authority or [have] prestige in society at large" and have a "feeling of solidarity." Every

tained as an "instrument of domination by dominant classes over subordinate classes" (p. 70). But he also refers to Mosca's view that in all societies there are two "classes": a "class that rules and a class that is ruled," which is a conception of command and obedience, thus elite domination, not class rule. Bottomore suggests that Weber is close to Marx in recognizing "social classes – and more generally various 'constellations of interest' in the economic bases of domination." But he regards Weber's emphasis on bureaucratic domination and legitimation as a "Marxist" element. Bottomore thus merges the class perspective into a managerial one by regarding class as "merely" another constellation of economic interests that seeks to dominate society. Whether or not Bottomore is right in reducing class rule to elite domination (that is, arguing that bureaucratic legitimation and coercion are more important than capitalist accumulation as forces shaping the state), he does not acknowledge the distinctive world view of the class perspective.

3 Stinchcombe argues, in his critique of the economic categories of neo-Marxist theories, that a synthetic theory requires consideration of the relations between levels of analysis, as we do. In his words, "monopoly capitalism as we know it is impossible without bureaucratic management, which is impossible without career incentives" (1983, p. 254). He criticizes economics for simply assuming that "incentive structures" exist and then not investigating them "in sufficient detail to see how specific modes of production work" (p. 255). But his general argument uses central managerial concepts. He asserts that "the political forms within which capitalism has grown has often been imposed against the will of the capitalists as a class: by feudal forces in late feudal times, by trade unions and socialist parties in the twentieth century, and by the military requirements and aims of national governments at all times" (p. 6). Stinchcombe redefines the class concept of forces of production into managerial terms: "patterns of combinations of energy and information in the production of a particular good with a particular kind of resources" (p. 128). This definition reduces the societal level of analysis to the organizational level. Information, resources, energy, technology, control, and constraint are the key concepts, not capital, labor, class, and production. The causal direction is reversed: "Relations of ownership and of authority in economic and military enterprises, then, depend in part on the exact shape of the technical system, how information is supplied, and what energy is used" (p. 129). Another key to his underlying world view is his abstraction of the concept of "administrative apparatus" from vastly different forms of society.

regime has a political class whether organized democratically or not, but not all societies have a unified ruling class.

Societies differ in the degree of cohesion of their elites (or "leading categories" or "leading strata"; Aron uses these terms interchangeably). Besides the political class, he distinguishes two other "categories of privileged persons, holders of . . . power [who] emerge from the economic system: *managers of collective labor*, owners of the means of production, directors, engineers, and *leaders of the masses*, heads of workers' unions, and eventually heads of political parties, anxious to organize an occupational group (the industrial workers) on the basis of a class affiliation" (1966, p. 205). Aron does not define these categories as classes, or even as class agents, because his concern is with societies both with and without private ownership of the means of production.

German sociologist Ralf Dahrendorf argues that the Marxian conception of class struggle must be replaced by the concept of conflict over authority relations. This fundamental shift in theoretical position has to be emphasized because Dahrendorf continues to use the language of classical Marxism – class, ruling class, class conflict – but with an entirely different meaning. By "ruling class," for example, he means not those who own the means of production but rather "the dominant groups in political conflicts" (1959, p. 303).

And by "class" Dahrendorf means not the division of society into those who own the means of production and those who must sell their labor but rather "social conflict groups the determinant of which can be found in the participation in or exclusion from the exercise of authority within any imperatively coordinated association" (1959, p. 138). This change of world view stems from the historical argument that "legal ownership and factual control are separated," institutionally, politically, economically. Once the legal owners no longer control production, classes fundamentally change their character. Authority or domination becomes the "more general social relation" (p. 137), and therefore a general theory of society and state must be concerned primarily with the conditions and consequences of political authority and rule and only secondarily with economic ownership and class struggle.

For Dahrendorf, following Weber, power has shifted in industrial societies from classes to bureaucratically governed states. This shift has made revolutions almost impossible (1959, p. 299). The key factor in the importance of bureaucracy is its "monopoly of specialized expert knowledge" (p. 298). Such a monopoly does not mean that bureaucracies as such are the "ruling class," although "domination without a bureaucracy is no longer possible" (p. 300). After considering this question, Dahrendorf concludes that "obviously we have to look for the ruling class in those positions that constitute the head of bureaucratic hierarchies, among those persons who are authorized to give directives to the administrative staff" (p. 301).[4]

Dahrendorf interprets the class perspective as arguing that "the governmental elite is part and parcel of a homogeneous and organized larger entity" (1959, p. 304). The goal of even a Marxist version of the ruling class is to "maintain the status quo of authority relations" (p. 304). Dahrendorf thus assimilates the class perspective to the managerial assumption that organizations, bureaucracy, and authority relations are the key aspects of the state.

Dahrendorf does not argue for a monolithic and homogeneous ruling class. The four elements of his ruling class (the bureaucracy, the governmental elite, the majority party, and the elites of dominant veto groups) vary in strength and composition from time to time and from country to country. But he believes the authority they exercise has almost completely superseded capitalist property relations as sources of conflict.

Daniel Bell disagrees with Dahrendorf's view that authority relations have become more centralized in both firms and government. According to Bell, "The nature of a market society is to disperse responsibility and to have 'production' decisions guided by the multiple demands of the scattered consumer. But a decision to allocate money to one scientific project rather than another is made by a political center as against a market decision" (1973, p. 263). Such a formulation stems from Bell's desire to contrast competitive markets with the rationality of conscious, planned decisions made at the political center with the guidance provided by "theoretical knowledge."[5] This is a debate within the managerial perspective over which institutions have become centralized.

In a later work, *The Cultural Contradictions of Capitalism*, Bell criticizes

---

[4] Dahrendorf distinguishes his position not only from that of Marx but also from those of James Burnham (1941) and C. Wright Mills. He rejects the position that "managerial or capitalist elites" constitute the ruling class. Such a view, he says, does not pay enough attention to the "evident seat of authority in the political state, and to its occupants. Managerial or capitalist elites may be extremely powerful groups in society, they may even exert partial control over governments and parliaments, but these very facts underline the significance of governmental elites: whatever decisions are made are made either through them or by them.... It is admittedly not sufficient to identify a ruling class solely in terms of a governmental elite, but it is necessary to think of this elite in the first place, and never to lose sight of its paramount position in the authority structure of the state" (Dahrendorf 1959, p. 302).

[5] Even aside from the inconsistency of this position with his final conclusion about the irrationality of politics, Bell's distinction between political and economic markets is arbitrary. Firms in a monopoly industry are making decisions from an "economic center," which may function much like a political center, a "private" state. Multinational firms often operate like private governments with their own security, intelligence, and lawmaking procedures to which their employees are subject. Conversely, government may be as fragmented and subject to multiple demands from scattered " political consumers" as is any competitive market.

the class perspective on the capitalist aspect of the state, as manifested in the work of James O'Connor, although Bell agrees that in western capitalist societies "private property has given a dominant economic class a disproportionate degree of political power," (1976, p. 231). But he asserts that the contradiction O'Connor sees between the accumulation of capital and the legitimation of the state exists in the Soviet Union as well as in the United States. He argues that it is not the "capitalist state" that runs the risk of losing legitimacy but the "democratic polity" (p. 231). Here he counterposes his own theory of the bureaucratic state to the class perspective on the capitalist state. "The sociological fact about modern western democratic polities is that the political system is a wider arena in which all kinds of interests – ethnic, economic, functional, bureaucratic – are claimants." The state must

> *manage* the double function of accumulation and legitimization; has to provide a unified direction for the economy, in accordance with some conception of the common good (as well as to have some unified conception of the national interest in foreign policy); and to adjudicate – on the basis of power, or by some normative philosophical criterion – the *conflicting claims* of the different constituencies. In its first task it has an *autonomous function of leading and directing*; in the second, it is at worst an arena of power, at best a normative umpire. [Pp. 231–2; italics added]

For Bell the state is thus torn by a contradiction between its bureaucratic aspect, which derives from its role in the economy and foreign policy, and its democratic aspect, which derives from its role of managing the demands of diverse interests. The basic contradiction is not between capitalism and democracy but between the state and democracy. Hence, to the extent that diverse interests can press their claims upon the state, this contradiction will characterize both capitalist and socialist societies. For pluralist theorists, such as Samuel Huntington, the state is subject not to external contradictions, only to the internal tension of achieving a balance between its consensual and its representative function.

Corporatism and state planning: the societal level

Unlike the class perspective, which tends to minimize the importance of differences in state structures among Western capitalist societies, the managerial perspective makes the state-economy relationship a chief theoretical focus. The degree of state intervention in the economy, and through what structural mechanisms, is a problem that assumes that state power is at least as important as capitalist power and that the public sector can be analyzed separately from the private sector.

Andrew Shonfield's book *Modern Capitalism* (1965) was a major work of the 1960s on the changes in the organization of the capitalist state.[6] The book analyzes institutional changes mainly in France, Britain, Germany, Italy, and the United States. Shonfield's definition of the relationship of the industrial economy to the bureaucratic state has been followed by a rich literature.

Shonfield rejects the class view that capitalist economies are still subject to uncontrollable swings from depression to boom, arguing that increasing "public power" has achieved the capacity to control the economy through comprehensive planning. Shonfield assumes that Western states potentially have the capacity to intervene effectively in the economy to prevent the worst consequences of uncontrolled competition. And, simply by omission, Shonfield rejects the possibility that popular movements, working-class organizations, or political parties are potentially important political forces affecting state policy.

Shonfield emphasizes several centralizing trends in all Western states: (1) increased regulation of private economic competition; (2) increased long-range national planning; and (3) increased publicly funded social welfare services. The growth of production, income, trade, and employment are in important ways the direct consequence of the increased managerial capacity of Western governments to regulate, plan, and provide services. But Shonfield raises the question of whether successful "continuing prosperity and uninterrupted growth . . . is . . . probable in the future." The answer to that question depends, he says, "very largely on political will and skill: specifically on the management of the institutional apparatus which guides Western economic life" (1965, p. 63). Elite capacity is furthered by a "variety of independent forces [which] have combined to increase the available powers of control over the economic system" (p. 64). The result of these forces has been a "vastly increased influence of the public authorities on the management of the economic system" (p. 66).

Several national cases illustrate his argument. France has a more centralized bureaucratic state than either Britain or the United States. The characteristic expression of the new capitalism – economic planning – is most explicitly expressed in France. Planning, "concerned with the attainment of specific objectives of a long-range character" (Shonfield 1965, p. 121), expresses the imperative of rationalization of the state and the economy.

Shonfield says that

---

[6] Political scientist John Zysman mentions Shonfield's work as a precursor of his own analysis of the relationships between the state and the economy, specifically financial systems. He says that Shonfield's "remarkable book . . . remains influential nearly twenty years after its publication precisely because it built on such a unified conception of the advanced countries" (1983, p. 299).

the development of French planning in the 1950's can be viewed as an act of voluntary collusion between senior civil servants and the senior managers of big business. The politicians and the representatives of organized labour were both largely passed by. The conspiracy in the public interest between big business and big officialdom worked, largely because both sides found it convenient. [1965, p. 128]

This coalition of business and the state presaged a corporatist solution to the problem of planning within a capitalist context. Some organized interests were coopted, others neglected. The French parliament "voluntarily handed over to the permanent administration the authority to get on with certain things, and denied itself the right to interfere with them" (p. 130).

Shonfield himself describes the process of French planning before the 1960s as an "elitist conspiracy, involving a fairly small number of people," but it was a conspiracy in the "public interest" (1965, pp. 130–1), as defined by the elites of key state and economic organizations. Shonfield does not deny that "the activity of planning, as it is practiced in France, has reinforced the systematic influence exerted by large-scale business on economic policy.... The Plan reflects, in large part, their ideas [those of large corporations] . . . or at least a compromise between their wishes and those of the officials responsible for government economic policy" (p. 139). This empirical observation is interpreted not as an indication of class rule but simply as the agreements reached between elites controlling the private and public sectors of the economy. For Shonfield, France represents the extreme of rationalized and centralized power in Western states.

The British state is capable of far less centralized economic planning than the French state. In Britain, neither the ministries nor the civil service supported either the principles or the instruments of "true" economic planning. Even in the policy areas in Britain that would seem to be the most highly centralized (the industries nationalized by the Labour government – coal, electricity, gas), each industry was set up with its own administrative board, with no provision for coordination of a national fuel policy. Even those functions already within the state's control are described as organized in a "pluralist" manner, Shonfield says, referring to an empirically observed fragmented organizational structure.

Planning's "essence" was seen as a bargain among interest groups, which was then given a formal definition as national economic policy and "occasionally tidied up by the professional staff" (Shonfield 1965, pp. 155–6). The outcomes of the political bargaining process were dressed in language that made it appear that the legislation or the administrative rule represented an independent assessment of the public interest. The traditional British doctrine was that government decisions are "simply the resultant of a series of pressures and counter-pressures among free associations of individuals." In such a state, "agreed action by communal organizations themselves is to be preferred to the exercise of governmental power" (p. 162), and "if the game of politics is being properly played, the other players will ensure that it [the state] has very little to do" (p. 162).

Shonfield holds, however, that the decentralized British state is under enormous pressure from the objective need for economic planning. And, given that pressure, the dominance of a pluralist ideology makes the emergence of oligarchic rule *more* likely, because there is little defense against rule by giant organizations. When corporations are treated as if they were voluntary organizations of individuals it is difficult to create countervailing power within the public sector. By comparison, "Continental practice . . . though much more tolerant of the privileged corporate body sometimes armed with para-statal authority, is also more insistent on public surveillance" (1965, p. 163). Shonfield attributes some of the differences between Britain and France to the political culture of Britain, but it is not a democratic virtue to be preserved. Rather, political and economic elites must deal with the empirical reality of pluralism as an obstacle to rational planning.

The state in the United States is both decentralized and fragmented, at the opposite extreme from France. Public power and authority are "uncertain," although the same long-range pressures toward central economic planning are present. Fragmenting power is seen in the United States as "the only firm guarantee of pluralism, the only defense against overwhelming private power. Public authority having been deliberately weakened by division, private power must be kept divided too" (Shonfield 1965, p. 329). Paradoxically, aggressive action by the U.S. state must be taken to maintain competition within and between industries, as well as within and between units of local and regional (state) governments. Antitrust legislation, designed to break up giant corporations reaching a monopoly position in their industry, almost has the status in the United States of a religion that worships divided power and authority.

The state in the United States, according to Shonfield, is marked by the division of authority not only between agencies but also within them. Federal agencies are a case in point: "*antiplanning* [is] deliberately elevated into a way of life." "Like some tireless primitive organism exclusively concerned with reproduction, these agencies divide themselves again into yet more parts, each with an independent body and soul" (1965, p. 322). If possible, additional authority is given to the courts, which play a policy-making role far more important than in Western Europe. Not only courts per se but even regulatory agencies tend to become quasi-judicial in their procedures, with hearings, briefs, and decisions. Both public and private power are divided to maximize the diversity of sources of authoritative decisions.

This fragmentation of authority does not mean that the state is not active. On the contrary, the Securities and Exchange Commission, to take one example, requires far more stringent reporting of data by corporations than does any European country (p. 299). The highly decentralized party system is part of the pluralist American system. Even a solid party majority in Congress does not provide the kind of "coherence" in policy making that is the "characteristic feature of modern planning, the treatment of all aspects of the economic activities of government, present and future, as interdependent parts of a single system" (p. 337).

Shonfield characterizes the American state as "riotous pluralism" (1965, p. 323). Even where power is seemingly centralized, it tends to fragment. In France, the situation is precisely the reverse. Even where apparently decentralized public agencies are created, decisions somehow end up being made in Paris (p. 318). Shonfield attributes this difference to the national political culture, an empirical category summarizing many differences of political and administrative structure. But even in the decentralized and fragmented American state the same centralizing pressures are at work as in France. Shonfield mentions some presumably rationalizing instruments, such as federal subsidies, stable bureaucratic careers, and requirements of comprehensive planning. He believes genuine national economic planning is not yet crucial for the United States because the country is not crowded and has such a highly productive economy that some inefficiencies could be tolerated, although "the same forces [are] at work" (p. 331).

These scanty tendencies toward internal rationalization of the state lead Shonfield to speculate whether the United States will follow the same path as other Western countries in moving toward comprehensive economic planning. The overall historical trend, he argues, is for a "new and much more intimate relationship between public and private power. This is the political meaning of planning in a mixed economy of the modern capitalist type. Its expression is the establishment of a single framework of long-range policy in unison between private enterprise and public authority" (1965, p. 333). In other words, some form of corporatist centralized structure is likely to develop in every industrial state.[7]

---

[7] Shonfield's last published book (1982), although not quite in finished form, shows that although he took account of the recent "backlash against government intervention" in the economy (p. 98) and retreated slightly on the issue of how detailed state planning could be he did not waver on the central issue of state intervention in the economy.

More recent dynamics of the capitalist state are illustrated by another study of the post–World War II evolution of economic planning in France (Hall 1982). The French state, in Peter Hall's view, has traditionally stood above society, claiming that only it could specify a "public interest." Since the first postwar plan in 1946, the French state has combined a policy of tight credit with its control over the capital market to provide cheap capital to those firms and sectors that would cooperate with its planning objectives. Initially oriented to overcoming bottlenecks and encouraging a high volume of domestic investment, these policies did not channel public or private investments in such a way that French firms could compete in a European economy increasingly open to international competition. The French state achieved high growth rates and also high inflation, which they had previously managed through devaluations of the franc.

To meet the challenge of international competition, French state elites had to change their strategy from macroeconomic sectoral planning to microeconomic planning. Whereas previously the French state had promulgated rules that applied to all firms within the economy or within a particular sector, now planning involved politically negotiated interventions between the state and individual firms. Whereas in the past the French state had negotiated with the entire French capitalist class, in part through a broad-based employers' association (Confédération nationale de patrons) or through trade associations, now it negotiated with the largest, most technically advanced firms in the leading industries – aeronautics, electronics, petrochemicals, pharmaceuticals.

To create internationally powerful firms, the state orchestrated a massive merger movement. The resultant corporate giants seized control in the employers' association, and new career paths swiftly emerged, linking the state technocrats charged with economic planning with the advanced corporations. As public authority fused with private, state elites and corporate elites faded into each other. As state regulation of a particular firm became more intensive, its dependence upon that firm became more complete. The objects of state regulation gradually become its subjects. The private corporations captured pieces of public power.

The planning structure was such that industrial sectors dealt with specialized government departments while the allocation of financial subsidies rested with the Ministry of Finance. Microeconomic state intervention made the departments into representatives of the firms upon

---

This was the "seeming paradox." The state had been "forced to recognize the limits of its capacity for short-term management" but was "called upon increasingly to take charge of its long-term managment. . . . The pretensions of the omnicompetent state have gone. But the interventionist state is more necessary than ever" (Zuzanna Shonfield, quoting Shonfield 1978; in Shonfield 1982, prolog, p. xxi).

which their policies depended, rather than agencies capable of controlling the behavior of a sector through incentives. The Ministry of Finance had previously controlled global policies and left specific firm implementation to the planning departments. Now single firms could short-circuit the departments and make demands on the ministry, demands for which it was not prepared. The state lost its capacity for macroeconomic coordination as private firms overloaded it with powerful demands. More importantly, the legitimacy of public economic policy was increasingly threatened, in part by factors over which the state had no control.

The French state, according to Hall, had traditionally legitimated its policies through its claim to speak for the public interest. Such a claim was based upon state autonomy and societal regulation through the implementation of rationalized systems of bureaucratic rules. As economic planning increasingly required political negotiation with private organizations, first industries and then firms, the basis of state legitimacy shifted to technical expertise: attempts to coordinate the solution of technical problems by state and corporate elites. Because of the political opposition of those who absorbed the costs of French economic policy, this technocratic ideology was insufficient. Increasingly, the state had to defend its policies in terms of their ability to achieve high rates of economic growth.

The state claimed responsibility for, and indeed rested its legitimacy upon, the performance of what was still a privately controlled economy. Such a basis for legitimation set the stage for massive political attack upon it once the oil crisis of 1974–5 initiated an economic downturn. As state intervention became more intrusive and more specific, the victims of the new economy – smaller corporations, which had formed a bulwark of the governing regime, and unemployed workers, who had not – claimed that their economic problems were state responsibility. The state had built the framework for its own delegitimation, according to Hall. The regime had set in motion policies that eroded the small-business basis of its support. In 1975 the French political executive restructured the state to attempt to recapture control over the planning process and began a program of "deplanification," attempting to disengage the state from economic management and return to a free-market ideology. French plans no longer even had targets for macroeconomic or sectoral growth, let alone unemployment. Although the disengagement from economic management was in part symbolic, given the high proportion of capital still allocated by the state, the size and autonomy of the planning apparatus were radically curtailed.

Hall's is a managerial analysis of the ways in which corporate organizations fragment the state and undermine the state's capacity, even in a powerful state such as France. These consequences are seen, however, not as the result of contradictions within capitalism, or between capitalism and the state, but as due to the power dynamics of a regulated economy.

One of the central contemporary dilemmas of the bureaucratic state under corporate capitalism, according to managerial theorists, is the tendency for dominant private firms to fragment the state as the state attempts increasingly to manage the economy. This undercuts the capacity of state elites not only to control the state but also to regulate the society.

Corporatism

The need to maintain state centralization in order to achieve economic planning confronts the growing organized power of those whose economic interests are at stake. Where a fragmented swarm of dominant organizations captures pieces of state power, the rationality of the whole is impossible. Referring to French planning, Henry Ehrmann writes:

In their common resistance to politics the technicians who collaborate in the subsystem hope to bring about, among other desirable results, that close union of public and private decision-making which in France has recently been christened *economie concertée*. Objectively, they may multiply states within the state and thereby reconstitute the technicalities of a feudal system. Should under such circumstances administrative creativity collapse, political decisions would amount to little more than an endorsement of the lowest common denominator of what the affected groups are willing to concede. [1968, p. 415]

Similarly, where unions have achieved power in the labor market, a rational economic policy may not be possible if a labor party does not have long-term control over the state apparatus. Referring to post–World War II Britain, Martin notes,

the shift in power to the labor movement organization in the labor market, resulting from the full employment begun during the war and continuing thereafter, was only sufficient to produce a stalemate over economic policy when the labor movement organization in the political arena was unable to control the state as well. Although this stalemate cannot protect the welfare state from erosion, it can protect full employment. But full employment can be protected this way only over the relatively short-run. The stop-go pattern of economic policy that results from the stalemate has destabilizing effects that make it progressively more difficult for full employment to be reconciled with a level of price increases that is politically tolerable and consistent with balance of payments requirements. [1975, pp. 33–4]

Martin argues that democratic control of a capitalist economy may be impossible if there is alternation in office. Fragmented alliances between corporations and segments of the state bureaucracy and the fragility of labor party control over state economic policy both undercut the rationality of central state intervention in the macroeconomic system.

One of the central mechanisms the managerial perspective offers to resolve this conflict between the functional requirements of rational state intervention in the economy and the increasing political power of well-organized interest groups, both corporate and labor, is the emergence of new "modes of interest intermediation" (Schmitter 1977). Managerial theorists have focused especially on the emergence of corporatism as a means of assuring continuous representation of dominant interests independent of partisan conflicts, while simultaneously adjudicating sectoral interests.

Whereas, in pluralist representation, the constituent units are unlimited in number, voluntary, competitive, nonhierarchically ordered, and not officially sanctioned in any way, in corporatist representation the constituent units are limited in number, compulsory, noncompetitive, hierarchically ordered, and are granted "representational monopoly" by the state (Schmitter 1977, p. 9). Schmitter argues that "societal corporatism" emerges out of the inadequacies of pluralist interest representation to deal with the problems of state planning and societal rationalization. Schmitter notes that

the decay of pluralism and its gradual displacement by societal corporatism can be traced primarily to the imperative necessity for a stable, bourgeois-dominant regime, due to the processes of concentration of ownership, competition between national economies, expansion of the role of public policy and rationalization of decision-making within the state to associate or incorporate subordinate classes and status groups more closely within the political process.

This view, that such planning and rationalization are even potentially possible in capitalist democracies, contrasts sharply with both pluralist and class perspectives.

Recent work has considered the historical origins of corporatist structures of power in Western states in the aftermath of World War I. Historian Charles Maier has analyzed the development of "corporatist" arrangements among business, labor, and the state after World War I in Italy, Germany, and France, emphasizing "domination of the capitalist order" by "political and economic elites" (1975, p. 1). Maier focuses on the changing ways in which the state maintained the existing class structure in Italy, Germany, and France after the upheaval of World War I, marked by a transition from "bourgeois" to "corporatist" rule. He uses the military metaphor of a fortress to connote the structures of power that political and economic elites were defending. His concern is to understand how the privileges of different elites remained intact and to investigate how elite strategies maintained the structure of corporate capitalism.

Maier is concerned with explaining the persistence of capitalist rule, not the rise of bureaucracy. In a lengthy footnote (1975, p. 9), Maier discusses why he chose the term "corporatist." He rejects "pluralism" as suggesting a "free competition among social forces." Similarly, he rejects "organized capitalism" as not emphasizing enough "the political [rather] than economic transition." In the emerging corporatist system, organized labor was integrated into a "bargaining system supervised by the state" (p. 11). The distinction between the "public sector" and the "private sector" eroded. "Political stability demanded a more bureaucratic and centralized bargaining. If Marx, in short, dictated the preoccupations of bourgeois society, Weber discerned its emerging structures of power" (p. 10).

Maier does not deal with the societal contradictions that might limit economic expansion. Although empirically recognizing the inflationary impact of corporatist bargaining among labor, business, and the state, Maier does not associate these trends with crises of capital accumulation. Political conflict has taken new forms and shapes control over and distribution of the social product. Both democracy and bureaucracy are seen as external conditions for the control by elites of the emerging corporatist organization of the capitalist economy. The state is the arena for these forces to play themselves out, but it is neither the executive committee of the bourgeoisie nor the scene of fundamental contradictions leading to crisis and transformation.[8]

Corporatist structures have again become of considerable interest as mechanisms for managing post–World War II capitalist democracies. In place of parliamentary determination of policy, centralized corporate and labor organizations in several countries have negotiated directly with each other and with the state in the determination of macroeconomic policy, particularly control over incomes. An incomes policy was made necessary by a strong union movement capable of winning relatively full employment. Increased international competition also made the relative rates of inflation critical factors in the fiscal capacities of the European states (Panitch 1976).

Corporatism has been explained by the failure of parliamentary politics to provide the political support necessary for effective macroeconomic policies (Schmitter 1974). Phillipe Schmitter's measure (in Berger 1981) of societal corporatism for fifteen Western European and North Amer-

---

[8] The concepts of class, elite, and interest groups are all used by Maier, in recognition of the three theoretical perspectives. But they are all interpreted in a managerial perspective. Class is defined (following Dahrendorf) as a "collective competition for power and the right to distribute rewards" (Maier 1975, pp. 19–20). Elites (following Mosca, Pareto, and Weber) are defined as a "privileged stratum enjoying power, wealth, and honor or combinations of all three." Interest groups are seen as concentrations of organized power, not as representatives of a constituency. Maier thus views individuals as having power when they command organized resources. Societal trends are significant as external conditions for organizational and elite actions.

ican countries is used to make that argument. Corporatism ranges from fairly voluntaristic mutual influence of interest groups and government bodies to firmly established partnerships among state, industry, and labor.[9] Faced with increasingly precarious rule, ruling elites in several Western European states adopted corporatist strategies – incorporating interest groups into the policy-making apparatus and shifting taxes away from such visible forms as income and property taxes to such invisible forms as value-added taxes. As corporatist states added more invisible taxes, there was less "tax/welfare backlash" and less government "unruliness" (Wilensky 1975; Schmitter 1981). Schmitter also develops measures of "fiscal ineffectiveness" and "governmental unstableness" to indicate the vulnerability of the ruling elite to dwindling tax revenues and shrinking electoral majorities.[10]

Unfortunately, Schmitter's data do not bear directly on the problem of the success or failure of corporatist strategies of the state in dealing with problems of fiscal ineffectiveness. His data show a correlation of − .63 between societal corporatism and fiscal ineffectiveness (Schmitter 1981, p. 312). This finding does not tell us whether a state elite suffering for revenues coopts interest groups and reduces their demands or whether a corporate elite has been able both to control popular demands for state expenditures and to dominate state agencies.

Another of his findings is that there has been more citizen "ruliness" in nations where voters are more likely to be "contained" within social group memberships (that is, where voting is highly predictable from occupation, region, and religion) (Schmitter 1981, tables 10.5, 10.6, pp. 312, 314). Structural change in the state (indicated by corporatism) has a strong relation to the containment of political participation within legitimate and orderly channels (pp. 311, 315).

Such studies, by compressing qualities of complex systems to a single number, in effect assume that the state is an organization, an instrument of elite strategies and goals. The unit of analysis and the conception of

---

[9] Schmitter (like Wilensky 1975) measured corporatism by two measures of labor union federation centralization, presuming that, "where workers' associations are highly centralized and monopolistic, other interests will be correspondingly organized" (Berger 1981, p. 293). The resulting measure is called "societal corporatism." The several indicators were the size of the central union federation bureaucracy, the existence of strike funds, the degree of control over member associations, the number of central federations, and whether or not blue- and white-collar associations were grouped in the same peak associations (p. 293).

[10] The indicators of "fiscal effectiveness" are the increase in government revenue between 1956 and reliance on indirect taxes (1956–74). The measure of "governmental unstableness" includes three components: (1) the number of changes in prime ministers or presidents and major ministries from 1960 to 1974; (2) the decrease in the governing margin between 1965 to 1975; and (3) change in the dispersion of voting preferences for different political parties between 1966 and 1975.

the empirical variables allow little analytic room for situational contingencies or systemic contradictions.[11] Both Schmitter and Wilensky convert an attribute of class structure – the organization of the working class – into an attribute of the state: corporatism. The origins of this structure in the history of class struggle or the ways fiscal "ineffectiveness" stems from the contradictions of capital accumulation are lost from view.

Politics also disappears as a situational activity in which outcomes are never quite predictable because of the ambiguous consequences of appeals to public opinion and the fragile calculations of political leaders about the outcomes of particular actions. Instead, those contingent qualities of politics become frozen strategies, a characteristic of a state or an organization that enables empirical correlations to be measured between "party strategy" and state policies. The key pluralist insight into the contingent nature of politics is also lost, given the empirical task of measuring organizational variables and the theoretical assumption that the outcomes of political debates and the impact on policy of shifting perceptions of leaders and voters are of minimal significance.

Corporate power: the organizational level

Economist John Kenneth Galbraith's *New Industrial State* is a paradigmatic example of the managerial world view on corporate organizations. Galbraith is a maverick within economics in much the same way that C. Wright Mills was in sociology: He rejects the dominant pluralist perspective cogently and wittily. Unencumbered, by his own admission, with the difficulty of dealing with empirical data, he constructs a forceful case for the managerial perspective on the capitalist state.

In the introduction to the second edition (1972) Galbraith makes this clear. "Power in the modern industrial society resides with the large producing organizations – the large corporations" (p. xiv). His focus is on the 2,000 largest industrial corporations composing the "industrial system," not on the economy as a whole (p. xxi). Galbraith rejects the

[11] Another empirical study in the same tradition is Cameron 1978, which finds the *growth* of state revenues in eighteen states, mainly Western European, between 1960 and 1975 to be associated with the partisanship of government and the "openness of the economy" (as measured by the proportion of GNP made up of exports and imports). Centralization of government, electoral competition, and the visibility of taxes and economic growth were important zero-order correlations with state expansion but disappeared with statistical controls. Cameron's basic empirical argument supports classic social democratic reform politics: Concentration of industry leads to concentration of labor, to labor organization, to class political organization, and then to leftist electoral majorities. Labor or social democratic control of government leads to greater expenditures for welfare state policies, lower capital accumulation, and greater income equality. The state is also, however, an organization functioning in a turbulent world economy.

pluralist emphasis on the market and the "ultimate power of the individual" (p. xvi), because it is simply wrong to presume that General Motors and the Pentagon are (respectively) "subordinate to the market ... and to ultimate citizen will" (p. xvii). He blames the "established structure of economics" for overemphasizing the "independent power of the consumer and citizen ... his immunity to persuasion and ... his power in the democratic process" (p. xvii).

But he is equally critical of the class perspective. Restating his thesis as associating "power with organization – with public and private bureaucracy," Galbraith says that his argument does indeed "obscure or even suppress the role of the capitalist" (1972, p. xix), seen by class analysts as still there "pulling the levers that motivate his managerial puppets." Galbraith's answer to the class critique of his argument is merely a repetition of his position: "The decisive power in modern industrial society is exercised not by capital but by organization, not by the capitalist but by the industrial bureaucrat" (p. xix). And, he continues, this is true for both the "Western industrial systems" and for the "socialist societies." The key assumption is that "organization – bureaucracy – is inescapable in advanced industrial technology" (p. xx). And the state is inextricably involved in maintaining corporate power. Not only do corporations control the market, but they "also obtain from the state such further action as is needed to insure a benign and stable environment for their operations" (p. xiv). Galbraith thus views the society from the vantage point of those organizations that have power: the largest industrial corporations. Capitalism is an organizational system, driven by science and technology. The themes of "planning, specialization, and organization" are dominant in Galbraith's argument (p. 20).

Galbraith's whole book is an elaborate embroidery on the threads of the above thesis. Given the world view, the argument flows inexorably. Technology requires large business organizations, which alone can "deploy the requisite capital; it alone can mobilize the requisite skills" (1972, p. 4). But this commitment of capital and organization "requires" foresight and planning. Given this requirement, "modern technology thus defines a growing function of the modern state" (p. 5). The corollary is the "regulation of demand by the state." There "must" be stabilization of overall demand. The scope of state activities and the most efficient organization of production flow from the dynamic of technology and science. Galbraith's work is a paean to the capacity of industrial corporations and the industrial state to plan.

The key concept Galbraith introduces to describe the "guiding intelligence – the brain" of the industrial organization is the "technostructure." Galbraith locates the key decision-making power in a specific elite, which has "specialized knowledge, talent or experience" (1972, p. 71). This emerging new elite, the technostructure, must have sufficient autonomy to be able to gather, test, and use the information necessary to make technically competent decisions (p. 77). Guarantees of corporate autonomy by the capitalist state, and the inability of the stockholders to assert their legal and formal control over the corporation ensure that autonomy. But the main source of autonomy is the sheer "complexity of modern technological and planning decisions" (p. 80).

Galbraith starts from the assumption that science and technology are the driving forces of change in industrial societies. Given that assumption, he can view different levels of analysis as in perfect alignment. The "Industrial State" (the alliance of giant organizations in economy and state) fits the "Industrial System" (the largest industrial corporations), which in turn fits the "Technostructure" (the managerial elites who actually control the corporations) (1972, p. 10).

Democratic socialism is not a possible alternative either to bureaucratic capitalism or bureaucratic socialism. "The technical complexity, planning, and associated scale of operations that took power from the capitalist entrepreneur and lodged it with the technostructure, removed it also from the reach of social control" (1972, p. 104). In effect, Galbraith has reconciled the contradictions among capitalism, bureaucracy, and democracy by ignoring the disruptive potential impact of democratic political demands upon capitalism and the state and by simply assuming that the state *must* function in accordance with the "needs" and "requirements" of the largest industrial corporations. What began as an analytic convenience becomes an intellectual straitjacket.

Galbraith gives no weight at all (in fact, hardly even mentions) institutions of democratic participation. They are dismissed out of hand as irrelevant to the exercise of power in the Industrial State. His critique of the class perspective is also practically nonexistent because he dismisses democratic socialism as an "overture to nostalgia" (1972, p. 104). All that Galbraith can see as worth salvaging from the classic socialist vision is the "autonomous public corporation" (p. 104). He is thus reacting, in effect, to the *politics* of class analysis – the slogans of public ownership or nationalization – in the absence of an adequate theory of societal contradictions that would theorize both democracy and bureaucracy as well as capitalism.

Galbraith gives little evidence of the actual behavior of any specific "technostructure," its use of information, response to complexity, or capacity to control its environment. Nor does he compare the technostructures of corporations in different Western societies. Galbraith hardly believes that such empirical evidence is necessary, so convinced is he of the managerial world view.

A completely different study of corporate power in the local state is one by political scientist Matthew Crenson (1971). His analysis of air pollution policy in East Chicago and Gary, Indiana, was a key "non-decision-making" challenge to pluralism within political science. Crenson's is an example of an empirical work within a managerial world view that is trapped by a pluralist epistemology. The systemic power of capital is not even visible because of an empirical focus upon participation as the measure of power.[12]

Crenson rejects the hypothesis that citizen preferences generate community issues. The pluralist argument is that citizen concern with air pollution is the best explanation for action. Crenson argues instead that the "political stratum" of a city decided whether or not an issue got on the political "agenda" of a city. Crenson views a local government as a political organization whose agendas for action manage conflict rather than represent individual citizens and the public interest. Issues do not arise from public opinion but are moved on and off the political agenda by political elites. Crenson accepts the pluralist empirical focus on decisions, however, by defining an issue as an "unresolved matter, controversial or noncontroversial, which awaits an authoritative decision" (1971, p. 29).

Crenson concludes that East Chicago exhibited speedy and effective action on air pollution; Gary slow and ineffective action. In East Chicago, government elites faced a fragmented corporate elite, while Gary's steel industry was dominated by a single firm, U.S. Steel. In Crenson's model, organizational differentiation of corporate elites was a critical determinant of the power of local state elites. East Chicago turned to industrial representatives immediately to help formulate a city ordinance. Gary's efforts were ignored by U.S. Steel, but the company's perceived interests were taken into account by the city even though the company chose not to be active on the issue. Gary still delayed implementation, and only under the threat of state legislation did the city finally act (in 1962). Even after that, the company refused to prepare a compliance schedule, after delaying two years and being threatened with legal action (Crenson 1971, p. 74).

---

[12] A challenge to the pluralist perspective developed in the debate, mostly in the 1950s and 1960s, on the issue of the "pluralist" or "elite" character of urban politics in the United States. A "nondecision" school arose, which argued that the special power of corporations was manifest in their ability to keep certain kinds of issues off the political agenda in the first place, so that challenges to business would seldom appear as public controversies. This was both a substantive and a methodological challenge to pluralism because it argued that the "population" of issues that pluralists regarded as adequate to measure power – those that became public and controversial governmental decisions – was already biased against the possibility of discovering corporate power. (See Bachrach and Baratz 1970.)

Despite the claim for East Chicago's effective antipollution action, its ultimate experience was practically the same as Gary's. The steel corporations were deeply involved in the preparation of the ordinance, partly because the chief advocate, the city attorney, realized the corporations had the capacity to resist with a variety of evasive actions. By including local businessmen in the negotiating sessions the city attorney felt business opposition to the measures would be lessened, because "if East Chicago corporations believed they had a hand in the writing of the air pollution ordinances, they would take a more lively and benevolent interest in the legislation than if the city administration snubbed them" (Crenson 1971, p. 47).

Later, in the implementation process, the corporations also had many points of access to get what they wanted. Local industries challenged the antipollution inspector for "misinterpret[ing] . . . the law." Then the scope of East Chicago's antipollution program was reduced by exempting "all pieces of equipment installed prior to the enactment of the dirty air ordinance" (Crenson 1971, p. 55). Finally, the explicit provisions providing for review of the emissions from new industrial equipment were apparently ignored when a steel-making technique was introduced. As a result, pollution was restored to its previous level. The strategy of the corporations was to keep regulation at the local level "where we can get at it" (p. 72). The East Chicago experience showed that corporate power affected not only the original language of the ordinance but also the implementation process, by either challenging it, delaying it, or simply violating the law with impunity.

Crenson was able to conclude that East Chicago was more effective because he restricted the empirical criteria of nondecisions to the actual political participation of different political and economic elites and the immediate consequence for whether or not a "decision" was made. That is, his empirical scope stops at the point when a decision is made or not made and when the actual participation or lack of it by a given elite is measured. His causal argument is not pluralist because he focuses on whether or not elites participated and whether any decision at all was made. By accepting the empirical focus on decisions but emphasizing elite strategies rather than public opinion, Crenson is able to point to differences in the decision-making style of urban governments. But his interpretation takes as given the boundaries of organizational power of corporate and political elites.

We can push Crenson's own analysis one step farther and argue, using his own evidence, that corporate elites had the capacity to prevent implementation of the antipollution ordinance in both cities. Crenson, by accepting pluralist criteria for effective participation, finds a distinction between East Chicago's allegedly effective action and Gary's allegedly ineffective action (its nondecision). Crenson discovers that there was corporate influence without corporate participation over what a local government decided *not* to do. In effect, he accepts the pluralist criterion for power without coming to a pluralist interpretation.

The paradox of the study, which Crenson does not make explicit because of a lack of clarity on different levels of analysis, is that corporate power ultimately won out in both cities, despite their difference in decision-making styles. The "effective action" of East Chicago was measured at the point (sufficient for the pluralist view of democratic participation) at which the local government made a decision. But if we regard actual implementation of antipollution controls as the test of effective challenge of corporate power, such efforts were stopped cold in East Chicago as well as in Gary. Formal democratic openness creates a special vulnerability to corporate power. This argument goes beyond Crenson's but is consistent with an extension of his managerial world view.[13]

Economic and administrative elites: the individual level

Individuals in powerful positions in the economic and administrative organizations of industrial societies are seen as elites within the managerial perspective. Structures of power are controlled by individuals who occupy the "command posts," to use C. Wright Mills's apt military metaphor.

The themes of political scientist John Armstrong's comparative study (1973) of European administrative elites are the "elite administrator's perception of his role in economic development" and the "processes by which role definitions are acquired" (p. 3). Armstrong derives his point of view from Shonfield's *Modern Capitalism* (Armstrong 1973, p. 4), given the assumption that a factor like "administrative intervention . . . may become crucial" in industrialization. His concern is with the "doctrines" (defined as "an articulated, coherent, and at least superficially consistent set of ideas") that favor "administrative intervention" in the economy, specifically "centralized initiative and planning in mobilizing and increasing economic resources" (pp. 47–50).

Armstrong defines elites as "roles in a societal control center" (1973,

---

[13] Clarence Stone, in his analysis of the conversion of business and neighborhood demands regarding urban renewal in Atlanta, studies all of the stages of the policy process (1976). Stone studied "demand conversion" under two mayors of opposing political orientations. He discovered that under both of them business demands had most impact at those stages least accessible to electoral influence – that is, where issues were originated and where they were implemented – and least impact where official decisions were made by elected officials.

p. 14). That assumes that "a small proportion of the individuals comprising a society exercises a very disproportionate authority in social control and allocation of resources." Further, "elite administrative roles are potentially crucial." Armstrong's theoretical criterion for the empirical selection of cases is "whether the positions are indicators of roles which have a high *potential* for participation in decisions significantly affecting major resource mobilization and allocation" (p. 23; italics in original). He rejects trying to determine "whether holders of positions actually participated in decision-making."[14]

Armstrong explains the nonintervention of the British state in the economy in terms of the institutional socialization of the administrative elite, not in terms of British values. Once that elite was established, "the administrators themselves acquired an interest in perpetuating the noninterventionist role definition. An interventionist position would have revealed the specific inadequacies of their training, disrupted their corporate solidarity, and reduced their status in the general elite" (1973, p. 301). Armstrong emphasizes the training, cohesion, and position of organizational elites in a larger elite structure, not their class functions or their service to societal values.

Another excellent study of the domination of an industrial society by "state-created elites" is Suleiman's study of France (1978). He interviewed "125 members of the organized elites holding top positions in the private sector (presidents and vice presidents of industrial corporations) and in the public sector (ministries, nationalized industries, and ministerial cabinets)" (p. 13). One of his main conclusions was that, although the elites he studied were "trained by the state and destined for state service," their importance today "transcends the public sector, for their members today dominate – in some cases monopolize – the key positions in the administrative, political, industrial, financial and even educational sectors" (pp. 11–12). State institutions guarantee the selection and training of elites and "concentrate the key posts in the major sectors of society in the hands of those who are able to make their way through these institutions" (p. 12).

Suleiman asserts that the "state . . . played a major role in the trans-

---

[14] Armstrong seems uncomfortable, and appropriately so, given his theoretical definition of elite positions, with mostly excluding "private sector elites," although he does present some comparative data on the "private managerial elite" (1973, p. 26). Although Armstrong says that his conception of ideology is drawn from Marx, he "detaches" that concept from the general class perspective. His concept of class is that of "collectivities with limited material or status interests," not, as in Marx, "antagonistic social forces defined by their ineluctable relationship to the production process" (p. 302). Armstrong also rejects a "total societal explanation" that explains the degree of state intervention in the economy in terms of the "need" of a society either to concentrate or to diffuse "achievement motivations." This explanation has the defect of assuming that "societies respond to a deficiency in one area by compensatory mechanisms" (p. 303).

formation of the French economy. . . . the agents of the state [the tech-
nocrats] . . . initiated and took responsibility for the changes that led
France into the industrial and postindustrial era" (1978, p. 252). It encouraged the "concentration of industrial firms [which] strengthened
the ties between big business and the state" (p. 253). Suleiman details
the symbiotic relationship between the *grandes ecoles*, which graduate
the elites of French society, and the *grand corps* in which they are placed,
the elite institutions of the state, banking, industry, and education. "[T]he
grandes écoles come to have strong ties throughout the society as a result
of the organizational structures which their graduates enter. Their graduates gain legitimacy because they are graduates of the *grandes écoles*,
and the *grandes écoles* reinforce their position because of the success of
their graduates" (p. 100). Individual elite power thus depends upon
what Suleiman calls the symbiotic relations between these institutional
sectors. The increased concentration of economic power has not diluted
the power of the grands corps to monopolize the highest posts in both
public and private sectors, according to Suleiman. Rather, "the expanding role of the state has actually allowed the organized elites to expand
their own rule" (p. 265).

Suleiman's is a study of the social psychology of elites, locating them
within the structural context of organizations that recruit, socialize, and
place them within the network of institutions that control French society.
As industrialization has occurred, facilitated by the state, it has changed
the "perceptions of managers of the private sector and those of the public
sector. . . . both the civil servants and the heads of the large industrial
enterprises [now] see themselves as managers" (1978, p. 234). Suleiman
emphasizes the conscious intentions of individual elites. When he says
the state "believes" (p. 257) or has "little interest" (p. 257) or has a
"desire" (p. 252) or has an "attitude" (p. 252) or "should encourage"
(p. 254) or is "aware" (p. 258) or has a "pattern of thinking" (p. 259),
he is attributing individual motives or beliefs to the elite organizations
composing the state, thus metaphorically fusing levels of analysis. His
analytic problem is to explain "the dominance and stability of France's
governing elites and their institutions," that is, the "way in which elites
are able to transform themselves in a manner that ultimately ensures
their survival" (p. 5). Suleiman draws upon the classic elite theorists
(Mosca, Pareto, Schumpeter) as well as Tocqueville, Mannheim, and
Weber. He rejects approaches that focus on the social origins of elites,
preferring to focus upon the organizational structures that train and
recruit them, and on those in which they operate.

Suleiman is not arguing that the state controls the economy; rather,
he says that the common elite structure shared by both public and private
sectors serves the interests of both. And he is not arguing that there is

no conflict between the various sectors of the elite. On the contrary, they are in continuous conflict over jurisdictions and turf, but they unite to defend the institutional principle of elite domination, that is, the basic existence of the interrelated elite structures of the grandes écoles and the grands corps. They share a common social psychology: "the elite is deeply committed to a certain view of the society – centralized, non-participatory, and fundamentally conservative" (Suleiman 1978, p. 249). Concrete policies are subordinate to, indeed are "judged according to their impact on the power and position of the elite" (p. 247).

The state is not capitalist, in the sense that the state's structure and policies must serve the long-range interests of capital accumulation. Rather, the economic and political interests of elites in the stability of the economy and the state merge, not because of any societal imperative but because of the mundane but pervasively powerful impulses to safeguard their institutional position at the command posts of French society. The interests of individual elites become the same as the goals of the institutions that recruit and train them.

Suleiman sees neither democratic values nor class contradictions as a potential challenge to elite domination. The parties of the left have been coopted by their elites, sharing in the "advantages which the elitist system offers" (1978, p. 28). Neither the Socialist nor the Communist Party, presumably ideologically committed to greater "democratization, participation and access to educational opportunities," has advocated abolition of the organizational structures that provide elites to French institutions. One member of the elite, himself a defender of the status quo, "readily acknowledged that 'our ENA [Ecole Nationale d'Administration] is an emanation of the bourgeois class, and its purpose is to extend the power of the class which exercises a hegemony over the lower classes' " (p. 77). But this societal function of the elite institutions is not discussed by Suleiman, except to say that the elite graduates have come to occupy elite positions within all political parties, both opposition and nonopposition. Suleiman is thus skeptical of the revolutionary pretensions of potential Left governments in France. He argues that a "left wing government would, when confronted with the problem of the need for order and stability, find itself an ally of the grandes écoles" (p. 88).

Suleiman makes the important point that the demand for "democratization" of the grandes écoles, even when expressed by reform parties of the Left, extends only to "greater representation of the lower classes" (1978, p. 277). He argues that "admitting a few more children of workers . . . would not be of much help to the working class and would not transform these institutions in any significant way. It would help, above all, to legitimize these institutions and ward off criticism against them" (p. 277). In other words, adopting pluralist criteria for democracy in terms of popular access would guarantee continued elite domination, as well as class hegemony. Suleiman's solution to the democratic demand for reform is an administrative one: "restrict the leaves of absence that entrants into these [elite] institutions are permitted to take" (p. 278). This proposal is a recognition of elite power and an accommodation to it. The distinctive fact about the elite structure in France is that members of the grands corps can leave any particular position without losing their membership in the grands corps. In effect, they constitute a freely circulating elite, which has come to "monopolize the function of elite certification and legitimation."

Suleiman offers both a managerial and an apparently class explanation for the centralization of both public and private institutions. The class explanation does not reject the empirical observation but argues that "rationality and efficiency are . . . subordinated to and defined by what serves the interests of the capitalist class" (1978, p. 269). Suleiman does not really take a stand on this explanation, reiterating that, regardless of how it is explained, members of the grands corps are dominant in both public and private sectors. Suleiman accepts, almost casually, the source of elite unity in their "common class origins," but "class" in this context refers to the interests created by an institutional location. Class interests in this sense are no different from the corporate interests of the grands corps; they are generic terms that cover any economic category: big business, farmers, shopkeepers, workers.

Suleiman rejects the class perspective as represented in the work of Nicos Poulantzas, which argues, in Suleiman's view, that "the distinction between the owners of production and the managers is meaningless [because of the common] class interests that are shared by the holders of power" (Suleiman 1978, p. 241). Suleiman does not directly deal with the issue of who benefits from the actions of state elites but poses another question instead: the extent to which "business and the state . . . share overlapping interests and . . . are independent of one another" (p. 241). "Business" and the "state" in this view have either "overlapping" or "independent" interests. Posing the alternatives in that way sets up *either* answer to support one or another position within the managerial world view, because in either interpretation "interests" derive from institutional locations that can be described and explained without analysis either of the open-ended choices made by individuals or of the grounding of those interests in the social relations between capital and labor.[15]

---

[15] Suleiman, in a footnote, also rejects the class language referring to the "production" of elites, arguing that elites are not produced on an industrial assembly line but are a craft trade, created in small numbers and "carefully trained, groomed and nurtured" (1978, p. 30).

Ultimately, Suleiman's explanation for the stability of a centralized system of recruitment of private and public elites in France, simply restates the fact of centralization. "The privileged position of the elite is closely tied to the centralization of the administrative and economic structure" (1978, p. 280). The problem of legitimacy is key. "What is essential, and what has been lacking in studies of governing elites, is an understanding of the elements on which the elite bases and in turn justifies its dominant position [especially when faced with the reality] of powerful democratic norms" (p. 126). He separates strategies of domination from the issue of whether or not the elite is accepted by non-elites as their appropriate rulers (p. 129). Here Suleiman draws upon Ralf Dahrendorf as well as Mosca and Pareto to support the importance of legitimacy: "The loss of confidence, followed by the society's withdrawal of support, leads to internal conflicts within the elite and so accelerates its demise" (p. 131).

Suleiman presents no evidence, however, that the French elite is in fact legitimate. He argues that its self-confidence, superiority, hierarchy, and authority are "essential factors accounting for the elite's survival," but that is a theoretical assertion stemming from the managerial world view, not an empirically grounded generalization. He assumes that, because of the institutionalized power of the elite, it must be legitimate. He says, for example, that a concern is to "understand how an ostensibly specialized elite is able to embrace, and to insist upon its acquisition of generalized skills, and *thus* to legitimize its diverse roles in the society" (1978, p. 158). We italicize "thus" to emphasize the theoretical leap he is making.

Suleiman recognizes that an elite monopoly in France "sets the conditions that determine the recognition of the elite," namely, the criteria of "efficiency and merit" that allegedly are the bases of recruitment, training, and placement of elite members. But he assumes, without giving any evidence, that "the severe competitiveness that entry into the elite involves serves to a very large extent to legitimize the elite for the society as a whole" (1978, p. 279). This argument derives from the managerial assumption that "the criterion of merit . . . has achieved a certain sanctity in all industrial societies" (p. 279). Rationality legitimizes power in industrial societies.

Suleiman also argues that "former civil servants provide the business community with an aura of legitimacy" (1978, p. 243) and that "organized elites have been able to survive and extend their positions in large part because of the legitimacy they acquire" (p. 241). Although this is a key conclusion of his whole argument, he gives no direct evidence of either the legitimacy of the elite or its consequences. It remains a theoretical assumption about the inevitable centralization of power in industrialized societies and the incapacity of counter-elites (such as Left parties) to challenge that power. The institutionalized power and stability of elites *cause* their legitimacy, not vice versa.

Conclusions

The capitalist aspect of the state is subordinate to the bureaucratic aspect in the managerial perspective, but both are best analyzed as if they were institutional arrangements commanded by elites. Whether administrative, political, or economic elites are most powerful varies from society to society, depending on the historical outcome of conflicts between them.

11

The managerial perspective on the democratic state

In the managerial view of democracy, state elites must manage political demands from below. Military and police control is the ultimate foundation of elite domination over potentially unruly populations. Democracy – if defined as an instrument of popular participation – is sometimes a fiction, a legitimation of elite control, sometimes a recipe for political disorder. An organized and limited elite competition, seeking mass support not out of solidary values but from more mundane motives of career and power, is the best approximation of democracy that can be hoped for in industrial societies. Even so, the democratic institutions of legislatures, parties, and elections are increasingly impotent in the face of powerful elite alliances.[1]

The managerial view of democracy

The classic statement on democracy is that by the economist Joseph Schumpeter (1943). For Schumpeter, democracy is not a process of popular participation and representation; rather, it is an institutional method for selecting leaders. It is not an *outcome* (representation of popular will) but a *structure* (elite competition). Competition between elites offering themselves for electoral choice is the only realistic kind of democracy possible for large-scale industrialized societies, whether capitalist or socialist. Democracy is a property of any unit – organization, community, society – in which elites compete for office.

Schumpeter, unlike some pluralists, does not see socialism as incompatible with democracy, partly because he defines socialism as a takeover of the giant business corporations by the state, as does Raymond Aron

---

[1] For a good summary of the literature within an explicitly managerial elite perspective on democracy, see Dye and Ziegler 1971. The authors cite C. Wright Mills and John Kenneth Galbraith favorably as representing an elite theory and say that the main goal of the book is to challenge the "prevailing pluralistic ideology" (p. vii).

(see Chapter 10). The same principle of operation – the bureaucratic criterion of efficiency – remains intact. No shift of class power, no working-class control of the workplace, no societal direction over technological change is entailed by socialism. Rather, bureaucratic control is extended even farther than it is in the era of monopoly capitalism. The socialist state is the ultimate bureaucratic power. It is thus not surprising that Schumpeter did not see elite competition as endangered by this kind of socialism.

Ralf Dahrendorf's view of the democratic aspect of the state (1959) is similar. He emphasizes that authority relations within the state are highly skewed. Most ordinary citizens have virtually no power. "In modern democracies the presumption of legitimacy has been converted into a continuous process of legitimation through regular elections and in some cases plebiscites." There is a clear division between ordinary citizens who possess only the right to vote and the elites who "are in the position to exercise regularly control over the life chances of others by issuing authoritative decisions... The citizens of a democratic state are not a suppressed class, but they are a subjected class" (p. 293). In democratic societies, "the conditions of organization are present for most subjected groups.... In fact there are organizations – political parties – representing the interests of the opposing quasi-groups" (p. 308). *Organization* is the potential instrument of democratic representation, not voting, public opinion, or even protest.

Dahrendorf emphasizes the continuity of rule when the administrative staff of the state survives the turnover of political regimes vulnerable to elections, particularly when political changes do not affect the "rules of the game agreed upon by both parties" (1959, p. 308; see discussion of Suleiman in Chapter 10, herein). Distortions of democracy do occur, but mainly in connection with the violations of stable rule by a governing elite. Such distortions occur when (1) there is an absence of *any* governing elite, (2) there is an absence of true elite competition (that is, a substantial minority party never wins), and (3) the public believes that elite competition has no consequences for their interests (that is, political conflict only leads to alternations in power between different elites).

The democratic state mainly regulates conflict. "The institutions of the democratic state reflect very nearly the model of effective conflict regulation; conflicting parties and interests are institutionally recognized; parliamentary bodies furnish the setting of regular conciliation between the parties; the rules of the game, including a constitution as well as statutory procedural arrangements, enable decisions to be made ... certain personages... may act as mediators ... the legal system [arbitrates] unsolved disputes" (Dahrendorf 1959, p. 308). The functions of democratic institutions to provide participation and benefits are thus secondary to their functions to maintain stable elite control over both state and society.[2]

The democratic aspect of the state is also secondary for Daniel Bell, who in *The Coming of Post-Industrial Society* never discusses democracy in a theoretical context. This is surprising, for one who writes that "the relationship between the social structure and the political order . . . becomes one of the chief problems of power in a post-industrial society" and "the axial principle of the modern polity is *participation*, sometimes mobilized or controlled, sometimes demanded from below." The conditions and consequences of participation are mentioned only in a context in which participation is seen as something that must be controlled and limited (1973, pp. 316, 366, 453, 469).

Bell cites several persons who believe that the bureaucratic aspect of the state will supplant and undermine its democratic aspect. One says that " 'real power' has shifted out of the hands of the elected representatives to the technical experts . . . now 'begins a new type of government, neither democracy nor bureaucracy, but a technocracy.' " Another says that technocracy is "undermining . . . the normal political framework of democracy." Bell does not take a clear position, perhaps because he does not want to face the implications for democracy, but he agrees that "in the society of the future . . . the scientist, the professional . . . and the technocrat will play a predominant role in the political life of the society" (1973, pp. 78–9). By implication, the democratic aspect will become secondary.

Bell's true opinion of democracy emerges when he discusses events of the 1960s in the United States. Criticizing the participatory concept of democracy, he says that

one may applaud the fact that the nature of the mass media increases the likelihood of a spectacular rise in "participatory democracy" but these instances are also more likely to arise out of emotional issues (drawing therefore from the extremes) so that the loss of insulating space may itself permit the setting off of chain reactions which may be disruptive of civil politics and reasoned debate. [1973, p. 316]

---

[2] Randall Collins presents a similar view of the democratic aspect of the state. He defines democracy as a collegial structure of authority, in which an assembly of equals meets to make decisions on state policies. He is critical of the view of democracy that emphasizes mass participation and says that his own view is an expansion of Max Weber's "organizational theory of centralization and decentralization." Collins also criticizes existing definitions of democracy for stressing mass participation without dealing with the "crucial difference in what kind of structure of power – autocratic or shared – there is to participate in" (1975, p. 394).

The event that triggered this almost apocalyptic comment was the civil rights march on Washington in 1963. For Bell, democracy must be confined to institutionalized channels of expressions of opinion to elites.

Bell analyzes the "participation revolution" in the 1960s as a reaction to the "professionalization" of society and the "emergent technocratic decision-making of a post-industrial society" in the universities, factories, and neighborhoods (1973, p. 366). But he argues that participatory democracy is not a panacea because the issue remains open of which majority shall rule, through what kinds of governmental forms, and for what kinds of decisions. He asserts somewhat despairingly that his vision of a "rational organization of society stands confounded" because of the challenge of democratic politics: "the cantankerousness of politics, the politics of interest and the politics of passion." What pluralists acclaim as the hallmark of democratic politics, Bell describes as its messiness. The endless bargaining and negotiation between interests moving in and out of the political arena Bell regards as a problem that the "adherents of rationality – in particular the planners and designers – " must face. Confronting democratic politics, rational planners must "rethink their premises and . . . understand their limits" (p. 366).

Bell stresses the contradiction between the democratic and the bureaucratic state. Sometimes he argues for the coming supremacy of technical criteria in planning the bureaucratic state, in the face of imperatives of foreign policy and economic productivity. Later, he retreats from his vision of a rational state. Postindustrial society requires "increasing amounts of coordination," but the costs of coordination have increased because of the "expansion of the political arena and the involvement of a greater number of persons" (1973, p. 469). Also, "the very increase in participation leads to the multiplication of groups that 'check' each other, and thus to the sense of impasse. Thus, increased participation paradoxically leads, more often than not, to increased frustration" (p. 469). Bell thus also perceives a contradiction within the democratic aspect of the state. Participation reduces the possibility of effective decision making and therefore reduces the impact of participation. Multiple group demands create stalemate.

These agonizing dilemmas are not apparent in Eric Nordlinger's more recent book on the autonomy of the democratic state (1981). Nordlinger minimizes the societal constraints upon the democratic state, whether seen as popular preferences or as class power, and substitutes a "state-centered" model. He places himself in the "realist" tradition of democracy, classically defined by Schumpeter, with elitist forebears in Mosca, Michels, and Pareto. Nordlinger argues that most of the empirical research since 1950 has confirmed the impotence of the mass electorate, the oligarchical character of most organizations, and the shift of state power from the legislature to the bureaucracy (pp. 208–9). Nordlinger's democratic state has "rules, procedures, and prescriptions that guarantee and provide for open, fair and regular elections, and the (minimally curtailed) freedoms of expression and organization upon which they depend" (p. 39). The state can be regarded as a single, homogeneous entity with goals and the power to make decisions.[3]

Nordlinger has begged some fundamental questions in the definition of his unit of analysis. His version of both class and pluralist perspectives redefines them in the managerial language of coercive domination and legitimate authority. He says that "in accounting for political stability, Marxism assigns far greater weight to the coercive domination of the subordinate class by both the state and the bourgeoisie, while liberal theory accords more importance to the legitimacy of state authority" (1981, p. 47). Nordlinger thus draws upon the competing theoretical traditions only to help him elaborate his core typology of different forms of state autonomy. He asserts that "the democratic state is frequently autonomous in translating its own preferences into authoritative actions, and markedly autonomous in doing so even when they diverge from those held by the politically weightiest groups in civil society" (p. 203). Because he rejects both pluralist and class interpretations of the state as being too "society-centered" (p. 42), it is not at all clear in what sense – except a managerial one – the state is democratic.[4]

Strategies of elite domination: the societal level

Authors within the managerial perspective also challenge the pluralist view of democratization as a smooth and uniform evolution of a national political culture. Rather, the major forms of political participation that Westerners

> now complacently refer to as "modern" are for the most part unintended outcomes of the efforts of European state-makers to build their armies, keep taxes coming in, form effective coalitions against their rivals, hold their nominal subordinates and allies in line, and fend off the threat of rebellion on the part of ordinary people. [Tilly, ed., 1975, p. 633]

---

[3] Nordlinger explicitly derives his view of the state from Weber, saying that "a Weberian type definition allows the state's relatively clear-cut empirical identification and delimitation. Moreover, it neither denies nor prevents consideration of those instances in which the state-society distinction is blurred" (1981, p. 12).

[4] Nordlinger rejects the views of "pluralists" Truman and Dahl, "neopluralists" McConnell and Lowi, and "Marxists" Miliband and Poulantzas, as well as those of the "social corporatists" Rokkan and Schmitter because they all accept some variant of the assumption that one looks to "civil society in order to understand what the state does and why it does so" (Nordlinger 1981, p. 44).

The authors in the volume edited by Tilly (1975) view the extension of rights of political participation, whether to nobles, bourgeois, or workers, as determined by their control over resources – capital, taxes, or military manpower – necessary for state power, the capacity of the state to repress demands for participation, and the concessions required to legitimate the tax burden on the population. As Finer points out, in an implicit critique of the pluralist interpretation of political culture:

Beliefs could inspire populations to sacrifices hitherto undreamt of. Hence, it could, and indeed it did become, an object of policy on the part of rulers to substitute beliefs for coercion, and benefits in return for sacrifices, in order to extract the vast resources needed. This helped forward the extension of citizenship and welfare services in the nineteenth and twentieth centuries. [Finer 1975, pp. 96–7]

The democracy of taxation was also the democracy of death through mass conscription. As Goldscheid, one of the first fiscal sociologists, said: "The 'just' tax and the 'just' war have the same social and rational roots" (cited in Braun 1975, p. 315). This analogy is typical of the tough-minded assessment of democracy in the managerial perspective.

The success with which state elites managed crises that occurred at critical junctures in each nation's history determined whether the society acquired and kept a democratic state according to the late Norwegian sociologist and political scientist Stein Rokkan. Rokkan divides European history into four periods, each characterized by a critical elite choice (Rokkan et al. 1970). During the sixteenth- and seventeenth-century Reformation, the central political issue revolved around national as opposed to supranational religion. The central cleavage was between a national center and religiously, culturally, and linguistically distinct peripheral territories. The second juncture occurred in the wake of the 1789 French Revolution, which secularized and democratized the state. The central cleavage in this period was between state and church. Political issues revolved around secular versus religious control over mass education. The third juncture was the Industrial Revolution in the nineteenth century, which brought people from the country to urban centers to work in factories. The central cleavage was between the landed agricultural classes and rising urban industrial classes. The central political issue revolved around agricultural tariffs and the extent of entrepreneurial freedom. The fourth historical juncture was the 1917 Russian Revolution. The central cleavage was between owner and worker, and political issues revolved around the integration of the working class into the national political system versus its commitment to an international revolutionary movement (Rokkan et al. 1970, pp. 130–1). Each cleavage created political dilemmas that emerging elites had to manage. Their degree of success determined the fate of democracy.

Depending on the success of the strategies of nation-building elites at each juncture, the party structures that subsequently emerged took on a different form. Rokkan argues that the three early cleavages (center–periphery, state–church, land–industry) were different in a crucial respect from the later owner–worker one. The first three "generated national developments in *divergent* directions," whereas the last cleavage "tended to bring the party systems" closer to each other in their basic structure (Rokkan et al. 1970, p. 113; italics in original). Working-class parties emerged in every country, whereas territorial, religious, and agrarian parties did not.[5]

Democracy thus meant the existence of competing elites, operating through political parties with different social, cultural, and territorial bases. Rokkan argues that center–periphery and state–church cleavages tended to be expressed as territorially based oppositions provoked by the growth of the state. "The growing nation-state developed a wide range of agencies of unification and standardization and gradually penetrated the bastions of "primordial" local culture. So did the organizations of the Church, sometimes in close cooperation with the secular administrators, often in opposition to and in competition with the officers of the state" (Rokkan et al. 1970, p. 101).

The conflicts based on land–industry and owner–worker cleavages could find political expression only "after some initial consolidation of the national territory" (Rokkan et al. 1970, p. 101). Because of the territorial location of cultural, religious, and linguistic groupings, conflicts with the state sometimes redefined the boundaries of the nation through civil war, secession, and mass migration (for example, in Norway, the Hapsburg empire, Ireland). The national revolution involved conflicts over cultural values between central elites and peripheral cultures. The elite solution to conflicts based on these cultural values established the legal framework of a state within which later economic conflicts between owners and workers became politicized as still another basis for party competition. Rokkan argues that the critical differences among national party systems emerged before mass suffrage and the electoral incorporation of the working class had been achieved (p. 113).

Where territorial and cultural conflicts were not "solved through secession or boundary change" but were contained within a unitary state, they frequently found expression in national partisan splits. Rokkan argued that regionally based political parties were most likely to emerge where a distinctive culture was concentrated in a regional territory that

---

[5] "Class" is here used in the Weberian sense of a material interest that forms one possible basis for political action. Owner-worker conflicts are not fundamental, as in the class perspective, but are only one of several bases of economic and political conflict.

had few economic or political links with the center (Rokkan et al. 1970, p. 121). Further, where religious and class conflicts reinforced these territorial cleavages, parties were more likely to express them. (See also Alford 1963.) In Britain, for example, the central culture was reinforced by a broad network of landed families, whereas in Scandinavia the central culture was maintained by "an essentially urban elite of officials and patricians" (Rokkan et al. 1970, p. 120). The historical consequence was that in the Nordic countries the conflict between urban and rural cultures was reinforced by conflict between urban and rural economic interests. In Britain, on the other hand, the dominant economic cleavage cross-cut the cultural cleavage, which both made the political "merger of urban and rural interests" easier and prevented the emergence of distinctive peripheral political parties in Wales and Scotland.

The failure of these territorial, religious, and linguistic cleavages to become politically expressed in Switzerland was due to their noncongruence with class conflicts, according to Rokkan. Within each territory in Switzerland, "the upper and lower strata . . . spoke the same language" (Rokkan et al. 1970, p. 125). In Belgium, on the other hand, the dominant urban industrial classes spoke an international elite language (French), whereas the rural peasantry spoke an internationally marginal language (Flemish). Thus, where culturally distinct groups were concentrated in a particular territory that had few political or economic links with the state, the efforts by central elites to create a national political culture met resistance from peripheral elites. Rokkan's argument is that a political culture becomes salient when elites select a cultural cleavage as a potential basis on which to mobilize support.

Although the cultural conflicts of center–periphery were historically the most resistant to change, especially when reinforced by urban–rural interest conflicts, Rokkan argued that owner–worker conflict was the most debilitating for democracy. The addition of class conflict to interest and value conflicts made the emergence and stability of democracy extremely problematic. Political elites managed the rise of working-class movements and parties with success depending on two main factors: First, if a national political culture was successfully created, class conflict did not become value-laden. It became an interest conflict susceptible to compromise. Second, whether or not parties backed by workers were politically repressed or were incorporated into a ruling elite also affected the impact of the owner–worker cleavage on the stability of democracy.

In countries where no national political culture had been created, the impact of the Russian Revolution on workers was greater (Rokkan et al. 1970, pp. 135–7). France, Italy, Spain, Finland, and Iceland developed strong left-wing working-class parties, whereas Denmark and Sweden did not (pp. 131–6). Rokkan suggests that in Catholic countries where intense conflicts between church and state occurred during the initial development of mass education and political mobilization and in Protestant countries where cultural standardization was most problematic, nonunified working-class movements with strong left-wing components were likely to develop.

Where repression of trade unions and parties supported by workers was intense (Germany, Austria, France, Italy, and Spain), the working class continued to be ideological and more susceptible to the influence of the Russian Revolution (Rokkan et al. 1970, p. 110). Party elites excluded from the state used the working class as a political base. But if a class-based elite was incorporated in a governing regime, the ideological bases of class conflict were undercut and domesticated labor parties developed (p. 110).

Rokkan thus differs with Almond and Verba's explanation (1963) of the cause of the instability of democracy in Italy and Germany and its stability in Britain and the United States. Rokkan explains democratic stability by the historical strategies of elites rather than by aggregated individual political orientations. This analysis is also an implicit critique of an emphasis upon the relations of production and class struggle in the economy and the state. Class ideology in the managerial perspective flows not from class conflict per se but from the political strategies of elites who base themselves upon working-class movements.[6]

Rokkan does not assume that popular mobilization would create an identification with the national political system. In fact, Rokkan argues that the political mobilization of peripheral territories, especially those coinciding with distinctive linguistic and religious groups, frequently occurred in opposition to the "agencies of unification and standardization" developed by the elites controlling the central state apparatus (Rokkan et al. 1970, pp. 98, 101). A national politics arises out of central state domination. Once culturally distinct territories were administra-

---

[6] Political scientist Giovanni Sartori has argued that the strategies of party elites actually create the symbols and identities of various groups, even including social class. According to Sartori, "it is not the 'objective' class (class condition) that creates the party, but the party that creates the 'subjective' class (class consciousness). . . . The party is not a 'consequence' of the class. Rather, and before, it is the class that receives its identity from the party" (1969, p. 84). The ideology of class, he says, takes hold only when there is a "firm organizational basis," when the elites of party or trade union can engage in "ideological persuasion" via a "powerfully organized network of communications." The political significance of beliefs in the importance of religious and class issues depends on the "relative strength of the *organizational support* of each belief system" (p. 87; italics in original). Sartori argues that one must not assume that a party system is a "response to a given socio-economic environment." Rather, various potential bases of social and political cleavages are "picked up as a resource by elite decision, and thereby come to reflect the channeling imprint of a structured party system" (p. 93). The causal imagery is the reverse of both pluralist and class arguments.

tively penetrated by the central state and economically penetrated by "networks of traders and merchants, of bankers and financiers, of artisans and industrial entrepreneurs" (p. 101), territorial political identities would quickly erode. Thus, territorial political movements would emerge if there were no "economic dependence" on the "political metropolis" (pp. 107, 99).

Rokkan views secret elections as a mechanism of state legitimation, the outcome of a struggle between organized groups for power and the state for authority. For the central elites, elections represented a mechanism both to control their political environment and to routinize the replacement of one political elite by another.

> The counting of votes was the administrative alternative to conflict and intrigue: the organization of electoral statistics was a direct product of the efforts to routinize the resolution of conflict within the body politic through the holding of regular elections under the control of formally neutral bodies of officials. To achieve legitimacy, the decisions of the electorate had to be documented and made available for scrutiny from all sides; the organization of regular electoral bookkeeping was a response to the widespread questioning of the electoral verdicts. [Rokkan et al. 1970, p. 170]

Electoral contest was thus an alternative to violent internal political conflict.

Even the secret ballot, formally introduced by the French law establishing the first legislative assembly in 1791, was at least in part a means to reduce the power of political organizations over working-class voters. The secret ballot made both bribery and social pressure less efficacious in determining how the individual voter would vote (Rokkan et al. 1970, pp. 153–4). On the one hand, the secret ballot channeled political participation into a routine ritual of selecting between alternative sets of political elites. On the other hand, it increased the political power of the central elites controlling the state, as opposed to counter-elites trying to mobilize the masses.[7]

Elite manipulation: the organizational level

The whole array of democratic institutions – elections, political parties, legislatures, forms of participation – is also seen in the managerial perspective as either symbolic (providing the forms of democracy without

---

[7] Historian Edward Jenks offers another managerial interpretation of the historical meaning of "representation" in his classic *State and the Nation* (1919). He criticizes the pluralist view that ordinary people wanted political representation, arguing that "the earliest political representatives were not agents, or delegates charged with asserting the claims of their constituents, but hostages, held to ransom for the satisfaction of claims put forward by the authority with the strong hand." The earliest political constituencies were quite unwilling to accept the honor of being represented (p. 185).

its content) or controlling (blunting mechanisms of participation that might otherwise lead to changes elites want to avoid). A classic statement is Murray Edelman's *Symbolic Uses of Politics* (1964). Edelman argues that in formally democratic states political quiescence must be induced in the masses of voters, and a main mechanism is symbolic reassurance that "something is being done." He offers several provocative hypotheses, illustrating them with many examples from regulatory legislation, administrative agencies, and a variety of other state policies. He asserts, for example, that "the most intensive dissemination of symbols commonly attends the enactment of legislation which is most meaningless in its effect upon resource allocation" (p. 26). One cannot tell from the name of legislation (Fair Housing, Clean Water, Full Employment Act) whose interests are affected and how. His hypothesis suggests that the impact will be the opposite of that advertised.

Edelman argues that formally democratic institutions preserve stability and order rather than respond to public opinion or class action. Elections, in other words, have very little to do with policy formation. "[T]he factors that explain voting behavior can be quite different from the factors that explain resource allocation through government" (Edelman 1964, p. 43). Edelman's hypothesis would be seen as paradoxical for the pluralist perspective. "The fact that large numbers of people are objectively affected by a governmental program may actually serve in some contexts to weaken their capacity to exert a political claim upon tangible values" (p. 43). The more people are affected by a policy, the more *unable* they are to act collectively. This accounts for the seemingly contradictory and "irrational" character of bureaucratic and legislative action and statements. The symbolism of an action contradicts its substance. In his words, "it is not uncommon to give the rhetoric to one side and the decision to the other" (p. 39).

A study of health-care planning in New York City comes to the same conclusion (Alford 1975a). The machinery of citizen participation through various forms – advisory boards, community action committees, task forces, and neighborhood elections – generated a lot of meetings and activity but very little power, in the sense of the capacity to control resources and outcomes. Consumer groups became absorbed in the process of negotiation, of gaining representation, of fighting among themselves for participatory crumbs from the head table. The political energies of activists were burned up in the process, with few tangible benefits for the community population.[8]

---

[8] For a summary of the literature on "participation without power," see Alford and Friedland 1975. See also Friedland 1983. C. Wright Mills's view of the "middle levels of power" as being impotent makes the same point (1956). Voluntary associations, political parties, even Congress, are increasingly powerless in the face of elite capacity to rule. In Mills's bleak view, there are fewer and fewer viable bases for political participation because most organizations to which ordinary people have access are losing power.

In the managerial perspective, the bureaucratization of democracy thus extends to such organizations as legislatures and parties.[9] The image of democracy is similar to stockholder control of a corporation. Andrew Shonfield redefines the meaning of democratic participation in these terms, saying that democracy has depended on a

limited suspension of judgment by the electors, on a willingness to clothe people with power and then give them a period of time for action, before reporting back to those from whom they derived their mandate. The principle has been further extended in postwar national planning; the plans formally recognize that decisions once made cannot be quickly unraveled. In the short or medium term they are irrevocable. [1965, p. 410]

A responsible board of directors is elected by the legitimate participants (the citizens or stockholders) to make decisions in the interest of the company. Participants have only periodic rights to review the consequences of the policies of management, in an election or an annual meeting (Herman 1981). If such a state is democratic, so are the largest multinational corporations.

Shonfield also proposes, as a solution to the problem of democracy, the "small specialist committee" of the legislatures, which can develop "a considerable degree of expertise, . . . supported by professional staff of its own sufficiently knowledgeable to talk to the professional civil servants on equal terms" (1965, p. 388). In other words, the legislature itself must be bureaucratized in order to deal with other agencies. Shonfield regards this as a new type of "political equilibrium," with one sector of the bureaucratic state offsetting the others. The increasing complexity of decision making requires long-range rational planning, which cannot be carried out by older forms of democratic institutions.[10]

Another functional perspective on representative institutions is offered by Ginsberg, who argues that "electoral outcomes have tended to reflect rather than affect the distribution of power in American society. Rather than provide those without power with a means to its acquisition,

---

[9] Robert Michels's study of the German Social Democratic Party (1962) is the classic analysis of bureaucratization of presumably democratic organizations.

[10] *Bureaucratic Democracy* by political scientist Douglas Yates (1982) consists essentially of advice for a would-be "bureaucratic controller" (p. 178). In effect, Yates is an advisor to an elite strategist seeking to manage the state and to use both competition and conflict to centralize policy making. Yates's view of bureaucracy is explicitly *not* of a "neutral, hierarchical machine." Bureaucracies must build in conflict. In this way their internal rules can be made compatible with his managerial concept of democracy. The new administrative role he envisages is significant: the "public manager" concerned with "how to improve the bureaucracy in terms of both democracy and efficiency" (p. 183). The key point is that managerial elites are now in charge of democracy, of defining its limits, and of deciding how and in what ways they respond to the preferences of the "man on the street." This is a democracy gutted of genuine participation and content, in sharp conflict with both the pluralist premise of open access by groups freely acting on their policy preferences and the class vision of struggle between fundamentally incompatible interests.

elections have more often allowed those with power in society to acquire political authority" (1982, p. 158).

Ginsberg explicitly distinguishes his concern with electoral institutions from pluralist studies of voters' choices (1982, p. vii). In his preface he says that "elections are among the principal mechanisms through which contemporary governments regulate mass political action and maintain their own power and authority. . . . the chief consequence of consent is the modern liberal state itself" (p. viii). Ginsberg turns the pluralist argument on its head. Rather than elections choosing governments, governments regulate mass action via voting. Representative institutions are an alternative to other methods of social control by elites. "Where at some critical historical juncture rulers lacked a preponderance of force, they tended to become much more concerned with acquisition of voluntary compliance through participatory and representative mechanisms" (p. 246).

State growth reduces the impact of elections, undermining the democratic aspect. "Though democratic elections initially promise to eliminate the adversary relationship between rulers and ruled, growth of the state's powers can . . . erode the possibility of popular influence through the ballot box" (Ginsberg 1982, p. 26).

Three fundamental historical changes have "given the governmental process a considerable degree of insulation from electoral politics . . . the expansion of rule through law . . . the growth of administration . . . and the conversion of policymaking to an institutional process" (Ginsberg 1982, p. 205). Rules of law commit the "government to specified courses of action over time" (p. 206). Public administration "in many areas of policy has become, in effect, the permanent government, substantially independent of congressional and presidential control" (p. 209). And even congressional decision making has become institutionalized, in the sense that "organization and leadership [are] based on internal, institutional criteria rather than external, political criteria" (p. 212). Many if not most "domestic legislative areas are dominated by 'subgovernments' composed of a congressional subcommittee and its subject matter counterpart in the bureaucracy" (p. 212).

Ginsberg offers several empirical generalizations whose interpretation could be either managerial or pluralist. For instance, he finds a correlation between voting turnout in the American states and the degree to which voting is legally facilitated (easy registration, low residence requirements, the hours polls remain open, and eight other measures). Ginsberg concludes that "legal facilitation . . . appears to considerably lessen both the motivation and resources needed to vote" (1982, p. 36). The causal direction of the relationship is interpreted as if actions by the state affect individual participation in elections. A pluralist interpretation might be that political mobilization of the electorate changed the electoral laws.

Democratic elections, according to Ginsberg, allow the state to extract revenues because they are more legitimate. Lack of democratic elections forces the state to rely on force to extract tax revenues. This is a managerial perspective on the impact of elections in states with greater or lesser repressive capacities. Voting turnout is seen here not as an instrument for achieving governmental responsiveness but as a tool for extracting revenues from a population that believes governments are responsive *because* of elections.

Alternatively, one could interpret the data as showing that democratic participation reduces the repressive capacities of the state and generates programs responsive to popular demands. Either interpretation is consistent with the data. Ginsberg chooses the first because he is constructing a case for the social control functions of elections.

Collective action: the individual level

The political explanation of democratic action stresses the inability of elites to successfully control mass action and the constant possibility of disruptive actions, often in reaction to state repression. Collective violence varies with the strength of the repressive capacity of the bureaucratic state and is not seen as either deviant behavior or potential revolutionary action. An important study of such collective actions is that by Tilly, Tilly, and Tilly (1975), which compares Italy, Germany, and France for selected periods in the nineteenth and twentieth centuries. The Tillys attempted to select "unbiased samples of all violent events – events in which more than some minimum number of persons took part in seizing or damaging persons or property" (p. 15). Collective violence is thus a set of actions by individuals, but it is significant only insofar as it is a "formation" – a group acting together (p. 313). Group formations vary in that they become "bigger, more complicated, more bureaucratized," and more oriented toward the state. The most modern form they call "proactive" collective action (p. 53).

The authors examine the "political basis for collective violence" in the course of the lengthy process of creating state structures in Italy, France, and Germany. But they resist the "temptation to call any government or any great concentration of power a state." States are a particular type of organization that controls the principal means of coercion in a well-defined territory. They are relatively independent from other organizations and are both centralized and internally coordinated. The conflicts between contenders for power within such states, differing in degrees of centralization and capacity for repression, create the conditions under which individuals join together in collective actions.

The Tillys argue that collective violence is not fundamentally different from "normal" institutionalized politics. With this fundamental assumption they part company with the pluralists.[11] But, by linking collective violence to "ordinary political structure and routine political process," they also part company with the class perspective (Tilly et al. 1975, p. 24). Their emphasis on the "struggle for power" (p. 289), on the "power positions" of conflicting interests (p. 285), on the "contention for power and of its repression" as a main cause of collective violence analytically severs power from its roots in class relationships. Class *interests* and class *conflict* remain important, in the Weberian sense of economic interests, but are not seen as deriving from class relations generating systemic contradictions that cannot be reduced to their organized expression.[12]

The Tillys' independent variable is the centralization of the state coupled with the possibility of the development of organizations making political demands. In France, the "centralization of politics [occurred] through the growth of a massive and powerful state apparatus" (Tilly et al. 1975, p. 45). This took place partly as a consequence, partly as a cause, of the particular form industrialization and urbanization took in France. Political conflict, as a result, "increasingly took the form of contention or coalition among formal organizations specialized in the pursuit of particular interests" (p. 44). The Tillys argue that this change is directly related to the character of collective violence, because "the groups . . . consist of populations perceiving and pursuing a common set of interests. And collective action on any considerable scale requires coordination, communication and solidarity extending beyond the moment of action itself" (p. 46). This theorization of politics as organized

[11] The Tillys reject Smelser's pluralist perspective on collective behavior. Action is taken not by "rootless" individuals but by the "mobilization . . . of masses around beliefs and programs which reject the beliefs and programs prevailing around them" (Tilly et al. 1975, p. 251).

[12] The Tillys argue that their "chief theoretical choices" are the same as those made by Marx. They stress that popular action "from below" is analogous to class struggle. But when they interpret Marx as emphasizing "industrialization as the shaper of organizational forms and hence of the forms of collective action" they are substituting managerial concepts. They generalize Marx's class perspective to a broader political argument when they say that "only Marx propounded an analysis of collective action in which the making of claims by solidarity groups organized around articulated interests played the central part" (Tilly et al. 1975, pp. 272–3). That is true but slightly misleading, because it diverts attention from the source of those interests in specifically *class* relations. The centralization of the state is empirically recognized by Marx but is not a theoretical category as it is for the Tillys.

conflict also differentiates their view from the home domain of both the pluralist and the class perspectives.[13]

Their concern is to trace the impact on patterns of collective violence as the French state became more centralized and as forms of political organization changed. The character of collective violence changed from "reactive" (food riots, machine breaking, resistance to conscription) to "proactive" (most demonstrations and strikes). The latter are "deliberate attempts to seize control of the state" (Tilly et al. 1975, pp. 50–1).

Empirically, the Tillys discover that "major bursts of violent conflict accompanied the largest realignments of the French political system" (1975, p. 56). Their argument is not that changes in the state cause collective violence but that they depended on each other. They reject explanations based on the "timing of population movements, changes in the organization of work, or the introduction of technological innovations." Rather, the "rhythm of collective violence . . . depended very much on shifts in the struggle for political power" (p. 61).[14]

Their concern is not with concrete political situations and the effect that violence (threatened or actual) has on a specific outcome. Historical events are the context within which acts of collective violence occur. Events are the units of enumeration, a basis for classification of time periods, but not the analytic units. Although the book is full of references to such concrete historical events as the February Revolution, the June Days, Louis Napoleon's 1851 coup, and hundreds of others, these events have no theoretical status, except as markers for the beginning and the end of periods of collective violence (Tilly et al. 1975, p. 55), as examples of one or another type of collective action, or as a manifestation of the centralization of the state.

---

[13] The Tillys deny derivation from Weber, citing his different theory of the routinization of charisma. They link Weber to Durkheim as viewing collective action as "innovative movements oriented to deviant definitions of reality, as irrational responses" (Tilly et al. 1975, p. 273). This minimizes Weber's analyses of class-oriented rational action, of party and political leadership, and of bureaucracy and status groups as sources of political action. Conversely, their own position, supposedly derived from Marx, seems to us more compatible with the heritage of Weber: "the social base, the organizational form, the prior claims and grievances, the present mobilization of the ordinary actors in political conflicts provide a major part of the explanation of their actions" (p. 274).

[14] Despite their concern to link "normal politics" to collective violence, the Tillys make some puzzling distinctions. They argue that the "usual strike is far too orderly to be a good representative of protest or violence and too marginal to politics to represent struggles for power accurately" (Tilly et al. 1975, p. 10). If their concern is to marshal evidence of struggles for power by organized contenders, then surely strikes, even totally peaceful ones, are part of the repertoire of tactics that are used by unions and political parties either to build their political base or to attempt to disrupt the political base of other interests. Yet the Tillys later compare the trends in strikes with those in collective violence, as parallel manifestations of "power" and "organization" variables (p. 71).

Their empirical analysis focuses upon "power" and "organizational" variables as explanations of both strikes and collective violence in France. Organizations (the "mobilizers of collective action") determined the "shape of the typical event." A "complex political process" determined the frequency of events. For both strikes and collective violence, "complex organizations... capable of mobilizing people for protest but also fairly effective in demobilizing them once the issue was decided... assumed a larger and larger role in the preparation of encounters between contenders and authorities" (Tilly et al. 1975, p. 71).

The Tillys correlate the time series for incidents of collective violence and strikes in France with various social trends, à la Durkheim's *Suicide* – price changes, suicides, criminal convictions – as well as with various "hardship" measures, such as food prices (Tilly et al. 1975, p. 81). They find relatively low correlations. Relationships with "power" and "organization" measures are higher: years in which the average days in jail were high, the national budget was being decided, national elections were being held, and cabinet changes were high. Violence is also associated with union membership. These are all regarded as indicators of the political or organizational state of affairs in a given year. The number of person days in French jails was assumed to reflect "changes in governmental repression more directly than changes in criminal activity" (p. 82). Their basic conclusion is that "power/organization" variables are more closely related to the number of violent incidents involving fifty or more persons, the number of participants, and the number of arrests than are "breakdown" or "hardship" variables.

In Italy, the nineteenth century showed a "dangerous dualism of popular participation and elite control." Each stage of state building involved "ordinary Italians in the national struggle," but then a small elite, in several successive cycles, "demobilized" those who had made victory possible. The cycle occurred several times because of three "recurrent features of the Italian political scene: centralized instruments of government; small and relatively coherent elites in control of those centralized instruments of government; exceptionally fragmented popular movements" (Tilly et al. 1975, p. 93). Popular participation is secondary in this analysis to elite strategies of control.

In the analysis of Germany, the Tillys use the metaphor of the "nationalization of relationships." As the autonomy of city life was reduced in the nineteenth century, "centers of power were shifting from local to national bases." If groups "wanted to retain control over their lives," they would have to "fashion national organizations to do so, not least of all, to influence the national state" (1975, p. 206).

Their logic of explanation stresses the centralization and "nationalization" of both society and the state, leading to the centralization of effective political organization as well.

The assumption embodied in these concepts and empirical procedures is that gross measures of the political and organizational conditions at the level of the national state are potentially significant causes of aggregated individual actions. Structural linkages through power and organization cause collective violence, not a breakdown of social control or individual deprivation. Deprivations and hardships can and do exist without political response.

The Tillys summarize the factors that account for the differences among the three countries as the "standard items of political analysis: the organization of contenders for power, the character of repression, the extent and form of political participation, rights in conflict" (1975, p. 259). With some caution, the Tillys argue that the presence of openly competitive elections reduces the payoffs of collective violence as a political strategy. "Even tightly controlled elections give some legitimacy to assembly, association and public discussion of the issues. To the extent that they are open contests, national elections give a peculiar advantage to interests organized in centralized associations." They agree with Michels that "the principle of organization is an absolutely essential condition for the political struggle of masses" (p. 276). Elections thus not only promote the "formation of durable political parties" but also "legitimized and promoted the growth of associations as vehicles for collective action" (pp. 276–7). The formal democratic apparatus of voting and elections is of secondary concern, both theoretically and empirically. They see democratic rights neither as deriving from a democratic political culture nor as part of "bourgeois" rights but as pragmatic and limited mechanisms of representation, safeguarded only by organizational capacity to compete and, if necessary, to make trouble for ruling elites.

Conclusions

In the managerial perspective, democratic states are political structures generated by conflict between organizations and elites who use available cultural identities and economic interests to create formal authority and legitimacy. The struggles between organizationally based elites located in states, churches, capitalist enterprises, and political parties had the consequence of mobilizing individual citizens, transforming social characteristics (religion, ethnicity, territory of birth) into political identities, and thereby shaping the political culture. The extent to which the social bases of political identities cross-cut or reinforced each other was determined by the strategies used by different elites at various critical junctures. Thus the role of voting, elections, political parties, and legislation is seen as a problematic outcome of elite strategies played out in interinstitutional conflict, rather than as a single evolutionary development.

The managerial perspective thus reinterprets the political role of democratic institutions in the state. The strategies of elites controlling organizational resources, some aiming to develop the central state and others to safeguard the territorial and functional organizations, determine whether a democratic state developed and how stable it would be. The commitment of mass publics or political leaders to democratic values is a secondary factor in creating and stabilizing democratic institutions. The struggles of the new working classes for political rights were seen as, at most, secondary factors. Even collective violence can be explained best by the opportunities created by varying forms of state organization.

PART III
The class perspective

12

State and society in class perspective

The "class" perspective might equally have been labeled the "Marxist" perspective because the relations of capitalist accumulation to class struggle have been largely defined by persons calling themselves Marxists. We choose the term "class" because it is a substantive word, like "pluralist" and "managerial," and refers to a core causal process and set of postulated relationships.

The class home domain

In the class perspective, individual actions and organizational interests must be understood via the societal contradictions inherent in the class relations comprising a mode of production. These contradictions must be specified if one is to understand the history of a society as a whole.[1] The internal laws of development of a mode of production provide the conditions under which certain types of organizations are likely to emerge and flourish whereas others never appear or die. Certain types of individual behavior – personalities, attitudes, and social roles – are similarly encouraged whereas others are not. The paradigmatic questions that identify the home domain are: How does class struggle affect the state and the nature of capitalist development? How is the contradiction between private appropriation and socialized production expressed in the state? How does it lead to crisis, revolution, and societal transformation?

The explanatory claims of the class perspective are relevant when certain societal conditions exist: (1) Individuals must sell their labor as a commodity to others who own the means of production; (2) the dominant economic organizations depend upon capital accumulation; and

[1] Our own approach is to retain the assumption of contradictory institutional logics but to drop the assumption that they are hierarchically ordered in a deterministic fashion, which actually incorporates elements of a managerial epistemology into a presumably dialectical method.

(3) the economy is dominated by privately controlled production for commodity markets. The classic works in the class perspective, back to Karl Marx, argue that these conditions penetrate both the organizational and the individual levels, although such theorists seldom analyze the linkages empirically. Like the pluralists, class analysts often assume that one can infer the operation of a system from its parts, although they differ on the level regarded as primary. For Marx the commodity relationship between capital and labor was the "cell" of a capitalist society, penetrating its every pore and creating conditions under which every capitalist organization and every individual worker and capitalist would have to sell or buy at a socially determined price. The class perspective does not predict whether or not a given capitalist will make the decisions that enable him to stay in business. The system as a whole selects out those capitalists with the capital, technology, and market timing to survive economic competition. Which individual capitalists or firms survive is irrelevant for the survival of the system. Similarly, which commodities survive the competition of the marketplace has nothing to do with the satisfaction of human needs.

The home domain of the class perspective is, at the societal level of analysis, focused on the conditions for accumulation and class struggle. Concern at other levels tends to be with organizational forms as segments or fractions of capital or as microcosms in which the class relation is revealed in the relationship of owner, worker, and machine. Capital also enjoys cultural hegemony over the definition of individual needs. Expressed preferences have no determinate relationship to objective interests and are seen as substitutes for or displacements of authentic human needs. Organizations and individuals act out the binary logic of the system – reproduction and transformation. The class perspective stresses the hegemony of the ruling class over the boundaries of the state and the definitions of the "political."

In the class world view, the state is fundamentally biased in its operations in favor of those who privately control the means of production. Such a system is neither natural nor inevitable but is a historical product of sometimes open, sometimes covert class struggle. In a capitalist society there is no public interest but only class interests. Social investments cannot be rationally planned because capitalism operates according to the logic of profitability, an increasingly irrational system for social production. The gap between what is produced and what could be produced grows ever wider.

The "normal" functioning of such a society is fraught with contradictions because social needs are unmet due to the logic of private profitability and because exploitation is the source of growth. Productivity increasingly expands in the midst of poverty. But class organization and mass education lay the basis for class-conscious political action. For the class perspective, neither the complexity of an industrial society nor the differentiation of a modern society can explain these developments. Class struggle and economic crisis are normal.

The capitalist whole is both constituted and torn apart by its contradictions: capital versus labor, socialized production versus private appropriation. Despite other differences, Marxists agree that superstructural institutions – including the state – can vary in many ways, but those variations are determined by the nonmarket requirements of capital accumulation. The forms in which capital and labor are organized affect the political mechanisms by which this reproduction takes place. The economic structure shapes both the political organizations of class conflict and what each class can win. This basic position leads to a characteristic silence within classic Marxism on both politics and the state, which are reduced to, at best, organizational and, at worst, purely situational phenomena, at the cost of ignoring much of the concrete history of capitalist societies.

The functional versus the political approach to the state

The contradiction postulated by the class perspective between accumulation and class struggle is linked to a major debate over functional versus political approaches to the state. In the functional (or structuralist) variant within the class world view, societal imperatives of production penetrate all institutions and levels of analysis. Althusser's argument (1970, p. 112) that individuals are bearers of class forces and that the state is structured by the political requisites of capitalism comes close to the extreme functionalist position.

Those Marxists concerned with retaining the classic distinction between base (the economy) and superstructure (the state and culture) tend to take a functional view of the state. Philosopher G. A. Cohen is concerned, for example, with the knotty problem of how to avoid defining production relations in terms of legal rights over property, which would seem to fuse base and superstructure irretrievably (1978, p. 218). He accomplishes the purification of the concept of production relations from the contaminating effects of the legal, moral, and political concept or property relations by distinguishing between "powers" (the effective capacity to do something) and "rights" (the legal, normative, moral, or legitimate – he uses these words interchangeably – claim to do something) (p. 220).

The example Cohen offers is that of the worker who must offer his labor on the market in order to survive. He does not have to offer his labor power to any particular capitalist, who therefore does not have the power (or the right either) to force the worker to work for him. Cohen cites Marx to the effect that "the proletarian is owned not by any given capitalist, but by the capitalist class as a whole." Thus the capitalist class as a whole has power over *every* worker but no rights over *any* worker. The power of capital is not manifest in any specific body of laws, no matter how detailed or how enforced, although a general system of laws defining property rights – that is, a capitalist state – may be necessary for the concrete implementation of this systemic power.

Cohen's distinction between a power and a right sees them both as *potential* capacities, not active powers or powers in use. Expressed as levels of power, the distinction might well be phrased in terms of a "capacity" (the systemic power of capital), a "right" (the structural power of firms), and a "use in action" (the situational power of businessmen). Here is the fundamental difference between the powers of capital and those of labor in the class perspective. Capital has systemic power; labor does not. Every person not possessing capital must offer his or her labor upon the labor market, or someone else who is willing and able to provide for that person must offer his or her own labor. Individual capitalists may lose their capital (their situational power to employ others or to enjoy the fruits of others' labor) and become laborers themselves, but capital as systemic power cannot "lose" in this sense.

The distinctive feature of the functional version of the class world view is that the assertion of the existence of the systemic power of capital is not regarded as simply a philosophic argument or a political stance or even a moral position that implies a condemnation of exploitation. Rather, the systemic power of capital constitutes the historically real environment of every organization in a capitalist society, as well as the context and even the content of individual behavior. Power is therefore observed in the reproduction of hegemonic social relations, that is, those that permeate every social institution and are unquestioned by most of the population. The efficacy of political participation and the structure of political authority are limited by the logic of a capitalist society.

In the class perspective, there can be no theory of the state per se, only a theory of the capitalist state. In a functional class approach, the state exists and is structured in particular ways because of the requirements of capitalism. Capitalism requires an independent state to absorb class conflict, prevent the politicization of production relations, and avert endemic tendencies to economic stagnation and crisis. As a result, the state absorbs the social and private costs of capitalist accumulation, leaving privately controlled profits untouched. These functional requirements delimit the creation of state structures and the possible benefits such structures allocate, and shape the range of conflicts over such allocations.

In a work by economist James Becker, *Marxian Political Economy* (1977), for example, the state is not seen as quasi-autonomous, let alone relatively autonomous, but is always an instrument of class domination. There is no entry in his index (or section in the book) for "state," none for "political" or "politics," none for "democracy." There are entries for "dictatorship, bourgeois," and "dictatorship, proletarian." Under the latter entry the only point made is that a "firm and sure socialist administration will be needed" after the revolution (p. 279). Becker does not consider the possibility of the state's reflecting either the political power of labor or even sectoral interests of capitalists. On the contrary, "a reduction in control by individual capitalists can result from increased control by capitalists as a class, e.g., through the state."[2] Even among contemporary Marxists, this position exhibits unusual belief in the subordination of the state to the requirements of class rule. The assumption that the main function of the state is either to guarantee individual capitalist rights or to maintain the powers of the capitalist class as a whole ("capital") is a pristine functional version of the class perspective on the state.

In contrast to these functional views, Nicos Poulantzas attempts to develop a "political" theory of the capitalist state. In his analysis of the crisis of the dictatorships of Portugal, Spain, and Greece, for example, he distinguishes between two Marxist views of the state, both of which he argues were incorrect, one viewing the state as a "subject," the other as a "thing." The former, analogous to the pluralist conception, derived from the "old Hegelian conception of a state that really is 'separate' from 'civil society,' and endowed with an intrinsic rationality as the embodiment of the general will in the face of atomized individuals." The Marxist version of this view, according to Poulantzas, is seen in statements about the state as an "organism independent of society and above it." The latter, analogous to the managerial conception, viewed the state as an "inert instrument . . . a machine, that can be manipulated at will by the dominant classes," although in the managerial image the state as an instrument has considerably more autonomy than that. But in both of

---

[2] Becker refers to the "managerial class" facing "administrative labor," in the economy and in the state (1977). In effect, by merging private capitalist owners with state managers, he accepts the classic Marxist hypothesis about the state being merely the "executive committee for the common affairs of the bourgeoisie." As he puts it, "managerial bureaucratizing is connected with the mode of production. It is an expression of the contradiction between the appropriation and the production of surplus value, between capital as property and functioning capital, between unproductive and productive labor . . . wasted administrative labor earns its living within mercantile establishments, within education, within the executive and policing agencies of the state judicial network, the latter holding together, by force when need be, the entire unwieldy amalgam of productive and of unproductive labor" (p. 253).

these Marxist images, he argues, "classes are seen as acting on the state only from outside" (1976, p. 81). Poulantzas asserts that, on the contrary, the state is a "relation" with internal contradictions. The contradictions of class struggle are expressed in the internal contradictions within the state. Poulantzas thus rejects the theoretical possibility of the "popular classes" being "enlisted" or "enrolled" in either democratic or fascist states as more than a transitory historical development.

For Poulantzas, dominant class political participation is neither necessary nor sufficient to ensure state reproduction of class relationships. As he argues in his earlier, more functionalist view,

The relation between the bourgeois class and the state is an *objective relation*. This means that if the *function* of the state in a determinant social formation and the *interests* of the dominant class *coincide*, it is by reason of the system itself: the direct participation of members of the ruling class in the State apparatus is not the *cause* but the *effect* and moreover a chance and contingent one, of this objective coincidence. [1972, p. 245; italics in original]

Even capitalist class political defeat – the loss of decisions that constitute powerlessness for the pluralists – may reproduce dominant class hegemony. Poulantzas writes,

The class struggle in capitalist formations entails that this guarantee of the economic interests of certain dominated classes is inscribed *as a possibility*, within the very limits imposed by the state on the struggle for hegemonic class leadership. But in making this guarantee, the state aims precisely at the political disorganization of the dominated classes; in a formation where the strictly political struggle of the dominated classes is possible, it is the sometimes indispensable means of maintaining the dominant classes' hegemony. In other words, according to the concrete conjuncture, a *line of demarcation* can always be drawn within which the guarantee given by the capitalist state to the dominated classes' economic interests not only fails to threaten the political relation of class domination but even constitutes an element of this relation. [1973, p. 191; italics in original]

Not only may capitalist political defeat be compatible with maintaining class power, but political disorganization of the capitalist class and its consequent inability to achieve hegemony also require the state to organize this class. In that way the state can function as a factor of cohesion in a society while disorganizing the dominated class (Poulantzas 1973). Poulantzas does not ignore the emergence of relatively autonomous bureaucratic organizations and diverse interest groups contending for influence over specific state decisions. And he views the legal and political identities of individuals as defined by the state, not merely by their class position. But, consistent with the class world view, all these processes occur within a societal totality defined by the capitalist mode of production.

Capitalist production requires individual labor. Individual persons become the private owners of their own means of production, that is, their labor power. This ownership is both economically real (in their roles as workers, producers, consumers) and politically real (in their role as citizens). Capitalist production is carried out both by organizations and by individuals: "the institutional materiality [that is, the organizations] of the capitalist state take root . . . in the individualization" of persons, in Poulantzas's words. "The specialization and centralization of the capitalist state, its hierarchical-bureaucratic functioning and its elective institutions all involve the atomization of the body-politic into what are called 'individuals' – that is, juridico-political persons who are the subjects of certain freedoms" (Poulantzas 1978, pp. 63-5). Capitalist relations of production and the labor process thus create a "material frame of reference" within which organizations and individuals must function.

State organizations also originate in societal factors. The bureaucratic aspect of the state is an "intricate decision-making structure of relatively autonomous bureaucracies." The resulting "political elaboration . . . takes the form of multi-level bargaining among administrative pressure groups and representatives of diverse interests." Here what pluralists see as the essential reality of the state becomes to Poulantzas a political mechanism for expressing varying situations of class struggle.

In his later work Poulantzas criticizes from within the class world view the functional approach to the capitalist state, which regards the state as having only economic, repressive, and ideological functions. (Althusser is the main target [Poulantzas 1978, p. 30].) But, even if one abandons such a monolithic view of the state, an alternate view that capital captures sectors of the state has the same defect. It has the virtue of being closer to the empirical reality of a fragmented state but still assumes that the structure of the state must express the overall needs of capital and the capitalist class. Poulantzas does not accept either of these functionalist alternatives.

His solution is to regard both the democratic and the bureaucratic aspects of the state (he does not call them that) as "relatively autonomous," with the extent of autonomy circumscribed by the reproductive requirements of capitalism coupled with class struggle. But Poulantzas avoids an adequate theoretical analysis of this issue by analyzing the other aspects of the state only with language borrowed from pluralist and managerial perspectives. He refers, for example, to influence and domination but does not theorize them. He links the individual, organizational, and societal levels by using such metaphors as "concretized," "crystallized," "inscribed," "institutional materiality," "elaborated," and "condensed." The phrase "take the form of" is his casual way of translating societal contradictions into presumed manifestations at other levels (1978, p. 132). Poulantzas's particular formulations rest heavily upon metaphors that are not logically related to either core concepts or empirical observations. The relationships between levels are not theorized.

This theoretical gap is also visible in the classic debate between Poulantzas (in an earlier functionalist stance) and Ralph Miliband. Poulantzas, arguing from the societal level, asserts that the epistemology of the totality must determine any analysis of "regions" such as politics and culture. Poulantzas argues that the participation of capitalists in state policy making was "chance and contingent," depending on structural and situational factors that did not affect the systemic dependence of the state upon capital. Poulantzas recognizes the empirical importance of factors affecting both the participation of capitalists in attempts to influence state action and the outcomes of such participation, but he dismisses such factors as *theoretically* insignificant. Miliband, operating at the organizational level of analysis, simply takes for granted the multiple functions of the state in a capitalist society and proceeds to theorize the concrete forms of control exercised by capitalists and corporations in particular states, including the process of legitimation of business as an interest group. Miliband introduced Weberian elements into his analysis and did not recognize the potential conflict between concepts located at different levels of analysis. This lacuna allowed Poulantzas, quite appropriately, to accuse him of un-Marxist epistemology, because he left the home domain of the class perspective.[3]

Political scientist Adam Przeworski (1977) rejects the division of the concept of class into "class-in-itself," defined by objective economic conditions, and "class-for-itself," defined by all other social relations that are seen as subjective, including both politics and ideology. Instead, classes are the "effects of struggles structured by objective conditions that are simultaneously economic, political and ideological" (p. 343). Przeworski has broken with the orthodox Marxist tradition that separates objective from subjective, base from superstructure, "economic foundations" from social institutions, material interests from consciousness, form from content, as different realms of causation and theory. We have labeled this basic dichotomy the distinction between functional and political approaches to the state and have found its manifestations within each perspective. Its significance and applicability go far beyond the state.

Przeworski appropriately locates the concept of "class" at the societal level of analysis but does not ignore the problematic nature of the relations of classes to individuals and organizations. "Individuals occupy places within the system of production; collective actors appear in strug-

---

[3] For the original debate, see Poulantzas (1972) and Miliband (1972). Miliband's more recent book, *Marxism and Politics* (1977), restates his position.

gles at concrete moments of history. Neither of these – occupants of places or participants in collective actions – are classes. Class is the relation between them, and in this sense class struggles concern the social organization of such relations" (1977, p. 388).

This formulation avoids the potential for reification of the societal level of analysis by seeing societal *relations* between organization ("collective actors") and individuals. Those relations are not tangible and visible, in the way that individuals and organizations are – or at least in the way their effects are. The "traces of their existence" are not as easily apprehended in the absence of an appropriate theory.[4]

Attempts by Marxists to revise Marxism to retain all of the original elements while simultaneously taking account of subsequent historical developments either not foreseen by Marx or not theorized have sometimes resulted in the hidden incorporation of non-Marxist concepts and assumptions, leading to a degree of theoretical incoherence. Basic to the class perspective on modern capitalist societies is an analytic emphasis on the penetration of the unequal social relations of capitalist production into institutions and behaviors seemingly far from the economy per se. Debates within the class perspective center around the functional claim that the state serves to reproduce capitalist social relations of production and the political claim that there is a systematic relationship between the state and capitalism but that the exact relationships depend upon class struggle and the historical exigencies of class rule.[5]

Capitalism, democracy, and the state: the class view

In all of these variants of the class perspective, capitalism is interpreted as a process through which class rule and capital accumulation are main-

---

[4] Przeworski opens up class analysis to consider the possible autonomy of "authority relations" and concrete organizations in conflict (mentioning Dahrendorf) and also the potential autonomy of the "value system" (mentioning Parsons). But he emphasizes that political power and culture values must be analyzed in relation to the accumulation of capital. He notes himself that this extension of his argument is both rudimentary and programmatic – pointing toward further theoretical argument and research and not a fully developed statement. His position, like ours, is that the most fruitful theoretical approach simultaneously considers the mutual relations of capitalist accumulation, political conflict, and cultural values (1977, pp. 388–9).

[5] Commenting on Theda Skocpol's work, Ralph Miliband agrees that the state is an "autonomous structure" and that the "Marxist tradition does tend to underemphasize or simply ignore the fact that the state does have interests of its own, or, to put it rather more appropriately, that the people who run it believe it has and do themselves have interests of their own" (1983, p. 60). This comment is an example of the conflating of two important issues central to the managerial perspective but peripheral to the class perspective, so that here they are seen not as different but simply as rewordings of the same question. In the first version, the state is seen as an organization (an "autonomous structure"). In the second, the state is seen as an apparatus controlled by elites ("the people who run it").

tained. Democracy is seen as a distorted outcome of class struggle, and the bureaucratic state is an instrument or structure of class rule, which becomes increasingly important in sustaining accumulation, partly by bearing the social costs of private production. As before, we do not cite particular works because we are presenting the basic elements of the class world view, not summarizing the debates in the literature.

Capital accumulation

In the class perspective, the state's role in the reproduction of capitalist relations of production is its most important aspect. The state is vital in the creation of the working class as a productive force and crucial in preventing its transformation into a revolutionary political force. The state must sustain the institutional conditions necessary for accumulation based upon noncoercive extraction of surplus value. State power is integral to a system of economic exploitation not based upon political force, although force must be available to deal with the inevitable class struggle that capitalist accumulation generates.

Capital accumulation is the driving force of capitalist economic growth. The source of profit is the surplus value extracted from the workers' labor, not a return to entrepreneurial risk or to corporate power. Surplus value is invested in machines, which increase the productivity of labor. Both mechanization and monopoly eliminate or reduce competition temporarily and maintain higher than average profits as long as the commodity being produced retains its privileged technological and market position. The development of capital accumulation is characterized by the concentration of capital (the increasing scale of production in large factories) and by the centralization of capital (the increasing control of profits by fewer and fewer corporations, banks, or families).

Capital accumulation transforms the social structure. From preindustrial societies composed of small landholding peasants, artisans, and shopkeepers, the social structure becomes polarized into a working class (proletariat) and an owning class (bourgeoisie), with a middle class (petit bourgeoisie) playing technical, service, professional, administrative, educational, and ideological roles within capital accumulation. From precapitalist production based upon simple handicrafts, small shops, and labor-intensive processes, production is increasingly carried out by machines owned and controlled by large capitalist corporations. From a maze of small firms competing to serve local markets, corporate organizations enlarge, producing for global markets. The class perspective views economic growth not as the consequence of the gradual acceptance by the population of modern values or as the increasingly efficient organization of industry but as a result of capital accumulation occurring simultaneously with class formation.

Marx predicted that the regulation of the economy by profit calculations based on the unpaid labor time of its workers would produce a persistent tendency toward economic crises. The class perspective stresses the tendencies toward "boom and bust." Economic crisis is generated by the tendency for the average rate of profit to fall with increasing mechanization and for the level of demand to be insufficient to absorb the ever-expanding absolute quantity of production available for consumption.

The capacity to produce grows faster than the capacity of workers to consume. Machinery becomes more important as capitalists compete to reduce labor costs to a minimum. Yet, because unpaid labor time is the source of all profit, there is a tendency for the rate of profit to fall. Finally, the fact that unpaid labor is the source of all profits makes the level of wages the object of intense, and often violent, class struggle. Overall, the economy experiences periodic economic crises due to an inability of producers to sell their goods, an unwillingness of capitalists to invest because of low profitability, or their inability to produce because the working class withholds its labor.

Capital accumulation progressively polarizes the class structure into those who own the means of production and those who do not. The organization of production is increasingly socialized through more complex and larger-scale interdependency among producers, and decision making remains in the hands of private owners who seek to maximize profits. Profitability, based upon the amount of unpaid labor time extracted from workers, continues to determine decisions to invest and produce, to hire and fire, to buy and sell. This contradiction between the socialization of production (which increases the collective capacities of the working class) and the continuing private appropriation of production lies at the heart of endemic tendencies toward economic, and therefore political, crisis. This contradiction is the source of the transformative potential of political class struggle, because the hegemony of capitalist production relations increasingly depends on maintaining political order.

Class struggle

The class perspective interprets the democratic aspect of the state as a distorted and partial outcome of class struggle. Trade unions and political parties win the right to organize or participate as a result of the struggles of workers around many kinds of issues.

The growing socialization of production in the process of capital accumulation creates an educated and potentially class-conscious working class. As a result, capitalist control is challenged through class struggle, sometimes taking the form of labor unions and mass political parties as instruments of working-class interests. Working-class political organizations are restrained by hegemonic ideologies that fragment workers' short-term interests into individual, occupational, or group interests. And, if demands challenge the prerogatives of private property or if legal forms of working-class participation do not achieve a response, participation takes illegitimate forms: social movements, demonstrations, strikes, riots, revolutionary activity. Therefore, demands must be channeled into forms of participation that do not threaten the state's role in sustaining capital accumulation. Otherwise, they may be met by state repression.

The class perspective views the changing structure of the state as a reflection of the historical organization of class struggle. As we explore in Chapter 14, capitalist development generates a complex succession of class struggles among crown, aristocracy, peasants, bourgeoisie, and workers. Where initial capital accumulation was least dependent upon active state support, the extension of mass suffrage rights did not threaten capitalism or the political power of the capitalist class, in contrast to countries where the economic power of the bourgeoisie was highly dependent upon the state. In the former countries, working-class struggles for the vote and for parliamentary representation were the easiest and most successful. In the latter, democracy was institutionalized later, after greater state repression and even fascism.

The achievement of mass democratic institutions is a result of working-class struggle, related to the strength of working-class organization in the labor market and workplace. The growth of the trade union movement in every capitalist country, the growth of socialist political parties or movements demanding welfare rights, health care, housing, and education, the growth of struggles for democratic political rights – all constitute interconnected strategies of class struggle. The political organization of the working class is regarded as the most secure basis for popular democratic institutions, not the accommodations of competing elites or the permeation of social groups by democratic values.

Capitalist development both unifies and fragments the working class, thus both enhancing and reducing its capacity to struggle. On the one hand, capital accumulation makes national organizations of workers possible, because of the creation of national capital. Capitalism depends ultimately on the authority of national states and is thus vulnerable to the organization of workers.

On the other hand, because capital accumulation occurs unevenly, the working class is composed of workers with different work experience, skills, unemployment histories, income, and working conditions. This economic and occupational heterogeneity produces internal political divisions within the working class. Some sectors of the working class may approximate a labor aristocracy, with higher incomes, greater job security, and greater status than most other workers, and consequently share few immediate material interests with less privileged sectors of the working class. Because capital is also fragmented – the "anarchy" of production, consumption, and investment – the conditions for the classic revolutionary struggle between capital and labor are not easily realized. The disorganization of capital lends to the disorganization of labor as well.

In addition, members of the working class tend to see themselves in the cultural categories produced by capitalism: as individual workers and citizens, whose preferences and interests are endlessly variegated. Further, the efficacy of class-based social movements and political parties has often proved of dubious value due to the systemic power of capital, which undercuts the viability of social reforms. The repressive power of the state is capable of effectively destroying the organizations that try to carry out those reforms. The potential costs of even reformist political mobilization therefore seem quite high. As a result, most working classes in Western capitalist societies fail to achieve unified, class-conscious socialist movements and parties.

Social classes have objective interests rooted in the relations of production. These interests are derived not from the distribution of income but from the control over the means of production and the resultant organization of production and distribution of commodities. The translation of these objective interests into political issues and into public policies of the state is contingent upon specific historical conditions of class struggle. The politicization of class interests is blocked by a combination of "false consciousness" (failure to identify with one's own objective class interests due to the hegemony of capitalist ideology), working-class disorganization, cooptation, and state repression. If working-class political organizations not only contest the distribution of the surplus product but also challenge capitalist control of production, democratic rights may be destroyed by a repressive state or undermined by "capital strike": the refusal of capitalists to invest.

Although class theorists see working-class organization as a safeguard for democracy, they also argue that the reduction of class struggle to party competition undercuts the potential impact of working-class political participation, in whatever form. Party competition erodes the ideological content of working-class parties and demobilizes the working class, for the sake of organizational power and strategic impact on particular issues and interests (Offe 1984). Thus party competition makes democracy compatible with capitalism. The class perspective frequently regards this outcome, however, as undermining the potential for socialist transformation, rather than as a historical achievement of democratic political culture in taming extremist political movements.

Socialization of the costs of production

The class perspective interprets the expansion and centralization of the state as a consequence of the socialization of production. The state must guarantee the conditions under which capital accumulation can continue.

Capital accumulation furthers expansion of the state because of the contradictory logic of capitalism: its inability to reproduce itself. The state must establish agencies to regulate competition between capitalists, guarantee the creation and reproduction of labor power, underwrite the social and private expenses of production, and guarantee effective economic demand via fiscal income, industrial, regulatory, and foreign policies.

The capitalist state is differentiated from the economy by the very nature of capitalism. Capitalism is a system of accumulation based upon free exchange, not upon political coercion controlled by the state. Yet the representative aspects of the state also provide the state with relative autonomy and ability to avoid direct control by the capitalist class.

The relative autonomy of the state and the economy also serves political functions for capitalism. The existence of a relatively autonomous state serves to generate policies that protect capitalism from the consequences of competition among individual capitalist interests. A separate state structure also helps to regulate class struggle and to deflect it from a direct challenge to the capitalist organization of production. Conflict is redirected from the shop floor and marketplace to the ballot box and courts. For the state to be considered an umpire of class conflict, it must appear autonomous, not as a captive instrument of capital. But the pressure to exclude the state from profitable production creates a dependence of state revenues upon taxation derived from capitalist economic growth. State efficacy also depends upon the cooperation of private capitalists. As a result of its institutional autonomy, the state nevertheless appears to represent general interests.

The state does not, however, have sufficient control over the economy. It must attempt to manage economic and political crises but lacks the authority to treat their causes. The state must buffer the intense conflicts between classes; yet it is unable to resolve these class-based conflicts over distribution and control of production. Because the state can treat only the consequences and not the causes of capitalist crisis, the internal organization of the state also becomes subject to crises of both insufficient public revenues and insufficient popular support.

As the state expands, this process of crisis and intervention also affects class struggle. The dependence of the state upon capital accumulation limits the nature of the political demands to which it can respond. Increasing public services for workers cut into profits. Investment slows, and public revenues fall. Popular demands for public expenditure are therefore always constrained by their effects on profitability. Because state legitimacy depends upon prosperity, some class theorists argue that a socialist transformation by democratic means is highly unlikely. State challenges to capitalist power will throttle private investment and thus economic growth. Mass support for a government that engenders such a response is unlikely. As the forms of state intervention change, political demands are also shaped. These processes create new possibilities for class struggle and also further fragment the working class as welfare recipients, public-sector, and private-sector workers seek their separate interests.

Conversely, the character of class struggle affects state expansion. Distributional conflicts over what share of the social product will be composed of profits or wages are transposed to the state. Because the state does not generate a substantial surplus itself, its expansion is determined by class conflict over the division of the surplus. On the one hand, both capitalist and working classes attempt to minimize the extent to which state activity is financed out of profits or wages, respectively. On the other, both attempt to maximize the extent to which state activity contributes to capital or wage formation. Conflicts over the level and distribution of private wages affect the expansion and distribution of social wages or state contributions to household incomes.

Conclusions

The class perspective sees individuals, organizations, and society as being simultaneously held together and torn apart by societal contradictions. Capitalism, democracy, and the state are seen in terms of the dynamic relationships between capital accumulation and class struggle, creating the imperative to socialize the private and social costs of production. The multiple contradictions of this process lead to crises, which threaten the hegemony of class rule.

Although structures of organized power are important to the class perspective, class power does not normally depend upon political organization of the class, even if the transformation of social relations does depend upon their political organization. Class power depends upon the state, and the state is shaped by class power. In this sense, class power is political. But accumulation, the systemic source of class power, does not require the existence of a politically organized ruling class.

The class perspective views the existence of a state apparatus as necessary to reproduce the conditions necessary for capital accumulation but as simultaneously undermining those conditions and creating the possibility of transformation. The state thus has a dialectical and contradictory relationship to the mode of production and thus to the population under its control. This relation is the *capitalist* aspect of the state.

The Marxist tradition deals most cogently and forcefully with basic contradictions that create the potential of long-term structural change and only intermittently and on an ad hoc basis with the emergence of organizations and leadership and with the conditions of action in particular situations by persons and groups playing specific roles. Precisely because the class perspective – in its ideological and political manifestations – sees itself as a guide to action, it is the organizational and individual levels of analysis that become important, but they are theoretically neglected or subordinated. The endless debates over what "Marx really meant" are testimony to the power of theory implicitly recognized by Marxists as a guide to action. The very intensity of those debates and their continuing consequences for the fragmentation of leftist parties of all stripes cannot be explained within the home domain of class analysis.

The diversity of contemporary Marxist theories of the state is shown in detail in Bob Jessop's recent exegesis and critique of "state monopoly capitalist," the "state derivation," and the "hegemonic" views within Marxism. His chapter dealing with Marx and Engels on the state makes distinctions that are parallel (within a general class perspective) to pluralist (the state as a "factor of cohesion") and managerial (the state as an "institutional ensemble") perspectives. The state is also, of course, an agent or instrument of class rule for all perspectives (1982, chap. 1).

If there was ever a hegemonic perspective called Marxism, there is one no longer. Debates rage about the falling rate of profit, the role of the working class, and – not least of all – the relative autonomy of the capitalist state. There are historical Marxists and functional Marxists, scientific Marxists and critical Marxists. As Karl Marx himself once said, "Je ne suis pas un Marxist," suggesting that dogma had no place in a theory presumably open to the understanding of any historical trend and committed only to human liberation from oppression and exploitation. Certain historical trends in the state cannot be fitted neatly within the prevailing interpretations of the class perspective as derived from Marx.[6]

---

[6] For some attempts to deal with the different tendencies within that history, see Anderson 1976; Gouldner 1980; Aronowitz 1981a; Giddens 1981; and Jacoby 1981.

One of the most creative English Marxists, Perry Anderson, acknowledges crucial gaps in Marx's and Engels's writings, which have left their legacy in contemporary debates within the class perspective. He says that "there are three areas where Marx's work appears centrally uncertain, from a contemporary perspective." First, "Marx never produced any coherent or comparative account of the political structures of bourgeois class power at all," that is, the capitalist state. Second, there is a "central theoretical silence on the character of nations and nationalisms," as well as on the "great shift in the international state system that accompanied the rise of the capitalist mode of production" (Anderson 1976, pp. 114–15). The third gap was in the theory of value and prices and the distinction between productive and unproductive labor, which Anderson links to Marx's "catastrophism" and the lack of a political theory. Anderson comments that these historical silences left "very damaging consequences [for] later generations of socialists" (p. 115). Anderson ends his survey of the multiple strands of "Western Marxism" with a series of "unanswered problems that form the most urgent agenda for Marxist theory today." They include democracy, the state, and bureaucracy.

To conclude, the contradiction that the class perspective postulates in the capitalist state is mirrored by the division of labor between functional and political approaches. Marxist political economists and sociologists, by and large, have taken a functional approach, arguing for the systemic constraints on the capitalist state by the "imperatives" or "requirements" of capital accumulation. Marxist social historians have, by and large, taken a political approach, stressing the active role of workers' resistance in shaping ruling-class strategies and the constant problems of maintaining workers' consent to becoming alienated objects in the production process. Both agree that systemic crises emerge from within such a contradictory social system.

13

The capitalist state and accumulation

In the functional class perspective, a state emerges with a form dictated by the requirements of capitalism as a unique form of political economy. The state must sustain, on the one hand, capitalist accumulation and, on the other, capitalist class rule. And yet, as we shall see, as an organization the state is hardly theoretically visible at all. In a more political view, because capitalism is a contradictory mode of production, the state must inherently endure crisis and class struggle. In this chapter, we shall present class analyses of the state as it developed historically to facilitate capital accumulation. In the following chapter, the state's relation to class struggle and crisis will be the focus of our attention.

Class and state formation: the societal level

The class perspective sees the origins of the capitalist aspect of the state in the political and economic requirements of capitalist accumulation. There can be no theory of the state abstracted from a particular mode of production. Class theorists agree that the capitalist mode of production, for the first time in world history, made the economy an institutional sphere autonomous from any other institution (for example, the family, the state, law, religion). Perry Anderson makes this point in his contrast of feudalism and capitalism: "The 'superstructures' of kinship, religion, law or the state necessarily enter into the constitutive structure of the mode of production in precapitalist social formations. . . . in capitalist social formations, the first in history to separate the economy as a formally self-contained order, they provide by contrast its 'external' preconditions" (1974, pp. 403–4).

Institutional separation of the state from the economy allowed capitalist accumulation to proceed without fundamental interference. Property rights to hire labor, invest capital, and sell in all available markets could then be exercised "freely" and did not depend upon the coercive powers of the state.

Historical studies within the class perspective emphasize the uneven character of the process of state formation, marked by continuous conflict between old feudal and new capitalist ruling classes, the forcible creation of a working class from a peasantry, and the destruction of old forms of precapitalist states that interfered with the exercise of property rights. In many of the historical studies (such as Hobsbawm's, summarized in this chapter), the theory is implicit, emerging through the interpretation of specific events.

There are relatively few historical studies of the development of the capitalist state, partly because of Marx's original assumption that the institutions within the superstructure reflect the needs of capitalist development in different stages and therefore, as subordinate social relations, do not need to be analyzed in their own right. The diverse actions of state agencies, political leaders, and parliaments are empirically recognized but the development of the capitalist state has not, by and large, been seen as a theoretical issue.[1]

One important exception is Perry Anderson's *Lineages of the Absolutist State* (1974), a country-by-country survey of the precapitalist state that contrasts the different forms of feudal and capitalist states in Western Europe. Anderson asserts that absolutist states, where the monarch was presumed to have absolute power, as in France, were fundamentally different from laissez-faire capitalist states like Britain. Two features of absolutist states contributed to the collapse of the feudal nobility and the emergence of capitalism: the emergence of sovereign power over a single territory, and the development of unconditional ownership of private property.

Anderson criticizes Marx and Engels for only casually alluding to the absolutist state and not theorizing its character and historical consequences. According to Anderson, Engels thought state power in the absolute monarchies had acquired a certain degree of independence from warring classes. Marx sometimes described the absolutist state as almost a kind of bourgeois state. That is, "the centralized State power" served "nascent middle class society as a mighty weapon in its struggles against feudalism" (Marx, quoted in Anderson 1974, p. 16).

Anderson considers this analysis simplistic. Many of the features of

---

[1] Another standpoint within the class perspective does not entail detailed historical studies of particular states. Recent French and German debates on the nature of the capitalist state share a common functionalist position, differing among themselves on the nature of state monopoly capitalism. Debate centers around the issue of the extent to which the state is directly controlled by agents of capital or must generate policies meeting the "needs" of capitalism without visible control. See Jessop 1982 for a thorough review, and Holloway and Piccioto 1978 for a selection of key articles from the "class derivation" school.

the absolutist state, including "standing armies, a permanent bureaucracy, national taxation, a codified law, and the beginnings of a unified market" (1974, p. 17), appear to be typical of a capitalist social order. Because all of these developments, which seem to mark the emergence of a capitalist state, coincided with the disappearance of serfdom, casual observers – such as Marx and Engels – might well assume that feudal class relations had also disappeared. According to Anderson, they had not. The feudal aristocracy remained the ruling class, the feudal social relations still dominated the countryside; thus the absolutist state was a "redeployed . . . apparatus of feudal domination" (p. 18).

This interpretation emphasizes the primacy of the dominant class in a given mode of production as the basic force shaping other institutions. The forms of the state are secondary, playing a role only within an emerging new form of class rule. Although this is Anderson's premise, he is critical of those who minimize variations in the form of the state. Anderson quotes historian Christopher Hill as having written in 1953: "The absolute monarch was a different form of feudal monarchy from the feudal-estates monarchy which preceded it, but the ruling class remained the same, just as a republic, a constitutional monarchy, and a fascist dictatorship can all be forms of the rule of the bourgeoisie" (1974, p. 18). Anderson willingly grants that the changing requirements of class rule are the principal explanation for the form of the state. He argues, however, that the historical transformation involved in absolutism and, by implication, variations among capitalist states as well must not be minimized. It was a "momentous change in the structure of the aristocratic state, and of feudal property" (p. 19).

Feudalism as a mode of production was "originally defined by an organic unity of economy and polity, paradoxically distributed in a chain of parcellized sovereignties" throughout the society (Anderson 1974, p. 19). At the bottom were the serfs, permanently attached to the land, owing dues to their lord in the form of labor, agricultural products, and service in his army. The nobility owed their obligations to the feudal king in a dense network of obligations, patronage, and responsibilities. Private ownership and a modern state with military control over a territory did not exist. "Ownership" rights were multiple and overlapping. The demands from the king and his leading vassals (lords of the nobility) had to be conveyed through subvassals who had control over certain populations and territories, rather than their being controlled through a state apparatus.

The result of the disappearance of serfdom was a "reinforced apparatus of royal power, whose permanent political function was the repression of the peasant and plebeian masses at the foot of the social hierarchy" (Anderson 1974, p. 19). This process was not smooth, and it was aggravated by sharp conflicts of interest within the aristocracy. One major change was reinforcement of the ownership of land in the modern sense. As the dense network of feudal obligations declined, the noble estates became more solidly established. "Landownership tended to become progressively less 'conditional' [that is, upon the services expected from vassals] as sovereignty became correspondingly more 'absolute' " (p. 20).

Another mechanism for the emergence of absolute monarchical sovereignty was the revival of Roman law, which also served the requirements of class rule. Commodity production and exchange had to reach a certain level before these "juridical concepts . . . could come into their own once again" (Anderson 1974, p. 26). Roman law fit the mercantile economy because of its "clearcut notions of absolute property . . . its traditions of equity, its rational canons of evidence, and its emphasis upon a professional judiciary" (p. 26). It was also consistent with a "drive of royal governments for increased central powers" and with its two sectors: "civil law regulating economic transactions between citizens, and public law governing political relations between the State and its subjects" (p. 27). In Anderson's summary, "the enhancement of private property from below was matched by the increase of public authority from above, embodied in the discretionary power of the royal ruler" (p. 28).

Anderson contrasts the feudal absolutist monarchical states with all subsequent capitalist states that share the following characteristics: an attempt to avoid war in the interests of expanded international trade; a rational-legal bureaucracy in the Weberian sense (offices cannot be bought and sold, nor can officials legitimately make a profit from their office); taxes based on *formal* equality of citizenship and thus their legitimate exaction from all citizens. Also, the international relations of capitalist states occur on the basis of the securely established sovereignty of each state over its territory and population (unless redivided as a consequence of war); and the "private" (economic) and "public" (governmental) sectors are rigidly separated – legally and institutionally. All these features differ from those found in the absolutist state.

The important aspect of his argument for our purpose is that the institutional transformation of the feudal absolutist states prepared the conditions for states with sovereignty over a territory and a guarantee of undivided ownership of property: capitalist states. Anderson asserts the symbiotic interdependence of the absolutist state with the emerging capitalist class: "Economic centralization, protectionism and overseas expansion aggrandized the late feudal State while they profited the early bourgeoisie. They increased the taxable revenues of the one by providing business opportunities for the other" (1974, p. 41). Thus the absolutist state had the double historical consequence of temporarily protecting the rule of the feudal nobility and creating the political conditions for the coming rule of the capitalist class. The state "accomplished certain partial functions in the primitive accumulation necessary for the eventual triumph of the capitalist mode of production itself" (p. 40). In conclusion, Anderson argues: "The rule of the Absolutist state was that of the feudal nobility in the epoch of transition to capitalism. Its end would signal the crisis of the power of its class: the advent of the bourgeois revolutions, and the emergence of the capitalist state" (p. 42). Anderson's study, although sensitive to variations in precapitalist states, nevertheless illustrates the primary theoretical assumption of the class perspective that the form of the state is fundamentally related to the mode of production and the requirements of class rule. The state does not play a truly autonomous or generative role.[2]

Another English Marxist, Ralph Miliband, praises Anderson's work but also admonishes him for minimizing the "relative autonomy" of the monarchs ruling the absolutist states and consequently minimizing the "policy choices which the Absolutist states often had to make, and the conflicting claims which these choices had to resolve." Miliband argues that Anderson's assertion that the state "simultaneously protected the rule of the nobility but also allowed the nascent bourgeoisie to operate . . . devalues this element of policy choices as between competing interests within and between classes" (1975, p. 317). According to Miliband, the state that the absolute monarch and his "advisers commanded was not the mere 'instrument' of aristocratic class power." More generally, he warns of the danger of overdeterminism in the class perspective, if the requirements of class rule are assumed always to explain the form of a particular state. Miliband is concerned that a class analysis not minimize the genuine political alternatives that rulers have within the general constraints of maintaining class rule. In our terms, societal and organizational levels of analysis should not be merged by theoretical fiat, nor should the potential contradictions between institutions be minimized.

An analysis of the transition from mercantile to industrial capitalism in Britain illustrates another class interpretation of the rise of the capi-

---

[2] Skocpol and Fullbrook argue that many of the empirical and historical analogies Anderson uses do not fit his essentially " 'class determinist' view of classical Marxism." A study concerned with "wide-ranging causal generalizations will find that military power and interstate competition assume a much larger and more theoretically independent role" (1984, p. 205). Skocpol and Fullbrook attribute Anderson's position to his world view (they call it his "intrinsic theoretical and political commitments"). Their argument for the centrality of land wars and state competition also stems partly from their world view.

talist state, which is simultaneously functional and political. (Hobsbawm 1968). Hobsbawm argues that early capitalism had to dismantle aspects of the precapitalist state that interfered with the process of capital accumulation. "To create the best conditions for the smooth operation of private enterprise meant [the elimination of] the numerous forms of existing government interference which could not be justified by the prevailing economic orthodoxy" (p. 227). Most important, the remains of traditional mercantilism (the "systematic fostering of national wealth through state power") had to be destroyed. Also, those state policies that prevented the nascent working class from being exposed to the cold winds of competition in the labor market had to be abolished: the traditional protections of a minimum wage and restriction on the number of working hours. The last remnant of these state protections was the Poor Law of 1834, which provided some semblance of minimum guarantees of subsistence.

Although eighteenth-century ruling ideology (Hobsbawm's term for the dominant political culture) advocated as little government as possible, the state had to tax and establish a currency (Hobsbawm 1968, p. 233). In the eighteenth century, revenue was raised chiefly by taxes on consumption (on both imported and home products), on property, and on legal transactions such as stamp duties. Tax policy did not develop out of any "systematic or rational view of the most effective or socially equitable methods" or their economic effects. Instead, "fiscal policy was dominated by three considerations: how to interfere least with businessmen; how to put the least burden on the rich; and how nevertheless to raise the necessary minimum for meeting public expenditure without going more heavily into debt." According to Hobsbawm, the "fundamental object of public finance was to keep expenditure low and the budget balanced" (pp. 234–5).

Britain was relatively successful in implementing laissez-faire ideology because it was in the enviable position of being the first nation in the world to industrialize under capitalist auspices and become the "workshop of the world." The British state abstained from two forms of economic intervention that no other capitalist society was able to avoid. It was "the only country which systematically refused any fiscal protection to its industries, and the only country in which the government neither built, nor helped to finance (directly or indirectly) or even planned any part of the railway system" (Hobsbawm 1968, p. 233).

Even Britain could not remain laissez-faire forever. As other countries industrialized, "the foundations of laissez-faire crumbled in the 1860's and 1870's." Britain lost its privileged position in world markets, and that forced a new role for the state. And after the working classes got the vote in 1867, but especially in 1884–5, "it became only too obvious that they would demand and receive substantial public intervention for greater welfare" (Hobsbawm 1968, p. 237).

Nineteenth-century state intervention was piecemeal, Hobsbawm argues, because political agents of class interests responded to immediate crises with improvised solutions that frequently exacerbated the crisis. His argument is that neither the logic of "rationalization" nor "political development" can explain the emergence and form of the capitalist state. Instead, the features of each such state vary in accordance with the twin historical pressures of the "class situation," that is, the double exigencies of capital accumulation and class struggle. These double circumstances are the constant reference point of Hobsbawm's analysis. His complex argument allows him to recognize both elite strategies and political culture, but he subordinates them to the primary process of the historical formation of classes as part of capitalist accumulation.

Wallerstein, a sociologist, defines the world economy as a capitalist system: a world division of labor for the production and distribution of surplus that does not have a single political system (1976). All states can be divided into three types: core, semiperiphery, and periphery, each with its distinctive role in the world system and type of class and state structure. The type of production required by the world system leads to distinctive and compatible patterns of labor control. In this functionalist class perspective, the multiplicity of states is explained by its consequences for the global accumulation of capital. Because capital operates globally, and states do not, capital has a "freedom of maneuver that is structurally based" (p. 230). Also, this system allows capitalism to flourish because "capitalism is based on the constant absorption of economic loss by political entities while economic gain is distributed to 'private' hands." Here the fiscal crises of the state central to O'Connor's political analysis (1973) are made into a systemic feature of world capitalism. Finally, the continuous political "turbulence" provides capital with the kind of environment that is conducive to technological change. Thus a system of nation-states exists because it is functional for the world capitalist system.

This world system theory, which has its roots in the dependency theories (Valenzuela and Valenzuela 1978), explains the geographical patterning of capitalist development, of class and state structure, based upon the positions different nations hold within the system. In this book, we focus upon what Wallerstein calls the "core" states, and this leads us to neglect how their position in the world economy affected their development and its impact on other states.

Maurice Zeitlin's analysis of the history of nineteenth-century civil wars in Chile is both a methodological and a theoretical challenge from a political class perspective to this functional world systems approach (1984). Rather than deriving Chile's eventual underdevelopment and domination by foreign capital from the logic of the world system, Zeitlin argues that Chile's pattern of industrialization and of penetration by foreign capital, and thus its position in the world system, derived from the history of class struggles *within* Chile. The decisive conflicts – in the 1850s against the centralized powers of President Montt and in the 1890s in defense of the industrializing statism of President Balmaceda – were between segments of the capitalist class, specifically the copper-mining industrialists against large estate owners of the central valley, bankers, and nitrate miners. The objectives of the copper capitalists were to use the state to protect their nascent industries, to provide the capital and the infrastructure necessary to industrialize based upon copper, to break up the enormous agricultural estates in order to modernize agriculture and expand the domestic market for domestic manufacture. The copper-mining families, who provided the bulk of the leaders in these civil wars, resisted the state's dependence upon their production for tax revenues and rebelled against the state's unwillingness to use those revenues and its authority to allow them to industrialize in the face of British competition. Because these two "bourgeois revolutions" failed, the first from below and the second from above, Chile was consigned to what Wallerstein would call a semiperipheral role in the world system. Yet, as a result, Zeitlin argues, Chile was provided with a structure of class power that allowed parliamentary democracy to survive until it was once again destroyed by a civil war facilitated by the Central Intelligence Agency in 1973. Thus Zeitlin's analysis of Chile reverses the logic of the world system, by deriving not only a nation's position in the world system but the very relationship between national states and international capital from the class struggles within them.

Thus, in the functional class perspective, the form of the state derives from the institutional requirements of reproducing capitalism rather than from the logic of state power. From a managerial perspective, Skocpol argues that Wallerstein incorrectly reduces the origins of the state system to its functions for capitalism (1979). How, Skocpol argues, can a system of states that predated capitalism be anything other than an "autonomous level of transnational reality"? States are more appropriately conceptualized as structures maintaining internal control and generating international conflict (p. 22).

In the political class perspective, the form of the state derives from historically specific patterns of class struggles rather than from the strategies of bureaucratic empowerment or group conflict. Thus Zeitlin argues that the conflicts between state elites and dominant classes, central to Skocpol's analysis, are in reality struggles between different segments of the dominant class in the case of Chile (see Skocpol 1979; Zeitlin 1984).

Corporate capital and state policy: the organizational level

Gabriel Kolko's analysis (1967) of the growing interdependence between monopoly capital and the state represents a self-conscious departure from not only managerial but also other class analyses of the dynamics of industrial concentration and state policy. Contrary to managerial analysts such as John Kenneth Galbraith (1967), monopolistic organizations do not naturally emerge because of the organizational and market requirements of innovative, technologically complex, and large-scale capital investments. Monopolies, Kolko argues, were a response by the largest and least innovative corporations to the technical challenge posed by smaller firms. Disagreeing with other class analysts, such as Paul Baran and Paul M. Sweezy (1966), Kolko maintains that monopoly did not evolve out of the competitive process in which capital became increasingly concentrated and centralized. On the contrary, monopolies were a *political* creation by oligopolistic giants who were often technologically sluggish, overcapitalized, and increasingly losing their share of the market.

Kolko's *Triumph of Conservatism* (1967) is a historical class analysis of successful corporate strategies in the Progressive era. Progressive reforms, in the pluralist perspective, were a response to popular demands in the early twentieth century to curb the rapacious powers of industrial capitalism. In the service of the "public interest," the state stepped in to regulate the excesses of capitalism. Kolko argues that, on the contrary, it was not popular opinion that shaped those state policies or public interests that they served. Rather, a politically advanced or "liberal" segment of the capitalist class used the political clamor to shape state policies that would increase their power and profits, rather than reduce them. Kolko argues that government regulation of industry was a corporate strategy to rationalize the industrial structure. State intervention was used not to break up ever more powerful industrial monopolies but to sustain, if not create, them. Kolko notes:

I use the attempt to preserve existing power and social relationships as the criterion for conservatism. . . . Only if we mechanistically assume that government intervention in the economy, and a departure from orthodox laissez-faire, automatically benefits the general welfare can we say that government economic regulation by its very nature is also progressive in the common meaning of that term. [P. 2]

Kolko argues that industrial monopoly was exceptional in the nineteenth and early twentieth centuries. Although between 1897 and 1901 a massive and short-lived merger movement developed, based on corporate desire to control increasing industrial competition, neither industrial concentration nor the merger movement was able to prevent the increasing competition with which new corporations threatened the established giants like U.S. Steel, AT&T, and J. P. Morgan and Company (1967, pp. 25, 26). Technological change, shifting markets and resources, internal financing out of profits, regional decentralization of financial control, and economies of scale at low production levels allowed competition to emerge that cut the market shares and stock prices of the largest corporations.

The largest capitalists turned to regulation by the federal government in order to eliminate "internecine competition," to create "calculable expectations," and to immobilize democratic "political attacks" (Kolko 1967, p. 3). Kolko refers to this new synthesis of state and economic power as "political capitalism." He argues that once the state comes to regulate capitalism there can no longer be any inexorable "laws of economic development." A theory of the economy now requires a theory of the state.

State intervention thus served corporate interests while seemingly serving the public interest. The Meat Inspection Act of 1906, for example, regulated the quality of products in this industry. Kolko points out that this act had strong industrial support, because of the industry's desire to reduce competition and gain access to a more hygienically restrictive European market (1967, p. 95). The federal government's role in forestry conservation is seen as a corporate-supported program to prevent lumber resources from "being permanently squandered by indiscriminate cutting" (pp. 110–11). The Federal Reserve Act of 1913 is seen as a form of rationalization of the banking system. It was designed and supported by the largest national banks, which faced increasing competition from state banks and industrial corporations able to finance their growth from internally generated profits.

Thus, contrary to the pluralist hypothesis, Kolko argues that "big business led the struggle for the federal regulation of the economy" (1967, p. 58). The largest corporations favored federal regulation, not only because of their desire for uniform political regulation in an increasingly national economy but also because, in comparison with national government, state and local governments were vulnerable to populist and socialist political demands for more democratic forms of state intervention in the capitalist economy. The political cohesion of the most powerful capitalists allowed them to coopt the democratic forces – including socialists and workers – who also wanted government reg-

ulation of business. The trouble, Kolko argues, was that radical leaders
"could not tell the difference between federal regulation of business and
federal regulation for business" (p. 285). In effect, the capitalist state
was created with the cooperation of the working class.

In some more recent empirical studies, corporations are analyzed as
the organizational mechanism of capitalist accumulation and class formation. The capitalist state is recognized as defining the legal possibilities for corporate relations, as empirically measured by joint directorships
on boards ("interlocks"). In one such study (Mizruchi 1982), the "concentration of power at the level of the system as a whole" is measured
by the concentration of corporate interlocks. The system is seen as dominated by the largest corporations (p. 91). The state is implicit. None of
the data or the hypotheses systematically deals with the role of the state.
A theory of the state is unnecessary to explain class structure.

This is not a criticism of a careful empirical study but only an observation that the inquiry is silent concerning the environment of the capitalist state surrounding the structure of relations between corporations.
The Clayton Antitrust Act of 1912, for example, "outlawed interlocks
between competing firms" (Mizruchi 1982, p. 182). Although Mizruchi
says that "the effect of legislation on interlocking is a crucial issue . . .
since it is possible that the decreased interlocking between 1912 and 1919
was primarily a result of the Clayton Act rather than indicative of actual
changes in intercorporate relations" (p. 182), he defines this as a measurement issue rather than a theoretical problem. Here a state action
appears out of the blue, so to speak, to affect the data but is regarded
as a factor exogenous to the empirical focus on corporate interlocks. Nor
are subsequent legislation and court cases either allowing or forbidding
further monopolization of industries taken into account. The state also
appears in Mizruchi's analysis as the collector of data on large corporations. The Securities and Exchange Commission, the Temporary National Economic Committee, and the House Committee on Banking and
Currency at various times and in various ways attempted to discover
who controlled American corporations (pp. 22–3). But the impact of
different federal and state laws regulating corporate ownership, mergers, or sales is not considered empirically as a major factor influencing
the scope and character of corporate interlocks.

Rather, starting from the vantage point of the corporations themselves,
seen as powerful economic actors, Mizruchi is concerned with whether
interlocks indicate a community of interest among corporations, the
dependence of one corporation upon another for necessary resources,
or the control by one corporation of another (1982, pp. 34–5). His historical data on changes in corporate structures allow him to analyze the
transformation of American capitalism from individual to institutional

intercorporate relations (p. 187), but he emphasizes that "the ascendance of a more bureaucratic form of corporate organization should not be confused with the transcendence of capitalism as a system. Corporations continued to maximize profits, to respond to the market, and to act in relation to one another" (p. 190). Mizruchi discusses several alternative positions within a general class perspective, which vary in their emphasis on managerial control, the role of banks, and the way to measure corporate as distinct from class power (pp. 178–81). He concludes that a "class hegemony" model, slightly modified to take account of the possibility of future expansion of bank control of corporations, fits the data on interlocking control best.[3]

The theoretical significance of corporate interlocking is not unambiguous. Class theorists use the interlocks among corporations to infer their class location (see Domhoff 1976, for example). This assumes that corporations link individual capitalists. Such interlocks are seen as a precondition for the creation of a politically coordinated capitalist class. Central actors in the corporate interlock network tend to be the most politically active capitalists in the formulation of public policy by the state (Useem 1979; Ratcliff 1980) because of their visibility and their capacity to represent global class interests.[4]

In another variant, the social relations of production within corporations are of concern, although production relations are not themselves often analyzed in relation to the state. Even so, the reproduction of the division of labor in production has been seen as a *political* process by some class theorists, using the metaphor "internal state." The politics of production has been addressed by Michael Burawoy (1979). With the rise of unionized workers and multinational corporations that are better able to insulate themselves from the market, the reproduction of production relations takes a new form, which Burawoy labels "hegemonic."

Burawoy is critical of both the "consensus" view of organizations (which he associates with Durkheim) and the "social control" view (which he associates with Weber) and argues that an "internal state" develops in factories that creates consent precisely because there is an area of

[3] Mizruchi ends his study with a comment on its implications for the managerial theory of democracy. He argues that his empirical discovery of an interlocking and centralized cohesive corporate elite – even without calling it a capitalist class – calls into question a theory of democracy based upon elite competition: "if democracy in our society depends on a divided elite, and if that elite is not essentially divided, then what does this say about the viability of the democracy?" (1982, p. 194).

[4] Managerial theorists, however, turn the relationship between corporations and individual directors around and analyze individuals as they link corporations (Friedland and Palmer 1984). This is the central thrust of resource dependency theory (Pfeffer and Nowak 1976; Burt 1983), which derives class formation from the logic of corporate adaptation to environmental uncertainty rather than from a societal logic of class formation.

choice allowed to the individual worker. An atmosphere is created in which individual workers compete with themselves to "make out" (create games of production). Burawoy makes the analogy of the behavior of workers in plants with their behavior as citizens. The autonomy of the plant and the choices allowed workers within it "constituted workers as industrial citizens with rights and obligations, and fostered competition, individualism, and mobility" (1979, p. 198), but Burawoy does not celebrate the outcome. Rather, "the internal state has the effect not only of disorganizing struggles but also of dispersing them among enterprises. It prevents struggles from reaching beyond the enterprise and coalescing in struggles aimed at the global state" (p. 198).

Trade union strategy was consonant with that of the corporations. Unions fought for collective bargaining with corporations that linked wages to the performance of the firm. Thus workers were organized around the interests they shared with the firm rather than with workers in less powerful firms. Unions also negotiated for grievance procedures, which gave workers in a particular firm a set of rights as industrial citizens. These rights were specific to the firm, and they attached to individuals, not collectivities. Grievances became individual, not collective. These negotiated structures of promotion, grievance, and collective bargaining within a firm are an internal state that regulates political conflicts over production relations. The efficacy of this internal state in securing the consent of workers to production relations prevents the development of political conflict in the external state over the organization of production.

Burawoy argues that the autonomy of the internal state in the major corporations in the United States and its definition of the industrial citizenship rights of workers as individuals prevent those internal political conflicts that do occur over production from having societal repercussions. Burawoy's argument is an ingenious application to workers' class situation of the pluralist categories of consent and citizenship and the "game" of making out on the shop floor. The outcome is seen, of course, as ideological hegemony rather than genuine participation on the basis of equality. Limited economic and political conflicts rarely challenge the terrain of production – namely, the game itself.[5]

[5] Braverman's study of the "labor process" under capitalism also takes as given the existence of a capitalist state whose fundamental role is to protect the "ever more unequal distribution of property which this system brings about" (1974, p. 284). His chapter on the role of the state simply asserts that this classic role for the state has become "greatly expanded and takes on a more complex and sophisticated form" in all capitalist societies (p. 284). Braverman hardly mentions class struggle, strikes, or resistance in any form to the growing alienation of the working class presumably created by the "habituation" of workers to the capitalist mode of production. Braverman's study severs consideration of accumulation and class formation from class struggle and crisis, focusing entirely on the first half of the dialectic.

The ruling class and the working class: the individual level

The work of G. William Domhoff was one of the first to analyze empirically the capitalist class as both a *social class* and a *ruling class*. Because of our focus on the state, we shall deal mainly with the latter aspect of his work. Domhoff makes inferences about class rule from an analysis of individual members of the ruling class and from particular events and decisions. Domhoff's work is one of the few that combines a class world view with an individual level of analysis. This discrepancy perhaps helps account for the controversial character of his work among some of those who hold a class perspective.[6] Domhoff also diverges sharply from C. Wright Mills's managerial world view in his conception of the "power elite" as

active, working members of the upper class and high-level employees in institutions controlled by members of the upper class. The power elite has its roots in and serves the interests of the social upper class. It is the operating arm of the upper-class. It functions to maintain and manage a socioeconomic system which is organized in such a way that it yields an amazing proportion of its wealth to a minuscule upper class of big business and their descendants. [Domhoff 1970, pp. 106–7]

An "upper class" is composed of families who are listed in social registers, attend exclusive private schools, and belong to select social clubs and thus share a distinctive life style and class consciousness. Domhoff suggests that the cohesion and consciousness of the upper class "provide a context for assessing the involvement of members of the upper class in government and politics" (p. 75). Members of the upper class "sit in pivotal government offices, define most major policy issues, shape the policy proposals on issues raised outside their circles, and mold the rules of government" (pp. 105–6).

Domhoff dissects the mechanisms through which the upper class exercises its political dominance by analyzing American foreign and domestic policy. Domhoff shows, for example, that a series of capitalist financed and controlled policy organizations – the Council on Foreign Relations and the Committee for Economic Development, for example – shape American foreign policy. Such corporate organizations set the

---

[6] Domhoff's approach to capitalist political power has been criticized as instrumentalist because it assumes that the privileged participation of capitalists and their agents is necessary to produce policies required by capitalist profitability (Esping-Andersen, Friedland, and Wright 1976). Domhoff responded: "Even though classes and institutions are the basic conceptual units, individuals are the basic elements for building the networks that make up the classes and that locate the institutions in sociological space. The questions asked in 'power structure' research about class cohesiveness, policy formation, and processes of state domination are best conceptualized in terms of networks, and the basic elements of most networks are individuals and institutions" (1976, p. 223).

ideological limits of foreign policy through mass education, generation of supportive technical information, and participation in governmental decision making.

Domhoff next shows that major foreign policy institutions within the state itself are staffed by members of the power elite: the National Security Council, the top positions in the Departments of State and Defense, government-appointed commissions and task forces.

The third step in showing power elite dominance of American foreign policy is to show that the initiatives among other potential groups that might influence policy are taken by civilian members of the power elite. Here he again challenges C. Wright Mills's more managerial view:

> In short, if the United States in the postwar era has adopted what Mills called a military definition of reality, it is because this was chosen by leading big business members of the power elite on the basis of their understanding of national goals and international events, not because it was somehow foisted on them by the military men with whom they interact at high-level military "colleges," promote and retire within the Department of Defense, and hire into large corporations upon retirement. [Domhoff 1970, p. 139]

Domhoff argues that Congress is reduced to legitimating and making marginal amendments to policies initiated elsewhere (p. 139). Indeed, Congress functions as a representative of last resort for dissident factions of the power elite (pp. 143–9).

Domhoff criticizes both the pluralist emphasis on interest group activity and the managerial emphasis on elite competition as determinants of state policy. For Domhoff, the reality behind the appearance of conflict between groups and elites is the internal disagreements within the ruling class about how to deal with challenges from below (1970, pp. 145, 185). He writes of such internal conflicts, particularly pronounced during the Depression:

> differences among these corporate organizations . . . are sometimes used as examples of the pluralism and diversity of our society. That these disputes were very real, and could have led to greater hardship for the underlying population if resolved more conservatively than they were, is not to be denied. However . . . these differences were primarily technical conflicts within the power elite over means to agreed ends, those ends being the maintenance of the wealth distribution and a private property system in which a very small percentage of the population enjoys great prestige, privilege and authority. [P. 185]

How does this analysis of power elite political domination relate to Domhoff's conception of a governing class? Domhoff defines a governing class as the members of "a social upper class which owns a disproportionate amount of the country's wealth, receives a disproportionate share of the country's yearly income, contributes a disproportionate number of its members to governmental bodies and decision-making groups, and dominates the policy-forming process through a variety of means" (1970, p. 109).

Domhoff includes in his operational definition of the governing class indicators of both political participation and economic benefits. The hypothesis is that members of the upper class control those policy organizations that form both popular and elite opinion and supply model legislation. Such control is seen as not only necessary for policies to serve class interest but as normally possible (Useem 1979).

Domhoff does not analyze the societal conditions under which corporate participation in policy formation is either necessary or possible. Class analysts starting from the societal level argue that in the absence of working-class political opposition, the structure of the state itself may produce policies benefiting capital, thus rendering capitalist political participation unnecessary. The exclusion of the state from surplus production and its dependence on economic growth for tax revenues may produce these results regardless of capitalist political participation (Friedland, Piven, and Alford 1977). The efficacy of capitalist political participation is also contingent upon the historical structure of capital and/or the state. For example, the concentration and regional diversification of capital provides a different economic base of power than does a less concentrated, more localized capital structure. Where financial capital controls industrial corporations, different kinds of policies are possible and different patterns of political participation are necessary (Hall 1982). The significance of capitalist political participation may also be contingent upon the nature of the policy at issue and the extent to which it affects profitability and the reproduction of capitalist social relations.

With his close empirical focus on the actions of individual agents of corporate organizations inside and outside of key government agencies, Domhoff and various studies he has inspired have specified the situational mechanisms of ruling-class control of state policy, taking as given a general class world view.

Turning to the working class, we note that analyses of individual strategies of worker resistance within the class perspective stress the failure of socialization into the values of work, citizenship, and community, unlike the pluralist view. The creation of "free individuals" capable of producing surplus value also creates human beings with a capacity to defy authority in a wide variety of militant and insurgent ways. But defiance can lead, seemingly paradoxically, to greater individual integration into the working class.

Paul Willis's study of the way in which working-class boys in England develop strategies of resistance against the school illustrates this argument. As Stanley Aronowitz summarizes the work in his preface,

working class "lads" create their own culture of resistance to school knowledge
... truancy, counterculture, and disruption of the intended reproduction outcomes of the curriculum and pedagogy of schools yield an ironic effect: the
"lads" *disqualify* themselves from the opportunity to enter middle class jobs ...
the students produce themselves as rebellious, "uneducated" workers whose
single choice is the unskilled and semi-skilled occupations found in manual
labor. [Willis 1981, p. xii; italics in original]

The schools as a state institution accomplish the reproduction of the
working class with the cooperation of the students/workers themselves.

Willis focuses upon twelve working-class boys at a secondary modern
school in the Midlands, observing and interviewing them for two years,
until they left school and got working-class jobs. He deals with the
tensions between teachers and students and the constant attempts by
teachers to legitimate their activities and control over the students.
Teaching is a "fair exchange – most basically of knowledge for respect,
of guidance for control. Since knowledge is the rarer commodity this
gives the teacher his moral superiority. This is the dominant educational
paradigm which stands outside particular teachers but enables them to
exert control legitimately upon the children" (1981, p. 64). This quotation
gives a sense of the way in which Willis analyzes the microexchanges
that constitute the way in which the reproduction of labor power is
facilitated by state employees: the teachers.

The power of Willis's analysis lies partly in the juxtaposition of the
individual level of analysis with a class world view. Without denying
(in fact, by exalting) the distinctively individual voices of his working-
class youths, he sees their location within a matrix of contradictory forces
that can be described only in the language of capital, labor, and the
state.

The attempt to find links between different levels of analysis within
a class world view – that is, never losing sight of the ways in which a
class society defines the conditions under which individual resistance
occurs – leads Willis to some seemingly convoluted formulations. He
says, for example, that there are "impulses within a cultural form towards the penetration of the conditions of existence of its members and
their position within the social whole but in a way which is not centered,
essentialist, or individualist" (1981, p. 119). Furthermore, a "specific
combination of cultural 'insight' and partiality which gives the mediated
strength of personal validation and identity to individual behavior ...
leads in the end to entrapment. . . . It is . . . only this contradictory double
articulation which allows a class society to exist in liberal and democratic
forms: for an unfree condition to be entered freely" (pp. 119–20). Willis
thus emphasizes the reality of free choice by manual workers to work,
to become labor power. This choice "represents both a freedom, election

and transcendence, and a precise insertion into a system of exploitation and oppression for working class people" (p. 120). Willis rescues the pluralist premise that individuals have preferences and make choices but relocates that premise in relation to its consequences for the class destination of individuals.

Willis levels an important criticism at traditional class analysis. So-called structural determinations, he argues, must have symbolic power, or they have no power at all. "Although it is a simplification for our purposes here, and ignoring important forms and forces such as the state, ideology, and various institutions, we can say that macrodeterminants need to pass through the culture milieu to reproduce themselves at all" (1981, p. 171). The metaphor "pass through" is an untheorized linkage concept, but it raises the issue of just how these cultural "mediations" operate if, simultaneously, there are other "important forms and forces" at work. By giving convincing and concrete evidence at the level of individual action, Willis mounts a major empirical as well as theoretical challenge to structuralist theories of the reproduction of capitalist social relations of production.

Structuralist theories of reproduction [here he cites Althusser] present the dominant ideology (under which culture is subsumed) as impenetrable. Everything fits too neatly. Ideology always pre-exists and preempts any authentic criticism. . . . All specific contradictions and conflicts are smoothed away in the universal reproductive functions of ideology. This study suggests on the contrary, and in my view more optimistically, that there are deep disjunctions and desperate tensions within social and cultural reproduction. Social agents are not passive bearers of ideology, but active appropriators who reproduce existing structures only through struggle, contestation and a partial penetration of those structures. [1981, p. 175]

But he also criticizes the pluralist concept of socialization for its image of the "passive transmission" of values.

In discussing the role of the state in relation to the simultaneously contested and reproductive character of working-class culture, Willis argues that "the huge growth of the state in welfare and education . . . is not necessarily in any 'best' interest of capitalism. It has to some extent been forced on it by competing groups using their own real freedoms for self-advancement as they have seen it." Although state agencies "have been utilized and modified to help cool out, or drive out, problems which capitalism produces but cannot solve," that is not their entire role or function. State personnel "solve, confuse or postpone [capitalism's] problems in the short term very often because of their commitment to professional goals which are finally and awkwardly independent from the functional needs of capitalism" (1981, p. 176). Willis's fundamental image is of the open-ended and contingent character of the reproduction of culture, even in reference to the bureaucratic aspect of the state.

The essence of the pervasive role of the state in reproducing individual working-class consciousness is that it is *not* explicit. Willis emphasizes that

it is of the utmost importance to appreciate that the exchange relationship in the educational paradigm is not primarily in terms of its own logic a relationship between social classes or in any sense at all a self-conscious attempt on the part of teachers to dominate or suppress either working class individuals or working class culture as such. The teachers . . . are dedicated, honest and forthright. . . . it would be quite wrong to attribute to them any kind of sinister motive such as miseducating or oppressing working class kids. The teacher is given formal control of his pupils by the state, but he exerts his social control through an educational, not a class, paradigm. [1981, p. 67]

Although Willis interprets the oppositional subculture in the school as evidence for the formation of a working-class consciousness that combines resistance with "freedom of choice," which leads to reproduction of exploited labor power, his evidence could be interpreted quite differently. The school may constitute a specific milieu of domination, like a prison or a factory, in which powerless people construct various defensive strategies to protect their sense of integrity. The subculture of resistance leads a self-contained existence, with no particular consequences for the formation of class consciousness. The children may pass through and pass on such a subculture in the same way that children's games are learned, passed on, and forgotten. Or, children in schools that train children for the ruling class (Eton, for example) may exhibit similar behavior – derisive gestures, cabals for planning disruptive actions – without interfering with their chances for elite positions. Here the methodology of sampling is critical, to establish the comparative consequences of different subcultures for the formation and reproduction of class consciousness and the condition of recruitment to different class locations.

One of Willis's most telling points, implicitly directed against a pluralist image of a universal political culture, is that the system would break down if everyone believed in the values of equal opportunity and acted on them, taking pluralism seriously.

The "transition" from school to work . . . of working class kids who had really absorbed the rubric of self-development, satisfaction and interest in work, would be a terrifying battle. Armies of kids equipped with their "self-concepts" would be fighting to enter the few meaningful jobs available, and masses of employers would be struggling to press them into meaningless work. [1981, p. 177]

The state, via the schools, would face a far greater "problem" of "careers guidance" than at present (p. 177). But, because "social reproduction of the class society in general continues despite the intervention of the liberal state and its institutions, it may be suggested that some of the real functions of institutions work counter to their stated aims" (p. 177).

Conclusions

We have drawn upon disparate studies within the class perspective to illustrate analyses of the process of development of a state necessary for capitalist accumulation and the formation of working and capitalist classes, a state capable of carrying out policies benefiting capital, with or without its direct participation, and one capable of reproducing a labor force of workers.

In Chapter 14 we deal with the other side of the tradition: the emphasis on class struggle; the ways in which the contradictions of a class society undermine its functioning and ultimately lead to its transformation into another mode of production. The paradox of the class perspective is that the two traditions are rarely brought together theoretically. Studies emphasizing capital accumulation do not normally deal with class struggle and vice versa.

14

The capitalist state and class struggle

Class struggle is the other side of accumulation in the class perspective. In this chapter we summarize several exemplary studies dealing with the sources and consequences of class struggle and the consequences for crises of capitalism.[1]

The debate over the nature of capitalist crisis

For a summary of different class theories of crisis, we rely upon a critique from within the class perspective by Erik Olin Wright (1977). Wright's treatment underlines the fundamental debates within the perspective. Crises are seen as stemming from within the sphere of production, but political and cultural factors explain responses to crisis. As Wright puts it, "all Marxist perspectives on economic crisis tend to see crisis as growing out of the contradictions inherent in the process of capital accumulation." But there is "very little general consensus on which contradictions are most central to understanding crisis" (p. 195). Capitalist accumulation faces "impediments" that are generated by the process of accumulation itself. Because the process as a whole is contradictory, the solutions to these impediments generate further impediments.

Wright distinguishes four types of impediments to accumulation in Marxist theory: the falling rate of profit, underconsumption, the profit squeeze, and fiscal crises of the state. All of these sources of crisis find

[1] We neglect here those analyses of class struggle that do not involve the state. An example of a study of class struggle in the workplace that hardly mentions the state is James Geschwender's study of the League of Revolutionary Black Workers in the Detroit auto industry (1977). His approach assumes that "power lies at the point of production" and that such collective actions as "a general strike of black workers would cripple [key] industries and, indirectly, cripple the entire American economy" (p. 225). The state's role and functions are simply taken for granted. Geschwender mentions concrete actions by the state (the Supreme Court desegregation decision, World War II, a Detroit police attack) but only as an environment within which the class struggle of black workers occurs.

their origins in the "contradictions in the sphere of production" (1977, p. 203). He stresses the internal tensions in the various theories of crisis. Some argue that the cause of crisis is excessive surplus value, others that it is inadequate surplus value. Some argue that the "reason for crises is a declining rate of exploitation caused by successful class struggle," others that it is the rising rate of exploitation (p. 222). Wright tries to integrate the seemingly inconsistent explanations of crisis by seeing them as appropriate to different moments in the history of capitalism itself.[2]

Wright criticizes Marxist theorists of economic crisis who stress the source of crisis in the squeeze on capitalist profits but ignore the "links between the dynamics of accumulation and class struggles over wages" (1977, p. 217). Separating those processes results in class struggle being "treated as a kind of deus ex machina that determines the development of the system" (p. 217). Wright agrees, in other words, that there has been a separation between analyses stressing capital accumulation and those emphasizing class struggle.

Wright says that, despite its theoretical centrality, there is virtually no empirical evidence supporting the theory of the rising organic composition of capital. Wright attributes that lack to the difficulty of converting that particular theoretical proposition into empirically testable form. "Because national income accounts are not figured in terms of embodied labor times, and because data on capital invested includes many entries that Marxists would not even consider capital, it is of course highly problematic to gather reliable data on the organic composition" of capital (1977, pp. 208–9). If central theoretical postulates in the class perspective are not supported by empirical evidence, their theoretical coherence becomes even more important.

The important point for empirical investigation is not "merely the forces that produce a general expansion of state activity, but also the extent to which those forces selectively expand the unproductive or indirectly productive activities of the state, and the extent to which either

---

[2] A limitation of Wright's account of the class theories of capitalist crisis is that it includes no consideration of "imperialism or the world capitalist system," seen by many as the "structural solution par excellence to a variety of impediments" (1977, p. 222). An exposition of a variety of explanations of crisis by class theorists committed to a global perspective shows their different concrete analyses of the sources and potential consequences of global crisis. They agree that "there is a social whole that may be called a capitalist world economy," that there is a "global crisis" of that social whole, and that there has been an "increasing organization of oppressed groups within the world-system and increasing opposition to its continuance" (Amin et al. 1982, p. 9). But they disagree on whether or not the present crisis is part of a cycle of "long waves" or is historically specific, on the nature of imperialism and the USSR, and on the different political roles of nationalist, ethnic, and racial movements.

surplus-expanding or surplus-absorbing taxation tends to grow more rapidly" (Wright 1977, p. 219). But, according to Wright, nothing is known about the relative consequences of different forms of state activity for surplus expansion or surplus absorption, even if we assume that the measurement of surplus itself were clear. This is a gaping hole in the empirical support for fundamental hypotheses in the class perspective. If the state is defined as only part of the superstructure, whose forms and activities are explained – in the last analysis – by the requirements of capitalist accumulation and class rule, then this issue is relatively unimportant for empirical inquiry.

Because most neo-Marxists, including Wright, assume that the state performs increasingly important functions, the issue of the consequences of state activity can no longer be avoided. The problem is that the classics of Marxism provide almost no clue to the answer. The class perspective has an inadequate theoretical or empirical basis for explaining the causes and consequences of the increasingly important role of the state in the accumulation process.

Discussing the contradiction between accumulation and legitimation, Wright assumes that state expenditures have the consequence of legitimating state activity in the minds of the working class (1977, pp. 219–20). As he puts it, "the legitimation function directs much state activity toward coopting potential sources of popular discontent by attempting to transform political demands into economic demands." And "the expansion of Keynesian programs beginning in the 1930s created a perfect political climate for dramatically expanding such legitimating state expenditures" (p. 220). Here a pluralist factor (the climate of opinion) is seen as a factor affecting state policies, with the consequences at the societal level assumed to stabilize capital accumulation. Pluralist concepts are introduced as exogenous but necessary explanatory factors because of the incomplete theoretical structure of class analysis.

Further, the consequence of such state expenditures is that the provision of a social service "becomes viewed as a right" (p. 220). Political consciousness is thus introduced as an explanatory factor. How important it is and at what stage of the process the "relative autonomy" of consciousness becomes politically important are not dealt with. Lastly, the establishing of a "right" to a state benefit or service is seen as a further explanation of the "constant pressure for programs to expand, *regardless of the requirements of the accumulation process*" (p. 220; italics added). As these examples indicate, Wright is attempting to deal simultaneously with different levels of analysis: political culture (what is "viewed as a right"), elite strategies ("conscious planning"), a very important elaboration of the classic categories of class analysis. But the political and cultural categories tend to be introduced as descriptions of specific events ("conjunctures").

Similarly, in discussing military production, Wright mentions the fact that corporations supplying military hardware "are guaranteed a given profit rate by the state . . . and are thus under relatively little pressure to introduce inexpensive, efficient innovations into their production processes" (1977, p. 220). The Vietnam War is also cited as an example of a "period where these two imperatives [of military spending generated by imperialism and that generated by underconsumption] were quite contradictory" (p. 220). These are examples of Wright's citing historical events and specific historical periods as if they were manifestations of societal contradictions. Wright also attributes some of the inability of the state to respond to the needs of accumulation to "pluralist interest group politics" and asserts that, until "new political forces" arise, it is difficult to see a way out of the growing crisis of the state. These political concepts, too, are exogenous to the theoretical argument.

Wright charts different stages of capitalist development, at which different crises and structural "solutions" arise. He is at pains to deny offering a "rigid" or "determined" causal argument, but his treatment of the accumulation process, regardless of what form it takes, as the overriding causal factor gives his argument a deterministic tone. Also, the way in which he treats the role of the working class is conducive to a deterministic view. Although he argues that the working class is "not merely a passive force, even in its most integrated and contained periods," it still must adapt "its strategies to the 'structural solutions' that emerge in the course of capitalist development" (Wright 1977, p. 230).

This argument, contained in a footnote, is an untheorized assertion about the consequences of *politics* and *consciousness* for working-class struggle. If class consciousness and class action are forces that have to be understood historically and if the forms and conditions of class struggle contribute both to crisis and to the solutions to the crisis, then they have to be introduced explicitly into the theory.

Wright locates the contemporary sources of capitalist crisis squarely in the new role for the state, as "active state involvement in the production process itself" becomes the emerging solution to the latest systemic crisis (1977, p. 226). He says that this will produce an "ever deepening politicization of the accumulation process." As this happens, the "ideological legitimations of the 'free enterprise system' will tend to become more and more tenuous" (p. 226). As a result, "class struggles around the state and around production (which increasingly become the same struggles) will thus tend to become more ideological, more politicized, and ultimately more threatening to the capitalist system" (p. 226).

The ultimate solution by a "full-fledged state capitalism" could be a combination of "repression and centralized planning" (p. 227). Wright says that this is a "highly speculative image of the future," but the point is that it flows directly from his overriding class perspective. All of these historical developments, he says, would "occur within the continuing context of capitalist social relations and a capitalist state that serves the function of reproducing the class structure of capitalist society" (p. 226). The conditions under which capitalists will demand such state actions and those under which the state "knows" what to do to restore a semblance of equilibrium, under which ordinary people lose their belief in the "system" are not clear. We believe that they cannot be derived from the categories of class analysis alone but require concepts of politics and culture, as Wright's own argument suggests.

In discussing the "mechanisms of crisis management," Wright also introduces untheorized factors from other perspectives. Monopoly capital reinforced by state regulation weakens the recovery from crisis, in part because of the "personal ties between the corporate elite and the state apparatus" and in part because of the "social dislocations" resulting from major corporate bankruptcies. The personal ties of elites in networks may be idiosyncratic features of particular corporations that do not affect the overall trajectory of the crisis and recovery. Thus the politics of individuals and organizations central to pluralist and managerial perspectives are impediments to the state's performing its class functions.

The conditions under which corporate failure is a contribution to the restoration of productivity and realization of surplus value and those when it is unacceptable "disruption" are not specified. Wright's article is an important attempt to confront the difficulties in class theories of crisis and shows the difficulties of theorizing different levels of analysis within a general class perspective.

Nicos Poulantzas formulates a theory of the capitalist state that tries to take into account the political and ideological "instances" in a way that would not merely subordinate them to the requirements of capitalist reproduction. The result of his attempt, as we have already indicated, is the invention of numerous untheorized concepts. But another consequence is a convoluted form of expression that seems almost necessary to carry his point, that a *systemic* crisis – one that involves the entire ensemble of social relations of a mode of production – cannot be identified with specific observable characteristics. As Poulantzas puts his point,

the transformations that affect the state apparatuses in the developed capitalist countries and that permit us to speak of new forms of the capitalist state are not reducible to specific characteristics. Certain transformations suggest general characteristics that come from the current crisis of capitalism and that concern the reproduction of capitalism; in other words, even if the crisis of capitalism and the crisis of the state were eventually reabsorbed, these profound modifications of the state apparatus would nonetheless persist. [1979, pp. 357–8][3]

The distinctive contribution of Poulantzas to the debate in the class perspective over the nature of the crisis of the capitalist state is to elevate political and ideological crisis to the same level as economic crisis.[4]

Crisis of the mode of production: the societal level

A major recent analysis of societal crisis illustrates both the home domain of the class perspective and the way in which other levels of analysis are not theorized (Castells 1980). Manuel Castells's book is one of the rare works that consciously grounds the theoretical argument in the best available empirical data. Still, political factors enter as a deus ex machina to explain particular events, the actions of individuals, and the calculations of elites. They do not follow in any systematic way from the theoretical categories that form the skeleton of the analysis.[5]

Castells agrees with Erik Wright's criticisms of the various class theories of crisis but disagrees with Wright's attempt to reconcile them by associating them with different stages of capitalist development. Castells regards Wright's effort as an ad hoc adaptation, not adequate to comprehend the new historical developments themselves (Castells 1980, p. 42). Castells restates the basic Marxist theory of "contradictory historical development of the modes of production," defining the mode of production as the "specific mechanisms" through which the "organizers of production" appropriate the social product, specifically through their "social domination, enforced politically, ideologically and militarily"

---

[3] In our terms, this is an argument that the observable actions of individuals and behavior of organizations are not the measure of the existence of a crisis, let alone its causes. No observable features of the state, the economy, or any other social or political institution can be used by themselves to identify the nature of the crisis or its outcomes, because they are contingent not only upon the multiple contradictions of the system but also upon the open possibilities of class struggle. The methodological problems of this argument are apparent at once, because there is no way to use methods that measure multiple interrelated factors to "test" the hypotheses flowing from such a theory of crisis.

[4] For a recent and important attempt to integrate cultural factors into a theory of capitalist crisis, see O'Connor 1984. O'Connor's distinction between "individualism" and "individuality" corresponds to our distinction between the pluralist conception of the individual (the dominant ideology of individualism in his usage) and living human beings as the individual level of analysis.

[5] It is important to emphasize that in singling out Castells we are purposely neglecting class analyses that do not even pretend to take into account political and cultural factors but remain at a level of abstraction that regards the mundane worlds of politics and culture, organizations, and individuals as mere appearance or, worse, sheer ideology.

(p. 43). In addition, capital "enforces this social organization of production, consumption and exchange through the state and through ideological apparatuses adequate to shape people's consciousness (family,
education, religion, mass media, everyday life institutions, etc.)" (pp. 43–
4). This formulation subordinates other levels of analysis and social
institutions to the requirements of capitalist reproduction.

Castells argues that "the systematic intervention of the state into the
economy constitutes the principal countertendency to overcome crises.
The state thereby becomes the main factor of structural change in advanced capitalism" (1980, p. 69). The state, like capital, is a generic,
societal phenomenon. Castells differentiates between the several principal forms of state intervention, "each of which is essential to the survival of the system" (p. 69–72). The state in advanced capitalist societies
must assume the "costs of unprofitable economic activities"; furnish
"indispensable equipment and services to monopoly firms"; assume
more and more of the "social costs of private capital," mainly science,
technology, and education; guarantee "unproductive activities that generate . . . demand" (particularly military expenditures and the state bureaucracy); and ensure the "reproduction of social relations" by regulating
and sometimes providing health care, housing, transportation, and other
services. Some of these state activities are "productive," in the sense
that they increase surplus value and the rate of profit; others are a drain
and therefore are "unproductive." But all of them are necessary counter-
tendencies to crisis.

Because "the social conditions necessary for the development of productive forces are increasingly contradictory to capitalist social relationships," the state is "used more and more as a basic mechanism to absorb,
smooth and regulate the contradictions that emerge in the process of
accumulation." Citing Habermas's *Legitimation Crisis*, Castells introduces
the democratic and bureaucratic aspects of the state, but, like Habermas,
he subordinates them to the capitalist aspect. "However, the state is not
a purely regulatory capitalist apparatus. It expresses the contradictions
of society and must also fulfill the functions of *legitimating* the dominant
interests and *integrating* the dominated class into the system" (Castells
1980, p. 58; italics added). Then Castells asserts, again agreeing with
Habermas, that this expansion of state activity is a source of crisis. "The
growing state intervention to support the capitalist logic in all spheres
of economic and social life undermines the basis for its legitimacy as the
representative of the general interest" (p. 58). However, the crisis-in-
ducing consequences of increasing state intervention are neither empirically demonstrated nor theoretically developed.

Castells's elaborate restatement of the class perspective does not theorize politics and culture. Innumerable empirical references dot the ar-

gument of the book, to the Democratic Party, George McGovern, the CIO, Chase Manhattan Bank, and a host of others. Both organizations and individuals are real for Castells, but their relations are defined only through the categories of class analysis. The "fragmentation of the labor movement," for example, is explained by a host of concrete "historical" factors, in a way central to the pluralist method. Deviations from the classic picture of capitalist development are explained by introducing ad hoc historical factors: the absence of feudalism, the frontier, early voting rights, the ideology of citizenship, the "fragmentation and decentralization of the state," and the "ethnic and social segmentation of a working class" (1980, p. 221). These multiple factors may indeed have contributed, as he argues, to the unusual combination in the United States of working-class militance and lack of class consciousness. Castells's argument is more flexible than that of many class analysts in accepting the "multidimensionality" of history and society, but he has not yet found the way to analyze democratic struggles and state centralization at the societal level.

Castells's theorization of the potential of "anti crisis policies" (1980, p. 220) suffers because he has changed his level of analysis, without a theoretical vocabulary to help him. Concepts that have theoretical status in the pluralist perspective (party, faction, voting, public sector, demand, interest group) have only empirical or ideological significance. Discussing the social movements that emerged during the sixties, he says that a pattern of "self-definition as an interest group" developed for blacks, minorities, students, and women, not to mention the ecological movements and the counterculture. Castells says that, "under these conditions, the political-ideological interests of the 'majority' including the unions and community groups, have been equivalent to the economic interests. Their political perspectives have been centered on the improvement of their bargaining capacities in relation to the distribution of the product" (pp. 222–3). The implication is that the level of political consciousness of these movements is quite low because it is at the level of distribution, not production, and is concerned only with immediate economic interests, not long-term class interests. Putting the word "majority" in quotation marks suggests that the political opinions of a majority of the population are superficial and will be superseded by the higher political consciousness of class. Interest group solidarity will be replaced by class solidarity, once the world crisis has deepened sufficiently, but the transition conditions are not theorized.

This is a classic argument. The problem is that it is an ad hoc one, not theoretically grounded in the kinds of categories Castells develops so carefully in the first part of the book. Except for the postulate that the experiences of ordinary people will teach them the essential nature of capitalist exploitation and their potential solidarity with others, there is no theory of why and how the interest group and economic consciousness of ordinary people will break down and new forms of class-based political action and organization emerge.

In hindsight, the specific political events that Castells regards as having rocked the foundations of American capitalism did not have quite the consequences he predicted. The general scheme does not explain political events. Watergate, for example, he says (writing probably in 1979), was a "major breach in the legitimacy of the highly integrated American political system," an event that showed that "its political foundations were being shaken" (1980, p. 78). And Castells has a tendency to collapse individual political strategies and global-system requirements into the same calculation. "Although Nixon paid a great deal of attention to his personal political interests, he also had to remember what the major requirements were for the reproduction of a system that structurally favored the large U.S. corporations in the international economy" (p. 83). The measures he implemented "had several immediate consequences that precipitated inflation and started the crisis." Under what conditions different state actions contribute to crisis or serve as counter-tendencies to crisis is not specified theoretically. Nor is it clear when the actions of individuals serve their own political or economic interests and when they are taken to further the global reproduction of capitalism – or how one can tell the difference.

The U.S. economic crisis of the mid-1970s and 1980s is explained by two main factors that led to severe inflation: the rise in both food and oil prices. The "decisive factor" in the former was the "support by the Nixon administration of food production for export" (Castells 1980, p. 83); in the latter, the "unstable political balance of forces" in the Middle East, leading to the possibility of OPEC power and shifting strategies by the big oil companies. Once again, political factors that are themselves not theoretically related to the "underlying" societal forces that work are called upon to explain the specific pattern of crisis. Nixon chose to support the export of grain in order to "allow the agricultural sector higher profit margins on exports" (p. 84). If that decision was structurally determined, the overriding importance of averting systemic crisis should have changed Nixon's calculations. If he "remembered" the "major requirements for the reproduction of the system" in other instances, he should have this time too.

Although the *primary* contradiction between capital and labor does not involve politics or the state, both class struggle and societal crisis are intrinsically political for Castells. "The only limit to this process of capitalist accumulation comes from the general crisis of the social relationships on which the process is based. As this limit is a political limit, it will depend ultimately on the power relationships generated in the overall process of class struggle" (Castells 1980, p. 48). And, when wages are reduced past a certain point, social and political "unrest" will occur. Unrest is an individual characteristic, which the dictionary defines as a "troubled or disturbed state, restlessness, disquiet and uneasiness" or (and this is the meaning Castells undoubtedly has in mind) "a condition of angry discontent and protest verging on revolt." Castells assumes that one of the *systemic* consequences intrinsic to the capitalist mode of production is the generation of individual "resistance" or "unrest," in other words, class struggle. Absolutely essential organizational and individual changes are assumed to develop out of societal processes inherent in the contradiction between capital and labor.

Accumulation versus legitimation: the organizational level

For some class analysts, the chief focus of contradictions, and therefore of both class struggle and crisis, has shifted from the point of production to the state. An example of this analysis is O'Connor's *Fiscal Crisis of the State* (1973), which combines an organizational level of analysis and a class world view. Its importance calls for detailed treatment.[6]

O'Connor takes as given the institutional separation of state and economy in a capitalist society, the imperative of accumulation, and the inevitability of crisis. The state must absorb the social costs of accumulation, which maintains the legitimacy of the capitalist mode of production. The distinctive feature of his study is that he looks at the specific organizational mechanisms that lead to crisis.

The U.S. post–World War II economy, according to O'Connor, can be divided into three sectors: competitive, monopoly, and state. The competitive sector consists of thousands of small firms producing for local and regional markets, which are likely to be seasonal and unstable. The firms employ largely nonunion workers at relatively low wages, and there is little capital investment per worker. Accordingly, both productivity and profits are low. Because such firms are highly competitive and any given industry is overcrowded, the rate of business failure is high. Wages, prices, and profits are determined chiefly by market forces. Prices

---

[6] Even appreciative appraisals of O'Connor's work distort it, if they are within another world view. Albert Hirschman (1981), for example, substitutes the term "entrepreneurial function" for O'Connor's "accumulation function" because he wants to emphasize the role of actors such as entrepreneurs. And he substitutes "reform" for "legitimation" function, similarly, because he wants to emphasize individual "reformers," who include "anyone determined to correct imbalances and inequities that have arisen in the course of [economic] growth" (pp. 124–5). He says that "legitimation" as used by O'Connor implies something about objectives of actors, which is an individual level, not O'Connor's organizational level of analysis.

are determined mainly by productivity. The extra profits gained by one set of capitalists through technical innovation are reduced in the long run as other capitalists adopt them and as increased production confronts a market that does not grow as fast. In the early 1970s, about one-third of the labor force in the United States was employed in the competitive sector.

The monopoly sector consists of relatively few large firms in industries such as auto, steel, rubber, and oil, producing for national and international markets that are relatively stable. The firms employ largely unionized workers at relatively high wages. Capital investment per worker is high, and firms are stable. Productivity and profits are high. Another one-third of the U.S. labor force was in the monopoly sector in the early 1970s.

The state sector consists of direct state production of services such as health, welfare, education, mail, and production contracted out to private firms to build military hardware, highways, and state buildings. The state sector, employing the last third of the United States labor force, has been expanding greatly since World War II to meet the changing needs of the economy and of political stability. Because the sole source of state revenue in the United States is taxation, ultimately drawn from private incomes and profits, the state is dependent upon private investment to finance ever-growing public expenditures.

Conversely, the private economy is increasingly dependent upon state action to increase the productivity of labor by providing infrastructure or specialized training ("social capital," in O'Connor's words). The state must also reduce the direct costs of labor through subsidized housing, health, transportation, social security, and so on ("social consumption"). Furthermore, the state must regulate the social conflicts that erupt both at home and abroad as a result of capitalist growth. Welfare at home and military intervention abroad are "social expenses." The state finances some facilities, manpower training, and education partly because they are necessary for the private economy but are not produced by the private economy. Roads and airports, for example, are either completely paid for or heavily subsidized by the state. Such facilities may also be used by the general public or consumers other than businesses, but those facilities that directly benefit business tend to be much more easily constructed than those that do not benefit business or whose financing actually cuts into profits.

Unemployment, poverty, urban sprawl, water and air pollution are regarded by O'Connor as typical indirect effects of private production. These social costs of production are not borne by the industries that produce them. The state either bears the costs, or they must be absorbed privately. These expenses of capitalist production are "owned" by the people as a whole, like the national debt.

The state expands welfare budgets in order to retain the support of the working and unemployed population. This is the "legitimation" function of the state. The state must also provide subsistence for those workers displaced because of the growth and decline of different sectors of the economy. Technological innovations lead to stagnating industries in some regions and shifting markets for products. Welfare – from food stamps to social security to unemployment insurance – reduces resistance to technological changes that increase profitability but displace labor. Because welfare support is geared to minimum market wages, these surplus workers tend to remain part of the labor pool competing for available jobs.

The maintenance of large armed forces also provides unproductive employment for millions of men and women (O'Connor 1973, p. 99). The goal of protecting the political stability of areas presently or potentially open to the investment of capital coincides with the goal of holding down domestic unemployment to a politically acceptable minimum. Attempts are made to stabilize the world capitalist order through arms sales, which maintain ruling classes in power in other countries, and through the military, which is trying to maintain the world balance of power and prevent revolutionary anticapitalist regimes in other countries.

The growth of the state is therefore both a significant cause and a consequence of the expansion of monopoly capitalism for O'Connor. The capitalist economy tends to produce both surplus labor and surplus capital. Surplus labor is produced because the monopoly sector relies on increasing capital investment in machines to increase production instead of hiring additional workers. Further, the monopoly sector's ability to control the prices of their commodities enables it to prevent productivity increases from being passed on to all workers in the form of lower prices. The real purchasing power of the workers does not increase, except in the monopoly sector. But the inability of the monopoly sector to generate increased employment floods the competitive sector with job applicants and keeps wages down. Poorly paid families in the competitive sector, plus unemployed workers and their families, are most in need of increased public services and increased public employment.

Surplus capital is also produced in the monopoly sector. Wages in the monopoly sector grow proportionately to productivity increases, but competitive sector wages lag behind. Competitive sector wages grow more slowly than monopoly sector productivity because of high competition, low unionization, and low productivity. Demand for monopoly sector goods is limited by their high prices, the low wages in the competitive sector, and the relatively high prices of competitive sector goods. Many of the competitive sector firms are engaged in the service sector. These labor-intensive services – barbers, repair people, doctors, cleaners – become relatively expensive when compared with the goods – calculators, drugs, vacuum cleaners, television sets – produced by the capital-intensive monopoly sector. Both low wages and low productivity limit growth of demand for monopoly sector goods and thus limit the sector's expansion. The high profits in the monopoly sector become surplus capital.

The welfare state thus expands because of the growth of surplus labor. The warfare state expands because of the growth of surplus capital. Welfare spending dampens political protest by the victims of economic growth and expands the level of demand for private sector goods. Warfare spending stimulates profitable investment at home and expands the area of the globe that is "safe" for foreign investment by United States firms.

O'Connor recognizes the impact on state expansion of both bureaucratic strategies and the political responsiveness of legislatures to popular political demands but emphasizes the primary importance of surplus labor and surplus capital as causal factors. Fiscal crisis – the tendency for government expenditures to increase faster than the tax revenues available to finance them – occurs because capitalist growth increasingly requires the public subsidy of costs, whereas profits remain privately controlled. This contradiction between public costs and private profits is an important cause of state crises. The generic label for the whole process is the growing contradiction between capital accumulation and legitimation of the state.

O'Connor argues that most state policies are the result of interest group politics, wherein particular class interests (both capitalist and working class) are represented in the decisions of particular state agencies. He then infers that many of those state policies create problems for the capitalist system and that these problems generate an attempt to create a coordinating executive agency (a class-conscious political directorate). His general argument assumes both that this new overall state agency will be able to create some internal coherence within the state (the executive function) and that it will be able to assess the consequences of alternative state policies for the capitalist class as a whole. The executive is assumed to be able to act effectively to carry out the policies in the interests of the capitalist class as a whole.

This argument collapses the organizational level of analysis into the societal level, assuming that state policies that satisfy overall system needs are generated almost automatically. O'Connor points out that even within the ruling class there are "conflicts [that] must be reconciled and compromised." Given the "complex and wide-ranging nature of the interests of this class, policy is dictated not by a single directorate but by a multitude of private, quasi-public, and public agencies," ranging from the Committee for Economic Development to the Business Council (1973, p. 68). He argues:

But the president and his key aides must remain independent: they must interpret class (as opposed to particular economic) corporate interests and translate these interests into action, not only in terms of immediate economic and political needs, but also in terms of the relations between monopoly capital and competitive sector labor and capital. Monopoly capitalist class interests . . . are not the aggregate of the particular interests of this class but rather emerge within the state administration "unintentionally." In this important sense, the capitalist state is not an "instrument" but a "structure." [Pp. 68–9]

But O'Connor fails to provide an explanation of the ability of this autonomous executive to develop effective class policies or to resist the political influence of particular industries, regions, or political blocs within the monopoly capitalist class. It is not at all clear what criteria could be used to assess when state policies further capital accumulation and when they do not.

O'Connor also assumes that state investment decisions are rational from the point of view of the objective interests of capital as a whole. Specific regions and industries may suffer from those decisions, but the interests of the total system are served. However, the difference between state policies that allow the system to function (the weakest assertion) and those that further the highest possible rate of capital accumulation (a much stronger assertion) is not clear, nor is the difference between those that lead to crisis and those that do not. Adequate information for predicting the consequences of a particular course of action is assumed to be available to the cohesive and "class conscious political directorate." Whether or not a given state investment decision is in the interests of capitalism remains an open question.

The theoretical issue is obviously not solved simply by asserting that the decisions actually made by state agencies further capital accumulation and the long-range interests of the capitalist class. Such an assertion accepts the ideology of capitalist rationality at face value, as if policies made by state organizations are capable of balancing the claims of one interest group against another to stabilize the system. In a curious sense, such an assertion inserts a functional version of pluralism into the class perspective by assuming that the state is above *all* competing interests, mediating, controlling, allocating, sometimes favoring one corporate sector or class interest above another, but always in the interests of the system as a whole. In the absence of criteria for the existence of contradictions between the representation of the interests (both short- and long-range) of specific industries or regions and the interests of the system as a whole, there is no explanation for why one state policy rather than another emerged from a particular situation of class struggle. Organizational forms and then policies are assumed to develop that reflect the need to respond either to a crisis or to class struggle (or both).

Implicit in O'Connor's position is the assumption that major developments in the state were *necessary* or even *required* by fundamental interests of monopoly capitalism. The phrase "the corporate ruling class learned to use the state" confuses the objective consequences of state actions with the "intentions" and perceived interests of various segments of classes and social groups. This blurring of the distinction between consequences and intentions has an important political implication, because it is then difficult to tell when the passing of a particular piece of legislation, for example, reveals political weakness in the capitalist class (a failure to anticipate consequences and thus a political situation of being off-balance) or when the situation fits neatly into the self-conscious strategies of ruling-class leadership. Surely it is important to be able to distinguish between state policies that are the carefully considered actions of self-conscious class leaders and those that are desperate compromises, negotiated to avoid jeopardizing the stability of class rule.

O'Connor's analysis of public expenditures also embodies assumptions as to their *effects* on the accumulation process. *Social capital* raises the productivity of labor. *Social consumption* reduces the cost of labor. These presumed effects are used to explain the existence and expansion of different public expenditures, a functional explanation. The categories themselves contain hypothesized consequences that are not the subject of empirical analysis. Whether or not a housing or health program lowers capital's cost of reproducing labor power is contingent upon the incidence of tax costs and expenditure benefits of the program and the opportunity costs of providing the same service through the private market. These costs are subject to complex contingencies, one of which is class struggle over private wages and the "social wage" (state transfer payments and other services that contribute to household wage incomes). Spending for public services is not determined only by the need to reduce direct wage costs, nor does it necessarily have the effect of reducing direct wage costs in this context.

Because of O'Connor's world view, he assumes that public expenditure variation can be explained by the societal requisites of capital accumulation and inserts those functional consequences into the very definition of the public expenditure categories. It is only then a small step to "explain" the variation in those expenditures by various problems of reproducing capital accumulation. In fact, O'Connor never demonstrates empirically the supposed consequences or causes of the public expenditures he studies.

Another study of the origins of the welfare state as a political response to working-class struggle is *The Corporate Ideal in the Liberal State* by James Weinstein (1968). Weinstein examines the class base and political role of the National Civic Federation (NCF) between 1900 and 1918, interpreting it as a key manifestation of capitalist political strategies to counter emerging forms of working-class organization. This "corporate liberal" organization was initiated and supported by some of the nation's largest industrial and financial capitalists, but it also included national labor leaders (Gompers of the AFL and Mitchell of the United Mine Workers), prominent educators, and public officials. Weinstein argues that the greater market control and higher levels of profit of the larger corporations made possible the emergence of a liberal corporate ideology.

One of the factors that made corporate liberalism necessary was the development of new forms of working-class political struggle. A national Socialist Party was formally organized in 1901 and was able at one time to elect 1,200 officeholders in 340 cities and control about one-third of the organizations of the American Federation of Labor (Weinstein 1968, p. 5). The AFL itself moved into partisan politics after 1905 (p. 22) and continued to lead unionization drives.

The National Civic Federation's political strategy was to develop social reforms that would preempt the emergence of the kinds of socialist union movements or independent labor parties that developed across Western Europe. Federation support for institutionalization of trade unions and collective bargaining was based on this premise. Thus federation member Louis Brandeis argued in 1905 that the survival of capitalism was dependent on the introduction of collective bargaining (Weinstein 1968, p. 17). Capitalist elites within the NCF increasingly came to see the trade unions as an "antidote for the socialistic propaganda" (p. 17). This differentiation of state and economy, celebrated as generic to the social system in pluralist theory, is here seen as a class strategy to insulate capitalism from political attack as it becomes increasingly dependent upon state intervention.

Through development of model legislation and the organization of liberal corporate and more conservative trade union leadership, the NCF successfully anticipated many programmatic socialist and militant labor union demands. This deprived socialist and union organizations of their immediate basis of mobilization and coopted progressive leaders. The NCF was frequently able to define the limits of reform. The reforms for which the NCF developed model legislation did improve working-class conditions but were structured in ways that headed off potential working-class political organization.

National Civic Federation strategy for social reform legislation – workmen's compensation or the minimum wage, for example – was primarily directed at the state (namely, California) level. Given the increasing role of the federal government in regulating the corporate economy, the NCF was eager to avoid attracting working-class attention to the federal level (Weinstein 1968, pp. 30–1). Reforms were designed to deflect working-class organization from the workplace and toward state bureaucracies. Workmen's compensation for occupational injury is an example. The labor unions opposed compensation laws on the ground that they would only pension off injured workers at less than full wages (p. 43). Instead, the unions favored legal changes that would make the employers liable for all nonnegligent injuries and place the cost and responsibility on capital rather than the taxpayer. The unions would rely on sympathetic juries to make high settlements.

Thus the new labor unions initially opposed minimum-wage, maximum-hour, and workmen's compensation legislation. The labor unions favored independent working-class organization within the corporation, not external bureaucratic administration by the state. This independent political working-class organization was precisely what the corporate leaders wanted to prevent. In addition, NCF leaders were fearful that the labor unions would move to reduce the political independence of the courts, given the increasing use of court injunctions against labor under the Sherman Act (Weinstein 1968, pp. 48–9). Because labor unions had been unsuccessful in their fight for employer liability legislation, they were eventually coopted into supporting the NCF drive for compensation laws. Union demands were reduced to coverage, benefit levels, waiting periods, and public versus commercial insurance (pp. 59–60). Legislation and bureaucratic machinery were put in place to deal with work-related injury, disease, and death as a matter of compensation of individual workers. Some of the costs of private production were therefore socialized.

These new state interventions ameliorated some consequences of exploitation, but they did not touch the systemic causes: lack of working-class control of production and the priority of profitability. Just at the time when the U.S. working class was organizing both in the workplace and in the electoral arena, the potential popular determination of policy was slipping out of the public arena. The agenda for reform was set by class-conscious capitalists anxious to coopt movements seeking more fundamental social change, not by the values of the public or the state's capacity to rationalize private markets.

Weinstein assumes that working-class political organization could have redirected its demands to production itself and developed a capacity for mass mobilization and resistance to state repression that this strategy would probably have entailed. But Weinstein does not analyze the institutional conditions under which such working-class politics might emerge. To analyze apparently progressive legislation as preemptive or cooptive on the part of the capitalist elites requires that one theoretically specify the political potentialities of the issues involved as well as the political capabilities of those who stand to win or lose by their alternative resolution. One must develop an analysis of the relative capacities of the different political actors in specific situations, without losing sight of the structural and systemic parameters.[7]

If the chief locus of contradictions has shifted to the state, which cannot simultaneously guarantee the conditions for capitalist accumulation and integrate politically the population, a reconstruction of class analysis is required. As Jean Cohen has put it:

Under the conditions of late capitalism, the growth of the administrative/political subsystem and its penetration of the economy implies the noncorrespondence of the contradiction between wage labor and capital and the constitution of social classes. In short, one cannot deduce all of the social strata or the conflict potential of groups from the contradiction within the capitalist economy, because this system is no longer isolated from political/administrative mediation. [1982, p. 197; see also Offe 1974, 1975, 1984]

In our terms, an adequate theory of class struggle requires the systematic introduction of categories to analyze structural and situational levels of power, something almost nonexistent in the class perspective.

Class consciousness and class culture: the individual level

A classic study of the making of the English working class stresses the interplay of consciousness and action among individual workers (Thompson 1963). Almost devoid of explicit theory, the work is a good example of the implicit capitalist state. Thompson sees capital accumulation and class formation as immanent in every event – the Leeds election of 1832 (p. 825) or the transportation of the Dorchester laborers (p. 825). It is not necessary to theorize capitalism and the state; they are present in every moment.

Thompson defines class as a process, not a structure, because he focuses upon individual experience. "Class happens when some men, as a result of common experiences (inherited or shared), feel and articulate the identity of their interests as between themselves, and as against other men whose interests are different from (and usually opposed to) theirs. The class experience is largely determined by the productive relations into which men are born – or enter involuntarily" (1963, p. 9).

---

[7] A parallel study of the ways in which working-class organizations acting in cooperation with the state coopted working-class militance in England is Panitch 1976.

Thompson's task is to describe, in extraordinary detail, the activities and experiences that constituted the English working class. The state is empirically recognized, through the actions of magistrates, members of parliament, and political leaders, but the theoretical framework is almost completely implicit.[8] In fact, Thompson even uses a biological analogy for the history of a class. "This book can be seen as a biography of the English working class from its adolescence until its early manhood" (p. 11).

When Thompson does generalize, there is no question about his world view. "The exploitive relationship is more than the sum of grievances and mutual antagonisms. It is a relationship which can be seen to take distinct forms in different historical contexts, forms which are related to corresponding forms of ownership and State power" (1963, p. 203). But Thompson simply assumes that the state has the appropriate form and operations to serve the needs of capital accumulation and class formation. His work is at the individual level of analysis from a class world view.

Thompson regards the Industrial Revolution as "truly catastrophic" for ordinary people, because they were "subjected simultaneously to an intensification of two intolerable forms of relationship: those of economic exploitation and of political oppression." At each point when the worker "sought to resist exploitation, he was met by the forces of employer or State, and commonly of both" (1963, pp. 198–9). But the Industrial Revolution should not be seen as an "external force . . . working upon some nondescript undifferentiated raw material of humanity" (p. 194). Rather, "the factory hand or stockinger was also the inheritor of Bunyan, of remembered village rights, of notions of equality before the law, of craft traditions. He was the object of massive religious indoctrination and the creator of new political traditions. The working class made itself as much as it was made" (p. 194). Such a statement is an important clue to Thompson's implicit theory of the emerging capitalist state. A multitude of concrete experiences, individual and shared, created the modern English working class, seen primarily as a *cultural* fact. It is appropriate that a work at the individual level of analysis should use the language of experience, of culture, of group. One of the reasons why Thompson's study is powerful is that he combines levels of analysis without losing sight of the conceptual language appropriate to his primary level of analysis. Concepts within the pluralist home domain are used, without

---

[8] It is relevant to note that Thompson makes withering comments on both Smelser (1959) and Dahrendorf (1959). Emphasizing that class is a relationship and not a thing, he says that "it" – the working class – does not exist and that the real question is "how the particular social organization (with its property rights and structure of authority) got to be there" (Thompson 1963, pp. 10–11).

adopting the pluralist world view. Thompson chronicles hundreds of incidents of protest, riots, and agitations that are not yet class struggle but manifold manifestations of the attempts to reclaim old rights or to win new ones, such as the vote or the right to strike. But these struggles for rights are seen not as part of an evolutionary progress toward universal citizenship but as an aspect of the creation of a working class within an intrinsically exploitative system.

Thompson's style is self-consciously concrete, full of evocative images and accounts of individuals. His quasibiography of William Cobbett reads as if Cobbett is a model for his own style and tone. Thompson wants to ground his argument in "commonly available experience," like Cobbett's political tracts. Comparing the "truly profound, democratic influence of Cobbett's attitude to his audience" (Thompson 1963, p. 749) with Hazlitt's style of "controlled rhythms," which "belongs to the polite culture of the essayist" (p. 748), Thompson clearly comes down on the side of Cobbett. He wants to start with the most concrete human experience of ordinary people and then expand to "wider social and political implications" (p. 749).

This view of Thompson's intellectual and political commitment to individual experience is consistent with his forceful rejection of abstract theoretical Marxism in his critique of Louis Althusser's structuralism (Thompson 1978). A good example of his theorizing, couched in the rhetoric of antitheory, is his view of law. Rejecting Althusser's elaboration of the notions of "relative autonomy" and "levels," Thompson asks, "Is law, for example, relatively autonomous, and if so, autonomous of what, and how relatively?" He answers his own question from a study of his own.

I found that law did not keep politely to a "level" but was at *every* bloody level; it was imbricated within the mode of production and productive relations themselves (as property-rights, definitions of agrarian practice) and it was simultaneously present in the philosophy of Locke; it intruded brusquely within alien categories; reappearing bewigged and gowned in the guise of ideology; it danced a cotillion with religion, moralizing over the theatre of Tyburn; it was an arm of politics and politics was one of its arms; it was an academic discipline, subjected to the rigour of its own autonomous logic; it contributed to the definition of the self-identity both of rulers and of ruled; above all, it afforded an arena for class struggle, within which alternative notions of law were fought out. [1978, p. 96]

This poetic quotation has been given at length because the very diversity of the manifestations of "law" is necessary to make our point. At the risk of incurring Thompson's ire for more abstract theorizing, it must be suggested that here is the class world view at work. Even in the act of rejecting the abstractions of Althusserian structuralism, Thompson sees embedded in every institution and every social practice of law and the state manifestations of the mode of capitalist production and class struggle.

Thompson regards Althusser's notion of

"levels" motoring around in history at different speeds and on different "sched-ules" as an academic fiction. For all these "instances" and "levels" are in fact human activities, institutions and ideas. We are talking about men and women, in their material life, in their determinate relationships, in their experience of these, and in their self-consciousness of this experience. [1978, p. 97]

Again, this shows Thompson's commitment to the analysis of individual experience, but it also shows the extent to which he shares a world view with Althusser. Thompson would not have taken the time or the energy to develop such an extensive critique if he did not share the same world view and see Althusser as competing in the same territory for theoretical domination. They share the same commitment to the view that law – the state – is in the last analysis a set of institutions maintaining capitalist accumulation and with it the owners and the working class.[9]

The state appears on almost every page of Thompson, not as the object of description or of theory, but as the context of the everyday experience of carpenters, spinners, weavers, field laborers, blacksmiths, and a host of other workers. But, "In the end, it is the political context as much as the steam engine which had most influence upon the shaping [of] con-sciousness and institutions of the working class" (1963, p. 197). Part of Thompson's achievement was to maintain an unwavering focus upon individuals and groups without losing sight of the economic and political context that shaped their experiences.[10]

Michael Hechter's *Internal Colonialism* (1975) is a different kind of class analysis of political culture. This is a statistical study of the origins and persistence of distinctive political cultures in peripheral territories in Great Britain: Ireland, Wales and Scotland. In Hechter's class world

[9] Perry Anderson, in turn, criticized Thompson for overemphasizing the role of experi-ence and consciousness (and therefore the methodology of historiography), reminding him of the fundamental premise of Marxism that "classes are constituted by the mode of production and not vice versa" (Anderson 1980, p. 55). Anderson says that Thompson relies upon the "persuasive everyday evidence that people go about their lives making all sorts of choices" (the individual level) but then merges that level of analysis with "collective projects" (the societal level) (Anderson 1980, p. 21). Anderson argues that this fusion of levels of analysis prevents Thompson from distinguishing "those actions which are indeed conscious volitions at a personal or local level" from the "variable role of different types of deliberate ventures, personal or collective, in history" (p. 21). We agree with that point.

[10] The question of how consciousness among individuals is reproduced and transformed remained for a long time beneath the surface, reflected only in unorthodox strands of Marxist thought, such as Georg Lukacs's analyses of commodity fetishism and reification (1971), Antonio Gramsci's views on cultural hegemony (1971), and the Frankfurt "critical school" analyses of capitalist culture.

view, the people of the Celtic periphery made use of distinctive cultural identities to defend themselves against economic exploitation.

After centuries of political and economic integration, the peoples of the Celtic periphery to this day have a distinctive cultural identity. Hechter analyzes the relationship between England and the Celtic periphery as one of internal colonialism, based upon economic exploitation reinforced by the power of the central English state. The original political incorporation of the periphery led to trade with the more developed British economy. Because the Celts were politically unable to protect their nascent manufacturing, their economy withered. A pattern of specialized, export-based growth resulted, growth that was highly vulnerable to English growth. English-controlled capital reinforced dependency upon industries that were complementary to the English economy and ensured that most of the new profits were exported back to England.

Hechter analyzes the changing economic structure of England and the Celtic periphery between 1851 and 1961. Contrary to what pluralist theorists of development would posit, the per capita income differential between the English core and the Celtic periphery persisted over the entire century, and industrialization remained highly localized in a few enclaves in the periphery.

Analyzing county data for England and its Celtic periphery, Hechter finds a persistent relationship between their cultural attributes – such as church affiliation – and their economic position. Thus counties that are culturally subordinate (non–Church of England) are poorer than those that are culturally dominant, even if we control for the level of industrialization. Although a pluralist might explain this relationship from the work habits that such cultural values inculcate, Hechter argues that English capitalists used these cultural attributes as a criterion for allocation of higher-income occupations to counties. Thus Hechter analytically fuses political domination, economic exploitation, and cultural subordination.

For both pluralist and managerial theorists, integration into a modern culture or control by the central state should erode subnational territorial and ethnic cultural identities. Hechter explains the strengthening of ethnic culture not as due to the persistence of primordial ties among premodern local cultures but as a reactive popular mobilization against foreign political and economic domination and as an aspect of working-class resistance to culturally distinct gentry and capitalists. Traditional ethnic and religious identities become tools of territorial and class resistance. Because the economic interests of the dominant gentry tied them to an alien culture, the legitimacy of their class power was reduced. Territorial resistance ultimately led to violent repression by the English state, the destruction and profanation of deviant religious institutions, and the forbidding of peripheral cultural practices. These in turn became the tools and symbols of resistance to that domination.

Hechter takes the development of class-based political identities as the normal "structural" path of societal development. A territory is nationally integrated to the extent that social structural characteristics determine its voting patterns. In Great Britain, the Conservative Party is most identified with London political elites, the Church of England, and the crown and is least likely to incorporate Celtic political elites.[11] Hechter found that in peripheral counties – those that were poor and had non-elite religious beliefs – per capita income had no relation to the level of Conservative Party voting. The structural model did not predict voting behavior where economic disadvantage was superimposed upon cultural distinctiveness. In peripheral counties, political identities were formulated in status, not class, terms. In the culturally and economically dominant areas industrialization led to class political cleavages.

Such peripheral cultural identities become political sources of resistance to what Hechter calls a "cultural division of labor" (1975, p. 340). An absence of identity with the national state and culture is due not to traditionalism, to be eroded by structural differentiation or state incorporation, but to political resistance to territorial economic exploitation and institutionalized racism. Hechter argues that territorial, religious, and ethnic identifications – the stuff of status group politics – have class content.[12]

Conclusions

The theme of crisis runs through many recent class analyses of the world capitalist system, regardless of how the state is analyzed. Ernest Mandel ends his *Late Capitalism* (1975) with a chapter called "The Crisis of Capitalist Relations of Production," linking that crisis explicitly to "the contradiction between the growth of the forces of production and the survival of the capitalist relations of production" (p. 562). The state plays a critical

---

[11] Analyzing eight elections between 1885 and 1966, Hechter finds that Celtic counties have the highest concentration of negative residuals (where industrialization overestimates Conservative vote) (1975, p. 223). Further, the proportion of nonconformist religious members, Celtic speakers, and Welsh-born persons is consistently negatively correlated with this voting residual (p. 222). Further, these results hold up in industrial and nonindustrial counties (pp. 231–2).

[12] Although Hechter has shown both theoretically and empirically how peripheral cultural identities are particularly modern forms of political mobilization, his data do not differentiate between territory and class as determinants of ethnic political mobilization. Thus it is impossible to distinguish the extent to which the ethnic political distinctiveness of the Celtic periphery is an expression of class consciousness or the territorial consciousness of an exploited area. Of course, it is likely to be an interaction of both, but the data do not allow an assessment of the additive and interactive effects.

role in this crisis. "[T]he strengthening of the state in late capitalism . . . is an expression of capital's attempt to overcome its increasingly explosive inner contradictions and, at the same time an expression of the necessary failure of this attempt" (pp. 580–1). And all of the recent historical developments show that "Marx's analyses have . . . been confirmed" (p. 582).

Geoffrey Kay ends his book on development and underdevelopment (1975) with a chapter entitled "Crisis and Recomposition," but he ends on the pessimistic note that the methods of political repression used in the underdeveloped world presage their adoption in the developed world. Politics and the state, which he rejects in his more formal theoretical argument, reappear at the end when he offers his prediction about actual historical developments, (pp. 186–7).[13] These studies subordinate the state and, with it, politics and culture to the exigencies of class rule, true to the Marxist heritage.

Perry Anderson blames "the absence of any political theory proper in the late Marx may . . . be . . . related to a latent catastrophism in his economic theory, which rendered the development of the former redundant" (1976, p. 116). But the opposite tendency to assume capitalist hegemony is also consistent with the absence of an adequate class theory of politics and culture. That is, the assumption that the capitalist class ultimately holds the reins of power and has manifold capabilities of creating false consciousness or creating a superstructure of educational, religious, and political institutions, which support or mystify class rule, also obviates the need for a theory of politics, because it is assumed that the institutions "needed" for class rule will be created. Both approaches reduce the need for systematic comparative study of different capitalist societies. If the underlying laws of development are the same, whether leading to crisis or to reproduction, then there is no need to understand the historical variations in the forms of politics, the structure of the state, or cultural values.

We now turn to class analyses of the democratic and bureaucratic aspects of the state. Bureaucratic and democratic aspects of the state are secondary to the capitalist aspect because of the assumption that the social relations of production penetrate all organizations and individual behavior. They do not *determine* them, in any simple causal sense, but the assumption is made that capitalist accumulation ultimately shapes other institutions, either in forms that reproduce capitalism or – because

---

[13] Trent Schroyer's analysis (1973) of the Frankfurt school ends with a chapter called "The Crises of American Capitalism" and a section called "The Structural Crisis of State Monopoly Capitalism," but he goes on to emphasize the "state-guided instrumental rationalization of society," as a new mode of "domination."

of the contradictions of capitalism – in forms that ultimately will lead to its transformation. In either approach, it is assumed that the state is an increasingly central institution for the reproduction or transformation of capitalism.

15

The class perspective on the democratic state

Democracy is a secondary aspect of the state within the class perspective; thus there are relatively few studies that single it out for explanation. Democracy is seen either as a direct consequence of class struggle, as a fictitious symbol mystifying the working class, as representing conflicts only among capitalist interests, or as a vision of the future, unrealizable under conditions of capitalism.

Democracy and capitalism

Class theorists admit that there is almost no serious class theory of the democratic aspect of the state. Swedish sociologist Goran Therborn said that "the entire Marxist tradition has had enormous difficulty in coming to grips with the paradoxical phenomenon of bourgeois democracy – a regime in which the exploiting minority rules by means of a system of legally free popular elections" (1978, p. 248). British sociologist Colin Crouch adds that "most Marxist theory [is reluctant] to admit any element of genuine pluralism within the polities of the liberal democracies" (1979, p. 13). One reason is a fear that the theorists will lose the distinctive political and theoretical commitments to socialism, the working class, and revolution and become mere reformists by using the tools of bourgeois democratic institutions. Political philosopher C. B. Mac-Pherson agrees with this possibility. "Pluralism had (and has) socialist advocates but its influence has not been confined to socialist ranks, and its effect has been to turn social thought away from class by emphasizing the multiplicity and moral value of group life." He adds that emphasis on the reality of plural interests, group formation, and the relations with state authority leaves "concealed or overshadowed the problem of getting men clear of the class relations of the market" (1973, p. 201).

When democratic institutions are taken seriously, they are usually regarded either as instruments for legitimating existing social institutions or as subordinated to the needs of capital. German sociologist Jurgen

333

Habermas, for example, considers the democratic state part of the "legitimation system": formal democracy, citizenship rights, diffuse mass loyalty expressed through elections ("institutions and procedures that are democratic in form" [1975, p. 37]). "Structural depoliticization" is justified by two ideologies: "democratic elite theories" (Weber and Schumpeter) and "technocratic systems theories" (Berle and Means, Rathenau) (1975, p. 37). Habermas argues that these different versions of the managerial perspective function to legitimate the capitalist state by reducing democracy either to a competitive elite or to an impossible ideal because of the technical complexity of decision making.

Ernest Mandel subordinates parliaments completely to the needs of capital:

the bourgeois parliamentary republic is indisputably the "ideal form" of the bourgeois State, because it best reflects the dialectical unity and struggle of the contradiction between the "competition of many capitals" and the "social interests and nature of capital in its totality." [1975, p. 481]

Furthermore,

every decision of the State concerning tariffs, taxes, railways or budgetary allocations affects competition and influences the overall social redistribution of surplus value. . . . all groups of capital are therefore obliged to become politically active, not just to articulate their own views on collective class interests, but also to defend their particular interests. [p. 480]

Mandel cites Marx as his authority and does not mention the possibility that parliaments might be used by the organized working class to defend its interests or that agencies and programs of the state can "represent" working-class interests and needs. On the contrary, suffrage, social democracy, welfare legislation, and the impact of the working-class movement in general "lent a further urgency and scale to the integrative role of the State" (p. 482).

Polish sociologist W. Wesolowski also finds in Marx and Engels the origin of the view that the chief mechanism of political domination by the capitalist class is the parliamentary republic. Quoting from Marx, he sees "bourgeois domination as the product and consequence of universal suffrage, an express act of the sovereign will of the people – that is the meaning of the bourgeois constitution." Political parties, elections, constitution, legislatures – all of the apparatus of the democratic state – mainly have the function of maintaining class rule (1979, p. 34; quotation is from Marx, *Class Struggles in France*).

A major class analysis of the democratic state is that of Nicos Poulantzas, who argues that "the celebrated social functions of the State directly depend . . . on the intensity of popular mobilization" and thus the penetration of the state by popular movements (1978, p. 184). But he rejects the separation of the state into two sectors, one responsive to the "popular masses" and the other to capital. "All measures taken by the capitalist state, even those imposed by the popular masses, are in the last analysis inserted in a pro-capitalist strategy or are compatible with expanded reproduction of capital" (p. 185). The phrase "in the last analysis" is an attempt to rescue the "ultimate" responsiveness of the state to the needs and requirements of capital. Much of *State, Power, and Socialism* (1978) suggests that, at the organizational level, different sectors of the state can be responsive to different class (and nonclass) interests, leaving aside the knotty question of whether or not the interests of capital are served at the societal level.

Poulantzas assumes, however, that democracy is expressed somehow in the outcomes of popular actions, that is, in class struggle. "However truncated by the dominant classes and by the materiality of the State," representative democracy "still constitutes a mode whereby popular struggle and resistance are inscribed in that materiality; and while not the only limit to the power of the State, it is nevertheless decisive" (1978, p. 73). Untheorized metaphors, such as "materiality," "inscribed," "molecular vessels," "truncation," are his attempt to recognize empirically different levels of analysis without integrating them theoretically.

He also argues that "the popular classes cannot hold such power within the State because of the unity of the state power of the dominant classes, who shift the center of real power from one apparatus to another as soon as the relationship of forces within any given one seems to be swinging to the side of the popular masses" (Poulantzas 1978, p. 143). The ruling classes have, in his view, sufficient control of the state to allow it quickly and effectively to centralize or decentralize the state if the requirements of class struggle make that necessary. Poulantzas postulates that popular movements can only influence specific state policies and that these demands can be easily countered by changing the location of state decisions. The autonomy of political and bureaucratic organizations, and thus their resistance to change, is minimized vis-à-vis capital, maximized vis-à-vis labor and popular movements. In effect, the democratic aspect of the state is confined to situational responses to collective actions by workers, who only sometimes gain benefits from specific state decisions.

The general skepticism about democracy does not mean that it is unimportant to class analysts. On the contrary, the principle of democracy must be extended from the state to the society. For Edward Thompson, for example, revising the visions of nineteenth-century English socialists, the goal was to democratize not the state but the society. The vision sought to "exert the collective power of the class to humanize the environment: by this community or that cooperative society, by this check on the blind operation of the market-economy, this legal enactment, that measure of relief for the poor. And, implicit, if not always explicit, in their outlook was the dangerous tenet: production must be, not for profit, but for *use*" (1963, p. 830; italics in original). This is a vision that goes far beyond the pluralist image of democratic participation.[1]

A last example is the important work of Adam Przeworski, who summarizes Marx's position, as stated in the *Eighteenth Brumaire* and *Class Struggles in France*, that democracy in a capitalist state is inherently unstable, because of the "fundamental political importance of the objective conflict of material interests" (1980*a*, p. 22). There is no way of reconciling the objective discrepancy between the economic interests of workers in higher wages and capitalists' interests in higher profits. But Przeworski argues that it does not follow that "conflict over material interests in the short run inevitably lead[s] to conflicts between classes over the form of organization of society" (p. 22). In our terms, he is asserting that conflict at the organizational level of analysis need not involve societal forces that lead to the transformation of the contradiction between capitalism and democracy. Nor need these conflicts of interest entail either rule by force or the inevitability of socialism. He argues that Gramsci's revision of Marxism starts from the premise that "capitalist relations of production can be perpetuated under democratic conditions; exploitation can be maintained with the consent of the exploited" (p. 23).

Przeworski and Wallerstein (1982) use pluralist concepts: consent, choice, compromise, effective claims, representation, preferences, norms. However, democracy for them is contained within a capitalist totality. It is real but limited. They reject those variants of a class perspective that believe that Western working classes have failed to vote in socialism because the working class is a "passive victim of repression, a perpetual dupe of ideological domination, or at best, as repeatedly betrayed by leadership" (1982, p. 236). Instead, workers have several real options in a capitalist democracy. One is "capitalist democracy without a compromise"; that is, a society with a democratic state engaged in a constant

---

[1] Sometimes pluralist democracy becomes a normative ideal, not a theoretical concept in the class perspective. Economist Richard Edwards, in a study of technical and bureaucratic modes of social control of workers, does not deal directly with the state, even in a chapter entitled "Capitalism or Democracy?". He asserts that "the rise of rule by the great state bureaucracies, the 'imperial presidency,' and government by executive order provides the undemocratic substance of modern democratic government" (1979, p. 22). He assumes that a challenge to capitalist hegemony would automatically serve democratic government, an instance of the implicit treatment not only of the state but also of democracy in the class perspective. Although he refers to democratic rule, government, traditions, and political democracy, he never defines democracy explicitly. Not only are elections important, but so are expansions of "popular participation" in the sense of "widespread discussion of issues, mobilizing of support, and expressing of interests." And the "government must be more immediately responsive, to ensure that state policy is kept in line with the expressed real interests of the citizenry" (p. 215).

and intense tug-of-war between conflicting interests. Such a tug-of-war, in our terms class struggle, is a possibility that flows from the nature of capitalist society. It is, of course, seen as pathological and disruptive by pluralists.[2]

Second, there is socialism. Workers could "claim the entire capital stock ('means of production') from capitalists and . . . reorganize the system of production so that the decision to withhold from current consumption would be made by all individuals qua citizens. The investment fund would be deducted directly from the gross product, profit having been abolished as a juridical and as an economic category." A variant of socialism would be to "claim the entire product or even a part of the capital stock without reorganizing the process of withholding from current consumption" (Przeworski and Wallerstein 1982, p. 217).

Third, the workers could "claim less than the entire product, thus leaving a part in the hands of capitalists as profit, in exchange for some assurance that future material conditions would improve as a consequence" (Przeworski and Wallerstein 1982, p. 217). The last option, they argue, is the class compromise with capitalism. It constitutes a genuine choice, not a fictitious or manipulated one, and is the typical pattern for Western capitalist states. Class compromise is the outcome of a bargain, in which workers expect capitalists to invest in productive ways that ensure economic growth, employment, and reasonable consumption in return for their allowing capitalists the temporary ability to realize a profit from their investments.

In effect, Przeworski and Wallerstein accept the pluralist argument about the nature of democracy but locate it within the class world view. Democracy is functional for both workers and capitalists, integrating the society and providing real material benefits. As they put it, "the logic of compromise must relate future wages to current profits. The only conceivable reason for workers to consent voluntarily not to claim the capital stock is to treat current profits as a form of workers delegated investment" (1982, p. 217). This is taking democracy seriously with a vengeance, by casually assuming that capitalism continues at the sufferance of the workers, as long as they calculate that capitalists are behaving in a way that serves their material interests. Socialism is a real and rational possibility, in this view. But the capitalists are in turn con-

---

[2] Przeworski has also challenged the pluralist thesis that rapid political mobilization of voters threatens political stability of democratic institutions, as enunciated most prominently by Huntington (1968, p. 4). Przeworski tests the thesis that political mobilization leads to "deinstitutionalization" on data from party alignments in a number of Western democracies. His basic argument is that demobilization ("group abstention from the political process") is more threatening to democratic stability than mobilization. Newly mobilized voters do not vote differently from already mobilized voters.

senting to democracy when they "consent to institutions that would permit workers to process their claims with some success: basically unions, parties, and a relatively autonomous state" (p. 218).

Their argument is analogous to a pluralist one in the sense that they equate workers with the citizenry, as an undifferentiated societal collectivity that chooses to maintain the system intact. "Consent" in their usage is not analogous to the pluralist concept of consensus because it derives not from deeply internalized values (what they call a "prior and immutable agreement about societal organization") but from a rational calculation of material interests.[3]

Przeworski and Wallerstein do not consider the character of differences of interest among both capitalists and workers, how those differences are organized, or how they relate to control of the state and to reactions to state decisions. They assume that both workers and capitalists can choose whether to be militant, economistic, or revolutionary. These choices enter their mathematical equations only as logically possible alternatives for two homogeneous entities.

Przeworski and Wallerstein criticize both the "instrumental" and the "structuralist" view of the state for being functionalist. Whether the state is "directly populated by capitalists or like-capitalists" or is "autonomous from particularistic interests of capitalists," the assumption is that it must perform the function of reproducing capitalist rule. As Przeworski points out, "ultimately even the state as an institution disappears from this functionalist analysis. . . . one can proceed from requirements to reproduction without bothering with the state at all. The very concept of the state is based on a reification" (Przeworski and Wallerstein 1982, p. 235). They properly criticize this functionalist form of the class perspective for not explaining "why conflicts among specific groups under concrete historical circumstances would regularly result in the state performing its functions" (p. 235). When such "conflicts" occur, the outcome is a "particular organization and a specific set of policies." And they properly criticize the functionalist version of the class perspective for assuming that such policies "have the function of reproducing capitalist relations" (p. 235).

It is ironic, given this critique, that Przeworski and Wallerstein do not escape a functionalist analysis. They reintroduce it with the added pro-

---

[3] The form of Przeworski and Wallerstein's analysis is not empirical but mathematical. They offer a series of equations on the conditions under which different choices are made by both workers and capitalists. Each class is seen as an undifferentiated collectivity. Their framework assumes certain historical facts as given and implicitly applies to all "capitalist democracies." For example, the "norm tying increases of wages to the growth of productivity became the foundation of the compromise established during the expansionist period between 1950 and 1970" (1982, p. 217).

viso that the workers, as well as the capitalists, have "chosen" to continue consenting to capitalism. They eliminate manipulation, repression, and betrayal as explanations of the continuation of capitalism, as well as the functioning of the state to guarantee capitalist class rule, but they have only added democracy as a feature of the state that reproduces capitalist social relations. As they put it, "the state *must* enforce the compliance of both classes with the terms of each compromise. . . . The state *must* induce individual capitalists to make the decisions required by the class compromise. . . . since the state of class compromise is a democratic state, it *must* see to it that the class coalition that forms the compromise can win popular support in elections" (Przeworski and Wallerstein 1982, p. 236; italics added). Przeworski and Wallerstein are here vulnerable to their own critique of instrumental and structuralist versions of the class perspective on the state. "The state as an institution" has disappeared from their analysis. Political and historical relations between classes have been broadened to include institutions embodying class compromises, but the image of the state as necessarily organizing that compromise remains intact.

Their argument is incomplete, however, when they refer to the "risks" workers must calculate in choosing to continue consenting to the existence of capitalist profits. One of the risks associated with uncertain political and economic conditions is "the institutionalization of labor-capital relations and the likelihood that a compromise would be enforced by the state. . . . Partisan control over the state and the electoral prospects would constitute an important consideration in evaluating this risk" (Przeworski and Wallerstein 1982, p. 221). This tangential, almost glancing, reference to politics is not just a risk that workers as a collectivity must evaluate but an essential element in the very structure of the working class, built into the fundamental relations of labor with capital. For one thing, the existence of political organization and political relations of labor and capital through the state means that the alleged choice that workers make is mediated through the state. It is not useful to postulate a homogeneous choice by the working class as a whole. The differentiation, not to say fragmentation, of the working class is a historical fact that cannot be ignored or defined away in order to achieve clear equations. Przeworski says in a footnote at this point that "to discuss this topic, as fundamental as it is, would be to open a can or worms" (1982, p. 231). Indeed it would, for an argument whose mathematical logic depends upon parsimonious assumptions.

Przeworski and Wallerstein agree that this is a "major limitation" of their model, because the "political arrangements that determine the class differential risks . . . may change in time, but such change is exogenous to our model" (1982, p. 231–2). The concrete historical and institutional arrangements that constitute the political relations of classes to the state are not theoretically incorporated in their model. They say explicitly that it is not possible in their model for "the players to trade off material gains for political power," although they conclude from their own equations that workers are "better off competing for political power than making deals with capitalists" (p. 231), because political power increases their certainty that a given class compromise will pay off with increased material benefits.[4]

Class alliances and revolution: the societal level

An important exception to the general lack of studies of the democratic state from a class perspective is historical sociologist Barrington Moore's monumental work, *Social Origins of Dictatorship and Democracy* (1966). Moore explained developments within each state in terms of internal class factors, and for that reason he has been criticized by others who emphasize political factors or the world capitalist context.[5] Moore's method is comparative and historical, attempting to explain why the most powerful states (Britain, the United States, France, Germany, Japan, Russia, and China) took alternative historical paths toward democracy, fascism, or communism. According to Moore, these different forms of the state developed after class struggles crystallized and were violently resolved. Whether or not a state became or remained democratic was determined by the pattern of class alliances and struggles among the landed upper classes, the peasantry, the commercial and manufacturing urban bourgeoisie, and the preindustrial central bureaucracy when they faced the transformation of precommercial agriculture.

[4] Przeworski's view of the societal level of analysis is that it specifies the basic constraints faced by actors. The organizational level specifies the collective resources that are forged within those constraints. The individual level specifies the forms of rationality and strategies that are adopted, using those resources within those constraints. Przeworski uses methodological tools from all three perspectives: game theory, mathematical models, detailed historical investigations, quantitative time series data, as well as concepts of class compromise, the dilemmas of party strategies, and historical transformations of the mode of production. Although clearly remaining within a class world view, Przeworski in his various works comes as close as any writer we have analyzed to integrating different levels of analysis. We are indebted to Erik Olin Wright for pointing this out to us.

[5] Charles Tilly taxes Moore with failing to deal adequately with "political decisions and political structure," arguing that, despite Moore's focus on "class structure as an explanation of alternative political paths to modernization," Moore introduces political factors to account empirically for different national alliances of economic interests and political interests. Moore, for example, mentions England's "reliance on a navy instead of an army, on unpaid justices of the peace instead of royal officials," and on a relatively weak "repressive apparatus" to explain the differences between Britain and Germany (Moore 1966, p. 444, quoted in Tilly, ed., 1975, p. 632). Such organizational factors as the military structure of the state are theoretically residual for Moore but central for Tilly.

In England the democratic capitalist form was assured through bourgeois revolutions (the civil war of 1640–60), where landed classes allied with the emerging bourgeoisie against the central bureaucracy. In Japan and Germany, the landed upper classes allied with the central bureaucracy, and a period of fascist politics ruled capitalist economic development. Fascism followed "revolutions from above": in Germany, the Stein-Hardenburg Reform of 1807–14 and Bismarck's Unification in 1860; in Japan, the Meiji Restoration in 1868. In Russia and China, the peasantry replaced the central royal bureaucracy with a revolutionary party apparatus, and industrialization took a communist form.

In each society the relations of agrarian lords and peasants to the central state apparatus changed with the rise of an agricultural market. The commercialization of agriculture and the penetration of markets into the agrarian sector to allocate land, labor, and crops both provided the impetus for political class struggle and explained the forms it took. Except for the United States, all of these societies began with royal absolutisms and/or agrarian bureaucracies established in the sixteenth and seventeenth centuries (Moore 1966, p. 417).

For Moore, the unique characteristic of the democratic state in a capitalist society is that, although the formal rights of property and citizenship are legally fused, their actual power is institutionally separated into private and public spheres. The historical genesis of this division between private economic and public political power is found in the ways in which the state was or was not used to extract a surplus, a portion of the product not consumed directly by producers from the agrarian sector. Moore recognized two forms of agricultural commercialization. The first is the market form, where commercialization was strong and agricultural land and labor were fully transformed into commodities. Agricultural surpluses could be accumulated, exchanged with an emerging urban bourgeoisie, as well as appropriated by the state through taxes with minimal direct state intervention in the developing economy. The second form is the labor-repressive form, where commercialization was weaker and agricultural surplus extraction was intensified through non-commodified forms (such as the reintroduction of serfdom in fifteenth- and sixteenth-century Germany). The production and accumulation of agricultural surpluses were thus more dependent upon continuous state intervention (Moore 1966, pp. 433–4). Strong, market forms of agricultural commercialization tended to produce democratic states. Weaker, labor-repressive forms of agricultural commercialization produced either fascist intervals or, where the agricultural commercialization was even weaker, peasant revolutions that led to communism (p. 460).

Moore argued that the dependence of the landed upper classes on the state to extract an agricultural surplus from the producers on the land (such as the French nobility's centrally reinforced intensification of feudal obligation or the southern U.S. slave system) had to be destroyed in order for a democratic state eventually to develop. In England, the civil war of 1640–60 destroyed the power of the monarchy that had been the last institutional obstacle to eliminating feudal tenure. Land was commodified by the enclosures of the "common" lands. In France, the revolution of 1789, led in the rural sector by commercially oriented peasants, destroyed a landed nobility that had attempted to exact a larger surplus from the peasantry through intensified feudal obligations. In the United States, the Civil War dismantled the slave system and thereby created a black agricultural labor market.

Why did market-based forms of agriculture commercialization produce – sometimes centuries later – a democratic state? First, the commercialization of agriculture tended either to destroy (as in England) or to transform (as in the United States and France) the peasantry into an economically atomized and internally stratified group of farmers producing for the market. As a result there was no rural mass base for later reactionary and fascist politics (as in Germany and Japan) or for peasant revolutions (as in Russia and China). Second, it generated a political struggle by landed classes to limit the repressive capacities of the central state and to create alternative institutions of representation. Limiting state power also reduced the ability of a politically powerful bourgeoisie to repress working-class demands for citizenship rights. Representative institutions provided a mechanism for the political adjudication of later class conflicts (Moore 1966, p. 29). Third, strong, market-based agricultural commercialization tended to be associated with the economically stronger urban bourgeoisie. In a later period, conflicts of interest between rural agriculture and urban industry and commerce were expressed in political competition among capitalists. This competition facilitated the political incorporation of the working class. Fourth, the development of an economically powerful urban bourgeoisie through market mechanisms meant that militarist nationalism was less necessary as a political and economic strategy to stimulate industry. Unlike England, France, and the United States, the state autonomy required by militarism in Germany and Japan assured the political cohesion of otherwise conflictual agricultural and industrial interests (pp. 440–2).

Lastly, market-based agricultural commercialization meant that the economic power of both agricultural and industrial bourgeoisie was less dependent upon the state and consequently less politically vulnerable. Where the state became and remained central in organizing production and distribution, the potential political power of those classes that produced the surplus threatened the economic power of those that bought their labor power. Where the economic power of the bourgeoisie was less dependent upon its own political power, the advance of mass de-mocratization was less threatening. Moore argued that the English landed upper classes used the state only for the expropriation of its peasantry and the creation of a labor market. The upper classes wanted the peasantry

out of the way in order to go over to commercial farming; by and large, economic measures would be enough to provide the labor force they needed. Succeeding economically in this particular fashion, they had little need to resort to repressive political measures to continue their leadership. Therefore in England manufac-turing and agrarian interests competed with one another for popular favor during the rest of the nineteenth century, gradually extending the suffrage while jeal-ously opposing and knocking down each other's more selfish measures. [1966, p. 444]

With respect to the political handling of labor supply and discipline by the English industrialists, Moore argues that "English industrial lead-ers could carry out [this task] on their own with a minimum of help from the state or the landed aristocracy. They had to do so because the repressive apparatus of the English state was relatively weak, a conse-quence of the Civil War" (1966, p. 32; see also p. 444). By contrast, a weaker industrial bourgeoisie in Germany, standing in the historical shadow of a more labor-repressive (and more labor-intensive) feudal aristocracy, responded differently. "[A] much weaker bourgeoisie leaned on the landed aristocracy to protect them against popular discontent and to carry through political and economic measures necessary for modernization" (p. 34).

Moore also focuses on the historical role of violent social revolutions in achieving a later democratic structure in which social classes peace-fully adjudicate their conflicts of interest (1966, p. 20). Social revolutions are not reduced to pathological forms of collective behavior but are seen as class struggles over the ways in which economic surpluses are pro-duced, appropriated, and distributed. Moore continually warns that we should not confuse the *form* with the *intensity* and *sequence* of violence. Institutionalized violence may be as horrific as the violence of institu-tionalization. And yet both may have been necessary to create subse-quently less violent political forms. In reference to the enclosure movement that pushed the peasantry off the land in England, leaving them suspended between town and country, Moore wrote:

for the "surplus" peasant it made little difference whether the pull from the towns or factories was more important than the push out of his rural world. In either case he was caught in the end between alternatives that meant degradation and suffering, compared with the traditional life of the village community. That the violence and coercion which produced these results took place over a long space of time, that it took place mainly within a framework of law and order and helped ultimately to establish democracy on a firmer footing, must not blind us to the fact that it was massive violence exercised by the upper classes against the lower. [P. 29]

Moore does not derive capitalist class power over the state from their direct political participation. This is nowhere more apparent than in his stress on the primacy of precapitalist strata – gentry, peasant, and artisan – as ideological and political agencies through which traditional absolutisms have been destroyed and capitalist economic transformation initiated.

Swedish sociologist Goran Therborn, in one of the few comparative analyses of Western democratic states from within a class perspective, argues that it is difficult to explain how a tiny capitalist class can "rule by means of democratic forms" (1977, p. 3). He analyzes seventeen of the "major capital-exporting states" that are members of the Organization for Economic Cooperation and Development (OECD), seen as the "broadest and most significant organization of the core capitalist states" (p. 7). Using two major variables constituting a democratic state, popular representation (the date at which an autonomous nation-state was established, with elections) and suffrage, he develops a fourfold typology. Dictatorships have "incarnate" representation, in which the army, a leader, or a party claims to incarnate the will or the interests of the nation, and can exist with elections. Authoritarian-exclusive, democratic-exclusive, and democracies (elective representation with universal suffrage) are the other three types. The United Kingdom excluded by class, the United States by race, Switzerland by sex, and Finland by politics (between 1930 and 1944 when the Communist Party was suppressed), for example. This typology incorporates the pluralist criterion of breadth of legitimate participation in the polity into a population of capitalist states.

Therborn does not deny the association of democracy with capitalism. "Democracy . . . did not appear anywhere prior to capitalism. . . . some capitalist countries have experienced a purely internal development of democracy; . . . all major advanced bourgeois states are today democracies" (1977, p. 28). Therborn argues that certain "intrinsic" tendencies of capitalism favor democracy, because the requirements for the development of capitalism are the same as the conditions favoring popular struggle, namely, "a free labor market, industrialization, concentration of capital . . . which simultaneously lay the basis for a working-class movement of a strength and stability inachievable by the exploited classes of precapitalist modes of production."[6] But Therborn rejects the argument that working-class militance directly won democratic reforms. In several cases it was "not the insurrectionary proletariat but foreign arm-

---

[6] Therborn argues that this relationship, in turn, explains the well-known correlations among wealth, literacy, urbanization, and democracy in studies by Lipset (1960) and subsequent research in that tradition.

ies that overthrew the existing regimes, whereupon the old internal democratic forces at last got the upper hand" (p. 29). Also, the franchise was sometimes extended as part of the process of national unification and liberation, seen as a "strategic necessity for the development and protection of trade and industry and the breaking of feudal dynastic power" (p. 30). Lastly, the impersonal character of rule in the capitalist mode of production is compatible with the creation of a separate sphere of "civil society," a state that "does not have to be managed personally by bourgeois" (p. 30).

As these examples indicate, Therborn is searching for factors internal to the dynamics of capitalism itself, because "the fight of the working class for universal suffrage and freely elected governments was never by itself sufficient to enforce the introduction of bourgeois democracy" (1977, pp. 30–1). He postulates that a major factor is the internal tendency of the capitalist mode of production to create an "*internally competing, peacefully disunited, ruling class*" (p. 31; italics in original). Only in instances of extreme crisis or threat, whether internal or external, is there a tendency toward unity, and thus, "in the absence of a single centre, some kind of elective, deliberative, and representative political machinery became necessary" (p. 31). In other words, democracy becomes the instrument used by competing economic interests to reach a workable compromise, through the various mechanisms offered by the state. This is still a functional view of the democratic state, within the class perspective.

Trade unions, parties, and movements: the organizational level

Working-class organization takes many forms – trade unions, working-class parties, and social movements. Such organizations and movements do not always represent explicitly class-linked issues, nor are they based upon obvious class membership or support. Economic dislocations and irrationalities stemming from the dynamics of the capitalist economy create the opportunities and interests that lay the basis for class organization and social movements. Many class theorists assume that protests have no secure political potential if they are not ultimately based on working-class organization.

For class theorists, working-class organization cannot be understood in isolation from the general political struggle between classes, in sharp contrast to the pluralist view that rights of unionization gave workers rights of "industrial citizenship" in the same way that universal suffrage gave them "political citizenship." If such dual citizenship became part of the political culture, workers would no longer connect workplace issues to community and national politics. Strikes would focus on narrow labor-market and job issues and would decline in intensity as a result of institutionalized channels of conflict adjudication.

In their class analysis of strikes between 1900 and 1976 in eighteen democratic nations (1980), Korpi and Shalev agree with this pluralist hypothesis but argue that this reflects a shift of working-class political participation from factory to state, an appropriate shift given the systemic power of capital. Because of the enormous power accorded capital in the organizations of production, workers in democratic states have a strong interest in shifting the locus of class struggle from the labor market to the state. Korpi and Shalev find that after World War II strike activity declined in those countries where the working class was highly unionized and left-wing parties maintained stable control over the government (see also Hibbs 1978). Thus Sweden, for example, had many strikes until the Social Democrats gained control of the national government. At that point, employers could no longer assume that the state would back their use of a lockout to break a strike. With the advent of centralized collective bargaining, class struggle increasingly moved to the parliamentary arena around issues of full employment, redistribution, and social control of investment. In France and the United States, where working-class organizations have not achieved political representation in the state, strike activity remained quite high in the postwar period.

Korpi and Shalev found that Socialist Party power in the national government was associated with redistributive government spending and lower unemployment. The working class responded to government redistribution with fewer strikes and to unemployment by more strikes. Working-class power in the labor market and in the state are mutually dependent.

This is a class analysis because it does not view working-class political representation in the state as the permanent achievement of modernization or as the integration of low-paid workers into the universal status of citizenship but views it as an alternative form of class struggle. The systemic power of capital defines the context for organized interest conflicts, sometimes in the workplace, sometimes against the state, sometimes inside the state, depending on varying historical conditions. However, the *political* evaluation of these alternative strategies varies considerably. Some socialists may regard parliamentary representation and the cessation of strikes as a defeat, as a sign of corporatist integration of the working class into the state, as a deflection of class struggle from the point of production. Working-class militancy was used by union elites to gain access to state power. But the cost of power sharing is the limitation of union demands to those consistent with capitalist social relations. Others see such reforms and benefits as a sign of working-class strength and solidarity. Still others see them as part of the transition to socialism (Stephens 1980). The answer partly depends on a theoretical question: To what extent can the democratic weapons available to the people modify the consequences of capital accumulation? About this issue there is little theoretical or empirical research in the class tradition.

A penetrating study of Chartist political agitation in Lancashire (Brown 1981) finds its sources in the organizational dynamics of class formation. The Chartists were a movement for working-class political and economic rights, directed at British Parliament in the mid-nineteenth century. In his study of the parishes of Lancashire, a burgeoning center of capitalist growth, Brown found that Chartist protests were lower in those localities where urban and industrial change was rapid. The most important determinants of local Chartist protest appear to be high levels of working-class organization and the ecological concentration of workers. The "plug plot" riots of 1842 ("plug plot" refers to the knocking out of boiler plugs to stop the machinery) were the first political mass strikes in Western history. Textile workers struck throughout the Lancashire region for the People's Charter. The National Charter Association began to recruit trade unions into their organization on the grounds that the unions could not protect their membership without formal parliamentary political power. The Chartist political elite argued that working-class interests were damaged by capitalist-class political power and "class legislation," not by their economic power per se. But, once working-class economic conflicts were fused with political conflicts, state repression soon followed. Under conditions of high unemployment and meager organizational development, working-class activists had to use coercion to stop production, sometimes directed at the workers themselves. Without local police, these early "turnout" actions flourished. As central police repression mounted, the working class was quickly and effectively demobilized.

As this study illustrates, class struggle is explained not by social disorganization, as in the pluralist perspective, but by working-class organization. Capitalist class relations make class struggles both possible and necessary. Brown's study analyzes class conflict as a series of events and explains the historical and geographical variation of these events by the organizational capacities of capitalists and working class, and the extent to which the working class challenged capital in both economy and state.

The apparent erosion in the 1970s of working-class support for the welfare state is a challenge to the view that workers receive benefits from and therefore support Socialist Party regimes. Some Socialist and Social Democratic parties lost support in the 1970s. Denmark and Sweden, for example, have equally large welfare state programs that were expanded by their Social Democratic parties. Yet the Danish Social Democrats lost considerable support among the working class, whereas the

Swedish ones did not. Esping-Anderson (1978) explains this difference in terms of organized working-class union and party strategies. Swedish labor unions, which encompass some 90 percent of all workers, have increasingly employed their pension funds to gain greater control over production by selective investment of these funds. Thus the state is assured a higher level of investment, less unemployment and poverty, and a greater ability to finance the growth of the welfare state without cutting into working-class income. As a result, the Swedish Social Democratic Party is less dependent on nonproductive sectors of the population than the Danish party.

In Denmark, by contrast, the less powerful unions have not developed instruments to intervene in production either to control the need for welfare assistance or to finance such programs without eating into working-class wages. As a result, the Danish Social Democratic Party is more dependent upon nonproductive populations. Serious disaffection has emerged among well-paid workers whose incomes are heavily taxed to pay for services for those who do not have well-paid work.

Historically, the capitalist economy inexorably organized the working class – through concentration in town and factory and through reduction to a common position of subordination dictated by an impersonal market logic. That such a working class could demand rights of economic and political organization coequal to men of property seemed to presage social disorder and revolution. Overt class struggle was necessary to secure working-class access to the democratic state. The conditions and limits under which trade unions and political parties can politically represent working-class interests in a capitalist society represent a critical issue for class analysts.

Democratic participation – at least of the poor – also occurs outside of the institutionalized channels of unions and parties. Piven and Cloward's study (1979) focuses on the strategies of organizational elites coopting popular militance. The work analyzes four "Poor People's Movements" since the 1930s in the United States: the unemployed workers' and the trade union organizing movements in the 1930s, the civil rights movement and the welfare rights movement in the 1960s. All of the movements sought to affect decisions or policies of the state. The unemployed workers' movement of the 1930s sought government relief. The sit-down strikes sought state recognition of unions and support for collective bargaining. The civil rights movement sought voting rights and the welfare rights movement welfare benefits.

Although Piven and Cloward do not theorize the democratic state explicitly, the first page of their introduction says that these movements reveal "much about both the limitations and the possibilities for power by the poor in the electoral-representative political institutions of the

United States." The "poor" are seen as a stratum within the working class: relatively impoverished, underemployed individuals and families. The whole is defined as "capitalist society" (1979, p. xvii) or "modern capitalism" (p. x), and institutions such as education are seen as ensuring "capitalistic ideological hegemony" (p. x).

Piven and Cloward's basic argument is that as individual consciousness changes protest becomes possible. Structural dislocations in the economy, coupled with political instability, lead people to realize that the old ways of living no longer work. People with common interests join together in a collective action of some kind, led by organizers who define the situation and develop specific plans of action. The protest leadership has considerable leeway, assuming the social conditions for protest are ripe, to decide whether or not to emphasize building an organization or to mobilize disruptive action for tangible benefits. Electoral-representative institutions are the targets of participation. Such institutions play a key role in defining the context and goals of action.

A cycle of protest, elite response, and cooptation begins. Specific victories are won, which for the moment encourage both leaders and members to make more militant demands. But, simultaneously, the movement leaders start to build a permanent organization. Mini-careers are envisioned and actions become moderate because of the need to respond to elite offers of benefits combined with concessions. As the organization grows, it becomes more dependent upon external resources – contributions, foundation grants, government contracts to support the staff and overhead costs. Organizers abandon militant actions to expand membership rolls. The overall result is to reinforce the stability of the social order and the state. Whatever tangible benefits have been won, they do not remove the systemic causes of inequality and injustice.

Piven and Cloward locate the situational causes of this process within historically developed institutional arrangements. Control over resources and the role of elections in legitimating the democratic state are the key causal factors that explain the emergence of specific situations and make possible certain actions. The occurrence of collective violence is the result of the structure of power rather than individual dissatisfaction, alienation, or personality. In any case, most violence is undertaken by the state in response to basically peaceful protests.

Piven and Cloward argue that the form and content of protest demands are shaped by the historical definition of legitimate demands and responses. "[P]olitical leaders proposed reforms that were in a sense prefigured by institutional arrangements that already existed, that were drawn from a repertoire provided by existing traditions. And an aroused people responded by demanding simply what political leaders had said they should have" (1979, p. 33). The dynamic of elite response is thus to "reintegrate disaffected groups . . . to guide them into less politically disturbing forms of behavior [and] to isolate them from potential supporters. . . . its leaders [are] attracted by new opportunities, its followers [are] conciliated, confused, or discouraged," and then the state can "demolish the few who are left" with repressive force (pp. 33–4).

The reforms won by the protest account for the disappearance of some mass support, but not because the state is so democratically responsive or the society so committed to the values of freedom and equality. Rather, the very actions of the democratic state transform the situation in which protest was possible in the first place. A "powerful image [is created] of a benevolent and responsive government that answers grievances and solves problems" (Piven and Cloward 1978, p. 34). Elite capacity to manage protest combines conciliations, symbolic responses, cooptation, and force against "unreasonable" and "extremist" elements within the protest movement.

The paradox of the National Welfare Rights Organization's history in the 1960s was that, precisely as its mass campaigns were faltering and the leadership itself was inhibiting the expansion of membership (for fear of creating damaging battles for succession), its national staff and budget grew and its support from outside sources was increasing (Piven and Cloward 1979, pp. 316–17). At the precise moment when the organization attained the greatest *appearance* of power – judged by staff size and budgets – it was the most vulnerable to the withdrawal of the external resources. The appearance was of public legitimacy and influence; the reality was gradual integration into a moderate politics of negotiation for incremental gains. But in the absence of a solid resource base, the NWRO became "enmeshed in a web of relationships with governmental officials and private groups," and it was "transformed from a protest organization to a negotiating and lobbying organization" (p. 317). The leadership was acting on behalf of a "constituency that was organized in name only."

Because there was no genuine and autonomous resource base, no mechanisms were available to the constituency to maintain its hold over the leaders. Genuine democratic participation requires a capacity to *represent* – because of clearly formulated demands, information about the consequences of leadership decisions, and clear channels of access to the leadership. The presumption of democratic politics is that the main channel of influence runs from the constituency to the leadership, not the other way around. Leaders may have a stake in their position, prestige, and various formal and informal rewards, but that stake must definitely be contingent upon the necessity of maintaining majority support within their constituency. Those conditions did not exist in the National Welfare Rights Organization.

The electoral system structures the form of protest, not because voting is an effective form of participation under normal circumstances but because elected leaders must respond somehow when challenged by nonelectoral defiance and the disruption of key social institutions. Voting and elections legitimate the state, and the electoral-representative institutions also mediate responses to protest. Criticizing the pluralist image of the role of political culture, Piven and Cloward argue that the "controlling force of the norms that guide political discontent into electoral channels" does not explain why it is so effective. The "pervasiveness of liberal political ideology in the United States and the absence of competing ideologies [still have] to be explained" (1979, p. 15).

Sometimes their empirical focus leads Piven and Cloward to offer explanations in terms of the motives of individuals. Discussing the threat of New York City's financial default in the 1970s, for example, they explain the absence of popular response in terms of the sense of fright, confusion, and helplessness of the urban pressure groups. As they themselves argue with reference to political culture, such psychological factors must themselves be explained and do not help explain the structural conditions that produce fright and confusion.

Piven and Cloward criticize the pluralist voting studies for neglecting the historical circumstances and social conditions that affect political choices. Pluralist explanations of voting assume that the process is more voluntary, more conscious, more informed, more "political" than it is. When pluralists discover that people are not very well informed, not very interested, not likely to participate effectively, they explain these empirical findings by individual characteristics, not by features of the social structure. Contrary to the pluralists, Piven and Cloward argue, "modes of participation and nonparticipation in electoral-representative procedures were not . . . the freely made political choices of free men and women" but were determined by the individual's location in the class structure (1979, p. 3).

Piven and Cloward also criticize a version of voluntarism in traditional class analysis, which assumes that protest and other forms of mass or working-class action occur spontaneously, in response to deep grievances that suddenly become unbearable. Protest, they argue, is as conditioned by specific political and organizational conditions as is more conventional and institutionalized forms of political behavior.

The authors also reject as incomplete the traditional explanations of the weakness of working-class organizations, mainly trade unions, in terms of the divisions among the working class. They do not deny ethnic and racial distinctions among workers, the oligarchic character of workers' organizations, and the weakening effect of social and geographic mobility upon the historical accumulation of political experience and solidarity. They emphasize both the cooptive and the coercive power of the state. Actively repressing worker efforts to organize prior to the New Deal, the state's posture changed during the extreme depression of the 1930s, when one-third of the work force was unemployed. Following the overwhelming Democratic victory for Roosevelt in 1932, unions became established and even government-sponsored, through the machinery of the National Labor Relations Board.

They see both action and *inaction* by the state, however, as a force maintaining the class structure generated by a capitalist economy that exists beyond and prior to the democratic state. The example here is of the blacks in the South, where the repressive role of all branches of the state created a docile political culture. State inaction reinforces the status quo, which then seems even more inevitable and "natural" because of a lack of any public concern with private repression. The southern state also had an array of specific laws regulating black participation. The exclusion of blacks from the southern electorate did not interfere with the "normal" operations of the democratic apparatus of voting, elections, and parties. Only when a popular protest movement changed the political terms under which elites had to function did the state have to respond. Not only were potential direct supporters of the movement activated, but noninvolved and previously uninterested persons also had to take a stand. Thus the protest movement, by disrupting key institutions, created reverberations throughout the democratic state.

Piven and Cloward assume that capitalist society has an endemic tendency to reproduce inequality and injustice, which creates a permanent basis for popular movements. Such movements arise from sources deep within capitalist society and cannot be responded to in a way that resolves the grievance, satisfies the need, or solves the problem. Also, even victories won by determined and persistent mass action and popular leadership tend to be eroded by the systemic power of capital. Analyzing the impact of the movement to organize trade unions in the 1930s, they say that by 1939 "the political tide had turned and measures to erode the concessions that labor had won began to be implemented." They see a permanent tendency toward domination of propertied interests over state policy and over the economy. Any strategies of workers and poor people that result in temporary victories are undermined by capital's continuing hegemony over economic and political institutions.

Piven and Cloward reject taking the organizational goals and interests of organizers and officials as an adequate explanation of the life history of movements and organizations. One must look, they assert, at the transformation of social structure and the economy for the ultimate explanation of the changing historical conditions under which particular kinds of demands can be translated into effective popular action. Organizations do have a tendency to develop oligarchical leadership, but that occurs in a societal context that allows certain kinds of organizations to develop in the first place. However, because their analysis is not at the societal level, the core terms referring to these processes are not theorized. Such phrases as "momentous changes in the institutional order," "historical circumstances," and "social conditions" (1979, p. 36) are used to refer to the underlying societal factors that create the conditions under which protest arises and elites respond.

Their theory of the state is also only implicit. Despite the fact that every one of their movements is directed against the state or in favor of state action, the state is hardly mentioned and enters the analysis only in concrete, "pluralist" language: decisions of governors, presidents, and specific agencies. They simply assume a theory of the conditions under which the state can contradict the interests of capital. In a sense, this silence reflects their pessimistic historical judgment that there are no conditions under which genuine democratic control of a capitalist state is possible, and therefore popular movements should get the most benefits for the most people while the momentum of the movement exists.

The language of class analysis when applied to concrete situations has tended to be either apocalyptic or spontaneous. Piven and Cloward cite Rosa Luxemburg as saying that it is difficult for the "leading organ of the proletarian movement" to anticipate moments of popular insurgency, which are like "explosions" or like an earthquake: "the crashing, crumbling, and displacing of all the social foundations" (1979, p. 14, n. 13). Similarly, the more recent language of political "conjunctures" or "moments" implies a convergence of multiple forces, which in the extreme case "overdetermine" specific political situations. Such terms are rhetorical language for untheorized processes at other levels of analysis.

The historical conditions of political choice: the individual level

Political scientist Adam Przeworski (1980b) has made an unusual attempt to integrate all of the levels of analysis of the democratic state within a class perspective, dealing simultaneously not only with societal contradictions but also with organizational strategies and differentiated individual interests.

Przeworski's concern is with the "logic of choices" faced by social democratic parties and socialist movements and with how "historical possibilities . . . are opened and closed as each choice is made" (1980b, p. 28). The issue as he poses it is whether "involvement in bourgeois institutions can result in socialism, or must strengthen the capitalist order" (p. 28). Such a definition of elections, political parties, and legislatures in a capitalist society as "bourgeois" already prejudges the issue to some extent and leads to the theoretical subordination of democratic institutions to the requirements of class rule. But Przeworski states the essential contradiction between democracy and capitalism in a way that few other class analysts have done, noting that "participation in electoral politics is necessary if the movement for socialism is to find mass support among workers, yet this participation seems to obstruct the attainment of final goals" (p. 28). In our words, electoral participation and the creation of parties seeking and obtaining working-class support lead to "consensus," not in the pluralist sense but in the sense of hegemony – a dwindling of class consciousness, not its heightening. Class is converted to economic interests; class struggle is transformed into political action; struggle against the state becomes conflict within the state. And all of these changes may occur while the rhetoric of socialism and class struggle blares ever louder, to conceal the transformation of content.

Both pluralist and class analysts agree on the *empirical* generalization that participation in a capitalist, democratic state "disaggregates . . . economic struggle . . . into a multitude of partial struggles" (1980b, p. 28). But pluralists see that as the crowning achievement of successful political modernization – the breaking up of the polarized identity known as "social class." Class analysts see the creation of individual citizens who perceive their separate interests and act on them as the victory of ruling-class hegemony. The difference is not at the level of empirical observation but rather in the theoretical interpretation. Przeworski even calls this "peaceful development, 'normal' for the bourgeois society" (p. 28), because this process of political representation functions to reproduce the capitalist social order. Because class relations become individualized, even the organizations presumably representing the working class, trade unions and parties with a distinct working-class base, must mobilize support from individuals who have different interests as consumers, workers, members or nonmembers of trade unions, and so on.

Przeworski fails to note, however, that representation in the sense that the "masses do not act directly in defense of their interests; they delegate this defense" (1980b, p. 29), will be as true of any conceivable form of socialism as it is of capitalism. Przeworski defines what we believe to be the contradiction between democracy and bureaucracy as subordinated to the contradictions within capitalism. We do not believe that one can understand the latter without analyzing the contradictions between democracy and bureaucracy as well.

Przeworski also assumes that democratic rights are important and that they create real political choices about whether or not to participate. "As long as workers did not have full political rights, no choice between insurrectionary and parliamentary tactics was necessary" (1980*b*, p. 30), or, we would add, possible. The historical context, in other words, in which working-class unions and parties must function – that is, its specifically capitalist context – undermines the conditions under which they can behave as *class* and not merely interest group political actors.

Przeworski explicitly links levels of analysis when he argues that "capitalism is a system in which workers compete with each other unless they are organized as a class" (1980*b*, p. 37). Organization is necessary to combat the very real objective differences of interest between individuals. "Similarity of class position does not necessarily result in solidarity since the interests which workers share are precisely those which put them in competition with one another, primarily as they bid down wages in quest of employment" (p. 37). Przeworski is here locating the contradiction at the heart of capitalism – individual workers have *both* interests in common with their fellow workers and interests in conflict with them. Therefore, the orthodox faith that common interests would lead to class consciousness, class organization, and finally class action was fatally flawed theoretically. Individual interests are *not* the same as those of the collective.

The failure of the working class to increase past a majority, indeed to remain at about one-third of the electorate in most Western European states, is the fundamental demographic fact that makes the electoral road to socialism impossible. Therefore, the historical issue of whether or not the bourgeoisie would accept electoral defeat at the hands of socialists is a possibility it has never had to confront, at least in Western Europe. The hard political fact is that "a party representing a class which has fewer members than the other classes combined cannot win electoral battles" (Przeworski 1980*b*, p. 39). Given that condition, socialists engaging in electoral politics must compromise, with all of the consequences that entails. The resulting choice is not between revolution and reform, because a party composed only of workers would not necessarily be revolutionary. Socialists, rather, must "choose between a party homogeneous in its class appeal, but sentenced to perpetual electoral defeats, and a party that struggles for electoral success at the cost of diluting its class character" (p. 39).

Przeworski rejects as simply historically wrong the assertion that the search of socialist parties for non-working-class allies is recent and a result of the failure of socialism. If one broadens the definition of a popular coalition to include not only the core industrial workers but also white-collar employees, petit bourgeois shopkeepers, housewives, retirees, and students, the "people" whose interests are not fundamentally antagonistic to socialism constitute three-quarters of the population of all advanced capitalist countries. This premise makes even more dramatic the issue of why social democratic parties, let alone socialist or communist ones, have not been able to gain consistent electoral majorities, and, more important, not even among manual workers. One of the problems, Przeworski argues, is a dilemma of electoral politics. Given the fact that workers are not a majority and that a socialist politics must engage in wider class appeals, class as a slogan, an appeal, a base for support becomes even less important. "By broadening their appeal to the 'masses,' social democrats weaken the general salience of class as a determinant of the political behavior of individuals" (1980b, p. 42).

Przeworski is explaining the behavior of individuals by the organizational imperatives of electoral competition. He assumes that intraclass and interclass conflict flows from the dynamics of capitalist accumulation. The organizational dilemmas of social democratic parties are explained by societal contradictions. Przeworski also explains a democratic political culture as a consequence of the inability of a class party to attain an electoral majority. "Differentiation of class appeal . . . has a fundamental effect on the form of political conflicts in capitalist societies since it reinstates a classless vision of politics" (1980b, p. 43). The inexorable consequence, however, is to reduce the capacity of the party to mobilize workers. Przeworski defines the essential contradiction well: "To be effective in elections [Social Democrats] have to seek allies who would join workers under the socialist banner, yet at the same time they erode exactly that ideology which is the source of their strength among workers. They cannot remain a party of workers alone and yet they can never cease to be a workers party" (p. 44). That is an internal contradiction of democracy within capitalism, but it would remain a contradiction within democracy even under socialism, if socialism is seen not as a monolithic political system in which a single party represents the collective interests of the entire population but rather as a society in which the inequalities generated by capitalist-class rule were eliminated but multiple differences of interest remained and can be freely represented.

The internal contradiction in bureaucracy is seen in the debate over the meaning of "socialization" (the turning over of industries to their employees) and "nationalization" (their "general direction by the state") (Przeworski 1980b, p. 49). Citing several Marxists worried about this issue, Przeworski summarizes their argument that "direct control of particular firms would not remove the antagonisms between producers and consumers, that is, workers in other firms. On the other hand, transfer to centralized control of the state would have the effect of replacing the private authority of capital by the bureaucratic authority of the government" (p. 49). Socialists in several countries were worried about the problem of "combining rationality at the level of the society as a whole with the control of the immediate producers over their own activities" (p. 49). Lacking any theory of bureaucracy, or subordinating bureaucratic contradictions to capitalist ones, the Social Democrats operated in a political and theoretical vacuum. The negative example of the Soviet Union as a form of bureaucratic or state socialism paralyzed them even more.

Przeworski argues that until the 1930s and the advent of Keynesianism, social democrats had no economic policy except nationalism. But Keynes and Wicksell found the solution in the active state, which was "not helpless against the whims of the capitalist market" (1980b, p. 51). Keynesian theory not only "justified socialist participation in government but... suddenly granted a universalistic status to the interests of workers" (p. 52). Higher wages were no longer seen as a cause of economic crisis but were seen as a source of increase in "aggregate demand, which implied increased expectations of profit, increased investment, and hence economic stimulation" (p. 52).

This theory became a "full-fledged ideology of the 'welfare state.' " The state no longer had to be either destroyed by the proletariat or taken over completely to become the instrument of working-class control but could devise new instruments of control over the chaotic capitalist markets. Defining what we call reform politics, Przeworski paraphrases economist Ernst Wigforss to the effect that "by indirect control the state could rationalize the economy as a whole and orient it toward the general welfare" (1980b, p. 52). The theoretical distinction is between the "concept of property as the authority to manage and property as a legal possession" (p. 52). Bureaucratization of both the state and private corporations thus separates managerial control from ownership.

Przeworski assumes that the present structure of the capitalist "welfare" state was "built by social democrats" (1980b, p. 54). It includes several features: (1) Activities "unprofitable for private firms but necessary for the economy as a whole" are operated by the state; (2) the private sector is regulated by the state, in ways desired by public opinion, expressed through both economic and political markets; (3) the "distributional effects of the operation of the market" are mitigated by the state through welfare measures (p. 54). Both pluralist and managerial perspectives are seen as different elements of social democratic ideology. The result is his political judgment that, "having made the commitment to maintain private property of the means of production, to assure efficiency, and to mitigate distributional effects, social democracy ceased to be a reformist movement" (p. 54). And this consequence, he argues, is a direct effect of the success of reforms. Unprofitable activities by the state deprive it of resources. Strengthening the market through regulation creates a permanent need for welfare payments to offset negative "distributional effects," that is, inequalities. Social democratic policies are therefore "contradictory since they are forced at the same time to strengthen the productive power of capital and to counteract its effects" (p. 55). This is not a contradiction of democracy but a contradiction between democracy and capitalism. As long as accumulation is privately controlled, the entire society is dependent upon private profit and thus economic growth.

Thus it is in the genuine, *individual* interests of particular wage earners that capitalists continue to make profits. As long as the democratic aspect of the state successfully individualizes the definition and political expression of interests, capitalism is reinforced, *by the very operations of democracy*. As Przeworski puts it, "the basic compromise of social democrats with private capital is thus an expression of the very structure of capitalist society" (1980*b*, p. 56). The implied bargain between social democracy and capital is that capitalists must appropriately invest in productive capacity and provide jobs and not attack the welfare state for mitigating the worst inequalities created by the capitalist economy. Consensus (or hegemony) rests as much on the political and economic behavior of capitalists as on the beliefs of ordinary people.

Here is where Przeworski's exclusive focus upon the "consent" of the working population given to the democratic capitalist state becomes only a partial view, and his pessimistic view of the conversion of social democracy from reformism is incomplete. In our terms, social democracy is still reformist politics; it is no longer *socialist* politics. The pluralists are right in that the inexorable pressure within capitalist democracies is toward liberal and conservative politics. In the absence of internally or externally caused crises, the incentives (winning elections) and the sanctions (losing power) for *all* significant political actors are toward gaining majorities, and that means finding an acceptable "political formula" that will satisfy all classes.

His argument is incomplete, however, mainly because he does not consider the complexities of the politics of the Right. Conservative and reactionary politics are either merged in his analysis or do not appear at all. In effect, Przeworski assumes that the politics of the Right are rational and effective and that capitalists always have the option of fascism – the destruction of the democratic state – if they do not like threatening actions by leftist parties and movements. In his last section, "Crisis and the Workers Government," he argues that the "crisis before socialism" will not be surmounted "under democratic conditions" (1980*b*, p. 56). Then he gives a scenario leading to crisis, in which social democrats win broadly based support and "attempt to use their position for a democratic transition to socialism" (p. 56). He spells out a dismal prospect of economic crisis, as "rational private capitalists" refuse to invest, "prices increase, nominal wage gains become eroded, and eventually output falls, demand slackens, unemployment reappears as a major problem" (p. 57). The result is that, "faced with an economic crisis, threatened with loss of electoral support, concerned about the possibility of fascist counter-revolution, social democrats abandon the project of transition or at least pause to wait for more auspicious times" (p. 58).

Przeworski ends his analysis with only two alternatives: accept social democratic compromises, or take the Leninist road to socialism, which accepts the potential gains of socialism at the cost of abandoning democratic institutions in order to create the political conditions of working-class rule.

This is an unpleasant alternative but theoretically unnecessary, because Przeworski has failed to take into account the full complexities of democratic capitalist politics. By invoking only the specter of fascism on the right and assuming that that political alternative is always available to capitalists if they calculate that fascism is the only way of maintaining class rule, he has ignored the ways in which conservative and reactionary politics differ from fascist politics, precisely because they are constrained by both democratic institutions and the bureaucratic state. He assumes implicitly that it is only the Left that is trapped by the requirements of democratic institutions and therefore unable to move from reformist to socialist politics. But conservative and reactionary politics are also constrained by the state, even if in some definition of the "last analysis" it serves their interests. An adequate assessment of the prospects for converting reformist to socialist politics must take into account not only the functions of social democracy for capitalism but also the functions of conservative and reactionary politics for socialism, as well as democracy. More generally, the multiple contradictions of democracy, bureaucracy, and capitalism must be seen in terms of the diverse politics they generate. Failing to see the diversities of politics from right to left, their mutual interdependencies, and their mutual constraints hampers both politics and theory.

Conclusions

The class perspective stresses a key contradiction in the state: It must maintain profitable accumulation, and it must attempt to satisfy the rising popular expectations of democracy. Capitalist states guarantee both property rights and political rights. In the capitalist democracies, states are organized internally to buffer the institutional contradiction between capitalism and democracy, as we shall see in the next chapter.

By its nature as a capitalist state bound to protect property rights, the legislature, courts, and executive cannot systematically control the investment and production decisions of private capital. Although votes are equally distributed, capital is not. Thus capitalism creates social conditions that may or may not become the source of political mobilization by an electorate in which the working class is dominant.

The state is forced to manage the conflict between democratic pressures for employment and adequate wages and an economy with inherent tendencies toward economic crisis, unemployment, and poverty. Because the working class is the first majoritarian class – the vast bulk of the population does not own the means of production – democracy is a constant threat to the prerogatives of capital. Because of the primacy of capitalist power, the democratic aspect of the state is always subordinated to its capitalist aspect in the class perspective. As we shall argue in Chapter 19, we do not agree with this extreme position.

16

The class perspective on the bureaucratic state

In the class perspective, state bureaucratization is also related to capitalism. According to Isaac Deutscher, the "massive ascendancy of bureaucracy as a distinct and separate social group came only with the development of capitalism" (1969, p. 15). But, Deutscher immediately adds that the classical Marxist writings approached bureaucracy "relatively optimistically – one might say lightmindedly," partly because bureaucracy was not seen as an independent force (p. 19). As capitalist states have become more centralized, the degree and consequences of bureaucratic rationalization have become topics of considerable debate.[1]

---

[1] The bureaucratization of Soviet state socialism has also challenged the traditional class view. Writing as far back as 1957, immediately after the first of several Polish "springs," sociologist Stanislaw Ossowski argued that (in our terms) the managerial perspective applied to the historical conditions of the Eastern socialist societies, the class perspective to Western capitalist societies. In his words, "in situations where changes of social structure are to a greater or lesser degree governed by the decision of the political authorities," social classes cannot be conceived of either as "relations to the means of production" or as "groups arising out of the spontaneous activities of individuals" (1963, p. 184). Under circumstances in which "the political authorities can overtly and effectively change the class structure" and in which "the majority of the population is included in a stratification of the type to be found in a bureaucratic hierarchy, class conflicts give way to other forms of social antagonism." But, in societies where "the social system approximates to the ideal type of a free and competitive capitalist society . . . the classes [are] determined by their relations to the means of production" (pp. 184–5). Ossowski has relativized the class world view, locating it within historical conditions that make different assumptions about the primacy of the capitalist economy or the bureaucratic state apparatus as societal forces. More recently, Michael Kidron argues, without using our language, that Ernest Mandel applies a managerial perspective to the Soviet Union by asserting that the Soviet "bureaucracy becomes the regulator and chief director of accumulation" and that the "central political, economic and military administration" has "controlling power over the surplus product." Kidron argues that the Soviet Union is still a class society, that "the people who organize and benefit from . . . the process of pumping out surpluses from the mass of producers . . . are under as oppressive a compulsion to fast economic growth as is any similarly placed class elsewhere" (Mandel 1968, pp. 631, 597; Kidron 1974, p. 86).

The point here is not to settle the issue of the class character of the Soviet state but only to illustrate that the categories of analysis are still within the managerial and class perspectives, even though there is no question that the means of production in the Soviet Union are no longer privately owned.

Within the general world view that changing class relations must affect the bureaucratic state there are a number of subthemes. Bureaucratization within and between agencies and levels of government is treated as a form of institutionalized intraclass organization within the state. State autonomy is seriously circumscribed by the instrumental demands of classes and class segments and by the requirements of sustaining capital accumulation. The concentration of state power in the executive and its administration is seen as caused not by the technical requirements of managing a complex industrial economy but by the need to bypass representative institutions in order to protect capitalist power and to overcome the political incapacity of the capitalist class. The difference in the managerial and class views of the bureaucratic state can be summarized succinctly. In the former view, class interests are one factor in the transformation of legal structures; in the latter, legal structures are one factor in the transformation of class rule.[2]

Bureaucracy and capitalism

There are two major variants of the class perspective on the bureaucratic state. The classic functional view is that the state is an instrument or structure outside the contradictions of capitalism but unable to overcome them. It is a rational agent in an irrational society, indeed, a formal rationality required by the substantive irrationality of capitalism. Bureaucratic rationalization is compatible, in fact necessary, for the state to function as a capitalist state, as the executive committee managing the common affairs of the bourgeoisie (Neumann 1957; Mandel 1975; Therborn 1978; Becker 1979).

The second, political view is that the state cannot be rationalized because the contradictions of capitalism are internalized within it. The state is torn by the contradiction between capital and labor. Rationality is an "appearance," an ideology. The state itself reflects and is the object of class struggle (Kidron, 1974; Offe, 1975; Poulantzas 1978).

---

[2] Erik Olin Wright has expressed our point in another way in his contrast of Weber – the father of the analysis of bureaucracy – and Lenin – a theorist of the capitalist state. "Weber has an elaborate theory of organizational contradictions, but an underdeveloped theory of social [in our words, societal] contradictions; Lenin has a relatively developed theory of social contradictions, but a limited theory of organizational contradictions" (1978, p. 213). As a consequence, in Lenin's analysis, there is a "partial fusion of his critique of capitalism as such, and a critique of complex organizations." In our terms, he collapses levels of analysis. It follows that Lenin conducts "virtually no analysis of the internal contradictions of soviet structures of organization" (p. 213). Weber, conversely, "tends to ignore or minimize the relationship of the growth of bureaucracy (and the development of the state apparatus in general) to class struggle in capitalist society" (p. 217). Wright offers "proletarian democracy" under socialism as the solution to the problem of "political mediations" that represent class interests inside the state.

Representing the first view, political scientist Franz Neumann links the formal rationality of law, the calculability of economic transactions, and thus the bureaucratization of the state to the basic requirements of capitalist competition. "Free competition requires the generality of law because it is the highest form of formal rationality. . . . It is the primary task of the state to create such a legal order as will secure the fulfillment of contracts" (1957, p. 40). The law governing private transactions becomes coequal with state law. Private interest, rather than public purpose, becomes the basis of legal rationalization. Workers and capitalists are treated as equal, as abstract individuals with the same rights of contract and property, each presumed to be free to follow their individual interests.

Neumann argues that the change in liberal law from Adam Smith's conception of a guarantee of equal competition and a prevention of monopolies to a bureaucratic concept of formal law was necessary to provide the legal underpinnings for monopoly capitalism. Political and economic competition in free markets was obsolete because freedom of contract meant freedom to conclude any kind of contract, "even such contracts as would mean the end of free competition" (1957, p. 41). "The transformation of the concept of the freedom of contract . . . into a formal, juridical concept contributed to the development of the system cf monopolistic capitalism, in which contract and general laws were to play a strictly secondary role" (pp. 41–2).

Neumann argues (writing in the 1950s) that

it now appears as if political power has begun to emancipate itself from its economic roots and, indeed, tends to become a base for the acquisition of economic power. In general, bureaucratization is believed to be the manifestation of that trend which culminates in doctrines of managerial rule: private and public managers eliminating property owners and parliaments. The trend toward bureaucratization has unquestionably two roots: the transformation of parliamentary democracy into mass democracy; and the transition of a predominantly competitive economy into a predominantly organized economy. [1957, p. 14]

Neumann accepts these historical trends as real and important but argues trenchantly that the growth of bureaucratic behaviors as well as the number of bureaucratic organizations do not mean that bureaucracies now have systemic power. Routine performance of tasks is now universal and necessary; bureaucratic organizations perform more and more functions, but from these empirical indicators one cannot infer that the system has changed. Rather, "the growth of the scope and number of bureaucratic structures may merely indicate that the social groups which rule now need more and more bureaucracies in order to cope with the exercise of political power" (p. 14). Although using the pluralist concept of groups, Neumann is arguing that bureaucratization is subordinate to the requirements of capitalist rule.[3]

Also representing the functionalist view, economist James Becker says that a "significant part of [the sphere of circulation of capital] consists of the juridical-administrative mechanisms that establish, maintain, and enforce the rules of the money-market economy. A portion of the management is realized through the 'invisible hand' of competition, but since the Civil War the visible administrative hand has become dominant" (1979, p. 35). Becker refers to "managerial capital" and "administrative labor" as if class relations were completely reproduced in the state (1977, p. 7). The bureaucratic state is not seen as even quasi-independent but simply reproduces the relations of production in the economy.[4]

Some of the recent class arguments about the successful contemporary efforts to centralize and rationalize the state are almost couched in Weberian language. According to sociologist Goran Therborn, in

the last few decades, a new mode of organizing the bourgeois state has developed alongside the legal bureaucracy.... Like the latter it is characterized by specialization, impersonality and stratified monopolization of intellectual knowledge by professionals. But it does not rely to the same degree upon calculable rules and fixed hierarchies. We may term this form *managerial technocracy*. Its rationality is substantive rather than formal; and instead of juridical knowledge, it promotes technical and scientific expertise, applied with discretion and consideration of actual effects, rather than with calculable legal precision.... In the internal control system, cost-benefit analysis and budgetary policy have overtaken legal reviews in importance. [1978, p. 54]

[3] Historian Gabriel Kolko has emphasized the specific interests and activities of capitalists in furthering the bureaucratization of the state (1967). Kolko argues that "the bureaucratization of the political machinery of society, to the extent it took place, was [not] as inevitable as the concentration of industry," although it was "logical" for the industrialists to "also welcome the intervention of a centralized state power to meet problems they could not solve themselves.... American capitalism was not merely interested in having law that operated like a piece of machinery, as Weber suggested, but in utilizing the state on terms and conditions which made bureaucratic functions class functions. Bureaucracy, in itself, needed a power base in order to operate in a roughly continuous, systematic fashion" (p. 303). Bureaucracy found that power base in support from "powerful economic groups," which bureaucrats in turn supported.

[4] Another functionalist version of the class view of the bureaucratic state interprets managerial ideology in class terms. Geoffrey Kay sees the emergence of a new "managerial caste" in both the state and the economy as the ideal agent, ideology, and organizational form for the next stage of capitalist development. "Its professional creed that commits it to abstractly defined goals such as growth, productivity, and efficiency is ideally suited to the needs of capital, but they serve the objective requirements of accumulation while mystifying its true nature and thereby lifting it beyond the range of criticism" (1975, p. 79).

Therborn gives no evidence for this empirical assertion that a rationalized bureaucratic state exists.[5] In discussing managerial technocracy, Therborn thus takes its rationalized efficiency as a genuine capacity of the bureaucratic state, not as merely a strategy of crisis management or an ideological construction. The technocracy is assumed to be able to calculate its policies in accordance with their predicted consequences. Contradictions within the state have disappeared in this functionalist view of bureaucracy.

Therborn regards not only the bureaucratic but also the democratic aspects of the state as "techniques of bourgeois rule." "Bureaucracy" and "parliamentary politics" were "two important novel elements . . . in the new political technology" of class rule. These older techniques of rule have been supplemented by two new ones: "plebiscitary politics" and "managerial technocracy" (1978, pp. 53–4). The former was "massively developed" by the fascist regimes. Nevertheless, in the industrialized countries, the traditional skills of politics are still important: "manipulation of agendas and procedures, horse trading, formation of unstable coalitions on a clique basis, and monitoring of confidence votes" (p. 53). Therborn recognizes these pluralist processes but does not assign them theoretical autonomy. The language derogates the operations of parliamentary bargaining, assuming that the outcomes are not significantly responsive to working-class interests.

A similar class view of the bureaucratic state assumes that organizational mechanisms arise to do what capitalists cannot: assure the reproduction of capitalism. According to Ernest Mandel, the three "functions of the State" are: (1) "Provision of those general conditions of production which cannot be assured by the private activities of the members of the dominant class"; (2) "Repression of any threat to the prevailing mode of production . . . by means of army, police, judiciary and prison systems"; and (3) "Integration of the dominant classes" (1975, p. 475). These functions are common to all capitalist states. However, the form in which they are fulfilled changes to fit the changing form of capital. As capital has become centralized within or between nations, the state or international system of states becomes politically centralized.

---

[5] A similar argument is presented by economist James O'Connor: "Program budgeting is a device for steering the economy as a whole and centralizing the allocation of budgetary resources – and for ameliorating the fiscal crisis." Citing another economist, Jesse Burkhead, approvingly, O'Connor says that the program budget "becomes a technique, not for management at the operating level, but for the centralization of administrative authority. . . . Overall budgetary planning based totally on monopoly capital's class needs is not an accomplished fact, but a future goal which will not be realized until administrative power is effectively centralized within the executive branch" (1973, pp. 77–8).

The alternative political interpretation of the bureaucratic state is that rationalization is neither necessary nor possible, given the nature of capitalism. Michael Kidron, for example, in a biting critique of Mandel, argues that "the dynamic of capitalism – accumulation – does not and never did require centralized control over the whole of society in order to function. It is a dynamic that operates within autonomous units, small or large, and for that reason it could coexist with the localism, the traditionalism and subsistence-orientation of feudalism" (1974, p. 88).

Kidron explains the organizational fragmentation of capital and the lack of any state mechanism that can regulate economic investment on different criteria than profit as essential features of capitalism. Capitalism is the only form of class society that lacks a "central, public arrangement to ensure that the process [of capital accumulation and exploitation] will go on in an orderly, continuous and predictable way. Key choices about the deployment of resources are left to individual capitals big and small, public and private" (Kidron 1974, p. 79). Kidron emphasizes the fragmentation into separate organizations as an essential quality of the whole society: "For the behavior of capital – its blind unconcerted compulsion to grow – derives directly from the central peculiarity of the system – its fragmentation into more or less autonomous competing units – while the mechanisms whereby the ruling class organizes itself to promote that behavior do not" (p. 81).[6]

Nicos Poulantzas also criticizes the view that part of the state is a technical apparatus for management controlled by the dominant class. He argues cogently that this view bears a strong family resemblance theoretically, although not politically, to the "left technocratic belief in the intrinsic capabilities of a rationalizing-managerial State" (1978, pp. 13, 190). Poulantzas argues that economic and political crises have ended the Keynesian illusions that a "rationalized, organized and planned capitalism has succeeded, by means of potentially unlimited state involvement in the economy, in suppressing or managing its own crises" (p. 190).

Poulantzas argues that the "dominant current of political sociology,"

---

[6] Kidron critiques the managerial perspective for inverting cause and effect by explaining rationalization as the goal of economic and state activity and industrialization as the means for rationalizing society. These views, he argues, are "typical inversions of the ruling ideology. . . . Instead of innovation and rationalization being seen as conditions for accumulation in a competitive setting they are presented as the ends and accumulation the means" (1974, p. 15). Similarly, Kidron reinterprets the pluralist argument about the relationship between economic growth and job opportunities, which stresses the need for economic growth in order to provide jobs. Not so, says Kidron, who calls this pure ideology. "Instead of the ability to work or labour power being seen as a saleable item, a commodity, because uncoordinated accumulation could not take place unless it were, the ruling explanation has it that accumulation must take place in order to enlarge the job market" (p. 15).

stemming from Hegel and Max Weber, assumes that the state enjoys an "absolute autonomy" relating both to the "peculiar power which the state is supposed to hold" and to the "bearers of this power and of state rationality: above all the bureaucracy and political elites" (1978, p. 129). Disagreeing with this position and offering the metaphor of "condensation," Poulantzas says that the "State is not purely and simply a relationship . . . it is the *specific material condensation* of a relationship of forces among classes and class fractions" (p. 129; italics in original).

Poulantzas contrasts this view to his own, which is that "class contradictions are the very stuff of the State: they are present in its material framework and pattern its organization; while the State's policy is the result of their functioning within the State" (1978, p. 132). Poulantzas thus rejects the image of the state as a "completely united mechanism, founded on a homogeneous and hierarchical distribution of the centers of power moving from top to bottom of a uniform ladder or pyramid" (p. 133). Even though the state "does possess a hierarchical and bureaucratic structure" and is "centralized," these structures do not resemble the features prescribed by constitutional law, administrative law, or statutes.

The changing needs of capital: the societal level

The bureaucratic state came into existence to meet the historical requirements of capital accumulation. Variations in bureaucratization from one capitalist society to another are significant to some class analysts. Sociologist Immanuel Wallerstein, for example, argues that strong, bureaucratic states came into being in Western Europe after the sixteenth century to protect the key interests of the new capitalist classes. "The evolution of the state machineries reflected precisely [an] uncertainty" about just which classes would come to dominate the new world system (1976, p. 236) that needed both "weak" and "strong" states. Weak states were needed to allow the "effective operation of transnational economic entities whose locus was in another state" (p. 237). That is, weak or nonexistent (colonial) states were needed to allow imperialist exploitation by the core states. Strong states were needed in the core areas of the world system to protect the capitalist classes who dominated those societies. Without such strong states, "the capitalist strata would have no mechanisms to protect their interests, guaranteeing their property rights, assuring various monopolies, spreading losses among the larger population, etc." (p. 237). The logic of uneven economic development produces a parallel political unevenness.

What is a "strong state" for Wallerstein? His answer recognizes the empirical existence of multiple group interests and autonomous state managers, within the context of a class world view.

A strong state ... is a partially autonomous entity in the sense that it has a margin of action available to it wherein it reflects the compromises of multiple interests, even if the bounds of these margins are set by the existence of some groups of primordial strength [for example, emerging capitalist classes]. To be a partially autonomous entity, there must be a group of people whose direct interests are served by such an entity: state managers and a state bureaucracy. [1976, p. 237]

Managerial bureaucrats emerge in a "capitalist world-economy because a strong state is the best choice between difficult alternatives for the two groups that are strongest in political, economic, and military terms: the emergent capitalist strata and the old aristocratic hierarchies" (p. 237).

Wallerstein goes on to emphasize strategies of elite domination of specific states within the capitalist world economy. "The skills of particular managerial groups make a difference" in whether or not a state becomes stronger or weaker. If the initial strategies of elites work, "strength creates more strength. Increasing tax revenues enable the state to have a large and more efficient civil bureaucracy and army which in turn leads to greater tax revenue" and so on, in either direction. "In those states in which the state machinery is weak, the state managers do not play the role of coordinating a complex industrial-commercial agricultural mechanism. Rather they simply become one set of landlords amidst others, with little claim to legitimate authority over the whole" (1976, p. 238).

For Wallerstein, the pluralism of competing groups arises in a particular state as a consequence of alternative strategies of managerial elites, but one cannot understand them without understanding the function of the state system within the capitalist world economy. Wallerstein is concerned to explain the overall state structure of the capitalist world system. He does not claim to have explained why a specific state became and remained strong or weak by the requirements of world capitalist development or why a particular group interest maintains its capacity to secure political access in a given leadership coalition. As he says, "the details of the canvas are filled in with the panoply of multiple forms of status-groups, their particular strengths and accents. But the grand sweep is in terms of the process of class formation" (1976, p. 236). The multiple status groups are empirically important in explaining particular actions but do not have theoretical status. Wallerstein's analysis of Europe in the sixteenth century is a prediction that in all capitalist societies the state is likely to take a bureaucratic form because that form provides the most predictable environment for capitalist calculations.[7]

[7] See Aronowitz 1981b for a similar view of Wallerstein.

Another recent study is one of the few within the class perspective to attempt to specify the stages of development of the internal bureaucratic structure of a capitalist state (Wolfe 1977). Alan Wolfe develops a typology of different periods of state development in the United States: accumulative, harmonious, expansionist, franchise, and dual. These types are untheorized metaphors, general symbols that seek to capture not only the key relations of the state with the capitalist class but also the particular forms of public and private bureaucracies encouraged within a particular historical period, as well as the hegemonic ideologies in each period. The types fuse the levels of analysis, starting from a societal vantage point on the relations between capital and the state.

The "accumulative state," he argues, in the nineteenth century represented the first state in which industrial capitalists shared political power (Wolfe 1977, pp. 20, 24). Its structure was a partial erosion of the previous compromise apparatus designed to protect aristocratic property while facilitating mercantile expansion (pp. 14, 19). The power of the capitalist class depended at first on its control of the state apparatus to make capital accumulation possible. Later its power rested on its control of capital accumulation alone. One of the striking features of the accumulative state was its creation of the legal possibility of a corporation, a privately owned economic organization, and the simultaneous limitation of its own regulation of corporation charters and destruction of the legal requirements that corporations be responsive to anything but the demands of capital (pp. 20–2). The state's withdrawal from critical areas of economic life required the active exercise of capitalist political power. State power included the power to decide to do nothing. Wolfe writes:

Nor did it necessarily follow that removing the state from the process of scrutinizing corporate charters was a triumph of laissez-faire. . . . Ironically, a political battle had to be fought in order to place an important . . . institution outside of politics. One had to have power in the state in order to make it impotent. Few clearer examples exist of how the struggle over legal parameters cannot be accepted as a given but becomes part of the activity of the state itself, how such struggles are often more important than the battles that take place after the parameters have been established. [P. 22]

The "harmonious state" represented the first "purely capitalist theory of legitimation" (Wolfe 1977, p. 54). An ideology based upon the inherent harmony of interests between capital and an emerging majoritarian working class, the harmonious state was based on a laissez-faire ideology wherever the industrial bourgeoisie was politically dominant (pp. 55–61). Wolfe argues that laissez-faire ideology denied the political power of capital as well as its dependency on the state at the precise moment that capitalist political power was achieved through the state

(p. 62). The harmonious state greatly expanded the state bureaucracies and engineered the rise of the bourgeois politicians to control them. The state was organized like a political market for public goods, depriving it of any effective tools of public administration.

As capital concentration and centralization proceeded, this method of public allocation proved dysfunctional. The movement to bureaucratize the state – civil service reform, executive reorganization, public administration – reflected the need for both predictability and neutrality in an increasingly monopolistic capitalist economy.

The "expansionist state" grew out of an intensification of the contradictory pressures of accumulation in the face of worldwide depression and surplus production in the late nineteenth century, on the one hand, and of legitimation in the face of an increasingly strike-prone and politically conscious industrial working class on the other (Wolfe 1977, pp. 81, 88–95).

In the aftermath of World War I, the "franchise state" arose, revealing the inability of the capitalist class to overcome vested interests voluntarily for the sake of industrial mobilization for war. A rapid escalation in working-class political activity resulted, including increased trade union membership, strikes and factory takeovers, and electoral mobilization (Wolfe 1977, pp. 108–18). The franchise state, whose heyday lasted from the Depression through the 1950s, was a strategy of delegating public power to private agencies.

Such arrangements reinforced the economic and political power of the largest corporations and reduced competitive processes within each industry and labor market segment (Wolfe 1977, pp. 129–33, 158–60). Private associations, both trade unions and corporations, were given public authority in exchange for self-regulation. In the case of United States labor, this meant internal political repression of the Left and control of wildcat strike activity (pp. 158–9). The franchise state structure possessed a bureaucratic aspect because public policy formation was delegated to informal elite negotiations between private and public agencies (pp. 143, 150–2). The growth of the franchise state was associated with the declining role of parliamentary institutions as more and more policies were informally decided by privately controlled public agencies (p. 153). In effect, many bureaucratic rules were decided upon by industrial associations, backed up by state authority.

The latest stage of development of the bureaucratic state is the "dual state," which emerged in the United States between the end of World War II and the mid-1970s. The dual state concept suggests the splitting of the state apparatus into segments that served capital accumulation and segments that were responsive to democratic pressures. The need to absorb a majoritarian working class into visible and politically accessible but essentially powerless sections of the state created this duality. The structural form of the dual state was a persistent enlargement of executive power, particularly in regard to matters of foreign policy. The rise of the centralized and bureaucratized executive branch of the state was marked by the abrogation of congressional power to scrutinize foreign treaties or declare war, a unification of the military services under civilian control, and the eventual concentration of military and foreign policy control in the president's staff (Wolfe 1977, pp. 177–93).

Wolfe's analysis is a plausible synthesis of diverse historical materials, fusing, as we already noted, different levels of analysis. He does not theorize the contradictions between different aspects of the state but argues that appropriate state bureaucratic structures will arise that serve the needs of the capitalist class, depending on the structure of class struggle.

Although all class analysts reject the possibility of transcending the contradictions of capitalism by means of the bureaucratic state, there is disagreement on the scope and consequence of bureaucratic rationality. One of the empirical debates centers around the issue of planning (Holland 1978). Shonfield's book (1965), summarized in Chapter 10, is an example of the managerial view that planning in Western Europe is real and important. New types of planning marked the transition from competitive to "modern" capitalism, superseding the old contradictions, according to Shonfield. Holland and his coauthors argue, on the contrary, that whatever planning capacity might have been attained by the early 1960s was destroyed by the new crises of the late 1960s and 1970s. Comprehensive public planning in conjunction with private capital is only a temporary response to the contradictions of capitalism. Capitalist planning, Holland says, was challenged both by the Right, for allowing "excessive public spending" and thus throwing the "self-balancing mechanisms of the capitalist market into disarray," and by the Left in Europe, which demanded a "transformation of planning itself" toward "socialist planned intervention in the market" (1978, p. 2).

In France, the contradiction within the state between its democratic and its capitalist aspects proved the downfall of planning. According to Jacques Delors (advisor to the Socialist Party leader François Mitterrand, president of France), "The Plan was not a good means for . . . conservative power" to solve this contradiction, since the Plan meant "transparency and coherence in objectives. But the dilemma could not be solved either through clandestine incoherence. The failure to resolve it resulted in aggravated inflation." Thus the Plan was "killed off . . . as the central institution in economic policy" (Delors 1978, p. 23).

In Italy, according to Franco Archibugi, the Pieraccini Plan (1966 to 1970) failed for similar reasons. Originally the Plan consisted of agreements between government and big business that were intended to solve the problem of

> coordinating corporate planning needs with the overall planning objectives of the government [yet] it proved unable to organize relations with small and medium enterprises. And, because of the absence on the government side of a clear, precise and consistent framework of references about targets, the government itself was not in a position to resist the entrepreneurial initiatives of big business, to control and stipulate its sectoral and locational direction, or to avoid its degeneration into the "patronage" system. [1978, pp. 51–2]

In other words, big business retained its autonomy to invest in what and where it saw the largest profits and to extract special subsidies and benefits ("patronage") from the state without reference to any overall "rational" criteria. Comprehensive economic planning is thus impossible. To the extent that planning takes place, capital is the main beneficiary. State intervention, even nationalization, would not transform state planning's capitalist character. "Without a socialization of control, [without] new forms of industrial and economic democracy, and new negotiations of changed ends for the use of resources, the institutions of state ownership and planning would tend to mean corporatism or state capitalism, rather than a transition to socialist planning and socialized development" (Holland 1978, p. 3).

Although the formal rationality of the bureaucratic state is fundamentally compromised by the contradictory character of capitalist accumulation, this sampling of diverse views shows that the class consequences and historical significance of state centralization and strategies of rationalization cannot easily be deduced from any set of theoretical premises but require systematic comparative and historical inquiry.

Public bureaucracies and class conflict: the organizational level

Some of the more creative analyses of public bureaucracies recently have been from a class perspective, viewing the evolution of state agencies as they have responded to changing class interests. We shall cite a few that deal with the Department of Labor, the U.S. Post Office, the Chicago public schools, and the courts.[8]

The Department of Labor

Specific state bureaucracies, according to sociologist Nancy DiTomaso (1980), emerge in a specific context of class struggle and the needs of

---

[8] See Heydebrand 1977 for an important attempt to develop a class theory of organizations. Heydebrand focuses upon the internal contradictions within bureaucracies that have their origins in societal contradictions.

the capitalist class. DiTomaso generalizes from the example of the internal structure of the U.S. Department of Labor, the tasks it has been given by legislation, its degree of centralization, and its subsequent reorganizations.

According to DiTomaso, the Department of Labor was created in 1913 originally as a response to demands from the Knights of Labor, the largest labor organization in the late nineteenth century, for a government bureau that would "put a stop to illegitimate profit-making." The state response was to create a Bureau of Labor Statistics in the Department of the Interior in 1884, rather than establish an autonomous agency with full cabinet status as demanded by labor. Although labor wanted statistics gathered on ownership, control, and employers' organizations, the bureau did not then and never has been able to gather such data; it has gathered data only on workers, according to DiTomaso.

Similarly, the agency's organizational structure has changed in response to the varying needs of capital. DiTomaso's study documents shifts back and forth between a more centralized and a more decentralized structure. She argues that these organizational changes, rather than being determined by considerations of rationality, were determined by the changing political strategies of the capitalist class, seeking to control a potentially troublesome agency because it represented a toehold for labor within the state. "The dominant class wanted a centralized organization structure as long as they were in control of it, but a decentralized organization structure whenever labor might gain control" (1980, p. 141). DiTomaso also asserts that the size of the agency is related to the balance of class forces in the state. She argues that the Department of Labor has remained the smallest and the weakest cabinet agency in the federal government because of its partial representation of the needs of labor.

The U.S. Post Office

In 1970 another federal bureaucracy, the U.S. Post Office Department, was reorganized into a government corporation: the United States Postal Service. A recent study by Charles Benda (1979) argues that this rationalization and centralization were taken in the interests of monopoly capital. The Post Office Department was faced with high and increasing costs, a militant and organized postal labor force, and demands from business for greater efficiency and speed. The old form of organization, directly responsible to Congress, was unable to respond to these problems, and in 1967 President Johnson appointed a high-level commission to recommend a reorganization plan. A bill introduced by President Nixon in 1969 was opposed by the postal labor unions, by the mailing industry, and by sections of Congress. A deal was worked out with the unions giving them a large pay increase and a "counterbalance" to their old access to Congress in the form of an arbitration panel in case of an impasse over a new contract. In return, the new Postal Service won the right to mechanize and to decrease the labor force through attrition.

Congress ultimately supported the rationalization of the mail system. The Post Office was no longer expanding, so the base of political patronage in the appointment of postmasters was gone. Postmasters who "distributed contracts and were party leaders" had given way to an urban clerical staff that was increasingly militant. The "political benefits of insulating themselves from the responsibility for postal policies" and postal deficits outweighed, for a majority of congressmen, the loss of control over yet another government agency.

The new Postal Service, which began operations in July 1971, significantly altered both the process of policy formation and actual operations. Policy formation shifted from a highly politicized one (bargaining with Congress) to a bureaucratized and technical analysis of costs and benefits. The proportion of mail handled mechanically rose sharply, and postal employment dropped by 9 percent.

The consequences of this reorganization were significant for the state and for large firms, as well as for labor. The state became more centralized.

Within the state, the corporate policy-making process appears to shift power relatively from the legislature to the executive. The corporate form essentially removes legislature involvement in policy authorization, appropriations and review, while the executive retains its power to appoint the managing board of a government corporation, and to remove board members if it should choose to do so, without legislative or judicial review. [Benda 1979, p. 129]

The power of large firms was also increased, according to Benda. Government corporations

shift power from competitive capital, and small, local pressure groups to more monopolistic capital. Congress is typically the domain of the former groups, with interests that are usually local, specific or "parochial" in concern. Given the geographic basis of legislative representation, legislators are particularly attuned to the demands of such competitive capital and its interests. [P. 130]

Monopoly capital supported and benefited from the plan for several reasons, according to Benda. Not only are monopoly firms large mail users who want delivery rationalized, but reorganization would improve access by firms to markets in the state sector, including post office machinery and managerial techniques. Monopoly capital was concerned about postal deficits as an increasing cost of operating state agencies and about the wage demands of postal workers. Also, the ideology of corporate rationalization was applicable to the public sector. Monopoly capital was involved in the reorganization in several ways: (1) It gave actual political support to the state managers' efforts to create a postal corporation; (2) big business dominated the presidential commission; and (3) big businesses were the major financial contributors to lobbying efforts.

Despite these convergences of interest and those public activities, Benda argues that "monopolistic capital did not instrumentally direct the reorganization" (1979, p. 147). In fact, he emphasizes the active role of the state managers in enlisting the support of monopoly firms and in orchestrating the political campaign. State managers used various strategies to inform monopoly capital of the "desirability of a major postal reorganization as well as to head off the formation of a congressional study commission possibly hostile to a major reorganization" (p. 147). Monopoly capital was an ally but did not trigger or execute the change.

The reorganization of the Post Office into a corporate form gave it the advantages of both private ownership and public authority. The private form gave it flexibility in operations, more management control, access to private bond markets to raise capital, and insulation from the political process governing public benefits. Public authority gave it some of the powers and privileges of government agencies: a legal monopoly over first-class mail, prohibition of employee strikes, some police powers, the right of eminent domain, tax-exempt bonds and property (Benda 1979, p. 129). The fiscal decisions concerning services and prices could be insulated "from groups demanding widespread and low-cost services from the state" (p. 128).

The political vulnerability of Congress to a well-organized, militant, and politically focused constituency had led to relatively high wage rates and continuing political pressure before reorganization. In opposition, the state managers behaved as good corporate managers would, "to weaken employee organizations, to limit wage increases, and to cover postal costs through postal revenues" (Benda 1979, p. 140). The conversion of the Post Office from a government department into a government corporation allowed the internal organization of the Post Office to approximate the management practices of large, monopolistic corporations.

Benda argues that the various attempts to resolve the recent fiscal crises of the state are not the "result of class-conscious and far sighted planning by enlightened capitalists. Rather, the state managers may have acted out of more limited and structured sets of interests and issues that they encountered due to their positions within the state" (1979, p. 150). The reorganization plans were part of a general response to specific situations in which certain organizational solutions – rationalization and centralization – seemed natural, because of the preexisting structure of the state, the affinities of the state managers to the ideology of corporate rationalization, and the fit of the interests of the state managers with those of monopoly capital. The organizational level of analysis is thus not reduced to the societal level, unlike some other class analysts, nor is the societal level reduced to organizations, unlike many managerial analyses of state–economy relations.

Benda's analysis is within the class world view despite his emphasis on the independent role of state managers and class organizations in shaping the reorganization of the Post Office. His concern is with the interests and role of both monopoly capital and postal labor in the political conflicts over the creation of the new government corporation.

The Chicago schools

Another study focuses on the perennial efforts to centralize and rationalize the operations of the American public schools: to raise the productivity of teachers and students, to conduct cost–benefit analyses of their structure, and to bring the behavior of both teachers and students under managerial control. Sociologist Julia Wrigley (1982) deals with the battle to centralize the administration of the Chicago public schools from 1900 to 1950 and focuses specifically on the labor movement's role in a self-conscious attempt to assess pluralist and managerial interpretations of the role of the working class in public education.

The drive to centralize the public schools was related to the "scientific management" movement in industry in the early twentieth century, a movement that was extended to all public institutions.

The enthusiasm for industrial efficiency helped to spawn a social counterpart in drives to transform public institutions to conform with efficiency principles. . . . The efficiency mania subsided by the 1920's, but in the deeper sense a movement ended only because the principles it espoused were incorporated into private industry and public institutions. [Wrigley 1982, p. 91]

As Wrigley summarizes,

the main principles of the social efficiency adherents were an emphasis on the need for direction by scientific experts, a desire for centralized control, and an impulse to standardize and test the methods and products of social institutions. In the educational sphere, business leaders and progressive reformers sought ways of restructuring public school systems in the name of these goals. In particular, business groups made repeated efforts to increase the power of the superintendent and to reduce the strength of the organized teachers. The labor movement viewed these actions as reinforcing business influence over the schools, and in Chicago this led to many skirmishes over school reorganization proposals. [Pp. 91–2]

Wrigley tells the story of the school administration's continuing efforts, supported by Chicago business, to rationalize and centralize the school system in order to control the behavior and productivity of teachers. Teachers and organized labor opposed almost all of these efforts.

This attempt at rationalization was related to the class content of education. Labor opposed vocational education, which would, as business saw it, inculcate the "morality of hard work." They also opposed the separate organization of vocational education, which would bring it under the direct domination of business, concerned to maintain a minimally educated and docile labor force. Labor by and large favored general liberal education in the arts and sciences. Thus the class content of education was linked to bureaucratic control of the schools. The struggle over teacher autonomy was a battle not merely for professional authority but over whether or not students would be challenged to become active, critical thinkers. The Chicago Federation of Labor

frequently argued that business wanted to make education monotonous and dreary in order to accustom students to monotonous and dreary work. The employers did not want the students to experience an interesting, challenging curriculum that would involve their minds because there would be no place for active intelligence in the jobs they would later occupy. [Wrigley 1982, p. 98]

By emphasizing the active role of the labor movement in supporting a certain content and structure of public education, Wrigley's conclusions differ from both pluralist and managerial interpretations. The pluralist view, exemplified by the work of Lawrence Cremin and Bernard Bailyn, is an optimistic one. Pluralists ascribed no special role to social classes or the labor movement, regarding the latter as "merely one of many forces, often internally fragmented, that competed in the pluralist arena for the attainment of the particular kind of school system" (Wrigley 1982, p. 5). Cremin's work exemplifies, according to Wrigley, the belief that "through the working-out of an immense variety of competing forces and pressures, the school system was developing and contributing to the growth of a democratic and successful society" (p. 5).

The managerial perspective on public education, sometimes called the revisionist school, is exemplified by the work of Michael Katz and Martin Carnoy. It is a theory of elite domination in public education, very close to a functionalist class analysis. Although they sometimes refer to the upper class, Wrigley argues that theirs is not a class analysis because it does not consider the possibility of working-class resistance and initiatives, nor does it see the possibility of education's fostering critical political attitudes and consciousness (1982, p. 9). In their research, the revisionists look at elite ideologies: the "ideological biases of educators and middle-class school promoters" but do not "explore actual working class attitudes and modes of political organization" (p. 10). They emphasize the "sophistication of the dominant elite," concerned with the maintenance of social control over the workers, without regard to the potential "destabilizing" role of the workers.

Wrigley argues that although the revisionists are critical of American public education they "seldom admit the possibility that public institutions could become new focal points of class conflict" (1982, p. 11). Her own standpoint is explicitly from a "political" class perspective: "Trade unions and public schools ... may serve at times to incorporate elements of the population into the industrial order, but they may also represent substantial popular victories that in themselves embody contradictions that may subsequently give rise to further conflicts" (p. 13).

The legal repression of consciousness: the individual level

The bureaucratic state individualizes political consciousness by treating persons as citizens with individual rights and duties. Under conditions of collective political revolt, however, the legal and political structures normally capable of routinely processing individual behaviors break down. A case study of state responses to the ghetto rebellions of the 1960s illustrates the contradictions within the bureaucratic state among legal rationality, political order, and organizational maintenance (Balbus 1973).

Political scientist Isaac Balbus analyzes the responses of the police, the courts, the lawyers, and political elites to the massive arrests of blacks in Detroit, Chicago, and Los Angeles from 1965 to 1968. In 1965, 4,000 blacks were arrested in the Watts area of Los Angeles. In 1967, 6,500 ghetto residents of Detroit were arrested and forty-four killed, most of them black victims of the police and national guard, in the "single largest instance of collective violence witnessed in this country" up to that time. In 1968, after Martin Luther King was assassinated, 2,700 blacks were arrested and nine persons died in Chicago. Balbus analyzes the police and court responses to the arrests and finds a breakdown of "normal" legal machinery under the double pressure of quickly restoring "order" by mass arrests and then reducing the enormous strain on the legal machinery by processing people quickly through the criminal justice institutions.

Balbus found that almost 80 percent of the 4,000 persons charged with felonies in Los Angeles who were convicted did not serve any more detention time than they had already served prior to trial. "In order to resolve the contradictions made manifest by such a massive instance of collective violence, then, Los Angeles court authorities not only drastically reduced the normal severity of their criminal sanctions, but also virtually abolished the distinction between guilt and innocence as a determinant of criminal sanctions" (1973, p. 85). Many "innocent" persons were jailed for just as long as "guilty" persons. The violations of legality included higher bail than normal (to keep persons off the streets), a longer detention than normal, but also lower sentences than normal.

In Detroit, as in Los Angeles, the courts imposed much lighter sentences than in equivalent cases in normal circumstances. Most charges were for misdemeanors, and lower bail was offered, to reduce the pressure on detention facilities. There were no serious plans for defense representation because neither the American Civil Liberties Union nor the black bar association would do it. The public defenders took over and tried to "guarantee that no serious challenges to the rapid and efficient processing of cases would occur" (Balbus 1973, p. 200). In Chicago, the same pattern of sentencing was found as in Los Angeles and Detroit: "not only did the overwhelming majority of convicted defendants escape imprisonment, but a majority also escaped *any actual penalties whatsoever following their conviction*" (p. 204; italics in original).

In all three cities, "the processes of arrest, charging, and bail-setting were characterized by serious and widespread abrogation of the dictates of formal rationality and organizational maintenance whose interplay ordinarily determines the nature of these processes" (Balbus 1973, p. 232). Arrests were characterized by a dragnet, no normal rules of evidence, no eyewitnesses, and no police recognition of individuals. In the charging process, there was no screening, and police requests for prosecution were routinely accepted. Releases before trial were dramatically fewer than normal in the first week but sharply higher than normal in all three cities thereafter. Under such extraordinary conditions as major rebellions by significant sectors of the black community, the responses of the political and legal systems were remarkably similar in all three cities, regardless of how the black community was organized or how centralized were political elites or local bureaucracies.

Balbus argues that his findings cannot be explained by the usual theories of political or bureaucratic organization (see Balbus 1973, pp. 40, 252). Hobbes's view of the primacy of social order would predict that elites would use more force where the threat to order was greater. Weber's view of the primacy of formal–legal rationality would predict that there would be no difference in the treatment of criminals behaving in the same way. Michels's view of the primacy of organizational maintenance would predict that the pressure upon the system of the sheer volume of cases would lead to lower proportions being brought in for the system to handle. None of these occurred. Instead, there was a far higher proportion of felony charges, which strained the organizational system. The courts acted in such a way as to make organizational maintenance extremely precarious, because of the conflicting requirement of social order.

Balbus analyzes the normal operations of the courts, seen as part of the bureaucratic state, showing how its changing organizational requirements created the conditions under which the mass arrests were managed in the way they were. Given the increase of crime but the lack of expansion of the legal and criminal system, there is enormous pressure generally for "administrative" treatment of offenders. Balbus discusses the organizational incentives and sanctions brought to bear on defendants to plead guilty and avoid a trial. The legal system cannot withstand the actual implementation of the principle of legal rationality. A facade of individualized treatment according to the "facts" of each case is created, even though the defense lawyer, the prosecutor, the police, and the judge are all involved in a "conspiracy" to maximize guilty pleas through plea bargaining. Even the prison warden is part of the game; when the prison load approaches riot levels, he pleads for no more inmates, so probation is granted even though the case is similar to another one that resulted in a prison term. Each actor in the court system knows that a certain quota of guilty pleas must be reached each day (Balbus 1973, pp. 18–23).

Given this imperative of even the "normal" functioning of the criminal justice system, "collective violence . . . simultaneously confronts American court authorities with a three-fold threat: a threat to their interests qua political authorities in *order*, a threat to their class interests in *formal rationality*, and a threat to their bureaucratic interests in *organizational maintenance*" (Balbus 1973, p. 25; italics in original).

The particular features of these rebellious acts – the number and intensity of the violent acts, the scope of participation they evoke in the community, and the amount of public attention that is aroused – overloaded the courts at precisely the time when it was most important to maintain their legitimacy; the sheer volume of individuals to be processed exceeded the system's capacity to manage them in accordance with legal norms. Balbus argues that one must take all these political and bureaucratic requirements into account in a dialectical fashion in order to explain what happened. "The . . . rather minimal sanctions following major revolts were a necessary, perhaps inevitable consequence of the extremely complex effort to manage the intensely manifest contradictions" (1973, p. 254).

The price of the deviations from both legal rationality and organizational maintenance was willingly paid because the benefit was the success in subsuming protest behavior under the rubric of "ordinary crime" (Balbus 1973, p. 255). The contradictory imperatives could be endured because "they encountered no sustained effort to prevent them from doing so on the part of the 'rioters' and/or their political and legal spokesmen." No major civil rights leaders challenged the effort to "criminalize" the revolts (p. 258). Nor did attorneys and defendants battle for legal rationality, which would have required a much higher level of solidarity and collective consciousness. This tactic reflected the level of black consciousness in this period, which sought "equal rights" (pp. 258–9). Balbus concedes that probably "few participants possessed coherent ideologies which might have served to explain or justify their participation. In the absence of such ideologies, the participants themselves were susceptible to a definition of their activities as 'ordinary crime,' or at the very least, had little basis on which to oppose such a definition" (p. 260). Balbus suggests that pervasive racism in American culture is also a factor and that white violence on such a scale and within the context of such exploitation would have created a far more serious crisis.

Balbus notes the striking absence of a *political* definition of the rebellions and thus a political response, which would have demanded amnesty and defied attempts to treat people as criminals. Both the defendants and the "defense community" lacked political and class consciousness. Balbus emphasizes that individualized participation in disorganized protests reflects the individualization of consciousness. The defendants accepted the "break" they were given, rather than insisting on either legal rationality (namely, equal treatment with other offenders) or their innocence on the grounds that the rebellions were political acts. The individualizing of reactions and the acceptance of criminal status, even though a felony charge was reduced to a misdemeanor, were critical to the success of political elites in managing the contradictions.

Balbus's analysis is within a class world view because he is trying to relate the "structural context of the criminal justice system of the American liberal state . . . to the historical dynamics of a specifically capitalist order" (1973, p. xiii). Also, Balbus rejects the reduction of the class concept of contradiction to conflict or differences of interests. "[The] category of 'contradiction' . . . must embrace the possibility, the potentiality, that *under certain conditions* the conflicts among elite interests necessarily become unmanageable, produce a 'breakdown' and hence the possibility of revolutionary transformation" (p. 261; italics in original). Balbus emphasizes that "the critical condition for the realization of this possibility is the development of consciousness." The political consciousness of the defendants was a key explanation for why the specific contradictions he analyzes did not become explosive but were successfully handled by violating bureaucratic rationality. What Balbus does not explain is how the class location of blacks affected the state responses they encountered, nor does he explain their capacity to threaten the class interests embodied in the bureaucratic state.

In the pluralist view, the courts and police acted in a way that could be interpreted as flexible responses by political leaders to a breakdown in social control. In the managerial perspective, these responses represented a breakdown in rationality, because of overwhelming environmental turbulence. Bureaucratic routines were simply insufficient to deal with the volume and nature of the demands on these agencies.

Conclusions

The debate within the class perspective over the timing and consequences of the bureaucratization of the state mirrors the managerial debate over the nature of centralization and fragmentation, with the crucial difference that all of these changes are subordinated to the contradictory imperatives of maintaining capitalist accumulation and managing class struggle. The theoretical debates can be reinterpreted in terms of alternative explanations of centralization and fragmentation at the organizational level of analysis.

Centralization sometimes occurs because of the need by the highest political executives to override specific capitalist interests (as well as labor) to secure the reproduction of the conditions of capital accumulation in the system as a whole. Particularly in situations of crisis, there is a need for overall political management of demands by centralized executive power. A second reason for centralization is to manage class struggle, partly by repression, but also to demonstrate via strong executive action that the state and the economy operate "efficiently." State centralization is not a universal imperative of modernization or industrialization but a class strategy that depends on the balance of class forces. Centralization also occurs because of the need to socialize the costs of production within the state when capital is unwilling or unable to bear the costs of certain types of infrastructure or services.

Fragmentation of the state occurs because of the extension of the "anarchy of production" into the state; because specific sectors of capital control various agencies whose support they need or who partly subsidize their costs of production; or because of the partial penetration of the state by working-class interests that are able to establish policies opposing those beneficial to capital. The state's vulnerability to multiple contradictory pressures makes internal fragmentation inevitable and cannot be eliminated by any conceivable reorganization plan.

Rationalization may thus be real at the organizational level but is always fictitious at the societal level, because the state cannot control the causes of the social problems it must manage. Because it imports efficiency criteria into the state apparatus, rationalization also has a strong ideological character, justifying minimum democratic participation. Given the hegemony of capitalism, the very language of planning, coordination, and rationality has an inherent ideological bias. Bureaucratic officials themselves are mystified about whose interests they are serving and the origins of the state structures in which they find themselves. More importantly, the general population comes to believe in the neutrality of public bureaucracies and their potential efficiency, if only reorganized with a professional staff of state managers.

These various arguments touch upon the debate within the class perspective over the origins and significance of the bureaucratization of the state. Bureaucratic organizations are seen by some as the instrument of specific class interests, by others as a mechanism for selecting certain kinds of state policies that are functional for the system, by still others as the political manifestations of contradictions within the state.

PART IV

Theory, politics, and contradictions in the state

17

The powers of theory

In this chapter we turn from a critique of other work to a presentation of our own synthetic framework. We translate levels of analysis into levels of power, using different terms to make the relationship clear. (Societal level becomes systemic power, organizational becomes structural, individual becomes situational.) In Chapter 18 we translate types of theories into types of politics. In Chapter 19 we translate tensions within theories into contradictions within the state. We use concepts drawn from each of the theoretical perspective's home domain for a larger theoretical purpose.[1]

In the previous chapters, we have analyzed the internal contradictions of the state as seen in different theoretical perspectives. Consensus versus participation, centralization versus fragmentation, and accumulation versus class struggle reflect the division between functional and political versions of the pluralist, managerial, and class perspectives. In the functional approach, the societal function of the state determines all other levels of analysis. In the political approach, the relations between levels of analysis and institutions are historically contingent and potentially conflictive. Thus, for example, in a political class approach, capitalism and democracy are contradictory, whereas in functional approaches, democracy is subordinate to and functional for the reproduction of capitalism. By rescuing both approaches and integrating all three levels of analysis, we are able, in this chapter, to redefine the powers of theory of the state in society. In the next two chapters, we apply this framework

---

[1] Model case studies of specific political events and class conflicts that explicitly contrast class, managerial (or elite), and pluralist theoretical perspectives include Stepan 1978, Gaventa 1980, McEachern 1980, and Krieger 1983. Several of them acknowledge a debt to Steven Lukes's typology of power relations (1974). All of them deal with the way in which institutional ("systemic") power at the societal level shapes organizational ("structural") power and situational power and attempt to integrate observations of specific events and individual actions with other levels of analysis.

to the power of politics and the power of contradictions to reproduce or transform the state in capitalist democracies.

Our own theoretical framework differs from each of the classic perspectives on the state in several significant ways. None of the perspectives recognizes multiple institutional contradictions in relation to different levels of analysis.

In our view, first, important contradictions exist besides the crucial one between capital and labor, emphasized by the class world view, which fails insofar as it does not take account of conflicts due to bureaucratic domination and cultural values. The hegemony of capital is not inscribed in all institutions and actions. Second, major causes and consequences of bureaucratic domination exist in addition to those stemming from the imperatives of complexity and technology stressed by the managerial perspective, which fails insofar as it does not take account of institutional contradictions and cultural values. Organized interests do not dominate all institutions and actions. Third, multiple sources of resistance – ethnic, religious, communal, national, gender-based – exist to both bureaucratic domination and class exploitation besides those grounded in a participatory political culture. Arguments within the pluralist world view fail insofar as they do not take account of both institutional contradictions and bureaucratic domination but assume that the internalized values of a democratic political culture influence all significant institutions and actions.

The powers of theory

Theories of the state have power. This is true in several senses. First, they can be used to interpret the causes and potential consequences of political, legislative, or administrative acts. Theory influences the interpretation of state actions. Second, theories shape the consciousness of social groups, telling them what actions are likely to be treated by the state as legitimate or illegal. A hypothesis about whether the police are likely to arrest someone for sitting-in at the mayor's office is a theory of probable state action. This is the domination of theory over behavior. Third, latent assumptions that certain behaviors are public while others are private rest upon an implicit theory about the boundaries between the state and the society. This is the hegemony of theory over the categories of language itself. Although we do not believe that the aspects of the state can be explained adequately by any single theoretical perspective, we nonetheless think that each perspective has power in all the above three senses.

If this premise is accepted, then the agenda must be to investigate the relations between levels of analysis and institutional orders. Focusing only on institutions – democracy, the state, capitalism – risks reifying them and fails to provide an adequate theory of societal change. Focusing only on levels of analysis assumes that individuals and organizations have properties that do not depend upon their institutional location within society, and therefore those properties cannot be used to construct theories of comparative institutional and societal change.[2]

Theoretical perspectives

We can now clarify our concept of a theoretical perspective, a fundamental category in the preceding chapters. A perspective is not merely a theory or a paradigm or a set of hypotheses but is all three, combining conceptions of the institutional logics of a societal totality, aspects of a complex structure, and dimensions of society.

First, a theoretical perspective contains assumptions about the latent institutional logics that compose a societal totality, independent of their particular historical manifestations.

Our central premise is that a theoretical perspective on society postulates a core institutional logic that defines the conditions for the operations of others. The institutional logics of accumulation, rationalization, and participation, for example, are potentially contradictory, sometimes leading to societal transformation. To identify this as the only characteristic of a perspective, however, would be to overemphasize the penetration of these institutional logics into all levels of analysis, assuming them to be determined by forces stemming from the society as a whole. The conditions of organizational and individual autonomy would not be theoretically problematic.

The second element, therefore, of a theoretical perspective is a conception of the aspects of a complex structure with potentially conflictual relations. The capitalist, bureaucratic, and democratic aspects of the state, for example, are not completely defined by the institutional logics at the societal level. That is, the specific relations between the aspects of a structure reflect only imperfectly the core institutional logics of the system. If, however, we focused only upon the aspects of complex existing structures, we would not be able to understand the ways the historical conditions of action transform them.

The third element of a theoretical perspective is a definition of the separate dimensions of society to which various concepts apply. The economic, political, and cultural dimensions, for example, become the

---

[2] Anthony Giddens's *Central Problems in Social Theory: Action, Structure, and Contradiction* (1979) deals with all three theoretical perspectives and all three levels of analysis. Giddens does not deal directly with the complex problem of assessing the counterparts of fundamental concepts within different world views.

conceptual referents of statements describing and explaining specific events and behaviors. If we regarded different dimensions of society as the primary components of a theoretical perspective, however, we would overemphasize the differentiation of fields and problems and exaggerate the role of individual choice in deciding what to study and how to study it.

We believe that it is a mistake to assume a priori that one logic, one aspect, and one dimension are primary and the others are secondary, peripheral, or transitory. Theories should not prejudge the relations between levels of analysis but should specify the conditions both of autonomy and of constraint. The traditional home domains of each perspective are inadequate.

If this general argument of this book is correct, it is not possible to answer the question: Is the theory of the state put forward by one perspective truer or more useful than the theory advanced by other perspectives? The three perspectives do not deal in the same way with the same levels of analysis and are not able to answer the same historical and empirical questions. By the same token, they cannot be "tested" as alternative explanations of the same phenomenon. It is neither useful nor possible to argue that one theoretical perspective is a complete and true one, in the sense that it alone can be an adequate source of concepts and hypotheses to explain *any* phenomenon. But, conversely, it is critically important to accept the potential autonomy of different levels of analysis. Thus we recognize the multiple types of relations among individuals, organizations, and societies under different historical conditions. Under some conditions, causally autonomous subsystems exist. Under other conditions, dominant causes generate multiple effects. Underlying both of these conditions, contradictory historical forces limit the circumstances under which subsystems interact and causes operate.

A multilevel approach to theory increases, we believe, the powers of theory in several ways. It potentially defines the relations between general presuppositions and specific empirical hypotheses. It has the capacity to bring to bear a wider variety of paradigms upon a problem without being limited by parochial or sectarian limits, which any one paradigm tends to place upon analysis. And it enables a recognition of the particular limits of argument set by the historical conditions under which knowledge is being produced.

Can a synthesis of the three theoretical perspectives be reached? From the standpoint of each perspective, the answer is no, although for different reasons.

For the functional version of the pluralist perspective, the perspectives are inconsistent because they derive from different intellectual subcultures concerning which problems are important to study, a reflection of the differentiation of society. A pessimistic version is that cultural diversity is so great that people simply do not see the world the same way. In the pluralist political view, points of view have proliferated, each defended by particular groups of investigators, each with some insight.

For the political version of the managerial perspective, the perspectives are incompatible paradigms, based on the power of organized disciplines to enforce their definitions of problems, appropriate data, and interpretations. Privileged positions and the resources to conduct inquiry are associated with control over particular theories. The functionalist call for coordinated and integrated scientific progress is a strategy of domination. The elite fields in the hierarchy of disciplines control the resources of a foundation or the funds of the research arms of state agencies. A faction of a field controls leading academic departments. Such power makes the issue of compatibility of hypotheses irrelevant – it never arises as a problem for inquiry.

For both versions of the class perspective, the perspectives are fundamentally contradictory because they are embedded in the contradictory social relations of the capitalist mode of production of knowledge. Both managerial and pluralist perspectives are "bourgeois" in the sense that they do not accept the fundamental reality of the class relation of capital and labor. In the political view, one cannot divorce philosophical and epistemological premises from the concrete historical circumstances of the theorist, who operates in a world torn by conflict between nation-states at different ("uneven") levels of economic development, with different internal forms of class struggle. The functional version sees the possibility of socialism's eliminating the contradictions of theory along with the contradiction between capital and labor.[3]

For each perspective, therefore, at this particular point in world history at least, theoretical reconciliation has receded to a despairing vision of a possible but not probable future. The images of intellectual consensus, of coordinating theoretical systems, of eliminating the social basis for

---

[3] Social and political relations under socialism are presumed by some analysts to be intrinsically rational and intelligible. Referring to the Soviet Union, G. A. Cohen says that, "though the rationality and thus the intelligibility of socialist production are immediately accessible, it is not the case that all of the facts of the socialist economy are present to perception. No peak in the Urals is so high that it affords a view of every factory, field and office in the Soviet Union. Data-gathering and data-processing are requisites of socialist planning, at any rate in the centralized socialism Marx envisaged when he emphasized the rationality of the future society in Volume II of Capital" (1978, p. 337). And "socialism dissolves the mysteries by abolishing the market" (p. 337). Cohen's argument exhibits the classic Marxist faith in the simplicity and visibility of social relations, once the production relations of capitalism are abolished. If our argument is correct, both democracy and bureaucracy exhibit contradictions that in no sense will disappear with the demise of capitalism.

bourgeois ideology can no longer be taken seriously, given the nuclear competition between the great powers, the cultural antagonisms that have reached unparalleled levels of hostility, and uncontrolled world-wide flows of capital and labor.

But this agreement on disagreement does not eliminate the issue before us: the grounds for deciding whether or not a genuine theoretical synthesis could be reached. Just because the historical conditions are not appropriate to argue that the synthesis is possible – within each perspective – is not an epistemologically adequate position. We must discover the grounds within our own framework to decide the issue. Here we return to our most fundamental argument, that theories themselves must be analyzed at different levels, which cannot be reduced to each other.

Our position is that each perspective has an implicit theory of knowledge, which in itself has a home domain and therefore a distinctive power. Explanations can be found that are better and worse for answering particular questions.

Empirical generalizations are plausibly true or false at the level of analysis of individual sentences and choice of the data corresponding to the assertions of that sentence, the relevance of which is established by the theory. At either the organizational or the societal level of analysis, such a position is the historically limited ideology of the intellectual marketplace, applied to truth, reason, and science.[4] To locate such a

---

[4] Our view here is compatible with that of Jeffrey Alexander, who describes positivism as holding that "social scientific development is basically progressive, and differentiation is much more a product of specialization, more the result of focussing on different aspects of the empirical world, than on a more generalized, nonempirical disagreement over the same pieces of observational evidence" (1982, p. 9). The assumption that the world is composed of causally autonomous subsystems, analyzed by multiple hypotheses, each of which can be adjudged as true or false in relation to evidence, is a pluralist epistemology appropriate to its home domain of individual concept/data relations. Significantly, Alexander goes on to argue that general scientific debate among genuinely different world views is "undermined in the absence of structured scientific conflict" (p. 9). Alexander's own fundamental presuppositions, however, are that sociology can be regarded as an autonomous field, with its own theoretical logic, and that there is a theoretical or presuppositional level, with *its* own autonomy. These assumptions make it impossible for him, in turn, to deal with certain kinds of epistemological issues, because he is not struggling with the problem of how evidence and observation are to be theoretically interpreted, as we have been interpreting the empirical and historical literature on the state. Thus we agree with his abstract formulation about the autonomy of levels but disagree with his use of that concept in the narrow context of the field of sociology. Also, he is theoretically concerned only with that type of knowledge regarded as science, which reflects his presupposition about the autonomy of different social sciences. Alexander does say, in a cryptic phrase outside his usual context of argument, that "proximity of the focus of social scientific analysis to the bases of political and cultural concern in social life heightens the inevitable methodological and substantive barriers to social scientific agreement" (p. 34). But he does not say why society is so torn apart by conflict that scientific agreement cannot be reached.

position historically and ideologically is not a rejection of its truth, however. We do not dismiss it as "bourgeois individualism" in science. Quite the contrary.[5] Every theory is also an ideology in the sense that ideas have social functions, create rationalizations for the power of dominant interests, and persuade people of a variety of nonempirically grounded beliefs. But we are not concerned here directly with the ideological origins or consequences of theories.

Nonetheless, we believe the perspectives to be incompatible at all three levels of analysis of the sources of truth and meaning. At the individual level, freedom of choice of the relevant data, hypotheses, and problems will in fact lead to a diversity of interpretations, which cannot be reconciled by any enforced interpretation of the truth. Faith that the incremental growth of knowledge fits within a general consensus on the value of truth is undermined, however, by the increasing recognition that the application of the "scientific method" to specific problems is systematically distorted by the "special interests" that benefit from the actions of individual scientists. At the organizational level, the fragmentation of fields and the command over scientific resources by elites in powerful foundations, government funding agencies, and departments in major universities prevent any coordinated definition of truth except within a dominant paradigm. And, at the societal level, the contradictions among the institutions of bureaucracy, democracy, and capitalism – not just the contradictions of the capitalist mode of production – prevent the achievement of any overriding "public interest" or "societal goal" that can override ideological incompatibility and bring about intellectual consensus.

To sum up, we believe that each level of analysis must be understood as having potential autonomy, which means that it must be understood both in its own terms and in relation to other levels. We therefore accept the power of the theory of knowledge implicit in each perspective's home domain.

We argue also that the functional and political approaches within each

---

[5] A recent article on the status-attainment literature in sociology applies the same logic we are using to studies of the state. As the authors put it, the "status attainment model not only describes a dimension of social relations structured around the commodity form, but it itself is also structured by the same logic" (Goldman and Tickamyer 1984, p. 205). The Blau/Duncan status-attainment model takes for granted the existence of a state (acting via the U.S. census) that generates data classifiable into individual attributes, thus mimicking the individualizing of persons into units of labor power, seeking work in a competitive labor market and developing signs of status that qualify them for higher positions. Analogously, the pluralist model of the democratic state individualizes political participation, assuming that the state is open and accessible to influence by all persons with the requisite status of citizenship. This is the political analog of the commodity form of labor. Pluralism is real but partial. This point does not imply that the logic of democracy is confined only to a capitalist society.

perspective exaggerate the importance of the specific relations defined by each world view and are therefore inadequate as a basis for a general theory of the state in society, as well as for a theory of knowledge about the state in society.

The postulate of ultimate reconciliation (via a "unified science" or "general systems theory" or "transcending contradictions") in theory, whether put in pluralist, managerial, or class rhetoric, is a projection from the actual historical diversity of interests, conflicts between centers of power, and the contradiction between capital and labor to an integrated, coordinated, harmonious society of the future. A theoretical synthesis that relies upon functionalist assumptions alone is not an appropriate beginning for an adequate theory of the state in society. But a total political approach is also partial and misleading. The possibilities for political action, whether defined as personal influence, elite strategies, or class struggle are not open-ended. A synthesis that ignores the institutional arrangements constraining and channeling both theory and action is also an incomplete starting point for analysis.

Concepts, science, and truth

Theoretical perspectives are "deep analogies" between empirical facts. The concepts we have associated with each perspective are entries in a theoretical "grammar" as well as generalizations to be disproved by evidence, as we argued briefly in Chapter 1. Concepts always contain a theory of the causes and consequences of the essential attributes of the phenomena located and defined by the concept. The concept of democracy, for example, contains a theory of democracy. Political participation may be seen as a cause of democracy (participation produces democratic outcomes), as a consequence (democracy allows participation), or as a logical attribute of democracy itself (no society can be democratic unless open and free participation is allowed).

Or, democracy may be seen as mainly a matter of due process: certain procedures or institutions (elections, legislatures, a free press, laws guaranteeing free speech, and so on). In this instance, due process may be seen as a cause of democracy (if the institutions guaranteeing due process exist, democracy is facilitated), as a consequence (democracies are most likely to have a legal system guaranteeing due process), or as a logical attribute of democracy itself (democracy itself means, in part, the existence of due process).

The same logic holds for a "definition" of democracy in terms of popular benefits from state action, which can be seen as the cause or the consequence or as intrinsically associated with the very meaning of democracy. Our point is that definitions of concepts are not theoretically neutral and are not simply the result of the individual taste or preference of the writer, although that is one important component of a definition. Definitions of concepts are also mandated by the dominant usages in a group or society, made authoritative by dictionaries, by sanctions against the "wrong" usage. And definitions are also part of the hegemony of language itself, the "deep structure" of meanings buried in the foundations of social order. To broaden the classic statement of Marx, the ruling ideas of an age are not only the ideology of its ruling class but also the vocabulary of dominant elites and the usages of ordinary people. These are not always the same.

Every level of the relationship of concept to reality involves both theoretical implications and empirical/truth components, from the most crudely descriptive (naming of an object) to the most general and abstract. The very categories of description contain hypotheses about relationships with other objects which define the *assumed* boundaries of this object with other objects. At the moment of classification or description, placing one's faith in the truth of these hypotheses constitutes a heuristic device, if only because one does not have the "facts" concerning the relation of these empirical predictions to other facts. The boundary between one category and another is based upon nonempirical predictions about similarities to and differences from *other* observations and classifications. That is, classification from fragmentary data that an observed series of events is a "battle," a "war," a "revolution," a "riot," or that from observed behaviors a "family," "organization," "community" exists, rests upon generalization from partial data. The basis for that generalization rests not only upon rational, empirical operations but also upon the criteria for choosing between alternative classifications of these data. These criteria are ultimately not empirical or factual but based upon theoretical premises that are *not* chosen on the basis of available evidence. At every stage of further investigation, one opens up new premises that in turn possess both empirical references and theoretical premises.

The different meanings associated with a concept are not necessarily consistent with each other and may differ in their importance in different social contexts and individual situations. The dominant theory within a social group will contain "natural" indicators that refer to the central meanings of the concepts in that theory. To the extent that a particular theory is dominant, the secondary meanings of a given concept associated with that theory will not be accepted or even debated, except within subcommunities that accept the main assumptions of a challenging or opposing world view.[6]

---

[6] An excellent example is Erik Olin Wright's definition of class (Wright et al. 1982), which draws upon Marx and Weber by including relations both to the means of production

Much, if not all, of the theoretical and empirical work on the state is done under the rubric of "social science." We have already criticized the differentiation of fields within the social sciences as arbitrarily partialing out different "factors" in the study of society. There is no good *theoretical* reason for assigning the "economic" dimension of society to economics, the "political" dimension to political science, and the "cultural" dimension to sociology. But, even more fundamentally, the conception of science as a differentiated institution with the function of discovering truth must also be seen as only one level of analysis.

Science in capitalist democracies is a differentiated institution like all others. The division of labor among scientific specialties generates "social facts," described by technical vocabularies that define hypotheses about the causal subsystems isolated by particular scientific theories. Science as a whole is ideologically integrated by the widely shared belief that science is an important human activity and also by the differentiation of scientific occupations into independent but related fields and subfields with their own reward structures and incentives.[7] Social science specifically is associated with the state. The very empirical tools – censuses, statistics, surveys – used to study society have a history bound up with that of the state, as the term "statistics" reveals.

But science is also a structure of power with its own mechanisms of control over the behavior of scientists: rewards and punishments for

and to the means of domination. Wright does not refer to the emphasis on consciousness, action, or culture in a third element within the Marxian tradition. Class struggle leads to the political creation of class unity around self-consciousness of common interests. Wright's definition seems driven by the empirical requirements of analyzing census data on occupations and firms. A definition based on consciousness and action would have to be much more historically specific. The occupations at the margins of an objectively defined working class would be essentially irrelevant, if the test of the existence of a class were based not on either empirical or theoretical criteria but on political and class *practices* and the outcomes of attempts to mobilize for class action.

[7] One of Robert K. Merton's early essays, "Science and the Social Order," written in 1938, illustrates the pluralist view of science. Science is simultaneously a social institution, a social function, and a social activity, giving rise to "cultural and civilizational products" and as such sometimes threatened by a centralizing state (1968, pp. 58–5). Merton, writing just before World War II, is mainly concerned with the challenges to liberal science by the Nazi state but generalizes the threat to any centralizing power. He argues that "in a liberal [read, pluralist] society, integration derives primarily from the body of cultural norms toward which human activity is oriented. In a dictatorial structure, integration is effected primarily by formal organization and centralization of social control" (p. 602). "The sentiments embodied in the ethos of science – intellectual honesty, integrity, organized scepticism, disinterestedness, impersonality – are outraged by the set of new sentiments which the State would impose in the sphere of scientific research" (p. 596). Here Durkheimian "sentiments" have become active societal and organizational forces (an "institutional complex") but also have the individual property of "outrage." Merton has reified science into an ideal type deriving from his image of a differentiated but integrated society. "Science must not suffer itself to become the handmaiden of theology or economy or state" (p. 596).

competent or incompetent science. Scientists in contemporary societies do not own the means of production of knowledge (computers and laboratories), and their work is increasingly bureaucratically controlled. Science fuses the material interests of scientists – career, reputation, income – with their ideological vision of the creation of new knowledge and the advancement of science.[8]

Science is also a social institution that is penetrated by the requirements of capitalist production and consumption. Scientific products – articles, books, discoveries, techniques – bring a price on the commodity market. The producers – the scientists – also have a price, which depends on their exchange value: whether they have a doctorate, how many articles they have published, and what their capacity is to produce more science and research grants in the future.

Knowledge is difficult to treat as a commodity, however. Once something is known, everyone can know it. And the ability to predict which knowledge will have profitable use is highly circumscribed. Because of the difficulties of turning knowledge into a commodity, basic research is likely to be done either by the state or by mega-corporations. The latter function like states in the sense of having resources for scientific investments that are not immediately "useful," that is, not marketable.

Scientific capital (knowledge and techniques) and labor (technicians and scientists) flow internationally with few boundaries except those related to the "profit" from such activity: the resources to solve problems, technical limitations of instrumentation, data storage and analysis, limitations on costs and availability of research staff, and a research infrastructure (the "forces of scientific production"). Embedded within national economies that support certain kinds of research and not others, a "scientific community" arises: organizations of specialists working on common problems, with defined tasks and orderly communication

[8] Max Weber exemplifies a managerial critique of pluralist epistemology. He contrasts his way of constructing concepts (ideal types) with simply aggregating the similar features of various empirical phenomena. Some concepts "merely summarize the common features of certain empirical phenomena," others contain judgment about the typical conditions under which the phenomenon will occur. Referring specifically to the concept of the state, he says that "when we inquire as to what corresponds to the idea of the 'state' in empirical reality, we find an infinity of diffuse and discrete human actions, both active and passive, factually and legally regulated relationships, partly unique and partly recurrent in character, all bound together by an idea, namely the belief in the actual or normative validity of rules and of the authority relationships of some human beings towards others" (Weber 1949, p. 99). The concrete contents can be abstracted from the multiple individual conceptions of those rules only by means of an "ideal type." The theoretical significance of concepts is imputed by the observer. To use our terms, the construction of ideal types is the action of the social scientist who "manages" concepts and is not limited to a pluralist description of correlated events and behaviors. Weber's position is a managerial epistemology at the individual level of analysis.

through journals, conferences, and informal exchanges. Theory in this sense is a property of a field or discipline; the constellation of concepts organized around problems actually defines the field or subfield. The beliefs, motives, and techniques necessary for individual scientists constitute the tools for their practical activity. They develop an empirical and practical language of inquiry, mostly data-linked concepts that constitute theory at the behavioral level of scientific practice and allow fast exchanges among problem, hypothesis, and test.

All of this is relevant to our argument because theorization of the state in society is a human activity, much of which is carried on by persons calling themselves social scientists. The nature of science critically affects the powers of theory.

"Truth" also has a very different meaning at different levels. The situational power of theory is "empirical validity": the correspondence of indicators of "reality" (evidence and data, events and behavior that are observable and measurable) and "concept" (words that correspond in a definable way to the inferred reality). The structural power of theory is "paradigmatic meaning," the location of both concept and evidence within an institutionally defined assignment of meaning. Selection of the concepts and the appropriate empirical indicators has to be legitimate within the correspondence rules that allow evaluation of whether or not a statement is empirically valid. The systemic power of theory is "historical significance," the location of perspectives and their institutionally structured embodiments within a societal totality.

Theories derive their plausibility from interrelated empirical hypotheses. Statements become "true" when the observations necessary to validate them can be specified. But at the same time the observations lose part of their theoretical relevance. Their "meaning" becomes unclear. Truth may have no necessary connection with meaning. To say that "Karl Marx was a founder of the International" may be a true statement, but it has little meaning outside of a theoretical context of interpretation of the historical significance of that action. Conversely, the statement, "Only under the historical conditions of the nineteenth century has political theory played a role in the transformation of a society," has considerable meaning, but its empirical truth would be extremely hard to agree upon, unlike the first statement.

If a theory focuses upon a particular factor as historically important, then the empirical manifestations of that factor become important, and they are singled out for investigation. The embedded rationale of assumptions that justified the focus on that factor in the first place may be invisible, contained within the vocabulary of empirical analysis.

In a world view, certain historical processes are regarded as temporary, others as more permanent. How they are regarded depends partly upon the empirical hypotheses within the perspective, partly upon the historical vision of social possibilities, partly upon their assumptions about the likely path of certain historical trends. Although the politics of theory is important, the political or value assumptions implied by assumptions and hypotheses can logically, although not historically, be separated from their empirical content. The interpretation of concepts is indeed theory-laden and politically charged, but it also has an irreducible empirical reference.

The "power of evidence" to settle an issue is analogous to the pluralist conception of winning in a controversial situation. When there is a debate over different possible explanations, the "weight of evidence" (the relevant resource) decides. Procedural rules of evidence and logic govern the interpretation of evidence by specific individuals. There are two types of scientific judgment: the market and voting. Generalizations are "bought" (and the double meaning is quite appropriate) in the scientific marketplace. And, scientific citizens – those persons adjudged competent to participate by the relevant criteria of professional standing, possession of an advanced degree, and so on – come to a majority agreement on which generalizations deserve to win on grounds of logic and evidence. A social process must take place, the outcome of which is a choice of the most "adequate" (that is, the most truthful or the most useful) conclusion about a hypothesis.

This image of the power of evidence applies only to particular statements around which data and observations can be marshaled. This criterion says relatively little if anything about *how* the procedural rules of science arise or how particular people get into the position to decide which rules apply to which kinds of evidence.

The "power of the paradigm" is analogous to the managerial conception of organized structures of power. A framework of scientific policy is established by the members of a scientific community or organized profession or discipline that controls the definition of problems, the selection of hypotheses, the rules for interpreting the relevant evidence, and the access of scientists to funding, tools, and equipment for research. The power to set the agenda for science and the explanatory priority of certain problems and hypotheses is not incompatible with the power of evidence – it is simply at another level. All of the organized agencies for the processing of information – the scientific professions and associations, the technical equipment, data archives, libraries – exist *before* the issue of the truth or falsity of a given hypothesis arises, and they condition in crucial ways the very possibility of devising an adequate test of the truth of a given empirical generalization.

The image of the power of a paradigm applies to existing scientific organizations and says relatively little about the "power of knowledge production," analogous to the class perspective's view of institutional contradictions. There is a fundamental asymmetry in the labor process of knowledge production. Institutions arise that define the realms of reality in which true statements are sought. These institutions are biased toward producing certain kinds of statements rather than others, even before the issue of their truth arises. Latent possibilities exist for the discovery of new knowledge that are not manifest in the public debates about evidence among scientists or in the organized intellectual life of fields, specialties, and disciplines. Transformation of the basic institutions of knowledge production would lead to the emergence of many new hypotheses not even perceived under present historical conditions.

The state in history

We must now return to the concept of the state. Although it has organized our entire argument, it remains a remarkably ambiguous one, once one departs from the simple, albeit classic, images of the state as the monopolistic agent of legitimate violence, as the political and legal framework that guarantees social stability. That image, if regarded as *the* definition of the state, is too close to the managerial perspective. The state in that structural imagery is, to adopt another metaphor, like the skeleton of a human being. It establishes the anatomy within which life functions. ("Join the United States Army.")

But the state also has the sense of "country" ("My country 'tis of thee"), which surely does not mean the bureaucratic, police, or military apparatus. The notion of a country is like the body of a human being – the territory, the "continent brought forth." A body must be fed and nourished. A territorial state must have an economy to sustain the population.

Further, "state" is also used in the sense of the "people," who have "brought forth a nation dedicated to liberty." The notion of a people or a nation is like the soul of a human being – that fundamental identity or personality, which grows and develops and which one does not abandon when moving to another country or even becoming a citizen of another state (in the first meaning). A state thus also has a cultural identity associated with peoplehood, usually in the sense of nationality. ("I am an American.")

In ordinary usage, we use terms that juxtapose the political, economic, and cultural aspects that constitute the historical reality of a given state, without worrying about these academic distinctions any more than we distinguish in everyday life among the skeleton, the body, and the personality of a living person. But, in periods of crisis, the distinctions become critically important, especially when the boundaries of state, nation, people, and country do not coincide. Struggle over the boundaries of states as well as over the activities that will be permitted, mandated, or proscribed within states has become one of the fundamental features of human existence on this planet. Conflict over the appropriate theories to understand these historical developments is therefore inevitable.

Public policy and the media: the invisibility of theory

Theories of the state are not merely topics for academic debate; they permeate a society's life. Two concrete examples ground our argument.

The first example is the case of the application of a radiation technique called "mammography" to 280,000 American women, in a program sponsored by the National Cancer Institute (*San Francisco Chronicle*, October 6, 1977). The program "was designed to detect unsuspected breast cancer in apparently healthy women." No one, however, told the women that "ionizing radiation may itself cause cancer a decade or more after exposure" or that no benefit had been demonstrated for those who had not yet reached the age of fifty. Although the twenty-seven mammography centers across the country discontinued treatment for "most" of their younger patients, by then 140,000 had had "at least two mammograms, many of which delivered far higher radiation than revised project guidelines permit." But the example of the program encouraged "thousands of other women under 50" to get mammograms.

Mammography has two further complications. It is capable of both false negatives and false positives. Some cancers were missed, and some detected were in fact nonexistent. Of the 506 tumors found, "most were treated with radical mastectomy," but the panel of inquiry that investigated the entire program found (via an "expert pathology team") that "more than 80 of the growths either were clearly not cancer or borderline."

Thus mammography "has been given credit for saving lives that were not endangered in the first place." And "the women in question, besides having unnecessarily lost a breast, have been living in needless fear of cancer recurrence." In addition, "they and their sisters and daughters have been automatically consigned by the erroneous or questionable diagnoses to the high risk categories and so are likely to have been repeatedly subject to (what else?) mammography."

The newspaper article from which this case is drawn, written by Judith Randal, ends by commenting that this "vicious circle will be difficult to break. Across the nation, mammography screening has become profitable for many radiologists not affiliated with the centers and they will be reluctant to give it up." The headline for the article is "Mammography: A Vicious Circle of Mistakes." The program is described as the "product of untempered scientific enthusiasm generously supplied with federal funds." Of course, a panel of inquiry, also with scientific expertise, had to discover the "mistake." The National Cancer Institute, the "program's principal sponsor, is now going to notify the victims of these mistakes."

This tragic example of state action can be analyzed in terms of three types of causes – market failure, bureaucratic disorganization, and institutional contradictions – which contain different implicit theories of the state and very different political implications.

If the cause is market failure, the problem is seen as a "vicious circle of mistakes." Individuals are at fault: scientists for not knowing enough about the side effects of radiation; doctors for not informing patients of the risks; public officials for not conducting adequate information campaigns or enough research before authorizing the program; patients for not investigating enough or for not paying attention to a doctor's warnings.

The solution is to patch up the market. The state informs the victims of what happened to them, so that they can act wisely in the future (that is, tell their daughters not to get mammography). If the National Cancer Institute issues a public announcement and the victims do not act on the information, the consequences are their own fault. Second, the state reduces the incentives to radiologists to give tests by stopping payment. (The implication of the article was that federal funds will continue to be used to pay radiologists for mammograms.) Third, articles like this one are written to educate the public about these mistakes so informed choices can be made.

If the cause is bureaucratic disorganization, the fragmentation of the organizations with jurisdiction over the problem must be corrected by more state action. Spend money on more scientific research aiming at reducing radiation. Set up a new coordinating agency to investigate and control the dissemination of these machines. Form more expert panels of inquiry. Reorganize the responsible agencies to control the approval process. Given the intrinsic complexity of scientific discovery and application, the failure lies in the lack of adequate public mechanisms to control the application of science. New knowledge is necessary to deal with the consequences of old knowledge.

If the cause is institutional contradictions, the problem is seen as lying deep within the institutions that have generated both market failure and bureaucratic disorganization. Markets and bureaucracies are symbiotically related to each other, sustaining the professional monopoly of the radiologists, organizational autonomy, and corporate profit. The American Cancer Society, the National Cancer Institute, the hospitals, the doctors, the scientists, and the manufacturers of mammography machines have forged a mutually beneficial strategic alliance, which maintains the powers and privileges of each institution but at vastly increasing costs, to individuals, the state, and society. Neither information nor changed incentives (the market solution) nor new agencies designed to coordinate the application of science to human needs (the bureaucratic solution) will succeed in correcting the misuse of that knowledge and the incentives to commit ever new "mistakes," even if old ones are corrected. Only a transformation of the fundamental institutional principles underlying the state and society will change these consequences. (See Alford 1975 for an analogous example in health planning.)

Our second example shows how theories about the democratic and bureaucratic aspects of the state are symbiotically related, in the sense that debates about their relative importance prevent the contradictory aspects of the state from becoming visible and thus potentially challenged. Public definition of issues by the mass media is almost exclusively based on pluralist or managerial perspectives. The point is, again, that the distinctions among these theoretical perspectives are not merely academic; they find their counterpart in dominant usages. In the United States, at least, the taken-for-granted vocabulary and assumptions underlying political discourse are drawn from either pluralist or managerial perspectives. The class perspective is found only in specialized academic monographs or in dissenting journals and small newspapers. The dominance of the language associated with the pluralist and managerial perspectives is an excellent example of ideological hegemony.

Two contrasting editorials, one from the *New York Times* and one from the *Washington Post*, nicely summarize the managerial and pluralist perspectives, respectively, on the role of the state.[9] Both editorials are critical of the Reagan administration's attempt to dismantle the structure of federal welfare programs built up since the New Deal.

The *Times* editorial stresses the strategies of elites, facing complex and difficult alternative policy decisions. The problems of administering a complex bureaucratic structure of block grants, local, state, and federal administrative agencies, and alternative private or public provision are the primary issues facing political elites. "President Reagan has a throbbing fiscal headache: the rising costs of Medicaid and Medicare." (But the subordinate elite is moving too fast.) "Secretary Schweiker of Health and Human Services is planning change at a reckless pace." The head of a bureaucratic agency has the capacity to "plan change." The expansion of health programs paid for by the state was a "historic act of compassion." (The motives of elites explain the policies of the state. And the goals and alternative means of achieving these goals are the main

---

[9] Both editorials appeared on the same day, November 27, 1981, and were reprinted in the *International Herald Tribune*'s edition of that date.

criteria to be used in assessing programs.) "The idea of block grants violates the fundamental premise that the poor are entitled to federally supported health care." (The "premise" is established not by public opinion but by political elites.) "The states need flexibility in financing different forms of treatment, but neither they nor patients should be abandoned by Washington." (Political elites at different levels of the state have different goals, which need to be recognized by the higher elites.) "[B]efore plunging ahead with budget-cutting reforms, the administration should learn more about their effects and about ways to encourage alternatives." (Policies can be controlled by rational assessment of the consequences of alternative policies, and political elites have the capacity to obtain the relevant information and apply it.)

The managerial perspective of the *Times* editorial is clear. The *Times* sees policies as being shaped by elite assessment of actual consequences of policies for cost, administrative efficiency, and rationality, as manifested by such terms as "flexibility," "effects," "careful experiments," and "clamp a lid."

The *Post* editorial, by contrast, stresses the responsiveness of the state to public opinion and assumes that the democratic aspect of the state is primary. As the "volume of [government] activities grew and the taxes needed to support them mounted, so did the *feeling among taxpayers* that too much was being spent on things they would rather not buy." (The Reagan policies were a response to public opinion.) But they went too far. "The *nation let the president know* in no uncertain terms that it places a high value on Social Security benefits." And the main problem for political leaders is to judge *"public reaction."* (The *Post* seems to approve of the massive budget cuts, with some programs then being restored in response to democratic public opinion.) "When all the budget cutting is done, it is not likely that the *nation would choose* to reconstruct the entire edifice of federal aid exactly as it was before." The phrases we have italicized indicate the assumption that the pressure of public opinion explains both the initial budget cuts and also the decisions to maintain or restore certain programs. The *Post*, unlike the *Times*, sees the president and federal agencies as simply responding to changing pressures in different directions from the public.

Both editorials accept the institutional parameters of the society and neglect the contradictions among capitalism, the state, and democracy as a source of crises. The primacy of capitalist growth as a constraint on the allocation of societal resources for public services that do not contribute to private profitability is not dealt with explicitly. Neither the distributional consequences of these funding cuts nor the swollen military budgets are mentioned. The ways in which human needs are defined or ignored in capitalist economies is invisible. Because the institutional structure is not in question, managerial and pluralist perspectives seem to be the only appropriate tools available for political analysis and action.

Conclusions

Our basic argument can be made clearer by contrasting it with that of Arthur Stinchcombe in a parallel effort (1978). Stinchcombe's distinctions between types of theory parallel our distinction between levels of analysis: "epochal interpretations" (the societal level), "causal structures" (organizational), and "narrative sequences" (individual). Stinchcombe rejects the usefulness of societal-level explanations and concepts, whether pluralist (Smelser) or class (Trotsky). His intellectual "strategy" (to use one of his favorite terms) is different from ours, because he is concerned to develop causal analogies useful in constructing "explanations" of specific sequences of historical events. He does not so much reject societal-level theories of differentiation and modernization, or the revolutionary transformation of a mode of production; he just regards them as unnecessary for the construction of a causal argument.

Stinchcombe's argument is based upon a managerial epistemology, applied to theory. Good theory is seen as constructed from analytic concepts, not produced from a whole set of assumptions that justify and make sense of those concepts. Concepts are to be judged by their adequacy in specific explanations, not by how they fit into or contribute to a general (that is, societal-level) theory. The power of theory for Stinchcombe is determined by the "realism and exactness of the lexicon of concepts, and not by the theoretical grammar" (1978, p. 225). Stinchcombe accepts two of our three powers of theory: those that result in truthful sentences and in fruitful causal arguments. What is striking is his strong, if not exclusive, emphasis upon cognition: "structural concepts – army, mode of production, nobility – have their causal force because they systematically shape people's cognitions" (p. 119). In our view, this emphasis seriously distorts the importance of processes both "above" the level of conscious cognition (worldwide migrations of capital, labor, and technology, for example) and "below" that level (deep-seated cultural attachments to ethnic and religious identities, for example). Stinchcombe uses such societal-level class concepts as revolution, capitalism, and the mode of production, but they are seen as empirical concepts, not theoretical ones. They are real and important historical realities, but they do not contribute to causal explanations.[10]

[10] Stinchcombe uses the three perspectives to illustrate different theories of epochal change: Marx's view of the transition from feudalism to capitalism, de Jouvenal's work on the growth of the "powerhouse state" from the French Revolution onward, and Parsons's view of progressive differentiation and modernization. He argues that they agree on the main facts but disagree on their relative causal importance as historical forces shaping contemporary societies.

Our fundamental argument about the powers of theory can be summarized as follows. Theories are simultaneously empirical generalizations, paradigmatic models, and critical ideologies (using the term "ideology" in a nonpejorative sense).

Theory seen as empirical generalizations alone (the conventional positivist model) operates within the paradigm of normal science, which differentiates among fields and disciplines. When a properly developed paradigmatic model is dominant, the empirical variables, the hypotheses linking them, and the data measuring them can be defined and analyzed without elaborate theoretical justification, although the world view is still present, albeit latent.

Operating at this level of theory, our study might have drawn a sample of works written in economics, political science, and sociology; coded the use of key concepts such as state, government, democracy, and bureaucracy; and computed the quantitative association of usages, developing an index of similarities, perhaps factor-analyzing the data to see if three main factors emerged. We could have then correlated the factors with a series of independent variables, such as discipline, prestige of institution, footnote citations to members of the same perspective, membership in multiple disciplinary associations, and so forth. We could have developed such indexes as theoretical cohesion, conceptual diffusion, and paradigmatic integration. Hypotheses such as "Studies that integrate different levels of analysis have more impact on their field" or "Studies that use the vocabulary of only one perspective tend to be cited only within the journals of one discipline" could have been tested.

Such a study would have allowed appropriate generalizations about many of our empirical assertions, which are not yet supported by the kinds of data required implicitly if we are generalizing to the "social science literature on the state."

Such a study could not have been done, because no paradigmatic model (the second level of theory) exists to analyze the powers of theory. In this book we have developed a paradigmatic model as an exploratory synthesis of the literature. Our argument has entailed a whole series of empirical generalizations about the coherence of institutions and the paradigms they enforce, the sources of internal debates between the functional and political divisions of labor in each perspective, and the different implicit models of theoretical differentiation, rationalization, and accumulation they contain. Theoretical models that accept certain assumptions and develop their logical elaborations are necessary before detailed empirical examination of the "facts" can be carried out. The latter have little meaning without an explicit paradigmatic model. Each of our "theoretical perspectives" is a paradigmatic model, or ideal type in Weber's sense, because it is not an empirical generalization, although each, as we have just suggested, could be disaggregated into statements that have the logical status of empirical generalization. Class, managerial, and pluralist perspectives are institutionally derived, politically bounded, and historically located.

Paradigmatic models presume still a third level of theory, for which we coin the term "critical ideology," explicitly incorporating but altering the term from the Frankfurt school: critical theory. We change the term in order to make clear that the term "theory" is not theory-free, any more than any other concept is. A critical ideology defines the potential historical force of general ideas to clarify or mystify the significance of massive societal transformations for ordinary people.

Theory as critical ideology is self-conscious of the societal functions of all ideas and locates itself historically and politically. Institutions, ideas, and history are a gestalt that must be seen as a totality within which individuals, organizations, and societies are particular "moments," isolated for analysis only at the great peril of failure to see the cultural, political, and economic matrix of social relations in which each element is embedded.

We believe that the best intellectual work in social and historical analysis must integrate empirical generalizations, paradigmatic models, and critical ideology. This injunction is obviously better heeded in "theory" than in "practice," but that is a contradiction we must live with.

18

The power of politics

We have used the terms "politics" and "political" up to this point as if they were not theoretically problematic, which of course is not true. Each theoretical perspective on the state in Western capitalist democracies has its own conception of politics. "Politics" in the pluralist view means a disagreement over alternative possible decisions in particular situations, in which individuals use their resources to attempt to influence the outcome. Possible outcomes are open-ended, at least from the point of view of the participants, so that political actors calculate the consequences of voting, forming a party, or joining a protest movement. Power is manifest in who wins in specific situations with contingent outcomes. Participation leads to power, via liberal and conservative politics, seeking to influence the actions of a democratic state.

"Politics" in the managerial view means organized conflict between political "parties" – relatively stable coalitions that compete for the chance to rule either the state or an organization. Power leads to participation, via reform and reactionary politics, seeking to control the bureaucratic state.

"Politics" in the class world view is not theorized directly. Insofar as the concept is theorized, politics is the embodiment of class forces, the actions of agents of classes. Politics is significant mainly when the social relations of production are at stake, being either reinforced or potentially transformed. Class politics is class struggle, transforming both power and participation in capitalist states via socialist and fascist politics.

The common element these conceptions share is a recognition of differences of interest and of the possibility of organizing to realize those interests in, through, or against the state. But each theoretical perspective assumes that its home domain defines the categories of political analysis. In this chapter we develop a framework that recognizes the autonomy of institutions, strategic alliances of interests, and contingent actions in situations, in order to show how the traditional categories of politics can be reinterpreted within our theoretical framework. Politics,

408

in other words, mediates between institutional contradictions and human action.

Theoretical conceptions of politics

Politics, like class, war, or love, is a conflictual relationship. No politics exists if there is genuine consensus or unchallenged rule. Communal sharing and totalitarian repression are extreme cases of an absence of politics. Politics is conjoined with power and therefore entails competition for influence, strategies for domination, and struggles for hegemony under different historical circumstances.

Given differences of interest, a politics is a *strategic alliance*, which creates the possibilities of action to reinforce or change institutional arrangements. The stability of a strategic alliance depends on how widespread the common interests are, what resources are available to define those interests in politically relevant terms, and how stable are the institutional arrangements favoring a given politics. If neither historical nor organizational conditions are favorable, political actions will stop and beliefs will fade, with little change in the "objective" conditions. Politics does not exist outside of a historical and institutional context, regardless of the consciousness of the participants. Political consciousness must be explained by that context; the context cannot be explained by individual consciousness.

Changes in the state's relationship to society are the outcome of political conflicts that constitute the concrete manifestations of institutional contradictions (see Chapter 19). The actions that constitute the visible aspects of a politics are surface phenomena that do not reveal the subterranean connections of politics to history. Politics alone does not make history. Power struggles among individuals and organizations using various strategies to shape the state and the economy in their interests are one factor in historical change but not the only one. Historical changes – whatever their diverse origins – create constantly new situations, in which individuals and organizations must make new calculations and devise new strategies.

The distinction between the causes of a politics and its consequences is critical, because we can understand the causes of a politics in terms of factors at each level of power – situation, structure, system – yet be unable to predict the outcomes of political action, because of the interplay of the same sets of factors. The complex and contingent character of politics prevents prediction. Thus the outcomes of political action are not clues to the basic character of politics, because the intentions of the political actors may be confounded by historical and structural factors over which actors have neither understanding nor control.

A type of politics cannot be understood simply in terms of a specific social base of support or a particular set of tactics. Political ideologies[1] frequently identify a "natural" social base expected to support a particular politics. The success of political leaders, elites, or class agents in actually mobilizing that social base is highly contingent, both historically and nationally. In North American history, workers have variously supported conservatives, liberals, reformers, socialists, racist movements, populist movements – and, more recently, have withdrawn from the political arena. Depending on the historical circumstances, socialist parties have been as likely to get support from white-collar and middle-class groups, or even peasants, as conservative parties are to get support from the blue-collar working class.

We choose to identify a politics by its ideology and the issues it emphasizes, leaving open the question of situational choices of tactics and the resulting success in mobilizing support. A given type of politics cannot be defined in terms of its specific tactics or means of influence in particular political situations because each politics may sometimes use voting, legislative bargaining, personal influence, bureaucratic maneuvering, or street demonstrations, depending on the strategic situation. The association between political strategy and specific tactics must remain an empirically open issue. The tendency to regard particular forms of political tactics as a sufficient basis for classifying types of politics (protest, violence, voting, for example) has prevented systematic analysis of the interplay between types of politics and of the substantive interests and visions of social possibilities and dangers about which politics revolves.

The political spectrum

Typologies tend, by their nature, to be static. The problems of transformation of one politics into another, or the overlapping and even seemingly incompatible associations of a given ideology or issue with a particular social or class base, are not dealt with by abstract types. Such seemingly irrational alliances are frequent in the real world of political conflict.

The normal political spectrum in the Western capitalist democracies ranges from socialist politics on the Left to fascist politics on the Right

[1] It should be noted that the concept of ideology also has a special meaning within each of the perspectives: as individual beliefs that influence action and may be either true or false; as the rationalizing symbols that unify an organized group and mobilize it for collective action; and as the historically embedded symbols that express the hegemony or resistance of a class. Here we use the term in the second sense. The logics of institutional contradictions are the theoretical counterpart of the political concept of ideology at the societal level.

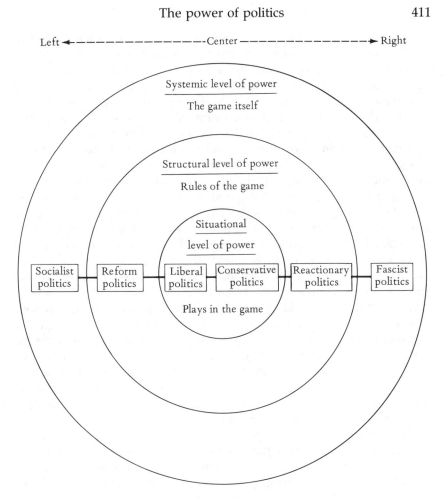

Figure 1. The political spectrum

(see Figure 1). Particular societies have only a certain range of politics within the whole spectrum at any given time.

The six types of politics differ in their typical strategies, the ideological principles they use to gain support, and the actors who rely upon those strategies in mobilizing support around certain kinds of issues. Each type of politics has its own distinctive qualities in particular historical situations and in a given society. We offer these types as the likely alternative ideological claims, as a basis for appeals for support, and as the structural components of significant strategic alliances in capitalist democracies. Our examples, similarly, are intended only to be illustrative.

Most political parties or social movements contending for power will center their ideology and strategy around one of these poles. However, political forces are frequently forced to move between types of politics as historical conditions change the potential bases of support, elite strategies, and institutional contexts. Conservative politics may move in a reactionary direction or vice versa. Socialist politics may become reform politics. The types developed here are meant as cross-sectional snapshots of a central tendency abstracted from the multiple pulls and pushes experienced by any given alliance and its elites in particular situations.

We believe that the ideologies and issues of a particular politics can be characterized by the situational, structural, and systemic levels of power at which such a politics operates. What we call conservative and liberal politics operate in those limited situations defined by an individual or group's position in existing political and economic markets. What is at stake is the distribution of income in the market and influence over decisions of an existing government. Reactionary and reform politics operate in structures defined by the organization of state authority and the institutionalized access to it that different organizations are able to achieve. What is at stake is the dominance of particular organizations over control of the production of goods and state policies. Fascist and socialist politics operate at the systemic level where the stakes are the institutional relationship among capitalism, the state, and democracy.[2] What is at stake is the hegemony of all of the institutions associated with capitalist democracies, not only the commodity form of social relations but also the bureaucratic form of domination and the parochialism of an individualized political culture of citizenship.

Liberal, reform, and socialist politics are more *democratic* than their counterparts, in the sense that their ideologies stress popular participation in political and economic markets, public control over social resources, and abolition of the systemic power of capital, respectively. This is the essential distinction between Left and Right politics.

Liberal and conservative politics

Liberal politics attempts to solve problems by transforming unmet social needs into marketable commodities (health services to be bought and sold, housing subsidies) and by assuring that all people will be able to participate equally in the labor market, whether through the elimination of racial and class barriers to occupational mobility or through special training or education. Liberal politics assumes that the market can be

---

[2] One of the lacunae of our approach has been to omit consideration of family, ethnicity, religion, and gender as central institutions. This task must be taken up in our future work.

made to work more democratically and hence more efficiently. Liberal ideology holds that there are barriers in poor education and discrimination to full participation as citizens in the political marketplace and as workers or consumers in the economic marketplace and that the state should do whatever is necessary to assure rights to enter the appropriate markets.

Liberal politics dominated the 1960s and the early 1970s in the United States. Large parts of the civil rights movement and the women's movement were liberal politics, even though they were sometimes associated with social movements using disruptive political tactics. These movements fought against the use of ascriptive criteria – race and gender – in the operation of the market. Social protests, which sometimes led to violent confrontations between police and counter-demonstrators, demanded that blacks and women be given equal pay for equal work, that housing and mortgage finance be allocated solely on the ability to pay, and that job advancement be determined by skills alone.

At a partisan level, liberal Democrats – like Kennedy and Johnson between 1960 and 1968 – pushed through various government programs to make the market work as it ideally should. A broad array of job training and special education programs was created to prepare people who had suffered generations of discrimination and poverty to compete effectively in the labor market. So, too, people were given special income supplements to purchase goods and services in the private market that they would otherwise be unable to afford. The code word that symbolically unified this politics was "equal opportunity" – opportunity for all individuals to compete equally and freely in the marketplace without regard to parentage, race, or gender. Equality would allow economic markets to operate more efficiently as well.

Conservative politics takes the operations of markets as self-regulating and attempts to limit the scope of state intervention in the belief that such interventions tend to undermine the efficiency of the market. Government efforts to support household incomes not only divert societal resources from more productive uses but encourage state dependency on the part of those who would otherwise work at lower wages. The result is a suboptimal level of economic growth and unemployment. Conservative ideology holds that people make their own choices to participate in political and economic markets. Individuals have the responsibility of deciding whether or not to acquire salable skills in the labor market that will give them higher-income jobs, and whether to save for a future day when they cannot find work or face extraordinary medical or educational expenses. State compensation reinforces habits and cultural values that erode both social integration and the boundary lines between state, economy, and family.

Recent examples of conservative politics are the tax revolts that occurred in many Western nations during the 1970s and 1980s. These movements, such as that which radically cut back state property and income tax revenues in California (Proposition 13 in 1978 and Proposition 9 in 1980), were nonpartisan, populist revolts against the growth of the state and its extraction of resources from private income, although the tax bite in the United States has been lower than in almost any other Western state. Although many interests were served by tax reduction, the prevailing ideology was that incomes earned in the private market should be protected from ever greater government demands.[3]

A more prosaic form of conservative politics is the effort to deregulate private industries (such as airlines and gasoline in the late 1970s under the presidency of Jimmy Carter). Conservative politicians, like President Eisenhower, are particularly wary of government–industry links. Thus it was Eisenhower, not a reformist or socialist politician, who first decried the "military-industrial complex" in the United States. Even though Eisenhower was a military commander, he feared the buildup of powerful bureaucratic empires that undercut representative democracy and the free market.

Although both conservative and liberal politics reflect the ideology that social values can be most efficiently and equitably produced and allocated through competitive markets, they differ in the extent to which

---

[3]   The conservative response in the 1970s and early 1980s to the reemergence of social movements – feminists, environmentalists, gays, the elderly, Chicanos – was both political and ideological. An example of an ideological response is one by political scientist Aaron Wildavsky (1982), who reinterprets the three theoretical perspectives, first into political responses, then into "cultures." Without dealing with the organizational and economic bases of these cultures, he distinguishes them in ways similar to our own usages. His equivalent to the managerial perspective is called "hierarchical collectivism," which "imposes order centrally through a division of labor.... From hierarchy comes order, including the rules for competition." Wildavsky's equivalent of the pluralist perspective is called "competitive individualism," which "imposes order by maintaining agreement on the basis of freedom of contract. Leaders are chosen like every other commodity, by bidding and bargaining. From individualism comes economic growth." Both of these cultures, in alliance, "constitute the modern social establishment," although there are "tensions" between the cultures (p. 47). Hierarchical collectivism and competitive individualism are "balanced [V. Almond and Verba] cultures; the strong group boundaries of strong prescription of behavioral norms in hierarchies reinforce one another, as do the weak boundaries and lack of prescriptions in individualistic markets" (p. 58). "Egalitarian sectarianism" is Wildavsky's bête noire because it believes in "equality of result." This culture is sectarian because it is not willing to compromise, does not believe in established authority, and is radical. Conservative groups cannot be sectarian by definition, because they believe in authority. The paradox of this argument is that Wildavsky believes that the egalitarian sectarian culture has enormous power to "coerce other interests" by successfully influencing government action to regulate and control them. The specific sectarian interests he mentions are those around which particular groups have mobilized: the young, women, the elderly, blacks, Chicanos, Native Americans. He does not mention corporations, except to note that they were among those coerced by regulation.

they wish to use the state to guarantee equal access to political and economic markets for those without skill or motivation. The issue is whether the state should be used to extend the market principle to more and more aspects of human activity, including residual compensation for those individuals who suffer disadvantages in functioning in various types of markets. Political participation is regarded by both as an extension of the rights for voters and citizens that workers and consumers have already achieved in the economic sphere: the right to offer oneself to an employer to be hired and the right to buy if one has the money.

Reform and reactionary politics

Reform politics attempts to replace markets with state authority over corporate and labor elites. The welfare state represents the form taken by efforts to centralize and plan economic growth and extend its benefits to more of the population.

One of the most advanced forms of reform politics was advocated by the Social Democrats in Sweden during the 1970s and 1980s. The Swedish Social Democrats, backed by the national labor organization, which comprises some 90 percent of all workers, has used the state to direct ever more extensively the operation of the capitalist market. The Social Democratic Party has used workers' pension funds to produce housing and to direct the flow of public capital into those industries that are likely to be the basis for long-term economic growth. Certain segments of the Social Democratic Party have supported a plan for gradual transfer of stock ownership to the labor unions. These collective wage-earner funds would accumulate by setting aside a share of profits each year into funds owned by the unions, eventually perhaps producing union ownership of a majority of stock in the largest firms.

The ideological assumption of this reform politics is that the working class and the general public can use public authority to supplant democratically the operation of capitalist markets. Like reactionaries, reformists believe that the market does not work by itself and will not by itself serve working-class or popular interests. Rather, workers and citizens must use the state to force it to serve these interests.

Reactionary politics also attempts to supplant the market, sometimes via policies and agencies controlled by and serving the interests of corporate elites. If reform politics is oriented toward minimizing the social costs of private production, reactionary politics is oriented toward maximizing its private benefits.

Corporatism could be either reform or reactionary politics, depending on the constellation of interests represented in corporatist structures and the balance of power between them. Corporatist arrangements tend to exclude unorganized groups, which often include large numbers of workers, as well as interests that are not organized through production, whether territorial, communal, or consumer, for instance. The political nature of working-class power means arrangements thus tend to be biased against working-class interests because of the systemic ("private") power of capital, a power untouched by all of the politically likely organizational arrangements usually described as corporatist. The political nature of working-class power means that working-class organizations have more control over their members than do capitalist organizations over any individual corporation (Offe 1984). As a result, corporatist politics tends to be reactionary.

France after World War II exhibited reactionary politics. With much of France's industrial plant in ruins from wartime destruction and much of its capitalist class discredited by collaboration with the Vichy regime, the Gaullists threw the state into the breach. The gradual elaboration of state planning was initiated by the state in collaboration with the elite of French industry. Through low-interest loans, tariff protections, tax credits, and cartel formation, the state reshaped the industrial structure of France. Basic sectors were modernized, capital was concentrated, and French industry regained its ability to finance investment from profits. Labor was largely excluded from the planning process, and its political marginality was evident in the lack of real emphasis of the plan on full employment, wage increases, and public services, including housing.

America is not immune to reactionary politics. During World War I, the United States experimented with corporatist arrangements (such as the War Industries Board), which allowed industrialists to set collaboratively their own prices, production levels, and production designs. Once again, labor unions were either excluded from the process or incorporated in a symbolic fashion.

The ideology and issues of the Reagan administration in the United States during the 1980s are a fusion of reactionary and conservative politics. The regime makes use of an ideology of a national security threat to expand the military budget, while silencing domestic opposition to draconian cuts in social programs. Military spending is in effect an industrial policy which benefits the profitability of America's largest corporations. Such use of state power to benefit corporate profitability is an example of reactionary politics. However, the regime is also involved in dismantling various forms of state support for household incomes and for corporate profitability. To the extent that the regime cuts back both on support for corporate farm prices and support for popular access to health care, it is an example of conservative politics.

For both reformist and reactionary politics, political issues in the society revolve around the failure to plan and regulate both market and political competition. The private market is irrational and chaotic and must be controlled by responsible state agencies acting in conjunction with the most powerful private interest groups, mainly business and labor. Both stress the importance of public expenditures made possible by privately controlled economic growth. The economy has changed rapidly, becoming ever more interdependent and dominated by large-scale organizations. Without sustained state intervention, economic growth and full employment are not possible.

Another major issue is created for both politics by demands from the citizenry, which are frequently irrational and disruptive, if not violent and narrowly self-interested. The proper kinds of channels for incorporated participation must be created, which leaves room for decisive action by political elites. These two issues are viewed as connected, in that an uncontrolled market generates excessive demands, both political and economic. The political strategy that follows is to reorganize the state and thereby plan the market and regulate participation. Both reform and reactionary politics argue that reorganizing the state will both prevent the excesses of a privately controlled economy from bringing disaster and prevent extreme forms of popular political demands from disrupting the orderly functioning of the state.

Reform and reactionary politics revolve around the principle of extending state authority and differ in the extent to which they will allow class conflict to continue openly. Both reform and reactionary politics regard the state as the central institution of control, not the "unseen" hand of the market. The regulation of the economy increasingly requires state intervention, which means that mass actions by mobilized social groups must be controlled by bureaucratic and political elites if the state is to function rationally. Reactionary and reform politics share the ideology that social values can be rationally produced and allocated through state coordination. Corporatist forms of authoritative bargaining among corporate, labor, and state elites are a major area of conflict between reform and reactionary politics.

Socialist and fascist politics

Socialist and fascist politics aim to politicize relationships between all institutions, including the state and the economy, through the use of mass political mobilization, by either expanding or reducing democratic participation. These politics aim to reduce the autonomy of the institutions of the state and the economy through the political instrument of a mass party.

Socialist politics has not flourished in the United States, although parties and movements using that label have sometimes won office or taken to the streets. Socialist politics has a longer history in a nation like

Italy, where large segments of the labor movement draw upon socialist and anarchist traditions, and yet where the state is a pervasive, but nonautonomous institution. In Italy, the rank-and-file labor movement, various leftist political parties and movements, and community groups created a powerful socialist politics during the late 1960s and early 1970s.

Through mass movements, workers and citizens in Italy attempted to create alternative institutions for the regulation of production and public services. Factory councils met to try to reshape the organization of production, and community groups, public workers, and clients tried to politicize public schools, hospitals, city planning, and public transportation. For a time at least, it seemed that the boundaries that had separated firm, government, and community were about to crumble. The ideological assumption of this socialist politics is that parliamentary representation alone cannot reshape either the state or capitalism in the interests of the working class or the people. Instead, mass movements must broaden the channels of political representation to create centers of popular power in the very operation of state bureaucracies and capitalist firms.

Fascist politics aims to politicize both the state and the economy through mass party control while minimizing democratic and, particularly, working-class influence. Fascist politics emerged in Italy and Germany in the 1930s and 1940s. The German National Socialists built up a mass party during the period of depression and hyperinflation, when class conflicts paralyzed the state and opposing political forces were taking increasingly to the streets. The Nazi movement was based on the symbolic unification of a national master race of Aryans. The party established a counter-state and used its police powers to crush political opposition and attempt the annihilation of Jews, homosexuals, Gypsies, and communists. Once in control of the government, the Nazis transformed the principles of law and bureaucratic rationality that did not conform to their political objectives of complete control over all aspects of social life.

Independent organizations, particularly the labor unions, were destroyed and rebuilt under control of the party state. Production and distribution were politically regulated, particularly for war. The power and profitability of capital were politically enforced by party and state. The ideological assumption of fascist politics was that parliamentary politics could not realize the national will or achieve national greatness. Rather, both the state and the economy needed direction by a nationalist mass party.

For both socialist and fascist politics, political issues in the society revolve around the symbiosis between capitalist production and the democratic state. They are not seen as separate institutions, changeable by incremental political demands. State planning cannot overcome the crisis tendencies in capitalism or provide the charismatic leadership needed to unify a society torn by class struggle. The demands on the state to compensate for the failures of the capitalist economy prevent the state from meeting social needs, push it toward fiscal crisis, and deprive the citizenry of any effective control over their government. The political strategy that follows is to transform political participation, by no longer recognizing the boundary between the public and the private sectors or that between bureaucratic and political authority. Neither the anarchy of capitalist production and markets nor the political limits of the state can be changed without a transformation of both institutions.

Although both socialist and fascist politics revolve around the issue of expanding party control over the society, they are in fundamental conflict over whether or not the state will be used to guarantee capitalist production relations or to transform those relations democratically. Both socialist and fascist politics view the creation of a politically organized mass electorate as the central historical tendency of democracy. Both view its political mobilization as potentially threatening to the state's capacity to reproduce capitalist production relations. The ability to transform the scope of democracy by expanding the authority of the mass political party is thus a central ideological question.

Both fascist and socialist politics are oriented to and supported by a wide variety of social movements. Socialist and fascist politics are associated with the social conditions that class theory takes as normal, that is, where class struggle and economic crisis are endemic, challenging the institutional boundaries that separate the state from the capitalist economy and from democratic participation. These politics both operate at the systemic level of power. However, because the class perspective has never successfully developed a theory of the structural and situational levels of power through which concrete politics operates, there has been a historic disjuncture between the internal languages and public ideologies of these politics. One important issue in assessing the powers of theory is the documentation of the extent to which their political strategies have been crippled because of this disjuncture.

Institutional tendencies and political types

Each pair of politics has a double relation with key historical processes, being shaped by them and in turn reinforcing them. Each type of politics finds particular institutional tendencies to be problematic because its ideologies, and the theories upon which they rest, cannot easily account for them and its political actors cannot easily adapt their strategies to deal with them. The historical tendencies that a given type of politics finds most worrisome provide the basis for the rhetoric concerning the pathologies of contemporary life from which the politics offers deliverance.

Liberal and conservative politics emerge within the context of political and economic markets, capable of converting political issues into incremental bargains around which individual preferences are compromised. Once in existence, liberal and conservative politics create political issues that can best be settled within political and economic markets in which marginal exchanges can be continuously transacted. When politics is focused around the kinds of issues that can be acted upon by incremental gains and losses, other kinds of issues tend to be defined as either illegitimate, unrealistic, or utopian.

For liberal and conservative politics, the growth of the public sector and the emergence of noninstitutionalized social movements are problematic historical developments. The accelerating growth of the public sector is seen as undercutting the private market, increasing inefficiencies, and reducing freedom of choice. The tendency for the state to absorb ever greater proportions of the total societal wealth and regulate market exchanges is defined ideologically as threatening to overwhelm and distort the operation of healthy economic and political competition.

Liberal and conservative politics also find the periodic eruption of social protest to be problematic. Such protests, particularly if they are class-based, suggest that political and economic markets do not work properly. On the one hand, protest implies that opportunities for individual advancement are structurally blocked and cannot be improved substantially by special programs of education or market support. On the other hand, the emergence of such protests implies that party competition has been unable to aggregate individual and group interests into policies the citizenry will accept. Such protests tend to thrust unnegotiable group interests into the political arena, reducing chances for incremental bargaining and resolution of conflicts through compromise.

Both liberal and conservative politics attempt to transform the working class into competing individuals and groups, in order to affirm and reinforce the market as the instrument by which individual, group, and societal goals can be achieved.

Reform and reactionary politics emerge within the context of a powerful and centralized bureaucratic state. Political actors and issues are oriented toward expanding or contracting the role of the state, and conflict revolves around the role of the peak associations of corporations, unions, and the state itself. Once in existence, as a result of the expansion of the bureaucratic state, reform and reactionary politics tend to convert the rationalization of the state into a central issue.

For reform and reactionary politics, the fragmentation of the state and political class struggle are problematic historical tendencies. The fragmentation of the state into multiple agencies and programs, each symbiotically dependent upon an external constituency of narrow interest groups, re-creates the anarchy of the market within the state. Such fragmentation makes it impossible to rationalize state activity and for the state to play a coherent and directive role in coordinating economic and social life.

Reform and reactionary politics also find political class struggle difficult to handle. Intense ideological conflict between classes prevents the state from rationalizing economic life and makes it enormously difficult for corporate and labor elites to coordinate their claims on the social product.

Both reform and reactionary politics try to convert class demands into party organizations and trade unions that control their members and become the instruments for negotiation between political and economic elites. Reform and reactionary politics also convert individual needs and preferences into visible organizational demands by controlling and screening them via interest groups and political parties. The leaders of social groups are coopted into becoming defenders of a negotiated order after political bargains are struck.

Socialist and fascist politics emerge when the institutional contradictions among capitalism, the state, and democracy become visible. Socialist and fascist politics convert institutional boundaries into central political questions and manifest themselves in class struggles and nationalist social movements that challenge the fundamental character of these social relations.

For socialist and fascist politics, the adaptability of the capitalist state to political and economic crises and the privatization and individualization of social life are problematic historical tendencies. The ability of the capitalist state to manage incipient mass movements with repression, cooptation, and symbolic reform and its capacity to manage economic crises through state planning tend to convert potential revolutionary movements into opportunities for either reform or reaction.

Socialist and fascist politics attempt to discover the "true" underlying interests of the population by creating a vision of a socialist community or a homogeneous nationalist state constructing a new basis for the organic unity of the population. The political relevance of social and cultural diversity is denied, and the boundaries between the legitimate jurisdictions of organizations are broken down to create a mass base for revolutionary parties.

The power of politics

Situational power, we remind the reader, exists where open and informed competition between relatively equal participants – individuals and groups – gains support from issue-oriented constituencies and exercises influence over responsive political leaders. Structural power is created in the course of elite conflict to create stable structures of domination – in the form of complex organizations with legal authority – that will be able to control the agenda of future political situations. Systemic power is made visible when the existing relations among capitalism, the state, and democracy are threatened and reproduced, or transformed. At stake are the institutional logics governing situational and structural power. Systemic power maintains or transforms the relationships among the capitalist economy, the bureaucratic state, and a democratic political culture.

These levels of power are not separable in the real world, in which conflict occurs precisely to *define* the kind of politics that will rule: the issues within the consensus or the social possibilities that are ruled out, so to speak, because of capitalist hegemony, elite domination, or group competition. The dominance of given types of politics may cause one or another structural element to function as if it were another type. That is, an organization (government agency, political party, corporation, labor union) may function in liberal and conservative politics as if it were a voluntary association of individuals and may be constrained to operate within certain parameters to which it would not be limited in reform or reactionary politics. Conversely, a similar organization may be forced to function in socialist or fascist politics as an agent of class stability or transformation.

We therefore cannot use ordinary descriptive language to explain the role of individuals and organizations functioning in different types of politics. The actions of Mayor Richard Lee of New Haven (Dahl 1961), Robert Moses of New York (Caro 1974), or Joseph Stalin of Tiflis (Deutscher 1949) in a given situation may represent their own personal careers and fortunes; serve the interests of Yale University, the Triborough Bridge and Tunnel Authority, the Communist Party of the Soviet Union; or be implicated in the transformation of the role of the state in capital accumulation. An individual may be an agent of personal influence, organizational domination, or institutional hegemony. Conversely, a person ideologically defined as an agent of an organization or class may only be acting on his or her own behalf or in behalf of the power and privileges of the organization – party, union, corporation – that gives him or her a position of authority. Concrete historical evidence as well as theoretical criteria must be used to make those difficult judgments.

The struggle to define the rhetorical character of a politics is an important aspect of the determination of the "cultural consensus" – the content of ideological hegemony – in a given historical period. Successful isolation of individual political actors as "voters" or "participants" from their organizational and class bases renders the pluralist perspective more plausible as an adequate theory of politics and power. But one can recognize situational influence and liberal or conservative politics as having real consequences without severing the links of that politics to theories that do not ignore elite conflict or class struggle.

Politics and institutions

The domination of particular institutions in a society will tend to strengthen the analogous types of politics. In the United States, where capitalist production and commodity markets, both political and economic, are ideologically and institutionally dominant, liberal and conservative politics, circling around the Center and seeking to maintain and extend the market principle of capitalism to the state and to democracy, have been historically most influential. The hegemony of capitalist social relations of production and the capacity of the state to repress political alternatives, coupled with its institutional weakness, have combined to constrain other politics from emerging. Other types of politics have been marginal.

Where the state has become the center of political and class conflict, as in post–World War II France and Sweden, reform and reactionary politics, seeking to extend the principle of the authority of the state to capitalism and democracy, have been strongest. Where the contradictions in capitalism and democracy have broken down the institutional boundaries that protect each from the other, as in early twentieth-century Italy, Spain, and Germany, socialist and fascist politics have emerged, seeking to transform the state and democracy in the interests of, or against, capitalist rule.

The stronger and more centralized states in European societies, coupled with much larger socialist and communist parties and movements, have combined to move the political spectrum farther both to the right and to the left and thus to a deeper critique of the role of the state in society. Issues of nationalization of industry, socialized medicine, state planning, democratic conditions of work have become important in many European countries, whereas they remain peripheral debates in the United States. Such issues spark abstract discussions of vague possibilities in the United States; they have been the immediate focus of mass political demands in Europe. Similarly, right-wing parties and fascist movements have been stronger in Europe than in the United States.

Obviously, social reality cannot be captured as neatly as these formulas suggest, but these are the theoretical connections between history and politics. Each politics, counting for help on the historical tendencies identified by an associated theory, extrapolates to the future, counting on history to help them win their debates and their battles.

The domination of particular types of politics may, under some conditions, transform the agents and issues of other politics. This is the "external" power of the politics. The dominance of liberal and conservative politics converts classes into competing individuals and groups, thereby affirming and reinforcing the market as the instrument that achieves individual, group, and societal goals and converts part of the state into a competitive, representative arena. The domination of reform and reactionary politics converts class demands into working-class parties and trade unions that control their members and become instruments of negotiation between political and economic elites. Political parties and pressure groups aggregate individual preferences into visible organizational demands. Leaders are coopted into defense of a hierarchical social order. When the hegemony stabilizing the institutional arrangements of a given society becomes visible or breaks down, socialist or fascist politics may break through and convert individualized and fragmented interests into political solidarity and class or nationalist movements.

Conclusions

In summary, liberal and conservative politics derive from the historical emergence of political and economic markets in which limited individual preferences can be freely exchanged. The pluralist perspective developed simultaneously as an ideology defending the politics of democracy and as a theory that tries to explain the role of political and economic markets. Reform and reactionary politics derive from the emergence of relatively autonomous economic and political bureaucratic organizations that attempt to rationalize societal wealth production and distribution. The vocabulary and hypotheses of the managerial perspective can be used to analyze the structure of bureaucracies that form the political base of reform and reactionary politics. Socialist and fascist politics derive from institutional breakdowns, which have the potential to transform both the economy and the state. The class perspective until now has provided the primary analytic tools with which to analyze the history of those class struggles that make the economy political and the polity economic.

Certain historical processes therefore correspond both to certain kinds of political theories and to certain kinds of politics. The success of these politics provides the corresponding theories with empirical data and historical evidence. The theories produced during those periods provide the corresponding politics with the ideological symbols and vocabulary that are most appropriate to their strategy of achieving political power. When historical processes are not compatible with a particular range of politics, the theoretical tools each politics has used historically are inadequate to inform the tactical and strategic decisions the politics confronts under these adverse circumstances. Thus the pluralist perspective is particularly ill suited to guide interest groups under conditions of polarized class struggle or massive state interventionism. Similarly, the managerial perspective is equally ill suited to inform elite strategies under conditions of class attempts to politicize public bureaucracies or where diverse social groups resist unitary political aggregation. Finally, the class perspective is at a loss to inform popular movements under conditions of particularistic interest politics or elite coalitions with other politically hostile parties. At such times, political practice tends to be ad hoc, opportunistic, violent, and often debilitating.

If such historical conditions are problematic for politics, they provide social scientists with a rich research opportunity. For it is precisely the conditions of *conversion* that are not apparent and require analysis. Thus the pluralist perspective alone cannot explain the conversion of classes or organizational interests into individualized political actors. The managerial perspective alone cannot explain the conversion of classes or individuals into organizational forces. Finally, the class perspective alone cannot explain the conversion of individuals and organizational elites into political classes. This reflects the partial nature of social theory, the autonomy of capitalism, the state, and democracy as institutional developments, and the periodic coherence of different kinds of politics. In the discrepancies and inconsistencies among historical processes, political actions, and abstract theories, one will find some of the most exciting problems for contemporary political analysis.

The ideological aspects of politics represent the appropriation or reshaping of theory for political ends. The political aspects of theory represent the conceptual identification of historical tendencies that provide the material basis for particular kinds of political strategies. Conversely, theories generated from historical tendencies that do not support that particular form of politics provide the concepts to explain the failure. Theories provide politics with a rational basis, whereas politics provides theory with an empirical basis. Pluralism can be seen, for example, as the political ideology of capitalist democracy but the political theory of communism.

The implication of the assertion that particular forms of politics must rely on the analytic tools of particular theories is that theories do *not* directly contain an implicit politics. Rather each politics contains an implicit theory. Theories of politics are partially validated by the relative success of different kinds of politics. Theory is political only to the extent that it is dependent upon the success of particular kinds of politics in changing history. To the extent that theory informs a given politics, thereby increasing its chances for success, and to the extent that theories can inform only a delimited set of politics, theory is political.

19

The power of contradictions

We can now summarize our argument, utilizing concepts drawn from all three perspectives. An adequate framework for an explanation of state actions, state structures, and the state's function in society cannot be derived from any one of the three classic theoretical perspectives.

Historical relations of capitalism, the state, and democracy

The institutional separation of capitalism, the state, and democracy furthered the development of each. Capitalist development was facilitated by a nation-state that guaranteed property rights. The requirements of capitalist accumulation were more likely to be assured by institutional separation than if the state were captured by specific industrial or class interests. Also, the inequalities created by the capitalist economy were concealed by the formal rights of all citizens to buy and sell all factors of production, including land and labor. The population was symbolically integrated by the emerging rights of citizenship, which established a form of universal equality – the adult franchise – as a substitute for the economic equality denied by capitalism.

Similarly, the expansion of the bureaucratic state was made possible by its institutional separation from the capitalist economy. Mass political participation could be limited to attempts to influence state actions, if the state had a considerable degree of autonomy, thereby propelling its expansion. And state autonomy allowed capitalists to use their political power to compensate for their growing inability to reproduce the commodity form through the market alone. State expansion was an alternative to politicization of the capitalist system itself. Autonomy allowed interest groups to capture particular pieces of public authority and others to compete with them. Both state and capital were therefore insulated from the full impact of mass democratic participation.

The state developed its own array of legal powers and was not constitutionally responsible for the operations of the economy, nor could it

427

threaten the bases of capitalist power. As long as the state was thereby safeguarded from overload, the autonomy of a capitalist-controlled economy was protected. In fact, "excessive" state intervention into the economy could be blamed for unemployment, inflation, recession, and recurring crises.

The establishment of democratic institutions was stimulated by capitalist and working classes struggling for political and economic rights but also was furthered by the growth of a state bureaucracy that found the extraction of taxes and military manpower from the population easier if mass participation legitimated its demands for resources. Those national capitalist classes that were more dependent on state authority were also more vulnerable to working-class mobilization. Some of them supported suppression of democracy, producing a historical legacy of violent class conflict in those states.

Insulating democratic institutions from the economy provided a political arena of formal equality alongside economic inequality. Democratic politics could then have a genuine, if limited, impact upon the state. Political participation could generate reforms, majorities could elect parliaments, and minorities could form parties and pressure groups to try to influence leaders and voters. Because of the bureaucratic autonomy of the state, issue-oriented minorities and voting majorities could have a real impact on state decisions within its legitimate sphere of action. The locus of class struggle moved from the market and workplace to parliaments and state bureaucracies as well.

Under historical conditions in which the state has not only bureaucratic and democratic aspects but also capitalist ones, the primary visibility of the leader-citizen relation and the official-client relation is an empirical indication of class hegemony.

The logics of institutional development

Once these separate institutional arrangements of capitalism, state bureaucracy, and democracy were established, each had its own internal logic of development. Although each historical process was dependent upon the others for its own development, each was incompatible with the others.[1]

---

[1] An "institutional logic" is an empirically and historically variable combination of explicit norms governing behavior ("Every citizen should vote"), a legal rule with a sanction attached ("Nonvoters must pay a fine"), and an implicit premise of action that permeates all social relationships ("All American citizens have the right to hire another American to work for them at whatever wage they will accept"). Where an institutional logic is reinforced by explicit norms, sanctioned law, and action premises, it is likely to be relatively stable.

The logic of capitalism

Following the logic of capitalist accumulation, private commodity production and market control are institutionalized into as many human activities as possible. The logic of accumulation makes the coordination of certain state policies both possible, because of institutional separation, and difficult, because the state cannot itself take over an anarchic process of capital accumulation that increasingly depends on state intervention.

The state is dependent upon capitalist growth, because not only does privately controlled investment generate the incomes upon which state revenues depend but the responses of capitalists to state policies provide an outer limit on the capacities of states. A conservative bias is built into a highly complex privately controlled economic structure, even if formal political rights exist to make changes if a majority desires them. Productivity and economic growth and, by direct extension, the welfare of the population come to be equated with a capitalist-controlled economy. State organizations come to represent the interests of different producer groups in the course of attempting to manage the capitalist economy. Invasions of property rights by the state require extraordinary political mobilization. Only with enormous difficulty, for example, can workers discover whether or not raw materials they work with are dangerous to their health, even if the corporations have the relevant data. State agencies find it difficult to discover, even when they want to, the real costs of safety measures and even to determine the degree of compliance with state regulations. During the oil crisis, the state could not get accurate information from the corporations on the actual supply of oil.

The logic of capitalism is also displayed in the everyday reproduction of political identities linked to roles and interests defined by the capitalist economy. Personal identities as producer and consumer become linked to political identities in ways that reinforce both types of identity. In this way, capitalist social relations become institutionalized in the organizational structures of state and democracy. Parties and voters come to define issues in terms of conflicts of interest generated within production, whether between buyers and sellers, workers and owners, or the organized and the unorganized. Contradictions between institutions are difficult to politicize, which helps reproduce the hegemony of capitalist social relations. But, by implication, a working-class politics defined *only* in terms of production relations is no more capable of transforming the relations among capitalism, the state, and democracy than a capitalist class is a priori capable of reproducing those relations.

Because of capitalist control over the economy, individual capitalists can behave in most normal situations as if they are just another interest group in relation to democratic institutions and just law-abiding citizens in relation to bureaucratic agencies. Their systemic power is not visible. The capital-labor relationship is hidden by the visibility of owner-worker relations in corporations and buyer-seller relations in markets. The media dramatize certain relations. Their silence about others, primarily the capital-labor relationship, is another empirical indication of class hegemony.

The logic of bureaucracy

Following the logic of bureaucratic rationalization, state elites increasingly attempt to coordinate the consequences of policy, utilizing professional staffs who try to allocate efficiently available resources to meet goals defined by political and administrative elites. This principle of organization creates difficulties for the capitalist economy because of increased regulation that constrains corporate responsiveness to changing markets and also because of the uncertainties created by unstable political control over the bureaucracy. And mass democratic participation is hampered because the state bureaucracies increasingly preempt major decisions, leaving to the public only periodic elections of the legislature and fragile appeals to public opinion.

The autonomy of the bureaucratic state means that the state is vulnerable to democratic demands and also has a capacity to establish policies facilitating capital accumulation. In this sense the state can both embody the "public interest" and serve as the executor of capital.

Public bureaucracies create an internal legal machinery for making and changing rules. An elaborate apparatus develops simply to manage the internal operations of the state, quite aside from its responsiveness to capitalist interests or democratic demands. This apparatus sets up significant institutionalized barriers to transforming the bureaucratic organizations of the state except through channels that themselves are controlled by state bureaucrats. External interest groups seek access to state agencies, creating interorganizational networks of considerable resilience and thereby political constituencies for state programs and agencies. Conversely, the external interest groups actually created by state action provide potential support for state programs. For example, social programs have created social workers and welfare clients, and arms contracts have given birth to defense corporations. Incentives and motives are also created for bureaucrats to maintain their positions, enhance their careers, mark off their jurisdictions from those guarded by other bureaucrats, and protect the integrity of a given project or seek funding for new programs.

The logic of democracy

Following the logic of democratic participation, the state is subjected to popular demands for public programs and benefits. The more social relations are democratized, the more rights of participation are extended into different institutions. Citizens come to demand participation not only in the selection of candidates for public office but even in the internal decision making of public agencies. The logic of participation makes it difficult for a privately controlled economy to function because of potential encroachment upon the property rights of private owners. The capacity of the bureaucratic state to function effectively is also hampered because of the continuous need to justify state actions. Considerable resources must be diverted to provide even fictitious mechanisms of public participation. The multiple potential targets of mass participation include direct demands not only upon political leaders but on every institution linked to the state.

Democratic institutions create channels of political participation and yet limit their targets and control their impact. The entire social order is stabilized if the population accepts the norms of genuine but limited participation. The incorporation of certain kinds of rights within the structure of the bureaucratic state itself serves to protect democratic institutions. Voting and elections render orderly the otherwise difficult process of succession of leaders and becomes a way in which the bureaucratic apparatus can tolerate the sometimes unruly exercise of democratic rights.

As with any organizational structure, democratic institutions also come to have a weight of their own. The complex institutionalized processes of candidate selection, primaries, elections, and party mobilization make it possible for majority preferences to have some impact on the state but also make it very difficult to change the process through which popular representation takes place. Due process and established democratic procedures must be used, which leads to endless meetings, consuming the energies of activists. Constant legislative and court challenges are undertaken by interests opposing many state decisions, even those presumably final. The very process of democratic participation, regardless of the substantive issue at stake, can become almost an end in itself.[2]

[2] Majority rule is a decision rule for a democratic consensus, which in principle is an action of the entire community governing itself. The minority accepts the decision of the majority, thereby accepting the popular will, as expressed pragmatically through the device of a majority vote, used only because in larger communities participation of all citizens in all decisions is not possible; at least, there is not time enough to allow discussions to proceed until a genuine consensus is reached. Thus agreement on the content of a decision must rest on the prior agreement to accept the outcome of a procedure. The fundamental premise is thus that all citizens accept as binding on them the outcomes of a decision-making procedure, as a surrogate for consensus. It is important to emphasize this point, because otherwise one can get lost in the debates about various devices for representation – federalism, two-chamber legislatures, preferential votes, second ballots, referendums and initiatives, primary systems, and so on. Debates over the relative degree to which various voting systems realize democratic representation are all likely to be within the pluralist world view.

Contradictory logics of the state

Concrete social practices manifest the institutional logics of capitalism, bureaucracy, and democracy. Inside each institution, the activities of individuals are symbolically defined by a historically developed vocabulary of motives and beliefs. Interests that cannot be converted to a particular vocabulary within a logic of action are difficult to express or to handle within that institutional sphere.

Commodity producers, for example, attempt to convert or homogenize all actions into the buying or selling of commodities that have a monetary price. Capitalist markets cannot exchange unpriced human activities that may be rational for an organization or useful to individuals. Bureaucratic organizations attempt to convert diverse individual situations into the basis for routine official decisions and cannot easily handle conflicting claims over the substantive ends toward which bureaucratic decisions are directed or demands for popular participation in them. Democratic institutions convert the most diverse issues into decisions that can be made either by majority vote or by consensus among the legitimate participants and cannot directly recognize claims of authority based on technical expertise or class privilege.

Societal interests that cannot be converted into the vocabulary and logic of action appropriate to capitalism, bureaucracy, or democracy are difficult to handle by that part of the state for which that aspect is dominant. This internal integrity of institutional logic protects each institution from actions it cannot handle, but the incompatibility of these logics is exhibited in conflicts among state bureaucracies, capitalist firms, and democratic institutions. The contradictory logics within the state reflect therefore the separate development of institutions of capitalism, bureaucracy, and democracy.

The autonomy of each institutional logic suggests that attempts to apply models developed for analysis of events and behavior in one institution should not be casually generalized to behavior in other institutions. Thus we question the attempt to apply market models to voting or participation in social movements, not to mention families and communities. Rational choice models that stress the difficulty of producing collective goods due to the ability to be a "free-rider" (Olson 1965) apply the logic of the market to non-market institutions. The conditions that allow such cross-institutional applicability have not been specified. For example, as profitability and wages become increasingly dependent upon state policy, models based upon either bureaucratic or democratic institutional logics may be increasingly applicable. The success of attempts to apply market criteria to state policies will be contingent upon the extent to which democratic and bureaucratic aspects of the state continue to be subordinate to its capitalist aspect. At present, these issues remain intractable ones for social theory and empirical research. If we are to be able to distinguish between ideology and theory, we must move toward answering them.

A contradiction is a property of a system. When the conditions required by a system at the same time undermine that system and lead to its transformation, then a contradiction exists. The basic contradiction of capitalism, as posited by class analysts, was that capitalist accumulation created and required a working class that would eventually develop the consciousness and the political tools to transform the social relation between capital and labor. Our argument accepts the fundamental importance of not only this contradiction but also those contradictions within and between democracy and bureaucracy at all levels of analysis.

Internal contradictions

Contradictions internal to the capitalist aspect of the state undermine its operations. We have summarized the basic contradiction as between accumulation and class struggle. Capitalist accumulation is based upon the private reinvestment of a surplus derived from employment of wage labor and the substitution of capital for labor. The rate of investment depends upon the rate of profit, which in turn depends on the relative power of capital as opposed to that of labor to secure for itself a larger share of the social product. Thus class struggle is an inherent determinant of the rate of capitalist growth. Capitalism generates a series of social costs – unemployment, pollution, occupational injury, and community dislocation – that are not priced in capitalist markets. The distributional struggle between labor and capital is necessarily transposed to the state. Workers compensate for their limited power in the labor market by attempting to increase benefits from the state (the "social wage"). Capitalists, in turn, adapt to working-class power in the private market by attempting to increase the state's absorption of their private costs. So, too, citizens push the state to absorb the social costs of capitalist growth. Market discipline loses its seeming inevitability.

If the state takes on increasing responsibility for both economic performance and its social and distributional consequences, it becomes increasingly vulnerable to all segments of the populace. As capitalists become more dependent upon state authority, their power also becomes more vulnerable to democratic influence. Property and production relations are politicized. As workers charge the state with responsibility for their standard of living and quality of life, the state must either increasingly intrude upon the rights of private property or disengage itself from the market and thereby fail to reproduce the capitalist economy. The distributional conflicts engendered within the capitalist economy are transposed to the state and threaten to overwhelm it with incompatible demands for which it lacks sufficient resources or authority to respond. Fiscal crises and expansion of public spending beyond what is compatible with continued capital accumulation threaten the capitalist state. Enormous deficits, which shift from one level of government to another as political pressures change, empirically index this contradiction in the capitalist state.

The class perspective locates the contradiction between accumulation and class struggle at the societal level, but because it subordinates the other aspects of the state to the capitalist aspect it does not theorize the contradictions among capitalism, bureaucracy, and democracy, nor is it sensitive to the internal dynamics of politics and culture.

Even neo-Marxist theories of the contradiction between accumulation and legitimation subordinate the bureaucratic and democratic aspects of the state. The legitimation process is often regarded as only the other side of the accumulation process: the need to conceal the reality of exploitation. Recognizing the importance of legitimation was an important critique of the classic Marxist theory of the state, but it did not go far enough in recognizing the institutional autonomy both of bureaucracy and of democracy. In effect, the concept of legitimation was imported from Max Weber into alien Marxist territory and was not adequately theorized.[3]

The recent work of an important class theorist, Claus Offe, explains societal crises in terms of institutional contradictions, as we do, rather than by the self-destructive dynamics of capitalist growth. Once a student of Jurgen Habermas, Offe locates the source of the ungovernability of modern states in the contradiction between two incompatible bases of social organization: norms that depend upon consciousness and individual conformity and economic laws and processes that do not (Offe 1984). The central problem of capitalism for Offe is that private exchange

---

[3] Jurgen Habermas has distinguished three "systems": economic, administrative, and legitimation. This distinction has the theoretical defect of mixing up consequences (legitimation) with structural properties and functions (economic and administrative). Further, his so-called administrative system "carries out numerous imperatives of the economic system" (Habermas 1975, p. 34). Although he discusses seven ways in which the state "actually replaces the market mechanism" (p. 35), his entire discussion of the administrative system assumes it is functional only for capital. Despite his use of the term "administrative," he ignores the bureaucratic aspect of the state and the process of rationalization. With respect to democracy, Habermas considers most of the democratic aspects of the state as part of the "legitimation system" (formal democratic institutions, citizenship rights, "diffuse mass loyalty" expressed through elections) (p. 37). Habermas thus subordinates both bureaucracy and democracy to the requirements of the capitalist state.

"neutralizes meaning" (p. 82), yet its reproduction increasingly depends upon collective actions for which meaningful and norm-oriented behavior is essential. Capitalist societies privatize production while socializing their reproduction. This contradiction results in ungovernability.

Briefly, Offe's argument is that capitalist societies lack mechanisms that allow them to adjust the consciously accepted rules governing social behavior ("social integration") to the unconscious laws of system integration. The capitalist economy depends not only upon the political reproduction of labor power (which, unlike all other commodities, must assent to its being used by others) but also upon the increasing use of noncommodified organization of social life to expand the commodified forms. In capitalist societies, crises derive from the contradictions between politicized and decommodified forms of social organization, particularly those organized by the state, and the "nonpolitical" organization of private production for profit. The capitalist economy must increasingly defend itself against intrusion from politically organized consciousness, so to speak. As the state increasingly organizes social life, political and normative criteria not derived from production or markets increasingly define the conditions for the functioning of all institutions, including the market. Capitalism requires state autonomy in order to sustain itself, yet that very autonomy creates the bases for politicization of consciousness (and therefore a challenge to "legitimacy") and potentially undermines capitalism itself.

In Offe's formulation, economic institutions determine systemic dynamics. Societal crises derive from the inability of the state to compensate for economic crisis. Offe draws heavily on the heritage of Habermas, distinguishing among capitalist exchange, state power, and "normative structures" (1984, pp. 49, 52). Noneconomic institutions (family, democratic politics, legal systems) are referred to as "flanking subsystems" (p. 49). He argues that state legitimation becomes increasingly difficult because of the commercialization of culture and the erosion of territorial, familial, and sacred symbols.

The state is torn between accumulation and legitimation, not primarily because it must conceal its role in sustaining an exploitative social order but because in order to sustain capitalism the state must create ever more social relations in which noncommodified forms of production prevail. The most intense political conflicts are increasingly located in these noncommodified institutions and not in the capitalist economy per se. These conflicts potentially threaten the commodity form as the primary social relation.

Offe's analysis ultimately subordinates the state's rational-legal legitimacy to the *consequences* of the application of those rules. Without market criteria, Offe claims, neither state efficiency nor its effectiveness has any clear meaning. Rather, they both depend on the extent to which the state can "universalize the commodity form" (1984, p. 137). The two sources of delegitimation are a failure to commodify, and a conflict between decommodified forms and their commodity function.

Although his analysis locates the origins of societal crisis in interinstitutional contradictions, noneconomic institutions are still subordinated to economic ones. The state's bureaucratic and democratic aspects, to use our terms, are seen as secondary to its capitalist aspect, which we believe begs the critical question of their relations. Our own thesis is that the contradictions are more usefully seen in terms of three components: *rationalization* (the bureaucratic aspect), *participation* (the democratic aspect), and *commodification* or accumulation (the capitalist aspect). The state must appear simultaneously to form policy rationally, to be responsive to popular participation, and to foster capitalist production and commodity markets.

If we are correct, state rationality and irrationality cannot be interpreted only in terms of the consequences of state activity for capitalism, nor can the bureaucratic and democratic aspects of the state be reduced to their services to capital. The rationality of the state is problematic because these three aspects are contradictory, but not only because capitalism has generic tendencies toward economic and therefore political crisis. The state is torn between the need to respond to politically organized demands, profitability as a premise of policy, and its own survival as an operating set of organizations.

The internal contradiction within the bureaucratic aspect of the state follows from the logic of rationalization. Each agency seeks to maximize its autonomy, to preserve its legitimacy, and to create a stable and broad constituency from clients, funding sources, and networks of influence with other bureaucratic agencies. The successful agencies expand, garnering more projects and larger budgets under their control. In this process of increasing the predictability of their specific environment, public bureaucracies incorporate external constituencies, blurring the boundary line between private and public sectors, as they establish powerful interest groups inside and outside the state with a stake in the preservation of the agency. Because conflicts between dominant interest groups cannot be solved by bureaucratic means, and because each fears the democratic political power of the other, powerful bureaucracies become insulated from electoral or legislative influence and hence from each other.

This process leads to a gradual depoliticization and fragmentation of public authority, and yet to an increasing fuzziness of the institutional boundary line between state and society. Central bureaucracies, like the state executive, gradually lose control over their departments, subbureaus, and regional offices as each seeks autonomous control over budgets, personnel, and implementation. The rationalization of each state agency renders the state bureaucracy as a whole increasingly irrational. Efforts are made to establish coordinating bodies, including corporatist structures, but because these bodies frequently lack sufficient authority to rationalize the total structure they become one more source of unpredictability. Finally, political elites may attempt to destroy whole bureaucratic systems, devolving responsibility for their functions to lower levels of government.

This contradiction within the bureaucratic aspect of the state we have summed up as between fragmentation and centralization. Within the managerial perspective, the contradiction is seen as a conflict of organizational goals. It tends to be reduced to problems of interorganizational relations: conflicts among agencies, corporate firms, labor unions, and political parties for resources and legitimacy. From an organizational level of analysis, the relations of these conflicts to societal contradictions are not visible. The problem is seen as one of coordinating and controlling fragmentation or maintaining the integrity of legal and programmatic commitments.

The internal contradiction in the democratic aspect of the state stems from the multiple incentives for participation created both by political rights and by the differentiation of the economy and the state. More groups form as more needs are perceived to be politically relevant and to require state action. As participation increases, so does stalemate, because of the difficulty of devising viable policies that accommodate all of the various competing interests. The multiple modes of democratic participation – hearings, publicity, delegations, demonstrations, petitions, advisory committees, legal challenges, alternative bills – take up more and more of the time of active citizens, political leaders, and public officials. Managing the process of participation becomes as important as the actual making and implementing of public policies. The impact of participation is reduced as it expands. Large publics are unorganized and unrepresented. The effective representation of collective majority interests suffers as intense and focused group interests organize to gain the legitimacy of state backing. Many citizens respond with political withdrawal or sometimes violations of democratic norms. Thus the very conditions that define the existence of the democratic aspect of the state undermine the conditions for its functioning.

Consensus versus participation has been our language for the basic contradiction within the democratic aspect of the state. The division of labor within the pluralist perspective reflects the attempt to reduce this contradiction to a "tension," an inconsistency, or even only differences of perception of interests by individual political actors.[4] Because political culture is located within individuals, pluralists see this tension as alternative individual responses to political issues, whether in terms of their conception of the public interest or in terms of their individual preferences.[5]

Two characteristics of the state absorb popular political participation without endangering the state's role in capital accumulation. In the long run, these intensify the basic contradiction between democracy and capitalism. First, there is a tendency to exclude the state from profitable activity (Offe 1975). Where the state is engaged in production, it is generally because a private market *fails* to supply some input necessary for accumulation. Although there are few technical barriers to nationalization, this development has been thwarted in the United States by legal prohibition of the use of equity financing of state enterprise, bank control of public capital markets, and other mechanisms. O'Connor argues that the resultant tax dependency reduces the "possibility that a popular government would reorder the allocation of material resources" (1973, p. 180). As long as state financing is dependent upon taxation, state policies are constrained not to impinge upon capital accumulation.

---

[4] It is important to emphasize once again that by rising to the societal level of analysis in this final chapter we do not reject pluralist concepts in their home domain. An analysis of the tension between consensus and participation within small decision-making groups is given by anthropologist F. G. Bailey (1965). Bailey gives examples from Indian villages, British local government, universities, and employers' and workers' associations of the conditions under which a committee is likely to make decisions by consensus or majority vote. Such groups are likely to make decisions by consensus when the decision is an "administrative" one (a routine one without any external sanctions), when the committee is in an "elite" position vis-à-vis an external public, and when the committee sees itself as under attack or in opposition to an external body. They are likely to make decisions by majority vote when they are making policy, when the committee is an "arena" group (that is, its members are representatives of outside groups), and when they are dealing with decisions that have only internal relevance. By extension, the internal process of influence in such committees is a classic instance of pluralist politics, when members of such committees try to persuade each other that a given decision has the characteristics that make it appropriate for consensus or a vote. The panoply of pluralist concepts of influence, logrolling, and bargaining are all appropriate to that level of analysis. Also, these processes and outcomes operate independently of the content or consequences of the decision. Bailey has abstracted away all aspects of the decision-making process except those that characterize the interaction of the group with other groups.

[5] Dahl takes account of how pluralist democracy is deformed by the existence of powerful organizations (corporations, unions, political parties), but he remains within the pluralist world view in several important respects, because he assumes that democracy is the overriding societal characteristic, and therefore rational public choice is ultimately possible. Democracy can be used to control the giant corporations. "[P]eople in a democratic country might also reasonably use the government of the state to regulate or prohibit transactions marked by unequal bargaining power" (1982, p. 200). But he rejects the equation of democracy with capitalism, arguing for a decentralized socialism that would maintain the autonomy of all social units, including economic ones.

To the extent that capital accumulation and public fiscal capacity depend on continued private control of investment and production, political issues questioning that control are extraordinarily difficult to raise.

A second mechanism that attempts to manage this contradiction is structural segregation. State functions most critical to capital accumulation are located in one sector of the state, whereas those that absorb social discontent generated by the same process of capital accumulation are located in another sector (see also Offe 1984). For example, urban renewal for profitable high-rise office and apartment construction is sponsored by one government agency, and public-housing construction and allocation for those poorly housed in the same city or area are handled by another agency (Friedland 1983). Public expenditures that condition the level and nature of private investment are located in one sector of government, and unemployment, welfare, and manpower programs that must absorb the inadequacies of employment generated by that investment are located in another sector. Not surprisingly, when unemployment, poverty, or skill-job imbalance becomes severe, political discontents are directed at the agencies that manage the consequences of economic processes over which *other* agencies have responsibility and leverage (Friedland et al. 1977). The consequences of such segregation are insufficient state revenues, vacillating mass support, and bureaucratic irrationality (Offe 1984).

Political and ideological battles occur to define concrete issues as within or outside the jurisdiction of specific institutions. This political process consists of juggling institutional jurisdictions and redirecting political demands toward different sectors of the state or away from the state. If actions of capitalists are seen as legitimately subject to state regulation, the state is burdened with an extremely heavy load. Because of the contradictions between capitalism and democracy, as well as the symbiosis between bureaucratic fragmentation and economic competition, the state is genetically incapable of rationalizing a capitalism that cannot reproduce itself.

Similarly, if political demands can be redefined as appropriately satisfied by voluntary action, or as appropriately performed by public officials without popular participation, or if they can be returned to private markets, the pressure on the state will be reduced. The conservative effort to reprivatize social welfare functions in the 1980s is illustrative. The functioning of democratic institutions requires multiple procedures often rife with conflict; these are evaded if possible by political and administrative elites.

The contradictions within the state that we have summarized are the systemic sources of conflict over the policies and structures of the state in Western societies. The existence of these societal contradictions in the state does not, however, predict specific conflicts between organizations or the outcome of any given political controversy. The assumption of the contradictory logics of capitalism, bureaucracy, and democracy allows a prediction that certain *kinds* of politics will exist with specific ranges of economic and political resources. Similarly, the existence of a specific network of organizations cannot explain which issues become important or when, or who will decide to participate. Theories with home domains at each level of analysis can be translated into empirical hypotheses about the *probabilities* of certain kinds of political processes and outcomes.

The democratic *aspect* of the state in a capitalist society must be distinguished from the *logic* of democracy – a principle of potentially unlimited participation by individuals and groups in state decisions that they perceive as influencing their interests. This definition of democracy is explicitly *not* tied to the structure of the state but is a normative or critical principle through which state policies, processes, and structures can be evaluated.[6] To put the point another way, no procedures or institutions are per se democratic. The *processes and consequences* – popular benefits from participation – are the crucial criterion: the conjoining of participation and power at all levels (Alford and Friedland 1975).[7]

Conclusions

The historical development of Western societies has changed the relationships among the capitalist, bureaucratic, and democratic aspects of the state. The time frame of this interinstitutional history is long-range, and we reject the usual implicit corollary of functionalism that history is an eternal parameter of analysis and the stable environment of politics.

[6] Joshua Cohen and Joel Rogers also see "capitalist democracy" as a single system. Their book *On Democracy* calls pluralism to account to defend certain principles of democracy rather than serve as an ideology for rationalizing whatever limited forms of participation are possible within the constraints of reproducing capitalism. They offer the principle of "democratic legitimacy" as a criterion to be used to criticize *any* contemporary society: the requirement that "individuals be free and equal in determining the conditions of their own association" (1983, p. 149), quintessential pluralist language.

[7] In offering this principle of democracy as a cornerstone of a critical theory of the state, we do not mean to minimize other knotty problems: how to ascertain the relevant persons or groups whose interests are affected; what modes of actual participation are possible; how information about the consequences of decisions can be learned by persons potentially affected by them; or what the modes of access might be to the organizations making decisions. In principle, these issues cannot be decided in advance by those who control the state, nor can any final institutional arrangements be constructed, because how important a given need or demand is and what modes of participation are appropriate can be decided only by the persons affected and concerned. This logic of democracy accepts the pluralist principle but does not identify any state structures or state-society relationship as approximating the democratic ideal.

The impact of history is seen directly in action and is not an unchanging context of action. Similarly, the institutional arrangements that constrain the situational level of political action are immanent in the reproduction of those situations. The system comprising interinstitutional contradictions may be both sustained and undermined by particular kinds of organized politics and contingent individual actions, which those structures make more or less probable.

An adequate analysis must be simultaneously political and functional in order to specify how action does or does not reproduce the interinstitutional relations composing a society. Ultimately, the contradictions between institutions are revealed through organizational structures and individual interactions. If the relations between these levels are adequately theorized, their study will prevent us from reifying the institutions of society.

Political and functional analyses must also be combined in order to integrate a theory of the origins and reproduction of particular institutions and their consequences for the larger society. These consequences are typically used by functionalists to explain their origins and persistence, but we do not believe that the internal structure and processes of organizations and institutions can be assumed to follow from their presumed consequences.

Finally, our analysis suggests that a class perspective centered on the economy has held the high ground of societal analysis for too long. We do not believe that the locus of class formation lies only in the economy, but neither do we think that the society can be rationalized by extending the control of the state. Nor can a common culture integrate all institutions. Societal analyses must find a way of understanding the larger institutional relations whose contradictory dynamics shape both state and society. It is time to reopen the theoretical debate central to classical social theory about the relations among class hegemony, organizational domination, and cultural integration.

The contradictory logics and the social relations typical of each institution, and the frequently conflictual interdependencies among them, must be charted historically and comparatively. To do so, we believe, will begin to open up both new theoretical possibilities of connecting different levels of analysis and the understandings necessary for innovative political visions.[8]

---

[8] See Elster 1978 for a similar view of contradictions in the capitalist state. He argues (at the individual level of analysis) that "the modern state and its officials certainly have a sincere wish to act as neutral brokers between the conflicting groups, rather than to further the interests of any particular group" (p. 148). In other words, individuals have a pluralist consciousness of their role. But "only organized groups can be admitted . . . to the negotiations" over decisions. And "owner and manager interests [are] better

We believe that the problems of domination and participation will exist regardless of the mode of economic production. There is no question that the specific forms of bureaucracy and democracy have been decisively affected by their historical relations with capitalism. But one of the critical defects of class analysis has been the refusal to define as theoretically problematic how bureaucratic domination can be avoided and democratic participation guaranteed under historical conditions in which the capitalist form of accumulation has been transformed (see Anderson 1984).

We are writing this book at a historical moment when the institutional structures of capitalism, the state, and democracy are all experiencing challenges that call into question the theories we have outlined. In part, these challenges derive from institutions not considered here – religious, ethnic, familial – as well as from interstate conflicts and even the increasingly fragile natural environment.

In addition, transnational capital and the forces at work in the world economy have reproduced in international form the system Marx envisaged in the nineteenth century – a "placeless" capital able to exploit national state boundaries, either remaining within them for protection or moving between them for competitive advantage, bringing with it mass migrations of labor. The human and social costs of these developments are incalculable. The capacity of democratic capitalist states to reproduce the conditions necessary for human life is also in question. The prospects of continued environmental degradation and nuclear annihilation have grown with the increased capacity to control nature. The point here is that particular states are losing their capacity to facilitate national capitalist growth, and the whole international state system, which almost all of the literature we have examined takes for granted, is being undermined.

Political conflicts are increasingly moving beyond production-based issues of class and toward interests and identities deriving from age, gender, family, community, church, and public policies themselves. Conflicts between the sexes, the generations, regions, as well as between public providers and their clients, increasingly dominate the political state. Perhaps this is a consequence of the state's growing regulation of

organized than worker interests, with a correspondingly greater impact on final decisions" (p. 148). "From the fact that capitalist class interests are over-represented in most mediations, it follows that the neutrality of the state between the various claims set forward, or even a slight bias in the favour of the workers (as in countries with social-democrat governments), will produce a set of final outcomes that is also skewed in the direction of capitalist interests" (p. 148). We agree with this argument but would modify it by arguing that the state is not only a capitalist but also a bureaucratic and a democratic state, each with its own distinctive contradictions as well.

as well as support for particular patterns of private life. The capacity of these new "interests" (and even that old term no longer seems applicable to social and individual identities that cannot easily be compromised and responded to with incremental benefits) to find expression in a parliamentary system increasingly subordinated to nonparliamentary representation and regulation around economic issues is in doubt. But, even if the state were able to guarantee continued growth of economic production, the instrumental rationality and possessive individualism that have been the cultural bulwarks of capitalism are increasingly insufficient to prevent crises in both state and society.

The capacity of existing capitalist and even socialist societies to counter this growing power of the bureaucratic state apparatus is likewise an important political and theoretical issue. Although genuine markets are a counterweight to bureaucratic domination and thus help to safeguard pluralistic democracy, capitalism has increasingly lost its marketlike character. As a result it is increasingly wrong to equate markets only with capitalism – and certainly not with socialist democracy. But it is also true that the elimination of capitalism has been associated with the rise of bureaucratic state domination. We are thus living in an age when the institutional conditions for the preservation of political democracy, not to mention its extension to new institutional locations, are more opaque than ever.

No theory seems to be able to adequately comprehend the conditions under which we might live, and no politics seems able to move toward them. In this desperate sense, theory is powerless. At no previous time has there been a moment when the powers of theory mattered so much as a guide to conscious, collective human action. For, today, human life literally depends upon it.

Glossary

This glossary contains the distinctive vocabulary of pluralist, managerial, and class perspectives. The concepts listed below are not definitions but meanings within each of the three theoretical perspectives. The concepts are not intended to be equivalent but are parallel in the sense that each locates some of the meaning of the concept but not all. Although some concepts contain contradictory meanings, we have attempted to use key concepts in clear and consistent ways. In certain important cases, we explicitly discuss the alternative meanings of a given word. In such cases, the discussion is referred to in the Index.

We divide the concepts into five major groups: (1) Society, (2) Capitalism, (3) State, (4) Democracy, and (5) Knowledge. Because every fundamental concept is theory-laden (including our own organizing categories), every usage carries with it a freight of theoretical baggage. The argument of the book as a whole defines the ground upon which we stand to examine the territory of other arguments.

Sometimes a given word is used by more than one perspective but given a different meaning. We do not attempt here to deal with those complexities. The text of the book deals with them in the appropriate context – showing how concepts are used to construct an empirical or theoretical argument. Sometimes a word is closely identified with only one perspective, and in that case we give the closest approximation within the other perspectives.

Each perspective theorizes its own central concepts and the relations between them. The ways those relations are conceived are the metaphors of knowledge of a perspective. Each perspective recognizes empirically and descriptively the phenomena central to the other perspectives but does not give them theoretical importance. They are explained away and subordinated or regarded as residual, random, obsolete, or exogenous phenomena. Concepts outside of the central theoretical vocabulary tend to be regarded as either empirical or ideological.

The usages of key concepts within different levels of analysis make up the microepistemology of each world view. All of these categories are presubstantive, in the sense that their use indicates theoretical and political presuppositions that precede the choice of a unit and level of analysis. The primacy of a given concept stems from the theory about its historical importance in understanding the relationships between state and society.

Reading from top to bottom gives a sense of the internal vocabulary of each perspective. Reading across the page gives a sense of the analogous usages across perspectives. We repeat the primary point that these concepts cannot be treated as if they can be innocently defined and used to describe and classify phenomena. Part of their meaning is associated with the theoretical context in which they play a role.

The monolithic list of concepts for each perspective does not imply that there are no debates within each perspective. Far from it. The most fervent debates are likely to occur within perspectives, not between them. But the issues are likely to be defined within this language of argument.

Society

	Pluralist	Managerial	Class
The social whole	Social system	Social structure	Social formation
Key society-wide characteristics	Culture	Legal order	Mode of production
Contemporary society	Modern	Industrial	Capitalist
Normal societal functioning	Integration and consensus	Rationalization and order	Hegemony and accumulation
Source of change	Disorganization	Rebellion	Class struggle
	Tensions	Conflicts	Contradictions
Social stability	Integration	Control	Repression
Societal level of analysis	Institutional relations	Interorganizational structures	Modes of production and reproduction
Key collective unit	Group	Organization	Class
Key level of power	Individual influence	Organizational domination	Societal hegemony
Who has power to act	Individuals	Elites	Class agents
Concept of polity	Government (institutions)	Bureaucracy (agencies)	State (apparatus)
Concept of culture	Values	Beliefs	Consciousness
Concept of economy	Preferences satisfied in markets	Networks of firms	Capital–labor relations
Institutions	Socialize	Constrain	Control
Organizational level of analysis	Mediating associations	Dominant and subordinate organizations	Agent of class interests
Patterns of social relations	Roles	Positions	Locations
Individuals	Make choices	Devise strategies	Engage in struggle
Individuals have	Preferences	Interests	Needs
Individual non-conformity is	Deviance	Dissent	Rebellion
Negative relations	Anomie	Illegitimacy	Alienation
Individual level of analysis	Actions in situations	Behaviors in positions	Practices in conjunctures
	Competing choices	Conflicting interests	Contradictory locations

Capitalism

	Pluralist	Managerial	Class
The whole	Market economy (modern)	Industrial society	Capitalist mode of production
Processes within the whole	Differentiation of social group demands	Complexity of organizations	Social division of labor
	Economies of scale	Centralization	Monopoly and concentration
	Supply and demand	Inputs and outputs	Forces and relations
	Economic development	Industrialization	Accumulation
Economic units	Entrepreneurs and firms	Managers and corporations	Capitalists and capital
	Employees and occupations	Labor force and masses	Labor and workers
	Professions	Staff	New middle class
Production	Goods and services	Products	Commodities
Inequality	Stratification	Hierarchy	Exploitation
Actors	Businessmen	Corporations	Class/segments
Individuals have	Economic preferences	Material interests	Class interests

State

	Pluralist	Managerial	Class
The whole	Democratic	Bureaucratic	Capitalist
Internal structure	Pluralist	Fragmented	Anarchic
Right-wing control	Authoritarian	Totalitarian	Fascist
Left-wing control	Extremist	Social democratic	Socialist
Political structure	Government (modern state)	State (industrial state)	Capitalist state
Those at top	Leaders	Elites	Ruling classes
Power	Influence	Domination	Hegemony
Who rules	Governing coalitions	Political elites	Power bloc
Ultimate means of deciding	Authority	Coercion	Repression
Who supports	Constituencies of individuals and groups	Clientele of elites and interests	Political base of class segments
Process	Institutionalization (political development)	Bureaucratization (rationalization)	Socialization (regulation of contradictions)
Consequences	Liberalism	Concessions	Reformism
	Social control (self-regulation)	Obedience (conformity)	Alienation (false consciousness)
	Integrated political culture	Legitimation	Hegemony
	Polarization	Delegitimation	Crisis
	Popular governance	Elite control	Class rule
	Public interest	Collective goals	Popular benefits
Outputs	Decisions of government	Policies of the state	Measures of the state apparatus
Individuals in power	Governing roles	Bureaucratic offices	Administrative labor

Democracy

	Pluralist	Managerial	Class
Population	Publics	Masses	People
Actors	Citizens	Subjects	Workers
Form of organization	Voluntary associations	Organizations	Class agents
	Interest group	Political party	Social movement
	Group	Faction	Sector
Basic process	Mechanisms of influence	Strategies of domination	Weapons of struggle
	Participation	Mobilization	Contestation
Mode of action	Persuasion	Acceptance	Solidarity
	Violence	Resistance	Revolutionary action
	Collective behavior	Collective action	Social movements
Source of action	Beliefs	Ideologies	Consciousness (false or true)
	Demands/prefer- ences, claims/ expectations	Organized interests	Needs
Result of action	Integration	Control	Rule
	Compromise	Cooptation	Sellout
Outcomes:	Electoral majorities	Mass base	Popular resistance
	Representation	Incorporation	Cooptation
	Disruption	Rebellion	Revolutionary situations
	Interest group demands	Popular movements	Class struggle
	Support	Submission	Hegemony
	Equilibrium	Domination	Transformation
Political relations	Leader– supporter	Elite–masses	Capital–labor
Power relations	Coalitions and contracts	Hierarchy and force	Exploitation and alienation
When interests are shared	Cooperation	Conformity	Solidarity
When interests are not shared	Competition	Conflict	Struggle
Situation requir- ing action	Issue	Dilemma	Imperative
Political situations	Historic opportunities	Critical junctures	Revolutionary conjunctures

Knowledge

	Pluralist	Managerial	Class
The whole	An aggregate of interdependent but autonomous parts	A structure with dominant elements	A totality determining internal relations
External system	Environmental factors	External constraints	Totality of relations
Image of general change	Evolution of systems	Manipulation of structures	Transformations of wholes
Source of change	Tensions	Dilemmas	Contradictions
Internal structures	Differentiated	Complex	Contradictory
Model of relations	Conditional processes	Causal structures	Dialectical relations
How relations described	Functions cause structures	Structures cause functions	Contradictory internal relations
Theory–method relations	Puzzle	Problem	Praxis
Science	Differentiated institution with a function	Technical resource	Force of production
Epistemological argument	Criticism of assumptions	Conflict over domain	Struggle over ideology
Causation	Interdependent influence of multiple factors	Dominance of forces in structures	Hegemony of imperatives
Knowledge	Incremental growth	Paradigmatic sequences of normal science and revolution	Historically relative
Unresolved issue	Paradox	Dilemma	Contradiction
Theory–reality relations	Theory of a phenomenon	Analytic framework of a problem	Ideology of a class
Empirical reference	Empirical indicator	Causal force	Historical manifestation
Truth	Consensus on the correspondence of hypothesis and evidence	Established by authoritative procedures	Human activity and experience (praxis)
Language	Correspondence of concept and object	Dominant usages	Hegemonic categories
Concepts	Abstract qualities of objects	Dominant vocabulary of a field	Categories of analysis

Knowledge (cont.)

	Pluralist	Managerial	Class
Definitions	Consensus after competition in intellectual market	Dominant usages	Historically relative
Observations	Empirical data	Social knowledge	Historical experience
Model of relations	Independent and dependent variables	Inputs and outputs	Forces and relations
Events	Situations	Critical junctures	Conjunctures
Social science fields	Functional division of labor	Fragmentation of problems	Bourgeois ideology
Individuals	Scholars	Employees of the university	Intellectual workers
Organizations	Fields of knowledge (disciplines)	Academic departments	Forces and relations of intellectual production
Consequences	Growth of knowledge	Rational information	Intellectual production

Bibliography

Aberbach, Joel D., Robert D. Putnam, and Bert A. Rockman. 1981. *Bureaucrats and Politicians in Western Democracies.* Harvard University Press, Cambridge, Mass.

Abramson, Paul R., and John H. Aldrich. 1982. "The Decline of Electoral Participation in America." *American Political Science Review* 76:502–21.

Aldrich, Howard. 1979. *Organizations and Environments.* Prentice-Hall, Englewood Cliffs, N.J.

Aldrich, Howard, and Jeffrey Pfeffer. 1976. "Environments of Organizations." *Annual Review of Sociology* 2:79–106.

Alexander, Jeffrey. 1982. *Theoretical Logic in Sociology.* Vol. 1, *Positivism, Presuppositions, and Current Controversies.* The University of California Press, Berkeley.

1983. *Theoretical Logic in Sociology.* Vol. 4, *The Modern Reconstruction of Social Thought: Talcott Parsons.* University of California Press, Berkeley.

Alford, Robert R. 1963. *Party and Society.* Rand McNally, Chicago.

1975a. *Health Care Politics.* University of Chicago Press, Chicago.

1975b. "Paradigms of Relations between State and Society." In *Stress and Contradiction in Modern Capitalism,* ed. Leon Lindberg, Robert Alford, Colin Crouch, and Claus Offe, pp. 145–60. Lexington Books, Lexington, Mass.

Alford, Robert R., and Roger Friedland. 1974. "Nations, Parties, and Participation: A Critique of Political Sociology." *Theory and Society* 1:307–28.

1975. "Political Participation and Public Policy." *Annual Review of Sociology* 1:429–79.

Allison, Graham T. 1971. *Essence of Decision: Explaining the Cuban Missile Crisis.* Little, Brown, Boston.

Almond, Gabriel A., and James S. Coleman, eds. 1960. *The Politics of the Developing Areas.* Princeton University Press, Princeton, N.J.

Almond, Gabriel, and Sidney Verba. 1963. *The Civic Culture.* Princeton University Press, Princeton, N.J.

Almond, Gabriel, and Sidney Verba, eds. 1980. *The Civic Culture Revisited.* Little, Brown, Boston.

Althusser, Louis. 1970. *Reading Capital.* New Left Books, London.

Altvater, Elmar. 1978. "Some Problems of State Interventionism." In *State and Capital,* John Holloway and Sol Piccioto, pp. 40–2. Arnold, London.

1981. "The Primacy of Politics in Post-Revolutionary Societies." *Review of Radical Political Economics* 13:1–10.

Amin, Samir, Giovanni Arrighi, Andre Gunder Frank, and Immanuel Wallerstein. 1982. *Dynamics of Global Crisis.* Monthly Review Press, New York.

Anderson, Perry. 1974. *Lineages of the Absolutist State.* New Left Books, London.

1976. *Considerations on Western Marxism.* New Left Books, London.

1980. *Arguments within English Marxism.* New Left Books, London.

1984. *In the Tracks of Historical Materialism.* University of Chicago Press, Chicago.

Apter, David E. 1965. *The Politics of Modernization.* University of Chicago Press, Chicago.

Archibugi, Franco. 1978. "Capitalist Planning in Question." In *Beyond Capitalist Planning,* ed. Stuart Holland, pp. 49–68. Blackwell, Publisher, Oxford.

Ardant, Gabriel. 1975. "Financial Policy and Economic Infrastructure of Modern States and Nations." In *The Formation of National States in Western Europe,* ed. Charles Tilly, pp. 164–242. Princeton University Press, Princeton, N.J.

Aristotle. 1962. *The Politics.* Penguin Books, Baltimore.

Armstrong, John A. 1973. *The European Administrative Elite.* Princeton University Press, Princeton, N.J.

Aron, Raymond. 1966. "Social Class, Political Class, Ruling Class." In *Class, Status, and Power: Social Stratification in Comparative Perspective,* ed. Reinhard Bendix and S. M. Lipset, pp. 201–10. Free Press, New York.

Aronowitz, Stanley. 1981a. *The Crisis in Historical Materialism: Class, Politics, and Culture in Marxist Theory.* Bergin, South Hadley, Mass.

1981b. "A Metatheoretical Critique of Immanuel Wallerstein's *The Modern World System.*" *Theory and Society* 10:503–20.

Arrow, Kenneth. 1951. *Social Choice and Individual Values.* Yale University Press, New Haven, Conn.

1974. *The Limits of Organizations.* Norton, New York.

Attewell, Paul, and Dean R. Gerstein. 1979. "Government Policy and Local Practice." *American Sociological Review* 44:311–27.

Auster, Richard D., and Morris Silver. 1979. *The State as a Firm: Economic Forces in Political Development.* Nijhoff, The Hague.

Bacharach, Samuel B., and Edward J. Lawler. 1980. *Power and Politics in Organizations: The Social Psychology of Conflict, Coalitions, and Bargaining.* Jossey-Bass, San Francisco.

Bachrach, Peter. 1967. *Theory of Democratic Elitism.* Little, Brown, Boston.

Bachrach, Peter, and Morton S. Baratz. 1970. *Power and Poverty: Theory and Practice.* Oxford University Press, New York.

Badie, Bernard, and Pierre Birnbaum. 1983. *The Sociology of the State.* University of Chicago Press, Chicago.

Bailey, F.G. 1965. "Decisions by Consensus in Councils and Committees." In *Political Systems and the Distribution of Power,* pp. 1–20. ASA Monographs. Tavistock, London.

Balbus, Isaac. 1973. *The Dialectics of Legal Repression.* Russell Sage Foundation, New York.

Baran, Paul A., and Paul M. Sweezy. 1966. *Monopoly Capital: An Essay on the American Economic and Social Order.* Monthly Review Press, New York.

Barnes, Samuel H. et al. 1979. *Political Action: Mass Participation in Five Western Democracies.* Sage Publications. Beverly Hills.

Baumol, William. 1965. *Welfare Economics and the Theory of the State.* Harvard University Press, Cambridge, Mass.

Bean, Richard. 1973. "War and the Birth of the Nation State." *Journal of Economic History* 33:203–221.

Becker, James. 1977. *Marxian Political Economy.* Cambridge University Press, Cambridge.

1979. "The Rise of Managerial Economics." *Marxist Perspectives* 6:34–54.

Bell, Daniel. 1958. "The Power Elite Reconsidered." *American Journal of Sociology* 64:238–50.

1973. *The Coming of Post–Industrial Society*. Basic Books, New York.

1976. *The Cultural Contradictions of Capitalism*. Basic Books, New York.

Benda, Charles G. 1979. "State Organization and Policy Formation: The 1970 Reorganization of the Post Office Department." *Politics and Society* 9:123–51.

Bendix, Reinhard. 1964. *Nation Building and Citizenship: Studies of Our Changing Social Order*. Wiley, New York.

Bendix, Reinhard, et al., eds. 1968. *State and Society*, "Introduction." Little, Brown, Boston.

Bendix, Reinhard, and Seymour Martin Lipset, eds. 1966. *Class Status and Power: Social Stratification in Comparative Perspective* 2d ed. Free Press, New York.

Benjamin, Roger. 1980. *The Limits of Politics: Collective Goods and Political Change in Post Industrial Societies*. University of Chicago Press, Chicago.

Berelson, Bernard R., Paul F. Lazarsfeld, and William N. McPhee. 1954. *Voting: A Study of Opinion Formation in a Presidential Campaign*. University of Chicago Press, Chicago.

Berger, Suzanne, ed. 1981. *Organizing Interests in Western Europe*. Cambridge University Press, Cambridge.

Berry, Jeffrey M. 1978. "On the Origin of Public Interest Groups: A Test of Two Theories." *Polity* 10:378–97.

Black, Cyril E. 1967. *The Dynamics of Modernization*. Harper & Row, New York.

Black, Cyril E., ed. 1976. *Comparative Modernization*. Free Press, New York.

Blau, Peter. 1964. *Exchange and Power in Social Life*. Wiley, New York.

1977. *Inequality and Heterogeneity: A Primitive Theory of Social Structure*. Free Press, New York.

au, Peter, and Otis Dudley Duncan. 1967. *The American Occupational Structure*. Wiley, New York.

Bollen, Kenneth A. 1979. "Political Democracy and the Timing of Development." *American Sociological Review* 44:572–87.

Bottomore, Tom. 1979. *Political Sociology*. Harper & Row, New York.

Boudon, Raymond. 1981. *The Logic of Social Action: An Introduction to Sociological Analysis*. Routledge & Kegan Paul, London. (Originally published in French in 1979.)

Braun, Rudolf. 1975. "Taxation, Sociopolitical Structure, and State-Building: Great Britain and Brandenburg-Prussia." In *The Formation of National States in Western Europe*, ed. Charles Tilly, pp. 243–327. Princeton University Press, Princeton, N.J.

Braverman, Harry. 1974. *Labor and Monopoly Capital: The Degradation of Work in the Twentieth Century*. Monthly Review Press, New York.

Brittan, Samuel. 1977. *The Economic Consequences of Democracy*. Temple Smith, London.

Brown, Brian R. 1981. "Industrial Capitalism, Conflict, and Working Class Contention in Lancashire, 1842." In *Class Conflict and Collective Action*, ed. Louise and Charles Tilly, pp. 111–41. Sage, Beverly Hills, Calif.

Brown, Thad A., and Arthur A. Stein. 1982. "The Political Economy of National Elections." *Comparative Politics* 14:479–97.

Bryce, James. 1921. *Modern Democracies*. Macmillan, New York.

Buchanan, James. 1975. *The Limits of Liberty: Between Anarchy and Leviathan*. University of Chicago Press, Chicago.

Budge, Ian. 1970. *Agreement and the Stability of Democracy*. Markham, Chicago.

Burawoy, Michael. 1979. *Manufacturing Consent: Change in the Labor Process under Monopoly Capitalism*. University of Chicago Press, Chicago.

Burnham, James. 1941. *Managerial Revolution*. Indiana University Press, Bloomington.

Burnham, Walter Dean. 1970. *Critical Elections and the Mainsprings of American Politics*. Norton, New York.

Burt, Ronald. 1983. *Corporate Profits and Cooptation*. Academic Press, New York.

Cameron, David R. 1978. "The Expansion of the Public Economy: A Comparative Analysis." *American Political Science Review* 72:1243–61.

Campbell, Angus, Philip E. Converse, Warren E. Miller, and Donald E. Stokes. 1960. *The American Voter*. Wiley, New York.

Caro, Robert A. 1974. *The Power Broker: Robert Moses and the Fall of New York*. Knopf, New York.

Castells, Manuel. 1980. *The Economic Crisis and American Society*. Princeton University Press, Princeton, N.J.

Child, John. 1972. "Organization, Structure, Environment, and Performance: The Role of Strategic Choice." *Sociology* 6:1–22.

Cohen, G. A. 1978. *Karl Marx's Theory of History: A Defense*. Princeton University Press, Princeton, N.J.

Cohen, Jean L. 1982. *Class and Civil Society: The Limits of Marxian Critical Theory*. University of Massachusetts Press, Amherst.

Cohen, Joshua, and Joel Rogers. 1983. *On Democracy: Toward a Transformation of American Society*. Penguin Books, New York.

Coleman, James S. 1974. *Power and the Structure of Society*. Norton, New York.
1978. *The Mathematics of Collective Action*. Aldine, Chicago.

Collier, David. 1978. "Industrial Modernization and Political Change: A Latin-American Perspective." *World Politics* 30:593–614.

Collins, Randall. 1968. "A Comparative Approach to Political Sociology." In *State and Society*, ed. Reinhard Bendix et al., pp. 42–67. Little, Brown, Boston.
1975. *Conflict Sociology*. Academic Press, New York.

Converse, Phillip E. 1964. "The Nature of Belief Systems in Mass Publics." In *Ideology and Discontent*, ed. David E. Apter, pp. 206–61. Free Press, New York.

Cook, Karen S., et al. 1983. "The Distribution of Power in Exchange Networks: Theory and Experimental Results." *American Journal of Sociology* 89:275–305.

Corrigan, Philip. 1980. "Towards a History of State Formation in Early Modern England." In *Capitalism, State Formation, and Marxist Theory*, ed. Philip Corrigan, pp. 27–48. Quartet, London.

Crenson, Matthew. 1971. *The Un-politics of Air Pollution: A Study of Non-decision-making in the Cities*. Johns Hopkins University Press, Baltimore.

Crouch, Colin. 1979. "The State, Capital, and Liberal Democracy." In *State and Economy in Contemporary Capitalism*, ed. Colin Crouch, pp. 13–54. Croom Helm, London.

Crozier, Michel, Samuel P. Huntington, and Joji Watanuki. 1975. *The Crisis of Democracy*. New York University Press, New York.

Cyert, Richard, and James G. March. 1963. *A Behavioral Theory of the Firm*. Prentice-Hall, Englewood Cliffs, N.J.

Dahl, Robert A. 1956. *A Preface to Democratic Theory*. University of Chicago Press, Chicago.
1958. "A Critique of the Ruling Elite Model." *American Political Science Review* 52:463–9.
1961. *Who Governs?* Yale University Press, New Haven, Conn.
1971. *Polyarchy: Participation and Opposition*. Yale University Press, New Haven, Conn.

1982. *Dilemmas of Pluralist Democracy: Autonomy versus Control.* Yale University Press, New Haven, Conn.

Dahl, Robert A., ed. 1973. *Regimes and Oppositions.* Yale University Press, New Haven, Conn.

Dahrendorf, Ralf. 1959. *Class and Class Conflict in Industrial Society.* Stanford University Press, Stanford, Calif.

Davies, James C. 1962. "Toward a Theory of Revolution." *American Sociological Review* 27:5–19.

Davis, James A. 1980. "Conservative Weather in a Liberalizing Climate: Change in Selected NORC General Social Survey Items, 1972–1978." *Social Forces* 58: 1129–56.

De Grazia, Sebastian. 1948. *The Political Community: A Study of Anomie.* University of Chicago Press, Chicago.

Delors, Jacques. 1978. "The Decline of French Planning." In *Beyond Capitalist Planning,* ed. Stuart Holland, pp. 9–33. Blackwell Publisher, Oxford.

Deutsch, Karl. 1963. *The Nerves of Government: Models of Political Communication and Control.* Free Press, London.

Deutscher, Isaac. 1949. *Stalin: A Political Biography.* Oxford University Press, New York.

1969. "Roots of Bureaucracy." In *The Socialist Register,* ed. Ralph Miliband and John Saville, pp. 9–28. Monthly Review Press, New York. (Originally delivered as a lecture in 1960).

DiTomaso, Nancy. 1980. "Class Politics and Public Bureaucracy: The U.S. Department of Labor." In *Classes, Class Conflict, and the State,* ed. Maurice Zeitlin, pp. 135–52. Winthrop, Cambridge, Mass.

Domhoff, G. William, 1970. *The Higher Circles: The Governing Class in America.* Random House, New York.

1976. "I Am Not an Instrumentalist." *Kapitalstate* 4:221–4.

1978. *The Powers That Be: Processes of Ruling Class Domination in America.* Random House, New York.

Domhoff, G. William, and Hoyt B. Ballard, eds. 1968. *C. Wright Mills and the Power Elite.* Beacon Press, Boston.

Dye, Thomas R., and L. Harmon Ziegler. 1971. *The Irony of Democracy.* Duxbury Press, Belmont, Mass.

Dyson, Kenneth. 1980. *The State Tradition in Western Europe: A Study of an Idea and an Institution.* Oxford University Press, New York.

Easton, David. 1965a. *A Framework for Political Analysis.* Prentice-Hall, Englewood Cliffs, N.J.

1965b. *A Systems Analysis of Political Life.* Wiley, New York.

Eckstein, Harry. 1961. *A Theory of Stable Democracy.* Princeton University Center for International Studies, Princeton, N.J.

Eckstein, Harry, and Ted R. Gurr. 1975. *Patterns of Authority: A Structural Basis for Political Inquiry.* Wiley, New York.

Edelman, Murray. 1964. *The Symbolic Uses of Politics.* University of Illinois Press, Urbana.

Edwards, Richard. 1979. *Contested Terrain.* Basic Books, New York.

Ehrmann, Henry W. 1968. "Interest Groups and the Bureaucracy in Western Democracies." In *State and Society,* ed. Reinhard Bendix et al., pp. 257–76. Little, Brown, Boston.

Elias, Norbert. 1982. *State Formation and Civilization: The Civilizing Process.* Vol. 2. Blackwell, Publisher, Oxford. (Originally published in German in 1939.)

Elster, Jon. 1978. *Logic and Society.* Wiley, Chichester.

Esping-Anderson, Gosta. 1978. "Social Class, Social Democracy, and the State: Party Policy and Party Decomposition in Denmark and Sweden." *Comparative Politics* 11:42–58.

Esping-Anderson, Gosta., Roger Friedland, and Erik Olin Wright. 1976. "Modes of Class Struggle and the Capitalist State." *Kapitalistate* 4/5:186–220.

Finer, Samuel. 1975. "State and Nation Building in Europe: The Role of the Military." In *The Formation of National States in Western Europe*, ed. Charles Tilly, pp. 84–163. Princeton University Press, Princeton, N.J.

Flanigan, William, and Edwin Fogelman. 1971a. "Patterns of Democratic Development: An Historical Comparative Analysis." *Macro-Quantitative Analysis: Conflict, Development, and Democratization*, ed. John V. Gillespie and Betty A. Nesyold, pp. 475–97. Sage Readers in Cross-National Research, vol. 1. Sage, Beverly Hills, Calif.

1971b. "Patterns of Political Development and Democratization: A Quantitative Analysis." In *Macro-Quantitative Analysis: Conflict, Development, and Democratization*, ed. John V. Gillespie and Betty A. Nesyold, Sage Readers in Cross-National Research, vol. 1. pp. 441–473. Sage, Beverly Hills, Calif.

Frank, Andre Gunder. 1967. *Capitalism and Underdevelopment in Latin America.* Monthly Review Press, New York.

Freedman, James O. 1978. *Crisis and Legitimacy: The Administrative Process and American Government.* Cambridge University Press, Cambridge.

Friedland, Roger. 1983. *Power and Crisis in the City: Corporations, Unions, and Urban Policy.* Schocken Books, New York.

Friedland, Roger, and Donald Palmer. 1984. "Park Place and Main Street: Business and the Urban Power Structure." *Annual Review of Sociology* 10:395–416.

Friedland, Roger, Frances Fox Piven, and Robert R. Alford. 1977. "Political Conflict, Urban Structure, and the Fiscal Crisis." In *Comparing Public Policies: New Concepts and Methods*, ed. Douglas Ashford, pp. 197–225. Sage Books in Politics and Public Policy. Sage, Beverly Hills, Calif.

Friedman, Milton. 1962. *Capitalism and Freedom.* University of Chicago Press, Chicago.

Galbraith, John Kenneth. 1972. *The New Industrial State.* 2d ed. Houghton Mifflin, Boston.

Gallie, W. B. 1956. "Essentially Contested Concepts." *Aristotelian Society* 56:167–98.

Gamson, William A. 1975. *The Strategy of Social Protest.* Dorsey Press, Homewood, Ill.

Gaventa, John. 1980. *Power and Powerlessness: Quiescence and Rebellion in an Appalachian Valley.* Oxford University Press (Clarendon Press), Oxford.

Geschwender, James. 1977. *Class, Race, and Worker Insurgency: The League of Revolutionary Black Workers.* Cambridge University Press, Cambridge.

Giddens, Anthony. 1976. *New Rules of Sociological Method.* Hutchinson, London.

1979. *Central Problems in Social Theory: Action, Structure, and Contradiction in Social Analysis.* University of California Press, Berkeley.

1981. *A Contemporary Critique of Historical Materialism.* University of California Press, Berkeley.

1984. *The Constitution of Society: Ourline of the Theory of Structuration.* Polity Press, Cambridge.

Ginsberg, Benjamin. 1982. *The Consequences of Consent: Elections, Citizen Control, and Popular Acquiescence.* Addison-Wesley, Reading, Mass.

Goldman, Robert, and Ann Tickamyer. 1984. "Status Attainment and the Commodity Form." *American Sociological Review* 49:196–209.

Gouldner, Alvin. 1954. *Wildcat Strike*. Antioch Press, Yellow Springs, Ohio.

　　1970. *The Coming Crisis in American Sociology*. Basic Books, New York.

　　1980. *The Two Marxisms: Contradictions and Anomalies in the Development of Theory*. Macmillan Press, London.

Gramsci, Antonio. 1971. *Selections from the Prison Notebooks*. International Publishers, New York.

Gurr, Ted R. 1970. *Why Men Rebel*. Princeton University Press, Princeton, N.J.

Habermas, Jurgen. 1975. *Legitimation Crisis*. Beacon Press, Boston.

Hagen, John, and Celesta Albonetti. 1982. "Race, Class, and the Perception of Criminal Justice in America." *American Journal of Sociology* 88:329–55.

Hall, Peter. 1982. "Economic Planning and the State: The Evolution of Economic Challenge and Political Response in France." In *Political Power and Social Theory*, ed. Maurice Zeitlin, pp. 175–214. JAI Press, Greenwich, Conn.

Hamilton, Richard. 1972. *Class and Politics in the United States*. Wiley, New York.

Hannan, Michael T., and John Freeman. 1977. "The Population Ecology of Organizations." *American Journal of Sociology* 82:929–64.

Haveman, Robert H. 1973. "Private Power and Federal Policy." In *The Political Economy of Federal Policy*, ed. Robert H. Haveman and Robert D. Hamrin, pp. 3–8. Harper & Row, New York.

Hechter, Michael. 1975. *Internal Colonialism: The Celtic Fringe in British National Development, 1536–1966*. University of California Press, Berkeley.

Hechter, Michael, ed. 1983. *The Microfoundations of Macrosociology*. Temple University Press, Philadelphia.

Heclo, Hugh. 1977. *A Government of Strangers: Executive Politics in Washington*. Brookings Institution, Washington, D.C.

Henderson, James M., and Richard E. Quandt. 1971. *Micro Economic Theory: A Mathematical Approach*. McGraw-Hill, New York. (Originally published in 1958.)

Herman, Edward. 1981. *Corporate Control, Corporate Power*. Cambridge University Press, Cambridge.

Heydebrand, Wolf. 1977. "Organizational Contradictions in Public Bureaucracies: Toward a Marxian Theory of Organizations." *Sociological Quarterly* 18:83–107.

Hibbs, Douglas A., Jr. 1978. "On the Political Economy of Long-Run Trends in Strike Activity." *British Journal of Political Science* 8:153–75.

Hickson, David J., et al. 1971. "A Strategic Contingencies Theory of Organizational Power." *Administrative Science Quarterly* 16:216–29.

Hirschman, Albert O. 1970. *Exit, Voice, and Loyalty: Responses to Decline in Firms, Organizations, and States*. Harvard University Press, Cambridge, Mass.

　　1981. *Essays in Trespassing*. Cambridge University Press, Cambridge.

Hobsbawm, E. J. 1968. *Industry and Empire*. Penguin Books, Harmondsworth.

Holland, Stuart, ed. 1978. *Beyond Capitalist Planning*. Blackwell Publisher, Oxford.

Holloway, John, and Sol Piccioto, eds. 1978. *State and Capital: A Marxist Debate*. Arnold, London.

Homans, George C. 1961. *Social Behavior: Its Elementary Forms*. Harcourt Brace & World, New York.

Hood, Christopher, and Andrew Dunsire. 1981. *Bureaumetrics: The Quantitative Comparison of British Central Government Agencies*. Gower, Westmead.

Horowitz, Irving Louis. 1983. *C. Wright Mills: An American Utopian*. Free Press, New York.

Huntington, Samuel P. 1968. *Political Order in Changing Societies*. Yale University Press, New Haven, Conn.

1981. *American Politics: The Promise of Disharmony*. Harvard University Press, Cambridge, Mass.

Hyman, Herbert H. 1959. *Political Socialization: A Study in the Psychology of Political Behavior*. Free Press, New York.

Inkeles, Alex, and David Smith. 1974. *Becoming Modern*. Harvard University Press, Cambridge, Mass.

Jackman, Robert. 1975. *Politics and Social Equality: A Comparative Analysis*. Wiley, New York.

Jacoby, Henry. 1973. *The Bureaucratization of the World*. University of California Press, Berkeley.

Jacoby, Russell. 1981. *Dialectic of Defeat: Contours of Western Marxism*. Cambridge University Press, Cambridge.

Janis, Irving. 1982. *Groupthink: Psychological Studies of Foreign-Policy Decisions and Fiascoes*. 2d ed. Houghton Mifflin, Boston.

Jay, Martin. 1973. *The Dialectical Imagination: A History of the Frankfurt School and the Institute of Social Research*. Little, Brown, Boston.

Jenks, Edward. 1919. *The State and the Nation*. Dutton, New York.

Jessop, Bob. 1982. *The Capitalist State: Marxist Theories and Methods*. New York University Press, New York.

Katz, Elihu, and Paul F. Lazarsfeld. 1955. *Personal Influence*. Free Press, New York.

Kavanaugh, Dennis. 1980. "Political Culture in Great Britain: The Decline of Civic Culture." In *The Civic Culture Revisited*, Gabriel Almond and Sidney Verba, pp. 124–76. Little, Brown, Boston.

Kay, Geoffrey. 1975. *Development and Underdevelopment: A Marxist Analysis*. St. Martin's Press, New York.

Key, V. O., Jr. 1961. *Public Opinion and American Democracy*. Knopf, New York.

Kidron, Michael. 1974. *Capitalism and Theory*. Pluto Press, London.

King, Anthony. 1973. "Ideas, Institutions, and the Policies of Governments: A Comparative Analysis." *British Journal of Political Science*, July (parts 1 and 2) and October (parts 3 and 4), pp. 291–313, 409–23.

Knight, Christopher. 1984. "L. A. Freeway: The Automotive Basilica." *Public Interest* 74:152–7.

Knight, Frank. 1965. *Risk, Uncertainty, and Profit*. Harper & Row, New York.

Kolko, Gabriel. 1967. *The Triumph of Conservatism: The Reinterpretation of American History, 1900–1916*. Quadrangle Books, Chicago. (Originally published by Free Press in 1963.)

Kornhauser, William. 1959. *The Politics of Mass Society*. Free Press, New York.

Korpi, Walter, and Michael Shalev. 1980. "Strikes, Power, and Politics in the Western Nations, 1900–1976." In *Political Power and Social Theory*, ed. Maurice Zeitlin, 1:301–34. JAI Press, Greenwich, Conn.

Krasner, Stephen. 1984. "Approaches to the State: Alternative Conceptions and Historical Dynamics." *Comparative Politics* 16:223–46.

Krieger, Joel. 1983. *Undermining Capitalism*. Princeton University Press, Princeton, N.J.

Kuhn, Thomas. 1962. *The Structure of Scientific Revolutions*. University of Chicago Press, Chicago.

Laclau, Ernesto. 1977. *Politics and Ideology in Marxist Theory*. Highlands Press, Atlantic Highlands, N.J.

La Palombara, Joseph. 1964. *Interest Groups in Italian Politics*. Princeton University Press, Princeton, N.J.

Lawrence, Paul R., and Jay W. Lorsch. 1967. "Differentiation and Integration in Complex Organizations." *Administrative Science Quarterly* 12:1–47.

Lerner, Daniel. 1958. *The Passing of Traditional Society*. Free Press, New York.

Levine, Robert A. 1972. *Public Planning: Failure and Redirection*. Basic Books, New York.

Lieberson, Stanley. 1971. "An Empirical Study of Military-Industrial Linkages." *American Journal of Sociology* 76:562–85.

Lijphart, Arend. 1975. *The Politics of Accommodation: Pluralism and Democracy in the Netherlands*. 2d rev. ed. University of California Press, Berkeley.

1977. *Democracy in Plural Societies: A Comparative Exploration*. Yale University Press, New Haven, Conn.

1980. "The Structure of Inference." In *The Civic Culture Revisted*, ed. Gabriel Almond and Sidney Verba, pp. 37–56. Little, Brown, Boston.

Lindblom, Charles E. 1977. *Politics and Markets: The World's Political-Economic Systems*. Basic Books, New York.

Lipset, S. M. 1950. *Agrarian Socialism: The Cooperative Commonwealth Federation in Saskatchewan*. University of California Press, Berkeley.

1960. *Political Man: The Social Bases of Politics*. Doubleday (Anchor Books), New York.

1963. *The First New Nation*. Basic Books, New York.

1976. "Political Sociology." In *Society and Politics: Readings in Political Sociology*, ed. Richard Braungart, pp. 41–60. Prentice-Hall, Englewood Cliffs, N.J. (Originally published in 1959.)

Lipset, S. M., and William Schneider. 1983. *The Confidence Gap*. Free Press, New York.

Lipset, S. M., Martin Trow, and James Coleman. 1956. *Union Democracy*. Free Press, New York.

Long, Norton E. 1962. *The Polity*. Edited by Charles Press. Rand McNally, Chicago.

Lowi, Theodore. 1964. "American Business, Public Policy, Case Studies, and Political Theory." *World Politics* 16:677–715.

1968. *Private Life and Public Order: The Context of Modern Public Policy*. Norton, New York.

Luhmann, Niklas. 1977. "Differentiation of Society." *Canadian Journal of Sociology* 2:19–53.

1979. *Trust and Power*. Wiley, New York.

1982. *The Differentiation of Society*. Columbia University Press, New York.

Lukacs, Georg. 1971. *History and Class Consciousness*. Merlin Press, London. (Originally published in 1922.)

Lukes, Steven. 1974. *Power: A Radical View*. Macmillan Press, London.

MacPherson, C. B. 1973. *Democratic Theory: Essays in Retrieval*. Oxford University Press, London.

Maier, Charles S. 1975. *Recasting Bourgeois Europe: Stabilization in France, Germany, and Italy in the Decade after World War I*. Princeton University Press, Princeton, N.J.

Mandel, Ernest. 1975. *Late Capitalism*. New Left Books, London.

Mann, Michael. 1980. "State and Society, 1130–1815: An Analysis of English State Finances." In *Political Power and Social Theory*, ed. Maurice Zeitlin, pp. 165–208. JAI Press. Greenwich, Conn.

Mantoux, Paul. 1961. *The Industrial Revolution in the Eighteenth Century*. Harper & Row, New York. (Originally published in 1928.)

March, James G. and Johan P. Olsen 1984. "The New Institutionalism: Organizational Factors in Political Life." *American Political Science Review* 78:734–49.

Marshall, T.H. 1964. *Class, Citizenship, and Social Development*. Doubleday, New York.

Martin, Andrew. 1975. "Is Democratic Control of Capitalist Economies Possible?" In *Stress and Contradiction in Modern Capitalism*, ed. Leon Lindberg, Robert Alford, Colin Crouch, and Claus Offe, pp. 13–56. Lexington Books, Lexington, Mass.

McConnell, Grant. 1966. *Private Power and American Democracy*. Knopf, New York.

McEachern, Doug. 1980. *A Class against Itself: Power in the Nationalization of the British Steel Industry*. Cambridge University Press, Cambridge.

McFarland, Andrew S. 1969. *Power and Leadership in Pluralist Systems*. Stanford University Press, Stanford, Calif.

Merton, Robert K. 1968. *Social Theory and Social Structure*. Free Press, New York.

Meyer, J. W., and B. Rowan. 1977. "Institutionalized Organizations: Formal Structure as Myth and Ceremony." *American Journal of Sociology* 83:340–63.

Meyer, Marshall. 1979. *Change in Public Bureaucracies*. Cambridge University Press, Cambridge.

Michels, Robert. 1962. *Political Parties*. Free Press, New York. (Originally published in 1915.)

Miliband, Ralph. 1969. *The State in Capitalist Society*. Basic Books, New York.

1972. "Reply to Nicos Poulantzas." In *Ideology in the Social Sciences*, ed. Robin Blackburn, pp. 253–62. Random House (Vintage Books), New York.

1975. "Political Forms and Historical Materialism." In *Socialist Register*, ed. Ralph Miliband and John Saville. Merlin Press, London.

1977. *Marxism and Politics*. Oxford University Press, Oxford.

1983. "State Power and Class Interests," *Class Power and State Power*, pp. 63–78. Verso, London. (Originally published in *New Left Review*, no. 138 [1983], pp. 57–68.)

Miller, Nicholas R. 1983. "Pluralism and Social Choice." *American Political Science Review* 77:734–47.

Miller, Warren E., and Teresa E. Levitin. 1976. *Leadership and Change: The New Politics and the American Electorate*. Winthrop, Cambridge, Mass.

Mills, C. Wright. 1956. *The Power Elite*. Oxford University Press, New York.

Mitchell, Neil J. 1983. "Ideology or the Iron Laws of Industrialism: The Case of Pension Policy in Britain and the Soviet Union." *Comparative Politics* 15:177–201.

Mizruchi, Mark S. 1982. *The American Corporate Network, 1904–1974*. Sage, Beverly Hills, Calif.

Moore, Barrington. 1966. *Social Origins of Dictatorship and Democracy: Lord and Peasant in the Making of the Modern World*. Beacon Press, Boston.

Moore, Wilbert. 1964. "Motivational Aspects of Development." In *Social Change*, ed. Amitai and Eva Etzioni, pp. 291–9. Basic Books, New York.

Mosca, Gaetano. 1939. *The Ruling Class*. McGraw-Hill, New York.

Musgrave, Richard, and Peggy Musgrave. 1959. *The Theory of Public Finance: A Study in Public Economy*. McGraw-Hill, New York.

Neubauer, Deane. 1967. "Some Conditions of Democracy." *American Political Science Review* 61:1002–9.

Neumann, Franz. 1957. *The Democratic and the Authoritarian State: Essays in Political and Legal Theory*. Free Press, Glencoe, Ill.

Nie, Norman H., Sidney Verba, and John R. Petrocik. 1976. *The Changing American Voter*. Harvard University Press, Cambridge, Mass.

Niskanen, William A., Jr. 1971. *Bureaucracy and Representative Government*. Aldine, Chicago.

Nordlinger, Eric. 1981. *On the Autonomy of the Democratic State*. Harvard University Press, Cambridge, Mass.

North, Douglas C. 1983. "A Theory of Economic Change." *Science* 219:163–4. (Review of Mancur Olson, *Rise and Decline of Nations*.)

Nozick, Robert. 1974. *Anarchy, State, and Utopia*. Basic Books, New York.

O'Connor, James. 1973. *The Fiscal Crisis of the State*. St. Martin's Press, New York.

     1984. *Accumulation Crisis*. Blackwell Publisher, New York.

Offe, Claus. 1974. "Structural Problems of the Capitalist State." In *German Political Studies*, ed. Klaus von Beyme, pp. 31–57. Sage, London.

     1975. "The Theory of the Capitalist State and the Problem of Policy Formation." In *Stress and Contradiction in Modern Capitalism*, ed. Leon Lindberg, Robert Alford, Colin Crouch, and Claus Offe, pp. 125–44. Lexington Books, Lexington, Mass.

     1984. *Contradictions of the Welfare State*. MIT Press, Cambridge, Mass.

Offe, Claus, and Volker Ronge. 1975. "Theses on the Theory of the State." *New German Critique* 6:139–47.

Olson, Mancur. 1965. *The Logic of Collective Action*. Harvard University Press, Cambridge, Mass.

     1982. *Rise and Decline of Nations: Economic Growth, Stagflation, and Social Rigidities*. Yale University Press, New Haven, Conn.

Ossowski, Stanislaw. 1963. *Class Structure in the Social Consciousness*. Free Press, New York. (Originally published in Poland in 1957.)

Padgett, John F. 1981. "Hierarchy and Ecological Control in Federal Budgetary Decision Making." *American Journal of Sociology* 87:75–129.

Panitch, Leo. 1976. *Social Democracy and Industrial Militancy: The Labour Party, the Trade Unions, and Incomes Policy*. Cambridge University Press, Cambridge.

Pareto, Vilfredo. 1963. *The Mind and Society*. Edited by Arthur Livingston. Dover, New York. (Originally published in 1935.)

Parker, Robert Nash. 1983. "Measuring Social Participation." *American Sociological Review* 48:864–73.

Parkin, Frank. 1979. *Marxism and Class Theory: A Bourgeois Critique*. Tavistock, London.

Parsons, Talcott. 1951. *The Social System*. Free Press, Glencoe, Ill.

     1959. "Voting and the Equilibrium of the American Political System." In *American Voting Behavior*, ed. by Eugene Burdick and Arthur J. Brodbeck, pp. 80–120. Free Press, Glencoe, Il.

     1960. *Structure and Process in Modern Societies*. Free Press, Glencoe, Ill.

     1967. *Sociological Theory and Modern Society*. Free Press, New York.

     1979. "The Symbolic Environment of Modern Economics." *Social Research* 46:436–53.

Parsons, Talcott, and Neil Smelser. 1956. *Economy and Society*. Free Press, Glencoe, Ill.

Patterson, Samuel, Ronald D. Hedlund, and G. Robert Boynton. 1975. *Representatives and Represented: Bases of Public Support for American Legislatures*. Wiley, New York.

Peacock, Alan T., and Jack Wiseman. 1961. *The Growth of Public Expenditure in the United Kingdom.* Princeton University Press, Princeton, N.J.

Peterson, Paul. 1981. *City Limits.* University of Chicago Press, Chicago.

Petrocik, John R. 1981. *Party Coalitions: Realignments and the Decline of the New Deal Party System.* University of Chicago Press, Chicago.

Pfeffer, Jeffrey, and P. Nowak. 1976. "Joint Ventures and Interorganizational Interdependence." *Administrative Science Quarterly* 21:398–418.

Pfeffer, Jeffrey, and Gerald Salancik. 1978. *The External Control of Organizations: A Resource Dependence Perspective.* Harper & Row, New York.

Piven, Frances Fox, and Richard A. Cloward. 1979. *Poor People's Movements: Why They Succeed, How They Fail.* Random House (Vintage Books), New York.

Poggi, Gianfranco. 1978. *The Development of the Modern State: A Sociological Introduction.* Stanford University Press, Stanford, Calif.

Polanyi, Karl. 1957. *The Great Transformation.* Beacon Press, Boston. (Originally published in 1944.)

Polsby, Nelson W. 1963. *Community Power and Political Theory.* Yale University Press, New Haven, Conn.

1968. "The Institutionalization of the U.S. House of Representatives." *American Political Science Review*, 62:144–68.

1969. "The Growth of the Seniority System in the U.S. House of Representatives." *American Political Science Review* 63:787.

Poulantzas, Nicos. 1972. "The Problem of the Capitalist State." In *Ideology in the Social Sciences,* ed. Robin Blackburn, pp. 238–53. Fontana, London.

1973. *Political Power and Social Classes.* New Left Books, London.

1976. *The Crisis of the Dictatorships.* New Left Books, London.

1978. *State, Power, and Socialism.* New Left Books, London.

1979. "The Political Crisis and the Crisis of the State." In *Critical Sociology: European Perspectives,* ed. J. W. Freiberg, pp. 357–93. Irvington, New York.

Powell, G. Bingham, Jr. 1981. "Party Systems and Political System Performance: Voting Participation, Government Stability, and Mass Violence in Contemporary Democracies." *American Political Science Review* 75:861–9.

1982. *Contemporary Democracies: Participation, Stability, and Violence.* Harvard University Press, Cambridge, Mass.

Przeworski, Adam. 1975. "Institutionalization of Voting Patterns; or, Is Mobilization the Source of Decay?" *American Political Science Review* 69:49–67.

1977. "Proletariat into a Class: The Process of Class Formation from Karl Kautsky's 'The Class Struggle' to Current Controversies." *Politics and Society* 7:343–401.

1980*a.* "Material Bases of Consent: Economics and Politics in a Hegemonic System." In *Political Power and Social Theory,* ed. Maurice Zeitlin, 1:21–66. JAI Press, Greenwich, Conn.

1980*b.* "Social Democracy as a Historical Phenomenon." *New Left Review* 122:27–58.

Przeworski, Adam, and Michael Wallerstein. 1982. "The Structure of Class Conflict in Democratic Capitalist Societies." *American Political Science Review* 76:215–38.

Putnam, Robert D. 1973. *The Beliefs of Politicians: Ideology, Conflict, and Democracy in Britain and Italy.* Yale University Press, New Haven, Conn.

Quirk, James, and Rubin Saposnik. 1968. *Introduction to General Equilibrium Theory and Welfare Economics.* McGraw–Hill, New York.

Ratcliff, Richard E. 1980. "Declining Cities and Capitalist Class Structure." In

Power Structure Research, ed. G. William Domhoff, pp. 115–38. Sage, Beverly Hills, Calif.

Rokkan, Stein. 1975. "Dimensions of State Formation and Nation Building: A Possible Paradigm for Research on Variations within Europe." In *The Formation of National States in Western Europe*, ed. Charles Tilly, pp. 562–600. Princeton University Press, Princeton, N.J.

Rokkan, Stein, with Angus Campbell, Per Torsvik, and Henry Valen. 1970. *Citizens, Elections, Parties*. McKay, New York.

Rose, Arnold. 1967. *The Power Structure*. Oxford University Press, New York.

Sartori, Giovanni. 1969. "From the Sociology of Politics to Political Sociology." In *Politics and the Social Sciences*, ed. S. M. Lipset, pp.65–100. Oxford University Press, New York.

Schattschneider, E. E. 1960. *The Semi–Sovereign People: A Realist's Review of Democracy in America*. Holt, Rinehart & Winston, New York.

Schmitter, Phillipe. 1974. "Still the Century of Corporatism?" *Review of Politics* 36:85–131.

　　1977. "Modes of Interest Intermediation and Models of Societal Change in Western Europe." *Comparative Political Studies* 10:7–38.

　　1981. "Interest Intermediation and Regime Governability in Contemporary Western Europe and North America." In *Organizing Interests in Western Europe*, ed. Suzanne Berger, pp. 285–327. Cambridge University Press, Cambridge.

Schroyer, Trent. 1973. *The Critique of Domination: The Origins and Development of Critical Theory*. Braziller, New York.

Schumpeter, Joseph. 1943. *Capitalism, Socialism, and Democracy*. Allen & Unwin, London.

Scott, Richard W. 1981. "Development in Organizations Theory, 1960–1980." *American Behavioral Scientist* 24:407–22.

Seidman, Harold. 1980. *Politics, Positions, and Power: The Dynamics of Federal Organization*. 3d ed. Oxford University Press, New York.

Selznick, Philip. 1949. *TVA and the Grass Roots*. University of California Press, Berkeley.

Sharpe, L. J. 1973a. "American Democracy Reconsidered: Part I." *British Journal of Political Science* 3:1–28.

　　1973b. "American Democracy Reconsidered: Part II and Conclusions." *British Journal of Political Science* 3:129–67.

Shonfield, Andrew. 1965. *Modern Capitalism: The Changing Balance of Public and Private Power*. Oxford University Press, New York.

　　1978. "Western Capitalism: A New Balance between Private and Public Power." *Executive* vol. 4, no. 2.

　　1982. *The Uses of Public Power*. Oxford University Press, Oxford.

Shoup, Laurence H., and William Minter. 1977. *Imperial Brain Trust: The Council on Foreign Relations and United States Foreign Policy*. Monthly Review Press, New York.

Skinner, Quentin. 1978a. *The Foundations of Modern Political Thought*. Vol. 1, *The Renaissance*. Cambridge University Press, Cambridge.

　　1978b. *The foundations of Modern Political Thought*. Vol. 2, *The Age of Reformation*. Cambridge University Press, Cambridge.

Skocpol, Theda. 1979. *States and Social Revolutions*. Cambridge University Press, Cambridge.

Skocpol, Theda, and Mary Fullbrook. 1984. "Destined Pathways: The Historical

Sociology of Perry Anderson." In *Vision and Method in Historical Sociology*, ed. Theda Skocpol, pp. 170–210. Cambridge University Press, Cambridge.

Skowronek, Stephen. 1982. *Building a New American State: The Expansion of National Administrative Capacities, 1877–1920*. Cambridge University Press, Cambridge.

Smelser, Neil. 1959. *Social Change in the Industrial Revolution: An Application of Theory to the British Cotton Industry*. University of Chicago Press, Chicago.

1963. *Theory of Collective Behavior*. Free Press, New York.

Stapleton, Vaughan, David P. Aday, Jr., and Jeanne A. Ito. 1982. "An Empirical Typology of American Metropolitan Juvenile Courts." *American Journal of Sociology* 88:549–64.

Stepan, Alfred. 1978. *The State and Society*. Princeton University Press, Princeton, N.J.

Stephens, John D. 1980. *The Transition from Capitalism to Socialism*. Humanities Press, Atlantic Highlands, N.J.

Stinchcombe, Arthur. 1968. *Constructing Social Theories*. Harcourt Brace, New York.

1978. *Theoretical Methods in Social History*. Academic Press, New York.

1983. *Economic Sociology*. Academic Press, New York.

Stone, Clarence N. 1976. *Economic Growth and Neighborhood Discontent*. University of North Carolina Press, Chapel Hill, N.C.

Stouffer, Samuel. 1955. *Communism, Conformity, and Civil Liberties*. Doubleday, New York.

Suleiman, Ezra N. 1978. *Elites in French Society: The Politics of Survival*. Princeton University Press, Princeton, N.J.

Therborn, Goran. 1977. "The Rule of Capital and the Rise of Democracy." *New Left Review* 103:3–41.

1978. *What Does the Ruling Class Do When It Rules?* New Left Books, London.

Thompson, E. P. 1963. *The Making of the English Working Class*. Random House (Vintage Books), New York.

1978. *The Poverty of Theory*. Monthly Review Press, London.

Tilly, Charles. 1975. "Revolutions and Collective Violence." In *Handbook of Political Science*, ed. Fred I. Greenstein and Nelson W. Polsby, 3:483–555. Addison-Wesley, Reading, Mass.

1978. *From Mobilization to Revolution*. Addison-Wesley, Reading, Mass.

Tilly, Charles, ed. 1975. *The Formation of National States in Western Europe*. Princeton University Press, Princeton, N.J.

Tilly, Charles, Louise Tilly, and Richard Tilly. 1975. *The Rebellious Century*. Harvard University Press, Cambridge, Mass.

Tipton, Frank B., Jr. 1981. "Government Policy and Economic Development in Germany and Japan: A Skeptical Reevaluation." *Journal of Economic History* 41:139–50.

Tocqueville, Alexis de. 1954. *Democracy in America*. Vols. 1 and 2. Random House (Vintage Books), New York.

Touraine, Alain. 1971. *The Post-Industrial Society – Tomorrow's Social History: Class, Conflicts, and Culture in the Programmed Society*. Random House, New York.

1977. *The Self-Production of Society*. University of Chicago Press, Chicago.

Truman, David B. 1971. *The Governmental Process: Political Interests and Public Opinion*. Knopf, New York. (Originally published in 1951.)

Tufte, Edward. 1978. *Political Control of the Economy*. Princeton University Press, Princeton, N.J.

Useem, Michael. 1979. "The Social Organization of the American Business Elite and Participation of Corporation Directors in the Governance of American Institutions." *American Sociological Review* 44:553–72.

Usher, Dan. 1981. *The Economic Prerequisite to Democracy*. Blackwell Publisher, Oxford.

Valenzuela, J. Samuel, and Arturo Valenzuela. 1978. "Modernization and Dependency: Alternative Perspectives in the Study of Latin-America Underdevelopment." *Comparative Politics* 10:535–57.

Verba, Sidney, and Norman H. Nie. 1972. *Participation in America: Political Democracy and Social Equality*. Harper & Row, New York.

Verba, Sidney, Norman H. Nie, and Jae-on Kim. 1978. *Participation and Political Equality: A Seven-Nation Comparison*. Cambridge University Press, Cambridge.

Vile, M. J. C. 1967. *Constitutionalism and the Separation of Powers*. Calderon Press, Oxford.

Wallerstein, Immanuel. 1976. *The Modern World System: Capitalist Agriculture and the Origins of the European World-Economy in the Sixteenth Century*. Text ed. Academic Press, New York.

Walsh, Edward J., and Rex H. Warland. 1983. "Social Movement Involvement in the Wake of a Nuclear Accident: Activists and Free Riders in the Three Mile Island Area." *American Sociological Review* 48:764–80.

Warwick, Donald P., Marvin Meade, and Theodore Reed. 1975. *A Theory of Public Bureaucracy: Politics, Personality, and Organization in the State Department*. Harvard University Press, Cambridge, Mass.

Weber, Max. 1949. *The Methodology of the Social Sciences*. Free Press, New York.

Weed, Frank J. 1977. "Centralized and Pluralistic Organizational Structures in Public Welfare." *Administration and Society* 9:111–36.

Weiner, Myron. 1966. *Modernization: The Dynamics of Growth*. Basic Books, New York.

Weinstein, James. 1968. *The Corporate Ideal in the Liberal State, 1900–1918*. Beacon Press, Boston.

Wesolowski, W. 1979. *Class, Strata, and Power*. Routledge & Kegan Paul, London.

White, Harrison C. 1981. "Where Do Markets Come From?" *American Journal of Sociology* 87:517–47.

Wildavsky, Aaron. 1974. *The Politics of the Budgetary Process*. 2d ed. Little, Brown, Boston.

    1982. "The Three Cultures: Explaining Anomalies in the American Welfare State." *Public Interest*. 69:45–58.

Wilensky, Harold L. 1975. *The Welfare State and Equality: Structural and Ideological Roots of Public Expenditures*. University of California Press, Berkeley.

    1976. *The "New Corporatism," Centralization, and the Welfare State*. Sage, Beverly Hills, Calif.

Williams, Raymond. 1976. *Keywords: A Vocabulary of Culture and Society*. Oxford University Press, New York.

Williams, Walter. 1980. *Government by Agency: Lessons from the Social Program Grants-in-Aid Experience*. Academic Press, New York.

Williamson, Oliver E. 1975. *Markets and Hierarchies: Analysis and Antitrust Implications*. Free Press, New York.

    1981. "The Economics of Organizations: The Transaction Cost Approach." *American Journal of Sociology* 87:548–77.

Willis, Paul. 1981. *Learning to Labor*. Columbia University Press, New York. (Originally published in 1977.)

Wolfe, Alan. 1977. *The Limits of Legitimacy*. Free Press, New York.

Wriggins, Howard. 1966. "National Integration." In *Modernization: The Dynamics of Growth*, ed. Myron Weiner, chap. 13. Basic Books, New York.

Wright, Erik Olin. 1977. "Alternative Perspectives in the Marxist Theory of Accumulation and Crisis." In *The Subtle Anatomy of Capitalism*, ed. J. Schwartz, pp. 195–231. Goodyear, Santa Monica, Calif. (A slightly revised version appears in Wright 1978.)

1978. *Class, Crisis, and the State*. New Left Books, London.

Wright, Erik Olin, Cynthia Costello, David Hachen, and Joey Sprague. 1982. "The American Class Structure." *American Sociological Review* 47:709–26.

Wright, James D. 1976. *The Dissent of the Governed*. Academic Press, New York.

Wrigley, Julia. 1982. *Class Politics and Public Schools: Chicago, 1900–1950*. Rutgers University Press, New Brunswick, N.J.

Wrong, Dennis H. 1979. *Power: Its Forms, Bases, and Uses*. Harper and Row, New York.

Yates, Douglas. 1982. *Bureaucratic Democracy: The Search for Democracy and Efficiency in American Government*. Harvard University Press, Cambridge, Mass.

Zeitlin, Maurice. 1984. *The Civil Wars in Chile*. Princeton University Press, Princeton, N.J.

Zysman, John. 1977. *Political Strategies for Industrial Order: State, Market, and Industry in France*. University of California Press, Berkeley.

1983. *Government, Markets, and Growth: Financial Systems and the Politics of Industrial Change*. Cornell University Press, Ithaca, N.Y.

Name index

Aberbach, Joel D., 81–2
Abramson, Paul R., 103n14
Aday, David P., Jr., 125n7
Albonetti, Celesta, 20n3
Aldrich, Howard, 163
Aldrich, John H., 103n14
Alexander, Jeffrey, 15n2, 20n3, 37n2, 392n4
Alford, Robert R., 191, 215n6, 260, 303, 403, 440
Allison, Graham, 219–22
Almond, Gabriel A., 42n8, 47n10, 56, 62–9, 76–7, 79–80, 84, 90, 258, 414n3
Althusser, Louis, 3n2, 273, 277, 305, 327–8
Amin, Samir, 309n2
Anderson, Perry, 3n2, 172n9, 286n6, 287, 288, 289–92, 328n9, 331, 442
Apter, David E., 47n12, 117, 173
Archibugi, Franco, 371–2
Ardant, Gabriel, 185n2, 188, 189
Aristotle, 41
Armstrong, John, 243–4
Aron, Raymond, 164n3, 224–5, 250–1
Aronowitz, Stanley, 286n6, 303–4, 368n7
Arrow, Kenneth, 44–5, 56n15, 70–2, 114–15, 128–9, 138
Auster, Richard D., 43

Bacharach, Samuel B., 93, 468
Bachrach, Peter, 181n12, 241n12
Badie, Bernard, 174n11
Bailey, F. G., 436n4
Bailyn, Bernard, 377
Balbus, Isaac, 55n14, 378–82
Ballard, Hoyt, 198n10, 200
Balmaceda (president of Chile), 295
Baran, Paul A., 296
Baratz, Morton S., 241n8
Barnes, Samuel H., 109
Baumol, William, 72, 114, 138
Bean, Richard, 189
Becker, James, 275, 362, 364

Bell, Daniel, 164n3, 165–8, 181, 182, 226–7, 252–3
Benda, Charles G., 373–6
Bendix, Reinhard, 50
Benjamin, Roger, 43
Berelson, Bernard R., 84, 102n12
Berger, Suzanne, 236
Berle, Adolf A., 334
Berry, Jeffrey M., 92n5
Beveridge, William Henry, 196n8
Birnbaum, Pierre, 174n11
Bismarck, Otto von, 341
Black, Cyril E., 47n12, 143
Blau, Peter, 38n3, 46n10, 393n5
Blondel, Jean, 194n6
Bollen, Kenneth A., 69n10
Bottomore, Tom, 223n2
Boudon, Raymond, 39
Boulton, Matthew, 144
Boynton, G. Robert, 73, 75
Brandeis, Louis, 323
Braun, Rudolf, 185n2, 186, 187, 188, 189, 255
Braverman, Harry, 300n5
Brezhnev, Leonid, 196n8
Brittan, Samuel, 157
Brown, Brian R., 347
Brown, Thad A., 128
Buchanan, James, 43
Budge, Ian, 80n19, 109n18
Burawoy, Michael, 299
Burnham, James, 226n4
Burnham, Walter Dean, 85n2
Burns, McGregor, 90
Burt, Ronald, 299n4

Cameron, David R., 238
Carnoy, Martin, 377–8
Caro, Robert A., 209n3, 422
Carter, James E., 100, 210, 214, 414
Castells, Manuel, 313–17
Castro, Fidel, 108
Child, John, 23

Subject index

absolutism (absolutist state), 205, 289–92, 341, 344
access, accessibility, 52, 69, 74, 114
accommodation, mechanisms of, 99
accountability, 113, 158, 175
accumulation, 185n1, 366, 370, 446, 447; capitalist state and, 288–307; in class perspective, 308; vs. class struggle, 271, 272, 281, 285–7, 387; and contradictory aspects of state, 436; contradictory pressure of, 370; impediments to, 308–9, 312; imperative of, 317; implicit models of, 406; institutional logic of, 389; and legitimation, 317–25, 434–6; privately controlled, 358; state and, 274, 359; transformation of, 442
accumulative state, 369
achievement, 40, 42, 48–9, 54
action(s), 4, 137, 163n2, 169, 195; collective, 44, 59, 110–11, 263–7, 349, 435, 449; formal/informal, 131–2; individual, 46, 446; political, 273; public, 45; responsible, 96; sources of, in theoretical perspectives on democracy, 449; Weberian categories of, 120n3
active state, 357
activism, activists, 68, 89, 111
actors: bureaucratic, 113; constraints on, 340n4; corporate, 164n5, 298–9; economic, 137; elite, 189, 191; political, 131, 132, 133, 134, 177, 195, 325, 355, 358, 408, 409, 411, 419, 420, 423, 438; relationships of, 142; state as, 185n1; subordinate, 170; in theoretical perspectives on capitalism, 447; in theoretical perspectives on democracy, 449
adaptability, 118
administration, 168, 170, 224n3, 262, 448; centralization of, 178
administrative officials, 113, 116
administrative strategies, 181–2
agency(ies), 169; in budget process, 216,
217, 218; cultures of, 125–8; functions of, 214–15; internal politics of, 216; rationalization of, 436–7; resources of, 214; see also bureaucratic agencies; state agencies
agrarian parties, 256
agrarian sector, 187
agricultural classes, 255, 256, 257
agricultural commercialization, 341–3; in development of bureaucratic state, 187, 188
agriculture, 255; modernization of, 203; precommercial, 340–4
air pollution policy, 241–3
alienation, 76–82, 118, 446, 448, 449
Allergy and Infectious Disease Treatment Agency, 126
allocation of benefits, 274; see also resource allocation
American Cancer Society, 402
American Civil Liberties Union, 379
American Enterprise Institute for Public Policy Research, 96n8
American Federation of Labor, 323
American Medical Association, 153
analysis(es), 3, 450; in managerial perspective, 5; potential of three perspectives of state for, xiii–xiv; simultaneously political and functional, 441; synthetic, 32, 135, 224n3; vocabulary of, 28
anarchy, 448; bureaucratic, 222; of market, 421; of production, 382
anomie, 51, 109, 118, 446
antitrust legislation, 230
apathy, 132
aspects of the state, 31, 32; potentially conflictual relations, 389; theoretical perspectives on, 388
assumptions (in theoretical perspectives), xiv, 2, 389, 450; central societal process, 23–6; class perspective, 292, 331, 353;

473

215, 219n8, 222, 227, 356–7, 362n2, 378, 391n3; of capital accumulation, 238, 308, 314; capital accumulation/class struggle, 382; capital accumulation/legitimation of state, 227, 320, 325; capital/labor, 316–17, 362, 388, 391, 394; within capitalism, 25, 332, 354, 355, 362, 371, 372, 423, 433–40, 441; capitalism/bureaucracy/democracy, 240, 393; capitalism/democracy, 152, 156, 336, 354, 358, 359, 438, 439; capitalism/state/bureaucracy, 404–5; in capitalist society, 272–3; of capitalist whole, 273; centralization/fragmentation, 437; of class, 17, 23, 246, 307, 367, 381; in class relations, 271–2, 285–7; concept, 20; consensus/participation, 40n5, 437–40; within democracy, 253, 356, 391n3; democracy bureaucracy, 210, 253, 354; democracy/capitalism, institutional, 24, 132, 292, 409, 410n1; interinstitutional, 441; internal, 433–40; latent, 23; in managerial perspective, 170, 171; multiple, 359, 388; participation/program goals, 212; in patterns of social relations, 26; political, 203, 205; power of, 388, 427–43; power/responsiveness, 66; private appropriation/socialized production, 271, 273, 281; is property of a system, 433; public costs/private profits, 320; between representation of interests, 321–2; societal, 11, 311, 356, 439–40; within state, 7–11, 276, 365, 387

control, 91, 161n1, 198, 446, 449; autonomy and, 55; of corporations, 139–40; through democratic institutions, 260; over means of production, 272, 283; in science, 396–7; separate from ownership, 357; by state, 5, 24, 147–8; of state policies, 163; strategies of, 162; see also social control

convergence, 146, 196n8

cooperation, 53, 449

Cooperative Commonwealth Federation (CCF), 86–9

Coopers & Lybrand (firm), 213

cooptation, 449; by business, 297–8; in class struggle, 283; by constituencies, 120, 123–5; by elites, 348–53; of labor unions, 324, 325; of left parties, 246; of social group leaders, 421; of traditional elites,185

coordinating bodies, 437

coordination, 169, 175, 198, 253, 382, 429

core states, 294

corporate capital: and state policy, 296–300

corporate interlocks, 175, 298–9

corporate liberalism, 323

corporate order, 181–2

corporate power: managerial perspective, 238–43; organizational level of analysis, 148–53

corporate rich (elite), 198, 199, 299n3

corporation(s), 141, 164, 175, 176, 298, 213, 420, 438n5, 447; in division of labor, 164–5; government, 374; legal possibility of, 369; multinational, 226n5, 261; organization of, 140; ownership and control of, 139–40; perceptions of influence of, 74–5; treated as voluntary organizations of individuals, 230

corporatism, 227–38, 372, 415–16, 417; societal, 237n9

correlation studies, 69–70

cost-benefit analysis, 364, 376

costs: public subsidy of, 314, 320; social, 442; see also socialization, of costs of production

Council on Foreign Relations, 222n9, 301

counter-elites, 249, 259

country: state as, 400–1

courts, 53, 230–1, 359, 380

criminal justice system, 380–2

crisis(es), 23, 24, 131, 158, 358–9, 428, 443, 448; adaptability of capitalist state to, 421; of capacity to rule, 183; capitalist, 156–7, 285, 308–13, 330–1, 435, 436; in class perspective, 271; concept of state in, 400–1; of confidence, 158, 208; of elite capacity to rule, 201, 202; fiscal, 1, 157, 294, 308–9, 320; inevitability of, 317; institutional contradictions and, 434–6; of legitimacy, 184; management of, 9, 255–9, 316, 366, 382; of mode of production, 313–17; organizational mechanisms in, 317–23; planning, 371; politics of, 316–17; sources of, 404; systemic, 287, 312–13; see also economic crisis(es); political crisis(es)

critical ideology(ies), 406–7

critical theory, 407

cross pressures, 48, 51

Cuban missile crisis, 218–20

Cuban Revolution, 108

cultural dimension of society, 25, 26, 289–90, 396, 400–1

cultural factors: in theory of capitalist crisis, 313n4, 314–15

cultural manipulation, 171

cultural values, 388; in democratic government, 54

culture(s), 16, 82, 165, 414n3, 446; of bureaucracies, 112; central, 257; commercialization of, 435; common, 441; concept, 17, 446; concepts in foundation